# Parents as Partners in Education

*Families and Schools
Working Together*

# Parents as Partners in Education

*Families and Schools Working Together*

**Eighth Edition**

**EUGENIA HEPWORTH BERGER**
Professor Emerita, Metropolitan State College of Denver

**MARI RIOJAS-CORTEZ**
University of Texas at San Antonio

Boston   Columbus   Indianapolis   New York   San Francisco   Upper Saddle River
Amsterdam   Cape Town   Dubai   London   Madrid   Milan   Munich   Paris   Montreal   Toronto
Delhi   Mexico City   São Paulo   Sydney   Hong Kong   Seoul   Singapore   Taipei   Tokyo

**Vice President and Editorial Director:** Jeffery W. Johnston
**Senior Acquisitions Editor:** Julie Peters
**Development Editor:** Bryce Bell
**Editorial Assistant:** Andrea Hall
**Vice President, Director of Marketing:** Margaret Waples
**Senior Marketing Manager:** Christopher D. Barry
**Senior Managing Editor:** Pamela D. Bennett
**Senior Project Manager:** Linda Hillis Bayma
**Senior Operations Supervisor:** Matthew Ottenweller
**Senior Art Director:** Diane C. Lorenzo

**Photo Coordinator:** Lori Whitley
**Cover Designer:** Wee Design Group
**Cover Image:** Fotolia
**Full-Service Project Management:** Norine Strang, S4Carlisle Publishing Services
**Composition:** S4Carlisle Publishing Services
**Printer/Binder:** Edwards Brothers
**Cover Printer:** Lehigh Phoenix/Hagerstown
**Text Font:** Garamond

Credits and acknowledgments for materials borrowed from other sources and reproduced, with permission, in this textbook appear on appropriate pages within text.

Every effort has been made to provide accurate and current Internet information in this book. However, the Internet and information posted on it are constantly changing, so it is inevitable that some of the Internet addresses listed in this textbook will change.

**Photo Credits:** Mari Riojas-Cortez, pp. 4 (top left), 5, 12, 43, 78, 113, 321; Cinthia Salinas, p. 4 (top right); Krista Greco/Merrill, pp. 4 (bottom left), 147; Todd Yarrington/Merrill, p. 4 (bottom right); Thinkstock, pp. 7, 44; provided by Eugenia Hepworth Berger, pp. 10, 13, 60, 61, 136, 178, 184, 322, 324, 339; Shutterstock, pp. 19, 33, 58, 62, 187, 325; Armando Cortez, pp. 20, 50, 281; Corbis RF, p. 24; Fotolia, LLC – Royalty Free, pp. 28, 32, 69, 117, 177; © Craig Cozart/Alamy, p. 42; RubberBall Productions, p. 45; Comstock Images/Thinkstock, p. 49; © Bettmann/Corbis, p. 64; Vanessa Davies © Dorling Kindersley, p. 75; Kim Cuero, p. 84; David Mager/Pearson Learning Photo Studio, pp. 87, 186; © Exactostock/SuperStock, p. 94; Annie Fuller/Pearson, pp. 96, 135, 182; iStockphoto.com, p. 120; Michael Newman/PhotoEdit Inc., pp. 123, 257, 282; © Blend Images/Alamy, p. 146; Mac H. Brown/Merrill, p. 162; Kathy Kirtland/Merrill, p. 167; EyeWire Collection/Getty Images–Photodisc–Royalty Free, p. 212; Jupiterimages/Thinkstock, p. 218; Ryan McVay/Getty Images, Inc.–PhotoDisc, p. 228; Andrea Berger, p. 229; Robin Sachs/PhotoEdit Inc., p. 231; George Dodson/PH College, p. 235; Scott Cunningham/Merrill, p. 246; Lori Whitley/Merrill, p. 251; Karla Broadus, p. 268; Barton D. Schmitt, M.D., courtesy of C. Henry Kempe National Center for Prevention and Treatment of Child Abuse and Neglect, pp. 287, 289, 295 (all), 296 (all).

**Library of Congress Cataloging-in-Publication Data**
Berger, Eugenia Hepworth.
  Parents as partners in education: families and schools working together/Eugenia Hepworth Berger, Mari Riojas-Cortez. — 8th ed.
    p. cm.
  Includes bibliographical references and index.
  ISBN-13: 978-0-13-707207-1
  ISBN-10: 0-13-707207-4
  1. Home and school—United States. 2. Education—Parent participation—United States.
  I. Riojas-Cortez, Mari. II. Title.
  LC225.3.B47 2012
  371.19'2—dc22                                                    2011001683

10 9 8 7 6 5 4 3 2 1

www.pearsonhighered.com

ISBN-13: 978-0-13-707207-1
ISBN-10:    0-13-707207-4

*To the memory of my husband, Glen Berger.*

*To the rest of my extended family—my parents, Gladys and Richard Hepworth and Anna and Henry Berger, my children, Dick, Debra, and John, my grandchildren, Jevon, Jeni, Caroline, and Andrea, and my sisters, Cora, Marian, and Jo.*

*It was through my participation in an extended family that I became aware of the importance of support, nurturance, and love.*

—Eugenia Hepworth Berger

*To my parents, Don Mario and Doña Elia Riojas, whose funds of knowledge taught me the value and the meaning of "familia." To my wonderful husband, Armando, and my three beautiful children, Marisol Isabel, Rodrigo Armando, and Miguel Fernando, with whom the practice of the meaning of a family has become the most significant reality.*

*Thanks to all the families and children with whom I have worked through the years. I also want to express a word of gratitude to my sister, Laly, who inspired me to become an educator.*

—Mari Riojas-Cortez

# About the Authors

 **Eugenia Hepworth Berger** became interested in parent involvement when she and her husband, Glen, became the parents of three children who attended public schools. A professional in early childhood education, sociology, family life education, and parent education for more than 35 years, she has two master's degrees and a Ph.D. in sociological foundations of education. Eugenia has been active in many professional organizations, including the Association for Childhood Education International, the National Association for the Education of Young Children (life member), and the National Council for the Social Studies. She served on the board for the National Association of Early Childhood Teacher Educators, the Colorado Association for Childhood Education, the Colorado Association for the Education of Young Children, and was president of the Rocky Mountain Council on Family Relations. After finishing her doctorate at the University of Denver, she became a faculty member at Metropolitan State College. She retired in December 1997 and is now professor emerita of education.

 **Mari Riojas-Cortez** became interested in parent involvement when she was a bilingual teacher working with young children in San Antonio, Texas. She learned early in her career that parents play a very important role in children's development, and she developed strong relationships with parents by welcoming families to her classroom and inviting them to participate in different aspects of their children's education. Mari understood the challenges that many Latino parents faced because her own parents faced the same challenges and barriers when they arrived in the United States from Mexico. After completing a master's degree in educational leadership, Mari's interests in early childhood education and bilingual education led her to The University of Texas at Austin, where she received a doctorate in curriculum and instruction with a concentration in early childhood education and multilingual studies (bilingual education) in 1998. Currently, as a faculty member at The University of Texas at San Antonio (UTSA), she has been able to create partnerships with local school districts and agencies in various capacities. Additionally, Mari's work has been published in journals including *Journal of Early Childhood Research, International Journal of Early Childhood Education, Young Children, Early Child Development and Care, Dimensions, Language Arts,* and the *Bilingual Research Journal,* among others. She has been a consulting editor for *Young Children* and reviewer for a variety of journals and served as a NCATE/NAEYC panel member/reviewer. Mari Riojas-Cortez was promoted to full professor in 2010.

# *Preface*

This edition of *Parents as Partners in Education: Families and Schools Working Together* highlights the changes in U.S. society and effective ways for teachers and other professionals to understand and work with families. For the last 25 years we have seen major changes in families. In particular, we have seen an increase in the number of culturally and linguistically diverse families. The beauty of this change reminds us of the diversity of our nation. Learning to work with culturally and linguistically diverse families, as well as those with diverse family structures, requires an understanding of who we are as individuals and educators, and that we acknowledge the values and beliefs that our own families have taught us.

Among other themes, this edition emphasizes the importance of *funds of knowledge* (Moll et al., 1992) for children's development and for effective partnerships with families. Throughout the book we make connections to this concept. It is not only important for educators to understand and know child development theories, but also how children develop within the context of their families.

Creating strong partnerships involves the understanding and willingness to work with all families, including families that are different than our own. Once educators understand the value of families for healthy development, they can begin to create strong partnerships to assist children in successful educational experiences. This edition continues to highlight important parent involvement programs and how such programs are often successful because of an asset-based view of families, particularly of those that are culturally and linguistically diverse as well as those with children with special needs.

## NEW TO THIS EDITION

This edition includes updated material and additional coverage of many subjects. Of particular interest are

- A focus on *funds of knowledge*, particularly as they relate to culturally and linguistically diverse families (Chapter 1).
- Numerous examples and scenarios that illustrate teachers' experiences working with parents and family members—to bring practices and insights to life.
- New statistics regarding issues that affect families, particularly those that are culturally and linguistically diverse (Chapters 1 and 2).
- Tips on how to work with culturally and linguistically diverse families (Chapter 3).
- Strategies for working with English language learners and their families, including a section on second language acquisition (Chapter 3).
- A newly streamlined history chapter, which explains how changing views of children and societal changes have affected how families have educated children throughout history and how school–family relations have evolved throughout history (Chapter 4).
- Descriptions of programs such as AVANCE that serve culturally and linguistically diverse families (Chapter 8).
- Expanded coverage of autism's effect on families (Chapter 10).
- An emphasis on national and international advocacy (Chapter 12).

## GUIDELINES AND STRATEGIES FOR WORKING WITH FAMILIES

The tried-and-true how-to ideas and means to help parents and educators join together include

- Communication, an essential element in providing an environment where learning and caring coexist.
- An understanding of diversity in different contexts.
- Ideas to help build a partnership of home and school.
- Ways to set up an ecology that is culturally and linguistically appropriate and where learning can take place.
- Historical development of views on children and how those views affect family life.
- Activities and programs to enrich parent–school collaboration.
- Awareness of the effects autism has on families.
- Methods needed to recruit volunteers for the school.
- Practices to develop working relationships with culturally and linguistically diverse families.

## ORIENTATION TO THE TEXT

*Interdisciplinary.* The text studies parent involvement from an interdisciplinary approach and looks at home–school partnerships from educational, anthropological, sociological, and psychological perspectives. In this edition there is a strong effort to view families from a diverse perspective.

*Theory and Research.* Theory and research underpin each chapter of the text. New research emphasizes the need for home–school partnerships, particularly as they relate to culturally and linguistically diverse families.

*Practical Application.* A parent, student, teacher, or administrator can pick up this book and find suggestions and descriptions of specific programs that will enable collaboration between families and schools.

*Readability.* Reviewers and students have commented on the readability of the text in its comprehensive coverage. It is written in an easy-to-read style.

*Figures and Tables.* Numerous helpful figures and tables are included in the text to help illustrate content.

*Photos.* Many new photographs that depict culturally and linguistically diverse children, families, and teachers as well as families with children with special needs enrich the content of the book.

## SPECIAL FEATURES

*Situational Vignettes.* Vignettes bring alive situations that typically occur in parent–school relationships. The new co-author, Mari Riojas-Cortez, has woven some personal vignettes through the book because of her experience as an immigrant from Mexico, as well as from her professional work with children and families.

*Diverse Families.* Suggestions and activities about how to work with diverse families, including a special focus on families affected by autism, are given.

*Advocacy.* Preparation and suggestions on advocating for children, plus facts about ombudsmanship for children in the United States, give parents and educators the knowledge they need to encourage them to be actively involved in advocacy issues.

*Historical Outline.* An outline of historical highlights of education and parent education succinctly illustrates parent involvement.

## NEW! COURSESMART eTEXTBOOK AVAILABLE

CourseSmart is an exciting new choice for students looking to save money. As an alternative to purchasing the printed textbook, students can purchase an electronic version of the same content. With a CourseSmart eTextbook, students can search the text, make notes online, print out reading assignments that incorporate lecture notes, and bookmark important passages for later review. For more information, or to purchase access to the CourseSmart eTextbook, visit www.coursesmart.com.

## INSTRUCTOR'S RESOURCES

The following ancillaries are available for download to adopting professors via www.pearsonhighered .com from the Educators screen. Contact your Pearson sales representative for additional information.

**Instructor's Resource Manual.** This manual contains activity ideas to enhance chapter concepts.

**Test Bank.** The test bank includes a variety of test items, arranged by chapter.

**Pearson MyTest.** This powerful assessment generation program helps instructors easily create and print quizzes and exams. Questions and tests are authored online, allowing ultimate flexibility and the ability to efficiently create and print assessments anytime, anywhere. Instructors can access Pearson MyTest and their test bank files by going to www.pearsonmytest.com to log in, register, or request access. Features of Pearson MyTest include:

Premium assessment content

- Draw from a rich library of assessments that complement your Pearson textbook and your course's learning objectives.
- Edit questions or tests to fit your specific teaching needs.

Instructor-friendly resources

- Easily create and store your own questions, including images, diagrams, and charts, using simple drag-and-drop and Word-like controls.
- Use additional information provided by Pearson, such as the question's difficulty level or learning objective, to help you quickly build your test.

Time-saving enhancements

- Add headers or footers and easily scramble questions and answer choices—all from one simple toolbar.
- Quickly create multiple versions of your test or answer key, and when ready, simply save to MS-Word or PDF format and print.
- Export your exams for import to Blackboard 6.0, CE (WebCT), or Vista (WebCT).

**PowerPoint Slides.** PowerPoint slides highlight key concepts and strategies in each chapter and enhance lectures and discussions.

**Test Bank in Blackboard and WebCT.** Also available are files containing test items converted for use in Blackboard and WebCT.

## A NOTE ABOUT CENSUS DATA

While this eighth edition was being revised, the U.S. Census was collecting and analyzing the nation's 2010 population data. Although every effort was made to include up-to-date information, we strongly suggest that readers check the American Fact Finder on the U.S. Census Web site at http://factfinder2.census.gov/main.html for the latest data.

## ACKNOWLEDGMENTS

This text developed over the years, and in this process I worked with many individuals. I would like to thank them all. Everyone was cooperative and gracious and their encouragement helped me to continue.

Professionals and organizations—Susan Blosten, Phyllis Levenstein, Joyce Epstein, Don Davies, Julia Herwig, Marion M. Wilson, Bettye Caldwell, Miriam Westheimer, Cynthia Franklin, Loretta Fuddy, Virginia Plunkett, Romie Tobi, Virginia Castro, Kevin Swick, Colorado Department of Education, Parents as Partners, Parent Education and Assistance for Kids (PEAK) Parent Center, and Utah Parent Center—all have shared materials with me. Kelly and Bruce Stahlman wrote about their experiences with twins who have cerebral palsy, and Bruce updated information about the children for the seventh edition. Clark E. Myers used his law expertise and contributed to Chapter 12. Pat Welch and David Denson of the C. Henry Kempe Center for the Prevention and Treatment of Child Abuse and Neglect gave me information and the Barton Schmitt photographs that appear in Chapter 11. Although I am no longer teaching, I am still indebted to my students; two of the case studies were written by Bretta Martinec and Rosina Kovar, students at MSCD. My family members have also been an essential ingredient in the entire project each time around, for they embodied what is best in families.

I also want to show my appreciation to the many organizations and government agencies for continued efforts to benefit children and share information with others.

Thanks to Karen Banks, an early childhood educator and consultant, who contributed revisions to several chapters in the seventh edition.

—*Eugenia Hepworth Berger*

Eugenia Hepworth Berger had a vision when she developed *Parents as Partners in Education: Families and Schools Working Together*. Her vision carried this book through seven editions—30 years of sharing ideas with educators and administrators on how to enhance parental involvement to strengthen home–school partnerships. I hope to carry her vision in this eighth edition where we further our understanding of working with diverse families, and I offer my sincere gratitude for trusting me with her book.

I want to thank all of the previous contributors to the book as well as my university students who provide me with opportunities to stay informed regarding the realities of many families. I also wish to thank my friends and colleagues who shared photographs that display the diversity of our society, including Cinthia Salinas from The University of Texas at Austin and Iliana Alanis, Karla Broadus, Kimberley Cuero, and Jenifer Thornton from The University of Texas at San Antonio.

I also want to thank my graduate assistant Erin Price, who came in at the end of the project to assist me in researching crucial information as well as other endeavors related to the book.

I want to thank the staff of Pearson for their guidance and support. Julie Peters, senior acquisitions editor, approached me regarding the idea of working on the revision of this book. I thank her for her trust, patience, guidance, and encouragement. I also want to thank Bryce Bell, development editor, for providing guidance and feedback on every aspect of the revision of the book and helping me find my voice as an author. I would also like to extend a thank-you to project manager Linda Bayma, for ensuring the accuracy of this edition, and to Norine Strang, senior project editor at S4Carlisle Publishing Services, and the copyeditors for the production services provided.

I also want to thank all the reviewers who took the time to read and provide feedback for this edition. Their diverse insights and expertise have strengthened it: Susan Baxter, El Camino University; Fredalene B. Bowers, Indiana University of Pennsylvania; Stewart W. Ehly, University of Iowa; Arminta L. Jacobson, University of North Texas; Sai Jambunathan, New Jersey City University; Barbara Kartz, Cleveland State University; Robert Moreno, Syracuse University; Ruth Piker, California State University, Long Beach; Kenneth E. Smith, University of Nebraska at Omaha; Susan Thompson, University of Northern Colorado; Steven Toepfer, Kent State University; and Heather Von Bank, Minnesota State University-Mankato.

Finally, I want to acknowledge my husband, Armando Cortez, for his support in taking care of our three children while Mommy was in her office revising this wonderful textbook about the reality of families today.

—*Mari Riojas-Cortez*

# Brief Contents

# Contents

# 3

## Working with Culturally and Linguistically Diverse Groups   40

# 4

## Parent Involvement: A Historical Overview   54

## 8

## School-Based Programs 176

## 11
## The Abused Child    286

# Parents as Partners in Education

*Families and Schools*
*Working Together*

# Family—Essential for a Child's Development

*Understanding the concept of funds of knowledge helps educators create an environment in the schools that helps children with their development because they feel respected and valued.*

Mari Riojas-Cortez

*This chapter stresses the importance of families, schools, and communities understanding, respecting, and valuing one another to assist children in their healthy overall development. After completing the chapter, you should be able to do the following:*

- Discuss the concept of **funds of knowledge** as it relates to families and how this helps to increase collaboration between families, communities, and schools.
- Explain how the Family Ecological Systems Theory provides opportunities for all families to learn to use the teachers, school, and community as resources to assist them in the development of their children.
- Identify and explain research on attachment that illustrates the need for early attachment of children with a parent or significant caregiver.
- Discuss breakthroughs in neuroscience research on brain development and what it means for families.

## :: STRONG FAMILIES, STRONG CHILDREN

Strong families are essential because they help to create a nurturing society, transforming the society by actively participating in different systems that in turn help them [families] have a healthy, successful life. Regardless of how nurturing the society, at times, even strong families face difficulties that test their well-being, such as parents working multiple jobs to ensure the basic necessities of the child are met. Although family stressors such as this are difficult for children, families that are strong are often resilient and learn to work out problems because they care for each other, particularly their children. When children have strong family members that continuously interact with them in a safe (albeit sometimes challenging) environment, they develop a positive self-concept and self-esteem, which helps them in many aspects of their development and in school experiences.

### Defining the Term *Parent*

Throughout this book, the term **parent** includes those who act in a primary caregiver or parent role whether they are the biological parent, a relative, adoptive parent, foster parent, or nonrelated caregiver. In fact, parents can be one person or a group of individuals (such as those that form part of support systems) who help meet the cognitive, linguistic, physical, socioemotional, and cultural needs of children.

### The Role of the Extended Family

Because families are so important, resources must be provided to support their needs, specifically their children's needs. Extended family members such as grandparents, who often are given the responsibility of taking care of the children, are an important resource of support for families. Because of their role as "parents," it is imperative that schools and communities help parents and families provide a caring environment for children.

A caring environment is one that promotes collaboration between school and families by providing adequate and supportive child care, ensuring small class sizes for individualized attention (especially for young children), and actively involving parents and caregivers in the children's development and education. Teachers must work together with parents by taking responsibility for children's linguistic, social, emotional, physical, cognitive, and cultural development, giving them the opportunity to develop skills and become educated citizens.

## :: FUNDS OF KNOWLEDGE

Caretaking and teaching other people's children are tremendous tasks. Teachers must have the desire to teach children who come from a variety of cultural and linguistic backgrounds as well as children who are not developing typically. Often teachers are told that they need to be aware of the differences in language and culture of the children they teach, but merely being aware of cultural and linguistic

Strong families nurture, socialize, and educate.

differences is not sufficient to work effectively with families. Awareness implies knowledge but no action. When working with culturally and linguistically diverse children, teachers must know about the children's families, including but not limited to their cultural practices, childrearing practices, traditions, and each individual family's funds of knowledge.

Really, families are a child's first teachers, passing on their concepts, or funds of knowledge, to help them grow and thrive (Moll et al., 1992). These concepts can be passed along from generation to generation, and new ones can be developed as new families are formed.

For early childhood educators, the importance of understanding the concept of funds of knowledge is crucial because they must understand why families do the things they do. Often educators criticize parents if their ways of raising their children are

different than theirs, and this creates a dissonance that prevents teachers from truly collaborating with parents. We must remember that parents are a child's first teacher, and the learning and teaching that occur in the home are great assets for children in school as long as teachers value the children's funds of knowledge.

## Examples of Funds of Knowledge

I (Mari Riojas-Cortez) have seen funds of knowledge "in action" in different settings. For example, while eating at a local restaurant, a father was observing his son (who had Down syndrome) figure out the amount of tip to leave for the server. This teaches the young man an important social skill while fostering his independence. In my husband's experience, his father, who was a carpenter, had my husband sort the screws needed when they worked on a project. This simple

Funds of knowledge can be passed along from generation to generation and new ones can be developed as new families are formed.

experience taught my husband to pay attention to detail, to be organized, and to have a strong work ethic.

My own experience growing up in Mexico allowed me to learn about how to solve issues of social justice through my father, who was actively involved in the *sindicato obrero,* or the "blue collar" union. My sisters and I were used to listening to my father talk about how to make sure the workers would get treated fairly, which is something that has become part of my philosophy of teaching (providing fair opportunities to learn).

Another example of funds of knowledge is derived from an interview with an African American family. The interview showed that the family wanted to teach their children about "Black pride"—they wanted their children to know their history so they would continue to advocate for each other. They taught their children about different African American historical figures, but they also talked about their own family and how they make a difference in their community. The funds of knowledge learned by the children in this family include the need to participate in advocacy for their community.

Families who immigrate to the United States often use their funds of knowledge to learn to live in a new culture, but oftentimes, the role of "teacher" is reversed. When visiting a school on the east side of Austin, Texas, I recall listening to a mother having a conversation with her young daughter, who was probably about 10 years old, regarding the papers that were needed to register her in school. The young daughter knew English and had to translate for the mother in order to register for school. Another time, I witnessed a family at an auto parts store, and the young son was

translating for his father what the salesperson was telling him in English. The father was a mechanic. In both instances, the children had knowledge of the vocabulary used in each occasion in their native language.

Examples of funds of knowledge vary between cultures as well as between individual families. As indicated above, funds of knowledge can be observed in different situations. In schools or child-care centers, examples can be found in children's play that include language, values and beliefs, ways of discipline, household care, and the value of education (Riojas-Cortez, 2001). Teachers can observe children during play, particularly sociodramatic play, to recognize the cultural traits and identify funds of knowledge. Another example includes a teacher who arranges the dramatic play area to reflect the children's experience such as setting it up as a neighborhood restaurant.

### Insights for Teachers and Administrators

1. Research and learn the cultural and linguistic background of the families in your classroom.
2. Use culturally appropriate ways to welcome all families in schools or centers.
3. Avoid saying things like "I only speak a little bit of _____ (language)—I just can't do it." It is offensive to parents because this gives a signal that their native language is not valued. Instead say, "I really like learning other languages even though it is difficult for me," and show interest by asking how to say a phrase in the parents' native language.
4. Make parents feel part of the classroom by treating them with respect, particularly by using their preferred name.
5. Where there's an opportunity, share with families and children your own funds of knowledge.
6. Create a "funds of knowledge" tree and display at the entrance of the school so that everyone can see what families value.

## :: CHILD DEVELOPMENT THEORIES

Child development theories often help us understand the basis for educational and childrearing practices (Charlesworth, 2011). Rosalind Charlesworth, Professor Emerita of Child and Family Studies, explains that in recent years, the cultural relevance of those theories has been criticized. The way to interpret the theory is to look at its premise and then adapt it to the child's situation in the United States. The theories described in this chapter focus on the role that the family has on child development, therefore making the theories relevant to the child's schema or experience.

## Family Ecological Systems Theory

Both children and parents are affected by the family system in which they participate. Family systems are guided and influenced by their cultural and historical backgrounds. When a family undergoes a transitional event such as the birth of a child, a move to a new location, or an illness of a family member, the system will need to adapt to accommodate the change. Change occurs in a variety of ways. It may be sudden or gradual, positive or negative. The change may be minimal or shattering. Divorce is one common change that causes children to lose the family system as they knew it and adapt to an

**FIGURE 1–1**
Bronfenbrenner's Ecological Theory.

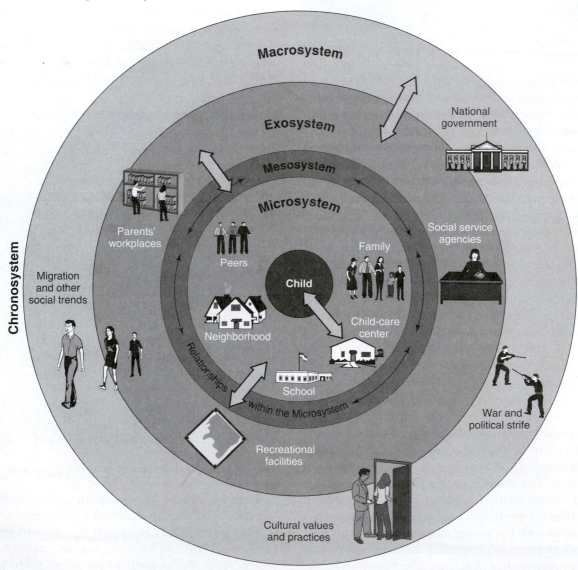

*Source:* Based on *Making Human Beings Human: Bioecological Perspectives on Human Development* by U. Bronfenbrenner, 2005, Thousand Oaks, CA: Sage.

entirely new one. Teachers need to know what is happening in a student's family so that they can respond in an appropriate manner and be helpful to the child.

**Levels of Ecological Systems.** The child's development is related to experiences in the entire environment. Bronfenbrenner (1979, 1986) recognized five levels, as shown in Figure 1–1.

1. The microsystem includes face-to-face relations with family and peers, with parents as the major influence on a child's interactive ecological system (O'Callaghan, 1993). Examples include interactions with parents, peers, or teachers.
2. The mesosystem involves face-to-face relationships with more formal organizations. Examples include school, family, peers, health-care services, religious institutions, and the playground.
3. The exosystem, which if further removed from personal interaction, still influences children through their parents and the parents' employment and government actions.
4. The macrosystem includes the attitudes and ideologies of the culture. Examples include environmental events and cultural traditions, laws, and customs.
5. The chronosystem includes the element of time as it relates to changes in a child's environment. Examples of the chronosystem include the child getting older and the aging or death of a parent or family member.

The parents' role in their children's early years is significant in many ways, but it requires the support of different systems as stated by Bronfenbrenner. This perspective seems to help families who face different types of stress like violence, homelessness, and chemical dependence (Swick & Williams, 2006).

Although this perspective has many positive factors, it is important to note that for children from culturally and linguistically diverse families, some of the systems may not work so successfully. For example, a study found that resiliency in nine Native American teenagers was influenced by individual and environmental factors related to the family and extended family support (Reclaiming Children and Youth, 2009), but there was no mention of how the mesosystem and exosystem have helped Native American children.

A criticism of this theory is that for culturally and linguistically diverse children, the mesosystem and the exosystem often do not value their culture, and their funds of knowledge are considered deficits.

## Attachment Theory

Ecological systems should be nurturing environments where children have opportunities to develop socially and emotionally. A nurturing environment allows children to create bonds and attachments. The development of positive parent–child relationships is based on the quality of attachments that the child has developed. Attachment is defined as a form of behavior that has its "own internal motivation

Eye contact between father and child fosters human attachment, a necessary component for healthy development.

distinct from feeding and sex, and of no less importance for survival" (Bowlby, 1988, p. 27).

Since the 1930s, there has been increasing research on bonding and attachment. Experts recognize attachment as an essential ingredient for a healthy personality. Attachment behavior is the behavior that a person exhibits to obtain and maintain proximity to the attachment figure, generally the mother but also the father, and in their absence, someone the child knows; in many culturally and linguistically diverse families, the grandparents may take that role. This attachment is strongest when the child is sick, tired, or frightened but is crucial throughout the life cycle.

Psychoanalysts Skeels, Spitz, and Bowlby recognized the importance of the first few years in the development of attachment, as evidenced through studies of children who did not thrive. These psychoanalysts did not conduct controlled studies that gave some children love and withheld it from others, but instead they looked at what had happened to children who had failed to thrive. Why had this happened? What did these children lack that the other children had?

**Skeels.** During the 1930s, questions about the importance of human attachment in the young children were raised. Harold Skeels, a member of the Iowa Group of child researchers, studied the effect of environment on the development of children during a period when most researchers (e.g., Gesell and Watson) were studying maturation or behaviorism. One study, a natural history investigation, had startling findings (Skeels, 1966). Skeels placed 13 infants and toddlers from an orphanage in an institution for people with mental retardation. The 13 children—10 girls and 3 boys—ranged from 7.1 to 35.9 months and had IQs from 36 to 89, with a mean IQ score of 64.3. Children in the control group of 12—also chosen from children in the orphanage, between 12 and 22 months old—had IQs of 50 to 103, with a mean IQ of 86.7 points. The children placed in the wards for mental retardation were showered with attention by the attendants and supervisors. They were cared for, played with, loved, and allowed to go along on excursions. Almost every child developed an attachment to one person who was particularly interested in the child and his or her achievements.

The control group of children in the orphanage, however, received traditional care with no special treatment. When retested, after varying periods from 6 to 52 months, the children in the institution for mental retardation had gained 27.5 IQ points, but those left in the orphanage had lost an average of 26.2 IQ points.

Although the research could be criticized because variables were not controlled—there were more girls than boys placed in the wards—and changes in IQ can be partially explained by statistical regression, the results were so dramatic and unexpected that the effect of early environment had to be considered. Skeels (1966) followed up on the subjects of this research almost 20 years later and found evidence to reinforce his initial findings. Of the 13 children in the experimental group who had been transferred to the mental institution, 11 had been adopted and reared as "normal" children. Twelve of the 13 had become self-supporting adults, achieving a median education level of 12 years of schooling. Of the control group children who had been left in the orphanage, 4 were still in institutions, 1 was a gardener's assistant, 3 were employed as dishwashers, 1 was a floater (performed different types of jobs as needed), 1 was a part-time worker in a cafeteria, and 1 had died. Only 1 individual had achieved an educational level similar to that of the experimental group—a man who as a child had received different treatment from the others. He had been transferred from the orphanage to a school for the deaf, where he received special attention from his teacher.

The children who had been placed in a mental institution and later adopted received love and developed human attachments; they had achieved a lifestyle more typical of children outside the orphanage, whereas those left in the orphanage had only a marginal existence. Evidence strongly supports the importance of a nurturing early environment and also indicates that a poor initial environment can be reversed by enriched personal interaction (Skeels, 1966). Interestingly, these findings also support (indirectly) the importance of funds of knowledge, which are gained through nurturing interactions between child and immediate and/or extended family in a caring environment (regardless of income level and mental ability).

## Spitz

In *The First Year of Life* (1965), René Spitz described his research and observations of the psychology of infants. He studied babies in different situations: private families, foster homes, an obstetrics ward, a well-baby clinic, a nursery, and a foundling home.

Both the nursery and foundling home were long-term institutions that guaranteed constancy of environment and dramatically illustrated the necessity of human attachment and interaction. Both institutions provided similar physical care of children, but they differed in their nurturing and interpersonal relationships. Both provided hygienic conditions, well-prepared food, and medical care. The foundling home had daily visits by a medical staff, whereas the nursery called a doctor only when needed. The nursery was connected to a penal institution where "delinquent girls," pregnant on admission, were sent to serve their sentences. Babies born to them were cared for in the nursery until the end of their first year. The mothers were primarily socially maladjusted minors. In contrast, some of the children in the foundling home had well-adjusted mothers who were unable to support their children. Others were children of unwed mothers who were asked to come to the home and nurse their own and one other child during the first 3 months.

Spitz (1965) filmed a representative group of the children he studied in both institutions. He studied 203 children in the nursery and 91 in the foundling home. The major difference in the care of the two sets of children was the amount of nurturing and social interaction. The nursery, which housed 40 to 60 children at a time, allowed the mothers or mother-substitutes to feed, nurse, and care for their babies. The infants had at least one toy, and they were able to see outside their cribs and to watch the activities of other children and the caregiving mothers. These babies thrived. In the foundling home, however, the babies were screened from outside activity by blankets hung over the sides and ends of their cribs, isolating them from any visual stimulation. They had no toys to play with, and the caretakers were busy tending to other duties rather than mothering the children. During the first 3 months, while they were breast-fed, the babies appeared normal. Soon after separation, however, they progressively deteriorated. Of the 91 foundling home children, 34 died by the end of the second year.

Spitz (1965) continued to follow up on 21 children who remained in the foundling home until they were 4 years old. He found that 20 could not dress themselves, 6 were not toilet trained, 6 could not talk, 5 had a vocabulary of two words, 8 had vocabularies of three to five words, and only 1 was able to speak in sentences. Spitz attributed the deterioration of the infants to lack of mothering. Although the children in the nursery had mothering, those in the foundling home did not:

> Absence of mothering equals emotional starvation. . . . This leads to progressive deterioration engulfing the child's whole person. Such deterioration is manifested first in an arrest of the child's psychological development; then psychological dysfunctions set in, paralleled by somatic changes. In the next stage this leads to increased infection liability and eventually, when the emotional deprivation continues into the second year of life, to a spectacularly increased rate of mortality. (Spitz, 1965, p. 281)

## Bowlby

In 1951, John Bowlby reviewed studies of deprivation and its effects on personality development. In a systematic review for the World Health Organization, he described those works that supported theories on the negative aspects of maternal deprivation. In a monograph, Bowlby (1966) stated: "It is submitted that the evidence is now such that it leaves no room for doubt regarding the general proposition that the prolonged deprivation of the young child of maternal care may have grave and far-reaching effects on his character and so the whole of his future life" (p. 46).

## Development of Attachment

Bowlby (1982) described attachment in a family setting. Most babies about 3 months old show more attention and are more responsive to their primary caregiver than to others by smiling at, vocalizing to, and visually following their parent or other primary caregiver. At about 6 to 8 months of age, infants develop stranger anxiety. They become concerned about being near their caregiver and fearful of those they do not know. This attachment to primary caregivers continues and strengthens in intensity from 6 to 9 months, although when the child is ill, fatigued, hungry, or alarmed, the intensity increases. During the same period, the infant demonstrates attachment to others as well, primarily the father, siblings, and caregivers. Attachment to others does not reduce the attachment to the mother or primary caregiver. At 9 months, most children try to follow primary caregivers when they leave the room, greet them on return, and crawl to be near them. This behavior continues throughout the second year of a child's life and on into the third. When children reach about 2 years 9 months to 3 years of age, they are better able to accept a parent's temporary absence.

Bowlby (1966) emphasized that the greatest effect on personality development is during the child's early years. The earliest critical period was believed to be during the first 5 or 6 months, while the mother figure and infant are forming an attachment. The second vital phase was seen as lasting until near the child's third birthday, during which time the mother figure needs to be virtually an ever-present companion. During the third phase, the child is able to maintain the attachment even though the nurturing parent is absent. During the fourth to fifth year, this tolerable absence might extend from a few days to a few weeks; during the seventh to eighth years, the separation could be lengthened to a year or more. Deprivation in the third phase does not have the same destructive effect on the child as it does in the period from infancy through the third year.

### Maternal or Human Attachment?

Prominent child psychiatrists Rutter (1981) and Bower (1982) questioned whether the term *maternal deprivation* was too restrictive to cover a wide range of abuses and variables. They suggested that maternal deprivation was too limited a concept—that human attachment and multiple attachments should be considered and that warmth as well as love be regarded as vital elements in relationships. Rutter argued that the bond with the mother was not different in quality or kind from other bonds. In addition, individual differences among children resulted in some children being more vulnerable to mother deprivation.

### Tizard and Hodges

Questions regarding the irreversibility of deprivation were raised. Would sound childrearing reverse early deprivation? It appeared that good childrearing practices and a good environment would help the child, but early deprivation continued to be a problem, and deprived infants often remained detached. Tizard and Hodges (1978) studied children raised in an institution to see if the lack of personal attachment had lasting effects. Children who were adopted did form bonds as late as 4 or 6 years of age, but they exhibited the same attention and social problems in school as those who remained in the institution: "Being one in a class of many other children may for the child have repeated some of the elements of the nursery 'family group,' leading to a similar pattern of competitive attempts to gain the attention of the teacher and poor relationships with other children" (Hodges, 1996, p. 71).

### Ainsworth

Ainsworth (1973) wrote that parent–child attachment is necessary for the development of a healthy personality, but that attachment may occur beyond the early "sensitive period." Ainsworth identified three classifications of attachment: avoidant/insecure, ambivalent/insecure, and securely attached (Shore, 1997).

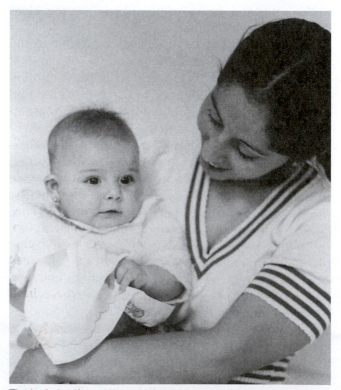

The brain is affected by nourishment, care, and stimulation. Early attachment and nurturing are essential for a child's development.

## Brazelton and Yogman

In their extensive studies of infants, Brazelton and Yogman (1986) analyzed the process of early attachment and wrote specifically about the interaction between infant and parent, covering even the effects of experiences in utero. The child appears to be born with predictable responses, including the ability to develop a reciprocal relationship with the caregiver.

Brazelton and Yogman (1986) described four stages vital to the parent-infant attachment process, which lasts from birth to 4 or 5 months. In the first stage, the infant achieves homeostatic control and is able to control stimuli by shutting out or reaching for stimuli. During the second stage, the infant is able to use and attend to social cues. In the third stage, usually at 3 to 4 months, the reciprocal process between parent and child shows the infant's ability to take in and respond to the information as well as to withdraw. During the fourth stage, the infant develops a sense of autonomy and initiates and responds to cues. If the parent recognizes and encourages the infant's desire to have control over the environment, the infant develops a sense that leads to a feeling of competence. This model is based on feedback and reciprocal interaction and allows for individual differences (Brazelton & Yogman, 1986).

## Brazelton Institute

The Newborn Behavioral Observation (NBO) is a family-centered observation set that is designed to be used by clinicians at the Brazelton Institute as they focus on individual infants and observe their individuality and competencies, as early months of infancy, from birth until the third month, are important periods in the infant's adaptation to his or her environment. In addition to strengthening the relationships between infant and parent as well as parent and clinician, the NBO provides information to the parents that helps them be better caregivers. The parents learn to read their baby's communication cues, understand their baby better, and are able to respond with appropriate care (Brazelton Institute, 2005).

## Concerns

Three groups of parents may pose particular concern when developing parent–child attachments. The first is made up of parents who have never had models of good parenting or have been reared in abusive homes. They need help in learning how to care for children. The second group contains parents who tend to be isolated and insecure and do not have a support system. These groups could be helped by home-based programs such as Parents as Teachers, HIPPY, and Project CARE. The third group includes parents who are busy and away from home for extended periods.

The importance of early bonding and attachment development is such that parents must be aware of the consequences of not devoting time to their young children. Children who lack attachment from infancy on may have enormous effects on their social interaction. It can result in dysfunctional relations not only between parent and child with insecure attachments but also with peers. These children are often aggressive in their relationships with other children in a school setting. The attachment process and the early life of a child are the first steps to the child's total growth. They provide the necessary emotional trust that allows the child to continue to develop relationships.

## :: BRAIN RESEARCH

Research on brain development emphasizes the importance of the first years of life (Brazelton & Greenspan, 2000; Carnegie Corporation of New York, 1994; Education Commission of the States, 1996; Greenspan, 2002; Newman, 1996; Shonkoff & Phillips, 2000; Shore, 1997; Zero to Three, 1998–2001). Brain research uses different technologies such as ultrasound to study fetal brain development and neural functioning and scanning techniques such as magnetic resonance imaging (MRI) and positron emission tomography (PET) to learn how the brain works after the child is born. "Functional MRI provides information about changes in the volume, flow, or oxygenation of blood that occur as a person undertakes various tasks, including not only motor activities, such as squeezing a hand, but also cognitive tasks, such as speaking or solving a problem" (Shore, 1997, p. 8). Another noninvasive way of studying activity in the brain can be through the use of neuropsychological tools such as electroencephalogram and magnetic encephalography. In these methods, the brain is studied indirectly by giving a child a task and examining which part of the brain is active as well as observing the child's level of activity in response to different stimuli (Shonkoff & Phillips, 2000).

A PET scan, employed when a child is thought to have neurological problems, requires an injection of a tracer chemical, making it an invasive procedure, which researchers generally avoid. Since PET scans cannot be considered noninvasive, the research comes from situations in which the child has needed the scan for medical reasons. By analyzing the results of PET scans, researchers have furthered scientific knowledge: "Scientists can visualize not only the fine structures of the brain, but also the level of activity that is taking place in its various parts" (Shore, 1997, p. 9). Prior to these technological advances, brain research was accomplished only when operations were performed or people had strokes, and neither situation revealed what was happening in the brain at specific times.

## Brain Development

The brain and spinal cord begin their developmental journey just a few days after conception and continue to develop in overlapping phases, with the brain cells multiplying and migrating according to where they are needed: "Once nerve cells are formed and finished migrating they rapidly extend axons and dendrites and begin to form connections with each other, called synapses" (Shonkoff & Phillips, 2000, p. 186). The nerve cells are able to communicate with one another. The synapses are refined through maturation and pruning followed by myelination, a protective and supportive tissue surrounding the cells.

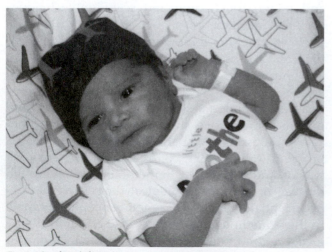

The brain of an infant develops at an exhilarating rate.

The brain does not develop one area and then the next in a straight, linear pattern. It develops in an integrated and overlapping fashion. Structures that control cognition (thinking), perception (sensing), and action (moving) develop at the same time but not in lockstep fashion. They are linked by a network of interconnections, separate but functioning parallel to one another (Goldman-Rakic, 1996).

The development of the brain proceeds at an exhilarating rate. The number of neurons peaks before birth (new neurons are produced throughout life though far less rapidly). Brain size also increases more gradually. A newborn's brain is only about one-quarter the size of an adult's. It grows to 80 percent of adult size by 3 years of age and 90 percent by 5. Its growth is largely due to changes in individual neurons, which are structured like trees. Thus, each brain cell begins as a tiny sapling and only gradually sprouts its hundreds of long, branching dendrites. Brain growth, measured either by weight or volume, is largely due to the growth of these dendrites, which serve as the receiving point of synaptic input from other neurons. Another way of measuring brain growth is speed processing. Newborns are considerably slower than adults—16 times less efficient—and the brain does not reach maximum size until about 15 years of age (Zero to Three, 1998–2001).

### Genes and the Environment.
The environment and the genes play a very important role in brain development. Interactions between the genes and the environment are crucial for brain development and they play different roles:

> Generally speaking, genes are responsible for the basic wiring plan—for forming all of the cells (neurons) and general connections between different brain regions—while experience is responsible for the fine-tuning of these connections, helping each child adapt to the particular environment (geographical, cultural, family, school, and peer group) to which he belongs. (Zero to Three, 1998–2001, p. 1)

According to Diamond (2009), it is experience that helps to wake up the dormant genes; therefore "the environment participates in sculpting expression of the genome" (p. 1).

### Early Interactions and Brain Development.
Engaging children from infancy is extremely important, as it is estimated that the number of synapses reaches adult level by age 2, and by age 3, a child's

brain is two and one half times more active than the brain of an adult. It is estimated that by age 3, the child's brain has a quadrillion synapses. The number holds steady for the first decade. After the child reaches 19, the synapses decline in density, and by late adolescence, half of the synapses have been discarded and 500 trillion remain (Shore, 1997). Elimination varies related to the area of the brain. Huttenlocher (1979, as cited in Shonkoff & Phillips, 2000) researched the production of synapses and the pruning that reduces the amount of synapses to adult level. He estimated that various areas of the brain have different patterns of synapse development and pruning. The visual cortex production occurs about midway of the first year, followed by a gradual reduction by the middle of the preschool period. The part of the brain responsible for language and hearing is similar but somewhat later. In the prefrontal area, which contains higher-level cognition, the proliferation of synapses begins around the first year, but adult level is not reached until middle to late adolescence.

A look at the development of vision illustrates one journey of growth. Infant vision is still developing when the child is born. At 1 month, the infant has poor contrast sensitivity and relatively poor color recognition. By 2 months, the baby can distinguish between many colors, including red, blue, and green. While their visual acuity and sensitivity to contrast at this age improves, it is still about 20 times less developed than adults' and has immature focus. By the third month, dramatic changes help the infant see shapes clearer, although depth perception is not fully developed. Color vision is similar to that of an adult's color vision. The baby has also developed a sense of recognition so that when a parent picks up and holds the infant, the child is aware and recognizes the parent. By 6 months of age, there is rapid improvement in eye development. The baby can focus at different distances as well as an adult can, and their motion detection continues to improve (Restak, 2001).

As infants continue to develop, their need for exploration increases. Soska, Adolph, and Johnson (2010) indicate that the infant's motor and perceptual abilities help with exploration. The more opportunities for exploration and movement the infant is given, the greater the chances for acquisition of new skills. Therefore, the early experiences that parents provide for their children are crucial for their development, though individual experiences for children will vary depending on their families.

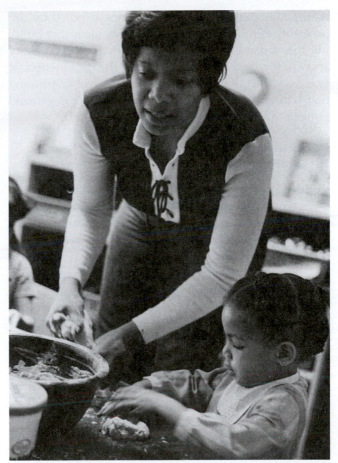

For children to achieve their potential, it is essential for families and educators to show support and caring.

## Wiring of the Brain

The proliferation of synapses occurs around the sixth month and reduces to adult amount later in early childhood. Experience is critical in the "wiring" of a child's brain. When a stimulus activates a neural path, the synapses receive and store a chemical signal. If synapses are used repeatedly, they are strengthened, reach a threshold level, and become permanent. If not used repeatedly, they are pruned and eliminated (Shore, 1997):

> In the first decade of life, a child's brain forms trillions of connection synapses. Axons hook up with dendrites, and chemicals called neurotransmitters facilitate the passage of impulses across the resulting synapses. Each individual neuron may be connected to as many as 15,000 other neurons, forming a network of neural pathways that is immensely complex. This elaborate network is sometimes referred to as the brain's "wiring" or "circuitry." (p. 17)

It appears that if synapses are not used, they are probably eliminated: "It is reasonably clear that building the organized neural systems that guide sensory and motor development involves the production of excess connections followed by some sort of pruning that leaves the system in a more precisely organized pattern" (Shonkoff & Phillips, 2000, p. 189).

## Importance of Family Interactions for Brain Development

Children learn and develop with their own developmental timetable, but they need interaction with their caregivers, mothers, fathers, and others to help in that development. When one realizes how rapidly the newborn infant's brain develops, a question emerges: How should the mother, father, and caregivers respond to best aid the development?

### Language Interactions with Parents or Caregivers.
Providing a safe environment helps infants and young children as well as families feel valued and respected. It is also important to develop a secure and positive relationship with the infant through holding him or her in a loving and comforting manner. Babies need cradling, gentle touch, and eye contact. They also need to hear a voice, whether singing or talking to them, while they are being dressed or fed. Be sure to respond to the baby's sounds; they too will try to imitate the sound that they hear. This will help them to develop a sense of language.

It is also important for families to continue to share their cultural values with their children because these values are assets to their children's development. For example, parents can play culturally significant music for their children. Interestingly, Soley and Hannon (2010) found that infants appear to prefer music that has culture-specific meaning—music from their native culture. Nursery rhymes in the child's heritage language assist young children to learn the sounds of that language. For example, parents can recite Mother Goose rhymes to increase language awareness because they are just fun to repeat. Young children also enjoy looking at colorful picture books and reading books with their caregivers, particularly when they can relate to the book themselves. A great example is Sandra Cisneros's book *Hairs/Pelitos*, in which the main character talks about the different types of hair that her family has.

Providing a safe environment is important so that infants and young children as well as families feel valued and respected. It is also important for families to continue to share their funds of knowledge with their children because these are assets to their children's development.

### Emotional and Cognitive Interactions with Parents and Caregivers.
According to Dowling (2010), there is a link between feelings and brain development that is crucial in the early years. Children who have healthy emotional development have supportive families that guide them through different emotions in order to develop strong cognitive skills such as problem solving, perception, and reasoning.

Six levels of developing emotional and intellectual health in children are described by Greenspan (2002). At the first level, when a familiar caregiver touches and talks with the infant, the child responds with interest and pleasure. This helps the child develop a feeling of security and also helps the child organize his or her senses and motor responses. When children do not receive interaction from their caregiver, they withdraw and become apathetic and despondent.

The second level of development occurs by 4 months, when infants begin to respond to a parent's smile. Emotional responses precede the child's motor ability. These emotional responses can be observed by watching a 4- or 5-month-old baby smile in response to another's smile. By 9 months, there are early forms of communication and thinking. Two-way communication with the mother talking and the baby responding occurs.

The emotional abilities developed earlier become the building blocks in the third level at 12 to 18 months. The child has greater ability to problem solve. The fourth level focuses on the toddler who needs to increasingly develop the use of emotional cueing, more often referred to as affect cueing.

The fifth level includes symbols that have purpose and meaning, as seen in preteen play. The sixth level finds the child able to use cause-and-effect thinking, recognizing others' ideas with his or her own intent and feelings. This level allows impulse control, judgment, and reality testing (Greenspan, 2002).

## Positive Environment, Healthy Families, and Children

As already discussed, a child's brain is not fixed at birth but rather is affected by the nourishment, care, and stimulation it receives. The interactions that children have with their families and other support systems are crucial for a healthy development:

- How a brain develops hinges on a complex interplay between the *genes* you're born with and the *experiences* you have.
- Early experiences have *decisive impact* on the architecture of the brain and on the nature and extent of adult capacities.
- Early interactions don't just create a context; they directly affect the way the brain is "wired."
- Brain development is nonlinear. There are prime times for acquiring different kinds of knowledge and skills.
- By the time children reach age 3, their brains are twice as active as those of adults. Activity levels drop during adolescence (Shore, 1997, p. 18).

Because the environment has an impact on the brain even before birth, trauma and abuse can harm it and interfere with its development. For example, exposure to nicotine, alcohol, or other drugs affects the child before and after birth. It influences not only the child's general development but also the wiring of the brain.

All this shows the importance of promoting nourishing, caring, responsive environments for healthy brain development.

## Early Experiences

Children are primed for learning during the early years. Their experiences in the first 3 years affect their growth and abilities for the rest of their childhood and as adults. According to Newman (1996), "Early stimulation is essential to normal development" (p. 15)—both normal brain development as well as emotional development. This is because when the environment is nurturing and stimulating, it results in both neurological brain development and human attachment (Brazelton & Greenspan, 2000). Parents must be able to read their babies' cues and respond to infants' feelings, knowing when they need stimulation, when they need to be left alone, and when they need comforting.

## Insights for Teachers and Administrators

1. Knowing different perspectives or theories regarding child development can help us understand parents' childrearing practices.
2. Strong attachments make strong children—give parents an opportunity to get used to leaving their children in the care of others.
3. Know the needs of the families, as this will enable you to assist families with their needs as well as their children's needs.
4. Find resources around the community that will help the center or school support children's development.

## SUMMARY

Strong families have strong parents who know how to meet the needs of their children regardless of the stressors that they face. Families need to know that what they offer their children—their funds of knowledge—are valued by the school and other extended systems. In order to identify funds of knowledge, teachers must know the family's cultural and social background. When working with diverse families in an early childhood program, it is very important to keep in mind ethnicity and national origin, language, religion or spiritual practice, special needs, socioeconomic status, and sexual orientation, as these characteristics of families help in the creation of funds of knowledge. It is important to keep in mind too that systems vary, and they change related to the circumstances in the family.

Parents are their child's first educators and as such are responsible for providing an environment that facilitates attachment and brain development in their child. All three responsibilities are extremely important for the child's subsequent development.

Child development theories help teachers and parents identify appropriate and quality environments for children. Theories of attachment help parents understand that when they provide children with strong attachments from birth, children will develop a healthy understanding of friendships and relationships that may last for a lifetime. The Ecological Systems Theory provides parent and educators a blueprint regarding how the community, the school, the teacher, and the family work together to promote children's overall development.

## SUGGESTED CLASS ACTIVITIES AND DISCUSSIONS

1. Make a list of the funds of knowledge that have been given to you by your family. Interview two families different than your own. Make a list of their funds of knowledge. Find similarities and differences between families. Share with the class.

2. Using the book *Cuadros de Familia* (or *Family Pictures*) by Carmen Lomas Garza, make your own book with your family pictures. You can draw the pictures or use real photographs. Write in the text that describes your family's traditions, beliefs, and cultural practices. Share with the class.

3. Using Family Ecological Systems Theory concentric circles, look for resources in your community that collaborate with families. Make a list including addresses, phone numbers, and Web sites to begin creating a Support Systems Resource Guide. Add information as needed.

4. Take the quiz regarding brain development on the Zero to Three Web site, www.zerotothree .org/, to examine your knowledge of brain development.

## USEFUL WEB SITES

**Engaging Diverse Families**
www.naeyc.org/ecp/trainings/edf
These family programs have been recognized by NAEYC for engaging diverse families.

**Funds of Knowledge**
www.learnnc.org/lp/pages/939
Teachers can use "funds of knowledge" to make their classrooms more inclusive.

**Learning from Language Minority Households**
www.cal.org/resources/digest/ncrcds01.html
An inaccurate assumption on the part of many educators has often led to lowered academic expectations.

**United Way Worldwide**
www.unitedway.org/worldwide/
This worldwide movement mobilizes millions in order to improve the conditions in which they live.

**Zero to Three**
www.zerotothree.org
This organization informs, trains, and supports professionals, policymakers, and parents in an effort to improve the lives of infants and toddlers.

# 2

# Diversity of Families

*Respect and value from teachers and administrators will help diverse families achieve emotional well-being.*

Mari Riojas-Cortez

*In this chapter on the diversity of families, you will find information that will help you examine the strengths and needs of families and enable you to do the following:*

- Define the term *family*.
- Identify different types of families.
- Examine different functions of families.
- List and explain parenting styles.
- Discuss the greater involvement of fathers in rearing their children.
- Discuss how poverty and homelessness affect today's families.

## ▪▪ FAMILIES

### Definition of Family

The U.S. Census Bureau (2010) defines a **family** as "a group of two or more people who reside together and who are related by birth, marriage, or adoption," while a **household** is defined as "all people who occupy a housing unit as their usual place of residence." A family is a socially constructed concept (Weigel, 2008). The definition of *family* fits many of the families today, particularly those who come from culturally and linguistically diverse backgrounds.

The importance of the family unit in the socialization of children cannot be overstated. It is essential that children have a supportive, interactive environment that provides loving, caring relationships so that children develop emotionally, intellectually, and physically. Families in the United States and around the world are living with change, but the essence of the family remains stable, with family members needing a permanent relationship on which they can count for consistency, understanding, and support. If the family provides for the basic needs of its members and is connected, reducing isolation and alienation, then the family will flourish—truly, as the provider for and socializing agent of children, the family has no match. Regardless of the structure, the family gives the nurture and support needed by its members and is a viable, working unit. Families need to be respected as such.

### Survival of Society Depends upon Families

Families across cultures have different ways of displaying affection, but children cannot thrive physically or emotionally without the nurturance

Unity helps families operate within a variety of systems.

of those who love and care for them; this is particularly true of children with special needs. For example, my son, who has autism, does extremely well when people who work with him praise him and respond to his hugs. This is important to note because in our family, we like to give hugs and praise one another as part of our funds of knowledge. Therefore, the caregiver must understand the family's socialization practices in order to collaborate with the family to provide safe and healthy experiences to assist in the child's development (Casper, Cooper, & Finn, 2003).

Parenting is challenging for any family, and extended family members such as grandparents often take on the responsibility of teaching child-rearing practices. In the Latino community, for example, this may be done through *consejos* (Valdés, 1996), or cultural narratives that elders

Immigrant families try to maintain traditions for the socioemotional well-being of their children.

within the family provide not only to maintain traditions but to help in the healthy development of children.

## :: STAGES IN FAMILY LIFE

The stages of family life, developed by Galinsky (1987), divide parenthood into six levels of development, much like the child's stages of development. Because each child has different needs for every stage, it is important for educators to understand the stages so they can provide families with the assistance needed to ensure healthy development of their children.

The first stage, **image making,** takes place before the birth of a child. Images are formed and preparation is made for the birth. This is where parents may get the nursery ready and buy clothes for the infant. Family members and others may help those parents who may not be able to provide for the infant. The second stage, **nurturing,** is when attachment develops during infancy. Parents and

infants begin to develop their relationship through different types of interactions such as breast-feeding, playing, reading, singing, and just holding the baby. In the third stage, **authority,** families help their child understand the norms of the society. As children get older, they begin to learn social rules, such as turn taking and sharing. During the fourth stage, from preschool to adolescence, parents offer **guidance** and children learn to interpret their social reality. Children throughout the elementary years practice social skills that are appropriate for their age. Families help children learn those rules by reinforcing expectations in the home and school. The **interdependent** years, the teens, make up the fifth stage of family development. When the children are ready to go out into the world for themselves, the family enters the last stage: **departure.** During the high school years, children develop a different type of independence that allows them to go out in the world to practice what they learned throughout their childhood. During each of these stages, parents provide the guidance necessary for that stage of development.

## :: DIVERSITY OF FAMILIES

The structure, stage of family development, family size, and ages and genders of the children all figure into the makeup of each unique family. According to Knopf and Swick (2008), families in today's society are very different than those from previous generations. The families presented in the following vignettes represent a few examples of the diversity, especially the diversity of structure, encountered in many families. Think about the families that you work with and see if any are similar to the ones presented in these examples.

### Single-Parent Family

Tina is a young divorced mother with one son, Tommy, age 3. They live with Tina's parents. In addition to working part-time at a department store, Tina takes 6 hours of classes at the community college. Each morning she prepares breakfast for Tommy and herself, bundles him into his coat during cold weather, hopes that her aging automobile will start, and heads into her long day. First, she drops Tommy off with her sister, who runs a family child-care home. She feels fortunate to have a relative who enjoys children to care for Tommy. He has been anxious ever since his father left, and the security of spending his days at Aunt Georgia's helps compensate for his loss.

Tina's ex-husband, Ted, does not send support money consistently, and Tina knows her parents can help only so much. As she works as a clerk in the department store, she dreams of the time when she will make enough to give Tommy the home and opportunities he needs. Tina figures that with family help and her part-time college work, she will be able to graduate in a little more than 2 years, just about the time Tommy will start school.

## Single Teenage Mother

As Sherrill thinks back, she can't remember when she didn't want a baby. "When I have a baby," she thought, "I'll be treated like an adult by my mother, and I'll also have a baby all my own who will love me." At 3 months, though, Gerald has already become a real handful.

Sherrill turned 15 yesterday, and instead of being able to hang out with her friends, she had to take care of Gerald. "If only my mother hadn't had to work," Sherrill complained, "I would have had a couple of hours between feedings just to get out. I never dreamed a baby would be so demanding. What makes him cry so much?"

The school down the street offers a program for teen mothers and their infants. Sherrill is on the waiting list and plans to enroll at the end of summer. "I never thought I'd want to go back to school," she says, "but they help out by caring for my baby while I'm in class and my mother says that I need to be able to make a living for Gerald. Temporary Assistance to Needy Families will help me for only 24 months. I really don't like school, but I guess I'd better go. If only Gerald would start being more fun."

## Two-Parent Family Experiencing Homelessness

When Barbara married Jed, the future looked good. Young, handsome, and hardworking, Jed thought his job at the plant would last forever. Who would have expected the layoffs? Jed's father worked at the plant for 25 years before he retired. Now Jed and Barbara, along with Jessie, age 2, and Bob, age 6, are moving west in hopes of finding work.

It's hard to live out of a car. Barbara worries about Bob because he is missing first grade. She and Jed put him in school whenever they are in a city for any length of time, but schools want his permanent address. It embarrasses Barbara to say their family is homeless, so she finds out the name of a street near the school and pretends they live there. Bob doesn't like school anyway. He says the children make fun of him and the teacher gives him seatwork that he doesn't understand.

Jed feels as if he has failed as a father and provider for his family. If he could just find a good job, his family would not be homeless. Minimum wage doesn't give him enough to pay for rent, let alone buy clothing and food. Last month they spent time at a church-run mission for the homeless. Jed was glad that they were in a town far from home so that none of his old school friends would recognize him and Barbara. Jed hopes that maybe a good factory job will turn up.

## Two-Income Family

"Joe, the alarm. It's your turn to get up and start breakfast," Maria says as she turns over to get 10 more minutes of sleep before the drive to school. Each day Maria teaches 28 second graders in the adjoining school district. Joe teaches mathematics at the local middle school. It works exceedingly well for them. Their children, Karen and Jaime, stay with a neighbor until it is time for them to walk to school. Joe and Maria take turns dashing home early enough in the afternoon to supervise the children after school.

At times, the stress of work and the demanding days get to Joe and Maria. Some days their schedules do not blend, and they scurry to find someone to care for the children after school. Karen and Jaime occasionally have been latchkey children, providing for themselves. Neither Joe nor Maria wants their children to be left on their own. They see too many children in their classrooms in similar situations who feel as if no one cares. Joe tries to be a nurturing father who helps with the home, but he relies on Maria to clean, shop, and cook.

Summers are the best time for the family. Joe works for a summer camp, but Maria is able to spend more time at home, enjoying the children and organizing for the coming year. Periodically, she thinks about how much easier it would be for her to quit teaching and be a full-time homemaker, but then reality sets in. They could not make the house payments if they were not a two-income family—and a family needs a home.

## The Immigrant Family

The Gonzalez family moved to the United States from San Luis Potosí, México, 10 years ago when their two older children were very young. After Juan and Leticia married, they decided to move to the United States to provide a better life for their children. Without proper documents, the newly-wed couple decided to venture to a new country where life is very different from their life in rural Mexico. Juan found work in construction while Leticia worked as a babysitter for children from an affluent neighborhood. Because Leticia and Juan work long hours, they have not been able to attend ESL classes at their local church, although they have tried. Their two oldest children have to translate for them when they receive notes from school or go to the doctor. Juan and Leticia have thought about going back to their home country, but they know life would be harder. Here, they live in a community close to family, and Leticia's aunt takes care of their youngest two children.

The above examples show some of the variety in family structure. Regardless of the structure, most families have support groups such as extended family to provide love and care when parents are not present. Even when families deal with difficult situations, strong families learn to cope with difficulties because they want to see their children succeed in school.

It is important for educators to understand how each of these structures (and others not discussed) affects families. Following are some suggestions for remaining sensitive to different family structures.

### Insights for Teachers and Administrators

1. Understand that there are different types of families.
2. All families need support and guidance but in different ways, particularly those who come from different countries and those with children with special needs.
3. Families that are not familiar with the school system are going to need more support in order to understand the school's expectations.
4. Provide a link to your center's or school's Web site with relevant information for each type of family.

5. Make school routines and procedures parent friendly by making things easy for parents. Avoid scolding parents if they have not followed procedures; instead, sit down and gently explain what needs to be accomplished.

## :: FUNCTIONS OF FAMILIES

Although their forms vary, families provide similar roles. Swick (1986) described these roles as "(1) nurturing, (2) guiding, (3) problem solving, and (4) modeling" (p. 72). Cataldo (1987) described similar roles: providing "care, nurturance, and protection"; socialization; "monitoring the child's development as a learner"; and supporting "each youngster's growth into a well-rounded, emotionally healthy person" (p. 28).

The first function of a family is to nurture by supplying the basic needs of nutrition, protection, and shelter as well as the emotional needs of interaction, love, and support. The family has a responsibility to see that the child receives adequate care but also a right to rear the child as it sees fit. This is important to remember, as many families in the United States are becoming more diverse as more families come from different countries and as American families (with children born and raised in the United States) develop new childrearing practices and beliefs. Educators need to understand these differences in order to better work with young children and their families. When differences are understood—particularly cultural differences—educators open the door to create partnerships with families that aid in the healthy development of children.

Part of understanding cultural differences is having knowledge of how parents socialize their children according to their native culture's norms. Socialization varies, depending on the culture. For example, respect for elders is a norm in most cultures, but in others, such as Latino and Asian cultures, it is even more important in the socialization process. Another example is the role the extended family plays in the raising of children—for some cultures, the role is very integral, whereas in others, this may not be the case. There are also variations within cultures that often result from how the parents were raised. For instance, in some African

American families, speaking Ebonics is very important (Boutte & Strickland, 2008). Whatever the rearing process, most children learn and internalize their parents' value system.

## :: PARENTING STYLES

Parents play a key role in ensuring that their family creates a strong bond regardless of the family structure. The roles that a parent plays are largely based on his/her parenting style which is also culturally-based. Parenting styles (some of which are more effective than others) are often identified as *authoritative, authoritarian,* or *laissez-faire* (see Table 2.1).

Each of these types has different ways of handling issues and concerns within the family. In addition, depending on the circumstance, responses even in

**TABLE 2.1**

**Parenting Styles** The manner in which families socialize their children varies. Three major styles—**authoritative, authoritarian**, and **laissez-faire**—include a multitude of styles.

| Family Type | Characteristics |
| --- | --- |
| Authoritative | Democratic decision making<br>Guidelines and parameters<br>Effective communication<br>Problem solving<br>Self-discipline and responsibility |
| Authoritarian (might be overprotective) | Demanding parent<br>Absolute rules<br>Restrictive environment<br>Punitive control<br>Strong guidelines |
| Laissez-faire (might be very indulgent) | Anything goes<br>Neglectful parent<br>No one cares<br>Withdrawal from parental responsibilities |
| Dysfunctional (includes authoritative, authoritarian, and laissez-faire families) | Alcohol- or drug-addicted<br>Neurotic or mentally ill<br>Abusive |

families with the same parenting style may vary. The style recommended by parent educators is the authoritative, democratic style because it is thought that children raised under that style will achieve, be dependable and responsible, and feel good about themselves.

Children raised with authoritative parents will be allowed to analyze and recognize the issues confronting them. Guidance will be available but will not be dictated. Children will learn to make decisions. Through working and talking together, they will be able to learn why angry, quick decisions are not effective.

Children with authoritarian parents are expected to mind their parents without any question about what precipitated the issue. The children do not get an opportunity to resolve a conflict or learn from actions, except to learn that punishment will follow no matter what the situation. They receive little training in decision making. Under this parenting style, children may learn to mind, but they also learn to avoid being caught and perhaps to lie when they are.

Children of laissez-faire rearing often think that their parents are not interested in them. The children may be depressed, act out, or take risks because they do not feel their parents care. In addition, they get little to no guidance to help them make decisions. While children may think they enjoy the freedom of a laissez-faire parenting style, too much freedom makes it possible for children to think that they do not matter.

There are also two subtypes that do not fit into the three major types. One is the overprotective parent, who can often become authoritarian. The other is the indulgent parent, who may not guide the child. Dysfunctional families—including those that are abusive or that have parents who are addicted to drugs or alcohol or are mentally unstable—may fluctuate between authoritarian (to the point of abuse) and laissez-faire, with abdication of parental roles. One of the most difficult issues that children in dysfunctional families face is the inconsistency. Dependable families in which children understand the guidelines and can communicate with and rely on their parents are extremely important to children's mental health.

If the types of families are multiplied by the number of configurations of families (single, two-parent, and blended) and the individual personality differences of each child and parent, it becomes apparent that to work effectively with parents, teachers and child-care workers must individualize their suggestions and responses.

### Insights for Teachers and Administrators

1. Realize that all parents are going to have different parenting styles, and each style will have its own needs. Get to know parents in order to better communicate with them regarding their children. Conduct a needs-assessment survey to identify the needs of parents depending on their parenting style. Provide 1-hour parenting workshops that target all parenting styles. Provide additional resources for those parents who need them.
2. Provide a variety of opportunities for parents to become involved in the school or classroom. Have a list ready for the first day of school.
3. Adopt before- and after-school programs that offer enriching activities for the child and safe child care for the family.
4. Keep the parents informed on the progress of their child. Set aside some time each week during which the parents can telephone you or contact you via e-mail.
5. Initiate telephone calls at a convenient time for both you and the parents to share something positive about the child. Texting a short message will brighten a parent's day. Hold a get-acquainted evening program for parents. Ask them to fill out a chart so they may share needs with others. Allow parents to decide on the extent of their participation.
6. Use the Internet to share class information. E-mail individual parents to share positive comments about the class or the child. Take digital photos during classroom activities and e-mail them to parents (make sure you have permission to photograph).
7. Videotape class activities or programs that are important to the children so that the parents who were unable to attend may view them later.
8. Make home visits at a time convenient for the family.

## :: GREATER INVOLVEMENT OF FATHERS WITH THEIR CHILDREN

From the Puritan times until industrialization, a "good" father was the breadwinner and provider of moral guidance. Fathers have long held these two roles, but in the 20th century, the importance of fathers' roles in their children's development underwent change based on social conditions and beliefs as well as research in child development. In the 21st century, fathers exhibit willingness to provide expanded roles as companions, standard setters, guidance counselors, play partners, teachers, providers, caregivers, and role models. The National Center for Fathering (2010) lists the following situations for many fathers in the United States today: adoptive dad, at-home dad, divorced dad, noncustodial dad, single dad, stepdad, traveling dad, special needs–kids dad, and urban dad. Also very important but not listed is the married dad.

The Children's Bureau, established in 1912, provides information to families about caring for their infants in the publication *Infant Care.* Historically, although fathers were mentioned in the publication, the advice was directed to mothers. Fathers were not considered as important to the child's development until the 1940s. Awareness of the father as a gender-role model came about toward the end of World War II, but it was not until the 1970s that the role of nurturant father was emphasized (Lamb, 1997).

Some advocates for fathers argue that in the 20th century, fathers were viewed as superfluous: "The retreat from fatherhood began in the 1960s, gained momentum in the 1970s, and hit full stride in the 1980s" (Horn, 1997, p. 24). In the 1990s, however, organizations that focused on fathers emerged, including the National Institute for Responsible Fatherhood and Family Development, Promise Keepers, National Centers for Fathering, and the

All children need a nurturing relationship with their fathers.

National Fatherhood Initiative. These groups responded to data about the negative aspects of being raised without a father, including that children are "three times more likely to fail at school, two to three times more likely to experience emotional or behavioral problems requiring psychiatric treatment . . . three times more likely to commit suicide as adolescents . . . five times more likely to be poor" (p. 27). Even when the families came from the same socioeconomic background, children without a father present had more challenges than those who had both parents (Horn, 1997). In two-parent families, it is important that family members are supportive of one another and that conflict and abuse be absent. For children growing up without a father, having a male as a father figure such as an uncle or grandfather seems to have a positive effect in their lives.

## Research on Father Involvement

If the parents have supportive relationships with one another and their children, the children thrive. But, as studies show, stressors such as drinking, marital conflict, and negative parenting are directly related to children internalizing problems (Schacht, Cummings, & Davies, 2009), and children "who have secure, supportive, reciprocal, and sensitive relationships with their parents are much more likely to be well-adjusted psychologically than individuals whose relationships with their parents—mothers or fathers—are less satisfying" (Lamb, 1997, p. 13). Current studies suggest that fathers' involvement may help offset negative effects on child development when mothers are not as supportive (Martin, Ryan, & Brooks-Gunn, 2010). Even when mothers are supportive, research shows that fathers' more physical style of interacting with their children supports and adds to the nurturing and verbal style of the mother (Horn, 1997; Lamb, 1997).

As a father's parental role grows beyond just that of a breadwinner, so do the father's attitudes toward parenting. In a national survey conducted by Zero to Three (2010), it was found that fathers today are not satisfied with work/family balance, they find challenges in a variety of parenting situations, and they need more information regarding social development. However, the National Center for Fathering and the National Parent Teacher Association (2009) surveys indicate that fathers today seem to be more involved with their children than they were 10 years ago.

High levels of father involvement indicate positive outcomes in cognitive and socioemotional development (Halme, Astedt-Kurk, & Tarkka, 2009). Indeed, the presence of a father indicates that a child will have the opportunity to have a healthy upbringing (The National Center on Fathers and Families, 2010). The Fathering Indicator Framework provides six positive fathering indicator categories: father presence, caregiving, children's social competence, cooperative parenting, father's healthy living, and material and financial contribution. Operational categories accompany the fathering indicator categories to be used by programs to guide research regarding the importance of fathers in a child's life, as well how fathers' participation creates a change in behavior in child and family, and how the effects are threaded together to help men become more positively involved in children's lives (National Center on Fathers and Families, 2011).

The research regarding father involvement shows that in any family, regardless of the structure, children will benefit from a positive involvement with their fathers.

## Importance of Fathers

Heightened interest in fatherhood goes hand in hand with the increasing number of women who work outside the home. Many young fathers see the expression of love toward their children as a way of fulfillment in their own lives through meaningful relationships. Some fathers are full-time homemakers and care for the children while their wives work outside the home.

Although fathers and mothers are similar in their connection with their children, fathers tend to be more physically stimulating through unpredictable play, whereas mothers tend toward containment and soft, repetitive verbal expression. Both the father's more physical and the mother's more verbal interactions are beneficial for the child (Lamb, 1997). Furthermore, fathers of children with special needs have a tremendous responsibility of making sure they bond with the child but that they also keep a strong bond with their other children (Huhtanen, 2009).

In the National Association for the Education of Young Children (NAEYC) accredited child-care programs, fathers preferred involvement in (a) family activities, (b) Daddy and Me programs, (c) activities for both parents to learn about their child's future, (d) activities for both parents to learn about child development, and (e) sporting events (Turbiville, Umbarger, & Guthrie, 2000).

### Suggestions for Fathers

1. *Be there.* Engage in activities with your child, from the early caregiving bathing and bedroom routine to the later reading, storytelling, and playing together activities.
2. *Accept your child.* Accept your child for who she or he is. Each child has an individual personality. Trying to change a quiet child into a boisterous one or an uncoordinated child into an outstanding athlete makes the child feel unaccepted.
3. *Use positive parenting.* Praise is better than punishment in guiding children. Help the child express anger constructively.
4. *Share parenting.* Work as a team with your spouse or with the mother of your children.
5. *See fathering as worthwhile and satisfying.* "Children need their fathers to help them with skills and decision making, and to feel competent and good about themselves" (Ballantine, 1999/2000, p. 105).
6. *Be there for your children.* Listen and be involved in their education from early childhood on.

### Involving Fathers in Schools and Centers

The first step in getting fathers, brothers, uncles, and other male role models involved is to keep in mind that the term *father* extends to all father figures. Because many children do not have a father in the home, inclusion of father figures is extremely important. Encourage family friends, uncles, grandfathers, stepfathers, and interested others to become support systems for children.

Many schools and centers have developed ways to involve fathers and other male role models. Fourteen of these programs are described in *Getting Men Involved* (Levine et al., 1993), but there are several others. For example, there is the National Fathering Network, which has affiliates in 35 states. Another example is the Kindering

Center in Bellevue, Washington, a support group for fathers raising children with special needs. The Parents as Teachers program in Ferguson-Florissant, Missouri, has established programs for teenage parents and parents-to-be. The FRED (Fathers Reading Every Day) program focuses on reading. AVANCE also offers a father involvement program that focuses on increasing father interactions with children and decreasing violence in the home (AVANCE, 2011).

### Insights for Teachers and Administrators

1. When fathers drop off or pick up their children at school, make an effort to talk with them, not just the mother.
2. Encourage fathers to participate in the classroom.
3. Send newsletters to fathers and other male relatives. Send a newsletter to noncustodial fathers, unless the courts object to contact with the noncustodial parent. Include a picture and an article about a father participating in the classroom.
4. Schedule conferences at times that are convenient for both parents. Encourage the father to come and participate.
5. Have a special conference with the noncustodial parent, if the courts permit and if it appears to be counterproductive for both custodial and noncustodial parents to be present at the same time.
6. Make telephone calls or send texts letting both parents know about something the child has done that was interesting and positive.
7. Ask a father who participates to recruit another, or pair up two fathers (one new and one "veteran") so that the more seasoned father can model for the father who is unfamiliar with the classroom.
8. Make home visits at a time when both parents will be there.
9. Videotape children in the classroom to share with parents. Include fathers working in the classroom in the video so that fathers see they are welcome to participate.
10. Include activities that appeal to fathers. Let them help with all types of classroom involvement, but also have activities such as games, exercise, or physical activities that fathers would feel comfortable overseeing.
11. Present a workshop that allows both parents to participate in the class so they become familiar with the expectations and activities.

> Encourage them to attend workshops on helping in the classroom, parenting skills, and conflict resolution.
> 12. Plan field trips such as visits to a zoo, farm, or museum. Ask both parents to accompany and participate.
> 13. Plan a family evening where both parents come and read with their children.
> 14. Learn from and listen to fathers. Appreciate their contributions.

## :: DIVORCE

The divorce rate in America has fluctuated between 2000 and 2009, with the highest rates in 2000 and 2001 (see Figure 2-1).

The economic status of parents who divorce changes drastically—about 1 quarter or 24.6 percent of all custodial parents and their children had incomes below the poverty level in 2007. Issues such as health care and child support that custodial and non custodial parents face affect their and their children's economic well-being (Grall, 2007).

### Divorce Causes Changes in Families

Divorce involves change for both parents and children but can be particularly difficult for children. Children are usually ashamed of the divorce and feel rejected because of a parent's departure, but the effects of divorce on children are related more to the previous situation and the subsequent events that affect the child than to the divorce itself. Despite most children's negative feelings about their parents' separation, divorce may improve the situation for a child in cases where a successful reestablished single-parent family or a remarriage provides the child with a good quality of life. Oftentimes, too, children's initial adverse feelings reduce over time; their risk at school is much lower even just a year after the divorce than immediately following it. How well and how quickly children adjust to a divorce depend on a few conditions (Shaw, 1992, p. 182):

- Relationships of parents following divorce. Are the parents amicable, or do they use the children as ammunition against each other?
- Separation from a parent who is significant to the child.
- The parenting skills and relationship of the children with the custodial parent.
- The relationship of children with the nonresidential parent.
- Economics and financial ability to keep a standard of living.

### Children's Responses

Children of all ages respond to the divorce of their parents. Wallerstein (1985) found that younger children seem to suffer the most at the time of the divorce, but in a 10-year follow-up, older girls still harbored feelings of betrayal and rejection by men, making commitment to their own romantic relationships difficult. Generally,

**FIGURE 2–1**

Provisional number of divorces and annulments and rate: United States, 2000 – 2009.

| Year | Divorces and annulments | Population | Rate per 1,000 total population | Year | Divorces and annulments | Population | Rate per 1,000 total population |
|------|------|------|------|------|------|------|------|
| 2009[1] | 840,000 | 242,497,000 | 3.5 | 2004[2] | 879,000 | 237,042,000 | 3.7 |
| 2008[1] | 844,000 | 240,663,000 | 3.5 | 2003[3] | 927,000 | 245,200,000 | 3.8 |
| 2007[1] | 856,000 | 238,759,000 | 3.6 | 2002[4] | 955,000 | 243,600,000 | 3.9 |
| 2006[1] | 872,000 | 236,172,000 | 3.7 | 2001[5] | 940,000 | 236,650,000 | 4.0 |
| 2005[1] | 847,000 | 234,114,000 | 3.6 | 2000[5] | 944,000 | 233,550,000 | 4.0 |

[1]Excludes data for California, Georgia, Hawaii, Indiana, Louisiana, and Minnesota. [2]Excludes data for California, Georgia, Hawaii, Indiana, and Louisiana. [3]Excludes data for California, Hawaii, Indiana, and Oklahoma. [4]Excludes data for California, Indiana, and Oklahoma. [5]Excludes data for California, Indiana, Louisiana, and Oklahoma.

*Note:* Populations are consistent with the 2000 census.

*Note:* The term "provisional" in this context indicates that the statistics are constantly changing.

*Source:* National Center for Health Statistics, CDC. www.cdc.gov/nchs/nvss/marriage_divorce_tables.htm

though, if the quality of life after the divorce was good, children did well. If parents continued to fight over the children or burdened their children with too much responsibility, "in short, if stress and deprivation continue after the divorce—then children are likely to suffer depression and interrupted development" (Wallerstein, 1985, p. 8).

Another part of helping children adjust to divorce is to reassure them they are not the cause of it. They also need to know by the parents' actions and words that they will continue to have their parents' love. Adapt your caring for children to their level of development—their understanding and response are related to their age and maturity (Leon & Cole, 2004):

1. Older infants and toddlers realize that one of their parents no longer lives with them. Infants need reassurance and tender caregiving.
2. Toddlers need reassurance of their parents' love. There may be evidence of regression in some of their skills but, with support, they can regain their development.
3. Preschool and early elementary children are more likely to blame themselves for the divorce. They need reassurance, support, and connection with the parent who no longer lives at home.

## Insights for Teachers and Administrators

1. Teachers and administrators must also recognize that during the period of divorce, the family may be in turmoil. Children will bring their distress with them to the classroom.
2. The school can offer the child a stable and sensitive environment—one the child can count on—during that period. Provide support and understanding by trying to meet the family's needs. Talk with both parents to see how you can help.
3. If parents use their children as part of their conflict, the children suffer. Ask the counselor to find resources close to the school or center that can help the family.
4. Children often yearn for their parents to reconcile and may blame themselves for the divorce. Provide a "Talk About Feelings" learning center where children can talk to you about their feelings or write or draw what they are feeling.
5. Keep positive expectations for the children. Be kind, but encourage them to keep up with their classwork. Find ways that the child can contribute to the class. Use special projects or activities that may interest the child.

6. Make phone calls to both parents to share a school activity or a positive contribution the child has made to the class.

## Single-Parent Families

Single-parent families are not a new phenomenon. From the 1860s until the mid-1960s, there was no increase in the proportion of single parents because the growing divorce rate was offset by the declining death rate. Young children in the last half of the 1800s and first half of the 1900s were raised in single-parent families, most often because the mother was widowed; 25 percent had lost a parent to death (Amato, 1994). Single-parent mothers worked hard to raise their children by taking in boarders, doing laundry, and somehow managing—with help from their children—to rear the family. Today there are about 13.7 million single parents in the United States. Grall (2009) indicates that 27 percent of custodial single mothers and their children live in poverty, whereas 12.9 percent of custodial single fathers and their children live in poverty.

Gender differences exist for mothers and fathers. For example, during the period that a mother is raising her children alone, she has a much higher risk of poverty. Twelve percent of single parents who work full time find themselves in poverty; 49 percent of those who work part time are also poor. Almost 74 percent of single parents who do not work are in poverty, and 79 percent of single parents are in the labor force (Litcher & Crowley, 2002). Most divorced parents remarry, however,

This single parent supports her child's education by coloring with him.

making it possible for 80 percent of children to live in two-parent homes with reduced risk of poverty.

## Insights for Teachers and Administrators

1. Schools must accept the fact that single-parent families can supply the components necessary for a flourishing, functioning family.
2. Increasing opportunities for talking with teachers and counselors or attending group sessions with other children who have lost a parent through or divorce can be helpful (Lewis, 1992).
3. Parents and teachers need to communicate throughout a child's education, but it is essential during periods of change to know what is happening both at home and at school and to help children overcome the isolation and distress they feel. Although only one in every five children will probably be from a one-parent family at any given time, half of all children will spend part of their childhood in a one-parent family.
4. Offer convenient times for parent–teacher conferences. Single parents (and many two-parent families) need early morning, evening, or weekend times for their conferences as well as for their child care.
5. Acknowledge and communicate with noncustodial parents. If noncustodial parents receive report cards and other information, they likely will be more interested in the child's work and better able to be involved with the child. Most noncustodial parents are men, and the percentage of men who pay child support is low. Schools can help sustain or even increase the father's interest by keeping him informed, if such communication is specified in the custody papers.
6. Learn parents' names. Always check the records to determine the names of the children and the parents because they may not be the same. This applies equally to two-parent families, as roughly half of them will have had a divorce. Calling the parents by their correct names is a simple gesture of courtesy.
7. Find ways that single parents can be involved without putting great stress on the family. Parents who work outside the home might be able to attend early morning breakfasts, especially if child care is provided and the children get breakfast too. Keep the number of parents at each breakfast small so you can talk with each parent individually. Find out how they would like to be involved, what their needs are, and if they have any ideas for their partnership with the school. Acknowledge

their suggestions for improved home–school collaboration.
8. Encourage communication among parents. Establish a newsletter that allows parents to communicate with other parents. Let the parents include what they want to say in the newsletter. Better yet, make it a parent-to-parent newsletter, so they can establish their own networks.
9. Use care in communication. In all partnerships with parents, one of the most important elements of cooperation and understanding is the ability to communicate. The first objective is to have effective communication. The second objective is to prepare written materials that project positive and knowledgeable feelings toward the parent. Take care when preparing invitations to programs. Perhaps you may wish to emphasize one group, but make sure the child and parent know that they do not need to have a father, mother, or grandparent to attend. For example, saying, "Bring your grandparent or a grand-friend to class next week" implies that the visitors, not their titles, are important. At the program, make sure you have some get-acquainted activities so that no one feels left out or alone. Activities also encourage networking among parents, and may be the best opportunity for new single parents in the neighborhood to become acquainted with others.
10. Reach out. To involve both single and working parents, Moles (1996a) suggests the following:

    Develop a single unobtrusive system to keep track of family changes, such as these examples: At the beginning of the year ask for the names and addresses of individuals to be informed about each child and involved in school activities. At mid-year send a form to each child's parents or guardians to verify that the information is still accurate. Invite the parents or guardians to indicate any changes. Work with local businesses to arrange released time from work so that parents can attend conferences, volunteer or in other ways spend time at their child's school when it is in session. (p. 49)
11. Be aware that if the parent remarries, the child is affected again, and concerns arise regarding the loss of the parent as the sole caregiver as well as the strong relationship that may have developed between parent and child. There could also be issues with relationships between the stepparent and the children.

## :: BLENDED FAMILIES

There is a complex social organization in blended families. In remarried families, some children may be offspring of the mother, some of the father, and the remaining may be born to the remarried couple. A child may be living in a home with a brother or sister, a stepbrother or stepsister whose biological parent is the mother or father in the home, and a half-sister or half-brother who is the child of the remarried couple. In addition, they may have a similar situation with their other biological parent and have another set of siblings, stepsiblings, and half-siblings when they are living or visiting there. In fact, families may have as many as 30 configurations (Manning & Wootten, 1987). In addition, there is an increase in families that have blended cultures.

## Blended-Family Cycle

When two people marry and one or both have children from a previous relationship, the road to a secure, happy family becomes more challenging. The members of the new family come with different backgrounds, have no family history together, and have no established way of doing things. Newly blended families need to recognize and mourn their losses, develop the ability to make decisions as a family, support each other, nurture the parent–child relationship, and foster new relationships among their new stepparent and other stepchildren as well as their own parent and siblings (American Academy of Child and Adolescent Psychiatry, 2004). Building a strong new family can be accomplished, but the initial excitement of the children and acceptance of the new arrangement by ex-spouses are complicated by the realities of the situation. One of the complications occurs because both parent and child have come from single-parent family status (even if the single-parent stage is short lived). During the single-parent stage, parent and child tend to become extremely close. The parent may have turned to the children for emotional support and decision-making help in the absence of the former spouse. Children of the newly married couple often see the remarriage as a double loss: First they lost a parent through divorce, and now they are losing their special relationship with the other parent by having to share their custodial parent with a new stepparent.

Papernow (1993, 1998) breaks down the development of the blended family into three stages: fantasy, which includes fantasy, immersion, and awareness; restructuring; and solidifying. In the first two stages, the family is generally divided according to biological lines, but by the third, the family has created a new bond. During the fantasy phase of the first stage, parents visualize that the new marriage will provide a supportive, loving family; however, the children often want their biological parents back together. Papernow (1993, 1998) explains that "because the adults in the new family adore each other, [they assume] stepparents and stepchildren will also" (p. 13). In the second phase of the first stage, immersion, the nonbiological parent becomes the outsider parent, not able to relate in the same way a biological parent does to the biological children. Because of this and other tricky situations in the immersion phase, the parents may be concerned about the family because of negative feelings occurring. It is a period of sinking versus swimming. During the last phase of the first stage, awareness, parents become more able to understand the dynamics of the new relationship. The bond between biological parent and child is acknowledged by the outsider parent, and they are ready to go to the next stage. If parents can recognize the areas of concern in the three phases and deal with them, the family will probably thrive, but if they get stuck in the first three phases, the family will probably dissolve.

The middle, or restructuring, stage includes mobilization—during which the airing of differences occurs—and action, during which power struggles are resolved and new agreements are made, with changes in family structure and new boundaries. In this stage, "Every family activity is no longer a potential power struggle between insiders and outsiders" (Papernow, 1993, p. 16).

The final stage, solidifying, includes contact, during which intimacy and authenticity in real relationships are forged: "The marital relationship becomes more of a sanctuary and source of nourishment and support, even on step issues" (Papernow, 1993, p. 16). Finally, resolution occurs. Although issues may recur and the family may reexperience the stepparenting cycle, the family is able to go forward. Differences no longer threaten the family.

Though by the final stage the family unit is set, the entire blended-family cycle affects the children. They may go through stages of grief similar to those experienced after divorce, death, or moving away from loved ones. During the first stage, while the children are still feeling a loss, their participation in school often suffers. Children may act out in class, they may be despondent, and they may have no interest in schoolwork. For school-age children, the school is a stable environment and can be a support for them. Staying in the same school with their friends can ease the transition.

The stages of the blended-family cycle affect the adults as well. During the early stage, stepparents become aware that they are not able to nurture children in the same way that biological parents do, because biological parents already have a strong bond with their children. Parents develop an awareness of these family pressures. Both partners recognize what they can handle and which attitudes need to be changed. In some cases the family is never able to restructure their lives, and many of these marriages do not succeed.

The restructuring period of stepfamily development allows for more openness in discussion of change. Parents and children continue to have strong biological ties, but the differences lead to action. In this action phase, family boundaries are clarified and the couple attempts to work together to find solutions.

Keep in mind that blended-family stages cannot be rushed, and that "learning how to work as a team is crucial to stepfamily integration, and usually essential for a close couple relationship to develop and grow" (Visher, 2001, p. 4). The biological parent can help the stepparent become part of the family by showing understanding of the stepparent's position: "Requiring civility within the household allows relationships to have the opportunity to develop, and demonstrating love and caring for both his or her children and new partner is an important element in the success of the family" (p. 3). Be patient with this process—Papernow (1993) found that from 4 to 7 years were needed to complete the entire cycle; without patience, some families may never be able to develop their blended family into a strong family. This patience will pay off, because when issues are resolved and the blended family develops into a strong family, children will rebound and will resume normal behavior, including being more engaged in school.

## Insights for Teachers and Administrators

1. Provide workshops for teachers to explain the varying configurations and the developmental stages of blended families. Review the possible effects on children according to age, gender, and needs.
2. Provide workshops on developing family traditions that strengthen families.
3. Eliminate the use of terms such as *broken home* that may offend remarried or single families. Survey the parents to determine whether *step* or *blended* are preferred terms or if there is another term that they value. Children can devalue themselves if they hear terms that appear to be derogatory. Other children might conclude that some students are different and inferior.
4. Mail report cards, newsletters, and other informational items to both custodial and noncustodial parents.
5. Include noncustodial parents on field trips, in special programs, and in school activities.
6. Be aware of days when the student is likely to visit the noncustodial parent. Time messages accordingly.
7. Encourage children to make more than one Mother's Day or Father's Day card if they have more than one parent of the same gender.
8. Appoint parents from blended and single-parent families to serve on advisory councils, Parent Teacher Associations, or other organizations.
9. Be sensitive to a child whose parent has just remarried. This is a period of stress for both the child and the family. Children may act out and need special handling during the transition.
10. Include family information and positive stories about children in blended families or single-parent families within the curriculum.
11. Provide peer support groups for stepchildren or single-parent children where they can meet and talk, helping them realize that they are not the only ones in a blended family. Allow children to question and express their feelings and concerns.
12. Offer books, articles, and lists of resources about stepfamilies and single-parent families for parents and school personnel.
13. Subscribe to the *Stepfamily Bulletin* from the Stepfamily Association of America.

(List adapted from American Academy of Child & Adolescent Psychiatry, 2004; Crosbie-Burnett & Skyles, 1989; Kelly, 1995; Manning & Wootten, 1987; Visher, 2001)

## :: FAMILIES HEADED BY GRANDPARENTS

Grandparent caregivers may also be an integral part of a family. In 2000, this role was acknowledged by the U.S. Census, which, for the first time ever, included questions regarding the grandparents' part in childrearing. Results of this census showed that the number of grandparents maintaining families doubled from 2.2 million in 1970 to 4.5 million in 2000, and care for grandchildren was maintained by 2.4 million grandparent caregivers. This equates to 3.9 percent of all households in 2000. Of these families, 19 percent had incomes below poverty. These are families in which parents may live with the family, but where the grandparents provide the financial support, different from families who have a grandparent move in with them (Simmons & Dye, 2003). These statistics mean that schools will have some families in which the children's grandparents are the primary caregivers, oftentimes for extended periods of time. Actually, only 12 percent had their grandchildren less than 6 months; 11 percent cared for their grandchildren for 6 to 11 months; 23 percent for 1 to 2 years; 15 percent for 3 to 4 years; and the most, 39 percent, for 5 or more years (Simmons & Dye, 2003). Thus, schools will have grandparents who are responsible for their grandchildren for differing lengths of time.

Families included different ethnic groups and differences in the proportions of the ethnic groups who had grandparents caring for grandchildren. The largest numbers of children living with their

Funds of knowledge are also transmitted by grandparents, who often take care of children.

### Insights for Teachers and Administrators

1. When grandparents drop off or pick up their grandchild or grandchildren at school, be available to talk with them, just as you would with other key figures in the child's life.
2. Send newsletters and other notices home to the grandparents.
3. Grandparents may need help in obtaining accurate information about and assistance with support services for themselves and their grandchildren. These issues may include counseling, mentoring, and tutoring for the children. The grandparents may need counseling as well as information on legal and financial aid. Information given should be easy to understand. The information needs to be geared so all grandparents, regardless of their ethnic, cultural, or educational background, can understand and use the information.
4. Make telephone calls to share something the grandchild has done that was a positive contribution. This could include such things as a painting, drawing, story, or just an interest in a subject.
5. Invite the grandparent to programs and "back-to-school night."
6. Invite them to visit the class and, if appropriate, share with a group of students.
7. Treat grandparents as you would treat other parents.
8. If there is a grandparent support group, encourage the grandparents with children in your class or school to attend. If there isn't a support group in your school, start one or find one nearby.
9. Teachers can "use projects to strengthen young children's motivation to master a wide variety of academic skills" (Helm & Lang, 2003, p. 97). They can also help their students begin to master their own environment by "maximizing opportunities for self-initiated learning" (p. 94). Grandparents' experience can be used as a great resource for projects.

grandparents are White, although the percentage is lower than that for other groups. These percentages are 2 percent non-Hispanic White; 6 percent Asian; 8 percent each for Black, American Indian and Alaska Native, and Hispanic; and 10 percent for Pacific Islanders. Today one child in 10 lives with a grandparent; about 41 percent of those are primarily raised by a grandparent (Livingston & Parker, 2010).

The research indicates that the majority of grandparent-maintained families differ from households maintained by parents. These differences

Grandparents play a significant role in raising children in different cultures.

include the educational level of the grandparent, who may not have graduated from high school, and the grandparent's profession, which may not be high income. Even when grandparents work and have health insurance, the insurance programs often do not cover grandchildren living with them.

## :: POVERTY

**Poverty** is defined in the United States according to the income of the person or family. Poverty implies that people lack resources relative to what they need (Cancian & Reed, 2009). In Figure 2–2 we can see how poverty (number of people and rate) has fluctuated in the United States from 1959 to 2009. The number of children living in poverty increased from 2008 to 2009, from 19 percent to 20.7 percent (DeNavas-Walt, Proctor, & Smith, 2010). Many families live in poverty due to loss of employment or unemployment, change in family structure, lack of education, addictions, or health problems, among other reasons.

The economic downturn in 2007 increased the poverty rate due to the loss of employment and earnings (Cancian & Danziger, 2009). According to Cancian and Reed (2009), researchers associated with the Institute for Research on Poverty, changes in family structure and single-parent homes also increased the likelihood of poverty. In fact, the researchers state

**FIGURE 2–2**
Number in poverty and poverty rate, 1959–2009.

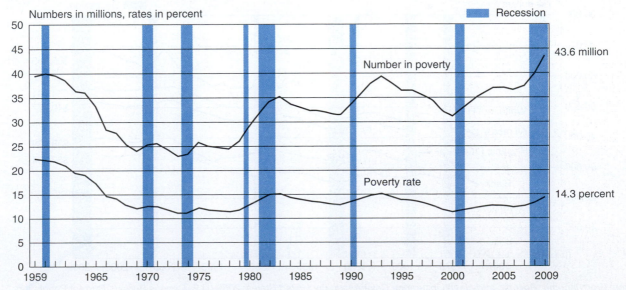

*Source:* From *Income, Poverty, and Health Insurance Coverage in the United States: 2009* (U.S. Census Bureau, Current Population Reports, P60–238, p. 14), by C. DeNavas-Walt, B. D. Proctor, and J. C. Smith, 2010, Washington, DC: U.S. Government Printing Office.

that single-mother families are five times as likely to be poor as married families. Most single mothers also qualify for government assistance programs, including income support programs such as cash welfare and food stamps. Furthermore, the high rate of divorce and the fact that more people are opting not marry increase the chances of a family living in poverty (Cancian & Reed, 2009). Policies that help such families increase their economic well-being, in particular, open the doors for young children to participate in experiences that will help them grow and develop as their parents struggle to find a better life by obtaining assistance through different programs and agencies. Following are a few of the nonprofit organizations that help people who are poor. An online search will easily locate their Web sites.

YMCA
Catholic Charities
Salvation Army
American Red Cross
United Jewish Communities
Goodwill Industries International
Boys and Girls Club of America
Feed the Children
Habitat for Humanity International
Shriners Hospitals for Children
Food for the Poor

## The Changing Face of Poverty

Throughout history, discrimination has had a negative effect on the social and economic well-being of culturally and linguistically diverse families such as African Americans, Latinos, and Native Americans. According to Cancian and Danziger (2009), half of the nation's poor are African American or Latino. From 2008 to 2009, the poverty rate increased for all groups except for the Asian population, as shown in Table 2.2 (DeNavas-Walt, 2010).

Few opportunities for better-paying jobs and education, particularly higher education, are reasons why Latinos and African Americans still fall behind in income level, as shown in Figure 2–3. Education

**TABLE 2.2**

**Poverty rate percentages by ethnic groups from 2008–2009.**

| Ethnic Group | Percent Increase |
| --- | --- |
| White non-Hispanics | 0.8% |
| Hispanics or Latinos | 2.1% |
| African Americans or Blacks | 1.1% |
| Asians | No significant change |

**FIGURE 2–3**

Real median household income by race and Hispanic origin, 1967 to 2009.

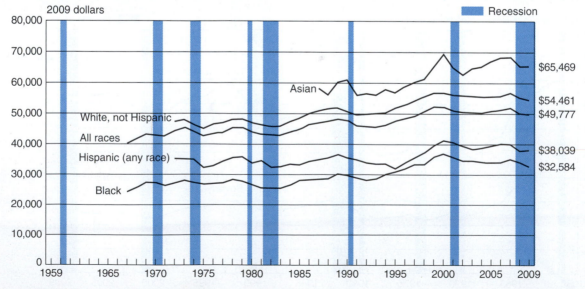

*Source:* From *Income, Poverty, and Health Insurance Coverage in the United States: 2009* (U.S. Census Bureau, Current Population Reports, P60-238, p. 6), by C. DeNavas-Walt, B. D. Proctor, and J. C. Smith, 2010, Washington, DC: U.S. Government Printing Office.

and job opportunities are essential for families to provide a better quality of life for their children.

## Poverty's Casualties

To exist in the culture of poverty often means to feel depressed, powerless to effect change, and unable to control one's destiny. Alienation, anomie, isolation, and depression are common partners of poverty. Although poverty has a look of despair, many families work together to provide the best for their children. Education and training appear to be the keys to help families in poverty, because many face such issues as lack of insurance and lack of medical care, may live in neighborhoods where crime is prevalent, and may have negative school experiences due to their socioeconomic status. Many government agencies, such as the Administration for Children and Families, under the U.S. Department of Health and Human Services, provide programs such as Head Start and Temporary Assistance for Needy Families (TANF) to help families survive and hopefully break the cycle of poverty.

### Insights for Teachers and Administrators

1. Find ways to involve parents—they need to know that they are important and wanted, regardless of economic situation.
2. Recommend community agencies for parents who need additional help.
3. Children in poverty are likely to have poor health and inadequate care. Before viewing a child as neglected, however, find out the source of the problem and offer solutions.
4. Families who have always been self-sufficient and suddenly find themselves without employment face tremendous psychological adjustments as well as difficulty in providing shelter and food. Have a resource guide posted on the school's Web site or on a bulletin board so parents can obtain numbers without feeling embarrassed or ashamed for doing so.
5. For some families, using social welfare is an acknowledgment of defeat and they would rather do without some necessities than accept such help. If they are open to suggestions, help by providing information on social services. The school can also provide exchange options where outgrown clothes may be substituted for ones that fit.
6. Teachers and administrators may help families by providing open-door policies so that families feel welcome in schools.

## Ways to Counteract Poverty

To counteract the stress of poverty on families, parents and children need at least the following:

- A decent standard of living (jobs that pay enough to adequately rear children).
- Flexible working conditions so children can be cared for.
- An integrated network of family services.
- Legal protection for children outside and inside families.

## HOMELESSNESS

The National Coalition for the Homeless (2011) states that each year 3.5 million Americans experience homelessness, and children make up 23 percent of the homeless population. A report from the U.S. Conference of Mayors (2009) points out that the three main reasons why people experience homelessness are lack of affordable housing, poverty, and unemployment.

Single mothers without homes lack more than just housing. In another report, only 38 percent of the young homeless single mothers had ever held a job for longer than 6 months. They were generally undereducated, had few job skills, probably had abused alcohol and other drugs, and were often the victims of domestic violence (Home for the Homeless, Institute for Children and Poverty, 2004). According to the Institute for Children, Poverty, and Homelessness (2011), currently there are over 1.35 million children who are homeless. Children who are homeless have acute and chronic health problems, experience emotional and behavioral problems, and have issues with school performance (Interagency Council on Homelessness, 2010).

Other people without homes, in addition to young single mothers with children, include unemployed two-parent families, single men and women, jobless people with mental illness, people with mental and physical disabilities, homeless independent children and young adults, alcoholics, and transients. It is estimated that families with children make up 40 percent of the homeless. Schools are directly concerned with single- or two-parent families with children who should be in school and runaway children who have dropped out of school, and federal legislation has been passed to aid with these concerns.

## McKinney-Vento Homeless Education Assistance Act

The Stewart B. McKinney Homeless Assistance Act of 1987 (P.L. 100-77) was reauthorized in January 2002 as the McKinney-Vento Amendment. The act was designed to ensure that homeless children have access to education. Although it offers incentives and nominal grants to encourage states to provide for homeless children, the responsibility is left to each state (National Law Center on Homelessness & Poverty, 2002b; Stronge & Helm, 1991). The authorized federal funding is $70 million. The minimum amount of funding any state receives is $150,000 (National Law Center on Homelessness & Poverty, 2002b).

## Authorized Rights for Students Who Are Experiencing Homelessness

The National Law Center for Homelessness & Poverty recognized some issues that need to be addressed to help persons who are homeless. Less than 30 percent of the people eligible for low-income housing receive low-income housing. Only 11 percent of the 40 percent eligible for disability benefits receive such benefits. Only 37 percent have food stamps, even though most are eligible for them. Similarly, most are eligible for welfare benefits, but only 52 percent receive them (National Law Center for Homelessness & Poverty, 2002a, pp. 1–2).

Children and youth who are considered homeless include those who are living with someone who cannot afford or has lost their home, be they a friend, relative, or someone else. It also includes those staying in a motel, hotel, or emergency shelter because they do not have adequate accommodations (National Law Center on Homelessness & Poverty, 2002b).

The McKinney-Vento Act states that children without homes must have the same educational services that are provided to other students. These include Head Start availability, Individuals with Disabilities Education and Child Find for early identification of needs, Title I for those at risk of failing in school, and free and reduced-price meals. Students in homeless situations also have the following protections in school selection (National Law Center on Homelessness & Poverty, 2002b, pp. 1–6):

- Local educational agencies (LEAs) must keep students in the school they attended when they had a permanent home or the school they last attended if at all feasible and if it is not against the parent's or guardian's desire.
- Students may stay at their original school until the end of the school year in which they move into permanent housing.
- If the LEA does not enroll the students in their school of origin, a written explanation to the parent/guardian is required and may be appealed. Dispute resolution is available.
- Students in homeless situations without a guardian or parent must be helped in choosing a school and enrolling.
- States must have a McKinney-Vento plan that describes how students in homeless situations will be given the same opportunity to reach academic standards as other students.
- Students in homeless situations should have access to education and services they might need to ensure that they meet the academic standards.
- Students in homeless situations must be enrolled even if they do not have all the required documents needed.
- At the parent's or guardian's request, transportation must be provided to transport the child to and from the school of origin. To ensure that children and youth in homeless situations are able to access the availability of education, the LEA must have a designated appropriate staff person to help them with information and assistance in obtaining services and education.

Regrettably, in spite of the law, 12 percent of homeless children are still denied their education (National Law Center for Homelessness & Poverty, 2002a, pp. 1–2).

## Concern for Children Experiencing Homelessness

When families are dislocated because of losing their home, they may move to various locations, such as shelters or relatives' homes, which may be in other school districts. Not only do the children lack the security of living in a stable environment, but if the school will not accept them because of residency requirements, they also lack the stability provided by attending the same school.

Children who are without homes also have a higher risk of nutritional deficiency and other health problems, including delayed immunization, poor iron levels, and developmental difficulties. In a study of children without homes compared with low-income children who had homes, it was found that the children without homes were delayed in their growth (Fierman et al., 1991). It may be a combination of factors—malnourishment, diarrhea, asthma, elevated lead levels, or social factors including family violence, drug exposure, alcohol abuse, mental disorders, and child abuse and neglect—that affect the child's growth (Bassuk, 1991; Fierman et al., 1991).

Administrators and teachers should be particularly aware of this and other special concerns of homeless children, including the opportunity for education, acceptance by staff and peers, and referrals as needed for special services. They should also be aware that homeless children may suffer from learning difficulties, speech delays, behavioral problems, depression and anxiety, short attention span, aggression, and withdrawal (Bassuk & Rubin, 1987; Klein, Bittel, & Molnar, 1993; McCormick & Holden, 1992). Children experiencing homelessness who come to school are usually ashamed of not having a home, instead living out of a car, tent, or shelter. They need support, not blame; they need acceptance, not rejection; and they need a curriculum that allows them to succeed. They may need special tutoring and a buddy assigned to help them learn the routine. If they are continuing in the same school that they attended before becoming homeless, they need to be assured that they are still valued. Administrators and teachers should keep in mind that because the family and children are under a lot of stress, it is better to let them offer information than to inquire into personal concerns.

## Parents' Desires

In a research survey (McCormick & Holden, 1992), parents without homes indicated they would like assistance with transportation, developmentally appropriate child care, opportunities to share with others, flexible opportunities to be involved, respite opportunities, mental health self-esteem groups, information on services, an easy intake process for preschool participation, and classes.

The McKinney-Vento Act (Sec. 722[g][4]) offers the following standards for parents:

> Standard 4. Parents or persons acting as parents of homeless children and youth will participate meaningfully in their children's education.

4.1. Parents or persons acting as parents will have a face-to-face conference with the teacher, guidance counselor, or social worker within 30 days of enrollment.

4.2. Parents or persons acting as parents will be provided with individual student reports informing them of their child's specific academic needs and achievement on academic assessments aligned with state academic achievement standards.

4.3. Parents or persons acting as parents will report monitoring or facilitating homework assignments.

4.4. Parents or persons acting as parents will share reading time with their children (i.e., parent reads to child or listens to child read).

4.5. Parents who would like parent skills training will attend available programs.

4.6. Parents or guardians will demonstrate awareness of McKinney-Vento rights.

4.7. Unaccompanied youth will demonstrate awareness of McKinney-Vento rights.

## Children's Feelings

Walsh (1992) depicted children experiencing homelessness through their conversations. Sam, for example, writes about how he felt about losing his pet dog, Ralphy, when he had to move to a shelter:

> I had a dog for a long time before I came here. We had to give him to a friend because we couldn't bring him down ere wit us. The shelter say "No animals." And, even if we move out of here, we can't get him back because he likes the people he's with right now. And me and him were best friends. His name was Ralphy. I always still remember him. I just hope he remembers me. (p. 77)

Juan expressed his feelings of sadness, not just for himself, but also for his parents:

> Being here makes me sad but I don't cry. I feel sad about it by myself. Sometimes I talk to my mother about it. I tell her how sad I am. She says she knows I'm sad. She knows because she feels the same way. I don't know if she cries about it. If she does I never see her. I think she does though. I don't like to talk about this stuff too much. (p. 82)

### Insights for Teachers and Administrators

1. Establish a buddy system in the classroom. Assign a buddy to all children new to the room (not just the homeless). Make it a classmate-friendly room.
2. Have clear, simple outlines that allow children to fit into the class schedule. (For children enrolling for the first time, let a buddy discuss the routine with the new child to mentor and guide the child through the procedures.)

3. Have a procedure for transitions from one activity to another. Music, rhythm, and movement give children extra creative activities as well as provide organized transitions.
4. Provide a place where children can keep their school materials and a supervised area where homework or enrichment activities can be completed at school.
5. Help the new child catch up, and individualize the assignments for the new child.
6. Provide health provisions (toothbrushes, soap, etc.) and clothes.
7. Encourage parents to become involved. Let the parents of homeless children participate in the classroom. As with all parents, they will need to know how you want them to participate. Plan a workshop for parents, or mentor them individually. Their involvement will not only provide extra help in the classroom, but it can also become an educational program for parents. They may learn more about how they can help their children.

All of these suggestions can help the family, but families need time to develop skills and stability. Due to the way homeless shelters are usually set up, the family can stay only a limited time. Some programs have begun to recognize that this does not provide homeless families enough time to gain skills for employment or enough stability to provide for the family. Homes for the Homeless (2011) developed the American Family Inns, where parents and children can live for a year, establishing stability in the family and allowing the parents to become self-sufficient. The American Family Inn meets the educational needs of each parent, children have supplemental help to compensate for skills they need to develop, and infants and preschoolers go to child development centers, giving the children a jump-start. Recreation and cultural programs are also provided. Similar programs have been established across the country. They provide single mothers and two-parent families time to develop skills and establish stable lifestyles.

The extra effort works. After a family moves from the American Family Inn to their own permanent housing, they are provided with aftercare services for an additional year. Studies show that approximately 94 percent of those who lived in an American Family Inn were still self-sufficient and living independently 2 years later (Nuñez, 1996, p. 76). The

continuing concerns for families and their children affected by homelessness require giving top priority to schools and programs that help these families survive and flourish. The United States has more of a challenge compared to many other nations: Although the United States provides many successful and effective programs to help the poor, more improvement is needed because the United States ranks 21st among industrialized countries for low birth weight rates, 28th in infant mortality rates, and last in relative child poverty (Children's Defense Fund, 2011).

## SUMMARY

The population of the United States has increased dramatically in the last 50 years. Along with growth in numbers, several trends are evident, such as the diversity within families that form part of the U.S. society. Diverse families include traditional two-parent, single-parent, divorced, blended, homeless, and immigrant families, as well as families living in poverty, among others. All families have the responsibility to provide for their children, so each family has functions it must exercise in order to ensure that children's needs are met. Parents also have different parenting styles that affect children's development. Grandparents play an important part in raising children in today's society, because not only do families depend on them for taking care of the grandchildren, but also many parents need the grandparents to take custody of their children. Fathers need to have a strong presence in their children's lives in order for children to have healthy relationships. Homelessness and poverty affect many diverse families, but there are laws that protect such families so that their quality of life can improve.

## SUGGESTED CLASS ACTIVITIES AND DISCUSSIONS

1. Survey your class and find out the different types of family structures represented.
2. Interview different types of families. Ask them questions, including what kinds of things help them be a family, some of their favorite things to do, the challenges that they face on a daily basis, and what keeps them together.

3. Who are the immigrant families in your city? Do a search for your city and discover where families live and the conditions in which they live. Compare your answers with another classmate and see what he or she found.

4. List ways that fathers can become involved in a school or child-care center.

5. Examine the Personal Responsibility and Work Opportunity Reconciliation Act (PRWORA). Is it working? Is it causing hardship for children? What are the changes to the PRWORA?

6. Count the number of residential moves the members of your class have made. Why have they moved? Where have they moved? How many times have they moved?

7. Research the effect of Temporary Assistance for Needy Families (TANF) on child care and families. What services does it provide? Has it been helpful? Are there any concerns? Learn where the TANF office is located in your community.

## USEFUL WEB SITES

**Association for Childhood Education International (ACEI)**
www.acei.org/
ACEI's Web site includes easy access to important childhood questions.

**Institute for Research on Poverty (IRP)**
www.irp.wisc.edu/publications/focus.htm
The IRP is an interdisciplinary center that examines the causes and consequences of poverty and social inequality in the United States and is based at the University of Wisconsin–Madison.

**Interagency Council on Homelessness (ICH)**
www.ich.gov/
The ICH's mission is to "coordinate the Federal response to homelessness and to create a national partnership at every level of government and with the private sector to reduce and end homelessness in the nation while maximizing the effectiveness of the Federal Government in contributing to the end of homelessness."

**McKinney-Vento Act**
www.nationalhomeless.org/publications/facts
   /McKinney.pdf
A more complete copy of the reauthorization can be obtained here.

**National Association for the Education of Young Children**
www.naeyc.org/
This national organization focuses on young children.

**National Fatherhood Initiative**
www.fatherhood.org/
The mission of this organization is to improve the lives of children by having involved fathers.

**Teachers First**
www.teachersfirst.com/fathers.html/
The site offers a list of programs, including programs for father involvement.

# Working with Culturally and Linguistically Diverse Groups

*Addressing issues that arise as a result of increased diversity demands both insight and care rather than arrogance and simplistic notions of unity.*

Sonia Nieto
*(2009, p. 150)*

In this chapter you will find information that will assist you on how to understand and work with culturally and linguistically diverse children and their families. After completing this chapter, you will be able to do the following:

- Explain the terms *culture* and *diversity*.
- Explain why examining one's own identity, including one's own ancestry, culture, and values is important before beginning to work with culturally and linguistically diverse families and children.
- Identify culturally and linguistically diverse children within the United States and the programs that best serve their needs.
- Discuss strategies for working with children and families who have a variety of linguistic and cultural backgrounds.

## :: WHAT IS IDENTITY?

My daughter has been exploring her own ethnic identity. She has heard the term *Chicana* and has been trying to figure out who can be identified as a Chicana or Chicano.[1] If you never heard the term, it is defined as a person who has Mexican ancestry. My daughter says that her skin is not "white" (fair) like her brother's who she says looks like he's from Europe because of the fair color of his skin. My daughter, like many children, often looks at the physical features of a person, but as she processes her understanding of ethnic identity, she realizes that this is more complex than just the color of someone's skin. Although teachers very often tend to think that all children are the same, it is important to note that not all children are the same and that their experiences are as varied as the color of their skin.

So why is it important for teachers to know how to explain issues of identity to children? Throughout this chapter you will see that the importance is based on the ability of teachers to offer quality experiences for all children and their families in the schools, particularly those who have often been marginalized because of their cultural and linguistic background. Knowing the children's identity will help teachers determine how to best meet the children's and family's needs in a supportive and nurturing environment where children

feel safe because teachers consider the color of their skin, language, national origin, and ethnicity. While reading this chapter, it will be important to keep in mind the previous discussion of *funds of knowledge*.

## :: WHAT IS CULTURE?

Our nation is diverse. Its diversity includes family configurations, ethnic groups, socioeconomic backgrounds, religions, as well as urban and rural settings. Very often the term *culture* gets confused with the term *diversity*.

> Diversity—differences in characteristics, qualities, traits, values, beliefs, and mannerisms in self and others based on predetermined factors (i.e., gender, race, etc.) and changeable features (i.e., language, citizenship). (Hernández-Sheets, 2005)

> Culture—the learned and shared values, a system of beliefs and attitudes or control mechanism (Geertz, 1973 as cited in Hernández-Sheets, 2005) that shape our behavior. (p. 15)

Knowing the difference between the two terms can help teachers better understand the diversity of the students they teach and their families (Nieto, 2008).

### Culture: A Way of Life

The term **culture** is most easily understood when viewed as a way of life. Other descriptions are "blueprints for living" and "guidelines for life." It is the knowing, perceiving, understanding, and learning one brings to a situation (Nieto, 2008). Although culture refers to the way life is lived—including

---

[1]The term was mostly used in the Civil Rights Movement of the 1960s and has remained part of the ethnic identity of many Latinos, mostly Mexican Americans.

housing, clothing, and utensils—it is much more than that. Culture is a way of life that is learned and that is shared. It is a process that is multilayered, connecting language, values, beliefs, and behaviors (Ovando, Combs, & Collier, 2006).

It is important for us as teachers of young children to understand the concept of culture because we are not only helping children to develop physically, socially, linguistically, and cognitively, but we are also helping them to develop culturally (Ovando, Combs, & Collier, 2006). How do we assist culturally and linguistically diverse children in our effort to make school relevant for them? Fisher (2006) suggests that "The challenge of cultural analysis is to develop translation and mediation tools for helping make visible the differences of interests, access, power, needs, desires, and philosophical perspective" (p. 363). This is particularly important because culture also includes the way in which life is perceived and, because of this, can be stereotyped.

Educators should focus on the following three approaches:

1. Focus on self. It is helpful when teachers know their own culture, beliefs, and biases toward others. Why do they feel the way they do? What do they value? What would they change? Teachers must examine their own lifestyles and beliefs so that they can begin to reflect on the differences between them and the children and families they teach.

2. Focus on culturally and linguistically diverse children. Encourage children, particularly those who are culturally and linguistically diverse and those who have special needs, to know themselves through an environment of acceptance, encouragement, and inquiry. Interactions with children should be based on knowledge of child development as well as the child's culture in order for the interaction among children and adults to be appropriate and enabling.

3. Focus on collaboration with parents and community, acceptance of others, and understanding of cultural history as well as individual family history. Recognize history and culture and their influence on the lives of children and families. Know the family's funds of knowledge. Find out the practices that have helped the child's family with his or her development. If you are not familiar with their culture or their language, find out the best way to make them feel welcome in school in order to create a truly nurturing community of learners. By opening the door to families, you may be providing opportunities for them to find out about community resources that will help them offer a better life for their children. Avoid the "tourist approach" to knowing a culture. A tourist approach is one that only focuses on the traditional tangible items of a culture such as Chinese lanterns or Mexican *sarapes*.

## :: CULTURAL IDENTITY

Who am I?

> *"I really don't have a culture. I'm just a simple American. I was born here and my parents are from here. I heard my grandmother's parents came from France but I never really thought about it. My last name is Morales but I am not Hispanic I was born in Louisiana. I don't speak Spanish."*

This quote represents a student's understanding of her identity. Note that the student is not prejudiced toward "Hispanics"[2] or people who speak

Culturally and linguistically diverse families adopt the traditions and values of the new culture.

---

[2]*Hispanic* is a term used by the U.S. Census, but a more appropriate term is *Latino*.

Latino families value all levels of education.

by examining our own ancestry, which allows us to begin to understand and explore the differences between diverse groups (Bekerman, 2009).

Taking a look at your own family history, you can begin to understand values, social practices, and traditions that your family has passed down from generations. What internalized values really came from childhood and the manner in which you were socialized? How much do you model after your parents, other relatives, or friends? Do you know your funds of knowledge? Examine the lives of those who have been significant to you—family, teachers, friends, or maybe even someone famous. What was their cultural background? What did they believe? What values did they live by? Have they influenced you? The questions you can ask yourself are endless. If you find some prejudicial feelings, you may be able to examine them, recognize that they are not based on fact, and work them out so that you can be more understanding of your students and their families. For teachers it is imperative that they look into the psychosocial factors that influence their perception and thinking such as beliefs, ethnic identity, acculturation, efficacy, and motivation (Flores, Clark, Guerra, Casebeer, & Sanchez, 2010).

## Practice Discovering Your Identity

One activity that may help you on your journey to understanding yourself is the answer to the question, "Who am I?" You may draw a picture of yourself and then on the back of the paper, make a list of who you are. List the points of how you see yourself, whatever comes to mind. Do not dwell on what the answers mean. List 5 to 10 items on your list. Now you can look at the list and see what you placed first. When you think of yourself, what roles are paramount? Was it teacher, mother, father, husband, or wife? Your view of who you are may change depending on what stage of life you are in. You may not even agree with the list you just made. Are there other roles more important to you? What is important is your review of the roles and thinking about what they mean to you. This is also an activity that you can do with your students, particularly those who are very young and who are learning about themselves. Parents might also enjoy this activity. The children's book *Hairs/Pelitos*, by Sandra Cisneros, can also be read to entice the children to

Spanish—in fact, in the same conversation, the student talked about how she wished she spoke Spanish. Yet her understanding of the Hispanic culture and her own was limited. Interestingly, she shared that she was from Louisiana and therefore couldn't be Hispanic. I asked her if she knew the history of Louisiana, which includes Spanish and French influence. The student said that she had never thought about it—she always thought that Hispanic people just came from Mexico. This conversation prompted her to begin looking for her own ancestry and thus her own identity.

**Identity** is defined as knowing who we are and to what groups we belong to (Hernández-Sheets, 2005; Dutro, Kazemi, Balf, & Lin, 2008). Knowing who we are very often helps us understand who others are. This is particularly important for teachers who work with diverse learners (Clark & Flores, 2001). However, since the majority of teachers in the schools are White (Marx, 2008), it may be difficult for them to see and understand "other people's children" (Delpit, 1996). One way around this is

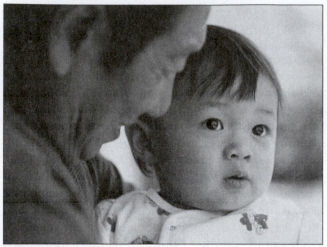

In many immigrant families, elders help children create strong bonds and attachments.

think about how everyone is different physically. Another children's book that can be used is *My People: My People with Photographs* by Langston Hughes. Langston Hughes wrote the classic poem, *My People*, used to create this book in the late 1920s, a time when Blacks were not accepted by society, as a way to celebrate the pride he felt about his people as a Black man.

Another activity both you and your students can work on is making a family tree. There are many Web sites that provide free templates to create one. In order to be sensitive to those children who are adopted, they can also make a tree with the people who are important in their life. After making the family tree, students may choose to make a family history album. Talk with relatives and find out what you can about the family. Record the stories they share. Even if the children are adopted or are from a foster family, they can write about their immediate family.

Children's literature is an excellent way to bridge commonalities between cultures. *Family Familia* (1999), by children's author Diane Gonzales Bertrand, is a good example of a book to read to children about family history because it touches on the topic through a family that is attending its family reunion. Although the book reflects the experience of a Mexican American family, it can be used for all children to discuss what their family is like. Similarly, *Aunt Flossie's Hats (and Crab Cakes Later),* by Elizabeth Fitzgerald Howard (1991),

describes two African American sisters who visit their great-great-aunt Flossie to try on her hats, hear her stories, and eat crabs. It is about learning about their family.

The Internet is an excellent source of information regarding ancestry. If you have a computer and Internet access, you can use a family history Web site to research your family tree. Using this information, you can write a narrative about your family. Use a scanner to include pictures of your ancestors and living relatives. You will learn a lot about your family and yourself. The parents that you work with can also do this activity to discover their ancestry.

### Insights for Teachers and Administrators

1. Examine your own cultural identity.
2. Identify the different cultural and linguistic backgrounds represented in your school or center.
3. Provide teachers with a variety of children's literature that represents the children in the classroom, school or center, and the community.
4. Provide teachers with real photographs of people in the community where your school or center is located.
5. Examine the existing curriculum and see how children's cultural and linguistic background is represented. If it is not, then discuss what provisions the school or center will enact to make sure that occurs. Bringing in experts in the field will help align the curriculum with Culturally and Developmentally Appropriate Practices or CDAP.

## :: CULTURALLY AND LINGUISTICALLY DIVERSE CHILDREN

Many children in the United States are considered culturally and linguistically diverse. We have children who are biracial, bicultural, and bilingual, meaning that they are growing up in two worlds (Pérez, 2004). Many of these children are minorities or are from traditionally underrepresented groups, such as Mexican Americans and African Americans. There are also those who are multicultural because their families are so varied in their ancestry. Also represented in the United States are children who are monolingual speakers of other languages, or what we know as **English language learners,** or **ELLs.**

**TABLE 3.1**
**U.S. population by race.**

| Race | Estimated Population 2006–2008 |
|---|---|
| Total: | 301,237,703 |
| Caucasian alone | 223,965,009 |
| Black or African American alone | 37,131,771 |
| American Indian and Alaska Native alone | 2,419,895 |
| Asian alone | 13,164,169 |
| Native Hawaiian and Other Pacific Islander alone | 446,164 |
| Some other race alone | 17,538,990 |
| Two or more races | 6,571,705 |
|   Two races including some other race | 1,338,960 |
|   Two races excluding some other race, and three or more races | 5,232,745 |

*Source:* U.S. Census Bureau (2006–2008). *American community survey.* www.census.gov/acs/

Immigrants come to the U.S. because it is a "land of opportunity."

Table 3.1 represents the estimated population from 2006–2008 and its ethnic breakdown. It also shows the individuals who are considered biracial or multiracial.

### Who Are English Language Learners?

If you examine Table 3.2, you can see the many different languages that are spoken in U.S. homes, though the table does not indicate how many of those families do not speak English. Many of the households represented on the table are English language learners, or ELLs.[3] The majority of the children who are ELLs are of Latino descent or immigrants. The second largest group of children who are also ELLs are of Asian descent.

The State of California has the largest number of ELLs, followed by Texas. Other states have also seen a growth in the number of children who are ELLs enrolled in their schools. Since the number of ELLs continues to increase, some school districts are realizing that effective programs and strategies need to be implemented in order to meet the needs of these students. When school districts do not comply with meeting the needs of English language learners, then the Office of Civil Rights gets involved in order to provide basic rights to language-minority students (Ovando, Combs, & Collier, 2006).

### Learning a Second Language

Understanding how a second language is learned becomes important not only for teachers but for parents as well, who very often want their children to quickly learn English at the expense of their native language (Wong-Fillmore, 1991). It is not that the parents want their children to lose their language—it is that they want their children to have better opportunities, and speaking English opens the door to many opportunities, such as education and employment.

Unfortunately, what happens to many children is that in an effort to learn English, their native

---

[3]Preferred term according to Honigsfeld (2009).

## TABLE 3.2
Languages spoken at home: 2007.

| Language | Number (1,000) | Language | Number (1,000) |
|---|---|---|---|
| Total population 5 years and over | 280,950 | Other Indic languages | 616 |
| Speak only English | 225,506 | Other Indo-European languages | 421 |
| Spanish or Spanish Creole | 34,547 | Chinese | 2,465 |
| French (incl. Patois, Cajun) | 1,356 | Japanese | 459 |
| French Creole | 629 | Korean | 1,062 |
| Italian | 799 | Mon-Khmer, Cambodian | 185 |
| Portuguese or Portuguese Creole | 687 | Hmong | 181 |
| German | 1,104 | Thai | 144 |
| Yiddish | 159 | Laotian | 149 |
| Other West Germanic languages | 270 | Vietnamese | 1,207 |
| Scandinavian languages | 135 | Other Asian languages | 625 |
| Greek | 330 | Tagalog | 1,480 |
| Russian | 851 | Other Pacific Island languages | 359 |
| Polish | 638 | Navajo | 171 |
| Serbo-Croatian | 277 | Other Native North American languages | 201 |
| Other Slavic languages | 312 | Hungarian | 91 |
| Armenian | 222 | Arabic | 767 |
| Persian | 350 | Hebrew | 214 |
| Gujarati | 287 | African languages | 700 |
| Hindi | 533 | Other and unspecified languages | 117 |
| Urdu | 345 | | |

*Note:* 280,950 represents 280,950,000. Covers population 5 years old and over. The American Community Survey universe is limited to the household population and excludes the population living in institutions, college dormitories, and other group quarters. Based on a sample and subject to sampling variability.

*Source:* U.S. Census Bureau (2010). American community survey table, P034: Language spoken at home for the population 5 years and over. *American Fact Finder*. Retrieved from http://facttcensus.gov.

language is lost. Language loss increases family challenges since parents (and other family members such as grandparents) can no longer communicate with their children, which brings issues of separation (Wong-Fillmore, 2000).

Still, learning English is crucial for the success of any individual in the United States; thus it is important to understand how children develop a second language so that the strategies used by teachers are appropriate and effective.

There are many theories of how children develop language, including behaviorist, nativist, cognitivist, social interactionist, and information processing (Hulit, Howard, & Fahey, 2011). Similarly, there are second language acquisition theories, including environmentalist theories, Schumann's Acculturation Model, nativist theories, and Krashen's Monitor Model (Freeman & Freeman, 2001). Krashen's Classic Monitor Model of Second Language Acquisition focuses on the importance of the learner to have low anxiety as he or she learns a second language. Krashen (1981) discusses five hypotheses regarding second language acquisition that have helped educators to understand the process: (1) acquisition/learning distinction, (2) the natural order hypothesis, (3) the monitor hypothesis, (4) the input hypothesis, and (5) the affective-filter hypothesis. This theory emphasizes the natural order of language acquisition and the importance of giving the learner time and support.

Another theory, proposed by Cummins (1979), indicates that there are two time periods that a child usually goes through when learning a second language: Basic Interpersonal Communication Skills (BICS) and Cognitive Academic Language Proficiency (CALP). In the BICS stage, children use language for social functions, to give information, to project situations or to guess future situations, to control themselves and others, and to direct attention and memory; in the CALP stage, children are listening, speaking, reading, and writing within a content area (Gonzalez, Yawkey, & Minaya-Rowe, 2006). These skills are usually practiced within a classroom setting and take 5 to 7 years to master (Gonzalez, et al.,).

These two skill stages have become guidelines for teachers to understand the process of second-language acquisition and the importance of teaching children in their native language in order for them to continue learning academic concepts. It is important also for teachers to explain to parents that their children will learn to speak English, but they need academic instruction in their native language as they learn English.

### Communicating with Parents Regarding Second Language Learning

Teachers can give parents the following tips to explain how to support young children's language development:

- Talk to your child in your native language.
- Sing songs to your child in your native language.
- Tell your child traditional stories from your culture in your native language.
- Read culturally relevant books to your child in your native language.
- Play traditional children's games from your culture.
- Have your child send letters or e-mails in their native language to family members, such as grandparents.

### Insights for Teachers and Administrators

1. Provide developmentally appropriate environments where children have opportunities for overall development (Duarte, 2008; Riojas-Cortez & Alanis, 2011).
2. Promote the use of the native language, particularly in the early childhood.
3. If a child's language is not common, find resources around the community and beyond to ensure that the family receives information in its native language.
4. Provide ample language-rich opportunities in the classroom, such as a music time where children practice their native language as well as their second language.
5. Engage children in environments that allow interaction with native-language peers as well as second-language peers, what Alanis (2010) calls bilingual pairs. Play in the learning centers is the optimal environment for this to occur.

### Programs for English Language Learners

The type of programs that research has shown to help ELLs not only learn English but learn academic content are bilingual programs with an English as a Second Language, or ESL, component. Bilingual programs are usually offered in school districts that have a large number of students with the same language background. Table 3.3 provides a list of Bilingual Education Program Models.

**Two-way Immersion, or Dual-language, Programs.** Two-way immersion, or dual-language programs seem to be getting more popular because of the inclusion of native-language speakers as well as English speakers. The programs are especially important because children who are growing up bilingually need to develop both languages, and these types of programs help facilitate that (Alanis,

**TABLE 3.3**
**Bilingual Education Program Models.**

| Program | Description |
|---|---|
| Transitional Bilingual Education | Instruction in the native language and English from kindergarten and an ELL component. Instruction in the native language decreases until about third or fourth grade, when the native-language instruction is replaced with English instruction. |
| Maintenance or Late Exit | Programs focus on maintaining the native language for instruction with ELL component very often up until fifth or sixth grade, depending on the school. |
| Dual Language | Emphasis is on the native language first in grades kindergarten and first. Gradual use of English begins in second or third, and both languages are used equally in fourth and fifth grade (90/10 model). The 50/50 model is one in which half of the instruction is in English and half in Spanish, but not simultaneously. Some subjects are taught in the native language and others in English. |

Ovando, C.J., Combs, M.C., Collier, V.P. (2006). *Bilingual and ESL Classrooms: Teaching in Multicultural Contexts* (4th ed.). Dubuque, IA: McGraw-Hill.

2006). Two-way immersion programs are beneficial for children. The children who are English speakers truly learn about their identity because they learn about the identity of others. Noteworthy is the fact that many children and families have lost their native language because historically language minority groups such as Chicanos were prohibited from speaking their language and were harshly punished (Valencia, 2002). Dual-language or two-way immersion programs seem to assist children in developing both languages (Alanis, 2006). The Center for Applied Linguistics provides guiding principles regarding Two-Way Immersion Programs (www.cal.org/twi/directory/).

**English as a Second Language.** Schools that do not offer bilingual programs often offer some type of ESL program, such as ESL (or English as a Second Language), ESL pull-out, sheltered instruction, and structured immersion (Ovando, Combs, & Collier, 2006). It is important for teachers to understand the difference between bilingual programs and ESL programs because one is asset-based, meaning that the native language of the child is valued for academic learning, while the other one focuses on rushing children to learn English quickly. The parents are the ones who decide if they want their children in a bilingual or ESL program. Therefore, it is imperative that the teachers assist parents in making an informed decision.

Additionally, programs should value and build a cultural and linguistic capital of English language learners. This means that the children's native language as well as their culture need to be respected in order to let parents know how they and their children are valued (Brooks & Karathanos, 2009).

**Bilingual Education Outlook**

There are a few states that have banned bilingual education (California, Arizona, and Massachusetts) because they are under the belief that bilingual education does not promote the acquisition of English. This belief is a misconception, though, as bilingual education promotes excellence and equity, allowing children to use their native language to learn academic concepts while at the same time learning English (which is one of the goals of bilingual education).

For very young children, bilingual education programs are crucial for their healthy development. When early childhood programs describe themselves as "developmentally appropriate," then they need to take into consideration the child's primary language. For example, in 2009, a Head Start program in Washington State decided to make changes in its curriculum to create a strong foundation in the children's primary language in order to help children succeed. Previously, they had used English immersion, but the teachers and administrators realized that English immersion was not helping children be successful in school (Youngquist & Martínez-Griego, 2009). The children's language increased as a result of allowing them to use their native language. This important finding supports previous research regarding the need for children to be allowed to interact in their native language in early childhood.

## :: CULTURALLY RELEVANT PEDAGOGY

**Culturally relevant pedagogy** has truly changed the way teachers work with students. It is defined as a "theoretical model that not only addresses student achievement but also helps students accept and affirm their cultural identity while developing critical perspectives that challenge inequities that schools (and other institutions) perpetuate" (Ladson-Billings, 1995, p. 469). Culturally relevant pedagogy is important for all culturally and linguistically diverse children because it provides opportunities to enhance learning, particularly for minority groups, such as African Americans and Latinos, who have been marginalized from the school system for many years, causing them to be less successful than White students (Howard, 2003). Culturally relevant pedagogy allows teachers to reflect on their practices and provide a curriculum that is relevant to all children. A curriculum that is culturally relevant means that it reflects the children's experiences, identity, culture, and abilities in the lessons. Such a curriculum also includes parents and sees families from an asset perspective.

Children's culture is an asset for school learning.

### Culturally Relevant Curriculum: Antibias

Antibias education focuses on the notion of "practice of freedom," which is how cultural consciousness has the power to transform reality (Lin, Lake, & Rice, 2008). An antibias classroom respects, values, and takes pride in the children and their families (Derman-Sparks & Olsen Edwards, 2010). One book (written for preschool teachers and their students) that can be useful in learning about and implementing antibias education is *Anti-Bias Education for Young Children and Ourselves* by Derman-Sparks and Olsen Edwards (2010). This book (in its second edition) has made an impact on issues of equity by providing ideas, questions, and strategies to use in the classroom. It encompasses what developmentally and culturally appropriate practices are all about: taking into consideration culture, language, religion, country of origin, and gender.

The foundation of antibias education is understanding how "young children construct their personal and social identities, [and] how they think about differences and absorb messages about prejudice and social advantage or disadvantage" (Derman-Sparks & Olsen Edwards, 2010, p. 11). The four goals of antibias education include the following:

Goal 1: Each child will demonstrate self-awareness, confidence, family pride, and positive social identities.

Goal 2: Each child will express comfort and joy with human diversity; accurate language for human differences, and deep, caring human connections.

Goal 3: Each child will increasingly recognize unfairness, have language to describe unfairness, and understand that unfairness hurts.

Goal 4: Each child will demonstrate empowerment and the skills to act, with others or alone, against prejudice and/or discriminatory actions. (Derman-Sparks & Olsen Edwards, 2010, pp. 4–5)

The antibias curriculum seeks to avoid the trap of the "tourist" examination of cultures, in which holidays and customs are the only ventures into cultural identity. An antibias curriculum also uses the children's funds of knowledge as a resource for learning. A preschool that follows the four antibias goals includes a curriculum that:

1. Uses children's books that reflect differences in gender, race, disabilities, geographic location, and socioeconomic class.
2. Offers opportunities for dramatic play with different peers.

3. Plays different genres of music that represent different groups in the U.S., such as rap, hip hop, jazz, *conjunto*, and country, among others. It is also a good idea to play traditional music from countries around the world.

4. Displays variety of art that represents different artists from the United States, allowing children to explore their own creativity.

5. Engages children in different types of traditional children's games from the United States and around the world.

6. Invites parents to join in the children's learning not only at home but at school as well.

In order for children to experience healthy development, social inequities and biases must be eradicated, and early on—Derman-Sparks and Olsen Edwards (2010) point out that children notice gender and racial differences as early as the second year of life and by age 3 may already have been exposed to biases that the authors call "preprejudice." For children to have an equitable education, it is important for educators and administrators to create antibias classrooms that focus on the reality of children's lives, taking into consideration the many cultural aspects of all of the children in the class. Building and maintaining strong relationships between teachers and families will help ensure the effectiveness of this antibias classroom.

## :: CULTURALLY AND LINGUISTICALLY DIVERSE PARENTS AND THE COMMUNITY

The first and most important thing to remember when working with culturally diverse groups is to avoid stereotyping. Very often, information about different ethnic groups is learned from the media, which may portray groups from just one perspective (Geneva, 2002). Unfortunately, this perspective leads to stereotypes that prevent teachers from communicating effectively with parents.

Culturally responsive teaching promotes active communication with parents by following the protocols of communication associated with the family's culture (Geneva, 2002). One way to get to know the families in the community, in addition to inviting them to the school, is to go out into their community. School personnel should get acquainted with the school neighborhood before school starts. Taking "block walks" or attending special events in the community can give teachers an idea of what the community is like. In order to get to know the community deeper, teachers can conduct a community study. A community study motivates teachers to look into different aspects of the community, such as the type of businesses, churches, schools, and other resources that are present. It also helps

Many culturally and linguistically diverse families are second, third, and fourth generations that have acculturated to a variety of traditions.

teachers understand other people's way of life (Ek, Machado-Casas, Sánchez, & Smith, 2010), including beliefs about how children develop and how they learn to assimilate and acculturate in a different world (Riojas-Cortez, 2008).

While learning about the community, it is imperative that teachers keep an open mind and begin by looking at positive aspects of the community and by avoiding stereotypes. For example, not all Latinos are immigrants from Mexico and other Latin American countries—Latinos have been in the United States for generations.

By getting to know the community, teachers can really use Bronfenbrenner's Ecological Systems Theory to understand how children are seen in the community and how each system supports their development. Rather than just giving information teachers can truly collaborate with culturally and linguistically diverse families by understanding the important role that parents have in their children's lives and how they truly want to participate in their children's education (Valdés, 1996), (Favela, 2007). The following list gives best practices regarding how to effectively communicate with culturally and linguistically diverse families (Araujo, 2009):

- Incorporate funds of knowledge—connect the children's world with the school by using the knowledge they gain at home within the curriculum.
- Practice culturally relevant teaching—use parents' knowledge to provide relevant lessons. Use native language for instruction.
- Foster effective communication—send newsletters in the student's native language, make phone calls to give positive feedback (use translator if necessary), make home visits, talk to parents about how you need their help reinforcing rules and policies, and ask parents to visit the classroom just to see how the school and the classroom operate.
- Extend and accept assistance—provide information regarding community resources, create parent liaisons within the school to assist parents who may not be familiar with the school system, and have a pool of translators who can readily communicate with parents.

## SUMMARY

Understanding the differences of terms such as culture and diversity will help teachers understand how to incorporate culturally relevant teaching in their classroom. Exploring one's own culture, ancestry, and values helps create empathy for others. Teachers and administrators identify the needs of culturally and linguistically diverse children by providing programs that promote the use of their native language for instruction, and when that is not possible, they provide programs that will help children achieve not only English proficiency but also academic proficiency. Culturally relevant pedagogy allows for teachers to use the children's *funds of knowledge* in their lessons therefore providing the opportunity for children not only to learn content but to learn it in a way that they can internalize it more effectively. The antibias curriculum shows teachers and administrators the importance of knowing how to effectively use developmentally and culturally appropriate practices with children and their families. Knowing how to work with culturally and linguistically diverse families will help teachers to enhance children's learning by using them as a resource for teaching.

## SUGGESTED CLASS ACTIVITIES AND DISCUSSIONS

1. List the values and strengths you look for in a family. Why did you choose them?
2. Discover your heritage by researching your family's past. If you were adopted and your heritage was not revealed to you, make up a heritage that you would like to have.
3. Invite parents of different cultures to share with the class family traditions.
4. Visit various places of worship. Invite ministers, priests, rabbis, or other clerics to share beliefs and ideas with the class.
5. Have a class discussion of family traditions and beliefs.
6. Visit museums in the area. What is revealed about beliefs or cultures of different time periods?
7. Investigate methods and curricula that schools are using to include culturally relevant pedagogy.

8. Complete the *Play Memories* handout on page 53 to understand differences and similarities in children's traditions.

## USEFUL WEB SITES

**Center for Applied Linguistics (CAL)**
www.cal.org/
This site addresses the needs of linguistically diverse students.

**National Association for Bilingual Education (NABE)**
www.nabe.org/
This site addresses the needs of bilingual students.

**Office for Civil Rights**
www.hhs.gov/ocr/
The Office for Civil Rights protects individuals from being or who have been discriminated.

**Pew Hispanic Center**
www.pewhispanic.org/
This site provides information regarding Latino issues in the United States.

**Southern Poverty Law Center—Fight Hate and Promote Tolerance**
www.tolerance.org/index.jsp/
The center discusses a variety of issues on tolerance and assault.

# Play Memories

**Directions:** Please complete the following form regarding how you and your family play(ed) together.

Who am I?


When I was young, I liked to play with…


When I was young, my favorite games were…


Today I like to play…


My parents' favorite games were…


When my parents were young, they used to play…


Today they play…


When my grandparents were young, they used to play…


Today they play…

# Parent Involvement: A Historical Overview

*Learning about the past gives us an opportunity to understand our future.*

Mari Riojas-Cortez

*In this chapter you will learn how parents' involvement in their children's lives has evolved over time. After completing the chapter, you should be able to do the following:*

- *Identify the contributions of Comenius, Locke, Rousseau, Pestalozzi, and Froebel to views of children and the family.*
- *Describe the growth of parent education and the development of women's associations.*

## :: SOCIAL CHANGES AND FAMILIES

As rapid changes, social problems, poverty, and political unrest produce turbulence for families, their need for stabilizing forces increases. In the 1960s, with the calls for the War on Poverty and the Great Society, there emerged a focus on the family as one institution that could affect the lives of millions of children. During the Civil Rights Movement, culturally and linguistically diverse families began to demand equitable opportunities for education. Thus a renewed interest in programs in child-care centers, home-based education, and combined home–school intervention projects began to emerge.

The history of parent involvement begins by understanding the differences between families throughout the world and in our nation. It would be a mistake on our part to view the history of parent involvement only from a Western lens. We must also understand parent involvement from a variety of cultural groups and how families' funds of knowledge have evolved over time.

## :: HISTORICAL VIEWS OF CHILDREN

History shows that perspectives regarding children vary depending on the era. For example, in primitive times, children were valued for their contribution to survival and for their implied continuance of society. Greeks also viewed children as a link to the future, the conveyors of culture and civilization, as well as valued members of the family. Artwork depicts Egyptians as holding their children in high esteem. In some societies, adults showed affection for their children by holding them on their laps and embracing them. Children were also portrayed in art as carefree—running, playing with balls, dolls, board games, and jumping at leapfrog and hopscotch (Bell & Harper, 1980; Osborn, 1991).

The views of children influenced education. Formal systems of education existed in ancient India, China, and Persia, as well as in the pre-Columbian Americas, especially in the cultures of the Mayas, Aztecs, and Incas. During the Middle Ages, about 400–1400, children were very low among society's priorities; therefore, there was no system of education and very little family life. Living conditions did not provide poor people with an opportunity for privacy or time with their families. European societies, emerging from a time of suffering and hardship and influenced by the Protestant Reformation and the Catholic Counter-Reformation, viewed the child as one in whom evil must be suppressed and the soul nourished (Bell & Harper, 1980). The modern parent educator did not begin to emerge until the 17th and 18th centuries, and the general population was not affected until the 19th century (Bell & Harper).

### The Influence of Social Thinkers

New ideas about education and the importance of the home in the education of children were developed by social thinkers such as Comenius, Locke, Rousseau, Pestalozzi, and Froebel. These theories help us understand how some views of children have evolved and how some still remain the same. It is important for teachers and other educators to understand these philosophical views because they need to understand the development of how the parents perceive children.

**John Amos Comenius (1592–1670).** Born in Moravia in 1592, Comenius was a member and bishop of the Moravian Brethren, who believed in the basic goodness of each child. These beliefs are reflected in his writing about education methodology. In *Didactica Magna,* a large treatise on education, he discussed the importance of the infant's education: "It is the nature of everything that comes into being, that while tender it is easily bent and formed, but that, when it has grown

55

hard, it is not easy to alter. Wax, when soft, can be easily fashioned and shaped; when hard it cracks readily" (Comenius, 1967, p. 58). In the *School of Infancy,* written in 1628, he emphasized that education begins at home and described in detail the manner in which young children should be educated. Comenius also wrote textbooks for children. *Orbis Pictus* (*The World in Pictures*) is considered the first picture book for children (Epstein, 1991). Still, although a prolific writer, Comenius was unable to change the direction of education during his lifetime.

However, Comenius's ideas as they relate to parental involvement are now extremely important. First, believing that children are inherently good helps families work with their children in harmony. It helps families understand that children go through phases and their behavior will change but that they can help mold that behavior through guidance and discipline (not necessarily spanking). Contrary to this, if families believe that children are born bad, then the undesired behavior becomes the focus, rather than teaching for teaching's sake. Such families often spend a great deal of time disciplining their children rather than spending time teaching their children. Often children who are playful, loud, or mischievous are categorized as "bad." I once had a student in one of my classes tell me that he believed that children were "bad." He told me that he spanked his 2-year-old because she had disobeyed him and had run away at the grocery store. He believed that his daughter disobeyed him on purpose.

Comenius also believed in the importance of infant education—perhaps not education in the formal sense of the word, but parents educating children, teaching them many things that we now define as funds of knowledge. This was a revolutionary premise because infants during Comenius's time were not believed to be able to do anything. Today we see parents praising their infants when they reach a milestone, and many look for different toys, books, and activities to help their children grow and develop, thus teaching their children from an early age.

**John Locke (1632–1704).** Locke, an Englishman, had far-reaching and innovative ideas concerning government and education. He probably is best known for the concept that the newborn's mind is a *tabula rasa,* or blank slate, at birth. All ideas develop from experience; none are innate. Therefore, it is up to the family and teacher to provide valuable experiences and the optimum environment for the child's mind to thrive.

Some parents still hold the belief that they have to "fill" their child's mind with much information, and thus some parents work with their infants steadily to get them to reach milestones sooner, while others send their infants to schools that emphasize academic development at an early age. I have often heard parents indicate that their child is like a "sponge," absorbing everything they see and hear. This idea shows their belief that infants need to be filled with ideas in order to understand and interact. Contrary to this concept is how children learn by doing and imitating because they have the cognitive skills to understand such concepts. For example, my infant son, Miguel Fernando, likes to give *besitos,* or kisses, to the pictures of family members. We never taught him to give kisses to the pictures, but we have taught him to love his family and to kiss to show affection. The baby is imitating his family's behavior and at the same time he is able to cognitively process the social interaction by showing his understanding of this cultural practice. When parents teach, they are more than involved—they are engaged.

Locke, who lived during the period when "hardening" the child was in vogue, was a staunch supporter of this concept. If children were exposed to cold baths and other methods of hardening, according to the belief, they would become more resistant to diseases and ailments. In essence this view tells parents that the more the child suffers, the better they are going to be equipped in life. We still see this idea when parents allow children to get hurt (but not harshly), such as letting them touch things that are hot so that they can learn not to do it again. I remember my father telling my sisters and me when we were growing up in Mexico that we needed to suffer to understand the value of things (i.e., studying and working), and if we didn't suffer to get something, we would not appreciate its value. Thus, the belief of the "hardening" of the child is one that helps children become "strong," and parents very often want their children to be strong. This thinking leads parents to be engaged in a different way, more as "watchdogs" over their children rather than people who believe and trust in what they do.

Although parents who value instilling this type of strength in their children ultimately have the children's best interest in mind, they should bear in mind that children should never be allowed to be in danger in order to learn something. It is our duty as parents and teachers to guide children to become strong and productive individuals who care for others, but it is also our duty to prevent harm and danger in their lives.

### Jean Jacques Rousseau (1712–1778).

Rousseau, a Frenchman, was another giant in the development of changing European social thought. As thoughts of greater freedom for human beings evolved, stirrings of freedom for children also emerged. As a political analyst, Rousseau wrote *Social Contract* (1762), in which he described government through consent and contract with its subjects. This desire for freedom extended into his writings concerning children. In *Emile,* written in 1762, he urged mothers to "cultivate, water the young plant before it dies. Its fruits will one day be your delights. . . . Plants are shaped by cultivation and men by education" (Rousscau, 1979, p. 38).

Rousseau's ideas began to show the importance of the mother teaching her children. There are many early childhood programs that work with mothers (and recently have extended to fathers) to show them how to educate their children. For example, the organization Zero to Three provides brochures and other resources for parents to work with their infants and toddlers (these materials are offered in English and Spanish). For parents who do not have access to the Internet, teachers and other caregivers can make copies or share the information during workshops.

### Johann Heinrick Pestalozzi (1747–1827).

Pestalozzi believed in the natural goodness of children, struggling for many years to teach and care for poor children in his home in Switzerland. Pestalozzi based his teaching on the use of concrete objects, group instruction, cooperation among students, and self-activity of the child. To teach mathematics, he used beans and pebbles as counters and divided cakes and apples to demonstrate fractions. The child's day also included recreation, games, and nutritious snacks and meals (Gutek, 1968).

There are many examples of how parents today use "manipulatives" to teach children, such as when they go to the grocery store to buy fruits and vegetables. They may teach older children measurement by using an infant's bottle to measure the milk. Parents, even those who have no formal education, use different methods. I recall a father who participated in one of my research projects teaching his child about weight using the tools from his mechanic shop.

Though his method of teaching through tangible objects is still prevalent, Pestalozzi is most remembered for his writings. In his first successful book, *How Gertrude Teaches Her Children,* he emphasized the importance of the mother and included teaching methods for parents. It was the first comprehensive education book for parents—Pestalozzi truly can be hailed as the father of parent education.

### Friedrich Wilhelm Froebel (1782–1852).

Froebel, known as the father of kindergarten, was born in Germany in 1782, 35 years after Pestalozzi. Froebel is most noted for his development of a curriculum for the kindergarten, but he also recognized the importance of the mother in the development of the child. He saw the mother as the first educator of the child and wrote a book for mothers to use with their children at home. The book, *Mother Play and Nursery Songs with Finger Plays,* included verses, pictures, songs, and finger plays still used today, such as "pat-a-cake." Froebel's plan for education grew around a concept of unity. He organized his curriculum to follow the natural unfolding of the child, with the mother assisting in the development. Froebel's *Mother Play and Nursery Songs with Finger Plays* was translated into English, giving a large number of parents an opportunity to use Froebelian activities in their homes. In 1870, there were only four books on kindergarten, but by the end of the decade, five more had been translated; four more had been written; many articles had been printed and distributed; and two journals, *The Kindergarten Messenger* and *The New Education,* were flourishing (Vandewalker, 1971).

Froebel's development of kindergarten curriculum had a significant effect on the current philosophy of education. Instead of a prescribed curriculum designed by the adult to teach the child to read, write, and be moral, the curriculum was developed from the needs of the child. The concepts of child development and teaching to the individual levels of each child were a radical departure from lockstep education.

Following the needs of their children is what many parents do today. When parents become aware of their children's needs, they can engage in their development by meeting those needs in different ways. Communication and awareness are two crucial skills to teach children social and emotional skills. For example, reading, singing, and even just conversing with their children are important for parents to do and oftentimes come naturally, perhaps because their parents taught them such skills (funds of knowledge). My mother, who only had a sixth-grade education and attended beauty school, taught us that talking and singing to infants were crucial for their language development. I still sing the same lullaby that my mother sang to us and all of her grandchildren. I have also heard my 8-year-old daughter sing it to her dolls.

## ∷ HISTORICAL INFLUENCES ON PARENT EDUCATION AND INVOLVEMENT

The perspectives mentioned in the previous section helped build the theoretical foundation for what has become known as parent education and parent involvement. The emphasis on childrearing and education helped to develop a climate in which the learning interactions between child and parent became important for children's development. For instance, the Child Study Association of America (CSAA) was formed in 1888 by a group of New York City mothers; the American Association of University Women (AAUW) was founded in 1882 by college graduates; the National Congress of Mothers, later changed to the National Congress of Parents and Teachers (the PTA), was organized by women who gathered from across the nation at a meeting in 1897; and the National Association of Colored Women was established in 1897.

The associations founded in the 1880s and 1890s had a lasting effect on parent education in the United States. Throughout its history, the CSAA has emphasized child study and parent education; it was the oldest and largest organization solely committed to the study of children. Its earliest programs were studies by authorities of the time: Spencer, Rousseau, Froebel, and Montessori (Brim, 1965). The organization engaged in a variety of activities and services—all related to children and parents (Brim, 1965; Fisher, 1933; National Society for the Study of Education, 1929; Schlossman, 1976). The AAUW implemented a diverse educational program including the study of children and parent education. The PTA has been concerned with parent–school relationships since its inception. The National Association of Colored Women has focused on civic service, social service, and education with committees on home and the child, mothers, and legislation. Another group, the General Federation of Women's Clubs, formed in 1889, ushered in an even greater interest in women's roles as leaders. These organizations, with the exception of the CSAA, are still actively involved in the field of education and provide resources for many parents.

Parent involvement in the 1800s focused on families working together for survival.

## ▪▪ THE EARLY 20th CENTURY AND CHILDREARING

The early part of the 20th century centered on the family, with well-defined roles for father and mother. The father's duty was to financially support the family while the mother's duty was to focus on the home. Mothers were idolized as the epitome of purity and goodness, and children were taught to model the mother in their character development. It was important then that the mother be the right kind of person. For this reason, women's clubs flourished. Well-to-do mothers were able to join the many clubs available to them, and those who were on a lower socioeconomic level were served by settlement houses and the Free Kindergarten Association.

Poverty-stricken children in the United States were often forced to work under horrendous conditions at a very young age. These children, who were undernourished, neglected, or abused, prompted a rising social concern. As a result, the first White House Conference on Care of Dependent Children was called in 1909. The Children's Bureau was created in 1912 as a consequence of the conference, a first step in government concern for children.

Soon after the 1909 White House conference, the government began disseminating information on child care. The first *Infant Care,* which would become a popular parent education book on child care for infants, was published in 1914 by the federal agency that is now the U.S. Department of Health and Human Services.

Interestingly, although the population of the United States was diverse, the study of childrearing focused mostly on Americans of European descent. Minorities' childrearing experiences were not taken into consideration until the Civil Rights Movement (i.e., African American slavery, reservations and boarding houses for Native American children, punishment for Mexican American children for speaking Spanish).

### Establishing High-Quality Child Care

Twelve faculty wives at the University of Chicago—with guidance from the university—established the first parent cooperative in the United States in 1916. The women wanted high-quality child care for their children, parent education, and time to work for the Red Cross during the war (Taylor, 1981). This cooperative, the only one established in that decade, followed the tradition of English nursery schools established in 1911 by Margaret McMillan.

McMillan originally designed an open-air school for the poor in England. She emphasized health, education, play, and parent education, rather than mere child watching. The concept of the nursery school was welcomed by middle-class American families, as illustrated by the first parent cooperative in Chicago. Thus, parent cooperatives and the growth of nursery schools in the United States strengthened and promoted parent education with an emphasis on social development.

### Change in Social Skills

While the period of 1890 to 1910 stressed love and freedom, the period of 1910 to 1930 emphasized strict scheduling and discipline. Changes in the philosophical view of children had prompted school authorities to suggest that in order to ensure character development, discipline through punishment was necessary. The increased attention to strict childrearing was illustrated by the first issue of *Infant Care.* Mothers were told to expect obedience, ignore temper tantrums, and restrict physical handling of their children. The recommended change started early, as seen in the shift in attitude toward breast-feeding. Although breast-feeding was still highly recommended, a supplemental bottle could be given at 5 months, and the child was supposed to be completely weaned by the end of the first year (Wolfenstein, 1953). These severe attitudes continued into the 1920s, when all magazine articles on the topic recommended strict scheduling of infants rather than responding to the infants' needs (Stendler, 1950).

## ▪▪ 1920s TO 1950s

As discussed above, early childhood as an important period for character formation was stressed in the 1920s. For example, the behaviorist theorists believed that parents should reinforce character formation from the beginning, "do it right early or else" (Schlossman, 1976, p. 462).

### Child-Care Beliefs

During the 1920s, many teenagers and young adults were viewed as reckless, overindulged, and spoiled

(Schlossman, 1976). To reverse this scandalous situation, children were to be trained early to be responsible, well-behaved individuals. Watsonian behaviorism, the belief that humans can modify behavior through environmental conditioning, was beginning to be felt (Trawick-Smith, 2010). This childrearing theory was mixed in the 1920s with the learning-by-doing theories of Dewey, a small portion of Freudian psychology, and Gesell's belief in natural maturation and growth. Although each theorist had a different approach, all recognized the importance of early experiences and the influence of the environment on the child's development.

The 1923 edition of *Infant Care,* issued by the Children's Bureau, admonished parents that "toilet training may begin as early as the end of the first month. . . . The first essential in bowel training is absolute regularity" (Vincent, 1951, p. 205). Although breast-feeding was recommended for 6 to 9 months, once weaning was commenced it was to be accomplished in 2 weeks. If the parents insist on substitution to "artificial food . . . the child will finally yield" (Wolfenstein, 1953, p. 125).

An explosion of parent programs accompanied the prosperity of the 1920s. The era reflected a swing from parent education offered by settlement houses for immigrants and free kindergartens for the underprivileged to the involvement of many middle-class parents in study groups for their own enlightenment and enjoyment.

## Parent Cooperatives

The parent cooperative movement, which developed rapidly in California but grew more slowly elsewhere until after World War II, was a way for parents to obtain high-quality education for their children (Osborn, 1991). Parent cooperatives emerged in five locations in the 1920s: Cambridge, Massachusetts; the University of California at Los Angeles; Schenectady, New York; Smith College in Northampton, Massachusetts; and the American Association of University Women in Berkeley, California. To participate, parents had to share responsibilities, which not only helped the cooperatives function but was an excellent example of parent involvement.

Rural families such as the one pictured here were the norm in the United States. Many immigrants also settled in the cities.

## Parent Education

Organizational membership growth also illustrated increased interest in parent education. PTA membership expansion depicted, in terms of sheer numbers, the growth in interest in parent programs. The organization grew from 60,000 in 1915 to 190,000 in 1920, to 875,000 in 1925, to nearly 1.5 million in 1930 (Schlossman, 1976). AAUW membership rose to 35,000 in the 1920s, and each issue of its journal contained a column on parent education. Concurrently, the Child Study Association of America, recognized as the educational leader in parent education during the 1920s, grew from 56 parent groups in 1926 to 135 in 1927 (National Society for the Study of Education, 1929).

## Child Study Manual

Across the country many school systems implemented parent education and preschool programs. The Emily Griffith Opportunity School (Denver public school system) initially funded a parent education and preschool program in 1926. Its early emphasis on health education for families expanded to childrearing theories and other parenting skills as interests and needs changed. Also in the 1920s Benjamin Gruenberg published *Outlines of Child Study: A Manual for Parents and Teachers,* a text on childrearing that many parent groups used as a study guide. Succinct discussions on issues of child development were included in each chapter (Gruenberg, 1927).

## The Coming of the Depression

As the 1920s drew to a close, middle-class parents were active in parent groups; optimistic about the future; and concerned about health, nutrition, and shaping their children's actions. That all changed with the financial crash of 1929, which forced a tremendous shift in the lifestyle of many families and set the stage for the Great Depression of the 1930s. Poverty made it very difficult for families to provide for their children during these years, and there was a need to support families by offering information on budget, clothing, health, physical care, and diet. The decade began with the White House Conference on Child Health and Protection in November 1930. Results included rehabilitation projects, such as the Works Progress Administration (WPA), which offered a forum for mothers who were not active in women's clubs or Parent–Teacher Associations to learn about home management practices. Established in October 1933, the Federal Emergency Relief Administration (FERA) authorized work-relief wages for unemployed teachers and others to organize and direct nursery schools; about 75,000 children were enrolled during 1934 and 1935 (Goodykoontz, Davis, & Gabbard, 1947).

This time of change also reflected varying viewpoints on childrearing, ranging from strict scheduling to self-regulation. *Character formation* began to take on broader meanings. Whereas it had meant moral development earlier in the 1900s, articles in magazines now included personality development (Stendler, 1950).

Regardless of their viewpoints, many parents maintained involvement with parent education, with numbers continuing at a high level during the first half of the decade. During this time, parents in the United States were receiving information through the mass media, including radio series, lectures, magazines, and the distribution of more than 8 million copies of *Infant Care.* The Pennsylvania Department of Public Instruction's (1935) Bulletin 86, *Parent Education,* reported that parents were also being reached through study groups, with more than 700,000 parents involved in group participation.

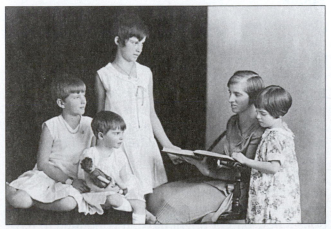

This mother reading to her children illustrates the emphasis on parent education, which expanded in the 1920s and continued into the 1930s.

Families struggled to survive in the 1930s.

Bulletin 86 stressed the importance of parent education, noting that

> The job of the school is only half done when it has educated the children of the nation. Since it has been demonstrated beyond doubt that the home environment and the role played by understanding parents are paramount in the determination of what the child is to become, it follows that helping the parent to feel more adequate for his task is fully as important from the point of view of public education and the welfare of society as is the education of the children themselves. Moreover, an educated parenthood facilitates the task of the schools and insures the success of its educational program with the child. (p. 12)

## Treatment of Minorities

Prejudice against minorities prevailed during this time. Much of the United States followed the separate-but-equal doctrine, operating separate, usually substandard programs for African Americans. It was not until 1954 that the U.S. Supreme Court declared the practice a violation of the Constitution. Latino children, mostly Mexican Americans, also suffered from prejudice, with many not being allowed to speak in their family's native language; in some schools, the teachers would even punish the children who spoke their native language by hitting them.

## Change in View of Children

The tendency of parents in the 1920s and early 1930s to follow the specific rules of behaviorists changed in the 1940s when parents began to recognize that no one answer could work for all situations (Brim, 1965): "The swing from the 'be-tough-with-them, feed-on-schedule, let them cry-it-out' doctrines of the twenties and thirties was almost complete" (Brim, 1965, pp. 130–131). The emotionally healthy child was the goal for professionals and parents, with a new emphasis being place on self-regulation, which allowed the development of trust and autonomy in the young child.

Vincent (1951) suggested that the decade between 1935 and 1945 could be called "baby's decade," with the mother "secondary to the infant care 'experts' and the baby's demands" (p. 205). By the early 1940s, mothers were told that children should be fed when hungry, and bowel and bladder training should not begin too early. Babies were to be trained in a gentle manner after they developed physical control. The latest version of *Infant Care* depicted children as interested in the world around them and viewed exploring as natural.

Mead and Wolfenstein later described the change in attitude toward the basic nature of human beings:

> One of the most striking changes in American thinking about children from the nineteenth and early twentieth centuries to the more recent past and the present is the radical change in the conception of the child's nature. From the 19th-century belief in "infant depravity" and the early 20th-century fear of the baby's "fierce" impulses, which, if not vigilantly curbed, could easily grow beyond control and lead to ruin, we have come to consider the child's nature as totally harmless and beneficent. (Mead & Wolfenstein, 1963, p. 146)

## Spock

Shifts in beliefs about children were reflected in the childrearing practices of the period. In 1946, Benjamin Spock, a best-selling author and parent educator, published *The Common Sense Book of Baby and Child Care*. He believed the rules and regulations imposed on parents during the 1920s and 1930s caused undue pressure, and he advised parents to enjoy their children and the role of parent.

Spock's book answered questions on feeding, sleeping, clothing, toilet training, management, and illnesses; he had answers for almost all the questions a new parent might have. It continued to have great influence on childrearing through the 1950s and beyond as children raised by Spock's methods became parents.

## Parent Groups

Both the Great Depression and World War II brought federal support for children's services at younger ages. FERA regulated the child-care funds originally, followed by WPA, and, during World War II, the Federal Works Agency (Goodykoontz et al., 1947). The need to provide child care for families during the Depression emanated from the necessity for parents to work to get back on their feet and support their families. During World War II, women needed child-care services so they could join the war effort.

The 1940s, although consumed by the outbreak of World War II, also saw no reduction in offerings in parent education, though research and training in child development did decline (Brim, 1965). Parent groups continued in public schools, and county extension programs prospered, and parent education found added direction in the 1940s through the mental health movement. In 1946, the National Mental Health Act authorized states to establish mental health programs and related parent education (Goodykoontz et al., 1947). The need to understand oneself and one's children was recognized as necessary for healthy parent–child interaction.

Many young adults had postponed marriage and family during the war, but the 1950s were years of relative calm, allowing for emphasis on children and family life. This is when the "baby boom" began gathering more steam. Schools were feeling the increase in numbers of children and were rapidly expanding to meet their needs. The PTA had more than 9 million members and thousands of study groups among its 30,000 local chapters. Parents were involved with the schools as "room parents" and fundraisers for special projects. The view "Send your child to school—we will do the teaching; your responsibility as a parent is to be supportive of the teachers and schools" prevailed as the basic philosophy between school and parents.

## Emphasis on Family Life

Parent education and preschool programs, part of adult education in many school districts, continued as a vital source of childrearing information. In fact, a survey by the National Education Association revealed that family life was the topic of 32 percent of adult education classes (Brim, 1965). Pamphlets from the Child Study Association, the Public Affairs Committee, Science Research Associates, and the Parent Education Project of Chicago, plus books by authorities such as Arnold Gesell, Erik Erikson, B. F. Skinner, Benjamin Spock, Lawrence Frank, and Sidonie Gruenberg, were used as curriculum guides.

This trend continued through the 1950s. During this time, James L. Hymes wrote his first book on home–school relations. *Your Child from 6 to 12,* published by the U.S. Department of Health, Education and Welfare (1949), illustrated the attitude that prevailed in the 1950s and beyond. The preface of the booklet reflected the change from the absolutism of the 1920s and 1930s: "There are many more things that we don't know than we know about children. . . . Every child is unique in temperament, intelligence, and physical make-up" (p. 39).

Orville Brim, sponsored by the Russell Sage Foundation and the Child Study Association, examined the issues involved in parent education in *Education for Child Rearing* (1965). His analysis of the effects of parent education continues to be relevant to the study of parent education today.

## Erikson

Erikson (1986) popularized the eight stages of personality development in *Childhood and Society,* first published in 1950. His neo-Freudian theories emphasized social and emotional development based on interdisciplinary theories from biology, psychology, and sociology. His theory outlines eight stages of growth from infancy to old age The stages begin with development of trust versus mistrust for infants, autonomy versus shame and doubt for toddlers, initiative versus guilt for preschoolers, and industry versus inferiority for school-age children. The later stages involve adolescents forming identity versus identity diffusion; for young adults, intimacy versus isolation; for adults, generativity versus self-absorption; and for mature adults, integrity versus despair. Erikson's developmental stages and the childrearing practices of the 1950s reflected the belief that social and emotional health were of utmost importance to the child.

## Analysis of Parent–Child Relations

The decades between the 1920s and the 1950s provided different ideas regarding child development and parental involvement based on the new ideas and beliefs shown by child psychologists and educational philosophers. In a content analysis of *Ladies' Home Journal, Good Housekeeping,* and *Redbook* from 1950 to 1970, Bigner (1985) found articles primarily concerned with parent–child relations, socialization, and developmental stages. Spanking was condoned by some in the early 1950s, but by the end of the decade, it was consistently discouraged and described as an inefficient and barbaric method that does no more than show the youngster that parents can hit. Most articles encouraged self-regulation by the child. Parents were told it was important that children feel loved and wanted and were advised to hold, love, and enjoy their children and to rely on their own good judgment in making childrearing decisions. Parents were also encouraged to provide a home life that was supportive of individual differences and allowed each child to grow into a well-adjusted adult. Development was a natural process, and maturation could not be pushed. Gesell's work on development in psychomotor and physical areas supported the theory that children proceed through innate developmental stages. As a consequence, parents were encouraged to provide a well-balanced, nutritional diet and an environment that allowed children to grow and learn at their own rate.

## ■■ THE 1960s: CIVIL RIGHTS AND THE FAMILY

Great changes in the American family took place between 1890 and 1960 as the country changed from a basically rural nation to an urban nation. The majority of families had been self-sufficient rural families with authoritarian parents in the earlier part of the century, and children were economic assets who helped their parents with the family farm or business; as the century progressed, children became financial liabilities, costing $20,000 to raise from infancy to 18 years of age (Hill, 1960). It was not just the children's role but also the roles of the parents that shifted during this time, including increased numbers of women entering the labor force to supplement their husband's income or increase their own economic freedom. For many women, who were single parents or were a supporting member of a two-parent family, working was an economic necessity. Because of the social

The Civil Rights Movement brought about changes in families.

climate during this time, it was common for all institutions—family, education, religion, economics, and government—to be questioned and to undergo change.

### Father Involvement

During the 1960s, the importance of the father's relationship with his children was also stressed and, although his expected obligations to his children were not the same as the mother's, early interaction with his newborn baby was recognized as very beneficial.

### Information for Parents

Parents of the 1960s had many child-care books and booklets from which to choose. Publications from the Child Study Association and Science Research Associates and public affairs pamphlets covered many of the problems parents faced. Benjamin Spock continued to publish books on child care, and in them he advised firm, consistent guidance of the child. Spock's efforts were aided by psychologist Haim Ginott (1965), who offered parents a method for talking about feelings and guiding the child in a manner that avoided placing guilt and helped the child understand the parents' feelings, thus disciplining the child in a positive manner.

### War on Poverty

Although prosperity was within reach for most U.S. citizens and the standard of living had steadily improved to the highest in the world, minorities, people with disabilities, and other groups were still underemployed, often poverty stricken, and largely ignored. The government had high hopes for the Great Society eliminating poverty for all citizens. The War on Poverty was legislation introduced by President Johnson to support his belief in increasing social welfare programs, including education and health care. In the War on Poverty programs, children of the poor—who were undernourished, in ill health, without proper housing, and lacking educational opportunities—as well as minority children in need, were chosen as a major target to realize hope for the future.

Works of behavioral scientists and educators presenting overpowering evidence that early environment has a profound effect on a child's development coupled with the national mood of equality and opportunity in the 1960s propelled the country to respond to the needs of the poor (Bloom, 1964; Hunt, 1961; Skeels, 1966; Spitz, 1965; see Chapter 1). One of the most effective responses was to provide educational intervention for the children of the poor. If children could be given equal environmental opportunities, the cycle of poverty could be broken. The stage was set for the birth of Head Start.

## Head Start

In 1965, the Office of Economic Opportunity began an 8-week summer program for preschool children from low-income families. The proposed projects had a two-pronged approach: The child would benefit from an enriched early education program, and the parents would be an integral part of the programs as aides, advisory council members, or paraprofessional members of the team. As a result of these beliefs, the first Head Start centers were opened in the summer of 1965 as part of the War on Poverty. Head Start was a comprehensive program of health, nutrition, and education as well as a career ladder for economically disadvantaged families. Migrant Head Start, a program for children of migrant workers, had the first center-based infant–toddler program.

## Elementary and Secondary Education Act

Shortly after the formation of Head Start, the Office of Education, Department of Health, Education, and Welfare, undertook direction for the Elementary and Secondary Education Act (ESEA) of 1965. Two of the title projects under ESEA were:

1. Title I, which assisted school districts in improving the education of educationally deprived children. From its inception, parents were involved in the program.
2. Title IV-C (formerly Title III), which promoted the innovative programs that enrich educational opportunities. Many of these projects included home visitation programs for preschool children, identification of children with developmental delays before school entry, and working with the parents for the benefit of their children.

Concern about continuity of educational success after Head Start resulted in the implementation of the Follow Through program as part of the 1967 Economic Opportunity Act. Designed to carry the benefits of Head Start and similar preschool programs into the public school system, parent participation was a major component of the program, and, as with the Head Start program, parent advisory councils were mandated.

## Developmental Continuity

Concern about the link between Head Start and the public school resulted in funding for developmental continuity. Two program designs were investigated. One was based on a cooperative model with both Head Start and the schools working out a continuous educational program for the child. The other caused change within the existing school system and included programs for children ages 3 years and up as part of the school system as well as a curriculum structured for preschool through age 8. Both programs involved parents throughout preschool and school years.

## Civil Rights Act of 1965

Although not directly connected with parent education, the Civil Rights Act of 1965 had great influence on the role of minorities and women during subsequent decades and, through this, affected the family. Affirmative action, requiring minorities and women to be treated equally in housing, education, and employment, resulted in psychological as well as empirical, observable changes in conditions for these populations.

## :: THE 1970s: MOVING FORWARD

The decade of the 1970s could be described as the era of advocacy. Groups were no longer willing to sit and wait; they had learned in the 1960s that the way to help is through self-advocacy and intensive activism. Parents of children with disabilities—individually and through organizations such as the Association for Retarded Children, the Council for Exceptional Children, and the Association for Children with Learning Disabilities—advocated equal rights for the special child and won. Advocate groups for children sprang up across the land with training sessions on political power and the means to implement change and protection for children.

The public schools were not immune. Parents began to question programs and their participation with schools and teachers. Forced integration and required busing were issues confronting schools and parents.

### Research

Studies conducted in the 1970s consistently demonstrated the importance of an enriched early home environment to the child's school success (Hanson, 1975; Shipman, Boroson, Bidgeman, Gart, & Mikovsky, 1976; White, Kaban, Attanucci, & Shapiro, 1973). Shipman et al. (1976) studied African American children of low socioeconomic status and found that the mother's educational aspirations and expectations were higher for children who scored high in reading than for those who scored low in reading. A higher level of parental education was also associated with children's overall academic success.

In 1975, the Consortium for Longitudinal Studies (1983) set out to determine the effect of the experimental early intervention programs of the 1960s on children. The consortium selected 11 research groups for analysis. Although the programs differed, they were all well designed and well monitored.

The consortium's findings emphasized the importance of early intervention (Consortium for Longitudinal Studies, 1983; Gray, Ramsey, & Klaus, 1982; Lazar et al., 1982; Levenstein, 1988; Spodek, 1982). In a summary of the findings, Lazar (1983) discussed two important points. First, a good preschool program pays off in two ways: benefits for children's development and financial savings

as a result of less special-education placement. Second, "closer contact between home and school and greater involvement of parents in the education of their children are probably more important" than generally realized by administrators (p. 464).

A follow-up study of Weikart's Perry Preschool Program vividly illustrated the effect that early educational intervention can have on children's lives (Berrueta-Clement, Schweinhart, Barnett, Epstein, & Weikart, 1984). The Perry Preschool Program followed children to age 19, 4 years beyond the report published by the consortium. Berrueta-Clement et al. compared children who had attended the Perry Preschool with children who had not. The researchers found that former Perry Preschool students grew up with more school success, placed a higher value on school, had higher aspirations for college, had fewer absences, and spent fewer of their school years in special education than children in a control group.

With the results of the research came increased programs. In 1972, 16 Home Start programs serving 1,200 families were launched, and 11 Child and Family Resource programs serving 900 families were started in July 1973. These programs promoted "continuity of service by including all children in the participating family from prenatal stage through age 8, and broaden[ed] the program focus from the age-eligible child, to the entire family" (U.S. Department of Health, Education and Welfare, 1974, p. iii).

Over the years, parent involvement in school decision making diminished, but when formal education joined with informal education, parents still had decision-making rights in regard to their child's schooling. The decade closed with school, government, social agencies, and families concerned with educational programs and support systems for children and parents.

## :: THE 1980s: A NEW DECADE OF HOPE FOR FAMILIES

The 1980s commenced with the White House Conference on Families, which took place in July 1980 at three locations: Baltimore, Minneapolis, and Los Angeles. Interest was high. Families were important to the citizens, but divisive interests complicated the work. Despite this, the conference approved 20 recommendations to support families, including flexible work schedules, leave policies, job sharing, more part-time jobs, and more child-care services. However, it did not have a great impact on reducing divorce or improving marital harmony.

## Family Concerns

Families in this decade were under stress caused by financial pressure, lack of available time, high mobility, lack of an extended family in proximity, drugs, abuse, violence on the streets and on television, health concerns, inadequate nutrition, and difficulty in obtaining or providing adequate child care. On the positive side, inflation steadied in the 1980s. Those who did not have housing, however, were caught in a crunch. Home buyers were faced with high down payments or extremely high monthly payments. Many could not afford any housing, and the number of homeless increased to become a national disgrace.

Poverty existed in all parts of the United States—32.5 million people were poor, 12.5 million of whom were children. One child out of five lived in poverty. The ratios were even higher for two minority groups: Nearly one in two African American children and one in three Latino children lived in poverty (Children's Defense Fund, 1989). Poverty was most evident in the inner cities. Relief came in the form of shelters and churches offering warmth to the homeless on cold nights and food lines set up by many private and church groups. In rural areas where poverty was not so evident, little hope was available. Many children attended school without their basic nutritional needs being met. Having access to school lunches was a means of survival for them.

Dealing drugs became more prevalent during this time. Children and families living in inner cities with high crime rates and widespread drug abuse needed comprehensive support to enable them to realize a more promising destiny (Schorr & Schorr, 1988). Social programs and education were intertwined in an effort to lower the high risk of poverty.

Along with drugs, two concerns that contributed to high risk for children were the increased numbers of teenage pregnancies. Very young mothers were not believed to be prepared physically, educationally, or mentally to rear children, yet one in five infants was born to teenagers (Hymes, 1987). The increased numbers of single mothers due to divorce, death of the husband, or preference also heightened the risk of poverty. In addition, acquired immunodeficiency syndrome (AIDS), first recognized in the early 1980s, frightened the entire society.

In sharp contrast, the 1980s were also characterized by greater affluence. High salaries were available for those in business, technology, and communication. In more than half of two-parent families in the United States, both parents worked outside the home (O'Connell & Bloom, 1987). This gave families a higher financial standard of living. However, time became a precious commodity, and some families found it difficult to save time for themselves and their children. Articles on handling stress and programs for stress reduction continued to grow in popularity. Parent education programs such as STEP, PET, and Active Parenting were offered by schools, hospitals, and social agencies.

## Parent Education

The country was divided throughout the 1980s, just as it had been during the White House Conference on Families: The far right decried public interference in rearing of children, but polls showed that most people favored family-life education.

The decade ended with little movement toward achievement of these recommendations. Few companies offered flexible work schedules and job sharing, and Congress defeated the Family and Parental Leave Act in 1988 (this later was approved and became the Family and Medical Leave Act of 1993).

## ∷ THE 1990s: FOCUS ON FAMILY INVOLVEMENT

The 1990s could be called the decade of Focus on the Family. Parent involvement changed to family involvement. From focusing on mothers in the 1950s and both fathers and mothers in the 1960s and 1970s, a shift occurred toward viewing the entire family environment as the most important factor in a child's education. The Department of Education emphasized the strengthening of families and issued a paper, *Strong Families, Strong Schools: Building*

*Community Partnerships for Learning* (1994). Family partnerships with school were encouraged, and in 1990, the Center on Children, Schools, Families, and Children's Learning was established.

Federal influence on schools continued with federal programs such as Title I, Even Start, and the Elementary and Secondary School Act. The introduction of *Goals 2000: Educate America* and the development of national standards were criticized by some as taking away the constitutional rights of states to control education, but, at the same time, parents were given more power to influence the education of their children. Many schools began restructuring and turned to site-based management, an educational design that had parents working with school personnel in the establishment of goals and direction. There was also a movement for choice in school selection. Charter schools became available in many states starting in 1996 and 1997. Parents could elect their own board and choose their own curriculum for their charter schools, funded by the school district in which they were located. Early childhood had great interest in constructivism and Reggio Emilio philosophy, which emphasizes the importance of children learning by doing.

## Family Resource Centers

During the 1990s, the creation and funding of family resource centers helped strengthen and empower families. The centers designed their programs according to the needs of their populations with offerings that might include parent education, programs for children, and literacy programs. Family literacy programs were established to help those who could not read, including immigrants who did not speak or read English or those who had not learned to read in school. Family literacy programs recognized that parents could help their children more if the parents themselves were able to read.

## Homeschooling

Homeschooling became more popular during the 1990s, and support groups helped parents who wanted to teach their children at home. States enacted certain requirements for parents to continue homeschooling. For example, children must take tests every 3 years and place no lower than the 19th percentile. It was recommended that schools work with homeschooling parents so that children could participate in activities that the home is unable to offer, such as band, chorus, and athletics.

## Family and Medical Leave Act

Congress finally passed the Family and Medical Leave Act in early 1993, providing 12 weeks of unpaid leave for employees with such family concerns as childbirth, adoption, or a serious illness of a child, spouse, or parent. The bill required all companies with 50 or more employees to guarantee jobs and provide health benefits to workers when they returned after the leave.

## Temporary Assistance for Needy Families

Welfare was revamped in 1996 with the Personal Responsibility and Work Opportunity Reconciliation Act. AFDC (Aid to Families with Dependent Children) had provided assistance for poor, single-parent families since 1935. It was replaced with Temporary Assistance for Needy Families (TANF), which provides block grants to states who run their own programs within federal guidelines. The law required mothers to join the workforce if they received assistance for more than two years. It placed a 5-year lifetime limit on eligibility for assistance. Some concerns have emerged as the law was carried out, including lack of child care, insufficient health care, poor job skills of some former AFDC recipients, and child-care workers who earn low wages.

## ▪▪ THE 21st CENTURY: EMPHASIS ON EDUCATION

The 21st century opened with continued emphasis on education. Programs that had originated in the 1960s from the War on Poverty, such as the Elementary and Secondary Education Act and Head Start, continued into the new century. The importance of families in the education of children was emphasized, and programs for the very young child were increased. A new law, No Child Left Behind Act of 2001, was signed into law on January 8, 2002. The new law was "considered to be the most sweeping reform of the Elementary and Secondary Education Act since it was enacted in 1965" (U.S. Department of Education, 2002).

Families that interact in different ways teach their children many skills and concepts.

## Partnerships for Family Involvement in Education

The U.S. Department of Education offered information and support through the establishment of Partnerships for Family Involvement in Education. In addition, the Center on Families, Communities, Schools, and Children's Learning, which was established at Johns Hopkins University, continued to provide research, policy, and the National Network of Partnerships. A number of Promising Practices policies put out during this time resulted in various improvements in the schools during the panel's existence, including goals around school readiness and parental involvement.

## Family and Medical Leave Act Revised

The Family and Medical Leave Act, which offers 12 weeks of unpaid leave from work, was favored by most citizens. It was found, however, that 78 percent of those who needed leave were unable to take it because one salary was not enough to support their families. Some states are looking at options that would supplement the one salary by allowing the parent staying home with the infant to take out unemployment benefits or temporary disability insurance. In 2000, the U.S. Department of Labor adopted regulations encouraging states to provide unemployment benefits to working parents who take leave to care for newborns or newly adopted children (Asher & Lenhoff, 2001).

## Technology

Technology in the 21st century exploded, with computers becoming "a reality no one can ignore" (Shields & Behrman, 2000). The number of computers in the schools increased from 250,000 in 1983 to 8.6 million in 1997. In 2008, 100 percent of all U.S. public schools had computers with Internet access (National Center for Education Statistics, 2010). Access to computers at home ranged from 22 percent of families with less than $20,000 income to 91 percent of families with incomes of $75,000, according to a 1998 survey (Becker, 2000). According to the 2010 U.S. Census, 68.7 percent of U.S. households owned a computer with Internet access in 2009.

With the iniquitousness of computer use and information available through the Internet, it is essential in the 21st century that older children become competent computer users. Parents can also be trained to use computers for a variety of purposes. Exposing younger children is wise as well, though teachers should keep in mind that making computers a useful tool in the early childhood classroom requires that the teacher also be knowledgeable and supportive. Children should be 3 or 4 years of age before they explore and use appropriate computer software. Kindergarten and primary-grade children continue with exploration, using developmentally appropriate software, but as they become more familiar with computers, their explorations may lead to composing a variety of visuals including stories and games.

## Living with Change

To understand the future, it is also necessary to understand the past. Table 4.1 offers an overview of important ideas about children over the centuries. In the new century, the United States faces issues of terrorist threats and conflict with different nations. Besides political unrest, social problems such as hunger, lack of health care, genocide, drug-infested communities, prejudice and racism, and lack of educational opportunities prevail around the world, affecting families and in our own backyard. Many families live in dire conditions that need to be eliminated. As challenges abound, it is important for us all to consider how we as well as our nation and the world will respond to create better experiences for all children.

**TABLE 4.1**

**Events and people who influenced ideas about children and childrearing, 6000 B.C.–A.D. 1800–2001.**

| | |
|---|---|
| 6000–5000 B.C. | Primitive cultures developed. Parents modeled behavior for children to learn. |
| 5510–3787 B.C. | Egyptian children were educated in their homes in the Old Kingdom of Egypt. |
| 3787–1580 B.C. | Schools outside the home developed in Egypt. |
| 427–347 B.C. | Life of Plato, who questioned theories of childrearing, suggesting that a controlled environment would promote good habits. Infanticide was practiced by Greeks, Romans, and others. |
| 384–323 B.C. | Life of Aristotle, father of the scientific method, who promoted childrearing and education by the state. |
| 204–122 B.C., | Life of Polybius, who noted the importance of the family in developing good Roman citizens. |
| 106–43 B.C. | Life of Cicero, who emphasized the family's role in the development of the Roman citizen. |
| A.D. 318 | Emperor Constantine declared infanticide a crime. |
| A.D. 400–1400 | The Roman Empire declined and the feudal system emerged. Wealthy children were apprenticed to nobles; commoners were apprenticed to tradesmen. Peasants worked in the fields. |
| A.D. 1450 | The printing press was invented, but books were available only to the wealthy. |
| 1483–1540 | Life of Martin Luther, who introduced the Ninety-five Theses and began the drive for all to learn to read the Bible. |
| 1500–1671 | Etiquette books began to include etiquette for children. |
| 1592–1670 | Life of John Amos Comenius, a Moravian educator, who wrote books on progressive educational theories. |
| 1632–1704 | Life of John Locke, who believed the newborn's mind was like a blank slate—everything is learned. |
| 1697 | Mother Goose tales were published. |
| 17th and 18th centuries | Wealthy European children were cared for by wet nurses. Colonial American children were taught to follow Puritanical religious beliefs and were trained to be obedient and faithful. |
| 1703–1791 | Life of John Wesley, founder of Methodism, who was raised by his mother, who believed in breaking the will. |
| 1712–1778 | Life of Jean Jacques Rousseau, author of *Emile,* who wrote that children should grow up untainted by society. |
| 1747–1827 | Life of Johann Heinrich Pestalozzi, father of parent education, who developed a curriculum based on concrete objects and group instruction, cooperation among students, and self-activity. |
| 1782–1852 | Life of Friedrich Froebel, who developed a curriculum for the young child based on the concept of unity. He is regarded as the father of kindergarten. |
| 19th century | American parents began to rely on American publications in addition to European ideas and the tenets of the church. |
| 1815 | Parent group meetings were held in Portland, Maine. |
| 1854 | Henry Barnard, U.S. commissioner of education, supported Froebelian concepts. |
| 1856 | A German-speaking kindergarten was established in Wisconsin by Margaretha Shurz. |
| 1860 | Elizabeth Peabody established the first English-speaking kindergarten in the United States. |
| 1860–1864 | During the Civil War, women were encouraged to replace men as teachers. |
| 1870 | The National Education Association was founded. |
| 1870–1880 | A great extension of the kindergarten movement and parent education occurred. |
| 1871 | The first public kindergarten in North America was established in Ontario, Canada. |

| 1873 | Susan Blow directed the first public kindergarten in the United States, opened by Dr. William Harris in St. Louis. |
|---|---|
| 1882 | The American Association of University Women was established. |
| 1884 | The Department of Kindergarten Instruction of the National Education Association was formed (later the Department of Elementary-Kindergarten-Nursery Education; dissolved in the mid-1970s). |
| 1888 | The Child Study Association of America was founded. |
| 1889 | The General Federation of Women's Clubs was founded. G. Stanley Hall began the first child study center. |
| 1890–1900 | Settlement houses were established to aid the poor and new immigrants. |
| 1892 | The International Kindergarten Union (now the Association for Childhood Education International) was established. |
| 1895 | Patty Smith Hill and Anna Bryan studied with G. Stanley Hall. |
| 1896 | The Laboratory School at the University of Chicago was started by John Dewey. The National Association of Colored Women was established. |
| 1897 | The Parent Teachers Association (PTA) was founded. |
| 1898 | *Kindergarten Magazine* was first published. |
| 1905 | Maria Montessori established Casa dei Bambini in Rome. Sigmund Freud wrote *Three Essays of the Theory of Sexuality.* |
| 1909 | The First White House Conference on Care of Dependent Children was held. |
| 1911 | Margaret McMillan designed an open-air nursery for children of the poor in England. Gesell started the Child Development Clinic at Yale University. |
| 1912 | The Children's Bureau was established. It published the first edition of *Infant Care* in 1914. |
| 1916 | The first parent cooperative was established in Chicago. |
| 1917 | The Smith-Hughes Act was passed. The Iowa Child Welfare Research Station was established. |
| 1920s | Twenty-six parent education programs were established. |
| 1920 | The Child Welfare League of America was founded. Watson, a behaviorist, believed that children should be strictly scheduled and should not be coddled. |
| 1922 | A nursery school was established in Boston by Abigail Elliot. Benjamin Gruenberg wrote the *Child Study Manual.* |
| 1925 | The National Council of Parent Education was established. Patty Smith Hill began the National Committee on Nursery Schools (now the National Association for the Education of Young Children). |
| 1927 | The first Black nursery school in the United States was founded by Dorothy Howard in Washington, DC. |
| 1928 | The nursery school movement expanded from 3 schools in 1920 to 89 in 1928. |
| 1930 | The White House Conference on Child Health and Protection recommended parent education as part of the public school system. |
| 1932 | Parent education courses were offered in 25 states. |
| 1933 | The Federal Emergency Relief Administration authorized work-relief wages for nursery school teachers. |
| 1934–1938 | *Parent Education,* the journal of the National Council of Parent Education, was published. |
| 1940s | A new emphasis on mental health for children emerged. |
| 1940 | The Lanham Act provided money for child care so that mothers could join the war effort. |
| 1946 | Benjamin Spock published *The Common Sense Book of Baby and Child Care.* |
| 1949 | *Your Children from 6 to 12* was published by the Children's Bureau. |

*(Continued)*

**TABLE 4.1**

**Events and people who influenced ideas about children and childrearing, 6000 B.C.–A.D. 1800–2001. (*continued*)**

| | |
|---|---|
| 1950 | Erik Erikson wrote *Childhood and Society,* which included the eight stages of personality growth. James Hymes wrote *Effective Home–School Relations.* |
| 1952 | Jean Piaget's work *The Origins of Intelligence in Children* was translated into English. |
| 1957 | After the launching of *Sputnik,* new emphasis was placed on children's intellectual development. *Parenthood in a Free Nation* was published by the Parent Education Project of the University of Chicago. |
| 1960 | The Golden Anniversary White House Conference on Children and Youth was held. The Parent Cooperative Preschools International was founded. |
| 1960 | The Day Care and Child Development Council of America was founded. |
| 1962 | J. McVicker Hunt wrote *Intelligence and Experience,* which questioned the concept of fixed IQ. |
| 1963 | The White House Conference on Mental Retardation was held. |
| 1964 | The Economic Opportunity Act of 1964 began the War on Poverty. |
| 1965 | The Civil Rights Act was passed. Head Start was established. The Elementary and Secondary School Act was passed; Title I provided money for educationally deprived children. |
| 1967 | The Follow Through program was begun to provide continuity for former Head Start students. |
| 1970 | The White House Conference on Children and Youth was held. |
| 1972 | The National Home Start program, which involved parents in teaching, was initiated. |
| 1975 | The Education for All Handicapped Children Act, P.L. 94-192, was passed. |
| 1980 | The White House Conference on Families was held. |
| 1987 | P.L. 99-457; designed to serve handicapped children with disabilities up to age 2, was passed. |
| 1990 | National Education Goals 2000 was established. |
| 1993 | The Family and Medical Leave Act of 1993 was passed. |
| 1996 | Temporary Assistance for Needy Families (TANF) replaced Aid to Families with Dependent Children (AFDC). |
| 1997 | The White House Summit on Early Childhood was held July 26 and 27. |
| 1997 | The Individuals with Disabilities Education Act of 1997 was reauthorized. |
| 2001 | The No Child Left Behind Act of 2001 was passed. |
| 2001 | On September 11, the Twin Towers of the World Trade Center in New York City were destroyed by terrorists. |
| 2008–2009 | Banking and housing crisis leave many families without homes. |

## SUMMARY

Historically, the family provided the first informal education for the child through modeling, teaching, and praising or disciplining. From the times of early Egyptian, Sumerian, Hebrew, Greek, and Roman days, parents were actively involved in the selection of teachers and the education of their children.

Family life in the United States was able to flourish from the early days. Childrearing practices varied according to country of origin, but they were basically tied to the religious background of the family. The parent education groups in the early 1800s were based on the need to rear children according to these religious principles.

The 1920s were the most productive in terms of the establishment of parent education programs. Change had also come in terms of childrearing practices. Although authorities in the 1890s and the early 1900s emphasized love and affection in the formation of character, the 1920s focused on strict scheduling and discipline. During the 1940s, parent education programs continued, bolstered by child-care money for mothers working in the war effort. The 1950s showed more concern for the mental health of the child.

In the 1960s and 1970s, Americans were confronted with great social change. The 1980s began with the first White House Conference on Families, attended by men and women representing diverse philosophical beliefs about families. Parent involvement was recognized as an important element in a child's success at school. Monetary support for family support programs, however, decreased in the 1980s. Societal problems included increased drug and alcohol abuse by school-age children and poverty for one in five children.

The 1990s saw the Family Medical Leave Act pass in 1993. Family resource centers, family literacy, and Even Start supported parents in their search for literacy and family strengths. In 1996, welfare was revamped as Temporary Assistance for Needy Families (TANF), which replaced Aid to Families with Dependent Children (AFDC). The 21st century arrived with many challenges.

## SUGGESTED CLASS ACTIVITIES AND DISCUSSIONS

1. Ask a librarian to help you find books from art museums throughout the world. Examine these for trends in childrearing practices and beliefs.
2. Find a library that has federal publications. Look through books published by the Children's Bureau. Examine the changes in beliefs about child development.
3. Get a copy of the *Twenty-Eighth Year Book, Parts I and II, Preschool and Parent Education* by the National Society for the Study of Education. Compare the programs on parent education in the 1920s with the programs in 2010.
4. Concern about the poor was strongest during the 1890s, the early 20th century, the 1930s, and the 1960s. What were the differing causes of poverty? Why did the concern seem to lessen in intervening decades?

5. Identify some of the Native Americans' nations. How has their way of life changed over the past 150 years?
6. Examine your community. How many types of programs for children have begun since Head Start was initiated in 1965?
7. Describe the changes in immigration. How have various immigrant groups differed in their treatment after arriving in the United States?

## USEFUL WEB SITES

When this chapter on history was originally written, Web sites were not as numerous as they currently are. Information was primarily acquired from books and journals, and the subject matter changed with each decade. I recommend that any specific information desired be found in individual Web sites such as those that accompany the rest of the chapters or in history Web sites.

**National Society for the Study of Education: Yearbooks**
www.nsse-chicago.org/yearbooks.asp/
The National Society for the Study of Education archives its yearbooks all the way back to 1900.

**On Writing Childhood History by Lloyd deMause**
www.psychohistory.com/
An interesting account of Lloyd deMause's (a psycho-historian rather than an early childhood educator) study of psychiatry. Written in 1988, deMause illustrates the challenge of childhood history.

**Smithsonian Education**
www.smithsonianeducation.org/
Site details school programs and tours at the National Museum of American History.

**Smithsonian National Museum of American History: Kids**
www.americanhistory.si.edu/kids/
Site offers child-centered activities and information related to American history.

**U.S. National Archives and Records Administration**
www.archives.gov/
The archives of the United States are quite extensive. The site allows you to select a subject. For example, there are 186 multipage letters received by teacher Clara D. True of Santa Clara Day School, a Santa Fe Indian School, from August 29, 1902, until September 17, 1906.

# Effective Home–School–Community Relationships

*That responsibility begins not in our classrooms, but in our homes and communities. It's the family first that instills the love of learning in a child.*

President Barack Obama
*(Winning the Future, State of the Union, 2011)*

*In this chapter you will learn how to ensure positive relationships between the home, school, and community, and enhance the education of young children. After completing this chapter, you will be able to do the following:*

- Create an environment that respects, values, and welcomes parents and the community.
- Develop a school, child-care center, or preschool that values parents' funds of knowledge, thus encouraging participation.
- List and explain community services that schools, child-care centers, and preschools can offer to support families with the task of parenting.
- List and explain services that need parents to help the center or school become successful.
- Create a family resource center to assist parents with different academic or development related tasks.
- Develop a parent advisory council.

In order to make discussion of parent, school, and community cooperation flow more smoothly, *schools* will often be used to include all levels of care and education.

## :: PARENT–SCHOOL COOPERATION

Parent–school cooperation brings the strengths of the home and the expertise of the center or school into a working partnership. As we have stated before, a family's funds of knowledge help children perform in life and in school. It is crucial for teachers and administrators to respect and value a child's culture and background because children bring the ideas, feelings, strengths, and weaknesses of the home into their life at school. Because of this, every school issue, concern, and educational goal should involve the child's family. If homes and centers are connected through the children, this partnership will strengthen the effectiveness of the center or school. Recent research emphasizes increased opportunities for children's success when the home and school work together. Parent–school partnerships are highly needed from birth through high school (Epstein 1996, 2001, 2005b; Epstein et al., 2002; Epstein & Sheldon, 2002; Loucks, 1992; Meyerhoff & White, 1986; Moles, 1987, 1996a, 1996b; National Association of State Boards of Education, 1988, 1991; Warner, 1991; Wherry,

2009). Truly, home–school partnerships are essential to moving education forward.

Support systems, such as schools and child development centers, recognize the importance of partnerships with families.

## :: SCHOOL CLIMATE
## AND PARENTAL ATTITUDES

When you walk into a school, preschool, or child-care center, are you able to sense its spirit? Does it seem to invite you in? Or does it make you feel unwelcome? Can you pinpoint the reasons for your feelings? Each school differs in its character (usually set by the administrators) and reflects the morale and attitudes of the personnel. Some say, "Come—enjoy this exciting business of education with us!" Others say, "You are infringing on my territory. Schools and child-care centers are the professional's business. Send us your children. We will return them to you each evening, but in the meantime, let's each keep to our own responsibilities." In the first instance, there is joy in the educational spirit. In the second, fear and avoidance are dominant.

Parents bring different attitudes into the home–school relationship. One parent may feel excitement and anticipation about a forthcoming visit to the school or center, whereas another may be struck with dread over a required conference. If past school experiences were pleasant and successful, parents are likely to enjoy visiting schools again. If the experiences were filled with failures and disappointments, the thought of school is depressing; if they do approach the school, it is with trepidation. To help make the idea of visiting the school exciting for parents, recognize, understand, and respect parents' cultural and social backgrounds. This will make you more likely to succeed at bringing those parents into a partnership with the school (Riojas-Cortez & Flores, 2009).

Coupled with the parents' past experiences are current pressures. In some districts, the burden of poverty will consume the parents. Parents concerned with mere subsistence may have little energy left for self-fulfillment or for meeting their children's emotional and educational needs; however, in my experience as a public preschool teacher, the poorest of parents were eager to help in any way they could because their children's education was very important. Parents contending with unemployment, inflation, and social change will need special understanding. In particular, immigrant parents face many challenges, and the schools need to provide an environment that respects, values, and welcomes them and their community (Suárez-Orozco, Gaytán, Bang, Pakes, O'Connor, & Rhodes, 2010).

The importance of parents' involvement in their child's growth and education has been recognized for many years. In a classic reading, Hymes (1974) eloquently described the parent–child–teacher relationship when he said that parents love their children, and if the teacher

> feels this same love, then parents are your friends. Show your interest in a child and parents are on your side. Be casual, be off-handed, be cold toward the child and parents can never work closely with you. . . . To touch the child is to touch the parent. To praise the child is to praise the parent. To criticize the child is to hit at the parent. The two are two, but the two are one. (pp. 8–9)

As stated before, all parents have had different experiences with schools—some positive, some negative. The following list and Figure 5–1 show how parents may respond to involvement in the schools based on their past experiences and current situations:

Parents who avoid schools like the plague
Parents who need encouragement to come to school
Parents who readily respond when invited to school
Parents who enjoy power and are overly active
Parents who are comfortable and enjoy involvement in school

It is important to note that in few instances, parents may appear to want to have control over every single aspect of the school or center, but the principal or director may guide that quest for power into more productive causes, such as giving the parents a special project in which they take the lead.

Each group requires a different response from the professional staff. The parents who tend to stay away will need time to overcome negative experiences and learn to appreciate that the school or center can be trusted to help their children. If the school has an inviting and responsive climate, the three groups of parents in the middle ground will feel welcome. These groups, which encompass the largest portion of parents, will soon begin contributing to the school's activities. They can also form a supportive advocacy for school plans.

Offering a variety of tasks and different degrees of involvement assures parents that they may contribute according to their talents and availability and allows all of them to be comfortable about coming to school and enjoying involvement in the educational process.

**FIGURE 5–1**

Parents respond to schools based on their past experiences and their current situations.

| Parents who avoid schools like the plague | Parents who need encouragement to come to school | Parents who readily respond when invited to school | Parents who are comfortable and enjoy involvement in school | Parents who enjoy power and are overly active |

It is up to the teachers and administrators to develop a school or center that welcomes parents. They must be aware of their own feelings and ability to work with and support parents as they develop their plans for the upcoming year.

## :: ROLES OF ADMINISTRATORS, CHIILD-CARE DIRECTORS, TEACHERS, AND PARENTS

Welcome to a new school year. We are excited that your child will be coming to our school. We ask you to drop her/him off and quietly leave the building. Teachers do not have time to speak with you since they are preparing for their instructional time. We hope that everyone has a great school year and expect to see you on our first PTA meeting.

OR

Welcome Bobcats! We are starting a new school year and we are happy to see everyone. Parents, we need your help—please come by the office and sign up for our volunteer opportunities.

Which vignette will your school or center represent? The attitude of the personnel is reflected in the way parents are met in the principal's or director's office, the friendly or unfriendly greetings in the hall, and the offerings in the school. If visitors walk into the school and the secretaries ignore them for a time, that body language and those attitudes reflect that the school would prefer that they not visit. If schools want to collaborate with parents, they must make sure the office is staffed by people who can make parents feel welcome. This, along with positive school policies and services, indicates whether the school recognizes families as important.

### The Administrator's or Center Director's Role in Parent Involvement

School ecology—the atmosphere in school or center—reflects the principal's or director's leadership style. Five aspects of school–parent interaction are affected by this leadership. First, the

**spirit** of the school or center and the enthusiasm of its staff reflect the administrator's role as morale builder. Supportive guidance, with freedom to develop plans based on individual school or center needs, allows the principal or director to function with productive autonomy. The principal or director builds staff morale by enabling staff members to feel positive, enthusiastic, and secure in their work with children and parents.

A second leadership role, **program designer,** involves implementing the educational program. The principal or director needs to recognize the importance of home–school–community relationships in the success of the educational program and strive toward implementation of such a working relationship. If the principal or director allows teachers the autonomy to work with parents using them as volunteers and aides in the development of individualized curricula, the school is on its way to an effective program of parent involvement.

The administrator's third role requires the development of an effective **principal–parent relationship or director–parent relationship.** The principal or director determines whether the school ecology makes parents feel welcome. Besides influencing the general spirit and morale of the school, the principal or director is responsible for maintaining an open-door policy, scheduling open houses, providing and equipping resource areas for parents, arranging parent education meetings, developing parent workshops and in-service meetings, and supporting the PTA, PTO, or family organization (Riojas-Cortez, Flores, Clark, & Smith, 2001).

Fourth, the principal serves as a **program coordinator.** Individual teachers may develop unique programs using the talents of parents, but the achievement of continuity requires the principal's or director's knowledge and coordination of parent-involvement programs.

Finally, the principal or director has a **leadership** role in developing site-based management and leading advisory councils and decision-making committees. This new role needs strong leadership ability to encourage and enable teachers, staff, and parents to work together and develop an educational program specific to their community's needs. Child-care center directors can develop a program that fits the center's individual needs.

In order to achieve these roles, an administrator who uses collaborative or shared decision making with other members of the staff and with the community, including parents, has others who have come to the same decisions and who will be comfortable with and supportive of the decisions. Principals become proactive participants in the development of strong school–family partnerships (Flynn & Nolan, 2008).

## The Teacher's Role in Parent Involvement

In order for teachers to engage parents in the education process, they must develop sociocultural consciousness. In other words, they need to understand the inequities in society (Villegas & Lucas, 2007). Teachers need to develop such understanding because they need to learn how to reach parents and how to get rid of negative stereotypes. Before teachers develop this type of understanding, they must understand the children they teach and their families. Family knowledge may include students' family makeup, favorite activities, concerns, strengths, and family history.

Teachers have different roles in the lives of children and their family. They can include facilitator, counselor, communicator, program director, interpreter, resource developer, and friend in addition to teacher. Because they touch the children's

Knowing children's favorite family activities will help educators strengthen family relations.

lives in so many capacities, being conscious of the background of children and their families becomes crucial in order to assist them to have a successful school experience.

## Teacher Attitudes and Feelings

The school needs personnel who accept parents, but sometimes teachers and administrators are unaware of how they feel toward parents. The questions in Figure 5–2 were developed to help teachers assess their attitudes toward parents.

It is also helpful for teachers to discuss their work with another person. Teachers can talk to a close colleague about what they value in their work with students and parents. They can then reflect on how their own ideal values compare to the values that they act on in their daily work. They should ask a close colleague to evaluate apparent values and compare their real with their ideal values. This will help teachers focus on their attitudes about working with parents. There are no right or wrong answers; the purpose is to recognize attitudes and perhaps anxiety about having parents in the classroom. An answer to anxiety about parents in the classroom is to organize activities in the classroom that allow parents to be involved and helpful. An example would be the parent who could go to a quiet spot with an individual child and let the child read to the parent or discuss their plans for an assignment or activity.

## FIGURE 5–2

Teachers can assess how they feel about collaboration with parents by answering these questions.

| As a Teacher I . . . | How You See Yourself | | How You Wish You Were | |
|---|---|---|---|---|
| | Yes | No | Yes | No |
| 1. Feel that parents are more work than help. | ❏ | ❏ | ❏ | ❏ |
| 2. Feel tense when parents enter my room. | ❏ | ❏ | ❏ | ❏ |
| 3. Prefer to work alone. | ❏ | ❏ | ❏ | ❏ |
| 4. Compare brothers and sisters from the same family. | ❏ | ❏ | ❏ | ❏ |
| 5. Feel threatened by parents. | ❏ | ❏ | ❏ | ❏ |
| 6. View parents as a great resource. | ❏ | ❏ | ❏ | ❏ |
| 7. Believe that low-income children have parents who do not care. | ❏ | ❏ | ❏ | ❏ |
| 8. Enjoy working with several outside persons in the classroom. | ❏ | ❏ | ❏ | ❏ |
| 9. Have prejudiced feelings about certain groups. | ❏ | ❏ | ❏ | ❏ |
| 10. Feel that parents let children watch too much television. | ❏ | ❏ | ❏ | ❏ |
| 11. Feel that parents are not interested in their children. | ❏ | ❏ | ❏ | ❏ |
| 12. Work better with social distance between the parent and myself. | ❏ | ❏ | ❏ | ❏ |
| 13. Believe parents who let their children come to school in inappropriate clothing are irresponsible. | ❏ | ❏ | ❏ | ❏ |
| 14. Feel that a close working relationship with parents is necessary for optimal student growth. | ❏ | ❏ | ❏ | ❏ |
| 15. Am pleased when all the parents are gone. | ❏ | ❏ | ❏ | ❏ |
| 16. Anticipate parent conferences with pleasure. | ❏ | ❏ | ❏ | ❏ |
| 17. Feel that parents have abdicated the parental role. | ❏ | ❏ | ❏ | ❏ |
| 18. Enjoy working with parents. | ❏ | ❏ | ❏ | ❏ |
| 19. Value my students' funds of knowledge. | ❏ | ❏ | ❏ | ❏ |
| 20. Work with parents of inclusion children. | ❏ | ❏ | ❏ | ❏ |

*(Continued)*

## FIGURE 5–2

Teachers can assess how they feel about collaboration with parents by answering these questions. (*continued*)

| | As a Teacher I . . . | | | As a Teacher I Believe That I Should . . . | |
|---|---|---|---|---|---|
| | Always | Sometimes | Never | Essential | Not Important |
| 1. Listen to what parents are saying. | ❑ | ❑ | ❑ | ❑ | ❑ |
| 2. Encourage parents to drop in. | ❑ | ❑ | ❑ | ❑ | ❑ |
| 3. Give parents an opportunity to contribute to my class. | ❑ | ❑ | ❑ | ❑ | ❑ |
| 4. Have written handouts that enable parents to participate in the classroom. | ❑ | ❑ | ❑ | ❑ | ❑ |
| 5. Send newsletters home to parents. | ❑ | ❑ | ❑ | ❑ | ❑ |
| 6. Contact parents before school begins in the fall. | ❑ | ❑ | ❑ | ❑ | ❑ |
| 7. Listen to parents 50 percent of the time during conferences. | ❑ | ❑ | ❑ | ❑ | ❑ |
| 8. Contact parents when a child does well. | ❑ | ❑ | ❑ | ❑ | ❑ |
| 9. Allow for differences among parents. | ❑ | ❑ | ❑ | ❑ | ❑ |
| 10. Learn what objectives parents have for their children. | ❑ | ❑ | ❑ | ❑ | ❑ |
| 11. Learn about interests and special abilities of students. | ❑ | ❑ | ❑ | ❑ | ❑ |
| 12. Visit students in their home. | ❑ | ❑ | ❑ | ❑ | ❑ |
| 13. Show parents examples of the student's work. | ❑ | ❑ | ❑ | ❑ | ❑ |
| 14. Enlist parent volunteers for my classroom. | ❑ | ❑ | ❑ | ❑ | ❑ |
| 15. Ensure a caring environment. | ❑ | ❑ | ❑ | ❑ | ❑ |
| 16. Encourage both mother and father to attend conferences. | ❑ | ❑ | ❑ | ❑ | ❑ |
| 17. Make parents feel comfortable coming to school. | ❑ | ❑ | ❑ | ❑ | ❑ |
| 18. Include parents in educational plans for their children. | ❑ | ❑ | ❑ | ❑ | ❑ |
| 19. Try to be open and honest with parents. | ❑ | ❑ | ❑ | ❑ | ❑ |
| 20. Send notes home with children. | ❑ | ❑ | ❑ | ❑ | ❑ |
| 21. Include students along with parents during conferences. | ❑ | ❑ | ❑ | ❑ | ❑ |
| 22. Let parents sit at their child's desk during back-to-school night. | ❑ | ❑ | ❑ | ❑ | ❑ |
| 23. Keep both parents informed if parents are separated. | ❑ | ❑ | ❑ | ❑ | ❑ |
| 24. Consider parents as partners in the educational process. | ❑ | ❑ | ❑ | ❑ | ❑ |
| 25. Encourage English language learners to use their first language. | ❑ | ❑ | ❑ | ❑ | ❑ |

## Roles of Parents

Within each school, parents may assume a variety of roles (see Figure 5–3). Most commonly, parents observe what the school does with their children in the educational process. But parents may also assume other roles simultaneously.

The room parent, for example, who provides treats and creates parties, is an accessory or temporary volunteer. Volunteers can provide needed services, but their involvement is geared only to a specific time and task. Furthermore, Figure 5–4, the parent questionnaire, asks the parents what they want to know about the school or centers well as how they would like to be involved. Each classroom can develop an appropriate questionnaire that would be based on the plans in the classroom and the opportunities available for parents as they volunteer in the school.

Increasingly, parents are serving as more regularly scheduled resources to the schools. Some parents spend a morning or a full day each week working in the resource center, developing materials, and sharing with other parents. You may find others making books with children's stories or listening to children read and discussing ideas with them. Still others work as unpaid aides in the classroom. Because many employed parents use a child-care center, their contributions will need to be geared to their availability. Some centers have an occasional activity on Saturday with those parents in mind.

Parents may also help make policies. For example, school boards have been composed of community leaders charged with making educational policy for many years. Early control of schools was accomplished by community leaders who were generally the elite of the area. At least 50 percent of the Parent Advisory Councils in Head Start must be composed of parents served by the program (U.S. Department for Health and Human Services, 2010). Parent involvement, including input into the program, is recommended. With this representative membership, policy control has reached down to the grassroots of the constituency being served, with the decisions of policy-making parents directly affecting the schools their own children attend.

Collaborative decision making brings parents of children in the schools into the decision-making process. Clearly, parents are teachers of their own children. Through funds of knowledge, parents teach children a variety of skills including language, problem solving, socioemotional, and physical skills. For example, setting the table and putting away the dishes involve classification of objects. Teaching children a traditional song from their culture helps children develop not only language awareness but also cultural pride and awareness. Very often parents are aware of their role in teaching their children but they may not be aware of the connection between home and academic learning; therefore, teachers must show parents how the two are connected (Riojas-Cortez & Flores, 2009).

## Ways to Enhance Center–School–Home–Community Relations

Why does one school or center have superb relationships with parents and community, whereas one nearby does not? Most often the leadership of the administration and individual teachers make the difference. Their leadership has made the school responsive to the parents and therefore the parents supportive of the school. The relationship with the community plays a very important role in the development of positive relations with parents.

Schools or centers usually do not change overnight, but gradually the school, home, and community can become united in a joint effort. Many of the techniques geared to improve center–home–school–community relationships are already in place. This chapter is a reminder to keep doing

**FIGURE 5–3**
Possible roles for parents in schools.

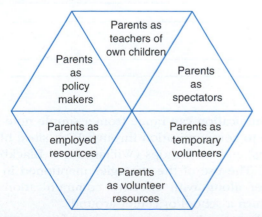

*Note:* These roles for parents in schools are typical of those that emerge in the interaction of parents and schools. It is important to have parents involved as more than spectators.

**FIGURE 5–4**

This questionnaire is a simplified needs assessment of what parents want to know about the school and how they would like to be involved. Asking these questions at the beginning the year shows interest in the parents and can help the school plan meetings and activities.

**PARENT QUESTIONNAIRE**

**1. What I want to know about the school:**

| | Very important | Somewhat | Not at all |
|---|---|---|---|
| 1. What curriculum will my child have? | | | |
| 2. How is the school organized? | | | |
| 3. What is the procedure for seeing school personnel? | | | |
| 4. If I have a problem with the school, not the class, whom do I see? | | | |
| 5. How is reading taught? | | | |
| 6. What books are used in the school? | | | |
| 7. What books should I use with my child? | | | |
| 8. How are subjects taught? | | | |
| 9. How should I help my child with different subjects? | | | |
| 10. Other | | | |

**2. How I would like to be involved with the school:**

| | Very interested | Somewhat | Not at all |
|---|---|---|---|
| 1. Be a classroom volunteer | | | |
| 2. Serve on policy committees | | | |
| 3. Make games for the classroom | | | |
| 4. Help with money-raising events | | | |
| 5. Collect resources for the classroom | | | |
| 6. Be a room parent | | | |
| 7. Organize a volunteer program | | | |
| 8. Share expertise or experiences | | | |
| 9. Work in family resource room | | | |
| 10. Other | | | |

Comments: _____

the positive activities that have helped, to increase attention to making a partnership, and to change negative attitudes. It focuses on five areas: (a) center–school atmosphere and involvement of parents, (b) activities and resources for parents, (c) contact early in the school year, (d) meeting the needs of the school or center area, and (e) volunteers.

Multiple methods of communications can increase contact between family, center, and school.

Communication can range from a simple note sent home to communication through Web sites, blogs, forums, and workshops (Williamson & Blackburn, 2010). The use of the strategies mentioned in this chapter along with effective communication can help turn a school or center around.

Welcoming is only one aspect of restructuring needs. Employment, elimination of discrimination, and inclusion of culturally and linguistically diverse groups and immigrants set the stage for all to participate meaningfully in a democratic society. Supporting and recognizing all families and children will be necessary before schools or centers can meet their challenge.

**Situation.** "I thought when we moved to this school district that Josi would receive an excellent education, but she is so upset over the way the children in her room are treating her that she cries when she comes home from school. I have to force her to go to school in the mornings. I wish we hadn't moved. Having a larger house just isn't worth the pain," Susan mournfully told her friend, Elizabeth.

"What's going on?" Elizabeth asked.

"The school just doesn't care about my child," Susan said. "I've talked with the principal several times, and I go visit every week and talk with the teacher, but she doesn't respond to my concerns at all. Miss Block, her homeroom teacher, thinks it is just natural for children to have a hard time in a new school. I think the children pick on Josi because she is small and defenseless, but Miss Block insists that Josi stands up for herself and just complains because she wants attention. She thinks Josi enjoys this attention. Oh, she also says that her self-esteem in the new school is not strong yet and that she doesn't have any friends, but that will come if we just let the children work it out for themselves."

"That attitude must really be hard on you and Josi."

"It makes me angry!" Susan's voice trembled. "I think that the principal and teacher hate me and my child." Here are some questions for reflection regarding Susan's situation:

1. Could this situation have been avoided? How?
2. What can the teacher and parent do to turn Susan's concerns into a collaborative effort rather than a confrontation?
3. What could Susan do to help Josi?
4. What could be done in the classroom to eliminate the concern?

## Open-Door Policy

An open-door welcoming policy is more an attitude of the school than a series of activities, although periodic open houses, forums, coffee hours, and interactive seminars can add to the receptive climate of the school. Parents are welcome at any time in schools with an open-door policy. Schools that have closed door policy and are unpleasant or that require appointments to visit the principal, teachers, or classrooms are saying, "Come only by request or when you want to discuss a problem." Schools and parents need to avoid the problem-conference syndrome. Dialogue between parents and schools should occur before a problem develops. This can be done through coffee klatches and seminars. Parents can give suggestions and get answers; school personnel can ask questions and clarify school procedures and curriculum long before an issue develops into a problem. By establishing an open-door policy early, the climate is set for parents and school to work together on behalf of, rather than suffer a confrontation over, a child.

## Parent Advisory Councils and Site-Based Management

Title I of the Elementary and Secondary Education Act was developed to improve the academic achievement of children of underrepresented groups and to "ensure that all children have a fair, equal, and significant opportunity to achieve a high quality education and reach, at a minimum, proficiency on challenging State academic achievement standards and State academic assessments" (U.S. Department of Education, 2002, p. l). All schools can establish parent advisory councils. Title I components establish two parent advisory councils: a districtwide council and a local council for each involved school. The councils give input on the planning, implementation, and evaluation of the Title I program. Head Start and Home Start have had participatory advisory councils since the 1960s, but public schools were not required to have such parent participation until 1974. Fifty percent of council members should be selected from among parents of students receiving Title I services U.S. Department of Education, 2002).

The success of parent advisory councils in Head Start, Home Start, and Title I programs has demonstrated that parents can be involved in policy and decision making in a meaningful and constructive way. Although schools can implement a parent advisory council related to their own situation, they can also learn from the Title I experience, in which schools actively solicit parents' participation and give them the information and training needed to become effective policy and decision makers. Working together with schools and centers through site-based management increases home–school–community relations.

Site-based management has been established in schools across the nation. The site-based management theory lies in the belief that those closest to an issue are the ones who can make decisions and find the most appropriate answer. Parents are on the team, which also includes teachers, school personnel, and community representatives. Site-based management, also known as school-based councils, seems to work best when the principal actively facilitates parental involvement (Shatkin & Gershber, 2007).

## Strategies for Supporting and Involving Culturally and Linguistically Diverse Families

A strong home–school connection is crucial for student success. Nelson and Guerra (2010) developed a plan for three of the most common types of home–school connections including involvement, engagement, and empowerment. Each of these connections varies depending on the backgrounds of the children and their family but will help teachers and principals or center directors to develop cultural awareness in their school or center:

*Involvement*—Actions at home provide support for children's education.
  *Example:* Encourage parents to use their funds of knowledge to teach children skills (i.e., singing, dancing, gardening, cooking, playing an instrument, or fixing things).
*Engagement*—Teachers and parents work collaboratively to meet school broad goals.
  *Example:* Meet regularly with parents to discuss children's progress and how they can help their children at home. Use native language for effective communication.
*Empowerment*—Parents, teachers, and school administrators participate in all aspects of decision making, working as partners.
  *Example*: All parents, particularly of those underrepresented groups, participate in giving input and taking action to create more educational opportunities for children in all aspects of learning. Parents work with one another, empowering themselves. One person should be working with the parents to ensure that the empowerment occurs.

## Home–School Continuity

Continuity between home and school is a necessary and important support system for families today.

President Obama eloquently explained the importance of continuity in his State of the Union 2011 address, "Our schools share this responsibility. When a child walks into a classroom, it should be a place of high expectations and high performance." Families cannot afford to be caught in an adversarial position with the school. They need cooperation, support, and facilities that make it possible to supply their children with a stable environment. If you do not know their needs, you will not be able to respond to them. For instance, the number of immigrant families has increased dramatically, and in order to better provide continuity for their children, it is important to understand their background.

A good way to improve relationships between school and home is to do a needs assessment or survey to determine what the families in the school area desire. The questionnaire shown earlier in Figure 5–4 is just an example. If you know several of the parents or have access to the parents' addresses, asking them what topics they want or need included on the questionnaire would make the assessment more meaningful.

Continuity needs to be a cooperative effort. Community outreach that continues to help families even when school is not in session is a positive step toward achieving continuity. Groups such as recreation program leaders, library services

Home–school activities should be culturally relevant.

personnel, special after-school teachers, and artists-in-residence should be enlisted to help extend the school day to accommodate parents' schedules. Parents who are not employed outside the home could volunteer or be paid to help with before- and after-school programs. The coordination of school programs with social agencies, recreation departments, and other community resources will greatly enhance the chance of successful continuity.

### Family Center

Parents need a place within the school where they can meet, share information, work, and relax. Ideally, parents will have a room similar to that traditional haven, the teachers' lounge, as well as a space within each classroom.

The family room can be equipped and stocked by the parents. Typical items include a sofa, comfortable chairs, table, coffeepot, microwave, telephone, computer, bulletin board, storage area, supplies, and reading materials. If a room is not available, a small area shared in a workroom, an area in an unused hall, or a large closet would give minimal space. In each, both storage space and a bulletin board for notices should be available.

Teachers can help parents develop a base in each classroom. An extra desk, corner, or bulletin board lets parents claim a spot within their child's classroom. If the area contains information on current assignments, new curriculum ideas, activities to be used at home, taped messages from the teacher, or a display of children's work, parents will make a point to stop by. Parents of preschool, kindergarten, and elementary children can use the corner to find activities to talk or work with individual children or small groups or to find ways to continue the educational experience in the home. Teachers can use the corner for short conferences with parents. The *parents' room* implies that parents are expected to be in the building—there is a place for them to stop and a base from which they can reach out in their involvement.

## :: SCHOOL ACTIVITIES AND RESOURCES

The following school activities and resources encourage parent participation. Parent involvement fosters interest and support of children's education. We encourage teachers and administrators to select those activities that will meet their parents' needs.

Very often schools continue to offer activities that are not of interest to parents or activities that parents cannot attend.

### Back-to-School Nights

A time-tested school event, the back-to-school night, has proved very successful. Teachers often complain that the parents who need to learn about the educational program are the very ones who do not show up, but this type of evening program nevertheless has improved home–school relationships from preschool through secondary schools. Parents enjoy sitting in the desk normally occupied by their child, viewing the curriculum materials, observing the displays in the room, and listening to the teacher tell them about school programs. Following a presentation of the course objectives, there is usually a period for questions and answers. Back-to-school night is not a time for talking extensively about individual children, although the teacher should identify which parents belong to which students. It is a good time to set up a special conference if you have concern about the progress of a student.

A variation on the back-to-school night is the Saturday morning session. Some working parents have difficulty attending evening programs, and offering an alternative time can increase parental participation. The Saturday morning activity can be a workshop with parents participating in their children's normal activities, or it can be a presentation and discussion similar to the evening session. Saturday morning programs work well for childcare centers and preschools as well as schools. The programs can become a meaningful educational experience for both children and families by involving a series of parent–child programs.

### Sharing Reading

A practice that has had promising results is inviting parents, community celebrities, and school personnel to share a book they enjoy with the children in the class. The book, of course, needs to be one that fits the developmental level of the children and short enough to be read in one session. It is also very important to select a book that reflects the children's culture as well as their native language. Parents and grandparents enjoy the opportunity to visit the class to read a story to the children during sharing time. Principals can use this as an opportunity to get to know children better. Afterward, children will be able to relate to the principal as someone who spent time reading with them and who respects them. Children are excited to meet a "celebrity" who comes to share with them. But most importantly, children's self-esteem will be positively affected if they see their parents or grandparents or any family member reading to them and their friends. Following the visits, letters by the children may be written to thank the contributor.

## Parent Education Groups

Parent education groups can be conducted in different forms. Meetings can range from a one-day workshop to an organized series of workshops throughout the year. Individual teachers use the parent group meetings for in-service training of volunteers in their rooms, dissemination of information to parents, or presentation of programs that answer parents' needs. Parents become real resources for the school through parent education meetings, which teach them to become effective tutors and school volunteers.

Parent education may be offered whenever the need arises. The school can have a list of workshops available or determine the needs of the community. If voice mail is available, parents could call any time for school-related information. Besides workshops, articles or individual conferences can be arranged to help the parents.

Parent education meetings offered by schools are viable for those with children at any age level. The parent of a young child may be interested in child development, enrichment activities, and promotion of creativity. Middle and high schools have very few parent education groups, but the parents of these students are vitally concerned about their children's futures. Parents of children of all ages are concerned about drugs and alcohol. Parent education groups are an essential part of the educational program because they allow parents to meet and discuss common concerns.

Schools need to offer parent education. In doing so, they strengthen parent–school–community relationships. An advocacy group for children and parents also can be formed to outline responsibilities and guidelines for students, as determined by parents and students in a specific community, that can support parents in the rearing of their children.

## Parent Networks

Parent networks may form naturally out of parent education groups, but many parents with no interest in parent education might want to join a network group of parents. When I was a teacher, there were many parents who were very interested and had the time to help, so the parents organized themselves to provide assistance to all of the teachers. Parents began to work together on bulletin boards, making games, and even going to the classroom to work with the children. In addition, the parents created a network of friends that provided support for one another, and they also learned how to share resources with those who needed them most.

## School–Home Activity Packets

Parents appreciate knowing activities and enrichment ideas that support the school curricula. Teachers can make calendars that describe what the child will be learning at school. Sending home packets with activities that support the curriculum enhances parents' involvement in their children's education (Riojas-Cortez, Flores, & Riojas Clark, 2003). The activities need to be relevant to the curriculum within each class and each school. These packets may be supported by workshops in which parents learn about the activities, or they may be ongoing informational packets related to what the child is learning at school.

One workshop could be developed in which parents make tote bags their children can use to bring ideas and materials for the activities to be done at home. At this workshop, the ideas behind the take-home activity kits could be explained and discussed. Some families have difficulty completing home-school activities. Communicate with them—develop quick activities for parents who do not have a lot of time, and try to encourage interactions between parent and child that are positive and fun. Some early childhood classrooms send home a stuffed teddy bear, asking the family to include the bear in their weekend and then write a story about the bear's adventures. Other schools send home fish, gerbils, or other live animals to be cared for during break. These activities are similar to those in school–home activity packets, but the kits usually include many educational activities, with some (but not all) related to the family. For example, children might measure their parents' height, design the week's menu, plan a garden, calculate the number of times each person can jump while playing jump rope, or write a story about their family. Think about the children and families with whom you work. Recognize their interests and their needs, and plan how to organize the school–home activities that are culturally appropriate for the children such as the ones included in the following list:

1. School–home activity packets should emphasize developmentally appropriate practice for young children and play.
2. Activities should be interesting and enjoyable for the parent and child. Stress that the activities are to be enjoyed; if they cause stress rather than a positive interaction, do not insist that they be completed.
3. Make sure that the activity is culturally relevant for families (for examples, see Smith & Riojas-Cortez, 2010).
4. Send home clear instructions included in English and the children's native language; be available to answer questions by telephone or e-mail.
5. The packets should include any special materials needed to complete the activity. Activities that do not require materials are often more fun than those that do because there is no stress related to finding the materials.
6. Activities that do not require materials are often more fun than those that do because there is no stress related to finding the materials.
7. Ask parents to complete an evaluation form that is included with the instructions that is easy to follow and complete.

Volunteering at school assists with home–school relationships.

8. If the activity kit has permanent equipment, make sure that it is returned within a timely manner such as a week.

## School Programs and Workshops

Parents from the community can plan and implement some of the workshops and speakers can be obtained from outside sources. Local universities may be good places to ask for resources. Often, professors are ready and willing to work on projects of interest to the families (Riojas-Cortez & Flores, 2009).

A project in which parents make books of their children's work can be a great success and also create memories to be kept for years. Simple construction-paper books as well as hardback books can be developed. Books containing stories and poems composed by parents or children can be placed in the library and classroom for all students to use. Using culturally appropriate activities during workshops ensures that parents continue to participate and attend (for examples, see Riojas-Cortez, Huerta, Flores, Perez & Clark, 2008).

Try to arrange alternate times to offer workshops. If you offer meetings during the day, in the evening, and on Saturdays, parents will be able to come to the ones that fit their schedules. In addition encourage parents to bring young children, allowing them to participate without the hassle of needing to find child care.

## District or School Conferences

Professionals go to conferences to gain information and be stimulated to try something new. Why not have the same kind of conference for parents? Instead of a workshop, plan a half-day or full-day conference where teachers and other professionals hold sessions for parents and community personnel to attend. These sessions could include such subjects as play, social development, literacy, math, music and movement, art, language arts, social studies, science, and computers. Other topics of interest for parents of young children include guidance, brain development, nutrition, and infant and toddler development, among others.

If a "mini conference" is planned, get resources from the district and the community to ensure that information from different organizations is given to parents. For example, a mini conference on how children learn and develop can involve district curriculum specialists but also pediatricians or nurses, speech and/or occupational therapists, education service centers, university professors, and even other parents and grandparents. Often, retired teachers and retired administrators are also willing to share their expertise with parents.

### School Projects

Enlist parent help if you plan to add to the playground or build a reading loft in your classroom. For example, at my daughter's public school, there was a nonprofit organization (Friends of Bonham) created by a group of parents to support the school's mission to provide a dual-language program, emphasize outdoor science, and support the arts. The organization works with the school administration and teachers to ensure that they provide the needed support to enhance children's learning.[1] Fundraising was very important to obtain items that otherwise the school would not be able to get, such as a new playground. With the help of all parents, this organization was able to replace the school's existing playground and donate it to another school. This is an excellent example of how schools with the help of the community can develop positive relations that enhance children's overall development and at the same time involve parents.

Most parents enjoy contributing their time for something permanent, and children will be proud that their parents helped build the jungle gym or plant the elm tree in the schoolyard. Many fathers find this the most comfortable way to contribute to the school. Working on a project can start a relationship that brings them into a partnership with the school such as when sessions are offered on different schedules to accommodate parents' busy schedules.

### PTO or PTA

The tradition of parent–teacher associations (PTAs) extends back to the 1890s, and their influence on parent–school relationships has been demonstrated over the years (National Parent Teacher Association, 2010). The PTA publishes material for parents and strives for parent–school cooperation. Many

---

[1]For more information go to the Friends of Bonham at www.friendsofbonham.org.

parent–teacher groups, generally called parent–teacher organizations (PTOs), do not join the national PTA but have similar structure and interaction with the schools. Both PTAs and PTOs can serve as avenues toward greater parent–school interaction. Many school PTAs have their own Web sites where they provide parents a variety of information. The national PTA's Web site provides grants, resources in Spanish, and ideas for fundraising (National Parent Teacher Association, 2010).

**Fairs, Carnivals, and Suppers.** Traditionally, the PTO or PTA sponsors spaghetti or enchilada suppers, potluck dinners, dinner theaters, or similar activities that promote a community spirit, give families a night of fun together, and usually increase the treasury. Parents and children flock to school to attend a carnival produced by parents and school staff. Money earned is generally spent on materials or equipment for the school program.

**Exchanges.** As children grow, new clothes are needed, toys get tiresome and books are read. Why not have an exchange? A popular exchange is to have children bring boots, heavy jackets, and raincoats to school to be traded or sold. Boots seldom wear out before they're outgrown, so a boot exchange works very well. Toys can also be exchanged. How often have you seen toys sit for months without being used? Some schools have children bring two toys, one for exchange and one to give to another child. Children swap the toy they brought for a different one.

Children also tire of some books and can exchange their old ones for books they have not read. A parent volunteer checks in the books and issues tickets to be used to "buy" another one. Children look through the books until they find a book they want and then use the tickets to buy it.

**Book and Toy Donations.** Teaching children the value of sharing can be practiced by asking them to bring the toys and/or books that they do not use to donate to a children's shelter or to donate to those children who may not have any. This can be done at the beginning of the school year and during the holidays. Parents can get involved by making sure that the toys and the books donated are in good condition and that the children actually get involved in taking the toys and books to children who need it the most.

**Caring-Cards Exchange.** Parents can organize a caring-cards exchange and take the cards to the children who are sick in hospitals. Parents can ask teachers to involve their children in a service learning activity in which they become "pals" with a child in a hospital who is ill. They can exchange cards that they each make, and the parents make sure that the cards get mailed out.

## Learning Centers

Parents or volunteers from the community can be put in charge of learning centers. Use the resource room to furnish ideas and supplies for parents, or have a workshop to demonstrate how to plan and prepare a learning center. Learning centers can include the following:

- A place for games
- A dramatic play center
- A reading center
- A center for writing and making books
- A puzzle center
- A center for problem-solving activities
- A science area
- A talk-and-listen center
- A place for music and tapes
- A weaving center
- An art project center

Rules and regulations for using the center should be posted. Parents can help create the poster.

## Telephone Tutor

The school can set up a tutor aide program through telephone calls in the evening. Volunteers or teachers can answer the telephone in the afternoon at the school. Later calls can be forwarded to the homes of a volunteer or paid aide working with the children that night. In a well-coordinated program, the volunteer could know what curriculum is being covered in the class. If the entire district uses the telephone tutor, special numbers could be assigned for mathematics and language arts.

## Internet

Many families have access to the Internet. E-mails may be sent to each child in each classroom or to all the children in the school if their families are willing to share their e-mail addresses. In addition, the school could have its own Web page with descriptions of upcoming school events or information about achievements and activities in the school and individual classrooms. They can also create blogs or chat rooms where they discuss their homework. Creating a LISTSERV helps to disseminate information pertinent for different classrooms.

## Resource Room

When parents see they can contribute to a project that has obvious benefits for their children, some will become more actively involved. A resource room can be beneficial to both school and parents. Resource materials located in an empty room, a storage closet, the corner of a room, or a metal cabinet can be a great help to teachers. Involve parents in developing a resource center by holding a workshop to describe and discuss the idea. Brainstorm with parents and other teachers on ideas that might be significant for your school. Parents can take over after the workshop to design, stock, and run the center. Later, as assistants in the classroom, they will use it. They can help supply the center with articles on teaching, ideas and materials for games, and recycled materials to use in activities.

**Articles on Teaching.** Parents and community volunteers check old magazines related to teaching and classify useful articles according to subject and student age level. These are filed for use by teachers and aides. In searching for and classifying the articles, parents learn a great deal about teaching activities for home and school, so the exercise is beneficial for the parent and the school. Internet access to academic journals and educational magazines provides parents opportunities to learn more about school and children's learning.

**Games.** Parents check books, magazines, and commercial catalogs for ideas for games and adapt them to the school's needs. Volunteers make universal game boards for reading, spelling, and math from poster board or tagboard. Felt markers are used to make lines and note directions; games are decorated with artwork, magazine cutouts, or stickers. Game materials should be laminated or covered with clear plastic.

**Recycled Materials.** Volunteers collect, sort, and store materials for classroom teachers. Items such as egg cartons, wood scraps, wallpaper books, cardboard tubes, felt, fabric remnants, and plastic food holders are used for many activities. Egg cartons, for example, can be used to cover a dragon, make a caterpillar, store buttons for classification activities, and hold tempera paint for dry mixing. Milk cartons are used for making items from simple computers to building blocks. Science activities are enriched by a collection of machines, for example, motors, radios, computers, clocks, and typewriters. The articles can be used as they are or taken apart and rebuilt. Recycling is limited only by lack of imagination.

### Libraries

A collection of magazines and books can be useful to parents or teachers in the development of teaching aids—such as games and learning activities—or for information on how children learn. From ideas therein, a toy lending library, an activity lending library, a book and magazine library, or a video lending library can be developed. Items can be checked out for a week or two. Checkout and return are supervised by parent volunteers.

**Toy Lending Library.** The toy lending library was developed with educational toys for young children (Nimnicht & Brown, 1972) or with a collection of toys for older children. The toys for young children can be built and collected by parents. Toys for older children can be collected from discarded toys left over after the toy exchange, or they can be built by parents and children.

**Activity Lending Library.** Games and activities developed by parents and children can be checked out for a week or two.

**Book and Magazine Library.** Discarded magazines and books can be collected and used to build a comprehensive lending library. Professional magazines have many articles on child development, education, and learning activities. Booklets distributed by numerous organizations can also be lent. Pamphlets and articles cut from magazines can be stapled to file folders and loaned to parents. To keep track of the publications, glue a library card pocket in each book or on each folder. Make a card that states the author and title of the publication, with lines for borrowers to sign their names. As each is taken, have the borrower sign the card and leave it in the card file. When the publication is returned, the name is crossed out, and the card is returned to the pocket.

**Video Lending Library DVDs.** DVDs made by teachers to illustrate their lessons on math, social studies, language arts, art, physical education, music, and other subjects or activities can be very helpful to parents. Homework or "homefun" assignments can be explained on the videos. Teachers can also share creative activities that families would enjoy together. This would be especially beneficial during breaks or weekends.

Actual classes can also be the subject of videos so that parents can see their child at work or play during the school hours. This type of video is often used to accompany parent–teacher conferences but could also be available in the family resource room. Selected videos and videos of student activities would offer a look at students at school; homefun or homework assignments; educational movies; videos on educational programs, such as language, writers' workshops, mathematics, geography, or science; and age-appropriate movies for entertainment. YouTube videos about lessons can be safely uploaded where only the intended participants can watch them.

Other educational DVDs can also be provided for parents to check out. These do not have to be commercial DVDs, but they can have educational value such as documentaries or National Geographic programs.

### Summer Vacation Activities

Parents can keep students, particularly elementary-age children, from losing academic gains during the summer. Research shows that the parents who are involved by teachers and child-care leaders become more positive about them and rate them higher in interpersonal skills and teaching ability. Activities differ depending on the age of the child. Let the parents of an infant child know how important it is to have eye and voice contact with their infant. Tell parents to hold one-way conversations and let the infant respond, read and sing with the infant, and move to music, engaging in dance with the infant (Trawick-Smith, 2009).

### Parents as Resources

Parents should be asked early in the year about their talents or experiences they would like to share with classes. Parents might share information about their careers, or they might have a hobby that would spark student interest or supplement learning programs. Storytelling is an art that is often overlooked. Invite some senior citizens to tell about their childhoods. The resources in the community are unlimited.

## Book Publishing

One of the most beneficial activities that has developed from the emphasis on reading, writing, and writing workshops is the opportunity for parents to be involved in helping children publish their own books. The activity may be done at home or at school. Some schools have the equipment that allows the parent to volunteer to be a book publisher. The child may develop a story during a writing workshop period, a language arts lesson, or traditional reading and writing sessions. After the story is completed, it can be published with or without editing, although editing helps the child learn conventional spelling and grammar in a positive situation. If parents are available, they can help with the process. The following steps are usually taken:

1. The story is written during a writing workshop or (for the younger child) the story is dictated to the parent.
2. The story is edited by the student, by the student and the parent, or by the parent alone. In some classes, an editing panel is established and students edit together.
3. The story is typed on a computer by the student or parent. If the story is to be published in handwritten form, this step is eliminated. Copies of the stories may be made on a copy machine.
4. If the book is going to be handled and read by many students, the pages should be laminated. A laminating machine or clear contact paper can help make the book permanent.
5. The book is bound. Many schools have spiral binding equipment available for the parent to use. In other schools, binding may be done by simply stapling the pages together and covering the book with heavy paper. Traditional bookbinding can also be accomplished by parents. A bookbinding workshop would show parents how to sew the pages together and make the outside cover. The outside sheet between the cover and the inside pages is a plain sheet of construction paper. The construction paper is glued to the outside cover. Depending on the material used, the outside cover can also be laminated.
6. The completed works should then be recognized and shared. Some schools have complete libraries of children's books displayed in the front halls or rooms. Others have classes that keep their published books in their own rooms. One school has the books circulate from room to room with an insert that allows children to write that they have read the book and to add a compliment so that. the young writer receives recognition for the work.

## Career Day

Plan a day or a series of days when parents and community volunteers come in and explain their careers. Rather than have parents talk to the whole class, let them work at a center. Have them explain their careers, the pros and cons, the necessary skills, and the satisfaction obtained from their work. If feasible, the parents can provide some activities the children could do related to the career. For example, a carpenter could bring in tools, demonstrate their use, and let the children make a small project, supervised by the carpenter and an aide or another parent.

## Talent Sharing

Let parents tell stories, sing folk songs, lead a creative theatre project, or share another talent. You might persuade some to perform before the class; some may wish to work with a few children at a time and let the children be involved. Some parents may have a collection or a hobby to share. Quilting is popular and could be followed by a lesson in stitchery. Basket making, growing orchids, stamp collecting—all these provide opportunities for enriching the classroom learning experiences. Bring those educational and fun lessons out to enjoy.

## :: PARENTS AS PARTNERS IN EDUCATION AT HOME

Reading at home throughout the year should be encouraged. Figures 5–5 and 5–6 illustrate a way to get parents involved in a home reading program. First, a letter is sent to parents describing the program (Figure 5–5). An explanation could also be given at back-to-school night or during a workshop. After the children read a book, they color in a book on the sheet sent home with the letter. When all the books on the sheet are colored in, a certificate is awarded (Figure 5–6). Each

teacher sends home a list of books that are appropriate for the child to read. Bookmarks with the titles of books related to the age of the child are a good idea. In addition, books from the school

**FIGURE 5–5**

Encouraging parents to be involved in their child's reading is a positive way to accomplish good reading habits and communicate with parents (sample letter).

**[School Letterhead]**

Dear Parents,

I would like to invite you and your child to participate in Read-Aloud Month during October. This statewide project is sponsored by the Colorado Council of the International Reading Association. The purpose is to encourage parents and children to read aloud together. Children who are read to become better readers—it's a fact!

Each student who participates in Read-Aloud Month will be given a time sheet to take home. This will be used to record time you or other adults spend reading aloud to your child. For every 15 minutes of read-aloud time, your child may color one book on the time sheet.

To successfully complete this project, all the characters on the time sheet must be colored in by the end of October. Each child who completes the time sheet will receive a certificate rewarding participation in the project.

Setting aside time to read with your child helps your child learn and develop an interest in reading. Take a few minutes each day to share the joy of reading with your child!

Sincerely,

*P.S. I'm also sending home a bookmark, an annotated bibliography with suggestions for good books to read aloud, and a Join the Read-Aloud Crowd poster for your refrigerator door or family bulletin board. Be sure to read the suggestions on the back of the poster.*

*Source:* Printed with permission. Colorado Council International Reading Association.

**FIGURE 5–6**
Attractive certificates, suggested books, and posters highlight the importance of reading.

*Source:* Art by Richard Florence.

library can be checked out and taken home. It is important to note that the books should be culturally and linguistically appropriate for children and their families.

Families need to be encouraged to use their first language when reading stories to children. A library with a variety of culturally and linguistically appropriate children's literature needs to be provided. The Barahona Center for the study of Books in Spanish for Children and Adolescents provides lists of recommended books and other resources for children and adolescents in Spanish. The North Central Regional Educational Laboratory provides listings and reviews of multicultural children's literature including African Americans, Native Americans, Asian Americans and Latinos (North Center Regional Educational Laboratory, 2010). The de Grummond Children's Literature Collection focuses on special collections of American and British children's literature with special collections and highlights of international fairy tales and folktales, African American Collection, and fables (Libraries, The University of Southern Mississipi, 2010).

## :: CONTACTS EARLY IN THE SCHOOL YEAR

Many teachers have found that early communication is well worth the time it takes, even if it is during summer vacation. It is quite common for kindergarten teachers to invite the new kindergarten class and their parents to a spring orientation meeting. Generally, these functions are scheduled in the hope that the strangeness of school will diminish and that, as a result, subsequent entry into kindergarten will be more pleasant. Just as important is the message to the parents that the school cares. This idea can be carried over into other levels of education with results that are just as gratifying.

### Letters in August

Some teachers send letters, with pictures of themselves enclosed, to each new student coming to their classes. The student and parents learn the teacher's identity and know that the teacher cares enough to write. A good rapport between teacher and home is established before school begins. E-mails are also beneficial for children and parents to begin to know the teacher and the school.

### Neighborhood Visits

Rather than waiting until the regular conference period arrives or a problem arises, teachers should contact each parent early in the year. Visits to the neighborhood are excellent ways to meet parents.

### Block Walks

Try a block walk while the weather is warm and sunny. Map the location of all your students' homes (this may be a class project) and divide the area into blocks. Schedule a series of block walks, and escort the children living in each block area to their homes on a selected day. Have the students write letters or notes in advance indicating that you will visit a particular block. Choose an alternate day in case of rain. On the appointed day, walk or ride the bus to the chosen block. Meet the parents outside and chat with them about school. You may also accumulate some teaching materials such as leaves, sidewalk rubbings, or bits of neighborhood history to be used later by the children in the classroom. This initial contact with parents will be positive and possibly make a second meeting even more productive. You can reinforce the positive aspect of an early meeting by making an interim telephone call to inform the parents of an activity or an interesting comment made by their child.

### Bus Trips

An all-school project, with teachers riding a bus to tour the school's enrollment area, allows parents and teachers to meet before the opening of school. A parent network can be used to approach all parents and create positive connections between them and the school. Parents that know the community are great assets to increase parental involvement.

### Picnics

A picnic during the lunch hour or while on a field trip during the early part of the year will afford teachers the opportunity to meet some parents. Plan a field trip to a park or zoo and invite the parents to a bring-your-own-lunch gathering. Have another picnic after school for those who could not come at lunchtime. After the lunch or picnic, call to thank those who came. Because some parents work and will be unable to attend either picnic, you might wish to phone them for a pleasant conversation about their child.

## :: WHAT WORKS

Parent behaviors that support the child's cognitive development include the following:

1. Talk with children and listen to their concerns.
2. Read to children and listen to them read.
3. Establish daily routines that include study time for homework in an area conducive to study (if the child is old enough to have homework).
4. Provide opportunities for exploring and play.
5. Eat meals together.
6. Have appropriate bedtime schedules.
7. Guide and monitor out-of-school time.
8. Model good values and positive behavior.
9. Have high expectations of achievement.
10. Gain knowledge of child development and parenting skills.
11. Use authoritative rather than authoritarian control.

Positive interactions from infancy help build strong relationships.

12. Take a strong interest in the schools.
13. Communicate with the teacher.
14. Acknowledge parents' diverse cultural and linguistic background.

Epstein's work at the Center for Families, Schools, Community, and Children's Learning found that:

- Children do better in school if their parents help them. The children also behave better and are more diligent than children whose parents do not involve themselves.
- Teachers and principals show greater respect to parents who participate in school activities and also have better attitudes toward the children of these parents.
- When teachers involve families, they rate the parents more positively and do not stereotype single parents or those with less education. The teachers recognize that parents are equally willing to help and follow through at home. When they do not work with single parents or parents with less education, they rate these parents as less willing to help and follow through at home.
- Work at home with one subject—for example, reading—resulted in increased scores in that subject but did not transfer to other subjects—for example, math.
- Parents are able to influence and make a contribution to the education of their children.
- Students, parents, and school personnel all agree that parent involvement is important.
- The way teachers work with parents is more important than the family background, including class, race, marital status, and whether both parents work (Epstein, 1996). Socioeconomic status is not the primary causal factor in school success or lack of success; it is parental interest and support of the child.

Parents can do many things at home to help their children succeed in school. They do this through their daily conversations, household routines, attention to school matters, and affectionate concern for their children's progress. Conversation is important. Children learn to read, reason, and understand things better when their parents use their funds of knowledge as well as

- Read, talk, and listen to them.
- Tell them stories, play games, and share hobbies.

- Discuss the news, TV programs, and special events.

  To enrich the "curriculum of the home," some parents:

- Provide books, supplies, and a special place for studying.
- Observe routine for meals, bedtime, and homework.
- Monitor the amount of time spent watching TV and doing after-school jobs.

Parents stay aware of their children's lives at school when they:

- Discuss school events.
- Help children meet deadlines.
- Talk with their children about school problems and successes.
- Build positive attachments that create strong relationships.

## :: MEETING THE NEEDS OF YOUR SCHOOL AREA

Schools can make a special effort to help families function more effectively. Some parents travel constantly; the stay-at-home partners in those families have many of the same problems that a single parent has. A parent with a disability may need help with transportation or child care. An early survey of families will disclose what parents need and suggest ways the school can encourage participation.

### Worksite Seminars

Meet the needs of parents by offering seminars and parent education at companies and businesses during the lunch hour. Some corporations hire a parent educator to set up a program for their employees. School personnel could coordinate with them and be a resource for the parent educator. Topics for seminars range from school activities and parent–child communication to child development. If the company does not have an employee to set up the program, the school could offer seminars on an ongoing basis.

### Telephone Tree, E-mail, Blogs, or Chats

A telephone tree set up by the PTO or PTA can alert parents quickly to needs in the community. One caller begins by calling four or five people, who each call four or five more. Soon the entire community is alerted. Depending on the availability of the Internet, e-mail can be used to send information to parents and children. Chats or blogs can be used to have multiple ways of communicating important information.

### Transportation

If a parent group is active, it can offer transportation to those who need help getting to the school or to places like the doctor's office. Those in need might include people with disabilities and families with small children or a child who is ill.

### Parent-to-Parent Support

Parents without an extended family living nearby can team up with other parents. The parent organization can set up a file on parents that includes their needs, interests, children's ages, and location, with cross-references for parents to use. Parent education group meetings tend to promote friendships within the group. Isolated parents are often the ones who need the help of another parent the most. One parent may be able to manage the home efficiently, whereas another needs tips and help. Some parents were not exposed to a stable home environment and need a capable parent as a model. Although educators may not want to interfere in the lives of parents, they must remember that they meet and work with all parents and thus have the greatest access to the most parents of any community agency.

### Child Care

Child care can be offered to families with young children during conferences. Older children can participate in activities in the gymnasium, while young children can be cared for in a separate room. It is difficult for some parents to arrange for child care, and a cooperative child-care arrangement with parent volunteers would allow greater participation at conferences.

### Crisis Nursery

A worthwhile project for a parent organization is the development of a crisis nursery. Schools would have to meet state regulations for child care to have a nursery within the school, but it provides a great service and a chance to meet parents

Providing child care helps families attend school events.

and children before school starts. An assessment program, similar to Child Find, might alert parents and schools to developmental problems, such as hearing loss or poor sight.

A neighborhood home can also be used as a crisis base. If a parent with several children must take one child to the doctor, the crisis center can care for the other children during the parent's absence. Abusive parents can use the crisis center as a refuge for their children until they regain control of their emotions.

### After-School Activities

Schools can become centers for the community. One step toward greater community involvement is an after-school program. With so many working parents, many children become latchkey kids, going home to an empty house. If schools, perhaps working with other agencies, provide an after-school program for children of all ages, a great service is accomplished. Teachers should not be expected to be involved in after-school programs. However, recreation workers, trained child-care workers, and volunteers can implement a program that supplements the school program. Children can be taught how to spend leisure time through participation in crafts, sports, and cultural programs.

Although it is generally recognized that young children need supervision, the needs of secondary students are often ignored. Older students may have three to four unsupervised hours between the time they are out of school and the time their parents arrive home, and that time may be in ways that will not enrich the child. If you look at community structure, it becomes clear that schools are the major link between the family and the community; therefore, it is important to include all parents, even the ones who may have limited educational experience.

### Family Literacy Programs

Parents who can read with their children are better able to help and encourage the children in their reading and learning. Family literacy programs are needed by families for whom English is a second language as well as by many parents who went through school without learning to read. Join a family literacy program and offer space and help in providing literacy development, or develop the school's literacy program. This program could be enhanced by including programs for those who are able to read. Expand by offering family literacy, workshops on great books for children. Solicit volunteers from the community, including retired teachers who might enjoy the challenge.

### Skills Training

Offer workshops that provide skills training for the amateur as well as for the person who needs a skill to get a job. Courses in computer training, carpentry, typing, financial management, and organizational skills would all be appropriate workshops to help the parents in the community.

Some underemployed parents may need to develop more skills to become self-sufficient. Offer life-skills training, such as classes on parenting, relationships, anger management, and leadership.

### Emotional and Educational Support for Parents Experiencing Homelessness

1. Attitude counts. Be sure the classroom accepts and values all children regardless of living conditions, including homelessness.
2. Make it easy for a family to enroll in the school with friendly, immediate, and trouble-free registration procedures.
3. Provide free or reduced-priced breakfasts, snacks, and lunches without stereotyping people who receive these meals.
4. Provide child-development centers for infants and toddlers.
5. Offer early childhood classes for preschoolers.
6. Provide parent education and parent participation programs.
7. Provide English as a Second Language (ESL) courses.
8. Provide family literacy programs in the families' native language.
9. Offer classes or find classes that can help the parent become ready for employment.
10. Provide support meetings that help parents deal with depression and anxiety.

### Advocacy

1. Assign a teacher, staff member, or liaison to help the child and family during crisis.
2. Advocate for the family, if necessary, to get needed services.
3. Help with job search and placement.
4. Mentor the family.

The preceding lists are adapted from Eddowes, 1992; Klein et al., 1993; McCormick & Holden, 1992; Nuñez, 1996; Swick et al., 2001; Stronge, 1992.

## :: BUILDING FAMILY STRENGTHS

All families have strengths, these are their funds of knowledge. They are expressed in a variety of ways, but the approach that schools and agencies must take when working with families is to focus on their strengths and, through this focus, eliminate their problems. Research shows that parents respond positively to schools that set out to collaborate with them. During 2001–2008 many families had breadwinners who were out of work or had difficulty finding work that allowed them to provide for their families. Other families have both parents working, so time becomes a scarce commodity. Schools can help make this dual role easier for parents by providing or allowing other agencies to use the school building to provide before- and after-school care.

We tend to look at the half-full glass as half empty. Even if a majority of both parents will be working outside the home, there are still many families who have one parent as caregiver at home with the children. Others can provide the needed security and support their children need to make the school's responsibility of educating easier. Programs such as the Building Family Strengths program, designed at the University of Nebraska, focus on areas that parents need to address to keep their families strong. These include the following:

- *Communication*. Effective communication in strong families involves clear, direct channels between the speaker and listener. Families develop complicated ways of communicating. Strong families have learned to communicate directly and use consistent verbal and nonverbal behaviors.
- *Appreciation*. Appreciation involves being able to recognize the beautiful, positive aspects of others and letting them know you value these qualities. It also means being able to receive compliments yourself.
- *Commitment*. Commitment in strong families means that the family as a whole is committed to seeing that all members reach their potential.
- *Wellness*. Family wellness is the belief in positive human interaction. This belief helps family members trust others and learn to give and receive love. Family wellness is not the absence of problems. Strong families have their share of troubles, but their trust and love enable them to deal with their problems effectively.
- *Time together*. Spending time together as a family can be the most rewarding experience for humans. Two important aspects of time together are quality and quantity. Members of a strong family spend a lot of meaningful time with each other. This gives a family an identity that can be had in no other way.
- *The ability to deal with stress, conflict, and crisis*. All the previous strengths combine to make an inner core of power for families. This core serves as a resource for those times when conflict and crisis come.

Developing these strengths takes time and energy, but realizing their significance can help a family focus on the important interactions within the family. Many families do realize the importance of spending time together, communicating clearly with one another, and showing appreciation. However, these last two strengths take no extra time; they may take practice, but clear communication and showing appreciation can become a natural part of family life.

Families benefit from programs offered at the school or from home visits by school personnel who are able to share ideas about developing family strengths, discipline, school activities, and "homefun."

## VOLUNTEERS

Parents want the best for their children; most will respond to an opportunity to volunteer if the options for working are varied and their contributions are meaningful. When both parents work, short-term commitments geared to their working hours will allow and encourage participation from this group. Although the world is a busy place, time spent at school can bring satisfaction and variety to a parent's life.

### Volunteers: Used or Users?

Volunteerism has been criticized by some as inequitable and an exploitation of "woman power." To avoid such accusations, try to choose volunteers who can afford the time, or allow busy parents to contribute in such a way that they enjoy the time away from their other obligations. If education and training are included in your volunteer program, the participants can gain personally from the experience. For many, volunteering in school may be the first step toward a career.

If you are alert to the needs of parents, using them as volunteers can become a means of helping their families. If you work with them over a period of time, listen and use your knowledge of community resources to support the families in solving their problems. Volunteerism should serve the volunteer as well as contribute to the school.

### Who Should Ask for Volunteers?

Volunteer programs vary in their scope and design. Individual teachers may solicit volunteers from parents, individual schools can support a volunteer program, or school districts can implement a volunteer program. A volunteer program can help parents create systems that will support children in families. For example, the school where I taught began developing their parent program because there were parents who would come to the school because they wanted to help but did not know how. It only took the tenacity of one parent to get everyone organized and assist the teachers to create more developmentally appropriate environments for the children.

All teachers can benefit from the services of volunteers, but they should first determine the extent to which they are ready to use the assistance. A teacher who has not used aides, assistants, or volunteers should probably start with help in one area before expanding and recruiting volunteers for each hour in the week. In preschools, the free-choice period is a natural time to have added assistance. In elementary schools, assistance during art projects is often a necessity. Add to this initial use of volunteer help by securing extra tutors for reading class. In secondary schools, recruitment for a special project provides an excellent initial contact.

Easing into use of volunteers may not be necessary in your school. Because most preschools and primary grades have used assistance for many years, their teachers are ready for more continuous support from volunteers. Yet, involving other people in the classroom program is an art, based on good planning and the ability to work with and supervise others. Successful involvement of a few may lay the groundwork for greater involvement of others at a later time.

## Recruitment of Volunteers by Individual Teachers

Many teachers have been successful in implementing their own volunteer programs from among the parents of their students. If you have used volunteers previously and parents in the community have heard about your program from other parents, recruitment may be easy. Early in the year, an evening program, during which the curriculum is explained and parents get acquainted, is an effective time to recruit parents into the program. If parents have not been exposed to volunteerism, encourage them to visit the room and give them opportunities to participate in an easy activity, such as reading a story to a child or playing a game with a group. Ask them back for an enjoyable program so they begin to feel comfortable in the room. Sharing their hobbies with the children introduces many parents to the joys of teaching. Gradually the fear of classroom involvement will disappear, and parents may be willing to spend several hours each week in the classroom.

## Invitations That Work

Suppose you write notes or publish an invitation in the newsletter inviting parents to visit the school or child-care center, but nobody comes. If you have had this experience, you need a "parent-getter." Judge your activity and invitation by the following questions:

- Does the event sound enjoyable?
- Is there something in it for the parents?
- Are the parents' children involved in the program?
- Does the program have alternate times for attendance?

The first criterion, making the event sound enjoyable, can be met by the wording of the invitation. The second and third vary in importance; one or the other should be addressed in each bid for parent attendance. Scheduling alternate times depends on your parents' needs.

One teacher complained that the parents at her school were just not interested in helping. Only three had volunteered when they were asked to clean up the playground. When asked if there were any other enticements for the parents to volunteer to help, the teacher said no. "Would you have wanted to spend your Saturday morning cleaning up the playground?" she was asked. The teacher realized she would not have participated either if she had been one of the parents. An excellent means of determining the drawing power of a program or activity is your own reaction to the project. Would you want to come? Had the Saturday cleanup project included the children, furnished refreshments, and allowed time for a get-together after the work was completed, the turnout would have been much better. Make it worth the parents' time to volunteer.

## Performances

Many schools have children perform to get parents to turn out. The ploy works—parents attend! Some professionals discourage this method because they believe that children are being exploited to attract parents. However, it is probably the manner in which the production is conceived and readied rather than the child's involvement that is unworthy. What are your memories of your childhood performances? If the experiences were devastating, was it the programs themselves or the way they were handled that led to disappointment? If the performance is a creative, worthwhile experience for the child and does not cause embarrassment, heartache, or a sense of rejection for the child who does not perform well and if all children are included, this method of enticing parents can be valuable for both children and parents. Experience in front of an audience can develop poise and heightened self-concept—and be fun for the child. Parents invited to unpolished programs enjoy the visit just as much as if they had attended refined productions. Small, simple classroom functions, scheduled often enough that every child has a moment in the limelight, are sure to have high parent turnout. The more parents come to school and get involved with the activities, the better chance you have of recruiting assistance.

### Field Trips

Use a field trip to talk with parents about volunteering in the classroom. Parents will often volunteer for field trips, during which teacher and parent can find time to chat. See if the parents' interests include hobbies that can be shared with the class. Be receptive to any ideas or needs that parents reveal. The informal atmosphere of a field trip encourages parents to volunteer.

### Want Ads to Encourage Sharing Experiences and Expertise

Parents have many experiences and talents that they can share. Who lived on a farm? Who just traveled to Japan? Who knows how to cook spaghetti? Who can knit? Who has a collection of baseball cards? Who can speak a different language? Who has some stories to tell? Who is a geologist? Who is a food server? Ask parents to share their talents, hobbies, and experiences with your class. Send home a want ad to parents (see Figure 5–7) and ask them to return a tear-off portion, or call them and ask them personally to come to the school. Schedule each parent at a time that is convenient for parent and teacher. If possible, a follow-up in class of the ideas presented will make the visit even more meaningful. After the presentations, write thank-you notes with suggestions

that parents might come to class again, providing another means of recruiting potential volunteers.

### Invitations to Share

Sending home invitations with the children asking parents if they are interested in volunteering is a direct way to recruit. Each teacher should design the invitation to fit the needs of the class. A letter that accompanies the form should stress to parents how important they are to the program. Let them know the following.

- Teachers and children need their help.
- Each parent is already experienced in working with children.
- Their child will be proud of the parents' involvement and will gain through their contributions.

Friendly requests along with suggestions enable parents to respond easily. Be sure to ask parents for their ideas and contributions. You have no way of knowing what useful treasures you may find! Let parents complete a questionnaire, such as the one in Figure 5–8, to indicate their interests and schedules. Perhaps a parent cannot visit school but is willing to make calls and coordinate the volunteer program. This parent can find substitutes when regular parent volunteers call in to say they must be absent. Others who are homebound can aid the class by sharing child care, making games and activities at home, designing and making costumes, writing newsletters, and making phone calls.

Parents who are able to work at school can perform both teaching and nonteaching tasks. Relate the task to the parents' interests. Nothing discourages some volunteers as much as being forced to do housekeeping tasks continually, with no opportunity for interaction with the children. The choice of tasks should not be difficult, however, because the opportunities are numerous and diversified, as the following lists indicate.

### Teaching Tasks.
#### *School, Preschool, or Child-care Center*

Supervise learning centers.
Listen to children.
Play games with students.
Tell stories.
Play instructional games.

## FIGURE 5–7

One way to solicit school volunteers is through a want ad.

---

**Help Wanted**
**Positions Available**

**Tutor for Reading**
Do you have an interest in children learning to read? Come tutor! We will train you in techniques to use.

**Good Listener**
Are you willing to listen to children share their experiences and stories? Come to the listening area and let a child share with you.

**Costume Designer**
There will be a class presentation next month. Is anyone willing to help with simple costumes?

**Tour Guide**
Do you have memories, slides, or tales about other states or countries? Come share.

**Talent Scout**
Some talented people never volunteer. We need a talent scout to help us find these people in our community.

**Good-will Ambassador**
Help us make everyone feel an important part of this school or center. Be in charge of sending get-well cards or congratulatory messages.

**Reader of Books**
Read to the children. Choose a favorite book or read one chosen by the teacher.

**Photographer**
Anyone want to help chronicle our year? Photographer needed.

**Collector**
Do you hate to throw good things away? Help us in our scrounge department. Collect and organize.

**Game Player**
We need someone who enjoys games to spend several hours a week at the game table.

**News Editor**
Be a news hound. Help us develop and publish a newsletter. The children will help furnish news.

**Book Designer**
The class needs books written by children for our reading center. Turn children's work into books.

**Volunteer Coordinator**
The class needs volunteers, but we also need to know who, when, and how. Coordinate the volunteer time sheet.

**Construction Worker**
Are you good at building and putting things together? Volunteer!

**Computer Programmer**
Share your expertise with the class.

SIGN UP IN YOUR CHILD'S CLASSROOM OR RETURN THIS FORM WITH YOUR INTERESTS CHECKED.

Tutor_____ Listener_____ Costume Designer_____ Tour Guide_____ Talent Scout_____ Ambassador_____
Reader_____ Photographer_____ Collector_____ Game Player_____ News Editor_____ Book Designer_____
Volunteer Coordinator_____ Construction Worker_____ Computer Programmer_____ Other_____

_____    _____    _____    _____
Name                       Address                    Telephone                  E-mail

---

Work with children with learning disabilities.
Help select library books for children.
Read to children.
Take children to the resource center.
Assist in learning centers.
Share a hobby.
Speak on travel and customs around the world.
Demonstrate sewing or weaving.
Provide computer training.

Demonstrate food preparation.
Show DVDs about subjects of interest

*School*

Help children prepare and practice speeches.
Supervise the making of books.
Show children how to use different software.
Supervise the production of a newsletter or newspaper.

**FIGURE 5–8**
Questionnaires are another way to obtain parents' interests and schedules.

**Please Share With the School or Center**

Dear Parents:

We need volunteers to help us with our school. You can share your time by helping while you are at home or at school. If you want to share in any way, please let us know.

Are you interested in volunteering this year? _____ Yes _____ No

Check the ways you want to help.

_____ In the classroom

_____ In the resource center

_____ At home

WHAT WOULD YOU LIKE TO DO?

| | |
|---|---|
| _____ Share your hobby or travel experience | _____ Tell stories |
| _____ Help children in learning centers | _____ Check papers |
| _____ Be a room parent | _____ Check spelling |
| _____ Work in a resource room | _____ Help with math |
| _____ Supervise a puppet show | _____ Read to children |
| _____ Go on field trips | _____ Make games |
| _____ Care for another volunteer's children | _____ Listen to children read |
| _____ Substitute for others | _____ Play games with children |
| _____ Develop a learning center | _____ Make books |
| _____ Tutor reading | _____ Share your recipes |

Any other suggestions? _____

_____

Comments _____

When can you come?

| Monday | Tuesday | Wednesday | Thursday | Friday |
|---|---|---|---|---|
| AM \| PM | AM \| PM | AM \| PM | AM \| PM | AM \| PM |

Can you come each week? _____ Other _____

What time can you come? _____

How long can you stay? _____

_____ _____ _____

Name                              E-mail                              Telephone

## Nonteaching Tasks.

Make games.

Prepare a parent bulletin board.

Repair equipment.

Select and reproduce articles for the resource room.

Record grades.

Take attendance.

Collect lunch money.

Plan a workshop for parents.

Grade and correct papers or write comments.

Organize cupboards.

Help with book publishing.

## Contributions from Home.

Serve as telephone chairperson.

Develop a classroom or school Web site.

Collect recycling materials.

Furnish refreshments.

Furnish dress-up clothes and costumes.

Wash aprons.

Make art aprons.

Design and/or make costumes.

Repair equipment.

Make games.

Care for another volunteer's child.

Write newsletters.

Coordinate volunteers.

Teaching embraces creative ideas and methods; volunteers, responding to the challenge, can provide a vast reservoir of talent and support. Book publishing is an excellent example of an effective volunteer activity that is both a teaching and a nonteaching role.

## Management Techniques

Use management skills in organizing and implementing your volunteer program. A parent coordinator can be very helpful in developing effective communication between teacher and parent. Two types of charts—schedules and volunteer action sheets—can clarify the program and help it run more smoothly.

### Schedules.
Schedules can be adjusted if weekly charts are posted at school and sent home to parents. When parents can visualize the coverage, the class will not be inundated by help in one session and suffer from lack of help in another.

### Volunteer Sheet.
Because volunteers are used in many ways, developing an action sheet that describes each person's contribution is helpful.

Figure 5–9 illustrates the scope of involvement within one classroom. With this list the parent coordinator can secure an effective substitute for someone who must be absent. If the teacher needs games constructed, the parent coordinator can call on parents who have volunteered for that activity. Special help in the resource center or with a student project may be found quickly by calling a parent who has already indicated an interest in helping this way. The responsibility for the volunteer program does not need to rest solely on the teacher's shoulders. Parents and teachers become partners in developing a smoothly working system.

## Increasing Volunteer Usage

Although permanent volunteers are more effective in establishing continuity in a program than periodic contributions by occasional volunteers, both are needed. As the year progresses, some parents may find they enjoy teaching immensely. These parents may extend their time obligation and, in doing so, bring more continuity to the program. Ideally, an assistant should tutor a reading group or a child for several sessions each week rather than just one. When initiating a program, it is best to start out with easily handled time slots and then expand the responsibilities of parents after they become secure and familiar with the class, the objectives, and the material.

## Volunteer Training

Suppose that several parents have indicated interest in being permanent volunteers in your classroom. What is your next step? The time spent explaining your routine, expectations, and preferences for teaching will be well worth the effort in the parents' abilities to coordinate with you in your classroom. Most teachers have specific preferences for teaching that they will want to share with the volunteers helping them. These, in addition to some general guidelines, will help prepare the volunteer. The following humanistic guidelines for working with children are appropriate for all volunteers:

- A healthy, positive self-concept is a prerequisite to learning.
- The act of listening to a child implies that you accept the child as a worthwhile person.
- The child will develop a better sense of self-worth if you praise specific efforts rather than deride failures.

## FIGURE 5–9

Volunteer action sheets help organize an orderly volunteer program.

| Name | Telephone or e-mail | Classroom Regularly | Classroom Substitute | Special Presentation | Child Care | Make Games at Home | Work in Resource Center — Help Students | Develop Resources — Type | Develop Resources — Make games |
|---|---|---|---|---|---|---|---|---|---|
| Names of volunteers | 555-5555 | | | | | | | Type | Make games |
| = | X | | | | | | | X | |
| = | | X | X | | | | | | |
| = | | X | X | | | | | | |
| = | X | | X | | | | | | |
| = | X | X | X | | X | | | | |
| = | | | | X | X | | | | |
| = | | | | X | X | X | X | | |
| = | X | | | | | | | | |
| = | X | | X | | | | | | |
| = | X | | | | | | | | |
| = | X | X | | | X | X | X | X | |
| = | X | | | X | | X | | | |
| = | X | X | X | | X | | X | | |
| = | | X | | | | | | | |
| = | | X | | | X | | | | |
| = | | X | | | | | | | |
| = | | X | | | X | | | | |
| = | | | | X | | | | | |
| = | | | X | X | | | | | |
| = | | | X | X | X | | | X | |
| = | | X | | | X | X | X | X | |
| = | | X | | X | | | | | |
| = | | X | X | X | | | | | |
| = | | | | X | | | | | |

- Provide tasks at which the children can succeed. As they master these, move on to the next level.

Many children who need extra help with their work also need their self-concepts strengthened. Volunteers can provide an extra touch through kindness, interest, and support.

### The Teacher's Responsibilities to the Volunteer

As teachers enlist the help of volunteers, certain responsibilities emerge. The teacher's responsibilities are as follows:

- *Make volunteers feel welcome.* Smile and reassure them.
- Explain class rules and regulations.
- Introduce volunteers to the resources within the school.
- Explain the routine of the class.
- Describe your expectations for their participation.
- Remember that volunteers are contributing and sharing time because of satisfaction they receive and to help the child.
- Give volunteers reinforcement and recognition.
- Meet with volunteers when class is not in session to clarify, answer questions, and, if needed, give instruction and training.
- Appreciate, respect, and encourage volunteers.

Awareness of these points will make the cooperative effort of teacher and volunteer more fulfilling for both.

### The Volunteer's Responsibilities to the Teacher

If parents or others in the community volunteer to help in the school, they accept certain responsibilities, which include the following:

- Be dependable and punctual. If an emergency requires that you miss a session, obtain a substitute or contact the volunteer coordinator.
- Keep privileged information concerning children or events confidential. Do not discuss children with people other than school personnel.
- Plan responsibilities in the classroom with the teacher.
- Cooperate with the staff. Welcome supervision.
- Be ready to learn and grow in your work.

- Enjoy yourself, but do not let your charges get out of control.
- Be fair, consistent, and organized.

Volunteer aides are not helpful if they continually cancel at the last moment, disrupt the room rather than help it run smoothly, or upset the students. They are immensely helpful if they work with the teacher to strengthen and individualize the school program.

### Recruitment by Schools and School Systems

Many schools and school districts assist teachers by recruiting volunteers for their classes. The first step in initiating a volunteer program for a school or school system is the development of a questionnaire to ascertain the teachers' needs. The teachers complete a form based on the curriculum for each age level of students. After the forms are completed, the coordinators can determine the requirements of each room.

After teachers have indicated their needs, the coordinator begins recruitment. Many avenues are open for the recruiter. A flyer geared to the appropriate age or level of children, asking people to share their time with the schools, can bring about the desired results. Organizations can also be contacted. The PTA or PTO, senior citizen groups, and other clubs have members who may want to get involved as volunteers in the school.

The points discussed earlier for obtaining volunteers for the individual classroom are also appropriate for volunteers who are solicited on a larger scale. The major differences are organizational and include the following:

- Teachers should contact the volunteer coordinator or reply to the coordinator's questionnaire if they want a volunteer.
- Districts usually require volunteers to fill out an application stating their background, giving references, and listing the hours they are available.
- Many school districts have an extensive compilation of resource people who have agreed to volunteer in the schools. An alliance with businesses encourages companies to allow their employees to visit schools and tell students about their careers. These resource people and experts can share their knowledge with classes throughout the school district. Lists of topics with resource

people available to share expertise can be distributed throughout the district. Teachers can request the subject and time they want a presentation.

- *Outreach, such as a community study hall, can be initiated and staffed by the volunteer program.* Volunteers can tutor and work with children after school hours in libraries, schools, or other public facilities (Denver Public Schools, n.d.).
- Certificates or awards distributed by the district offer a way to thank the volunteers for effort and time shared with the schools.

Individual teachers tend to use parents as aides and resource people in the room. The district most often furnishes resource people, drawn from the total population, in schools throughout the district. The school's volunteer coordinator uses both approaches, enlisting volunteers to tutor and aid in the classroom and recruiting resource people from residents of the school's population area to enrich the curriculum.

## SUMMARY

Understanding parents' feelings and concerns provides the basis for creating effective home–school relationships. Schools have character—some invite parents to participate while others suggest they stay away. Parents have feelings about schools that range from a desire to avoid the school to such a high interest that they are overly active. Parents participate in schools as spectators, accessory volunteers, volunteer resources, paid resources, policy makers, and teachers of their children.

Schools can develop attitudes that welcome parents and conduct activities that invite them into the school. Personnel in the school need to understand and examine their own attitudes toward parents. The use of questionnaires helps in the recognition of these attitudes.

An open-door policy with open forums, coffee chats, and seminars invites comments from parents. Initial contact should be made early in the year or even during the summer before the school year begins. Suggestions for early contact include neighborhood visits, telephone calls, texting, school and/or classroom Web sites, home visits, and breakfasts.

A resource room, established and staffed by parent volunteers, makes parents significant educational resources. The resource room includes articles on teaching, games, recycled materials, and a lending library for toys, books, and games. A family center gives parents a place to stop and a base from which they can reach out to help children.

Parents today are more involved as policy makers than in the past. Parent advisory councils are part of Title I, and parents confer with school administrators on program planning, implementation, and evaluation.

Schools can become community centers and meet the needs of families in the area by organizing parent volunteers for parent-to-parent groups, child-care centers, crisis centers, and after-school programs. If schools focus on family strengths, they will help families develop and keep effective communication, commitment, wellness, time together, and the ability to deal with stress, conflict, and crises. Parents and others from the community can also be included in the schools as volunteers. Teachers need to develop skills to recruit, train, and work with volunteers as part of an educational team.

## SUGGESTED CLASS ACTIVITIES AND DISCUSSIONS

1. Interview a school principal and ask him or her about ideas regarding school–community relations.
2. Contact the president of the PTA or PTO in a neighborhood school. What are his or her goals for parent involvement in the school? Which programs have been planned for the year? Which direction would he or she like the PTO or PTA to take?
3. Discuss why some parents may feel intimidated by schools and why some teachers may be reluctant to have parents involved. Role play the teacher and parent roles and share your feelings.
4. Describe an ideal parent–teacher relationship. List five things a teacher can do to encourage such a relationship. List five ways a parent can work with the school.
5. List what makes you feel comfortable or uncomfortable when you visit a center or school.
6. Visit a school and look at bulletin boards, notices, and family centers that might welcome parents. Make a list of things that might

invite parents as well as things that might intimidate parents.

7. Examine the offerings of a school system or an individual school. What programs or activities does the school offer? List and describe the offerings, including programs such as Head Start, family literacy, telephone tutoring, resource rooms, exchanges, prekindergarten programs, and parent advisory council.

8. Do a community study in which you analyze the different families you might find in the school in your neighborhood and in a different neighborhood. What are their living arrangements, their values, their ambitions, their hopes for the future? What businesses are around the school/center that provide services to families? Are there other community resources that families from the neighborhood use?

9. Design a want ad or letter that invites parents to become volunteers in the classroom.

10. Search the community for resources that can be used in the school. Include specialists, materials, and places to visit.

11. List the strengths that help families. What other strengths might you add? How would you help families build their strengths?

## USEFUL WEB SITES

**Clearinghouse on Early Education and Parenting (CEEP): ERIC/EECE Archive of Publications and Resources**
http://ceep.crc.uiuc.edu/eecearchive/
CEEP maintains the ERIC/EECE elementary and early childhood archive. Many useful publications are available.

**National Center for Family Literacy**
www.famlit.org/
Focuses on the advancement of literacy for families.

**Parents as Teachers National Center (PATNC)**
www.patnc.org/
PATNC and MELD have joined resources and both have literature and many positive programs helpful to parents and those working with parents.

**Reading Is Fundamental**
www.rif.org/
The site offers a monthly calendar with activities that enhance reading.

**Zero to Three**
www.zerotothree.org/
Zero to Three focuses on the very young child and has an excellent program and information on children aged 0 to 3.

# Effective Teacher–Family Communication: Types, Barriers, Conferences, and Programs

*To really communicate one must listen, one must share true meaning, and one must reflect upon the message being shared.*

E. H. Berger

In this chapter on communication, you will find methods for effective communication that will enable you to do the following:

- Discuss effective communication.
- Identify and use one-way and two-way communication.
- Describe roadblocks to communication.
- List elements of effective communication with parents.
- List and describe parent education programs.
- Develop a plan for an effective parent–teacher conference.

What do you have in mind when you think of effective communication? Is it the transmission of feelings, information, and signals? Is it the sending and receiving of messages? Is it a verbal exchange between people—for example, parents and teachers?

## :: COMMUNICATION

Most definitions of **communication** encompass more than mere interchange of information. Communication entails the active participation of the sender to convey a message or thought to the receiver who, in turn, may or may not reciprocate the action by acknowledging that information. Communication is achieved when an understanding, but not necessarily an agreement, is reached. Is the message received with the meaning that the sender intended to convey? In working with parents, it is essential that messages are sent and received as intended for all parents, particularly if we don't speak their language or know their culture.

### Messages

Each message has at least three components: (a) the words or verbal stimuli—what a person says; (b) the body language or physical stimuli—the gestures; and (c) the vocal characteristics or vocal stimuli—the pitch, loudness or softness, and speed (Gamble & Gamble, 1982). All cultures will vary in the way that they convey their messages; therefore, it is important for teachers to know the families that they work with in order to know appropriate ways to send messages because this will help increase communication and relations.

The sender gives a message, which is received and interpreted by the receiver. If the intent of the message is accurately received, effective communication has occurred. For this to happen, the listener must be an active participant. The listener must be able to hear the message, the feeling, and the meaning of the message.

Communication includes speaking, listening, reflection of feeling, and interpretation of the message. It is a complicated process because so many variables come into play. The sender's voice and body language, the message itself, the receiver's reaction to the sender, and the receiver's expectations all affect the message and are all culturally based. To be effective in communication, speakers need to understand their own reactions and the reaction of others to them, and they must listen to the meaning of the message.

The receiver must correctly interpret the meaning of the message and the sender's intent. If the message—or the receiver's response—is misinterpreted, miscommunication occurs (this very often occurs in parent–teacher conferences). Miscommunication can be overcome, but the sender or the receiver must understand how to recover from it. The receiver may check out understanding by rephrasing and recycling the conversation or by further questioning within the context of the subsequent discussion.

### Miscommunication

Interpersonal communication may be visualized as messages within an ongoing circle or oval configuration. As pictured in Figure 6–1, the message (filtered through values and past experiences) goes to the receiver (where it also is filtered through values and

## FIGURE 6–1

Messages are filtered through the receiver's value system and experiences before they are decoded and responded to. Communication is a dynamic, continuous process.

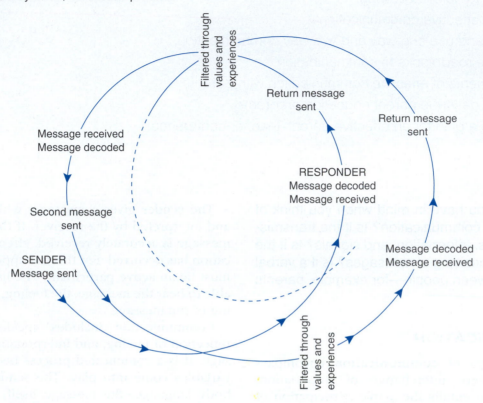

past experiences), is decoded, responded to, and sent back to begin the cycle again. Communication is a dynamic, continuous process that changes and evolves.

### Visual Messages

When talking with one another, it is easy to assume that what one says is the most important element in the conversation. However, research shows that oral, verbal messages (the spoken words) account for only 7 percent of the input; vocal and tonal messages (the way in which the words are spoken) account for 38 percent; and visual messages (body language) account for 55 percent (Miller, Wackman, Nunnally, & Miller, 1988). If this is the case, teachers, principals, and child-care professionals need to focus on their total communication system and be aware of their body language and tone of voice as well as their verbal messages. It is the power of words—what we do with the words (Bloome, 2007)—that transforms

communication by considering the context and the words in how we communicate (Enciso, Katz, Kiefer, Price-Dennis, & Wilson, 2007).

### One- and Two-Way Communication

One-way communication from the school merely informs parents about the school's plans and happenings. Two-way communication, which requires interaction among participants, allows parents to give feedback to the school on their knowledge, concerns, and desires. Both the school and parents gain. The steps to achieve effective communication among school, home, and community are easy to implement once the importance of effective communication is acknowledged. A number of strategies for establishing improved communication are described on the following pages. Choose the ones that fit your individual needs, and add others that work for you. The strategies used should be the ones that work best for parents.

**FIGURE 6–2**
Newsletters may take many forms, ranging from this informal design to very sophisticated publications.

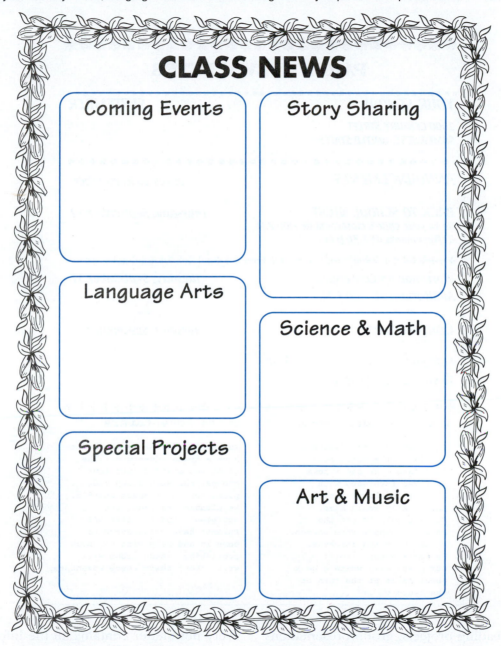

## :: ONE-WAY COMMUNICATION

A newsletter may be sent by the school as a message from the principal, or it may be sent home by each teacher. It is a simple form of one-way communication. The format varies with the goals and objectives of each newsletter, with designs ranging from a very simple notice to an elaborate and professionally written letter.

### Simple Newsletters

The more newsletters you write, the easier they become. The design may vary from a simple notice that is handprinted and photocopied (see Figure 6–2) to a letter created through a desktop publishing program on the school computer (see Figure 6–3). Items may include the children's activities in curriculum areas such as math contracts

**FIGURE 6–3**
If you regularly collect anecdotes and children's work, you will easily have enough material for a four-page newsletter for parents.

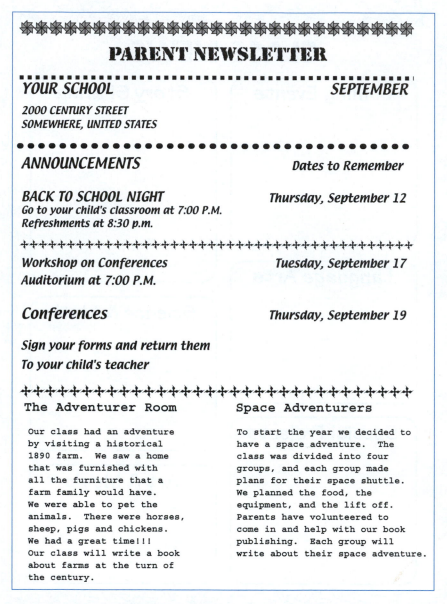

# PARENT NEWSLETTER

*YOUR SCHOOL*                                    *SEPTEMBER*

*2000 CENTURY STREET*
*SOMEWHERE, UNITED STATES*

## ANNOUNCEMENTS                              *Dates to Remember*

**BACK TO SCHOOL NIGHT**                      **Thursday, September 12**
*Go to your child's classroom at 7:00 P.M.*
*Refreshments at 8:30 p.m.*

*Workshop on Conferences*                     **Tuesday, September 17**
*Auditorium at 7:00 P.M.*

## Conferences                               **Thursday, September 19**

*Sign your forms and return them*
*To your child's teacher*

### The Adventurer Room              ### Space Adventurers

Our class had an adventure        To start the year we decided to
by visiting a historical          have a space adventure.  The
1890 farm.  We saw a home         class was divided into four
that was furnished with           groups, and each group made
all the furniture that a          plans for their space shuttle.
farm family would have.           We planned the food, the
We were able to pet the           equipment, and the lift off.
animals.  There were horses,      Parents have volunteered to
sheep, pigs and chickens.         come in and help with our book
We had a great time!!!            publishing.  Each group will
Our class will write a book       write about their space adventure.
about farms at the turn of
the century.

or contests, reading projects, group presentations in social studies, hands-on work in science, practice in music skills, art experiences, field trips, care of classroom pets, contributions by resource people, creative drama experiences, and accomplishments or remarks by individual children (teacher must ensure that parents give permission to use their child's work in the newsletter). In addition, items may include information important to parents, such as parent–teacher conferences, back-to-school nights, and parent breakfasts. Not

every newsletter contains all the information, for it is an ongoing communication.

Newsletters may also be used at the secondary level with sections blocked for each course of study. Newsletters at the secondary level also provide parents with information regarding deadlines, such as those related to testing dates, scheduling, and financial-aid submission dates.

For both elementary and secondary schools newsletters can also provide parents with a means of staying in touch with each other. Selected parents can be identified as liaisons for particular school events or just as resources when parents have questions. This is particularly helpful when many parents speak languages other than English and need assistance with translations more quickly than the school can provide. Communication between home and school is essential. This type of communication allows parents to see the messages that the school needs for them to know. Often parents post the newsletter in a place where they can easily access it.

Students who are old enough can be given the responsibility of writing the periodic newsletter. This way, the newsletter serves two purposes: curriculum and communication. The students are challenged to write neatly, spell correctly, and construct a readable newsletter. Younger children can make individual contributions by painting a picture or making a comment that can be shared. Newsletters can also be done electronically. They can be posted on the school's Web site and also distribute through a LISTSERV.

Consider using the following in your newsletter:

- Clear headlines that identify the topic
- Colorful paper
- Calendar of the week or month
- Book suggestions
- Recognition of birthdays
- Children's or students' work
- Quotes from children
- Artwork

**Preschool.** Publication of newsletters in preschool is an excellent way to include children in the development of literacy. The newsletters should reflect the diversity of children in the classroom. Children can contribute by selecting a topic and interviewing one another about the things they like. They can also take pictures of projects that they have worked on using digital cameras and include any other artifacts to enhance the newsletter. The teacher can ask a parent to organize the classroom newsletter and then seek volunteers each month to create the newsletter. Parents are often very willing to contribute their knowledge and time to their child's classroom. If parents are not literate, the teacher can team them up with another parent. This creates endless opportunities for all parents to create networks that will help them increase their own literacy level.

Try collecting newsletter ideas throughout the year. Excellent sources for information include federal, state, and local agencies that provide interesting and

Include photos of favorite family activities in newsletters.

relevant information for families. Commercial newsletters are available that can be used with inserts from your own center to reflect your concerns and news. As you collect interesting comments by the children or complete special projects, make a short note for the newsletter. If you choose a "very important person" each week, include information about that child in the newsletter. If you include articles about individual children, be sure to include each child before the end of the term. When time comes for publication, you will have more than enough news.

Keep in mind that it is more important to have a newsletter than to worry about its design. Recruit a parent who is interested in communications to help you develop the newsletter. Recruiting other parents to help with the newsletter also helps create community within the classroom and school. Subjects that parents will find interesting include nutrition, child development, communication, and activities for rainy days, as well as events specific to your center or class. A picture drawn by a child to accompany the news is an attractive addition.

**Elementary.** A newsletter is an excellent curriculum tool in elementary school. Make the newsletter an ongoing project, with a center set up to handle the papers and equipment. Assign a group in each subject area to be responsible for the newsletter. Let them collect the news and determine the content and design of the letter. You can have the children develop the newsletter on the computer. Different children could add messages or articles. You can ask parent volunteers to make copies of the newsletter or you can have the children create an electronic copy of the newsletter and post it on the classroom or school Web site as well as distribute it to parents through e-mail.

**District Newsletter.** Many school districts use newsletters to keep the community up to date on school events. Often produced by professional public relations firms, they may display excellent style and format and contain precise information, but they may also lack the personal touch and tend to be viewed as a communiqué from the administration. District newsletters do have a place in building effective home–school–community relations, and some districts want all press releases to originate from administration; however, these may be supplemented by individual class reports (newsletters). In this way,

parents receive both formal and personalized communication about their children's schooling.

### Notes and Letters

An "upslip" is sent home when a child is doing well to inform parents about a child's performance in different aspects of school (see Figure 6–4). It is a good idea to buy small sheets of paper with space enough for a one- or two-line note. If you write too much, you may be forced by time limitation to postpone the incidental note, and the positive effect of timeliness is lost.

Letters sent prior to the beginning of school also help establish good communication. They should include significant dates, reminders, and school events (see Figure 6–5).

### FIGURE 6–4
Happy grams, "upslips," and short notes are appreciated by parents and child.

**FIGURE 6–5**

Friendly letters sent prior to the opening of school can set the stage for a cooperative and pleasant school year.

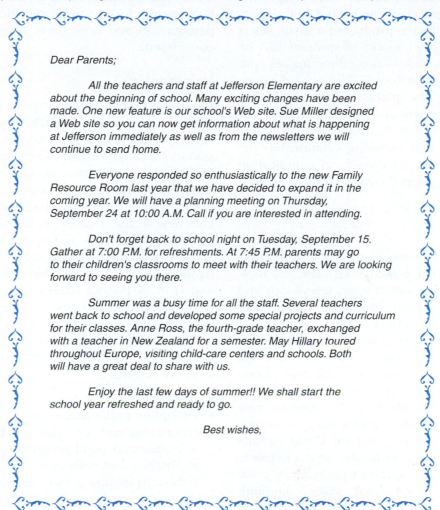

> Dear Parents;
>
> All the teachers and staff at Jefferson Elementary are excited about the beginning of school. Many exciting changes have been made. One new feature is our school's Web site. Sue Miller designed a Web site so you can now get information about what is happening at Jefferson immediately as well as from the newsletters we will continue to send home.
>
> Everyone responded so enthusiastically to the new Family Resource Room last year that we have decided to expand it in the coming year. We will have a planning meeting on Thursday, September 24 at 10:00 A.M. Call if you are interested in attending.
>
> Don't forget back to school night on Tuesday, September 15. Gather at 7:00 P.M. for refreshments. At 7:45 P.M. parents may go to their children's classrooms to meet with their teachers. We are looking forward to seeing you there.
>
> Summer was a busy time for all the staff. Several teachers went back to school and developed some special projects and curriculum for their classes. Anne Ross, the fourth-grade teacher, exchanged with a teacher in New Zealand for a semester. May Hillary toured throughout Europe, visiting child-care centers and schools. Both will have a great deal to share with us.
>
> Enjoy the last few days of summer!! We shall start the school year refreshed and ready to go.
>
> Best wishes,

Many teachers like to use "good news notes," happy faces, "happy grams," or similar forms periodically to report something positive about each child. The concept behind each of these formats is the same—to communicate with parents in a positive manner, thereby improving both parent–teacher relations and the child's self-concept. Make a concerted effort to send these notes in a spirit of spontaneous sincerity. A contrived, meaningless comment, sent because you are required to do so, will probably be received as it was sent. Preserving good relations requires that the message have meaning.

## Newspapers

Most school districts have newspapers, yearbooks, and other school-sponsored publications. These, along with the district newsletter, are important school traditions and effectively disseminate information. Don't stop publishing them, but always remember that the newsletters that touch on their children are of greater importance to parents. Those most affected by yearbooks are those whose children are pictured in them. Parents most affected by newspapers are those who find articles in them concerning activities in which their children are involved.

Relying solely on newspapers and yearbooks for communicating with parents may promote complacency; some administrators and teachers assume communication is complete because a newspaper comes out periodically and a yearbook is published when seniors graduate. Yearbooks have very little effect on school–home relationships. They arrive after the student's school career ends, they often picture a small segment of the school population, and they are generally the product of a small, select group of students. The majority of students may be omitted or ignored, unless the editor makes sure that all children are included. The school newspaper cannot take the place of individual class newsletters. Newspapers and yearbooks meet different needs and are significant in their own way, but to establish a real, working relationship between parents and schools, the school's publication must concern the parents' number one interest—their own children.

## Media

A formal and effective means of reaching parents is through the Internet, e-mail, Web sites, text messages, the community newspaper, television, and radio stations. Television and radio often make public service announcements. Use the format of "who, what, when, where, why, and how" information to send to television and radio stations. Be brief but include a contact name and phone number. The Internet is probably the fastest way to reach parents. Many districts also connect with their families sending text and e-mail messages. Paper media may still be used for those parents who may not have access to the new electronic media. Use these opportunities to inform the community about events at school. Many communities have access to a cable information line that alerts the community to upcoming events. These may include conferences, sports events, musical performances, debates, theatre, school board meetings, community meetings, back-to-school nights, and carnivals. For example, the San Antonio Independent School District provides short video clips to highlight activities throughout the district. The video clips allow parents and the community to learn more about their school district.

## Suggestion Box

A suggestion box placed in the hallway encourages parents to share their concerns and pleasures with the school anonymously. Although this is really a one-way communication system, it effectively tells parents, "We want your suggestions. Let us know what you feel" and encourages them to respond.

A way to let parents know that their suggestions were read is to have a "response corner" on a bulletin board close to the suggestion box. That way parents can see how their suggestion has been considered.

## Handbooks

Handbooks sent home before the child enters school are greatly appreciated by parents. If sent while the child is a preschooler, the school's expectations for the child can be met early. If given to parents at an open house during the spring term, they can reinforce the directions given by the teacher at that time. Handbooks can help parents new to the area by including information on community activities and associations for families. Many school districts and centers are sending the handbooks electronically for parents to download and read. A district handbook designed to introduce parents to the resources in the area—with special pages geared to each level of student—can be developed and used by all teachers in the district. Moles (1996a) suggests the following handbook inclusions:

- Statement of school goals and philosophy
- Discipline policy and code
- Operations and procedures regarding
  a. grades and pupil progress reports
  b. absence and tardiness
  c. how to inquire about student difficulties
  d. emergency procedures for weather and other events
  e. transportation schedules and provisions for after-school activities
- Special programs at the school, such as after-school enrichment or child-care programs
- Parent involvement policies and practices at the school, with items that describe
  a. "Bill of Rights" for parents
  b. "Code of Responsibilities" for parents
  c. open house and parent–teacher conferences
  d. involvement opportunities, such as volunteer programs, advisory councils, and PTAs
- A calendar of major school events throughout the year: holidays, vacations, regular PTA meetings, report card periods, open houses, and other regularly scheduled school–home contacts
- Names and phone numbers of key school contact people

- Names and phone numbers of parent leaders (e.g., members of advisory councils, key people in parent organizations, and room parents)
- A tear-off response form allowing parents to ask questions, voice concerns, and volunteer at the school

In addition, consider the following items when you compile your handbook:

- Procedures for registration
- Invitations to visit the school
- Conferences and progress reports
- Testing and evaluation programs
- Decision-making process, advisory committees, site-based management
- Facilities at the school (cafeteria, clinic, library)
- Special programs offered by the school (band, chorus, gymnastics)
- Summer programs
- Recreation programs
- Associations related to families and children
- Community center

**Specialized Handbook.** A special handbook related to the child's grade level and academic program can be an effective way to gain parents' cooperation. If it is sent out early in the school term, include the teacher's name and a short autobiography.

The handbook can include a special section related to the curriculum in the child's grade level and can be developed by classroom teachers at each level and inserted for children assigned to their classes. This is especially important when the school is changing the manner in which the curriculum is taught. For example, for early childhood classrooms, an explanation about the importance of play for children's development can be included to inform parents of the benefits of play. Another section of the handbook can include ideas for parents to do at home with their children that will support the school's curriculum. A list of developmentally and culturally appropriate children's literature complements the specialized handbook.

**Summer Handbook or Note.** If a handbook does not give individualized personal information, a note from the teacher mailed to the home during the summer will be appreciated by the family and will set the tone for a successful home–school relationship.

## ∷ TWO-WAY COMMUNICATION

Although one-way communication is important, two-way communication is essential. It is possible only when school personnel meet the children and their parents. The school principals or center directors set the climate of acceptance within their institutions. Their perceptions of the role of the school in communicating with parents permeate the atmosphere, making parents feel either welcome or unwanted.

Increased involvement is necessary for a true partnership. Telephone calls, e-mails, home visits, parent visits at the school, parent–teacher conferences, and school activities encourage continued parental involvement. Use of the Internet capabilities on computers allows schools and parents to have immediate opportunities for information exchanges. Sharing e-mail addresses makes this possible.

Visits to the classroom allow parents to become acquainted with their child's educational environment, the other children in the room, and the teacher. Parents need to feel welcome at all times. The teacher can send parents a calendar letting them know of special projects, testing dates, and other important events so that they (the parents) know the best time to visit. If a teacher finds a parent that always wants to be in the classroom, put that parent to work and officially name him or her the "homeroom parent." Ask this parent to assist you in the classroom doing things like working in a learning center, making classroom games, or working on the newsletter—the possibilities are endless. Participation in school activities allows parents to become working members of the education team.

Two-way communication improves partnerships.

## Homework Hot Line

The telephone system allows for many inventive ways to serve the student. This includes such services as call forwarding, recorded responses, voice mail, text messaging, and having people available at the school's telephone number. The traditional use of the telephone requires volunteers or paid professionals to answer the phone at school. Some schools have a hot line open each day after school for students to call when they have questions about homework. If specialists in each academic field are available, the hot-line call may be transferred to the appropriate specialist to answer questions about homework. In individual schools, teachers can leave their assignments with the hot-line specialists so they have the information available for each class. Using call forwarding, people responding to homework hot-line calls can work out of their homes. The school can work collaboratively with the local university (or colleges) to recruit students to volunteer with this task.

Some communities have the homework hot line connected to local celebrities and others who volunteer for a set number of hours at a special telephone number. Details of individual assignments are more difficult to handle in this type of setup, but it serves well as a public-relations format, and general questions about homework may be answered.

Enlist a TV station as a partner in education. Some stations sponsor tutoring programs. Students are encouraged to call designated numbers to talk to someone about homework. The station commits funds to hire tutors to answer questions children or parents might have about homework. It also works to have recognizable personalities take turns on the telephone. Watch the tutor service take off if parents and children know that local celebrities are willing to help.

## Computer Information Line

Computers can be used in a variety of ways. Each school would have to determine if computers were available to the families in its area. Families would either own their own online computers or community libraries can provide them. A questionnaire could be used to determine if the family has accessibility and if they want to use computers for information access with the school. There are plenty of homework help Web sites that families can use to help their children; a Google search will help identifying the appropriate local hotlines.

**E-mail.** Individual messages can be used for specific correspondence between the school and the student or the student's family. Sending e-mails to families whose children have been ill and unable to attend school would help the children keep up with schoolwork. When children are ill, it is often difficult for parents to get to the school to get assignments. A teacher could e-mail an assignment that would be printed and used by the child.

**Chats.** Safe chat rooms can be set up by the school or school district for children to communicate with one another regarding their homework. The chat rooms should include security devices to make sure that children can safely discuss their questions with other friends, teachers, and volunteers.

**Background Material and Assignment Explanations.** Permanent explanations and discussions of academic assignments could be available on the computer. This would be similar to an online course, as offered by many institutions of higher education. Although it would be time-consuming to set up the programs, they could be easily revised and used again.

## Telephone Calls

If it is impossible to visit a parent in person, rely on a telephone call. A telephone call early in the school year produces many benefits from appreciative parents. Beware, however, that most parents will wonder what is wrong when their child's teacher calls. This is quite an indictment of our communication methods; parents are generally contacted only when something is amiss. Change that practice by setting aside a short period each day for making telephone calls to parents. Begin the dialogue on a positive note. Early in the year, calls can include information about who you are, why you are calling, and a short anecdote about the child. If each call takes five minutes and you have 30 children in your class, the calls will consume two and a half hours—a small amount of time for the results you will see. Divide the time into segments of 20 to 30 minutes each evening. Parents also

**FIGURE 6–6**

Asking parents when they are available for telephone calls and letting them know when they can call you encourage communication.

---

Dear _____:

    During the school year, I will be making periodic telephone calls to parents of my students. I am able to call on Tuesday evening from 7:00 P.M. to 9:30 P.M. or on Wednesday afternoon from 3:30 P.M. to 5:00 P.M. Could you mark the time that would be most convenient for you?

    Should you want to call me, you will find me available on Thursday evenings from 7:00 P.M. to 9:00 P.M. Feel free to call my home at _____ if you have questions or would like to talk.

    I am looking forward to visiting with you this year.

Best wishes,

_____

Telephone call preference

Tuesday:  ❑ 7:00 to 8:00 P.M.      Wednesday:  ❑ 3:30 to 4:00 P.M.
          ❑ 8:00 to 9:30 P.M.                     ❑ 4:00 to 5:00 P.M.

If none of these times are convenient, please let me know.

---

appreciate a note sent home saying you hope to call and asking for a convenient time. A sample letter is shown in Figure 6–6.

### Home Visits

Some teachers make the effort to visit their students' homes early in the fall. This may be the only way to reach parents who have no telephone. It is also a rewarding experience for any teacher who can devote the time required. Not all parents are receptive to home visits, however, and some are afraid that the teacher is judging the home rather than coming as a friendly advocate of their child. Take precautions to avoid making the family feel ill at ease. Always let the family know you are coming. It is a good idea to write a note in which you request a time to visit or, possibly, give parents the option of meeting at another place. Once home visits become an accepted part of the parent-involvement program, they become less threatening, and both parents and children look forward to them.

### Visits to the Classroom

The traditional visit with parents invited for a specific event works very well in some school systems. In other schools, special events are complemented by an open invitation to parents to participate in ongoing educational programs.

Outside the classroom or just inside the door, hang a special bulletin board with messages for parents. It might display assignments for the week, plans for a party, good work children have done, requests for everyday items to complete an art project, requests for special volunteer time, or just about anything that promotes the welfare of the room. Parents can plan and develop the bulletin board with the teacher's guidance.

### Participation Visits

Directions for classroom participation are necessary if the experience is to be successful. Parents or other visitors feel more comfortable, teachers are more relaxed, and children benefit more if parents or visitors are given pointers for classroom visits. They can be in the form of a handout or a poster displayed prominently in the room, but a brief parent–teacher dialogue will make the welcome more personal and encourage specific participation.

The best welcome encourages the visitor to be active in the room's activities. Select activities that are easily described, require no advance training,

Visitors can encourage children to work together.

and contribute rather than disrupt. You may want to give explicit directions on voice quality and noise control. If you do not want the parent to make any noise, request that a soft tone be used when talking with students in the room. Or you might want to ask the parent to work in a specific area of the room. Most visitors are happiest when they know what you want.

If it bothers you that some parents tend to give answers to students rather than help the students work out their own problems, suggest the method of instruction you prefer. You might give them a tip sheet for working with students describing your favorite practices. Making activities simple for "drop-in" participants will keep problems to a minimum. If some parents prefer to sit and observe, don't force participation. As they become more comfortable in your room, they may try some activities. Selecting and reading a story to a child or group, listening to a child read, supervising the newsletter center, playing a game chosen from the game center with a student, supervising the puzzle table, or talking with students about their work are appropriate activities for new volunteers.

## Visits by Invitation

A special invitation is sent to parents of a different child each week asking them to visit as "Parents of the Week" or VIPs—very important parents. A memo from the administration that explains the objective of the visit accompanies the invitation, which is written by the child or teacher. Have the child bring in information about brothers and sisters, favorite activities, and other interesting or important facts about the family. Place a picture of the family on the bulletin board that week. The family could include parents, grandparents, special friends (young or old), and younger siblings. Parents and guests are asked to let the teacher know when they plan to visit.

You could also improve a child's self-concept by making the child "Student of the Week." Not only do the children have a chance to feel good about themselves on their special week, but it also helps children get to know one another better. Feedback from parents after a visit is important. A reaction sheet is given to parents asking them to write their impressions and return it to the school. Comments range from compliments to questions about the school. This process encourages two-way communication.

## Student–Parent Exchange Day

An idea similar to the student visiting the parent's place of employment is to have the parent take the place of the student at school. This can be done in several ways. The parent may accompany the student to class and spend the day with the child, or the parent and child may exchange places for the day. Exchanging places for the day works best for an older student who can fulfill some obligation at home or go on a field trip while the parent goes through the student's exact schedule. The parent is responsible for listening to the lecture or participating in the class and doing the homework. The parent learns about the school program, becomes acquainted with the teacher, and is better able to relate to the child's school experience. If the child is young and the school and parent prefer to participate in the school day without the child, the process is possible if the parent hires a babysitter or if the school provides a field trip for the children in the class.

## Breakfasts

If you have a cooperative cafeteria staff or volunteers who are willing to make a simple breakfast, you can invite parents to an early breakfast. Many parents can stop for breakfast on their way to work. Plan a breakfast meeting early in the fall to meet parents and answer questions. Breakfast meetings tend to be rushed because parents need to get to work, so schedule a series of breakfasts and restrict the number of parents invited to each. In this way, real dialogue can be started. If a group is too large, the personal contact that is the prime requisite of two-way communication between school and home is prevented. Breakfasts also support parent-to-parent communication. It is important that parents get an opportunity to meet the parents of their children's friends. It should be made clear to parents the potential advantage of attending the breakfasts.

## :: ROADBLOCKS TO COMMUNICATION

The goals of those who work with young children are to meet the needs of the children, educate them, and help them reach their potential as children and develop into productive adults. What is the challenge to parents? They have the same goals! Because parents and school personnel have the same goals in mind, it would seem that communication would be quite easy. Such is not the case. There are many roadblocks to good communication between school personnel and parents. Both school personnel and parents set up roadblocks. Some roadblocks are used to protect positions, and others occur because the participants are unable to understand one another's positions.

The roadblocks that hinder communication between parents and school personnel are similar to those that affect any communication, but different concerns emerge. Some of the most common parent–school roadblocks will be described so we can work to overcome them.

### Parent Roadblocks

Roadblocks to communication often occur because as parents and teachers we have different characteristics that may hinder the process. It is important as you look at this section to think of the roadblocks not as something negative or a way to criticize parents, but as a way to identify those traits that hinder effective communication. In the following sections, you are going to read about parents' and schools' characteristics that may hinder communication.

**"My Own and My Child Guardian" Role.** Many parents, often subconsciously, view their children as extensions of themselves. "Criticize my child and you criticize me" is their message. They may also think things like "Are you saying that I did not rear my children correctly?" or "Is my child slow in school because I am the parent?" or "Is there something that I should have done differently in my childrearing?"

When a parent puts up a shield against perceived criticism, it becomes very difficult to communicate. When parents are hurt by a child's inability to progress satisfactorily in school, they may withdraw from open, honest communication in an effort to protect their child and their own self-esteem.

A parent's vested interest in the child can be channeled in a positive direction. Effective communication, with positive suggestions for encouraging the child, can help the parent become a partner with the school.

**"I Don't Belong" Role.** Many parents do not feel comfortable talking with school personnel. These parents avoid going to civic events—including events that take place at schools—because they do not feel as if they belong. If parents feel inadequate, they avoid coming in contact with the schools. If they do come, they find it difficult to communicate their desires or feelings to the staff. These parents can benefit from encouragement so that they can contribute and be involved.

**Avoidance Role.** The avoidance role may include self-assured parents who do not respect the school or the way it treats parents and students. It also includes parents who had a difficult time in school when they were growing up. Perhaps they dropped out of school—the building might bring back bad memories. Schools must reach out to these parents by caring and offering activities and services that the parents need and desire.

**"Indifferent Parent" Role.** It seems more difficult today to be a concerned, involved parent because of financial and time pressures. Although most parents want what is best for their children, some are willing to shift their parental responsibilities to others. The institution where children spend most of their working hours is the school. When children are reared by indifferent parents, their futures can be devastated. If no one cares, why should the children care? Parents may be facing problems that prevent them from focusing on the children. Drug and alcohol abuse, divorce, financial troubles, and criminal behavior may be evidence that parents are facing major problems in their life.

**"Don't Make Waves" Role.** Many parents are unwilling to be honest in their concerns because they do not want school personnel to take it out on their child. They believe that the teacher or principal might be negative toward their children if they make suggestions or express concerns. This represses communication.

**"Club-Waving Advocate" Role.** Sometimes parents get carried away with their devotion to their children, and they exhibit this through a power play. These advocates often become abrasive in their desire to protect their children or change school policy. These parents are the opposite of the "I don't belong" or the "don't make waves" parents. "Club-waving" parents express their concerns through confrontation. Schools must acknowledge these concerns and change the situation when it is sensible to do so. In addition, give the parents opportunities to be leaders in areas where they can contribute.

### School Roadblocks

Many times schools install roadblocks to effective communication without even realizing it. Sometimes they do so intentionally. The stress of educating and working with many children and families, the pressure to accomplish many tasks, and the desire to be seen as efficient all get in the way of unhurried, effective communication. The following roles describe some of the roadblocks that hamper communication between home and school.

**"Authority Figure" Role.** School personnel who act as chief executive officers all too often hinder communication. These teachers and administrators claim to be the authorities, ready to impart information to the parent. They neglect to set the stage for the parent to be a partner in the discussion. If staff members take all the responsibility of running the school without considering the parents' backgrounds and knowledge, there seems to be no reason to communicate. Parents are locked out of the decision-making process. Schools that ignore or criticize parents destroy communication between parents and schools.

**"Sympathizing Counselor" Role.** School personnel who focus on the inadequacy of the child in a vain attempt to console the parent miss a great opportunity for communication. Parents want to solve their concerns through constructive remediation or support. Parents and schools both need to focus on the achievements that can be attained through cooperation and collaboration.

**"Pass the Buck" Role.** Communication stops when school personnel refer the concerns of the parent to another department. They may say things like "Sara may need help, but we cannot schedule her for tests for five months" or "It is too bad that Richard had such a bad experience last year. I wish I could help, but he needs special services." Sometimes parents think the school is deliberately stalling while their child falls further and further behind.

**"Protect the Empire" Role.** A united, invincible staff can cause parents to think no one cares about their needs. School personnel need to work together and support one another, but they also need to listen to the parent and should advocate for the parent as they formulate an educational plan for the student.

**"Busy Teacher" Role.** Perhaps the greatest roadblock to good communication between parent and teacher is time. If you are harried, you do not have time to communicate with your students or their parents. Both teachers and parents need to reduce stress and set aside time for communication. Reorganize schedules to include on-the-run conferences, telephone calls, and short personal notes to parents and children. Principals and directors might take over the classroom occasionally so teachers could make telephone calls to parents. The principals and directors would get to know the children in the classes and the importance of teacher–parent interaction would be emphasized. Roadblocks can be overcome.

### Communicating with Culturally and Linguistically Diverse Families

Because communication is culturally based, teachers and administrators need to learn the culturally appropriate ways to communicate with families who are culturally and linguistically diverse.

Teachers and administrators need to find translators who can communicate with the parents the information that needs to be given. An idea would be to recruit other parents who speak different languages to become translators because not only would they know how to talk with the parents, but they would encourage these parents to participate and become involved in the school even if they don't speak English. Although some carefully planned events such as "Parents' Night" may work for a group of parents, for those parents whose background is different,

Teachers need to effectively communicate with culturally and linguistically diverse parents.

these types of activities may not work (Guo, 2009). Therefore, it is imperative that teachers and administrators find ways to increase communication with parents that are of diverse backgrounds but have been marginalized by society as well as those who are not familiar with the education system.

### Insights for Teachers and Administrators

1. Research the cultural and linguistic backgrounds of families.
2. Develop an understanding of the cultural rules and norms in order to increase communication.
3. Understand the gender differences in communication from each cultural group in your school.
4. Treat the family with respect.
5. Conduct a simple needs assessment in which you ask parents how they would like to receive information from the school. Provide them with a variety of options so that they can select one that best fits their family needs.
6. Conduct home visits with the classroom teacher and other resource teachers to get to know the family. Before conducting the home visit talk with other families of same cultural background to follow appropriate etiquette from their cultural group.

## :: EFFECTIVE COMMUNICATION WITH PARENTS

Effective communication starts with effective leadership. Effective administrators recognize that in order for children's school experiences to be successful,

the parents must be informed to be involved. To achieve effective communication, parents and teachers need to recognize roadblocks to their success. At the same time, they can increase their communication skills by practicing positive speaking, rephrasing, and attentive listening. Frequent communication builds a sense of trust between the teacher and the parent (David & Yang, 2009).

When teachers talk with parents, they communicate in many ways—through their words, their body actions, and their manner of speaking. Every contact communicates whether the speaker respects the other person, values that person's input, and is willing to collaborate. The self-fulfilling prophecy works with parents as well as with students. If teachers treat parents as if they are incapable of being partners, the parents will not work with teachers effectively.

### Effective Communication Skills

Teachers can establish rapport with parents by using effective communication skills. Effective communication is honest and open and takes time. Good communicators listen, rephrase and check out, and avoid criticizing and acting superior.

Teachers are good communicators when they do the following:

1. Give their total attention to the parents. They establish eye contact and clearly demonstrate through body language that their interest is focused on what is being said.
2. Use culturally appropriate communication.
3. Listen and restate the parents' concerns. They clarify what has been said and try to discern the speaker's meaning and feeling to be sure that they received it correctly. They avoid closed responses or answering as a critic, judge, or moralist.
4. Show respect for the parents. They recognize that their concerns, opinions, and questions are significant factors in mutual understanding and communication.
5. Recognize the parents' feelings. How much can they discuss with parents? Perhaps they need to establish a better parent–teacher relationship before they can completely share their concerns for the child.
6. Tailor discussions to fit the parents' ability to handle the situation.

7. Do not set off the fuse of a parent who might not be able to handle a child's difficulties. They don't accuse but instead spend more time with the parent in other communication and conferences.

8. Emphasize that concerns are no one's fault. Teacher and parents have to work on problems together to help the child. They use concerns as forums for understanding one another.

9. Remember that no one ever wins an argument. Calmly, quietly, and enthusiastically they discuss the *good* points of the child before bringing up any concerns.

10. Protect the parents' egos. Teachers don't make parents believe they are to blame for their child's deficiencies. On the other hand, they give parents credit for their child's achievements. They focus on the future.

11. Focus on one issue at a time. They are specific about the child's progress or concerns.

12. Become allies with parents.

Parents become partners in the educational process when they do the following:

1. View the teacher as a source of support for their child and themselves.

2. Listen carefully and give total commitment to the teacher.

3. Show respect for the teacher—recognize that the teacher's concerns, opinions, and questions are significant to mutual understanding and communication.

4. Recognize that the teacher has a difficult challenge to meet the needs of all students. They help the teacher succeed.

5. Rephrase and check out understanding of messages during conversations or conferences.

6. Speak openly and honestly about the child.

7. Use concerns as forums for understanding the school and teacher.

8. Become allies with the teacher.

## Positive Speaking

If your message is positive, the parent is more likely to want to listen. The relationship between teacher and parent is enhanced. A positive statement needs to be accompanied by attentive behavior, good body language, and a warm tone of voice. Add clear articulation, and you have the recipe for effective communication between parent and teacher.

## Listening

**Listening** is the heart of effective communication. Listening is more than hearing sounds. It is the active process of interpreting, understanding, and evaluating the spoken and nonverbal speech as a meaningful message. Listening, not speaking, is the most-used form of communication. Forty-five percent of verbal communication is spent listening; 30 percent, speaking; 16 percent, reading; and 9 percent writing.

In education, much attention is given to the ability to write, yet there is very little training for listening. Greater understanding and retention of information would occur if an appropriate amount of time were spent on helping people listen effectively. Smith (1986) recommends these steps to improve listening skills:

1. *Be receptive.* Listeners encourage the speaker by being receptive and providing an environment where the speaker feels free to express ideas and feelings.

2. *Pay attention.* Make an effort to concentrate on what is being said.

3. *Use silence.* Communicate that you are listening through attentive behaviors while remaining silent.

4. *Seek agreement.* Look for the broader meaning of the message rather than focusing on isolated facts.

5. *Avoid ambiguity.* Ask questions to clarify, look for main ideas, and focus on intent as well as content.

6. *Remove distractions.* Eliminate daydreaming, remove physical barriers, and delay other important messages to make the climate clear for listening.

7. *Be patient.* Don't rush the speaker. Allow time for the message to be completed.

Teachers and parents communicate when they use communication that helps them work together to help the child. Although most effective communication traits are culturally based, the following list provides some examples of what is often valued and practiced in American society. Good listeners:

- Listen carefully to the other person.
- Have good eye contact.
- Encourage the speaker by using body language and verbal expressions such as "yes."
- Observe the speaker and have a facial expression that shows interest.

- Respond with attentive body language, such as leaning forward or touching.
- Rephrase the substance and meaning of the message they receive from the speaker when appropriate.

### Open Responses and Closed Responses

An **open response** encourages communication to continue. Open responses can vary from positive body language—demonstrated by a nod of the head or a smile indicating that you wish the speaker to continue—to a verbal response in which you indicate your interest. If a child comes into a home or classroom with a caterpillar in hand, ready to display the treasure to mother or teacher, an open response would be a smile, a nod, or a question such as "Where did you find such a marvelous caterpillar?" A closed response would be a frown or a comment such as "Take that caterpillar away this very minute." What child would dare to explain that the caterpillar was a treasure?

Should a child be a problem to a teacher, the easy response to a question by the parent would be a **closed response**. For example, a parent asks, "Why does John have trouble with math?" A closed response would be "If you would help him with his homework, he wouldn't have so much trouble." The conversation is ended. No one has sought to communicate and find out the best way to handle the situation.

### Reflective Listening

**Reflective listening** is the ability to reflect the speaker's feelings. The listener's response identifies the basic feelings being expressed and reflects the essence of those feelings back to the speaker. Reflective or active listening is used in several parent programs, such as the Parent Effectiveness Training (PET) (Gordon, 1975, 2000), Active Parenting (Popkin, 2002), Parent's Handbook, Systematic Teaching of Effective Parenting (STEP) (Dinkmeyer, McKay & Dinkmeyer, 1997), and Teaching and Leading Children (Dinkmeyer, McKay, Dinkmeyer, & Dinkmeyer, 1992). These programs are described in the next section. The examples illustrate the use of active or reflective listening.

**Reflective Listening and Reflective Responses.** Reflective listening encourages open responses. A reflective response is effective if the listener recognizes the feelings of the speaker and is able to respond accordingly. The parent asks, "Why does John have trouble with math?" A reflective response would be "You are concerned about John's ability to do his math?" The parent at that point probably would agree.

To practice reflective listening, think of the following three steps:

1. Use attending behavior. Make eye contact. Lean forward and be interested.
2. Listen for the feeling behind the message.
3. Respond with a statement of that feeling.

**I–You–We Messages.** One useful communication skill relies on **I messages** instead of **you messages**. A "you" message places the responsibility on the person receiving the message, and it is often a negative message. With a parent, it might be used in the following way: "If you would just help John with his homework, he would be more successful at school." To change that statement to a more positive "I" message, use words like those described in the following three steps:

1. "When [describe the behavior that is bothering you],
2. I feel [state how you feel about the concern]
3. Because [describe what you think might happen]."

For example, you might say, "*When* John does not finish his homework, *I feel* worried *because* I am afraid he will fall behind and not be able to catch up." Gordon (1975, 2000) introduced the "I" message, and Dinkmeyer and McKay (1983, 1997) and Popkin (2002) use "I" messages in their parenting programs. There are times when a "we" message is more appropriate than an "I" message (Burr, 1990): "When Mary does not finish her homework, we have real concerns because she may fall behind her classmates." By using a "we" message, the teacher acknowledges that the parent is also concerned.

**Rephrasing.** **Rephrasing** is restating the intent of the message in a condensed version. There are three steps in rephrasing. First, the listener must determine the basic message and the intent of the message. Second, the listener restates the intent of the message. Third, the listener checks out the accuracy of the rephrasing.

When listeners seek to check out or clarify a statement by saying something like "It sounds as if you feel ..." or "I'm hearing you say ...," they are rephrasing the statement. With rephrasing, communicators can avoid misunderstanding the message by checking the accuracy. Confusion and ambiguity in communication are avoided. The interest displayed by rephrasing also shows caring and builds trust (Center for Family Strengths, 1986).

**Reframing.** **Reframing** involves taking the sting out of the negative description of a child. When communicating with parents, if your answer reflects your understanding of parents' concerns, the conversation will remain open, but the words you choose can bring either desirable or disastrous results.

A teacher with good intentions and great concern for a child once opened a conference with a parent by referring to the child's "problem" of not staying on task. The antagonized parent struck back: "I think you're obnoxious!" The family was already overwrought by strain and worry over the child. The rest of the conference time had to be devoted to rebuilding a working relationship, allowing no time for productive dialogue about the child and leaving both teacher and parent with emotional scars.

Instead of focusing on the negative aspects of an individual, start with positive comments. Then reframe the child's troublesome quality into an acceptable or even positive trait. Had the teacher started the conference with some friendly remarks and then stated, "I have some concerns about John that we should work on together," the parent might not have responded with such anger.

Examples of phrases that reframe a "problem" as a concern about the child include the following:

| Problem | Concern | Examples |
|---|---|---|
| loud and boisterous | very active | "Linda seems to be very active." |
| gives others' answers | can't help sharing | "Juan is so excited about participating that sometimes he can't help himself…" |
| steals | takes without asking | "When Britanny plays, she takes toys without asking." |
| won't follow rules | has own agenda, or is determined | "Tanya is very independent even when she needs to follow my lead." |
| shy | self-contained | "I noticed that Izumi likes to play by herself." |
| talks too much | likes to share with others | "Isabella has a lot of information to share." |
| does not pay attention | is preoccupied | "Amira seems to be preoccupied with other things during circle time." |

It is particularly important in parent–teacher conferences and other communication between parent and teacher to couch the annoying behavior in terms that allow for dealing with it. There may be times, however, when the teacher's concern has reached such proportions that it must be faced squarely and openly but with respect. After several fruitless attempts at communicating, it may become obvious that the parent does not recognize that the behavior is hurting the child's progress. In such cases, you may have to use more forthright terms. Just beware of the terminology you use—harsh terms may completely cut off communication.

## ∷ PARENT EDUCATION PROGRAMS—PET, STEP, AND ACTIVE PARENTING

Many parent education programs incorporate the resources of childrearing suggestions in Parent Effectiveness Training (PET), Systematic Training for Effective Parenting (STEP), or Active Parenting. Excerpts from these programs illustrate the materials and communication techniques each uses.

### Parent Effectiveness Training: The Proven Program for Raising Responsible Children

In Parent Effectiveness Training (PET), Gordon (1975, 2000) discusses many topics, including active listening, "I messages," changing behavior by changing the environment, parent–child conflicts, parental power, and "no-lose" methods for resolving conflicts. The following excerpt relates to problem ownership and active listening:

In the parent–child relationship, three situations occur that we will illustrate with brief case histories:

1. The child has a problem because he or she is thwarted in satisfying a need. It is not a problem for the parent because the child's behavior in no tangible way interferes with the parent's satisfying his or her own needs. Therefore, *the child owns the problem.*

2. The child is satisfying his or her own needs (he or she is not thwarted), and his or her behavior is not interfering with the parent's own needs. Therefore, *there is no problem in the relationship.*

3. The child is satisfying his or her own needs (he or she is not thwarted). But his or her behavior is a problem to the parent because it is interfering in some tangible way with the parent's satisfying a need of his or her own. *Now the parent owns the problem.*

It is critical that parents always classify each situation that occurs in a relationship. Which of these three categories does the following situation fall into? It helps to remember this diagram (see Figure 6–7).

When parents accept the fact that problems are owned by the child, this in no way means that the parents cannot be concerned, care, or offer help. Professional counselors have real concern for, and genuinely care about, each child they are trying to help. But, unlike most parents, the counselors leave the responsibility for solving the child's problem with the child. They allow the child to own the problem. They accept the child's having the problem. They accept the child as a person separate from herself or himself. And they rely heavily upon and basically trust the child's own inner resources for solving the problem. Only because they let the child own the problem areas, the professional counselors are able to employ active listening.

Active listening is a powerful method for helping another person solve a problem that that person owns, provided the listener can accept the other's ownership and consistently allow the person to find the solutions. Active listening can greatly increase the effectiveness of parents as helping agents for their children, but it is a different kind of help from that which parents usually try to give.

Paradoxically, this method will increase the parent's influence on the child, but it is an influence that differs from the kind that most parents try to exert over their children. Active listening is a method of influencing children to find their own solutions to their own problems. Most parents, however, are tempted to take ownership of their children's problems, as in the following case:

*Johnny:* Tommy won't play with me today. He won't ever do what I want to do.

*Mother:* Well, why don't you offer to do what he wants to do? You've got to learn to get along with your little friends. *(advising; moralizing)*

*Johnny:* I don't like to do things he wants to do, and besides I don't want to get along with that dope.

*Mother:* Well, go find someone else to play with, then, if you're going to be a spoilsport. *(offering a solution; name-calling)*

*Johnny:* He's the spoilsport, not me. And there isn't anyone else to play with.

**FIGURE 6–7**
When the child's behavior is a problem to the parent, the parent owns the problem.

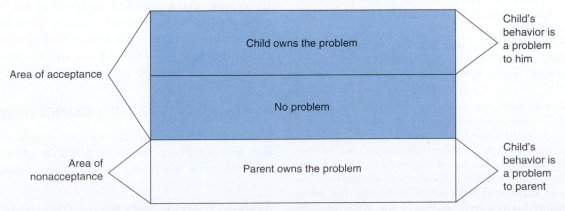

*Source:* Gordon, T. (1975). *P.E.T./Parent Effectiveness Training* (p. 64). New York: Wyden.

*Mother:* You're just upset because you're tired. You'll feel better about this tomorrow. *(interpreting; reassuring)*

*Johnny:* I'm not tired, and I won't feel different tomorrow. You just don't understand how much I hate the little squirt.

*Mother:* Now stop talking like that! If I ever hear you talk about one of your friends like that again, you'll be sorry. *(ordering; threatening)*

*Johnny: (walking away and sulking)* I hate this neighborhood. I wish we would move.

Here is how the parent can help the same boy with active listening:

*Johnny:* Tommy won't play with me today. He won't ever do what I want to do.

*Mother:* You're kinda angry with Tommy. *(active listening)*

*Johnny:* I sure am. I never want to play with him again. I don't want him for a friend.

*Mother:* You're so angry you feel like never seeing him again. *(active listening)*

*Johnny:* That's right. But if I don't have him for a friend, I won't have anyone to play with then.

*Mother:* You would hate to be left with no one. *(active listening)*

*Johnny:* Yeah. I guess I just have to get along with him some way. But it's so hard for me to stop getting mad at him.

*Mother:* You want to get along better, but it's hard for you to keep from getting mad at Tommy. *(active listening)*

*Johnny:* I never used to, but that's when he was always willing to do what I wanted to do. He won't let me boss him anymore.

*Mother:* Tommy's not so easy to influence now. *(active listening)*

*Johnny:* He sure isn't. He's not such a baby now. He's more fun though.

*Mother:* You really like him better this way. *(active listening)*

*Johnny:* Yeah. But it's hard to stop bossing him—I'm so used to it. Maybe we wouldn't fight so much if I let him have his way once in a while. Think that would work?

*Mother:* You're thinking that if you might give in occasionally, it might help. *(active listening)*

*Johnny:* Yeah, maybe it would. I'll try it.

In the first scenario, the mother used eight of the "Typical Twelve" categories of responding. In the second, the mother consistently used active listening. In the first, the mother "took over the problem"; in the second, her active listening left ownership of the problem with Johnny. In the first, Johnny resisted his mother's suggestions, his anger and frustration were never dissipated, the problem remained unresolved, and there was no growth on Johnny's part. In the second, his anger left, he initiated

problem solving, and he took a deeper look at himself. He arrived at his own solution and obviously grew a notch toward becoming a responsible, self-directing problem solver.[1]

Gordon clarifies active listening and problem ownership through examples such as these. Parent groups follow up with a parent notebook and discussion within the group. Open discussion, led by a person knowledgeable about PET, allows parents to apply the methods to their own experiences in childrearing.

### Systematic Training for Effective Parenting

The Systematic Training for Effective Parenting (STEP) program offers a variety of training programs. Offered in English and Spanish, these programs focus on children 6 to 12 years of age. They furnish videos, a parent's manual, and a leadership and resource guide used to facilitate parent meetings. The child's goals in behavior, which include attention, power, revenge, and displays of inadequacy, are examined. Parents learn to understand their child and themselves through engaging in topics that include listening, encouraging, learning to cooperate, and understanding emotions and beliefs.

### Active Parenting

The Active Parenting program is similar to both PET and STEP in that it is also based on the theories of Alfred Adler and Rudolf Dreikurs. Goals of misbehavior, logical consequences, active communication, exploring alternatives, and family council meetings are described. A handbook and workbook supplement the group meetings, and a leader's handbook gives detailed instruction on how the class should be conducted. Each session has a corresponding portion of a video that illustrates the child and family issues under discussion. Online delivery of the course is also available.

## :: PARENT–TEACHER CONFERENCES

A parent–teacher conference is a collaborative effort to coordinate the best possible effort for the education of the child in the classroom. It is a

---

[1]Gordon, T. (1975). *P.E.T./Parent Effectiveness Training* (pp. 64, 66–68). New York: Wyden.

time for listening and sharing on the part of the school staff and the parents (Manning, 1985; Moles, 1996a; Elmore, 2008). To accomplish the greatest cooperation between home and school and the greatest benefit for the student, the conference needs to continue the communication between the parent and school, based on agreed-upon goals for the child throughout the year. Teachers and parents need to build a "relationship of respect and cooperation" (Saylor, 2007). "Personalizing" the school can help increase partnerships with parents (Esparza, 2007).

Start the school year with a positive interchange between teacher and parent by an early telephone call or a block walk to initiate the parent–school partnership. Stephens (2007) shares that it is important to ask parents what they would like to talk about and where they can hold the meetings. Some alternative ideas for parent conferences include meetings online. A preconference discussion can then be used to set goals and direction for the child during the school year. The goals should reflect what parents want and what is best for the child (Akers, 2005). The first conference can be a progress and planning session based on those goals.

Parent–teacher conferences are personal opportunities for two-way communication between parent and teacher or three-way communication among parent, teacher, and student. Parents as well as teachers recognize the conference as an excellent opportunity for clarifying issues, searching for answers, deciding on goals, determining mutual strategies, and forming a team in the education of the student. Most schools schedule conferences two or three times a year for typical-developing children; for children with disabilities, it is important that teachers conference with parents more often (Kroth & Edge, 2007). How can conferences be as productive as possible and yet nonthreatening to parents, teachers, and students?

## Collaborative Conversations

Collaborative conversations can help develop cooperation and resolution of issues. Koch and McDonough (1999), using an example of a young child who hit and bit other children, describe five stages to improve parent–teacher conferences through collaboration of all parties part of the team:

**Stage 1.** *Development of trust.* It is essential that a trusting relationship be developed. This can be enhanced prior to the conference at back-to-school nights, home visits, and informal interactions at school.

**Stage 2.** *Invite.* Extend an invitation that promotes cooperation and involvement. For example: "When would be a good time for us to talk together about Mary? Would you prefer to talk at school or at your home? Is there anyone else involved with Mary who could join us? Between now and the time we meet, let's all notice when Mary expresses her feelings safely" (p. 12).

**Stage 3.** *Set a mutual goal.* Facilitate or have a facilitator establish a cooperative atmosphere. Focus on the positive actions of the child when he or she appropriately handled the situation. Come to an understanding of your goal to enhance the positive.

**Stage 4.** *Listen to all viewpoints and expand understanding.* Allow all participants to express their feelings and ideas. The discussion moves from "identification of and observations about the effects of the problem to a dialogue about the unique outcomes/exceptions and the significance of these for all persons concerned" (p. 14).

**Stage 5.** *Restate the goal, measure it, and decide what to do about it.* Collaborative conversations "create an atmosphere filled with possibilities and ideas that enhance the lives of children and the adults that care for them" (p. 14).

## Invitations and Schedules

The invitation to attend a conference sets the tone. If it is cordial, shows an awareness of parents' busy lives and obligations, and gives the parents time options for scheduling the conference, the teacher has shown consideration of the parents and a desire to meet with them. Most school systems have worked out procedures for scheduling conference periods. Release time is usually granted teachers. Originally, most conferences took place in the afternoons. Children attended school in the mornings, and classes were dismissed at noon, with conferences between school personnel and parents—usually mothers only—occurring in the afternoon. With the increase in the number of working parents and single-parent families, plus the growing number of fathers becoming more directly involved in their children's education, many schools are scheduling more evening conferences, while retaining some afternoon conferences.

To prepare the schedule, notes are sent to parents asking for their time preference. The formal note should be direct and list specific options for the time and place of the conference. A sample note is found in Figure 6–8. After the responses have been returned, staff members, including teachers in special areas of education, meet to schedule back-to-back conferences for parents with more than one child attending the school.

A telephone call from the teacher to each parent adds a personal touch. These calls, made either before or after the invitation has been sent, may clarify questions and let the parents know they are really welcome.

Notes confirming the exact time and date of the conference should be sent home, whether the parent has been contacted or not. This ensures that both teacher and parent have the same understanding of the conference time. This confirmation note from the teacher to each parent could be personal, or a form could be used (see Figure 6–9).

A personal note might read:

I am looking forward to meeting _____ 's parents. I enjoy her contribution to the class through her great interest in _____. The time and date of the conference are _____.

## Private and Comfortable Meeting Place

How often have you gone into a school, walked down the halls, and seen parents and teachers trying to have a private conversation in the midst of children and other adults? To achieve open, two-way communication, parent and teacher need to talk in confidence. Select a room designed for conferences or use an empty classroom, and attach a note to the door so people won't interrupt. Give the parents adult-size chairs so they can be comfortable and on the same level as the teacher. Place a table in front of the chairs so materials, class projects, and the student's work can be exhibited. The parent, teacher, and student (if it is a three-way conference) can sit around the table and talk and

**FIGURE 6–8**
Send a note home to schedule a conference.

Dear _____:

    We are looking forward to meeting with you and discussing _____ experiences and progress at school. Will you please let us know when a conference would be most convenient for you? Please check the date and time of day you could come.

                                        Thank you,

                                        _____
                                        Teacher or principal's name

Could you give a first and second choice? Please write "1" for your first preference and "2" for your second.

|                          | Afternoon<br>1 to 4 P.M. | Evening<br>6 to 9 P.M. |
|--------------------------|--------------------------|------------------------|
| Tuesday, November 12     | _____             | _____           |
| Wednesday, November 13   | _____             | _____           |
| Thursday, November 14    | _____             | _____           |
| Please return by _____ |  |  |

**FIGURE 6–9**
This note confirms and reminds of conference times.

Dear _____:

   Thank you for your response to our request for a conference time about your child's progress. Your appointment has been set for _____ (time) on _____ (day, month, and date) in room _____ .
   We have set aside _____ minutes for our chance to talk together. If the above time is not convenient, please contact the office, and we can schedule another time for you.
   We are looking forward to meeting with you.

                                             Best wishes,

                                             _____
                                             Teacher

exchange information. The room should be well ventilated and neither too warm nor too cold.

Teachers also should be alert to psychological and physical barriers. People conducting interviews often set up such barriers to maintain social distance or imply a status relationship; an executive may sit behind a desk to talk with a subordinate. When teachers set themselves apart from the parents, a barrier is created.

### Two-Way Communication in Conferences

Conditions necessary for effective communication during conferences include an attitude of caring shown through attentive behaviors, smiling, touching, and body language. Along with warmth is empathy, the ability to listen and respond in such a way that the parent knows you understand. Respect is key to the success of building a collaborative connection between parent and teacher. If teachers and parents respect each other and enter the conference with a warm, caring attitude, able to listen effectively and understand the other's meanings and feelings, the stage is set for a successful conference (Rotter & Robinson, 1986; Esparza, 2007).

Some school administrators and teachers make the mistake of seeing parent–school communication as the school informing the parent about the educational process, rather than as a two-way system. During a conference, the teacher should spend only about half the time speaking. If teachers recognize the conference as a sharing time, half the

burden has been lifted from their shoulders. They can use half the time to get to know the parent and child better.

During conferences, communicators need to believe that what they have to say is important to the listener. Body language can reflect feelings contrary to the spoken word, causing the verbal message to be misunderstood or missed altogether. It is important to be aware of what you are communicating. If you are rushed, pressured, or concerned about your own family, you will have to take a deep breath, relax, and concentrate on the conference. Just as important is to know cultural gender boundaries in order not to offend families.

Just as some physical gestures communicate distraction or lack of interest, so does some body language convey your interest and attention to parents' concerns. Use appropriate, attentive behavior to signal your interest, such as the following:

1. *Eye contact*. Make sure you look at the person as you communicate. Failure to do so could imply evasion, deception, or lack of commitment.
2. *Forward posture*. Leaning forward creates the image of interest in what is being said. Be comfortable but do not slouch, which can indicate that the whole process is boring or unimportant.
3. *Body response*. A nod in agreement, a smile, and use of the body to create an appearance of interest promote empathy. If you act aware and interested, you will probably become interested. If you do not, perhaps you are in the wrong profession.

## Understandable Language

Specialized language gets in the way of communication. Each year, new terms and acronyms become common language in the schools, but they freeze communication when used with people not familiar with the terms. Imagine a teacher explaining to a parent that the school has decided to use the SRA program this year in second grade, but the first grade is trying balanced literacy instruction; or one who says, "I've been using behavior modification with Johnny this year, and it has been very effective, but with Janet I find TA more helpful." Jargon can create misunderstanding and stop communication.

Sometimes terms have meaning for both communicators, but the meanings are not the same. Hymes (1974) declared that lack of communication, superficial communication, and "words and vocabulary, without friendship and trust and knowledge, get in the way of understanding" (p. 33):

> Look, for example, at "progressive education." Use those words and you have a fight on your hands. People get emotional, and wild charges fly. Yet parents will be the first to say, "Experience is the best teacher"—and there you have it! Different words, but a good definition of what progressive education stands for. (Hymes, 1974, p. 33)

## Practice

To achieve the ability to listen reflectively and respond in a positive manner, practice until it becomes natural. You can practice alone, but it is more effective if you can role play the conference. Having an observer present provides both practice and feedback. Teachers can choose a typical case from among their records or invent a hypothetical one. For example:

> Andy, a precocious third-grade child, spends most of the class period doodling ideas in a notebook. Although he completes his assignments, Andy takes no pride in his work and turns in messy papers. Special enrichment centers in the classroom do not attract him. Andy participates positively during recess and in physical education and music.

Each participant in the role play has basic information: the child's sex, grade assigned, and background. Assign one participant to act as the parent, another as the teacher. The third member of the team observes the interaction between the parent and teacher to check on the following:

1. Reflective listening
2. Attentive behavior (eye contact, forward posture, etc.)
3. Sensitivity to parents' feelings
4. Positive language
5. Cooperative decision making

Because no two teachers or parents are identical, there is no prescribed way to have a conference. The dialogue will be a constant flow, filled with emotions as well as objective analysis. You can prepare yourself, however, by practicing good reflective listening and positive communication. Look forward to sharing together.

## Preparation for the Conference

Two types of preparation will set the stage for a successful conference. The first, an optional program, involves training teachers and parents for an effective conference. The second is essential—analyzing the child's records, current performance and attitude, and relationship with peers and gathering examples of work along with recent standardized test results.

## Preconference Workshops and Guides

Workshops for parents, teachers, or a combination of both are fruitful. A discussion of what makes a conference a success or a calamity can bring forth an enormous number of tips for both parents and teachers. If parents and teachers form small groups, many ideas will emerge that can be recorded on the board for discussion later by the total group. Encourage parents to ask questions about their part in conferences. Clarifying objectives and expectations will help parents understand their responsibilities. Parents and teachers attending a workshop together can learn the art of reflective listening and communication. Role playing during conferences can elicit discussion. Many participants will see themselves in the roles portrayed and will attempt to find alternative methods of handling conference discussions. Videos or YouTube video clips that illustrate common communication problems can also be used as starters for discussion.

At the close of the workshop, handouts or conference guides may be distributed to the participants. The guide should be designed with the school's objectives in mind. Parents can be told what to expect in the school's report and what the school expects from them. If your school does not schedule preconference workshops, put the handout in a newsletter and send it home to the parents before the conference. Questions in the conference guide should be those the school would like answered and also ones the parents might be interested in knowing. Typical questions include the following:

1. How does your child seem to feel about school?
2. Which activities does your child talk about at home?
3. Which activities seem to stimulate your child's intellectual growth?
4. How does your child spend free time?
5. Is there anything that your child dreads?
6. What are your child's interests and hobbies?

Some schools might also include questions about current concerns:

7. What concerns do you have?
8. What kinds of support or collaboration would you like from the school to help your family?

A similar memo suggests questions the parents might want to ask:

1. How well does my child get along with other children? Who seem to be my child's best friends?
2. How does my child react to discipline? What methods do you use to promote self-discipline and cooperation?
3. Does my child select books at the proper reading level from the library?
4. Does my child use study periods effectively?
5. Are there any skills you are working on at school that we might reinforce at home?
6. Do you expect me to help my child with homework?
7. Are there any areas in which my child needs special help?
8. Does my child display any special interests or talents at school that we might support at home?
9. Does my child seem to be self-confident, happy, and secure? If not, what do you think the home or school can do to increase my child's feelings of self-worth?

Supplying questions before the conference is helpful in preparing parents, but it can also limit questions that develop naturally. In addition, if these questions are strictly adhered to during conferences, they can limit the scope, direction, and outcome of the conference. A checklist (Figure 6–10) can help ensure everything is covered.

## Teacher Preparation

Throughout the school year, teachers should make a practice of accumulating anecdotal records, tests, workbooks, art projects, and papers that represent both academic and extracurricular areas. Folders created by students, an accordion file, or a file box or cabinet can store the papers until conference time. Students may then compile a notebook or folder of samples of their work to share with their parents during conferences. The file is worked on periodically throughout the term, with papers placed in chronological order, thus illustrating the progress in each subject. The child's work is an essential assessment tool.

Standardized tests that reveal the child's potential compared with actual performance level are useful in tailoring an education program to fit the student. With this information, parents and teachers can discuss whether the student is performing above or below potential. Parents and teachers can use the information to plan for the future.

One word of caution on the use of standardized tests: These tests are not infallible. One child might not feel well on the day of testing; another might freeze when taking tests. Standardized test results should be used to supplement informal assessment tools, such as class papers, notebooks, class observation, and informal tests, but not to replace those tools. With the increasing number of tests children are now mandated to take at every grade level, it is very possible that children will "burn out" or simply refuse to complete the standardized tests. Therefore, it is important to be selective in administering tests.

If standardized test results and your informal assessment are congruent and the child scores high on aptitude tests and shows moments of brilliance in class but consistently falls short on work, you can be fairly certain that the child is not working up to ability. If the child scores low but does excellent work in class, observe closely before deciding that the child is under too much pressure to achieve. In that case, the test may not indicate the child's true potential. Should the child score low on the test and also show a high level of frustration when working, you may want to make plans to gear the work closer to the child's ability. The standardized test, used as a backup to the informal assessment, can help teachers and parents plan the child's educational program.

**FIGURE 6–10**
A checklist reviews important conference practices.

---

**Conference Checklist**

*Yes*  *No*  *Did You*
❏  ❏  1. Review information about the child's family? Did you know the parents' last names? Were you aware of the child's educational experience?

❏  ❏  2. Prepare ahead by collecting anecdotal records, tests, papers, notebooks, workbooks, and art materials from the beginning to the end of the reporting period?

❏  ❏  3. Provide book exhibits, displays, or interesting reading for parents as they waited for their conferences?

❏  ❏  4. Make arrangements for coffee or tea for parents as they waited for their conferences?

❏  ❏  5. Prepare your room with an attractive display of children's work?

❏  ❏  6. Welcome the parents with a friendly greeting?

❏  ❏  7. Start on a positive note?

❏  ❏  8. Adjust your conference to the parents' needs and levels of understanding?

❏  ❏  9. Have clear objectives for the conference?

❏  ❏  10. Say in descriptive terms what you meant? Did you avoid educational jargon and use of initials?

❏  ❏  11. Listen reflectively?

❏  ❏  12. Keep the communication lines open? Were you objective and honest?

❏  ❏  13. Avoid comparing students or parents? Did you discuss other teachers only if it was complimentary?

❏  ❏  14. Check your body language? Were you alert to the parents' body language?

❏  ❏  15. Plan the child's educational program together?

❏  ❏  16. Summarize your decisions? Did you make a record of your agreements and plans?

❏  ❏  17. Begin and end on time? If you needed more time, did you set up another appointment?

❏  ❏  18. Follow up with a note and a telephone call?

If you had the student lead the conference, in addition to the above

*Yes*  *No*  *Did You*
❏  ❏  1. Work with the student to develop goals and objectives?

❏  ❏  2. Encourage the student to achieve his/her goals and objectives?

❏  ❏  3. Have the student prepare a portfolio with projects, papers, research, tests, and other achievements?

❏  ❏  4. Have practice sessions in which the student developed the ability to explain objectives and progress? (Students may work with partners and/or other peers.)

❏  ❏  5. Make yourself available to discuss the student's progress with the family during the conference period?

---

## Congruent Beliefs About the Child

Have you ever had a child who constantly disrupts in class only to discover that the child behaves well during Scouts? Sometimes the disparity makes one wonder if it is the same child. It is difficult to discuss a child on common ground if the parents' and teacher's perceptions of the child are completely different. Teachers and parents may need to compare their perceptions of the child. It is often meaningful to have students sort their own views so the perceptions of teacher, parents, and student can be compared.

## Conference Membership

When children are taught by more than one teacher or have contact with numerous specialists (such as a speech teacher or physical therapist), including all professionals involved with the child is appropriate and requires cooperative planning. Beware of the effect on the parent, however, because a ratio of four professionals to one parent may be foreboding. If special care is taken to assure parents that all specialists are there to clarify and work with the teacher and parent as a team, the cooperative discussion and planning can have worthwhile results.

An alternative plan allows the parent to talk individually with each involved specialist. In some schools, the homeroom teacher reports for all the specialists, but personal contact with each person involved with the child's education is more satisfying to the parents. If time is short, the entire group could meet with the parents once in the fall and assure the parents they will be available whenever the parents have a concern.

Consider including the child in the conference. Who is better equipped to clarify why the child is doing well or needs extra help? Who has more at stake? Preschoolers make less sustained conference members, but as soon as the child becomes interested in assessment and evaluations and recognizes the goal of parent–teacher conferences, the teacher should consider including the child in the process. Initially, the child may attend for a short portion of the conference, but as interest and attention span increase, the child might be present for the entire conference. If portions of the conference need to be conducted without the child present, have a supervised play area available. If older students are included as members of the team, issues can be clarified and goals set. The student is part of the discussion and helps in setting realistic goals.

Bjorklund and Burger (1987) describe a four-phase process for collaboration with parents. *Phase 1,* scheduled early in the year, sets the stage with an overview of when conferences will take place, techniques for observation of the children, and a detailed account of the curriculum based on developmental goals. During this phase, both the teachers and parents are encouraged to consider the developmental goals of the program. *Phase 2* is based on the goals. Parents, teachers, and administrators meet and set priorities using observation, testing, anecdotal records, and work samples. Two to four goals are given priority for each child. In *Phase 3,* observations, anecdotal records, checklists, and rating scales are collected for review.

*Phase 4* involves the child. The teacher sends a progress report home in which all the developmental areas are reviewed. A guide for the conference is also sent, with three questions that parents should discuss with the child before the meeting: (a) What do you like best about school? (b) Who are some of the special friends you like to play with at school? (c) Are there any things at school you would like to do more often? The teacher "begins the progress conference by sharing examples of the child's growth through anecdotes which describe some of the child's best skills or characteristics. This leads into a discussion of the three questions with the child" (Bjorklund & Burger, 1987, p. 31). The conference promotes a good self-image for the child by emphasizing the child's positive growth.

## Student–Teacher–Parent Conferences

Many schools have conferences that give the task of deciding about objectives and goals to students. The advantage of this approach is that it empowers students to be responsible for their own learning. The conference planning involves the teacher, any special professionals, and the student. In a private setting, the teacher and student decide what the student is going to accomplish. Young and Behounek (2008) describe an interesting program where kindergarten students use PowerPoints to lead the parent–teacher–student conference. Every slide of the PowerPoint focuses on the child's day. The children answer questions for each slide. For example, "What do you like to do at school?" or "What's your favorite job in kindergarten?" PowerPoints provide an opportunity for young children to visually and verbally share their progress in school.

When conference time arrives, the student and teacher(s) meet in advance to decide what they

A child may participate in a parent–teacher conference.

will talk about at conference time and what they will put in the portfolio to share with the parents. These conferences involve more planning with the student than the traditional conference. At conference time, the student leads the discussion of what has been accomplished, what needs to be worked on, and what the future goals are. The concept behind this conference is similar to the Individualized Education Plan in that plans are made for individual students, but the pupil is more responsible for determining the objectives and goals.

Some schools organize student–teacher–parent conferences into a participatory situation with four sets of parents and children meeting at the same time. Each set discusses the child's achievements and goals. The teacher enters the discussion whenever a parent or child has questions or comments or when the teacher has a reason for participating in their conference. At some point during the session, each set of parents and students include the teacher in their discussion.

Different issues arise with this change in the format of the conference. With this type of conference, the child and parents are responsible for its success. Teachers must have good organizational and leadership skills so that the student has established goals and direction before the conference. During the conference, the teacher will not have the opportunity to monopolize the discussion, but the student and parents must take the teacher's responsibility seriously if the conference is to be successful.

## Congruent Expectations

Conferences go more smoothly when the teacher and parents have congruent expectations about the performance of the child. If the child is an excellent student and both teacher and parents are pleased with the evaluation, it is easy to accept the report. If the child has a disability and both teacher and parents recognize the disabling condition, they can work together to plan an appropriate program for the child.

Too often the outward signs of good marks and pleasant personality and behavior fail to uncover how the child feels and whether the teacher can make the educational experience more satisfying and challenging. In working with a successful student, parents and teachers may fail to communicate about the child's potential and the need to have a good self-concept. Special interests of the child, friends,

To promote the well-being of this child, conferences need to be cooperative with the teacher and sensitive to the parents' feelings.

reading preferences, experiences, and needs are important for the teacher to know. Bring the child into the decision-making process. Together, the parents, teacher, and child can plan activities that will encourage growth and improve self-concept. Let these parents and children communicate too.

**Situation.** Denzel is one of those students every teacher loves to have in class. He is enthusiastic, stays on task, completes his work, and never causes a disturbance. A quiet, attractive boy with his long brown hair pulled back in a ponytail, Denzel always does the correct thing. He is polite to everyone and avoids fighting or taking sides when others are arguing.

Mrs. Jackson relaxed in her chair as she prepared for the conference with Denzel's parents. "What an easy conference," she thought. "I really don't have to talk with Denzel's parents because he fits into the routine, is well adjusted, and is progressing nicely." As she looked up, she saw Mrs. Johnson, Denzel's mother, standing outside the door. She rose to greet her and led her into the room, offering her a chair. As they sat side by side, Mrs. Jackson remarked, "It is really good to see you, Mrs. Johnson. I enjoy

Denzel in class, and he is having no problems. Here are some of the papers I have collected. You can see that he completes his work and does a good job. I wish all my students were like Denzel."

After looking over the papers, Mrs. Johnson looked up and said, "It is nice not to have to worry about Denzel. I wish that Tanisha were as conscientious. I'm dreading that conference. I've really enjoyed having you be Denzel's teacher."

Mrs. Jackson and Mrs. Johnson glanced at Denzel's papers and leaned back, satisfied.

"Look at the time; we finished in 10 minutes," Mrs. Johnson said. "You have five minutes to spare. Have a good day."

"You have a good day, too," the teacher said as she escorted Denzel's mother to the door.

1. What did the conference accomplish?
2. Could there be a problem? How does Denzel feel?
3. What should Mrs. Johnson and Mrs. Jackson consider as they think about Denzel? Does Denzel feel good about himself? Is he a class leader? Does he get along well with the other children?
4. What does he enjoy doing the most? Is there anything that might make his school career even better?

**Situation.** "Welcome, Mrs. García. We are so pleased to have Jaime with us this year," said Jaime's preschool teacher, Mr. López, greeting the boy's mother.

"He's just so happy to be here," Mrs. García said. "He was a little anxious at first, but you have made him feel welcome."

"I'm pleased Jaime is beginning to feel comfortable. I noticed that he is interacting with the other children more—he played on the jungle gym today. His coordination is improving, and he is much more outgoing than he was three weeks ago when he first started. Let me share some of his paintings and some stories we have recorded. He illustrated this story. Look at the detail. What a great imagination!"

Mr. López and Mrs. García looked at the papers together.

"What does Jaime enjoy doing at home?" Mr. López asked.

"He becomes very involved in building with his LEGO set," Mrs. García said. "He loves to have us read him stories. We share stories together each afternoon and in the evening before he goes to bed. I try to limit his television viewing, though he does get to watch *Sesame Street* and *Mister Rogers* occasionally."

"Does he have any children to play with in his neighborhood?"

"There are no 4-year-old children, but Beto, who lives down the street, is in kindergarten, and he plays with Jaime about three times a week."

"I'll bet they play hard too!" Mr. López said and then turned to the current class activities.

"Our theme for this month is the sun," she said. "We're studying about shadows, reflections, and how the sun helps flowers to grow. These are some of the collages we have made. As you can tell, a lot of the pictures were made by tearing the paper, but we are also working on cutting. Let me show you how we are having him hold his scissors. Do you think you can help him with this at home? I'll be sending home activity suggestions and notes that let you know what we are doing at school."

"Thank you," Mrs. García said. "That way, I'll be more able to help Jaime at home if he needs it."

"Why don't you go into the observation room and watch him for a while before you leave," Mr. López said. "Don't forget that you can observe anytime, and you might want to volunteer to help in the preschool."

Jaime's mother looked surprised and answered, "I hadn't thought about that, but it might be enjoyable.

"What haven't we covered? Do you have any questions that we neglected to discuss?" Mr. López asked. After a pause, he added, "It was nice to be able to share with you about Jaime's experiences here. Be sure to call if you have any concerns or if something is happening at home that we should know about. We want to keep in touch."

"I enjoyed talking with you. I can see why Jaime enjoys school so much. Gracias, thank you. Goodbye," Jaime's mother said as she walked toward the observation room.

1. What was effective in this conference?
2. Did the mother get to share enough?
3. What would you suggest to make it better?

**Situation.** Ashley, a charming 7-year-old with big brown eyes, curly black hair, and a sparkling smile, seemed older and larger than most children her age. When she came into the classroom before school started, she always went up to Miss Allen and told her about what was going on in her neighborhood. The stories were usually about fights, guns, holdups, gangs, and anger. There was reason to believe that she was relating what she had actually witnessed or heard. Ashley lived with her father; her mother had disappeared several years earlier and, although Ashley knew she was still alive, she had no contact with her. At one period in Ashley's life, she lived in a cardboard box. Life had not been easy for this child, who had experienced much change and abuse.

When school started, Ashley was unable to stay on task. She seemed to crave attention, whether it be from sharing, describing a story in the author's chair, or acting out. Her primary method of obtaining attention was through acting out. She spoke out of turn, took pencils from other children, and shoved and pushed. Because she was large for her age, she could hurt another child with a shove.

One day, Ashley threatened an aide working in the classroom by suggesting that her older sister would beat her up. Time-out did not help because she did not oblige, but she did seem to be threatened by a trip to the office. The school year was in its fourth week and there had been no parent–teacher conferences.

1. What would you suggest the teacher do to obtain parent collaboration?
2. Do you believe that parent–school cooperation is feasible? Why or why not?
3. What could you do as a teacher to help Ashley become a productive child?
4. Would a conference that included Ashley and her father be a good idea? Why or why not?
5. If you believed that Ashley comes from an abusive home, would you change your approach? Why or why not?

## Preconference Preparation

Before the day of the conference and throughout the reporting period, you, as the teacher, prepare by getting to know the student, conducting ongoing assessment, and developing a portfolio. Before the conference, review the child's history, cultural background, family situation, successes, and concerns. Depending on which records are kept by the school, try to learn about the student's educational experience. Review the papers in the current portfolio so that you can know the student's growth or delay that has occurred under your guidance.

Try to have three- to five-minute individual conferences with each child to talk about what you are going to cover in the conference. Determine if there is anything that the child would like to see

included, thus providing you insight into the child's thoughts. If you recognize the child's thoughts as important, you increase the child's respect for self and belief in the teacher or a caring ally.

## The Day of the Conference

Relax before conference time. It is important to establish a cooperative climate. If the teacher is relaxed and poised, parents will be able to relax too, and the climate for communication will be improved. Meyers and Pawlas (1989) recommend developing a form to use for record keeping for planning as well as keeping records for future conferences. The teacher is able to focus on one or two predetermined issues and keep records of the collaboration. Multiple concerns can be overwhelming; time does not allow all issues to be resolved. When determining the issues to be discussed, however, parents should have the option of helping determine the agenda. Perhaps they have a concern that is not known by the teacher. They can either share their concerns by sending back an information sheet suggesting what they would like to discuss, or during the conference the teacher can encourage them to bring up their concerns or comments.

Why do parents enter into parent–teacher conferences with apprehension? Some are worried because they want the best for their child but do not know how to achieve it. They are unsure of themselves in the discussion and might be threatened by jargon. The parent–teacher conference should be an opportunity for the exchange of ideas and information and a chance to support each other; both can enter into the conference with enthusiasm and confidence.

## The Conference

Begin the conference in a relaxed, positive manner. During the conference, review your objectives, use effective communication skills, discuss concrete examples of work, and plan together.

Besides being adept at reflective listening, you need to listen intuitively to determine if parents have problems within their homes or are themselves emotionally immature. Such problems make it difficult for the child to have the home support needed for educational success. Remember that you, as the teacher, can gain a great deal of knowledge and understanding of the child from the parents and the conference is a good way to gain that knowledge.

When indicated, invite other professionals, such as the school's social worker or principal, to the conference to support and help the family and child. We want to learn more from the parents in order to understand the child's needs (Cannella, 2002).

**Sandwich Approach.** Use the sandwich approach for the conference (Manning, 1985). Start the conference with pleasant and positive items. If you have negative comments or concerns to be discussed, bring them up during the middle of the conference. Always end with a positive summary, spend time planning with parents, and make a pleasant comment about the child.

**Clear Statement of Objectives.** Some objectives may be universal; others will be specific for the individual conference. Use the following objectives as a guide:

1. To gain a team member (the parent) in the education of the child
2. To document the child's progress for the parent
3. To explain the educational program you are using as it relates to the individual child
4. To learn about the environment in which the child lives
5. To allow the parents to express feelings, questions, and concerns
6. To get a better understanding of the expectations the parent holds for the child
7. To set up a lasting network of communication among parent, teacher, and child
8. To establish cooperative goals for the education of the child

**The Parent as Part of the Team.** After you have made sure the room is comfortable, two-way communication will be uninterrupted, and you are ready to listen and be responsive to the parent, it is easy to recognize the parent as a part of the educational team. Parents arrive at conferences as experts on their children's history, hobbies, interests, likes and dislikes, friends, and experiences. Explain to the parents that all participants in the conference are members of a team looking at the progress of the child and working together to benefit the child. How can *we* help the child who is having a difficult time? How can *we* enrich the program for the child who is accelerated? How can *we* get the child to do the task at hand? How can *we* promote self-esteem? If the teacher and parents work as a team to answer

these questions, the conference will be far more productive than if the teacher simply dictates answers to the parents. Here are some tips that will help parents feel they are part of the team:

- Review your file and know enough about the child before the parent arrives that the parent can tell you have taken a personal interest in the child's welfare.
- Know the parent's name. Do not assume that the child and parent have the same last name. Look in the record for the correct name.
- Ensure the privacy of the conference.
- Begin on a positive note. Start by praising an accomplishment of the child or a contribution the child has made to the class.
- Know the time limitations.
- Do not use terminology that may have meaning for you but not the parent.
- Do not refer to organizations, forms, tests, materials, or ideas by their initials or acronyms. Do not assume that everyone knows what the initials or acronyms mean.
- Have some questions about and show interest in the child.
- Remind parents that they may ask questions at any time and that you will be pleased to explain anything that is not clear.
- Keep on the subject: the child's schooling and development.
- Encourage the parents to contribute. Allow parents to talk for at least 50 percent of the time.
- Show that you understand the parent by checking periodically during the conference. For example, you might ask, "Would you agree with this?" or "Do you have suggestions to add about this?"
- Make note of an idea suggested by a parent, but do not get so involved in writing that you lose the flow of the conversation.
- Keep in mind the parents' cultural background and follow culturally appropriate rules.
- Use attentive behaviors—that is, lean forward, look interested, and nod when in agreement.
- Do not ignore a parent's question.
- Be honest yet tactful and sensitive to the parent's feelings.
- Base your discussion on objective observation and concrete examples of work.
- Deal in specifics rather than generalities whenever possible.

- Evaluate needs and select methods of remediating difficulties.
- Evaluate strengths and select methods of enriching those strengths.
- Plan educational goals together.
- Talk about how you have modified your teaching to meet the needs of the child.
- Clarify and summarize the discussion.
- Make plans to continue the dialogue.

## Concrete Examples of Child's Work and Development

Both parent and teacher are interested in the child's accomplishments. By making objective observations of the child's classroom behavior with anecdotal notes collected throughout the reporting periods, the teacher documents the child's social as well as intellectual achievements. Anecdotal records of significant behaviors are especially valuable for conferences with parents of young children. Papers and tests may not be available, so the anecdotal records become tools for evaluating the child's social, intellectual, and physical progress. In the case of children with behavioral difficulties, it is also important to be able to cite specific incidents rather than vague generalizations about incidents. Keep anecdotal records in electronic files.

The accumulated examples of the child's work with a few words from the teacher also illustrate to parents what their child is doing. It is not necessary to state when a child has not progressed, for that will be obvious. If another child has made great progress, that too will be evident from the samples collected. Consider asking parents if they have come to the same conclusion as you when comparing early and subsequent papers.

Some teachers supplement papers and anecdotal records with videos of children in the classroom. Although time-consuming, a video report is enjoyable for parents and encourages interaction between parent and teacher on the child's classroom participation.

Bringing concrete examples to the conference illustrating the child's work may prevent a confrontation and allows parent and teacher to analyze the work together. Include anecdotal records and samples of the child's work in comparison with expected behavior at that age level. In preschool this may include fine-motor control, large-muscle activities, art, and problem solving. For school-age children, examples may include papers, artwork, projects, work in academic subjects, tests, notebooks, workbooks, and anecdotal records. It is also helpful to parents for the teacher to collect a set of unidentified "average" papers. If parents want to compare their child's work with that of the "average" child, they have a basis for this comparison.

Whatever the level of the child's performance, the parent and teacher need to form a team as they evaluate the child's educational progress and work together for the good of the child.

Use the conference form recommended by Meyers and Pawlas (1989) to keep a record. Parents and teacher—and student, if in attendance—decide on goals, highlights, or accomplishments and plans for the future. All attendees should read and sign the conference form and retain a copy.

## Postconference Plans

After the conference, write a note thanking the parents for their participation. Later, in a follow-up telephone call, let the parents know how the conference plans are being implemented and how the student is participating. Each contact increases the parent–school collaboration.

A checklist may be used for self-evaluation, as shown in Figure 6–10. If you are able to answer yes to these questions, you are ready to have productive parent–teacher conferences.

## Working with Angry Parents

What do you do when an upset and angry parent confronts you? Most professionals face such a situation at one time or another. Margolis and Brannigan (1986) list seven steps to help you control the volatile situation and allow the parent to regain composure. If you understand the dynamics of anger, you can engage in reflective listening. As a result, you can redirect the wrath and empathize with the parent. The steps include the following:

1. Remain calm and courteous, and maintain natural eye contact through the barrage. After the parents have expressed their anger, usually dominated by emotion, ask them to repeat their concerns so you can understand the situation better. The second time around, the statements are usually more comprehensible and rational.
2. Use reflective listening and give reflective summaries of their statements. You can explore the

content of their messages later, but during this stage attempt to establish a more relaxed and trusting atmosphere.

3. Continue with reflective listening, and ask some open-ended questions that allow them to talk more as you gain greater understanding.

4. Keep exploring until you have determined what the underlying critical issues are. Do not evaluate, and do not be defensive.

5. After the issues have been fully explored, rephrase and summarize, including points of agreement. Check to see if your summary of their concerns is correct. Offer to let them add to what you have summarized. When you clearly define the concerns, they often seem more manageable.

6. Margolis and Brannigan (1986) point out that by now, listening has been used to build trust and defuse the anger. You are more likely to understand the problem from the parent's perspective. When the first five steps "are followed in an open, sincere, and empathetic manner, disagreements frequently dissolve and respect emerges" (p. 345). If such is not the case, go back and allow free exploration again.

7. Use a systematic problem-solving approach to any issues that remain unresolved. The steps in collaborative problem solving include (a) understand each other's needs and the resources available to help satisfy those needs, (b) formulate a hypothesis that might solve the problem, (c) brainstorm other solutions, (d) combine ideas and solutions to create new solutions, (e) together, develop criteria to judge the solutions, (f) clarify and evaluate solutions, and (g) select the most likely solution. At the end of the confrontation, the result should satisfy both educator and parent.

**Situation.** "I've never come to a school conference without having to wait 45 minutes to talk with you. Then, when I get in, you rush me, never let me ask questions, and just tell me how poorly Mary is doing. I know that Mary is doing poorly! I have my hands full just trying to go to work and feed my four children. Can't you do something to help Mary? Do you care?" Mary's father breathlessly expressed his anger and frustration.

"Hold on, Mr. Washington," Mr. Bonner said. "You're responsible for Mary, not me. She does poorly because she doesn't pay attention; she's more interested in her friends than in school, and she cuts class. I can work with students who come to school ready to learn. I just don't have the strength or the patience to take on your daughter until she changes her attitude."

"I waited 45 minutes to hear that?" Mr. Washington asked. "What's going on here? No wonder Mary skips school. Where's the superintendent's office? I need to talk with your supervisor." Mr. Washington stalked out of the room.

1. How could Mr. Bonner respond in a manner to reduce Mr. Washington's anger?

2. What kind of interaction should take place to promote problem solving?

3. Is there anything Mr. Bonner can do to help this situation?

4. What can Mr. Washington do to help resolve his daughter's problems?

5. What responsibility does Mary have?

## Making a Contract—Parent–Teacher Communication

Most teachers have experienced working with children who do not stay on task, daydream, act out in class, or seem to be wasting their potential. Parents of these children are usually just as concerned as the teacher. In a contract arrangement, the parents are empowered to get involved in the child's school behavior. In an effort to increase the student's positive participation in school, teachers and parents have an ongoing communication system that acknowledges how the child does in school. Parents and teachers work together to establish the goals and parameters of the contract. Usually a note is sent home each day detailing how the student performed at school. This includes schoolwork as well as classroom behavior. The parents reinforce the positive behavior and help diminish the negative. By communicating each day with a focus on the goals of the contract, parents and teachers form a team to help the child become successful in school.

Kelley (1990) describes a home-based reinforcement method in her book on school–home notes. It is based on behavioral theory and is similar to the contract method. This approach is beneficial for children who have difficulty staying on task or are not performing up to their abilities. The school–home note, or daily report card, is an intervention method that requires the participation of parents as well as teachers. Together they collaborate on problem solving and determine their approach. Each day, the teacher completes a simple form and sends it home, letting the parents know how the child behaved and participated in class that day. The parent follows up with consequences. It is important that the consequences fit and that they have the desired result: "The goals in any contingency management system are to reinforce appropriate behavior (so as to increase its frequency) and to ignore or punish inappropriate or unacceptable behavior (so as to decrease its frequency)" (p. 16).

If the school–home contract or notes are not working, the teachers and parents should meet again and revise their plan.

## :: HANDLING CONCERNS THROUGHOUT THE YEAR

The following principles, proposed by Franklin (1993), will help facilitate good home–school communication as issues emerge throughout the year.

1. Approach the parents at every meeting with the assumption that you have a common goal—a good environment in which the child can learn and develop.
2. Try to facilitate the best in the parent, just as you support and try to develop the best potential in the child.
3. Avoid confrontation and defensive responses. Model working together as partners.
4. Assess your motives before giving negative feedback to parents. Why are you telling this to the parent? What do you hope will come out of the exchange? Will it help the child's learning? Do you expect a positive outcome?
5. Avoid setting yourself up as an authority figure with parents. Work toward establishing a partnership with the parents. Respect the parents' knowledge of their child and ask them to share information with you. Parents and teachers can learn from each other and provide different perspectives.
6. Try to avoid judging the parent, just as you hope they are not focused on evaluating you.
7. Give a careful and thoughtful response to parent concerns. Be available and unhurried in your interaction.
8. There are no typical responses from parents. They are as different from one another as teachers are from one another. Be an active listener, and remain open to different perspectives.

## SUMMARY

Effective communication between parents and schools allows parents to become partners in education. Communication includes speaking, listening, reflection of feelings, and interpretation of the meaning of the message. If the message sent is not correctly interpreted by the receiver, then miscommunication has occurred. It can be overcome by rephrasing and checking out meanings. Talking is not the most important element in communication. The way a message is spoken and the speaker's body language account for 93 percent of the message. Teachers and administrators must know and understand cultural ways of communicating for all families but especially for culturally and linguistically diverse families.

It is essential for schools to have good communication with families. One-way communication describes the method that schools use when they offer parents information through newsletters, newspapers, media, and handbooks. Two-way communication allows parents to communicate with school personnel through telephone calls, home visits, classroom visits, and school functions. It continues through the year with classroom visits and participation, back-to-school nights, parent education groups, school programs, projects, workshops, PTA carnivals, exchanges, and a suggestion box.

Parents and schools both put up roadblocks to communication. Parent roadblocks include the following roles: "my own and my child guardian," "I don't belong," avoidance, "indifferent parent," "don't make waves," and "club-waving advocate." Roadblocks put up by schools include the following roles: "authority figure," "sympathizing counselor," "pass the buck," "protect the empire," and "busy teacher."

Effective communication and trust building between parent and educator are important. The areas of communication that can be developed include positive speaking, listening, reflective listening, rephrasing, reframing, and attentive behavior. PET, STEP, and Active Parenting all include communication with an emphasis on reflective or active listening in their parent education format.

Parent–teacher conferences are the most common of two-way exchanges. Conferences can be effective if educators and parents prepare for them in advance. Teachers need to make parents feel welcome; materials and displays should be available. Two-way conversations will build cooperation and trust. Teachers can develop expertise in conducting conferences by relating to the parents, developing trust, and learning from them about the child. A checklist is included to analyze the effectiveness of the conference.

The chapter includes suggestions for dealing with angry parents and how to deal with concerns parents may have throughout the year.

## SUGGESTED CLASS ACTIVITIES AND DISCUSSIONS

1. Develop a simple newsletter, a note to parents, and a detailed newsletter.
2. Practice speaking positively. Develop situations in which a child has average ability, has a learning disability, or is gifted. Role play the parent and the teacher. Make the interaction focus on positive speaking. Then reverse your approach and become negative in your analysis of the child. How did you feel during each interchange? You can videotape the role playing, so you can analyze the results objectively.
3. Practice listening. Divide the class into groups of three. One person is the speaker, another is the listener, and the third is the observer. Exchange roles so each person in the group gets to play each role. Have each person select a topic of interest, from something as simple as "my favorite hideaway" to something as serious as "coping with death in my family." Each person tells a story; the listener listens and then repeats or rephrases the story. The observer watches for body language, attentive behavior, interest, and correct rephrasing. A checklist is an excellent way to make sure the observer watches for all elements of listening.
4. Visit a school and obtain a copy of the school's newsletter. Analyze it. Does it communicate with parents effectively? How would you improve it?
5. Consider your beliefs and value system. What beliefs might be blocks to communication with parents, particularly those with a different value system?
6. Brainstorm in class for words to use in rephrasing. For example, what words could you use to describe a child who hands in sloppy work?
7. Role play the parent putting up roadblocks to communication.
8. Role play the roadblocks that schools put up that hinder communication.
9. Sit in on a staffing or a parent–teacher conference. Observe the parents' and the educators' interaction.
10. Compose situations that need constructive, positive answers. Make up several answers that would be appropriate for each situation.

## USEFUL WEB SITES

**Frank Porter Graham Child Development Institute**
www.fpg.unc.edu/
The institute, housed at the University of North Carolina, Chapel Hill, offers a wide range of information and knowledge on a child's development.

**Harvard Family Research Project**
www.hfrp.org/family-involvement
Committed to find effective ways to support family's involvement in children's learning and development.

**National Coalition for Parent Involvement in Education**
www.ncpie.org/
The focus is to advocate the involvement of parents in their children's education.

**Reading Is Fundamental**
www.rif.org/
This site describes how reading is fundamental to communication and the importance for children and families to engage in meaningful reading activities.

**Teaching Strategies**
www.teachingstrategies.com/
Teaching Strategies offers information, training materials, and parenting resources to help children birth through 8 years of age.

**Zero to Three**
www.zerotothree.org/
Zero to Three provides support and information for parents of infants through age 3. Included is BrainWonders, which has information about brain development.

# 7

# Collaborative Leadership— Working with Parents

*A leader is best*
*When people barely know that he exists*
*Not so good when people obey and acclaim him*
*Worst when they despise him*
*Fail to honor people,*
*They fail to honor you,*
*But of a good leader, who talks little*
*When work is done, his aim fulfilled*
*They will all say, "We did this ourselves."*

Lao-tze, ancient Chinese philosopher

In this chapter on collaborative leadership, you will find procedures that will enable you to do the following:

- Describe types of leadership.
- Use collaborative leadership skills as you work in site-based or community management, charter schools, classroom management, cooperative education, or parent involvement and parent education.
- Cite research that supports parent involvement and parent education.
- Plan and develop a needs assessment.
- Organize the format of a meeting.
- Recognize roles that develop when participating in meetings.
- Select meeting formats that meet the needs of the participants.
- Select appropriate topics for meetings.
- Evaluate meetings.

Leadership ability is a skill that helps in all facets of human interactions. School professionals find it essential whether they are parent educators, principals, or teachers. Principals provide leadership in community or collective collaboration in site-based management of schools. Teachers need leadership skills to encourage problem solving and critical thinking and to set the stage for learning. In-group decision making and leadership skills are essential to accomplish the goals of the group. This chapter expands your thinking to visualize how good collaborative involvement and leadership can be used in classrooms, family meetings, professional meetings, and group activities.

## :: DEVELOP COLLABORATIVE LEADERSHIP SKILLS

Good collaborative leadership skills are beneficial in many areas of life. Whether it be the home, school, or the wider arena of the community, information on group leadership and processes is very useful. Students of all ages can participate in a family meeting, and those in middle school and high school often have presentations about a project they have developed.

Professionals and/or classroom teachers who can support and motivate the group can accomplish the goals of the group without undermining the responsibilities of the participants. The style of the leader is determined by the individual's training and personality as well as the makeup of the group, which hopefully represents the diversity of learners in the school or center. Group management can be enhanced by collaborative leadership training sessions where members of the group can be introduced to group methods, curriculum, and resources. It helps if participants have a basic understanding of group processes and communication, whether the group is being led by students, parents, principals, or professionals.

In collaborative decision making for the school and child-care center, the principal or director is usually the leader. Because the approach is collaborative, the designated leader should be a facilitator, one with information and background material that can be used by the entire group. School counselors may also be able to fulfill this role because they often have access to community resources that benefit families (Griffin & Steen, 2010). The leader also should be aware that those on the committee have much to share and must be willing to encourage interaction. Leadership skills go beyond administrators to those with whom they work. These leaders, along with teachers, must collaborate with parents and other community members to establish the management and objectives of the school. In site-based management, members of organizing committees who understand group dynamics, growth, and leadership responsibilities will be more effective than those who flounder trying to develop meaningful and effective group decision making. Using a collaborative approach with site-based management typically proves to be very effective.

## :: LEADERSHIP IN PARENT EDUCATION

Leadership in parent education may be viewed along a continuum (Figure 7–1) that ranges from a lay leader, or nonprofessional with little training, to a knowledgeable expert trained to expedite group processes, a professional who lectures as an authority. As you begin a parent education program, keep in mind that groups can be organized in different fashions. A trained professional should not dominate the group with specific, didactic teaching, nor should the lay group be left without direction.

The use of lay leaders—parents leading their own groups—encourages parents to be actively involved. Because educational growth and positive change are what is wanted in parent education groups, active involvement is highly desired. More change will occur if the parent formulates some of the educational suggestions and acts upon the information. Parents are more able to develop ways of handling parent–child relationships if they develop their expertise from their own research and interact with other members of the group. This does not mean excluding experts in the field. At times, it is necessary to have an authority give background material. After the information is received, however, parents need to discuss and act upon it themselves.

Various types of meetings and group processes serve as guides in the development of new

The background and experience of the parents provide an opportunity for sharing expertise and knowledge and an impetus for self-directed learning.

parent-group programs. The types of meetings discussed here range from those led by a person without formal training, on the left of the continuum in Figure 7–1, to the professional person on the right. At the center of the continuum is the parent education group that is most appropriate for achieving parental self-determination, attitudinal change, competence, and educational gains—that of parent leadership with professional support. Descriptions of meetings that illustrate each of the types include the following:

1. Unstructured meetings with no goals, curriculum, or trained leader.
2. Meetings led by lay leaders to get comments, solve a problem, study an issue, or become better acquainted.
3. Meetings led by lay leaders who follow a curriculum devised by professionals, such as Active Parenting, Parent Effectiveness Training (PET), and Systematic Training for Effective Parenting (STEP).
4. Meetings called by a parent or a professional that involve members and respond to their concerns with professional support. In the case of site-based management, the professional (principal) involves

**FIGURE 7–1**
Continuum of leaders in parent education.

| Parent leader with no training | Parent leader with leadership training | Parent leader with a structured curriculum | Parent leader with professional support | Professional leader with parent participation | Professional |
| --- | --- | --- | --- | --- | --- |

members of the committee and leads them to a consensus or a decision by majority vote.

5. Meetings called and led by a professional, with participation by lay members.
6. Meetings called, led, directed, and controlled by the professional, with members of the audience as observers only.

The aims of traditional parent education are furthered in the recent restructuring trend and collaborative decision making in public education. Parent involvement includes shared goal setting and decision making (Comer, 1988; Seeley, 1989; Swick, 2001). Encouraging parents to be involved calls for active parent collaboration that includes the parents in "mutual accountability. . . . This brings a power into the relationship that supersedes the power of bureaucratic control" (Seeley, 1989, p. 48). Belief in the autonomy of parents inspires the promotion of their decision making abilities and allows them to be full partners in the education process. Educators must help instill a sense of trust to build strong interactions with parents (Bolívar & Chrispeels, 2011).

Mutual collaboration enhances children's possibilities to perform successfully in academic tasks such as reading and math as well as in socioemotional issues such as behavior (Powell, Son, File, & San Juan, 2010). It is important to note that for many parents, the extended family also plays a crucial role in school involvement; in other words, not only the parents are involved in the child's education, but others such as the grandparents may also be involved (Ryan, Casas, Kelly-Vance, Ryalls, & Nero, 2010).

## :: NEEDS ASSESSMENT

Before you begin a parent education program—and periodically during the program—you should determine the interests and needs of the community. In order to determine the needs of families, administrators and teachers must respond to their interests by having conversations about how to make connections in children's learning contexts and by providing leadership training (Darragh, 2009). A brainstorming session is an ideal mechanism for eliciting many ideas. Write down the ideas or questions that concern and interest the families. It is important to remember to provide the sessions in the language that parents understand or have translators that know the community in order to better communicate your thoughts and their thoughts (Buysse, Castro, & West, 2005).

Once you have developed your basic list of interests and concerns, give it to a trial group and ask the members to add new ideas and concerns. Next, construct a needs-assessment tool, listing possible topics or formats for parents. Disseminate the questionnaire to adults in the school or center community. Finally, choose from the questionnaire those items that received the most requests and develop a program to meet the needs of the community.

Needs assessments are necessary when new programs are developed as well as when established

A needs assessment helps to discover topics of interest for parents.

**Insights for Teachers and Administrators**

1. Brainstorm ideas for concerns and interests.
2. Collect as many ideas as your group can generate.
3. Show the group a similar list that might provide inspiration for other ideas to add to their list.
4. Form buzz groups, and let the participants discuss the lists.
5. Let the members list their choices in order of importance.
6. Generate your programs for the year from the group responses.
7. If a new issue arises that concerns most of the group, find a space or add a session to cover the important topic.

parent groups reassess their needs. Less formal assessments are used frequently by ongoing groups.

## Interest Finders

If a parent group is already established, members may use a number of informal methods to indicate their interests. These range from brainstorming among the members to soliciting ideas in a suggestion box.

**Brainstorming.** For a brainstorming session, choose a recorder and encourage all members to contribute ideas for programs. A list of past successful programs may be distributed. Write ideas on a whiteboard (you can use chart paper, a chalkboard, or an overhead projector if a whiteboard is not available). Caution members not to judge any suggestions, good or bad—all suggestions are valid at this point. After all suggestions are listed, have members choose (in writing) three to six ideas that interest them most. Keep in mind the parents' cultural background and funds of knowledge. Develop your program from the interests that receive the most votes (or are most frequently mentioned). If the group has difficulty thinking of items, you may be able to generate responses by having participants complete statements such as these:

My greatest concerns are . . .

My greatest happiness comes from . . .

If I had three wishes, I would . . .

If I could eliminate one problem from my home, it would be . . .

Questions that concern me about my child's education are . . .

Questions that concern me about my child's development are . . .

As a parent, I hope to be . . .

**Open-Ended Questions.** Parent groups can solicit requests for a wider knowledge of the community and possible ways for parents to become more involved in schools and the community. The leader asks parents to respond to such topics as:

- What do I want to know about my school?
- What do I want to know about my community?
- What would I like to do about my school and/or community?

**Questionnaires.** Develop a questionnaire, such as *Test Your Know-how as a Parent,* that will bring out differences in opinions in the group and show where interests and room for learning occur.

**Question Box.** Some parents are hesitant to make suggestions in an open meeting. They might feel more comfortable dropping questions and comments into a box that is available throughout the year. Make sure that the box is visible enough for parents to see but that is also in a place where they know their input will be anonymous. For example, do not place the suggestion box by the administrative assistant desk; instead, place it on a table in the school's entrance.

During early planning, it may also be advisable to let the members anonymously write their ideas on a small sheet of paper. Parents may be concerned about alcohol and other drugs, for example, but hesitate to mention that lest they reveal they have that problem in their homes.

## Development of Objectives

After the group's interests have been assessed, the program is developed. Within most programs, at least two aspects should receive attention: the content of the meeting and the changes in behavior and attitudes of the participants.

Most parents know when they want help with parenting skills, although reticent parents may need special encouragement. When a new family is formed and the first baby comes home to live, parents are intensely interested in knowing how to care for the baby. An opportune time for parent education is before the birth and during the child's first 3 years of life.

Parents are also ready for sharing information during the child's preschool years. Parent education and preschool programs bring the professional and the parents together to share concerns and experiences.

During the child's school-age years, parent education programs that focus on learning activities, building family strengths, and concerns specific to the group are beneficial. The needs of school-age children differ from those of young children; therefore, parents need help to meet those needs. Parents need to share, ask questions, and be a part of the decision-making process.

## :: HOW PARENTS LEARN BEST

Parent educators facilitate the learning experience for parents. They design the program and the environment so that the parent is an active participant in the delivery of knowledge. Families will be more apt to become involved in the learning process and thereby change their attitudes more easily if:

- A positive climate is established.
- Their culture and language (including funds of knowledge) are valued and respected.
- Risk is eliminated.
- Parents are recognized as having something worthwhile to contribute.
- Parents are actively involved in their own education.
- The curriculum addresses their concerns and needs and is culturally relevant.
- Parents discover the need for change on their own.
- Respect and encouragement are present.
- Real situations and analogies are used to bring theories to life.
- Positive feedback is used.
- Different approaches (role playing, short lectures, open discussion, debates, brainstorming, workshops) allow them to learn to use a variety of techniques.
- Different approaches use a variety of sensory experiences (sight, sound, touch, taste, and smell).
- Problem solving and analysis enable the learner to continue learning beyond the personal contact.
- Parents are considered part of the learning–teaching team.

You may have noted that the way parents learn best can apply to students, professionals, or even young children. Most everyone learns better when in a positive environment with relevant material.

In addition, it is important to note that parents will have difficulty focusing on their children if their own immediate needs are not met. Therefore, it is important to provide support, resources, and referral information to parents to help them meet their own needs. Once this has been accomplished, they will be able to focus their energy on the children.

## :: GROUP DISCUSSIONS

Most meetings involve group discussion, which can range from the use of open discussion as the total meeting format to a short discussion after a formal presentation.

The following examples, an informal discussion plan and a problem-solving format, illustrate two uses of group discussions. The first focuses on the informality of the process, and the second requires prior development of expertise and a resolution of the issue.

### *Informal Discussion Plan*

A. Stems from interest or needs of group.
   *Example:* How can parents be more involved in their child's school?
B. Establishes goals and objectives.
   1. Goal—parental involvement.
   2. Objectives.
      a. To determine why parents do not feel comfortable coming to school.
      b. To encourage parents to participate in school.
      c. To initiate a plan for getting parents involved.
      d. To suggest activities in which parents can be involved.
C. Provides for informal group meetings.
   1. Allows parents to speak freely.
   2. Emphasizes the clarification of feelings and acceptance of ideas.
   3. Encourages participation.
   4. Includes keeping a record of suggestions.
D. Selects and analyzes relevant information that emerges during the discussion.
E. Outlines a plan for action, if the group desires.

### Problem-Solving Format

A. Recognition of the problem—state the hypothesis.
  1. The problem should be selected by the group and reflect its needs and interests.
  *Example:* Does violence on television impact our children and cause more violence in the country?
  2. The leader writes the question or problem for discussion on a chart, chalkboard, or whiteboard.
B. Understanding the problem—discuss the nature of the problem.
  *Example:* Is television viewing a problem and, if so, why?
C. Data collection—gather a wide range of ideas and determine which are relevant.
  1. Prior development of expertise—identify resources and read before meeting.
  2. Nonjudgmental acceptance—accept and record comments and ideas from participants.
D. Analysis of the problem.
  1. Focus on the subject so that it can be discussed thoroughly by participants.
  2. Establish criteria for evaluation of a solution.
  3. Keep participants focused on problems.
E. Conclusion and summary.

  1. Suggest solutions.
  2. List possible conclusions.
  3. Seek an integrative conclusion that reflects the group's goals and thinking.
F. Appropriate action.
  1. Develop a timetable.
  2. Determine a method of accomplishing tasks.
  3. Delegate tasks.

## :: LEADERSHIP TRAINING

Lay leaders benefit from having guidelines to follow in developing their leadership skills. The leader's goal is to establish an environment that facilitates and guides members in achieving the objectives.

Group members can participate more effectively if they are aware of their rights and responsibilities within the group. A handout on communication skills, given to members early in the school term, helps eliminate problems and encourages a relaxed, productive group (Figure 7–2). Use the handout as a guide. This handout, along with a description of group roles (Table 7.1), will enable group members to grow into productive participants in group interaction. As a leader, it is your responsibility to share these communication tips with the group membership.

**FIGURE 7–2**
Criteria for group communication.

---

**CRITERIA FOR GROUP COMMUNICATION**

1. Come to the meeting ready to ask questions and share your ideas.

2. Once your ideas and thoughts are given to the group, do not feel compelled to defend them. Once shared, they become the group's property to discuss and consider. Clarify meaning if it would help the group proceed, but don't feel responsible for the idea just because you suggested it.

3. Speak freely and communicate feelings. Listen to others with consideration and understanding for their feelings.

4. Accept others in the interchange of ideas. Allow them to have opinions that differ from yours. Do not ignore or reject members of the group.

5. Engage in friendly disagreements. Listen critically and carefully to suggestions others have to offer. Differences of opinion bring forth a variety of ideas.

6. Be sincere. Reveal your true self. Communicate in an atmosphere of mutual trust.

7. Allow and promote individual freedom. Do not manipulate, suppress, or ridicule other group members. Encourage their creativity and individuality.

8. Work hard, acknowledge the contributions of others, and focus on the objectives of the group's task.

**TABLE 7.1**
Role interaction. Both task and maintenance roles are necessary for effective group participation.

| Task Roles | Group Building or Maintenance Roles | Dysfunctional Roles |
| --- | --- | --- |
| Initiator–leader | Encourager | Dominator |
| Facilitator | Harmonizer | Aggressor |
| Information giver/seeker | Listener | Negativist |
| Clarifier | Follower | Flirtatious |
| Questioner | Tension breaker | Blocker |
| Asserter | Compromiser | Competitor |
| Energizer | Standard setter | Recognition seeker |
| Elaborator | Observer | Deserter |
| Orientator | Recorder | Challenger |
| Opinion giver | Gatekeeper | |
| Opinion seeker | | |
| Summarizer | | |

## General Qualifications

The following pointers emphasize the leader's personality, interpersonal relationships, and skill in handling group discussions:

A. Leader's personality.
1. Ability to think and act quickly. The leader may need to change plans on the spur of the moment.
2. Ability to get along with others, be well liked, and not have a tendency to "fly off the handle."
3. Respect for the opinions of others. The leader should be a good listener and avoid telling others what to think.
4. Willingness to remain in the background. Instead of voicing opinions, ask questions and guide but do not dominate.
5. Freedom from prejudice.
B. Leader's knowledge and skills.
1. Knowledge of the discussion method. The leader must know the purpose and the procedure agreed upon if the meeting is to be successful.
2. Knowledge of the opinions of authorities on the subject so that conclusions will be based on evidence rather than on the leader's opinion.

3. Skill in asking questions. The leader should present questions that bring out the opinions of others. He or she should use questions to avoid hasty decisions or the acceptance of conclusions not based on good evidence. Throwing out a question to the group can help the leader avoid expressing personal opinions. The following suggestions give examples of how to handle certain situations that may arise in a discussion:
a. To call attention to a point that has not been considered: "Has anyone thought about this phase of the problem—or about this possible solution?"
b. To evaluate the strengths of an argument: "What reasons do we have for accepting this statement?"
c. To get back to causes: "Why do you suppose a child—or a parent—feels or acts this way?"
d. To question the source of information or argument: "Who gathered these statistics that you spoke of?" or "Would you care to identify the authority you are quoting?"
e. To suggest that new information has not been added: "Can anyone add a new idea to the information already given on this point?"

f. To register steps of agreement or disagreement: "Am I correct in assuming that all of us agree [or disagree] with this point?"

g. To bring a generalizing speaker down to earth: "Can you give us a specific example?" or "Your general idea is good, but I wonder if we can't make it more concrete. Does anyone know of a case . . . ?"

h. To handle the member who has "all the answers": "Would your idea work in all cases?" or "Let's get a variety of opinions on this point."

i. To bring an individual back to the subject: "I wonder if you can relate your ideas to the subject we are discussing?"

j. To handle a question directed to the leader:
   (1) If the leader knows the answer but does not wish to be set up as an authority, the question can be redirected to the group.
   (2) The leader can quote from resource material and ask for additional opinions.
   (3) If the leader is a specialist in the area, occasional questions may be answered.
   (4) The leader can say, "I don't know. Who does? Shall we research this?"

k. To cut off a long-winded speaker: "While we're on this point, let's hear from the others," or "Shall we save your next point until later?"

l. To help the members who may have difficulty expressing themselves: "I wonder if I am interpreting you correctly—were you saying . . . ?" or "Can we tie in what you are saying with our subject something like this . . ."

m. To encourage further questions: "I'm glad you raised that question. Can anyone answer?"

n. To break up a heated argument: "I'm sure all of us feel strongly about this. Would some of the rest of you care to express opinions?"

o. To be sensitive to body language of the group, watch for people who want to speak and bring out their contributions.[1]

---

[1]From "Pointers for discussion group leaders" in *Parent Education and Preschool Department Leadership Handbook,* by Denver Public Schools. (n.d.). Denver, CO: Author.

Leaders initiate, plan, guide, and build group norms; give support; challenge; and encourage group growth. In building the group norms, special attention should be paid to the feelings of people in the group.

1. Each person is respected, listened to, and recognized.
2. The meeting is a safe place to be; no one will be ridiculed or put down.
3. Feelings are important, and the expression of feelings helps the group solve problems.
4. Feelings may be discussed.
5. The participants and leader are encouraged to be objective. (Adapted from Denver Public Schools, n.d.)

Leaders who show a caring attitude are most effective. They offer protection, affection, praise, and encouragement as well as friendship. But caring is not enough. The effective leader is there to give support, explain, and clarify if needed.

## USING TECHNOLOGY

The increased use of communication through the Internet allows parents, leaders, teachers, and students to interact virtually. The process allows participants to respond to one another with the added convenience of flexible schedules and immediate discussion. This is especially true for those parents who live a distance from the school or meeting place and for those whose work schedule or children at home make it impossible for them to attend meetings.

### E-mail

E-mail may be used to communicate and provides an opportunity for an immediate response. It can be used to give information and to receive parent responses and questions.

### Web Sites

Schools can develop Web sites that communicate with parents about the happenings at school. Emergencies can be explained, assignments may be posted and explained, and links that include articles about educational ideas and procedures for improving academic achievement may be included. Articles that concern education and child development can be placed on the Web site for the parents or students to read. If the school has had some difficulty with bullying and rejection of some students by others, information from the school can help set up programs and encourage both parents and the school to work on the concerns.

For parents who cannot attend meetings because of their schedules, the Internet expands their opportunities to be involved with the school. Chat rooms or blogs are particularly helpful for parents who want to be informed but who cannot attend meetings. Schools can also become more technologically efficient by allowing parents to join in meetings online through communication Web sites such as Skype. By working with the district's technology department, schools not only are using technology to communicate with parents, but can create communities or practice by thinking outside of the box.

## :: ESTABLISHING A POSITIVE ATMOSPHERE

### Icebreakers

To create an accepting, warm atmosphere, get-acquainted activities help people relax and become involved in the group. These icebreakers range from introductions of the person to mixers during breaks.

### While Members Gather

**Signature Sheets.** Make a form before the meeting that includes statements about people. Following each statement is a signature blank. These sheets can be made specifically for the group or can be broad enough to be used in any group. It is important to select activities that are culturally relevant to parents so that they get to enjoy the activity. The kinds of signature sheets are not limited—create original ones. As the group arrives, give one to each participant. Encourage mixing and meeting new people. By the time the period is completed, the members will have an opportunity to meet and talk with a large number of people. A typical signature sheet is shown in Figure 7–3A. Figure 7–3B illustrates another design for a signature sheet.

A word of caution regarding signature sheets: if a parent refuses to sign, have her or him pair up with another parent—it may just be that the parent may not know how to read or write. In my experiences working with parents, I have met parents who did not know how to read or write in their home language much less English. I recall one parent signing with an X and sitting in the back of the room. If the parents stay quiet and in the back of the room, this may be an indication that they may not feel comfortable with opening activities that require them to be literate. This activity can also be used as a needs-assessment activity because it is showing the need to provide literacy classes for adults.

**Bingo Card.** Give each member a card that contains 12 to 25 squares, as shown in Figure 7–4. Ask members to fill each blank with a signature.

### FIGURE 7–3A
Use a get-acquainted activity such as a signature sheet at the beginning of a meeting.

Find people who meet the qualifications listed below and have them sign their names.

1. Find someone who is wearing the same color clothes as you. _____
2. Find someone who has the same color eyes as you. _____
3. Find someone who has the same number of children as you. _____
4. Find someone who lives in the same area as you. _____
5. Find someone who has a child the same age as yours. _____
6. Find someone who likes to go hiking. _____
7. Find someone who plays the piano. _____
8. Find someone who has the same hobby as you. _____
9. Find someone who has lived in this state as long as you have. _____
10. Find someone who was brought up in the same area you were. _____

## FIGURE 7–3B

During the next few minutes, you are to find people who have the same attributes as you. Have them sign their names in the wheel of friendship between the wheel spokes.

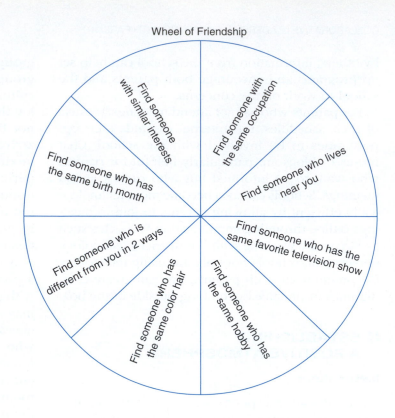

Wheel of Friendship

- Find someone with similar interests
- Find someone with the same occupation
- Find someone who lives near you
- Find someone who has the same favorite television show
- Find someone who has the same hobby
- Find someone who has the same color hair
- Find someone who is different from you in 2 ways
- Find someone who has the same birth month

## FIGURE 7–4

Find a person who can sign the squares. When you have completed an entire line, you can call "Bingo!" Bingo games can use initials or attributes of the members of the group.

| I watch television regularly. | I enjoy reading. | I have more than two children. | I like to dance. | My favorite color is orange. |
|---|---|---|---|---|
| I have dark hair. | I like to go shopping. | I enjoy skiing. | I enjoy hiking. | I enjoy biking. |
| I have red hair. | I have blonde hair. | I have brown eyes. | I have blue eyes. | I have a son. |
| I have two children. | I live near here. | I have lived in this area for more than one year. | I enjoy music. | I enjoy helping in school. |
| I exercise regularly. | I have a daughter. | I have a brother. | I have a sister. | I work outside the home. |

Signatures may not be repeated. This encourages interaction with all members. For English language learners, make sure that the bingo cards are in their language.

A variation of the bingo card includes a letter within each square. Find someone whose name begins with that letter. Check the roster ahead of time and use the members' initials in the squares. Another variation is similar to the signature sheet but asks for the signature of someone who fulfills the attribute.

**Who Am I?** Attach a piece of paper with the name of a famous person to the back of each person. Members go from person to person asking questions until they determine who they are. Questions must be phrased so that a yes or no answer is adequate. Variations include changing the famous person to an event, an animal, or an educational statement.

**Scrambled Name Tags.** Make up name tags with letters out of order, for example, *Ilaehs* (Sheila). Have the members try to figure out each name as they talk with each person. Obviously, this has to be done at the first or second meeting, before the group becomes acquainted.

### After Members Are Seated

**Dyad Introductions.** Have members talk to each other in pairs with the idea that they will introduce each other. You may give specific instructions, for example, to ask the number of children in the family and what the member expects from parent education, or you may leave the discussion completely up to the two individuals. Following the discussion, go around the room and have members introduce their partners.

It is interesting to have the dyad discuss memory questions, such as something the partner remembers that happened before the age of 5 or the person's happiest experience. This activity can be used later in the year as well as at the beginning. Allow members to introduce themselves. Topics they might use include the following:

My secret hiding place was . . .
As a child I liked to . . . best.
Summertime was . . .

If I had my wish, I would be . . .
What I liked most about school was . . .
What I remember about walking or riding the bus home from school was . . .

**I've Got a Secret.** After people have become acquainted, ask each participant to write a secret on a piece of paper. (Be sure that the person does not mind having the secret revealed.) Place the pieces of paper in a bag, and as they are drawn and read, group members try to guess who has that secret.

Activities that promote good relations and allow members to get acquainted are limited only by the planner's imagination. The chairperson or leader may be in charge of this part of the program or may delegate the responsibility to a number of persons charged with the task of discovering new means of interaction.

## ▓ GROUP ROLES

Within each group, roles emerge that are functional and task oriented and that move the group forward; others that are group sustaining, expressive, and maintain the group; and still others that are negative and dysfunctional and reduce the effectiveness of the group. Group members should be given descriptions of group roles to help them identify their participatory roles or roles that they would like to develop (see Table 7.1).

Roles emerge within groups and influence the interactive process. A **role,** defined as the behavior characteristic of a person occupying a particular position in the social system, influences the actions of the person and the expectations of others toward that person. Parent groups (in this text) are the "social system"; members of the group expect certain norms or standards of behavior from the perceived leader of the group. These role expectations are projected in members' role behavior toward the leader. Likewise, the leader's own interpretation of the role influences the resulting role behavior or role performance.

Role continuity is easier to obtain in parent education groups with ongoing memberships. Parents are encouraged to participate for at least 2 years. New officers and leaders, already familiar with the standards of the group, may be elected in the spring and be ready to take over leadership in the fall. Although this system ensures greater continuity than the establishment of a new group each year, the returning members must be careful to be flexible, open to new ideas, and sensitive to the desires of new members.

Early in the year, a session may include a discussion of roles and group dynamics. Role playing is an excellent mechanism for clarifying role behavior. If group members are aware of the effects that roles have on the functioning of a group, they will not fall into dysfunctional roles so readily.

A leader can deter or eliminate the problem of domination or withdrawal by group members if members are aware of roles and how each member of the group can influence the group's functioning, either positively or negatively. Most people do not want to be viewed as dysfunctional members and will, therefore, refrain from acting in ways that are detrimental to group interaction. I have used this technique of discussing roles in parent groups and classes for many years and have found that the group discussion and the role playing of group roles greatly enhance the productivity of the group.

Knowing how to handle the situation stated in the previous paragraph will encourage some members, but it can also inhibit others who worry about which role theory they are enacting. Although this is a possible negative result of a discussion of group roles, role definition can benefit the total group in the elimination of one common problem in groups—domination of the discussion by a few participants. It is also beneficial to reticent communicators to learn that they can become productive group members despite the inability to express themselves. Asking questions, being an active listener, and being a positive member of the group are shown to be valuable contributions to a well-functioning discussion group. When balanced out, the positive aspects of discussing group roles overshadow the negative ones. One word of caution, however— do not wait until a problem has become obvious before discussing dysfunctional roles. That would embarrass and alienate the person who has been a negative contributor. It is best to handle such a problem through the leadership techniques discussed previously in the chapter.

## DYNAMICS OF ROLES WITHIN GROUPS

Observation of interaction within groups shows that role behavior influences the cohesiveness and productivity of the group. Observation will be facilitated if analysis of the group is based on role interaction (Table 7.1), wherein behaviors within a group are divided into task, group building and maintenance, and dysfunctional roles.

### Task Roles

The roles related to the task area in Table 7.1 are attributed to members of the group who initiate, question, and facilitate reaching the group's goals or objectives. The roles related to group building or maintenance are attributed to members of the group who support and maintain the cohesiveness, solidarity, and productivity of the group.

### Dysfunctional or Individual Roles

The roles in this area are attributed to members who place their own individual needs, which are not relevant to group goals, above group needs. These individual goals are not functional or productive to group achievement, but if such members are brought into the group process, they can become contributing participants.

Members of groups generally do not fit into only one role category. Members may participate in a task role and switch to a maintenance role with the next action or comment. For example, Elena is anxious about absenteeism and suggests that the group might improve attendance by organizing a carpool. Lisa responds by suggesting a telephone network to contact members. Elena welcomes the idea, saying, "Good thought, Lisa. We might be able to start right away." Elena, within the space of 2 minutes, has initiated an idea, acting in a task-oriented role, and has then supported Lisa's contribution with a group-building or maintenance statement. There may be moments when members lapse into a dysfunctional role, but as long as the mix of interaction remains primarily positive and productive, the group will be effective.

## ROLE DESCRIPTIONS

The following role descriptions are based on Beal and colleagues (1962); Benne and Sheets (1948); Borchers, (1999); King (1962); and MSU Extension (1999).

## Task-Oriented

Task roles are the roles that initiate and keep the group discussion meaningful and ongoing:

*Initiator–leader*—Initiates the discussion, guides but does not dominate, contributes ideas or suggestions that help move the group forward.

*Facilitator*—Helps the group stay on track and encourages member participation.

*Information giver*—Contributes information and facts that are from authoritative sources and are relevant to the ongoing discussion.

*Information seeker*—Asks for clarification or expansion of an issue from additional relevant, authoritative information.

*Clarifier*—Restates the discussion of an issue so that points are made clear to the group and relationships between ideas are clear.

*Orientator*—Takes a look at the group's position in relation to the objectives of the meetings and where the discussion is going and as a result may refocus the group discussion.

*Questioner*—Asks questions about issues, requests clarification, or offers constructive criticism.

*Asserter*—States a position in a positive manner; may take a different point of view and disagree with opinions or suggestions without attacking them.

*Energizer*—Stimulates and facilitates the group to action and increased output and problem solving.

*Elaborator*—Expands an idea or concept; brings out details, points, and alternatives that may have been overlooked.

*Opinion giver*—States own opinion on the situation, basing the contribution on personal experiences.

*Opinion seeker*—Requests suggestions from others according to their life experiences and value orientation.

*Summarizer*—Brings out facts, ideas, and suggestions made by the group in an attempt to clarify the group's position during the meeting and at the conclusion.

## Group-Building and Maintenance Roles

**Group-building** and **maintenance roles** help the group develop and maintain the existence and quality of the group. The first six roles will emerge within the group:

*Encourager*—Supports, praises, and recognizes other members of the group; builds self-confidence and self-concept of others.

*Harmonizer*—Mediates misunderstandings and clarifies conflicting statements and disagreements; adds to the discussion in a calming and tension-reducing manner.

*Listener*—Is involved in the discussion through quiet attention to the group process; gives support through body language and eye contact.

*Follower*—Serves as a supportive member of the discussion by accepting the ideas and suggestions of others.

*Tension breaker*—Uses humor or clarifying statements to relieve tension within the group.

*Compromiser*—Views both sides of the question and offers solutions or suggestions that move group to a position that fits conflicting viewpoints.

The following four roles are appointed or elected positions:

*Standard setter*—Sets standards for group performance; may apply standards as an evaluative technique for the meeting.

*Observer*—Charts the group process throughout the meeting and uses the data for evaluation of group interaction.

*Recorder*—Records decisions and ideas for group use throughout the meeting.

*Gatekeeper*—Regulates time spent and membership participation during various parts of the program; keeps communication open and the meeting on schedule.

## Dysfunctional Roles

**Dysfunctional roles** interfere with achievement of the goals of the group:

*Dominator*—Monopolizes the meeting and asserts superiority by attempting to manipulate the group.

*Aggressor*—Shows aggression toward the group in a variety of forms; for example, attacks ideas, criticizes others, denigrates others' contributions, and disapproves of solutions.

*Challenger*—Challenges other group members' ideas and suggestions.

*Negativist*—Demonstrates pessimism and disapproval of suggestions that emerge within the group; sees the negative side of the issue and rejects new insights.

*Flirtatious*—Spends time mostly getting the attention of the opposite sex.

*Blocker*—Opposes decision making and attempts to block actions by introducing alternatives that have already been rejected.

*Competitor*—Competes with other members of the discussion group by challenging their ideas and expressing and defending his or her own suggestions.

*Recognition seeker*—Needs recognition and focus on himself or herself.

*Deserter*—Leaves the group in spirit and mind but not in body; doodles, looks around the room, appears uninterested, and stays aloof and indifferent to the group process.

## :: PRODUCTIVE GROUPS

In productive groups, members of the group are both active and productive:

1. Members listen and pay attention to one another.
2. Members discuss the subject at hand.
3. Everyone's ideas and suggestions are welcomed.
4. Everyone has a chance to state his or her views.
5. The group uses its agenda as a guide for discussion.
6. One or two members are appointed to summarize the discussion and to see that everyone has had a chance to speak.
7. Members know and use problem-solving steps.
8. Members are clear about group decisions and committed to them (MSU Extension, 1999).

Less-productive groups often do the following:

1. Members do not listen and everyone tends to talk at the same time.
2. The discussion jumps from one idea to another.
3. Some members' ideas don't seem to count, so they feel that they don't belong.
4. One or two members do all the talking.
5. The agenda is not clear, and there is no written guide for discussion.
6. No one summarizes or checks to see if everyone who wants to speak has actually spoken. Discussions go on and on until people get tired.
7. No order is followed for identifying and solving problems.
8. Decision making is muddy and people are not committed to the plan (MSU Extension, 1999).

### Role-Playing Group Roles

Early in the formation of a group, members can benefit from a session in which they role play task, maintenance, and dysfunctional roles while discussing an issue of high interest. This exercise will illustrate to members how role performance can support or destroy a group. It is practical to arrange seating in two concentric circles, allowing the inner circle to discuss an issue in light of the roles assigned, whereas the outer circle observes and analyzes the roles being demonstrated. The session will be humorous, with members enthusiastically playing dysfunctional roles, but it should end with the understanding that each member is important to the effectiveness of the group process. It is also important to observe the course of the session. If there is any indication that a participant is having difficulty functioning within the group, the leader needs to provide support and redirect the activity.

**Observer.** Analytical observation of group interaction reveals patterns that are not always obvious to the casual observer. A systematic observation can pinpoint problems and illustrate strengths to the members. One simple technique for analytical observation is the construction of a discussion wheel. A diagram of the participants is made, with names or numbers reflecting individual members. If the participants are sitting in a circle, the diagram would be similar to the one in Figure 7–5.

As members speak, the observer uses arrows to record the direction of each interaction. An arrow pointed toward the center indicates that the communicator is speaking to the group; an arrow pointed from one member to another represents a statement made to an individual rather than to the group (Beal et al., 1962). A glance at Figure 7–5 shows that Ralph did not make any suggestions; he had either withdrawn from the group or lacked its supportive encouragement. Most members contributed to the group process rather than making side comments to individual communicators. As interaction continues throughout the meeting, the observer can make cross marks on the arrows to reflect duplication of communication, eliminating an overabundance of lines in the observation circle (Figure 7–6).

## FIGURE 7–5
Group interaction recorded on an observation wheel.

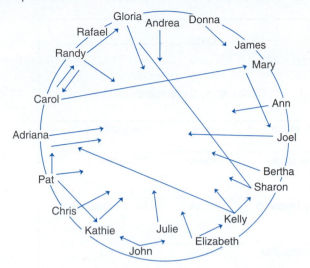

## FIGURE 7–6
Group interaction is anonymously recorded on an observation wheel. Each time a person speaks, a mark is added to the interaction line. In this manner, one can see how often and to whom each participant communicates.

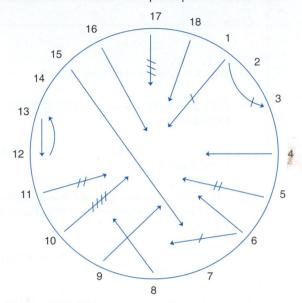

**End-of-Meeting Evaluations.** Evaluations are used effectively by many groups to see if the needs of the group are being met. Because every group is somewhat different, evaluations should be constructed to meet the needs of the group and should be based on the goals and objectives of the meeting. Sample evaluations are helpful, however, to guide the group in its development of evaluative methods that work for that particular group. The example in Figure 7–7 may be adapted to any group's needs.

## :: TYPES OF MEETINGS

Meetings can range from formal lectures to informal buzz sessions. In parent groups informal meetings are used most often to reinforce the active involvement that proves so critical to understanding concepts and changing attitudes. The formal meeting has its place; however, if the group needs a specialist to give an organized background lecture on a specific topic. Figure 7–8 illustrates types of meetings that can be used as needs, time, space, subject, and resources dictate. On the right are meetings that are the most informal and require active involvement by the participants; in the center is the panel meeting; on the left is the most formal lecture where the only audience participation is listening to the speaker. Although each type of meeting has its place in parent group meetings, the informal meeting elicits more participation by group members—a

necessary ingredient for attitude clarification, learning, and change.

## :: ARRANGEMENTS FOR MEETINGS

All parent group meetings require certain procedures, regardless of the meeting format. Also, parents need to feel physically and emotionally comfortable at every meeting, whether formal or informal. To ensure this, the person in charge of the meeting should do the following for all meetings:

1. Check the meeting room to be sure the temperature is appropriate, the ventilation and lighting are adequate, and the room is large enough to accommodate the group.
2. As members or guests arrive, make them feel welcome. Greet them, offer name tags, and suggest that they have refreshments, look at a book display, or participate in an icebreaker activity before the meeting begins. Call members or guests by name as soon as possible.
3. Have refreshments available before the meeting, during the break, or at both times. A 15-minute refreshment period before the meeting gives latecomers an opportunity to arrive

**FIGURE 7–7**

A meeting evaluation form lets you know exactly how the participants viewed the program.

Topic: _____     Date: _____

Group: _____

Check along the continuum.

1. Was the meeting of interest to you?

| Very much | Some | Very little |
|---|---|---|

2. Did you receive any pertinent ideas that will be helpful to you?

| Many ideas | Some | No ideas |
|---|---|---|

3. Did the group participate and seem involved in the meeting?

| Very involved | Some | No involvement |
|---|---|---|

4. Did the meeting give you any new insights, or did you change any of your attitudes as a result of the meeting?

| New insights | Some | No effect |
|---|---|---|

5. Were you encouraged to contribute as much as you wanted?

| Participation encouraged | Neutral | Left out |
|---|---|---|

6. Did the leader respond to the needs of the group?

| Good leadership | Neutral | No leadership |
|---|---|---|

7. Was there adequate preparation by the members?

| Excellent preparation | Some | Poor preparation |
|---|---|---|

8. Were group members encouraged to participate?

| Strong | Average | Poor |
|---|---|---|

9. Was there enough time for discussion?

| Too much | Just right | No time |
|---|---|---|

10. Was the atmosphere conducive to freedom of expression?

| Safe environment | Neutral | Felt threatened |
|---|---|---|

11. Do you have any suggestions for improvement?

12. What were the strong points of the meeting?

13. Comments:

You do not need to sign this sheet.

**FIGURE 7–8**

Types of meetings range from the informal on the right to very formal on the left.

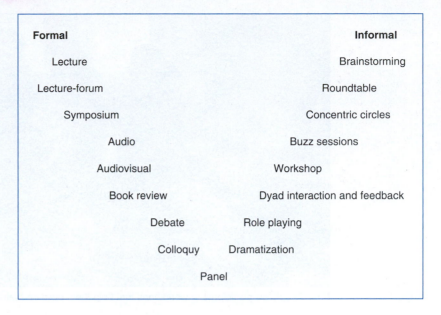

| Formal | | Informal |
| --- | --- | --- |
| Lecture | | Brainstorming |
| Lecture-forum | | Roundtable |
| Symposium | | Concentric circles |
| Audio | | Buzz sessions |
| Audiovisual | | Workshop |
| Book review | | Dyad interaction and feedback |
| Debate | Role playing | |
| Colloquy | Dramatization | |
| | Panel | |

before discussion commences. It also sets a relaxed tone and gives members a forum for informal interaction.

4. As participants arrive, involve them in an informal discussion through an icebreaker activity. Get-acquainted activities are important, but choose an appropriate one. For meetings at which few people know one another, it may prove beneficial to use a signature sheet or the dyad-introductions technique of asking the entire group to form into pairs, with each partner introducing the other one to the group.

5. In large groups where icebreakers are not appropriate, the participants can respond to group questions—where they live, what they do, how many children they have, what their interests are, and so on. Responses to the questions (by a show of hands or verbal answers) help the speaker know more about the audience to be addressed, and audience members feel they have been recognized.

6. After the group feels comfortable, the meeting can commence. Open discussion is part of all but the most formal or informal meetings, so it is important that all group leaders are able to conduct discussion sessions. Debates, panels, audiovisual aids, buzz sessions, workshops, role playing, book reviews, dramatizations, and observations can precede open discussion. The leader should gauge the time and conclude the meeting.

7. After the presentation and discussion (or question-and-answer session), thank the presenters and give appropriate recognition for their contributions.

8. Announce any specific instructions necessary for the next meeting before the group disperses.

The descriptions of the types of meetings that follow are compiled from Eugenia Berger's experiences with parent education (Since she directed a parent-education and preschool program for nearly 4 years). Additional information can be found in Applbaum et al. (1979), Denver Public Schools (n.d.), and Kawin (1970).

### Roundtables (Open Discussions)

Although not the most informal meeting available, the **roundtable** is a true open discussion, the mainstay of group interaction (see Figure 7–9). It is used to complement most meetings, such as panels, symposiums, role-playing sessions, or buzz sessions. The roundtable discussion is also used for decision-making meetings and parent councils.

In a roundtable discussion, all members are encouraged to participate throughout the meeting. Care must be taken to promote good communication among all members of the group. To facilitate good group interaction, leaders should keep in

Parents actively participate in workshops that help them build on their leadership skills.

**FIGURE 7–9**
The roundtable is the basic open discussion group.

mind the following suggestions from the Denver Public Schools:[2]

1. Have a clear understanding of the topic as defined by the group.
2. Obtain materials.
3. Get a general knowledge, through reading, to be able to direct and add to the contributions from the group.
4. Be sure to plan an introduction that will stimulate interest of the group.
5. Prepare a logical, progressive list of questions to start the ball rolling and keep it moving.
6. Keep the discussion on track; keep it always directed, but let the group lay its own track to a large extent. Don't groove it narrowly yourself.
7. Be alert to adjust questions to needs of group—omit, change, reword.
8. Remember—the leader's opinion doesn't count in the discussion. Keep your own view out of it. Your job is to get the ideas of others out for airing.
9. If you see that some important angle is being neglected, point it out: "Bill Jones was telling me last week that he thinks. . . . What do you think of that?"
10. Keep spirits high. Encourage ease, informality, good humor. Let everybody have a good time. Foster friendly disagreement. Listen to all ideas with respect and appreciation, but stress what is important and turn discussion away from what is not.
11. Take time every 10 minutes or so to draw loose ends together: "Let's see where we've been going." Be as fair and accurate in summary as possible. Close the discussion with a summary—your own or the secretary's.
12. Call attention to unanswered questions for future study or for your reference back to speakers. Nourish a desire in group members for continuing study and discussion through a skillful closing summary.

Problems that could emerge in a roundtable meeting include domination of the discussion by one or two members, withdrawal from the group and side discussions by two or three people, or lack of preparation by the members. Good leadership

makes it possible to avoid these pitfalls. If the leader is prepared for the meeting and if members come to the meeting prepared, have relevant experiences, or have background expertise on the subject, the meeting can be a most effective means of changing attitudes and educating members. It allows all members to contribute and become involved in discussion, clarification of issues, and decision making.

### Arrangements Before the Meeting

1. Select a topic for open discussion and announce it to the membership.
2. Provide members with materials and bibliography.
   a. Duplicate and distribute background information on the topic through a distribution system or at a meeting before the roundtable.
   b. Select members to read relevant material before the meeting.
   c. Come to the meeting well prepared and ready to guide but not dominate.

### Setup

1. Arrange chairs in a circle or semicircle or around tables so that all participants can see each other and eye contact is possible.
2. Check the room for comfort—ventilation, lighting, and heat.

### Procedure

1. The leader starts the meeting with a thought-provoking question or statement of fact. Throughout the discussion, the leader tries to keep the meeting from wandering. Before the meeting, the leader has prepared a list of questions or statements that may keep the discussion moving forward.
2. During the meeting, the leader avoids dominating the discussion. Instead, the leadership role brings others into the discussion, helps clarify, and keeps the meeting on the topic.
3. The leader summarizes at the conclusion.
4. If the members want to take action on the conclusions, the leader should call for appropriate action, help the group make plans, and assign tasks.

### Appropriate Topics

1. Learning activities that work
2. Behavior and misbehavior

---

[2]From *Parent Education and Preschool Department Leadership Handbook*, by Denver Public Schools. (n.d.). Denver, CO: Author.

3. Influence of Internet, videogames, and television on children
4. Rivalry between brothers and sisters
5. Problem solving
6. Bullying in the schools.
7. Helping children cope with terrorism.

## Concentric Circles

The **concentric-circle arrangement** is a variation of the open discussion or roundtable meeting. Instead of one circle, there are two—one inside the other—with everyone facing the center. The dialogue among members is similar to that of the open discussion, only the smaller circle within the larger circle contains the communicators at first (Figure 7–10). Divide the group so that the smaller group has six to 12 people. The members of the smaller group discuss the issue; those in the larger group listen to the discussion. After a designated time of five to 10 minutes, the meeting is opened to the entire group. If you have 24 to 30 people, with people who are reticent in a large group, the concentric circle will help solve the problem. Those within the inner circle form a small group with which to interact. This arrangement precipitates more discussion from them and succeeds in getting the total group interested in the discussion. Those sitting in the outer circle are required to listen,

**FIGURE 7–10**
Concentric circles encourage those who might not participate freely to get involved.

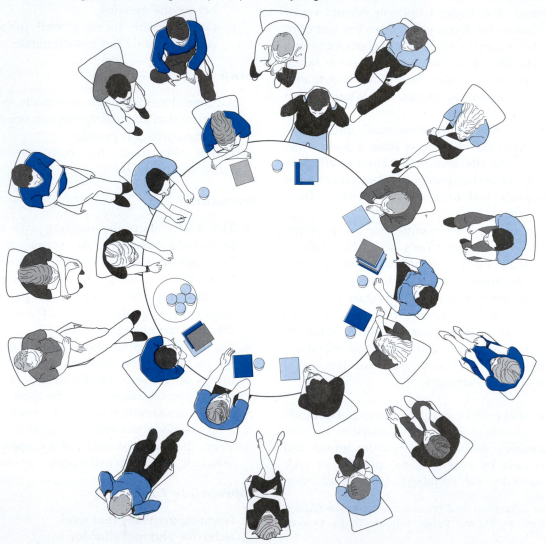

but the statements, questions, and ideas offered usually promote their interest as they listen. This method is surprisingly effective in getting groups to discuss. By the time the discussion is opened up to the entire group, many ideas have emerged.

### Setup

1. Arrange chairs with one large circle on the outside and a smaller circle within the larger circle.
2. Review the "Arrangement for Meetings" section and make appropriate preparations.

### Procedure

1. The leader of the total group may request a volunteer leader for the inner circle, or the leader may take that role.
2. The session is started with a statement or question to promote interest and dialogue.
3. The inner circle discusses the topic, using a small-group, open-discussion format. The outer circle listens. At the end of a designated period (for example, six minutes), the discussion may be opened to all in the room. At that time, the leader continues to control the meeting but does not dominate it.
4. For variation, reverse the roles. Those now in the outer circle move to the inner circle and have the opportunity for more-involved discussion, while those from the outer circle listen to this discussion. A separate issue or different questions concerning one issue may be used for each group in its discussion.

### Appropriate Topics

1. How to build self-esteem in children
2. What to expect of 2-, 3-, 4-, or 5-year-olds
3. Problem solving
4. Living with change
5. Positive uses of the Internet, video games, and television
6. Courses and workshops that could be offered at school
7. Issues and concerns of children

## Buzz Sessions

**Buzz sessions** are an excellent means of eliciting participation from all members of the group. They must be small enough to allow interaction among all participants. The smallest session consists of two people, and the maximum size should be six to eight. This makes it possible for all members to have the chance to express their opinions easily. Even in a large group, the audience can divide into smaller groups and discuss. The latter is called a 6–6 discussion, with six people discussing for six minutes. Because the session time is limited, it does not allow thorough examination of issues, but it does bring forth ideas from all involved in a very short period of time—an objective that is not accomplished in an open discussion with a large group.

### Setup

1. Up to 24 people.
   a. Arrange chairs in a circle or semicircle.
   b. When the smaller group session is to begin, six people turn their chairs together to form their group. It is also possible for a group to move to another area for a quieter meeting.
2. Large auditorium.
   a. If people are seated in rows, three people turn around and discuss with three people behind them.
   b. Use some other technique to form groups of six throughout the auditorium.

### Procedure

1. Buzz sessions may be formed at the beginning of the meeting, or they may be initiated later. The leader announces the formation of buzz groups either by proximity of chairs, a common interest in specific discussion areas, or by a mechanism to distribute members, such as counting off 1 through 6 and having those with common numbers form a group.
2. Each group chooses a leader and a recorder.
3. The topic is introduced to the group for discussion, and people are encouraged to participate much as they would in any other small-group discussion.
4. The recorder keeps relevant thoughts ready to report back to the larger group. In the smaller meeting (24 people), each group might have the time to give a short report to the total group. In an auditorium 6–6 meeting, it might not be possible to have everyone report back. Allow a specific number of groups that indicate interest in doing so to report back to the total audience.

## *Appropriate Topics*

1. Home-management tips
2. Feelings about childrearing
3. Discipline
4. Moral values
5. Vacation ideas on a budget
6. Solving problems around the home
7. Issues concerning school
8. Decisions that should be made concerning education

## Brainstorming Sessions

**Brainstorming** is a unique method of active interaction by all members of the group. It promotes interchange, encourages lateral thinking, and facilitates expansion of thought. In brainstorming sessions, all contributions are accepted. Everyone is encouraged to suggest ideas and solutions. The participants may add to, combine, or modify other ideas, or they may introduce something new. There are no value judgments on the quality of suggestions.

The free and open brainstorming session provides an environment that facilitates the production of a variety of ideas from the participants. Members who are reluctant to contribute during an open discussion because they are not sure their ideas are worthy have a guaranteed safe environment in which to contribute during brainstorming. Quantity of ideas is the object. Later, the ideas may be analyzed, judged as to quality, and reduced to selected items. The brainstorming technique, therefore, is excellent for stimulation of diversified thought and solutions to issues and problems. It also reinforces the socioemotional aspects of a group by accepting the contributions of all people freely.

### *Setup*

1. Arrange chairs in a circle if the group has fewer than 30 members. A small group allows for more interaction.
2. Brainstorming may be used in a larger group with an auditorium arrangement of chairs. In that case, the entire group has difficulty participating, but the mechanism is effective for bringing forth a quantity of ideas and thoughts.

### *Procedure*

1. The brainstorming session requires a leader and a recorder.
   a. Appoint a recorder or ask for a volunteer.
   b. Appoint a leader or assume the leadership role.
2. The leader begins the brainstorming session by explaining the rules and emphasizing that all contributions are wanted and accepted. Even if ideas seem unusual, all members should contribute. Ideas should be interjected as they occur.
3. The topic or issue is explained to the group.
4. The session is opened to contributions from the group.
5. The recorder writes on a board or piece of paper all the ideas that come from the group.
6. After a selected amount of time—4, 6, or 10 minutes, depending on the issue and the flow of ideas—the group may turn to analyzing all the suggestions and pulling out the ones that seem to answer the issue or problem best.
7. A summary of the solutions and ideas gained from brainstorming is reported by the leader.
8. If this is an action meeting, plans for action should be identified at this time.

### *Appropriate Topics*

1. Ideas to solve problems—for example, subjects for meetings, summer activities
2. How to get your child to . . . (eat or go to bed, etc.)
3. Creative activities
4. Exploring your environment
5. Nutrition
6. Ways to improve relations at the school
7. Summer offerings for families

## Workshops and Centers

**Workshops** are a superb means of achieving involvement by members. Most useful for demonstrating programs and curricula, they can also be used as an effective means of explaining procedures, illustrating the learning process, and developing understanding. The major ingredient in a workshop is active participation by members, whether through making puzzles and toys, working on mathematics, painting, modeling with clay, editing a newspaper, composing music, writing poetry, or planning an action.

Although often confused with workshops, **centers** are different in that they do not require participants to be actively involved in the project. Centers allow subgroups of the membership to gather simultaneously in various areas of the room, where they might see a demonstration, hear an explanation of an issue or program, or watch a media presentation. If time allows, more than one center may be visited. The variety of centers is limited only by the imagination and productivity of the planning group. The advantages of this diversified meeting are that (a) it reduces group size and thus promotes more interaction and allows individual questions, (b) participants are able to select topics of interest to them, and (c) tension and anxiety of the presenters are reduced because of the informal format.

### Setup

1. Depending on available space, workshops and centers may take place in separate rooms or in one large room with designated areas.
2. Each presenter might have different requirements. The amount of space and number of tables and chairs requested should be set up according to those requirements.

### Procedure

1. The chairperson explains the variety of workshops or centers available and procedures to be used.
2. Participants choose a workshop or center. These may be assigned according to several Procedures: free choice, numbers on name tags, or preregistration.
3. Participants attend one or more workshops depending on time available. If plans include a time limit for each, the groups proceed from one to the next at a signal.
4. Members may gather together at the close of the meeting, or it may conclude with the final workshop or center.

### Appropriate Topics

1. Learning activities
2. Art activities
3. Bookmaking
4. Games and toys
5. Math activities to do at home
6. Science activities to do at home
7. Rainy-day activities
8. Leadership training session
9. Writers' workshop
10. Learning to read
11. Guidance
12. Outdoor play
13. Traditional children's games
14. Music and songs for young children
15. The environment

## Observations and Field Trips

Although **observations and field trips** can be quite different in their objectives, they are similar in theory and procedure. The active viewing of a classroom, like a visit in the community, encourages the participant to be involved in observing activities. The opportunity to see an activity in process clarifies that process as no written or spoken word can. It is imperative, however, to discuss objectives and points to consider before the field trip or observation. It is also essential to analyze and discuss observations after the visits, to clarify the experience and bring it into focus. Many times, the end of a field trip can be the beginning of a new, expanded project for the individual or group.

### Arrangements Before Observations or Field Trips

1. Select the time and place for the observation or field trip.
   a. Plan classroom visits in advance. Specific objectives may be discussed prior to the observation.
   b. If the classroom has an observation area, observers can easily watch without disturbing the class. If there is no observation area,

Parents work with one another, enchancing collaboration between them.

those going into the classroom should know the teacher's preferred procedure.

  c. Field trips must be planned and permission for visiting obtained.

2. Participants learn more and receive more satisfaction from field trips if background information and items to be aware of are discussed before the visit.

3. If the members are going to a place different from their regular meeting area, group travel arrangements should be made.

## Procedure

1. The leader plans and conducts a previsit orientation.
2. The observation or field trip is completed.
3. Discussion of the experience clarifies the issues and focuses on the learning that has taken place. Many field trips tend to be an end in themselves, but that omits the most important follow-up, where new ideas and greater understanding are generated.

## Appropriate Observations and Field Trips

1. In classroom observations, look for the following:
   a. How children learn
   b. Play—child's work
   c. Interpersonal relations
   d. Aggression
   e. Fine- and gross-motor control
   f. Hand–eye coordination
   g. Stages and ages
2. Field trip options include the following:
   a. Children's museums
   b. Art museums
   c. Parks
   d. Special schools
   e. Newspapers
   f. Hospitals
   g. Businesses
   h. Farms
   i. State legislature

### Dyad or Triad Interaction and Feedback

During structured programs such as STEP and PET, interludes that allow the audience or participants to clarify, practice, and receive feedback on their interaction with others are beneficial. For example, if parents and teachers were working to improve interaction during a conference, sample statements would allow them to practice listening and other communication skills. If the topic were reflective listening, one member of the dyad or triad would share with the others an aspect or concern. The second person would answer with a reflective listening response. The third then would critique the response. Each member of a triad would have an opportunity to play each role: the speaker, listener, and observer.

## Setup

1. Small group (up to 24).
   a. Arrange chairs in a circle, semicircle, or around tables.
   b. Have participants arrange their chairs so that two or three can communicate with each other.
2. Large auditorium.
   a. Start at the beginning of the row and have the aisle person turn and discuss with the person to the right. Dyads or triads can be formed all along each row.

## Procedure

1. After a topic has been described or a video shown, stop the program and have the participants form dyads or triads.
2. Have the dyad or triad decide who will be the speaker, the listener, and the observer.
3. Describe a situation or problem that needs to be clarified or solved. Handouts describing situations are effective in large meetings.
4. Have the participants play out their parts.
5. The observer then critiques the statement and response using positive reinforcement as well as suggestions.

## Appropriate Topics

1. Communication
2. Behavior and misbehavior
3. Determination of problem ownership
4. Reflective and active listening
5. Natural and logical consequences

### Role Playing

**Role playing** is the dramatization of a situation where group members put themselves into designated roles. Role playing is a very informal type of meeting, similar to presenting a drama, so it can be adapted to a variety of situations. The roles that people play can be initiated by the players, or players can follow a set format or enact a specific situation. In either situation, the people playing the roles are to put themselves into those roles. They are to feel that they are the characters in the roles and respond with appropriate reactions and emotions. For this reason, spontaneous role playing is advantageous over the planned drama.

Role playing can be used to demonstrate a problem or develop participants' sensitivities to a situation. In demonstrating a situation, the group members discuss their feelings and reactions and offer solutions. It is an excellent means for getting many people involved in a situation and is easily used to illustrate parent–child interaction.

In development of sensitivity, role reversal is often used. For example, a teacher plays the role of principal while a principal plays the role of teacher. Not only do participants begin to understand the obligations of the other role, but through their playing of the role they also are able to demonstrate their feelings. This clarifies feelings for both parties. Another role-reversal situation that can be used is the parent–child relationship, with one participant playing the child's role and another playing the parent's role. The parent in the child's role develops sensitivity to the child's position.

Participants in role playing feel free to communicate their feelings and attitudes because they are not portraying themselves. This encourages greater openness and involvement. When group members begin role playing, they tend to be hesitant to get involved emotionally with the part. After using role playing for a time, hesitancy and reluctance to be involved disappear and people enjoy the opportunity to participate. If the group progresses to a therapeutic enactment, professional counselors should be included and consulted.

### Setup

1. Role playing can be used in a variety of formats: (a) within the circle of participants—the center of the circle is the stage; (b) with chairs arranged in semicircles and the stage at the front—this is appropriate for larger groups; (c) in a large group meeting with an auditorium stage for the actors.

2. If the role playing is planned for participation by the entire group, allow members to meet first in a circle arrangement and then break into smaller groups after an introduction.

### Procedure

1. A short discussion of the topic or situation is introduced by the leader or panel.
2. The situation that will be role played is introduced. This may be done by (a) volunteers, (b) people selected before the meeting to start the initial role play, or (c) breaking up the total group into groups of four or five, giving each group a topic with an outline of the role situation or a challenge to develop its own role situations.
3. The role can be played in two ways:
   a. It can be done in front of the entire group with members watching and listening to the dramatization and interaction. After the role play, the members use the open discussion method to clarify issues, study the problem, and make decisions.
   b. If the members are divided into smaller groups, it is beneficial to let each group play its roles simultaneously and have each small group discuss the feelings and attitudes that arose while they were playing their roles. After this, the small groups may discuss alternative means, ideas, and solutions.
4. If the small groups have all met and developed specific situations, it is also meaningful to have each group perform its role playing in front of the full group. Afterward, the larger group may discuss the role playing openly. Clarification, questions, and solutions are brought forth at this time.
5. The leader thanks those who participated in role playing.

### Appropriate Topics

1. Parent–teacher conferences
2. Behavioral problems
3. Building self-esteem
4. Reflective listening
5. Roles within groups

### Dramatizations

**Dramatizations** or **short plays**, written by group members or selected from those available from commercial companies, mental health organizations, or social agencies, can be used as springboards to discussions. There is an advantage to using skits composed by members. First, the skit can be kept short with parts that are easy to learn. Second, the action may be specifically related to the group's needs. Third, the preparation of the skit encourages group participants to become actively involved in the process and in the material that is presented.

A variation of the drama can be the use of puppets. Many participants like to use a puppet because it takes away the threat of performing.

### Setup

1. Depending on the number of people at the meeting, the room can be arranged as follows:
   a. Use a circle for a small group, with the dramatization performed as a play in the round.
   b. If the group is small, chairs may be arranged in a semicircle with the "stage" at the opening. The stage may be raised or on the same level as the group members.
   c. If the group is large, an auditorium arrangement is appropriate. The dramatization can be performed on a stage.

### Procedure

1. The leader convenes the meeting and introduces the drama and the cast of characters.
2. The dramatization is presented.
3. Open discussion ensues, which clarifies feelings, emotions, and information presented.
4. The leader thanks the performers.

### Appropriate Topics

1. Family violence
2. Handling the stubborn child
3. Rivalry between children
4. Family rivalry
5. Family conferences
6. Communication among family members

## Panels

A **panel** is an informal presentation by four to six presenters who discuss an issue or idea. Panel members come prepared with background material on a selected subject and, seated behind a table or in a semicircle, discuss the subject among themselves. The presentation allows informal interaction and conversation among the members.

The chairperson, although a member of the panel, has different responsibilities from the other members. The chairperson introduces members, presents the topic, and then encourages participation by the other members. Like a leader, the chairperson can clarify, keep the panel focused on the topic, and summarize the closing.

### Setup

1. Place a table, or two tables slightly turned toward each other, in front of the audience. Set chairs for the panelists behind the table, allowing members to see and converse with one another easily.
2. Seat the audience or remaining members of the group in a semicircle, with the panel facing them. If the audience is large, auditorium-style seating may be used with a panel presentation.

### Procedure

The chairperson does the following:

1. Clarifies the panel procedure to the audience.
2. Presents the topic for discussion and the relevance of the topic to the group's concerns.
3. Introduces the panel members.
4. Starts the discussion with a question or statement. The panelists begin a discussion, freely interacting and conversing with one another.
5. Asks for questions from the audience. Questions are discussed among panelists.
6. Summarizes the major points and the conclusions of the panel.
7. Thanks the panel members for their contributions.

### Appropriate Topics

1. Child development—social, intellectual, emotional, and physical
2. New methods of classroom teaching
3. Bias-free education
4. Exceptional children
5. Influence of drugs and alcohol on children
6. Discipline
7. Emotions in children

8. Managing a home with both parents working
9. Nutrition

## Colloquies

The **colloquy** is a panel discussion by an informed or expert panel where members of the audience are encouraged by the chairperson to interject questions or comments during the presentation. This allows information pertinent to the audience's interests to be discussed during the main part of the presentation instead of waiting for a question-and-answer period after the presentation.

A second form of the colloquy includes two sets of panels, an expert panel and a lay panel. The lay panel uses the procedures for a panel discussion. The expert panel gives advice when called upon by the lay panel or when it thinks pertinent information is being overlooked.

### Setup

1. For a single panel, place chairs behind tables that are turned so the members of the panel can make eye contact with one another.
2. For two panels—lay and expert—seat the chairperson in the center with one panel on the left and one on the right. Both sets of panel members should be facing slightly toward the center so they can see each other and the audience.

### Procedure

1. Single-panel colloquy:
   a. The leader or chairperson explains and clarifies the colloquy procedure to the audience.
   b. The topic for discussion is introduced.
   c. Panel members are introduced.
   d. The chairperson offers a stimulating comment or question to start the discussion.
   e. The chairperson encourages free interaction among panel members and takes questions and comments from the audience.
   f. An open forum follows the conclusion of the panel discussion.
   g. The leader summarizes and concludes the meeting.
2. Dual-panel colloquy:
   a. The chairperson explains and clarifies the two-panel colloquy to the audience.

   b. The chairperson introduces the subject for discussion.
   c. The expert and lay panels are presented to the audience.
   d. The leader starts the discussion with a stimulating remark or question.
   e. As expert advice is needed, the second panel is called upon to contribute.
   f. A question-and-answer period follows the presentation, with comments and questions from the audience answered and discussed by both the lay and expert panels.
   g. The chairperson summarizes, thanks the participants, and concludes the colloquy.

### Appropriate Topics

1. Dealing with your child's fears
2. Handling stress
3. Drug addiction and alcoholism
4. Helping exceptional children
5. Nutrition

## Debates

When an issue is of a pro-and-con nature, a **debate** is an effective means of presenting both sides. The debate team presents opposing views of a controversial issue.

### Setup

1. Place enough chairs for the members of each debate team on either side of a podium or table.
2. Place chairs in a circle for a small audience; if the group is large, use an auditorium formation.

### Procedure

1. The question to be debated is announced by the chairperson, and the issue is turned over to the speakers for each side.
2. One speaker for the affirmative begins with a two- to four-minute speech. The next speaker is from the opposing position. The teams alternate until each member has spoken.
3. Rebuttal following each speech is optional, or leaders of both debate teams may conclude the debate section with rebuttals.

4. The chairperson entertains questions from the audience, and the debate teams answer and discuss the issue.

## Appropriate Topics

1. Sex education—home's or school's responsibility?
2. Behavior modification versus logical consequences.
3. Open education versus traditional education.
4. Encouragement toward achievement versus "don't push my child."
5. Back to basics versus inquiry and/or literacy-based education.

## Book Review Discussions

**Book reviews** by group members or experts provide a format that brings out stimulating new ideas or acknowledges expertise. The review may be given by one presenter or several members. An open discussion by the entire group follows.

### Setup

1. Place chairs for book reviewers behind a table in front of the group.
2. Arrange chairs for the audience in a circle or semicircle.

### Procedure

1. The chairperson tells a little about the book to be reviewed and introduces the book reviewer or book review panel.
2. The book reviewer discusses the author of the book.
3. The book review is given.
   a. If the book is to be reviewed by panel discussion, the group discusses issues and ideas in a conversational format.
   b. One person may give the book review.
   c. Two or three people may each review a portion of the book.
4. After the review, the entire group joins in an open discussion of the book.

### Appropriate Topics

1. Values
2. Decision making
3. Building self-concept
4. Communication

5. Divorce
6. Role identification
7. Single parents

## Audiovisual Presentations

Visual stimuli, programmed material, and film presentations can be catalysts for a good open discussion. The audiovisual format is directed toward two senses—hearing and sight—whereas an audio presentation relies solely on hearing. The addition of visual stimuli is beneficial to those who learn better through sight than sound. Accompanying charts, posters, or pictures always help clarify ideas. Video presentations can present information in an interesting and succinct manner.

### Techniques

1. CDs and MP3s
2. Audiovisual:
   a. DVDs
   b. PowerPoints with running commentary
3. Visual:
   a. Charts
   b. Posters
   c. Computers

### Arrangements Before the Meeting

1. The teacher or group decides on information needed by members through interest finders.
2. Review and select DVDs. (Choose only programs that are relevant, interesting, and presented well.)
3. Choose a member to give a presentation.
4. Reserve equipment—laptops, LCD projectors, chart stands, projection carts, extension cords, outlet adapters, screen, and so on.
5. Preview audiovisual and audio materials to be sure of quality and develop questions and comments relevant to the presentation. Do not use audiovisual materials as fillers; use them only as relevant additions to the curriculum.
6. Review the "Arrangements for Meetings" section and make appropriate preparations.

### Setup

1. Check and prepare equipment before the meeting. Have DVDs ready to begin and have charts and posters set up.
2. Arrange chairs so everyone can see the presentation.

## *Procedure*

1. The chairperson introduces the topic and the presenter.
2. The presenter gives background information on audiovisual material and points out important aspects of the showing.
3. After the presentation, the presenter leads an open discussion and question-and-answer period.

## *Appropriate Topics*

1. Foundations of reading and writing
2. Emotional growth
3. Dealing with fears
4. Exceptional children, for example, those who are gifted or those with learning disabilities
5. Autism spectrum disorder
6. Attention-deficit/hyperactivity disorder
7. Drugs and alcohol
8. Drop-out problems
9. Teenage pregnancies

## Symposiums

A **symposium** is a formal presentation by several speakers on various aspects of a topic. Each symposium presenter develops a specific talk of five to 15 minutes in length. The symposium is similar to a lecture, but information is given by several lecturers rather than just one. Its value—to share expert information—is the same.

## *Setup*

1. Place chairs for the presenters behind a table in front of the audience.
2. Chairs for the audience may be in a circle or semicircle for a small group, or auditorium arrangements can be made for a large group.

## *Procedure*

1. The chairperson or leader introduces the symposium speakers.
2. Each presenter gives a talk.
3. The chairperson or leader provides transitional statements between each speaker's presentation.
4. At the end of the presentations, questions directed to a specific speaker or to the entire

symposium are entertained by the chairperson. A discussion of questions follows.
5. The chairperson summarizes the main points of the meeting.
6. Symposium presenters are thanked for their contributions.

## *Appropriate Topics*

1. Nonsexist education
2. Single parenthood
3. Gender-role identification
4. Multicultural understanding
5. Consumer education
6. Death and dying
7. Safety in the home (e.g., toys, storage of hazardous materials, home arrangement)
8. Special education services
9. Drugs and alcohol
10. Suicide
11. Restructuring schools

## Lectures

A **lecture** is a talk prepared by an expert or lay presenter. No interruptions or questions are allowed during the presentation, but there may be a question-and-answer period afterward. The lecture without a forum following it results in a formal presentation with no interaction between speaker and audience. A lecture forum that includes a period for questions and answers at the end of the address permits some interaction and allows the audience an opportunity to ask questions, clarify points, and make comments.

The lecture is an excellent vehicle for dissemination of specific information. As a result, care must be taken to choose a speaker who not only knows the subject but also presents unbiased material.

## *Arrangements Before the Meeting*

1. Select a topic and obtain a speaker who is recognized as an unbiased authority.
2. Communicate with the speaker on group interests and needs, time limit for speech, and forum period.
3. Prepare an introduction that is based on the speaker's background and expertise.
4. Review the "Arrangements for Meetings" section and make appropriate preparations.

### Setup

1. Place a podium or table at the center of the stage if the audience is large. Place chairs in a circle with a small table in front of the speaker if the audience is small.
2. Check the sound system if the area is large.
3. Obtain a glass and a pitcher of water for the speaker.

### Procedure

1. The chairperson introduces the speaker and topic.
2. The speaker gives a talk for a specific period of time.
3. The chairperson conducts a forum for questions with the guest speaker responding to comments and answering questions.
4. The chairperson thanks the speaker, and the meeting is concluded.

### Appropriate Topics

1. Money management
2. Specialists in different areas of child development, for example, psychiatrists, pediatricians, dentists, nutritionists, obstetricians, special educators, speech therapists, occupational therapists, and physical therapists
3. How to manage stress
4. Dealing with illness and death
5. Preventive health measures
6. Childhood diseases and disorders
7. School finances
8. Preventing violence

Select the meeting format that fulfills your needs and is most appropriate for the topic. Members of the group have responsibilities to themselves and to the group. After a positive group meeting, the participants should feel supportive and supported as well as fulfilled and productive.

## SUMMARY

Parent group meetings are among the most efficient and viable forms of parent education. Positive leadership skills are essential to facilitate productive parent groups. Included in this chapter are a description of a needs assessment and a discussion of the formation of parent groups.

Leadership skills and good group interaction can be developed if groups are aware of leadership and group roles. Roles that emerge within groups affect the interaction among participants. Knowledge of task, maintenance, and dysfunctional roles improves the productivity of group interactions through the concerted elimination of dysfunctional roles. An analysis of group discussion illustrates the interaction in process.

Group meetings use a variety of meeting formats, either individually or in combination. The formats include roundtables, concentric circles, buzz sessions, brainstorming sessions, workshops, field trips, dyad or triad interaction and feedback, role playing, dramatizations, panels, colloquies, debates, book reviews, audiovisual presentations, symposiums, and lectures. Choice of topics for the meetings should fit the interests and needs of the groups.

Evaluations are necessary in ongoing parent groups because they provide a basis for improvement of group interaction and suggestions for the continuing program.

## SUGGESTED CLASS ACTIVITIES AND DISCUSSIONS

1. Conduct an opening period of a parent meeting. Include icebreakers and interest finders.
2. Attend a parent-education meeting in a community different than your own. Visit with the members. Note how the meeting is conducted, the involvement of the parents, and the feelings of the members. Talk with the director about the goals and objectives of the group. Talk with parents about their desires for the group.
3. Conduct a needs assessment in a familiar school or child development center. From the needs assessment, develop a workshop or meeting for parents. Include the objectives of the meeting, questions to be answered, background material on the questions, and a list of additional resources.
4. Attend a board meeting of a local district. Make note of the items that relate to family engagement.
5. Attend a parent-advisory council meeting. Present your findings to your class. How does this group promote family engagement?
6. Attend or participate in a site-based or community management meeting. Does this group promote family engagement?

7. Participate in a session from the Harvard Family Research Project Webinar series www .nationalpirc.org/engagement_webinars/register .html). Click on Webinar Sessions to make your selection.

## USEFUL WEB SITES

**Center on School, Family & Community Partnership, Johns Hopkins University**
www.csos.jhu.edu/
The center's site has many articles and programs concerning family and school partnerships.

**Council for Exceptional Children**
www.cec.sped.org/
The CEC has information on children with special needs, including those with autism.

**Harvard Family Research Project**
www.hfrp.org/
This center promotes excellence and innovation in family, school, and community engagement.

**MALDEF Leadership Programs**
www.maldef.org/leadership/programs/index.html
The primary objective of this leadership program is to promote the educational attainment and leadership advancement of Latinos through free community workshops across the nation.

**National Center for Educational Statistics**
http://nces.ed.gov/
This is the primary federal center for analyzing data, including early childhood education. It is located in the U.S. Department of Education and the Institute of Education Sciences.

**National Dropout Prevention Center**
www.dropoutprevention.org/
This network, provided by the U.S. Department of Education Office of Special Education Programs, promotes networking for parents, policy makers, and researchers to help children at risk find and receive the programs they need.

# School-Based Programs

*Providing information about school's expectations helps parents understand what is expected of their children to be successful in school. Parents and educators must engage in meaningful dialogue to convey the valores (values) that will build school success.*

Riojas-Cortez & Flores
(2009)

In this chapter on school-based education, you will read about effective parent–school programs. After completing the chapter, you should be able to do the following:

- Describe a school where parents are active partners.
- Explain how parents can be actively involved in schools.
- Develop activities that strengthen family and parent–school collaboration.
- List and describe successful programs related to early childhood and parent involvement.
- Identify educational and community resources.
- Identify the importance of family literacy programs to promote parent involvement and help overcome illiteracy.

Assume the role of a parent who visits a school committed to the involvement of parents. As you open the school door, you notice a sign that welcomes you in your native language. The staff greets you with smiles when you check in at the office. If you want to have a cup of tea or coffee, look through the school's curricula, or read an article, you can visit the family center.

There, several parents are developing curriculum material for the school's resource room. One parent is making a game for the third- and fourth-grade classes. Another is clipping curriculum-related articles to be filed for reference. As you sip your coffee, the sounds of young children echo down the hall from the west wing of the building. Parents and their children are arriving for parent education classes, parent–child meetings, and ESL classes. The school offers programs for parents of infants, toddlers, and preschool children. Both parents are invited and included in the programs. For those who cannot come during the week, a Saturday session is available. On the fourth Tuesday of every month, the school has a breakfast for students' fathers and/or friends.

You came to school today to visit your child's classroom, so, after a brief visit in the family center, you walk to your child's room. On the bulletin board outside the door is a welcome notice that shows in detail what the children have been accomplishing. Here the teacher has described the happenings for the week, listed volunteer times for parents, and asked for contributions of plastic containers to be used in making tempera-paint prints.

Parents are active partners in education.

Immediately aware of what is happening in the room, you make a note to start collecting "scrounge materials" for recycling in the classroom. An invitation to an evening workshop reminds you that you have saved next Tuesday evening for that very event. In the space for notes to and from parents, you write a short response to the message you received from the teacher last week.

Also attached to the bulletin board are "Tips for Visiting." These let you know that you can become involved in a classroom activity rather than spend your time passively observing. The teacher smiles and acknowledges your presence but, being involved with the class, continues teaching. The class greeter, a child chosen as a "very important person" this week, comes up and welcomes you. Later, during a center session or break, you have an opportunity to talk with the teacher and your child. Recruitment of volunteers is under way, so you are encouraged—but not forced—to contribute. Flexible hours, designated times, child-care services, and a variety of tasks make it easy to share some time in this classroom.

Knowing that the principal holds an open forum each week at this time, you stop by and join a discussion on school policy. Parents are being encouraged to evaluate the "tote bag" home learning activities that have been sent home with children. In addition, plans are under way for an after-school recreation program. The principal will take the comments to the Parent Advisory Board meeting later this week. As you leave the school, you feel satisfied that this school responds to the needs of both you and your child.

A positive view of children and parents creates a healthy ecology in any school or center.

The preceding scenario shows a school or center that reaches out to families and the community thus creating collaboration in children's lives. See Figure 8–1 for an illustration of schools reaching out and collaborating with families and communities.

## :: INVOLVING PARENTS

Parent involvement is expressed by many schools and described in a voluminous number of articles. Family and community involvement in the schools has been linked to improved school programs and quality, better school attendance, and increased academic achievement of children (Michael, Dittus, & Epstein, 2007). Involvement ranges from offering breakfasts for fathers to recognizing the school as one part of a community that must meet the needs of the family to creating change through leadership and advocacy.

The implementation of strategies for parent involvement is based on the strengths of families and their knowledge of their children. Identification and implementation of preventive strategies that recognize the stresses affecting many families today—financial, emotional, social, and personal—to make the school family friendly and supportive are crucial for the development of school-based parent involvement programs. Collaboration with community agencies offers the opportunity for families and children to use new resources as necessary. Exploration of different models help schools reach out to families; models that meet the needs of the community and school or development of programs based on community and family needs provide opportunities for family engagement.

It is important to find the model that will help families understand their role as it relates to parental involvement. In some cultures, parent involvement in the schools is limited because of the parents' strong beliefs that the teacher and the school know more than they (the parents) do. Although evidence exists that parental involvement makes a difference in the academic lives of children, considerations regarding how parents become involved and children's reactions to parental involvement must be taken into account (Pomerantz, Moorman, & Litwack, 2007).

## :: MAKING PROGRAMS HAPPEN

How can parent programs get started? Parent programs begin from the need to create partnerships with families in order to provide the best

**FIGURE 8–1**

The spokes of the wheel radiate from the school and reveal opportunities for involving parents, children, and the community.

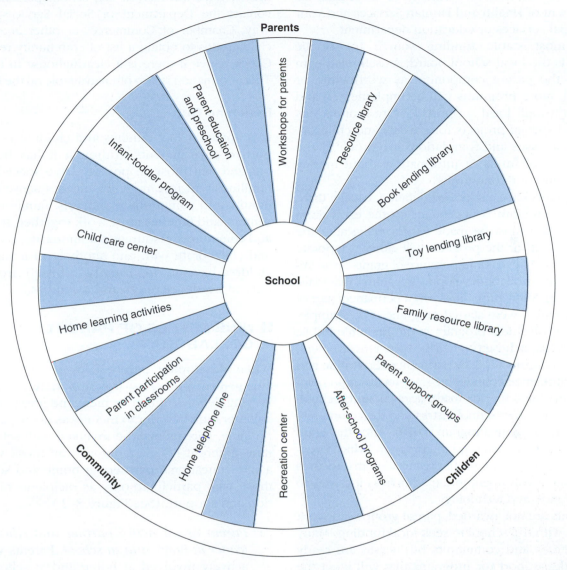

opportunities for children in the schools. When parent-involvement programs are planned, they usually focus on an identified need (Epstein, 2005; Riojas-Cortez & Flores, 2010). After the need is identified, community resources and funding are explored. It is important to remember that funding is not necessary to begin a parent-involvement program. Resources from the school, school district, and community may be used in order to begin a program. If funding is necessary, then there are options to look into the individual district or the school as well as community resources such as

businesses and organizations that want to support education efforts.

**Funding**

Funding for school-related programs comes primarily from three major sources: (a) government grants, either federal or state; (b) private foundation awards; and (c) local school budgets. A public school's budget is based on local taxes and state distribution of funds. Private schools rely primarily on tuition and private sources to provide their budgets, although they are eligible for some federal grants. Current information on funding and grants can be obtained from your regional Department of Education or Department of Health and Human Services and your state social services or education department.

The most stable funding source for public schools is the local school board. As schools begin to view the parent component as worthwhile or essential, more programs will be implemented and funded through local support. Private foundations also fund special projects for parents and children. Local businesses and foundations are probably the best source of funds or information about money available in your community.

Most grants have a specified duration, usually three years. If a program is dependent on the extra grant funding, plans must be made for financing after the grant runs out, or the program will either deteriorate or disappear. The major importance of grants is the impetus they provide for developing programs, materials, and services. Many programs, now a permanent part of the community, were started on grants. For example, a parent-involvement program in the Braintree Public Schools in Massachusetts called the Parent Involvement, Inc., initiated from a U.S. Department of Education and a National Science Foundation grant focusing on helping parents advocate for math, science, and technology reform for their school district and the community (Parent Involvement Program, 2010). After the grant ended, parents helped fund the program, which eventually turned into a nonprofit organization that focuses on parental involvement in the schools as it relates to math, science, and technology.

If grants are not awarded, parent groups can work together with the school to seek local funding. Many organizations and community businesses are ready to provide support for programs that will meet the needs of the children and their families. Teachers can work together with parents to discover the type of programs that families need and want. Develop a unique approach to bring about a partnership. For example, volunteers can be an alternative to funding in making programs happen. Using volunteers in a positive way can help teachers and enable the school to enrich its educational offerings.

### Resources and Social Agencies

Collaboration between schools and social agencies helps develop continuity and supply the support that families need. Teachers as well as administrators can make referrals to social services, recreation districts, libraries, and other public agencies. If the school district does not have a list, school personnel may contact the Department of Social Services, United Way, Chamber of Commerce, or other agencies or civic groups to obtain a list of community resources. Check to see if there is a clearinghouse in the area. This information is also often available on the Internet.

### Reaching Out

It is apparent that families and children need supportive environments. Although it has been recognized that those in poverty have special needs, families at all income levels need a sense of community and commitment. Schools, family resource centers, and families must work together. If schools and community resources communicate, cooperate, and collaborate with one another, all families and children have an opportunity to benefit from a variety of needed services and resources.

## ∷ NINE LEVELS OF PARENT COLLABORATION

When developing parent-involvement or parent-engagement programs, it is important to allow for varying degrees of involvement and levels of parent collaboration in order to include as many parents as possible. Parents may be involved with schools on nine different levels, ranging from those who are active educational partners at home and school to those who participate only as recipients of education and support. (See Figure 8–2.)

1. *Parent as an active partner and educational leader at home and at school.* Parents who are actively involved at home and at school have the time and availability to participate in both aspects of their children's lives. These families want to support their children through active involvement at home as well as in the school. Their roles may end with their commitment to their children, or they may also be involved in the second level.

2. *Parent as a decision maker.* The second role goes beyond active involvement to include decision making. These parents may serve on the school board, on a site-based management team, or on an advisory council. With decision making comes the power to affect the offerings

**FIGURE 8–2**
Parents relate to the schools in ways ranging from support of their children's education to decision making.

---

**Parent Collaboration with Schools**

Parent as an active partner and educational leader at home and at school

Parent as a decision maker

Parent as an advocate for the school

Parent actively involved as volunteer or paid employee

Parent as a liaison between school and home to support homework

Parent as supporter of the educational goals of the school

Parent as a recipient of education and support

Parent as member of parent educational classes

Parent as representative and activist in the community

---

and climate of the school. Power and decision making are seen in the use of policy committees, site-based collaborative decision making, advisory task forces, and school boards. The trend toward site-based management, collaborative decision making, and charter schools shows an emerging shift in position. If this trend continues, decision making in public schools will include parents. Charter schools, financed by the public school systems, will continue to increase in numbers with parents acting as the decision makers.

3. *Parent as an advocate to help schools achieve excellent educational offerings.* Some parents are primarily involved with the schools as advocates for the school and as fund-raisers. Think of the parent who spends hours setting up the booths for a school fair to earn money to buy computers or some other equipment the school needs. Think of the parent who writes letters to newspapers or administrators supporting school programs or who advocates forcefully for educational principles. Advocacy has spurred the development of programs for special-education students. Case advocacy, in the hands of individual parents, can give parents the opportunity to state their case and get it resolved to their satisfaction. There are many levels of advocacy and a variety of ways parents can advocate for their children and the concerns they have.

4. *Parent actively involved with the school as a volunteer or paid employee.* Parents who work in the school enjoy a special position there.

Through their work they can view the operations of the school, learn about the curricula, and become acquainted with teachers and administrators as friends and colleagues. They can also help as advocates for the school in the community. However, it is important for the school and parent to have specific guidelines on duties and responsibilities.

5. *Parent as a liaison between school and home to support homework and to be aware of school activities.* Parents who act as liaisons between school and home do not become involved in power or advocacy and are most interested in the school as the agency that educates their children.

6. *Parent, though not active, supporting the educational goals of the school and encouraging the child to study.* These parents, similar to those who serve as liaisons, are supportive of the schools. Perhaps they are too busy to be involved, or perhaps they do not remember schools with fondness and prefer to keep their distance, but they do not undermine the school's objective to educate their children. Schools should reach out to these parents and make them feel welcome.

7. *Parent as recipient of support from the school.* Schools reach more families than any other agency, and so it becomes expedient to look to schools for support. Parent involvement and family education can help mothers and fathers become better informed and offer support that enables them to strengthen their families. Offerings

in the school may include family literacy classes, a crisis nursery, before- and after-school programs for children, a family resource room, clothes and shoes/boot exchanges, free breakfasts and lunches for children, and parent education. Schools can also serve as referral agencies for community services if families are in need.

8. *Parent as member of parent education classes.* If parents can be encouraged to attend classes, knowledge of child development may help with their raising their children. For example, knowledge of the importance of language development, based in the first four years of life, is essential for later school success. During parent-education classes, it has come as a surprise to many parents that talking and reading with their young child are important. It is important for parents who are English language learners to know that speaking in their native language to their children builds a stronger foundation for biliteracy (Perez, 2004). This small amount of parent education can help turn a child into a capable student.

9. *Parent as a representative and activist in community.* Parents with knowledge of community offerings and active membership in community endeavors may have the ability to solicit information and help from organizations in the community. These community offerings may be able to help the family who is homeless, the child whose parents are on drugs, the family who needs help in obtaining employment, the child who needs protection, or the child who needs extra help with lessons. Parents who know the community strengthen the school's ability to use community offerings, but the school must value their knowledge to increase collaboration.

Families need agencies to collaborate with each other and to help them [the families] grow or, in some cases, to survive. With the large number of parents working, all agencies involved with the family (recreation, health, social agencies, businesses, schools, and churches or synagogues) must work together to ensure continuity. Employers must reevaluate their structure to allow more part-time, shared, and flexible hours and release time for parents to visit and volunteer in the schools. They should also collaborate with high schools to

Teachers are important resources to support culturally and linguistically diverse familiies.

provide occupational internships. Social agencies can provide support for parents that are unable to provide adequately for their families or that might be neglectful or abusive if they do not have support. Schools cannot be expected to solve all of society's problems and answer all the questions involved in change, but they should work with other agencies and provide education and facilities to help strengthen families.

The emerging family resource centers and the increasing number of schools offering family literacy classes are steps in the right direction. For parents who are English language learners, it is important that the schools together with family resource centers offer English as a second language classes at times that are convenient for parents. Parents need to be given the opportunity to enhance their literacy skills so they can participate in society successfully, earn a living, and better assist in their children's development.

## :: SIX TYPES OF PARENT INVOLVEMENT

Epstein (1995, 1996, 2001, 2006) shares a framework of six types of involvement that schools may implement to increase collaboration among schools, families, and community:

1. *Parenting*—Help parents with skills and give them an understanding of child and adolescent development that enables them to have a home environment that supports learning and school success.

2. *Communicating*—Communicate effectively, school to home and home to school, about children's progress and school programs.
3. *Volunteering*—Involve parents as volunteers but be sure to provide training and flexible schedules so that parents can be involved.
4. *Learning at home*—Provide information and activities that parents can use in learning at home, connecting the family and school.
5. *Decision making*—Include parents in school decisions and governance and strengthen the parents' leadership skills.
6. *Collaborating with the community*—Integrate services and resources of the community with the schools to strengthen families, school programs, and children's development and learning.

Epstein suggests that the six-component framework be used to further knowledge about parent involvement. This framework also shows a gap in knowledge about parental involvement. Epstein has suggested that there are more questions to be answered regarding parental involvement including the teachers' views of parents and how those are different from parents' views of themselves.

Teachers who reach out to parents are more accepting of and more knowledgeable about the families than those who hesitate to be involved with parents. Studies show that teachers' involvement with families is more critical than family background in determining how students progress: "At the elementary, middle, and high school levels, surveys of parents, teachers, principals, and students reveal that if schools invest in practices that involve families, then parents respond by conducting those practices, including many parents who might not have otherwise become involved on their own" (Epstein, 1996, p. 217).

Teachers who involve and work well with parents tend to evaluate the parents without stereotyping them, whether the parents are single or married, educated or lacking in education. When teachers involve parents, they find that the parents are helpful. When teachers do not involve parents, they often stereotype single parents and those with less education as not being helpful (Epstein, 1996).

The Center on School, Family, and Community Partnership focuses on elementary, middle, and secondary schools in their research and publications. They have guidelines to assist schools in building school–family–community partnerships.

## ▀▀ CHARACTERISTICS OF EFFECTIVE COLLABORATION

The characteristics of effective parent–school collaboration include the following:

1. Principals, teachers, child-care providers, staff, and parents who believe in parent involvement.
2. Schools and child-care centers that encourage parent collaboration by encouraging parents to participate at the level that best fits their interests and time.
3. An open-door policy and climate that respond to parent concerns with effective communication.
4. Pairing children new to the school or center with a classmate to help new children with routines.
5. Conferences, with child care available, held at times that make it possible and convenient for parents to attend.
6. A feeling of family, schools, center, and community joined together in a cooperative effort to support children's health and educational growth.

## ▀▀ REACHING ALL FAMILIES

All parents want to help their children succeed in school. They need to know they can help their children by fostering emotional competency at a very early age (Ray & Smith, 2010). Schools or centers can develop strategies that are culturally and developmentally appropriate for families to help children develop. Moles (1996a) describes methods and strategies to reach families that include early fall mailings, home–school handbooks, open houses, school–parent compacts, personal contacts, parent–teacher conferences, home visits, parent liaisons, homework, resource centers, family gatherings, special programs for children with special needs, and positive communication.

### Partnership for Family Involvement in Education

Family School Partnership was established to encourage families, local school-board governance, administration, teachers, and school staff to form a partnership to bolster children's learning. They made the following pledge:

▪ We will share responsibility at school and at home to give students a better education and a good start in life.

Developmentally and culturally appropriate programs provide culturally and linguistically diverse children with opportunities for play, problem solving, and social development.

- Our school will be welcoming to families; reach out to families before problems arise, offer challenging courses, create safe and drug-free learning environments, organize tutoring and other opportunities to improve student learning, and support families to be included in the school decision-making process.
- Our families will monitor student attendance, homework completion and television watching; take the time to talk and listen to their children; become acquainted with teachers, administrators, and school staff; read with younger children and share a good book with a teen; volunteer in school when possible; and participate in the school decision-making process.
- We will promote effective two-way communication between families and schools by reducing educational jargon and breaking down cultural and language barriers and by families staying in touch with the schools.
- We will provide opportunities for families to learn how to help their children succeed in school and for school staff to work with families.
- We will support family–school efforts to improve student learning by reviewing progress regularly and strengthening cooperative actions. (U.S. Department of Education, 1997)

## Communication Through the Internet and/or Telephone

Telling the family about the child's accomplishments or contributions is almost always a positive interaction. Teachers need to let the parents know at the beginning of the school year that phone calls will be made to keep the communication open throughout the school year. Some children contribute with an unusual idea or a friendly smile. Others may have had a particularly successful day participating in class or finishing work. For the many parents who own a computer and have access to the Internet, communication can be easy. E-mail addresses can be given to parents who want to contact the school or a particular teacher with questions or comments. Parents can furnish their child's or their own e-mail address for information that needs to go home, such as an explanation of assignments or an invitation to a school event.

## ▪▪ WORKSHOPS AT SCHOOL FOR PARENTS TO USE AT HOME

A workshop is one vehicle for introducing parents to home–school learning activities. Ann Grimes, a first-grade teacher, invited her students' parents to such a workshop. She greeted them, gave them name tags, and passed out a get-acquainted signature sheet for a signature game.

After the signature game, during which parents enthusiastically talked with one another, the make-and-take workshop began. Mrs. Grimes explained the program, its philosophy, and what the school expected of parents. She assured the parents that close, two-way communication helps ensure the program is meeting the needs of the child, parents, and school. If parents were interested in participating in a home–school learning project, she assured them that she would like to work with them as a member of the team.

Mrs. Grimes reminded the parents of how important it is to listen to children, ask open-ended questions, and allow children the opportunity to predict and problem solve. She also reminded the parents that children, like adults, work best when they have a quiet, private work area and a regular time to work. She stressed that children should enjoy and succeed at home assignments. If a child struggles with more than 20 percent of the projects or problems, the activity selection should be re-assessed and new activities better geared to the child's level can be chosen. Many home activities can be recreational and enriching to family life. As she concluded her talk, Mrs. Grimes explained the plans for the evening. Parents were asked to participate in the activities located in different areas throughout the room. "If you will look at your name tag, you will find a number. Go to that activity first," she instructed the parents.

The centers included games and activities as well as directions on how to play them. Materials and guidelines were also available for activities that parents could make and take home. Some parents played Concentration (Figure 8–3) and made game boards. They found that game boards could be

**FIGURE 8–3**
The game of Concentration may be designed, constructed, and played at home or at school.

TASK SAMPLE—"CONCENTRATION"

AIM: To play a matching game with pairs of cards.

WHY: To practice visual memory, remembering the position of matching cards. To follow rules and take turns are skills used in most games.

MATERIALS: Grocery sack or small cards, five pairs of matching pictures, magazines, sales pamphlets, paste, scissors.

PROCEDURE:

1. Cut pairs of like pictures (10) from magazine and paste on circles cut from paper sacks or cards.

2. Encourage child to talk about pictures and name them. Then, together, place them in pairs.

3. Collect cards, turn them face down, and mix them.

4. Place cards in rows without looking at pictures.

5. Have child pick up one card and turn it over and say what it is. (Repeat the name if the child cannot say the name.) Then choose another card trying for a match. If no match, then both cards are turned over. Say, "That's your turn; now it's my turn."

6. The play continues until all the cards are matched. Count the matched pairs to see who is the winner.

EXTENDING THE CONCEPT:

1. Add more picture cards for pairs.

2. Play game using colors instead of pictures.

3. Use pictures of sets of objects.

TASK SAMPLE—"CONCENTRATION"

*Source:* Project Home Base, Yakima, WA.

easily made from cardboard, poster board, or a file folder. Mrs. Grimes furnished decorative stickers that the parents could place on the game boards. To protect the completed board, some parents used the laminating machine, and others spread clear adhesive paper over their work. Each board was different, yet each was based on the same format— that is, squares on which the children placed symbols as they used a spinner or die to tell them how many spaces to move. Some parents wrote letters or numbers on the spaces; others developed cards that children could take as they had a turn. If the spaces were left empty, the board could be used for many skill activities by developing sets of cards for phonics, numbers, or other basic skills. While some parents were busy with the game boards, others worked on language and math concepts, constructed books, or plied their creativity at the art center.

After a busy 2-hour session, the group met again, and an animated discussion of the activities began. Two parents volunteered to make canvas tote bags for the class, and another promised to make a silk-screened print of the class emblem on each. They decided the tote bags would be reserved for home-learning adventures. "Please be sure to evaluate

School activities can be reinforced in the home.

the home-learning activities as you use them. And, please contribute your own ideas," encouraged Mrs. Grimes. "I'll keep track of each child's activities on these record sheets. If you have any questions, be sure to write or call me."

After refreshments, the parents began to leave. Some stopped by the table to sign up to volunteer in the program. Mrs. Grimes announced that she would need help implementing the home-learning program and that she could use help in the room as well. A volunteer training session was planned for the next week; the work toward a productive home–school endeavor had just begun.

## Implementation of Home-Learning Activities

Home-learning activities can be useful as enrichment projects, or they can be valuable as a sequential educational curriculum. If they are used to complement learning that is occurring simultaneously in the school, it is necessary to monitor the child's work at home and keep track of what is accomplished.

The process varies according to the availability of a parent coordinator. If parent coordinators are available, it will be their responsibility to keep track of the home-learning activities. They can contact parents, make home visits, and report on the progress of each child. It is the teacher's responsibility to advise the parent coordinator about the child's progress in school and recommend appropriate learning activities. If a parent coordinator is not available, a parent volunteer can help with record keeping and provide contact between the parents and the teacher. The following steps are appropriate for either situation:

1. Offer an orientation workshop.
2. Send learning activities home in a tote bag, deliver them personally, or give the responsibility of the delivery system to a parent coordinator.
3. Keep records of activity cards the child has taken home. Make a record card for each child with a space to indicate when each activity went home and a space for response to the activity. This way you will know which activity the child should be given next.
4. Get feedback from parents via notes, reports, phone calls, or visits. Find out their reactions to the activities and their assessments of their child's success.

5. Continue communicating with parents. Include supplemental ideas and activity sheets on a skill that proved difficult for a particular student. Ask parents to reinforce skills up to the too-difficult level. Have them refer to previous activity cards for related projects.

6. Diversify your program to meet the needs of the parents and keep interest levels high.

7. Meet occasionally with parents or make home visits to support the monitoring system.

Communication is a basic ingredient in the success of home–school cooperation. Through talking with parents, you will know whether they consider home-learning activities to be a joy or a threat. You will want to adapt your program according to each parent's desires.

Projects around the home can furnish experiences in math, language, art, music, science, and composition. The process of exploring an idea and carrying it to fruition requires problem solving. The Ferguson-Florissant School District developed a home curriculum to help parents of young children with problem solving (Figure 8–4). Ideas for activities around the home and in the community are restricted only by the imagination.

## :: REACHING RETICENT PARENTS

Parents who feel good about themselves and who feel validated by the school participate. There are some parents, however, that have a difficult time getting involved for a variety of reasons. This situation is especially true for low-income and culturally and linguistically diverse parents who may be made to feel inferior by school personnel, but it is also true for many middle- and upper-class parents who receive negative feedback on their involvement in the schools.

The initiative of parent involvement must come from the school; the school must reach out to the home. It is also important to remember that engagement of parents in children's learning in the home has a greater impact than the amount of time they spend participating in school activities (Harris & Goodall, 2008).

### Parent Involvement Program

Twenty years ago in the New York City school system, there seemed to be a need to reconfigure their parent involvement programs. A grant for $800,000 was given to the system to develop strategies for parent involvement. The program by that name, the Parent Involvement Program, found that 10 factors seemed important in their efforts: leadership from the schools, accessibility—and open lines of communication, time to plan and implement changes, cultural awareness, active teacher roles, continuity, public recognition of those involved, broad-based support, adolescent focus, and recognition of parents as people (Jackson & Cooper, 1992).

### Empowerment

A research project at Cornell University first worked with parents and later tied parent involvement to the schools. Working with 160 families, the parent teams helped parents become more confident of their abilities. The group used a series of activities, such as role playing, to help parents feel secure when they became involved with schools. They developed a

Outdoor activities at home or school help children develop creativity.

## FIGURE 8–4
Home activities that help the child learn and solve problems.

Early Education
Ferguson-Florissant
School District

# Lifelong Values
# Problem-Solving

**Problem-solving** is the ability to take what you know and come up with a new solution to a problem. Problem-solving is the foundation that helps children think, reason, and make their own decisions. It enables children to accomplish the goals they choose in life.

One of the ways children learn is by watching and listening to others. As problems crop up in everyday life, by thinking out loud we are modeling problem-solving skills.

Examples:
• "We are having eight people for dinner, and there is only room for six people at the table. I wonder what we should do."

• "We have bird seed but our bird feeder broke. What can we use to build a new bird feeder?"

As you and your child are solving problems together you might ask:

• "Does it work?"
• "What else can I do?"
• "What's going to happen?"
• "How did we do?"

## Ways to Encourage Problem-Solving:

1. **Age-appropriate activities and materials**
Giving children materials that can be used in many different ways helps children understand that there is more than one way to accomplish a task. Materials such as Play-Doh (letting children decide what they want to make with the Play-Doh), blocks (how many different ways can the blocks be used to build with?), and collage materials (paint, scissors, tape, paper, paste) offer opportunities for children to explore, create and experience solving problems. Children are making judgments about size, cause and effect, and special relationships.
    "How can I make the paper stick together?"
    "What happens if I put this block on top?"
    "How can I build a ramp for my cars?"
    "What size does it need to be?"

2. **Take advantage of everyday opportunities**
The following are just a few examples:

• You're planning a birthday party—"What can we use to decorate cupcakes for our party? What kind of decorations can we make?"
• It's time to clean up and your child can't reach the sink to wash his hands. You might ask, "What are you going to do?"
• You've been to the grocery store and you have a heavy bag of groceries to put away. You ask your child to help but the bag is too heavy for him to pick up. See if your child can think of a different way to get the bag of groceries to the pantry.

program titled Cooperative Communication Between Home and School (CCBHS), which included teachers and administrators. Including the school along with the parents provided even more positive attitudes. Parents need to view themselves as worthwhile participants to truly be able to interact with teachers and administrators, while the school personnel need to respect the parents and recognize their importance as they collaborate. In this way they work for the greater good of families, schools, and communities (Cochran & Dean, 1991).

Perseverance, patience, and true interest in the parent are the most important factors involved in overcoming parents' reticence. Understanding,

**FIGURE 8–4**
(Continued)

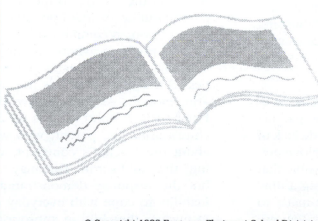

**3. Time to think and act on their ideas**
For children to become successful at solving problems, it's important to give them plenty of time to think and act on their ideas.
It is even more important to accept all ideas. If we don't, they will be afraid to try again. We all learn from our mistakes. Children need that trial-and-error process to learn.

**4. Bedtime stories**
When reading a bedtime story, ask your child to think of another way the story could end. Ask your child to make predictions about what we think the character will do.

**Ways to Encourage Self-Evaluation**
Learning is more valuable to children when they evaluate their own performance.

Questions to discuss with children:

1. "What happened?"

2. "Why did or didn't it work?"

3. "What works best?"

4. "What else could you try?"

5. "What would you change?"

When children aren't given the opportunity to solve problems and use materials creatively, they aren't able to take charge of their own learning and make appropriate decisions.

Looking to the Future
Today's problems are very complex. We are concerned about jobs, the environment, and our economy. We need people with creative ideas to help solve these complicated problems.

No one knows what the future holds for our children. But we do know if we help them to make decisions and become independent thinkers and creative problem-solvers, they will be able to handle what the future has in store.

*Source:* From the Ferguson-Florissant School District, St. Louis, MO.

support, and interest usually will encourage a parent to take that first step toward collaborating with a teacher for the good of the child. However, a few parents may refuse to be involved regardless of the teacher's efforts. Some may have serious social adjustment problems and need professional help in that area. One challenging parent or one bad experience should not destroy the commitment of the home visitor or teacher toward working with others. Do what can be done and acknowledge the impossibility of reaching all parents. Do this with grace, understanding, and no recriminations. One way of involving the parents is through empowerment. **Empowerment** is a process of adult development, enhanced through participation. Family empowerment benefits parents and teachers and therefore children because it helps create a school that is responsive to the needs of all of its stakeholders (Nelson & Guerra, 2010). Dunlap (2000) studied family empowerment in a preschool cooperative and found that "Through involvement with the family component of this preschool, caregivers acquire cultural capital. Over time they translate cultural capital into human capital, or economic gain" (p. 5). This process of developing cultural capital into human capital is the process of empowerment. Dunlap found this can be accomplished without giving up the participant's sense of ethnic identity.

## Necessary Communication and Support

Teachers' ability to communicate with parents provides opportunities for parents and teachers to develop a collaborative partnership of support (Schecter & Sherri, 2009). By establishing communication early in the school year, the teacher can ensure parents will be ready to receive messages throughout the year. A call from the teacher or home visitor should not always mean that a child is in trouble. If good communication and support have been established, that call could mean the child is a strong leader or is working hard on a research project. Keep in mind that establishing communication early on does not guarantee an easy path to parent involvement. Involving parents may remain difficult for a few reasons:

1. *Families and parents might be under a lot of stress.* In our fast-paced society, many parents are under stress. Problems might include lack of money, illness of a loved one, unemployment, or an argument with a friend. It is possible that they cannot be actively involved during a time of hardship, and they should not be made to feel guilty about this. Let them know you are supportive and whenever they want to be more actively involved, they may. Keep communication open through telephone calls or e-mails.

2. *Many hard-to-reach parents feel out of their element whether coming to school or receiving home visitors.* They are unsure of themselves. They do not have confidence in their own ideas, or they believe someone else will not value them. They need their self-esteem and level of trust raised. If they have the time, let

them contribute in a small way. Accept their ideas and enlist their help in an activity at which they will succeed. Build slowly; it takes time to make a change.

3. *The parents do not realize their importance in their child's education.* Many parents, from those in programs such as Home Start and Head Start to those whose children are involved in accelerated programs, do not recognize their importance as educators. The parents' knowledge about the child is important, as they are the best experts on their child. Starting with parent–teacher conferences or home visits, the teacher needs to help parents understand that the parents' interactions with their children are part of the child's education and that the teacher values the parent as a true partner.

4. *Many teachers do not know the parents' interests, strengths, and abilities.* Keep in mind that some parents cannot help with schoolwork. They may become frustrated and angry, and the child can respond with dejection and hurt. Rather than helping the child, the parent creates a battleground. It is part of your role as an educator to try to prevent this sort of situation from occurring. Suggest projects and activities that lend themselves to the capabilities of the parent, but be aware of possible misinterpretations of your recommendations. For example, in one program where a home visitor was working with an abusive parent, it was suggested that the child was not using the right arm enough. At the next week's class, the home visitor found bruises up and down the child's arm. The parent, who was concerned about the teacher's comment, was "developing" the child's arm. This may seem extreme, but the response demonstrated the parent's inability to cope with everyday problems and to nurture the child in appropriate ways. The parent actually wanted the child to do well.

It is helpful to offer training sessions for parents where techniques and suggestions for working positively with the child are discussed. The STEP, PET, and Active Parenting programs suggest methods for communicating with children, using planned programs for parents. YouTube video clips, MP3s, and DVDs can also be helpful for illustrating parenting skills and the role of parents as teachers. These resources can serve as guides in setting up sessions on working with children. Parents also learn through modeling. Helping in the classroom can be an effective learning experience. Methods of teaching that permit observation, demonstration, and role playing prove useful. Parents, like children, learn best through active participation.

Engaging reticent parents in this way when their children are young is very important because prevention is far better than trying to find a cure. If parents can be involved from the start, their resistance to programs and partnerships can be reduced or eliminated. Different approaches that meet the needs of the individual communities are essential.

Minnesota Early Learning Design (MELD), which started in Minneapolis in 1973 but later merged with Parents as Teachers National Center, is one such approach. This program focuses on increasing parents' self-confidence, supporting parents' connection with their children, and helping families set goals in their work and family life (MELD, 2006). MELD's mission is to provide support and information that strengthens families at critical periods during the parenting process. Initially it focused on early childhood education, adult education, and family management (Parents as Teachers National Center, 2006), but as needs emerged, it expanded to include New Parents (for first-time parents); MELD Special (for parents of children with special needs); MYM, Young Moms; MELD for parents who are deaf; Nueva Familia/La Familia (for Hispanic parents); MELD's Young Dads; and MELD's Young Moms Plus (for parents of 3- to 6-year-old children) (MELD, 1988).

## :: COMER PROCESS

Over 30 years ago in New Haven, Connecticut, the Yale Child Study Center and New Haven Public Schools collaborated to bring change to two public schools. Comer, founder of the process, analyzed issues and problems in the schools, drawing on his own childhood experiences and his professional background in medicine and psychology. The process Comer used to develop nurturing and successful schools has succeeded and been copied throughout the United States.

Comer's School Development Program (SDP) is based on three principles—consensus, collaboration, and no fault—needed to develop a climate that allows schools, children, and parents to thrive

(see Figure 8–5). Consensus allows discussion, brainstorming for ideas, and decision making without requiring a vote that might cause divisiveness. Collaboration allows the schools, families, and community to move forward to develop a viable, responsive environment for children (Comer, 1997, 2004, 2005; Comer, Haynes, Joyner, & Ben-Avie, 1996). In using these principles, school personnel and parents can review aims and concerns without fault being assigned to anyone. The focus is on making decisions at the school and the individual student level (Fields-Smith & Neuharth-Pritchett, 2009).

Comer recognized that children's behaviors were determined by their environment, and hence they need to have positive interactions in order to develop physically, socially, and emotionally. With this in mind, he based the framework for school change on Field Theory, Human Ecological Systems Theory, the Population Adjustment Model, and the Social Action Model. SDP schools therefore place the child at the center, striving to meet his or her needs through the curriculum, social activities, and teaching methods, while reinforcing the positive aspects of home and building social networks. The foundation of Comer's framework is illustrated in Figure 8–6, with brief descriptions of the theories behind the school reform.

The child-centered environment is facilitated by planning and collaboration between professional and community. To do this, three teams guided by the three principles plan and work to develop a school climate that nurtures the children. The three teams, as shown in Figure 8–5, are as follows:

1. *School Planning and Management Team* (SPMT). The School Planning and Management Team plans and coordinates school endeavors, including curriculum, assessment, and instruction.
2. *Student and Staff Support Team* (SSST). First called the Mental Health Team, the Student and Staff Support Team works to prevent concerns from becoming problems and responds to the issues and needs of individual students.
3. *Parent Team* (PT). The Parent Team involves parents at all levels of the school and integrates the school with the community. (Comer, 2004; Comer, Haynes, & Joyner, 1996; Emmons, Comer, & Haynes, 1996; Haynes, Ben-Avie, Squires, Howley, Negron, & Corbin, 1996)

**FIGURE 8–5**
The foundations of Comer's theoretical framework of school reform.

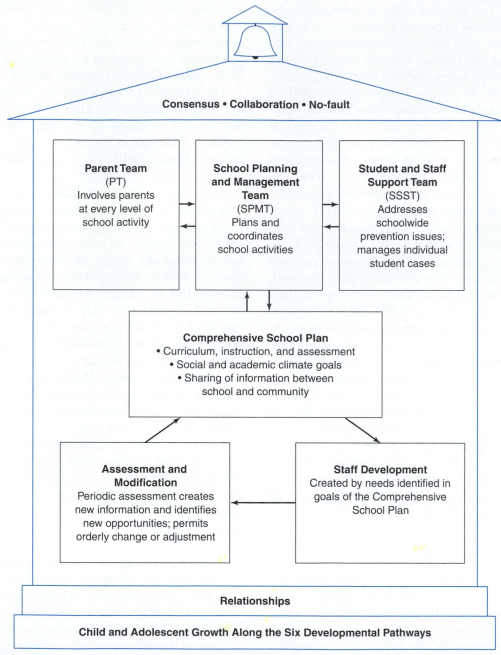

**Consensus • Collaboration • No-fault**

**Parent Team**
(PT)
Involves parents
at every level of
school activity

**School Planning
and Management
Team**
(SPMT)
Plans and
coordinates
school activities

**Student and Staff
Support Team**
(SSST)
Addresses
schoolwide
prevention issues;
manages individual
student cases

**Comprehensive School Plan**
• Curriculum, instruction, and assessment
• Social and academic climate goals
• Sharing of information between
school and community

**Assessment and
Modification**
Periodic assessment creates
new information and identifies
new opportunities; permits
orderly change or adjustment

**Staff Development**
Created by needs identified in
goals of the Comprehensive
School Plan

**Relationships**

**Child and Adolescent Growth Along the Six Developmental Pathways**

*Source:* Reprinted by permission of the publisher from Comer, J. P., Haynes, N. M., Joyner, E. T., & Ben-Avie, M. (Eds.). (1996). *Rallying the Whole Village: The Comer Process for Reforming Education* (New York: Teachers College Press, © 1996 by Teachers College, Columbia University. All rights reserved.). Figures 1-1 & 2-1.

To develop an SDP school, participants must build trust; plan well; empower parents; and continually monitor, assess, and modify as necessary (Haynes et al., 1996). For more information refer to *Rallying the Whole Village: The Comer Process for Reforming Education* by Comer, Haynes, Joyner, and Ben-Avie (1996); or *Leave No Child Behind: Preparing Today's Youth for Tomorrow's World* by Comer (2004); or contact the School Development Program in New Haven, Connecticut.

**FIGURE 8-6**
Model of the SDP process.

**Population Adjustment Model**
Becker, Wylan, and McCourt (1971)
Hartman (1979)

- Identify populations at risk for developing mental illness.
- Intervene through modifying the environment to promote mental health.

**Social Action Model**
Reiff (1966)

- Program planning should be a collaborative effort between professionals and community members.
- Professionals should have an integral knowledge of the community in which they are working.

**Comer's Theoretical Framework of Child Development**

- A child's behavior is determined by his or her interaction with the physical, social, and psychological environments.
- Children need positive interactions with adults in order to develop adequately.
- Child-centered planning and collaboration among adults facilitate positive interaction.
- All planning for child development should be a collaborative effort between professionals and community members.

**Comer's Framework Applied**
*The School Development Program*

- Three Guiding Principles
- Three Mechanisms (Teams)
- Three Operations

**Field Theory**
Lewin (1936)

- Everything an individual knows, feels, and perceives is done in a subjective reality.
- This subjective reality is known as a person's psychological field or life space; only those things present in the life space influence behavior.

**Human Ecological Systems Theory**
Kelly (1966)

- Behavior is an interaction of human beings with the physical, social, and psychological environments, making behavior adaptive.
- The theory's four principles are:
  — The community is the client.
  — Reduce those community services that maintain the status quo.
  — Strengthen community resources.
  — Plan for change.

*Source:* Reprinted by permission of the publisher from Comer, J. P., Haynes, N. M., Joyner, E. T., & Ben-Avie, M. (Eds.). (1996). *Rallying the Whole Village: The Comer Process for Reforming Education* (New York: Teachers College Press, © 1996 by Teachers College, Columbia University. All rights reserved.). Figures 1-1 & 2-1.

## REGGIO EMILIA

The importance of parent involvement in education extends beyond the United States, of course. One example can be seen in the Reggio Emilia program in Italy. Malaguzzi, the founder and former director of the program, described it this way: "Our proposition is to consider a triad at the center of education—children, teachers, and families. To think of a dyad of only a teacher and a child is to create an artificial world that does not reflect reality" (Malaguzzi, 1993, p. 9). The Reggio Emilia program believes that the interaction of children with adults (both parents and teachers) and other children is essential for their development: "Interaction among children affects social, emotional, communicative, and cognitive behavior and development . . . different from those usually reached by children working in isolation" (Malaguzzi, 1993, p. 12).

Teachers in the Reggio Emilia approach have different roles that go beyond being a "pedagogista or pedagogue" but teachers are facilitators, researchers, and reflective practitioners (Hewett, 2001). If you add *parent* to the roles of the teacher, you will be able to visualize the triad of child, teacher, and parent in the total development of the child, particularly through aesthetic activities (Piazza, 2007).

## THE PROJECT APPROACH

Similar to the Reggio Emilia program would be the **Project Approach,** which involves the child as a constructor of knowledge and research. The project approach was not formally recognized until 1918, when W. H. Kirkpatrick and colleagues, players in the progressive education movement, used the term *project method* to describe what we now think of as the *project approach*. Infant Schools in England had active involvement of children using projects as early as the 1970s. More recently, the constructivist approach in the United States and the Reggio Emilia program in Italy have revived the interest in education revolving around projects.

The term *project approach* describes the focus of the lesson without any need for other descriptive terms. It does not, however, describe the in-depth construction of learning that can be achieved by being involved in the planning, discovery, conducting of research, or the describing and writing the results of the project. This approach can be adapted

so that it is appropriate for children of all ages, including very young children. It is important to incorporate this kind of learning because children grow socially when they can work cooperatively and share both the excitement and challenge of learning about their chosen project. It is important to remember too that whether the idea for a project comes from the teacher, child-care provider, or child, it is essential that there be an opportunity for the child to succeed in its development (Harris Helm & Katz, 2010).

A good example of a project appeared in *Young Children* in an article by Helm, Hebner, and Long (2000) titled "Quiltmaking: A Perfect Project for Preschool and Primary." In most project approaches, there are three phases: (a) planning, researching, and organizing; (b) investigating, discovering, constructing, and working; and (c) completing the project and celebrating its success. The authors showed how both preschool and primary classrooms could use the same project theme, quilting, to successfully complete these three stages. Using quilts also provided a bridge to home and parent involvement. Children made class quilt squares using paper, fabric, Velcro, and tie-dye; and the squares put together created a banner. The curriculum was enhanced using this project idea. The preschool room had language, art/music, drama, science, and math quilt squares. The primary room had reading enrichment, math, social studies, and art/music quilt squares. Throughout the project, children were communicating, cooperating, and constructing a knowledge base. Articles about projects can be found in the *Early Childhood Research and Practice* journal edited by Lilian Katz.

Projects also allow teachers to invite parents to help with the different phases, perhaps by providing their expertise. They can also be invited to assist the teacher in guiding the children in the project; to chaperone on project-related field trips; or to attend a culminating event, such as in the project "Cheese Pizza" (Gallick & Lee, 2010).

## SCHOOL AND CENTER PROGRAMS

The tradition of involving parents has been strong in the early childhood profession for years, as exemplified in the parent-cooperative movement and carried forth by many child-care providers and educators. The following sections describe programs for early childhood–age children.

### Effective Programs—Research Briefs

Early childhood education programs are extremely beneficial. They benefit education progress and academic achievement, reduce delinquency and crime, and improve ability in the labor market. According to research reported by Koraly, Kilburn, and Cannon (2005), the following early childhood education programs were found to be effective when combined with parent education and/or home visitations: Head Start, High/Scope Perry Preschool Project, Carolina Abecedarian Project, Project CARE, Syracuse Family Development Research, Houston Parent–Child Development Center, Early Training Project, Chicago Child Parent Center, Oklahoma Pre-K, and AVANCE.

Findings concluded that early intervention has more favorable results if the caregivers are well trained. There is also evidence to suggest that center-based programs with smaller child-to-staff ratios are more successful.

**Head Start.** Head Start is a federally-funded program that has served over 27 million children since 1965 (U.S. Department of Health and Human Services, 2011). It is a comprehensive early childhood program that provides child-development initiatives for low-income children. Although the related Early Head Start program serves infants and toddlers, Head Start is best known as a preschool program. From its inception, Head Start involved the family in its outreach, with spokes of the wheel covering education; health care, including medical, dental, and mental health; nutrition; social services; staff development; and parent involvement. Head Start makes a significant difference in the lives of children and their parents through these services.

During the 2009 fiscal year, the American Recovery and Reinvestment Act appropriated an additional $2.1 billion for Head Start and Early Head Start Programs to increase enrollment by 64,000 children and families (U.S. Department of Health and Human Services, 2011). Research indicates that the services of Head Start improve vocabulary, math, and social skills. In addition, Head Start parents are more involved with their children's education. Two-thirds of these parents read to their children three times a week or more, three-fourths attend parent–teacher conferences, and most volunteer in the classroom (U.S. Department of Health and Human Services Fact Sheet, 2002).

*Parent Involvement.* In 2004, revised Head Start Performance Standards (HSPS) were implemented. The standards reinforce previous practices of family partnerships. Parent involvement policies, HSPS 1304.40, Family Partnerships, include the following:

### *Family Goal Setting*

- Grantee and delegate agencies must engage in a process of collaborative partnership building with parents to establish mutual trust and to identify family goals, strengths, and necessary services and other supports. This process must be initiated as early after enrollment as possible, and it must take into consideration each family's readiness and willingness to participate in the process.

### *Parent Involvement—General*

- Grantee and delegate agencies must provide parent-involvement and education activities that are responsive to the ongoing and expressed needs of the parents, both as individuals and as members of a group. Other community agencies should be encouraged to assist in the planning and implementation of such programs' opportunities in policy making, parent involvement, and education.
- Early Head Start and Head Start settings must be open to parents during all program hours. Parents must be welcomed as visitors and encouraged to observe children as often as possible and to participate with children in group activities. The participation of parents in any program activity must be voluntary and must not be required as a condition of the child's enrollment.
- Grantee and delegate agencies must provide parents with opportunities to participate in the program as employees or volunteers.

### *Parent Involvement in Child Development and Education*

- Grantee and delegate agencies must provide opportunities to include parents in the development of the program's curriculum and approach to child development and education.
- Grantee and delegate agencies must provide opportunities for parents to enhance their parenting skills, knowledge, and understanding of the educational and developmental needs and

activities of their children and to share concerns about their children with program staff.

- In addition to the two home visits, teachers in center-based programs must conduct staff–parent conferences as needed, but no less than two per program year, to enhance the knowledge and understanding of both staff and parents of the educational developmental progress and activities of children in the program.

### Communication with Families

- Grantee and delegate agencies must ensure that effective two-way comprehensive communications between staff and parents are carried out on a regular basis throughout the program year.

The thrust of this information is to enable parents to help themselves. Parents can do this only with more education, more options, more knowledge, greater self-esteem, and more empowerment. Although Head Start parents have had more access to parent involvement than parents in most early childhood programs (with perhaps the exception of parent cooperatives), the task force and standards encourage a more active commitment to ensuring true parent involvement.

Before initiating any parent program, it is wise to ask parents how they perceive their needs. Although needs will change throughout the life of any program, early assessment with periodic review will show the initial needs and the progression of later needs. Develop a needs assessment specific to the population.

After Head Start parents complete a needs assessment, plans for parent participation can be devised with better understanding. As parents become more familiar with the program and more sophisticated in their learning, their needs and requests will vary, so provide ongoing assessment by continued use of questionnaires. Head Start, initially conceived with a parent component, has integrated parents into every aspect of its program. Because the center is located in the community it serves, parents usually drop off and pick up their children. As they enter the school, teachers and parents exchange pleasant greetings. On some days, the parents stay and help.

In the area of decision making, Head Start programs involve parents at two or three levels: the Head Start Center Committee, the Head Start Policy Committee for the delegate agency, and the Head Start Policy Council (for the grantee funded by the federal government). The first is initiated by each center, which should have a committee composed of parents whose children are enrolled.

Two of the most essential and greatest strengths of the Head Start philosophy are the involvement of parents and the belief that parents can achieve. Through a Head Start career ladder, many low-income parents are hired to assist in the program. The teacher may be a college graduate from another neighborhood, but, just as often, the teacher is a local parent who had children enrolled in the Head Start program or a parent who has a college degree and who has earned Child Development Associate (CDA) credentials. The aide typically lives in the neighborhood and perhaps also has children in the program. The person responsible for lunch is another community parent. After lunch, the parent coordinator drops in to check on a child who has been ill. The parent coordinator was chosen by the policy committee because the parents respected and liked this neighbor. This person has succeeded in establishing rapport with and support for the neighbors.

Even if the parent does not work in the classroom, the quality of the parent–teacher relationship as well as parental participation in the program are very important components to increase children's social and linguistic competence, which are some of the goals for Head Start (Mendez, 2010). In essence, the importance of parents as leaders of their children's development is a key component of the Head Start program (National Head Start Association, 2011).

**Early Head Start.** Early Head Start, a program that serves low-income families who have infants and toddlers, was created with the reauthorization of the Head Start Act in 1994. From 68 programs in 1995, it grew to 635 programs serving 45,000 children in 2001. In 2002 and 2003, Early Head Start (EHS) received 10 percent of the Head Start appropriation. In January 2001, a national evaluation that covered the first two years of 3,000 children showed that EHS children performed significantly better on cognitive, social–emotional, and language development. In addition, the parents scored higher than the control group on knowledge of infant–toddler development, parenting, and home environment. It was also found that parents of children were more likely to go into job training or attend school, and that family conflict declined (Fenichel &

Mann, 2001). Parents' contributions to children's linguistic and social development through a positive early learning environment appear to have positive correlations with emotion regulation and vocabulary development whereas depressive symptoms and parenting stress were associated with behavior problems (Chazan-Cohen, Raikes, Brooks-Gunn, Ayoub, Pan, Kisker, Roggman, & Fuligni, 2009).

Families may be served in center-based or home-based environments or a combination of the two. Programs need to meet or exceed federal Head Start performance standards (Buell, Hallam, & Beck, 2001). For children from birth to 36 months who are enrolled in out-of-home programs, the EHS standard is a maximum of eight children and a child ratio of one to four. This standard helps ensure the high-quality care and nurturing environment that infants and toddlers need.

**High/Scope Perry Preschool Program.** In November 2004, High/Scope reported a long-term study of adults at age 40 who, as low-income 3- and 4-year-old children, had participated in a 2-year early education and care program provided by High/Scope. From 1962 through 1967, High/Scope operated the High/Scope Perry Preschool Program with a limit of eight children per teacher. A sample of 123 low-income African American boys and girls were randomly assigned to five preschools or to a group who received no preschool program. Classes were held 5 days a week for two and a half hours. Teachers were college graduates certified in early childhood, special education, or elementary education.

*Research Results.* High/Scope Educational Research Foundation staff studied these children every year from the age of 3 until they were 11 and then at ages 14, 15, 19, 27, and 40. They found that more students who had preschool graduated from high school than did those in the no-program group (65 percent versus 45 percent), with women significantly higher than men (84 percent versus 32 percent). Sample comparisons of the High/Scope Program versus no program at age 40 showed that 70 percent program versus 50 percent no program were employed; 37 percent program versus 28 percent no program owned their own home; 76 percent program versus 50 percent no program had savings accounts; 2 percent program versus 12 percent no program committed violent felonies; and 3 percent program versus 20 percent no program were cited for having dangerous drugs.

*Curriculum Research.* High/Scope conducted a High/Scope Preschool Curriculum Comparison study after the High/Scope Perry Preschool study and found that the High/Scope model was successful. The researchers studied the direct instructional model, in which teachers taught the children academic skills and rewarded them for correct answers. They also examined the traditional nursery school model in which teachers responded to the children's self-initiated activities in a supportive and loosely structured environment. In the High/Scope model, teachers design their classrooms with both large- and small-group activities, emphasizing self-initiated learning. The children, with help from the teacher, plan their own activities and review these activities after they have carried out their plans (Schweinhart, 2009). When research was conducted of the participants of nursery school and High/Scope at 23 years of age, it showed that the nursery school and High/Scope had similar outcomes (Schweinhart & Weikart, 1997). Although the direct instructional model shows early improvement in academics, it is temporary, and it loses the opportunity for improvement in long-term social behavior improvement (Schweinhart, 2005). These two programs, Head Start and High/Scope, illustrate successful programs that continue to be actively effective.

*Parent Involvement.* The spring 2006 issue of *Resource: A Magazine for Educators* highlights the Head Start performance standards as they relate to High/Scope and points out the ways in which it has involved parents in its program. Suggestions include the following:

1. Include parents through conversations during arrival and departure time. Ask the parent to leave a note if special instructions are needed.
2. Provide parents with copies of the daily routine and furnish a bulletin board for messages. A welcome packet lets parents know that the caregivers want to keep parents informed.
3. Write daily notes, share observations through phone calls, keep pass-down logs, have daily news sheets and newsletters, take and give digital photos of the child participating in preschool (remember to have parents' permission

to do this), and use e-mail for parents who have Internet capability.

4. Hold open house at a time when parents can participate, learn more about the setting, and talk with staff.

5. Include parents in the program if they are able to volunteer.

6. Supply an information sheet that includes suggestions for learning experiences at home. (Kruse, 2006)

**The Carolina Abecedarian Project.** The North Carolina Abecedarian Project was a program in which children from low-income families had high-quality full-time educational intervention, infancy through age 5, with the recruited children being born between 1972 and 1977. The development was achieved through individualized education with the activities consisting of "games" included in the children's regular day. The activities had an emphasis on language development with social, intellectual, and emotional development also included (Campbell et al., 2008).

The Woodcock-Johnson Achievement Test was given children in the Abecedarian Project in the fall and spring of their third year of school. The children were monitored and had follow-up studies during the summer following their seventh-grade year (age 12), tenth-grade year (age 15), and at 21 years of age. It was found that high-quality intervention and education during early childhood can carry over academically as the child progressed through school. The children had higher cognitive test scores beginning as toddlers, and the scores continued through until the last study at age 21. Improved language development seems to have enhanced the resulting cognitive test scores. Other major findings included the following: intervention children on the average were older when they had their first child, academic achievement in both reading and math was higher from early grades to young adulthood, and the children were more likely to attend a four-year college (University of North Carolina, FPG Child Development Institute, n.d.).

**Carolina Approach to Responsive Education (Project CARE).** A related study to the Abecedarian Project was the Carolina Approach to Responsive Education (Project CARE). Recruited children who were born between 1978 and 1980 were randomly assigned to one of three groups: educational child care plus home visits from 6 weeks until school entry, home visits from 6 weeks until school entry, and the control group. The first two groups received home–school resource services during the first three years of school. Extensive testing was done during the period the children were in school, with testing including quality of family environment, maternal measures (mother's characteristics and other information), and cognitive and academic achievement. The Woodcock-Johnson was administered fall and spring during the first three years of school, and in the summer after their seventh year of school. Based on Woodcock-Johnson test scores, Rand Corporation identified Project CARE as a successful program (Karoly, Kilburn, & Cannon, 2005). This evidence along with evidence from the Abecedarian Project strengthen the case to provide quality early childhood intervention, particularly for families in need (Campbell et al., 2008).

**Syracuse Family Development Research Program.** The Syracuse Family Development Research Program (FDRP) was a comprehensive early childhood program that included home visits, parent training, and a children's center with a program of education, health, nutrition, and other human services, prenatal to the beginning of elementary school. The targeted program participants were low-income families of young African American single parents. Honig, Lally, and Mathieson assessed the program in 1982, finding that the FDRP kindergarten children had emotional functioning superior to those in the control group and were more flexible, purposeful, energetic, social, relaxed, and affectionate to others than the children in the control group. In addition, those in the FDRP groups had more children who attained an IQ score above 89. The first-grade group continued to have positive behavior toward other children, but they had more negative and positive behavior toward adults than the control group (Promising Practices Network, n.d.). In 1988, the research found that by eighth grade, none of the FDRP girls had failing averages, whereas 16 percent of the control group did. Seventy-two percent of the FDRP girls maintained a C average or better, compared to only 47 percent of the control group. There were no significant differences in achievement between FDRP boys and the control group. Research on delinquency reported by Lally, Mangione, and Honig in 1988 found that three of the control group compared to none of the FDRP had committed violent crimes. An analysis reported in 2001 by Aos, Barnoski, and Lieb found that the FDRP children committed fewer crimes than the comparison, but of those who committed crimes, there was no difference in the number of offenses that had been committed (Promising Practices Network, 2011).

**Houston Parent–Child Development Center Infant Health Development Program.** The Houston Parent–Child Development Center focused on very young Latino children. The first year included 25 home visits. Each 90-minute visit focused on infant development. Small groups met together on weekends for family workshops in which they discussed communication, decisions, and issues chosen by the participants. English as a second language classes were also offered to the mothers of the children. Information on child and public health was furnished by a visiting nurse. Transportation and information on ways to obtain resources were provided.

During the second year, there were center-based classes for mothers and their 2-year-old for four hours, four mornings a week. Transportation and lunch were provided, and the group discussion and information of home management and child care continued. Fathers attended monthly meetings, which strengthened their paternal roles (Johnson, 1990).

**The Early Training Project.** The Early Training Project was an early (1962–1965) research project in which 65 African American children who were 4 to 5 years old were chosen to participate in a study to improve educational achievement. The children were chosen from families based on education, occupation, housing, and income. The children were randomly assigned to a 10-week summer program for either two summers, three summers, or a control group (no program). Those in the intervention programs also received weekly home visits throughout the school year. Assessments of the program were conducted during the intervention period and in 1965, 1966, 1968, 1975, and 1978. In 1965, at the end of first grade, the children scored high on three of the four subtests of the Metropolitan Achievement (Karoly, Kilburn, & Cannon, 2005). Significant

differences were found, but they faded as the children matured. Participants were less likely to be placed in special education, be retained in grade, or drop out of high school (Karoly et al., 2005). The reduction of special education at age 12 showed that only 5 percent of Early Training Project students were in special education compared to 29 percent of the control group and that 8 percent graduated compared to 52 percent of the control group (Currie, 2000).

**Chicago Child–Parent Center.** Chicago Child–Parent Centers are centers integrated with primary schools in Chicago. When it began in 1967, the program was a half-day preschool program for 3- to 4-year-old children. Using federal Title I funds, the center provided health services, social services, and a preschool and encouraged parent participation and involvement. The preschool program was designed to prepare children for school with a focus on language skills and preparation for reading.

In 1978, with the addition of state funding, the kindergarten was increased to full day and the program was extended through third grade. The children also received free breakfasts, lunches, and health screenings. Class sizes were kept relatively small, with the adult-to-child ratio in preschool being one to eight in a class of 17 and in kindergarten, 1 to 12 in a class of 25. The class size was further reduced, with the primary program additionally offering coordinated instruction and parent involvement. Findings based on children at 9 years of age showed that CPC children had significantly higher math and reading achievement scores, less retention, and more significant parent involvement. There was no difference in special-education placement, but the number of years spent in special education was significantly lower (Karoly et al., 2005).

It is important to note here that the parent involvement aspect was strong. Activities included parenting classes, clerical assistance by parents, and parent involvement in school activities such as developing resources and coordinating school projects (Chicago Longitudinal Study, 2004).

**Oklahoma Pre-K.** Oklahoma has been a leader in providing public school prekindergarten offerings. As early as 1980, Oklahoma was considering standards for a program for 4-year-old children. In 1990, Head Start–eligible students could attend prekindergarten without cost and, if space was available, others could pay tuition and attend. The standards for a pre-K program include early childhood–certified teachers who have a bachelor's degree and who pass an early childhood education–subject-area competency test. The pre-K teachers are also paid on the same salary scale as the K–12 teachers. Pre-K has small class sizes of 20 students and an adult-to-child ratio of 1 to 10. Family involvement is also encouraged. Developmentally appropriate curriculum and continued professional development of certified personnel are required (Garrett, 2004; Gormley, Gayer, Phillips, & Dawson, 2004).

In September 2003, the Woodcock-Johnson Achievement Test was given to 1,567 pre-K children and 3,148 kindergarteners in Tulsa, Oklahoma. The pre-K students were ready to begin their pre-K program for the year, and nearly half of the kindergarten students had participated in the pre-K program the year before. Key findings included a 52 percent gain in letter word identification, a 27 percent gain in spelling test scores, and a 21 percent gain in applied problems. These are percentages above the average gain that occurs over one year. Gains for minority students were even more impressive. Hispanic students showed a 79 percent gain in letter and word identification. There was also a 39 percent gain in spelling, and a 54 percent gain in applied programs (Gormley et al., 2004).

**AVANCE.** This program is one of the oldest and most distinguished parenting and early childhood programs in the United States. The word *avance* in Spanish means "to advance," and that is what the program strives for through parent education. The program assists parents in creating cognitively stimulating environments that allow children to develop their five senses in order to explore their world. It uses a wide variety of methods of reaching families and their children, including weekly three-hour class time consisting of play and toy curriculum, a parenting-education curriculum, and community-resource awareness (AVANCE, 2010). The AVANCE model also teaches participants that the home must provide a language-rich environment because through language, learning occurs. AVANCE shows parents how they can transmit the values associated with their culture to encourage appropriate behavior within their family and the large society. In addition

AVANCE trains parents in developing homes that are safe havens for children, free from violence and abuse. Many AVANCE parents have been victims of abuse and neglect; therefore, it is imperative that the parents attend the scheduled classes for their optimal success. Johnson, Walker, and Rodriguez (1996) found that mothers who participated in the program with their infants became highly skilled teachers even after a one-year follow-up. In fact, after participating in the training, AVANCE parents become center teachers themselves.

**Other Examples of Successful Programs— School on Saturday.** The Ferguson-Florissant School District in St. Louis, Missouri worked with parents to offer a Saturday school. This included 3 (3-hour) preschool sessions for 4-year-olds on Saturdays throughout the school year. Although the program is no longer available in the school district, the concept behind it is appropriate for districts that could have a Saturday program, especially if they were unable to furnish full-time preschools. The program had three major objectives:

- To provide an education program that will help 4-year-old children succeed in school.
- To involve parents in the education of their children.
- To provide support for families.

These objectives were accomplished by providing the following:

- Diagnostic screening at the beginning of the school year to establish appropriate goals.
- Half-day preschool each Saturday in a public kindergarten.
- Opportunities for participation by parents in the preschool. (Parents had to participate every 4 to 6 weeks as a parent helper in the preschool.)
- Home visits, one hour each week, with a group of two or three children and their parents.
- Home activity guides that provided ideas for projects and other activities for the 4-year-old child—and younger siblings, if any—to do at home; these activities fostered skills needed for success in school.
- Consultants in child development, who were available to consider specific concerns as well as provide parent meetings

Although the program was ended in Ferguson-Florissant, Saturday school seemed to work because children gained in cognitive, language, and eye–hand coordination. Parents gained in their ability to communicate with their children, use appropriate reinforcement techniques, and sense a child's learning readiness. The program reached out to fathers as well as mothers. The curriculum, dealing with motor-coordination development, goes hand in hand with positive interaction between child and father. See Figure 8–7 for an example of activities for father and child.

What can other programs gain from the Saturday school? These aspects seem especially important:

- Active participation by both parents in teaching their own children.
- Diagnostic and prescriptive activities for children with disabilities.
- Observation and participation by parents in a school setting.
- Guidance and activities that support parents' efforts.

**FIGURE 8–7**
Fathers are an integral part of the Saturday school.

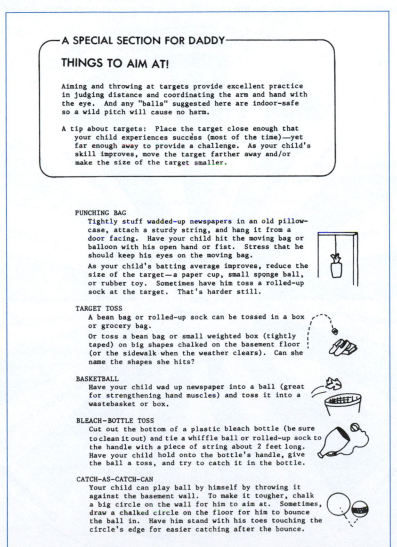

*Source:* Reprinted with permission from the Ferguson-Florissant School District, St. Louis, MO.

- Teacher visits to the home, establishing a team rapport between teachers and parents.
- Opportunities for the child to experience routine school activities and an enriched curriculum each week.
- Home-learning activity booklets to be used by parents of children from birth through age 3.

The varied approaches of the Saturday school met many more needs than a program with only one dimension—for example, preschool without the parent component.

**Brookline Early Education Project.** An excellent example of how the public school system can collaborate with a health organization was the Brookline Early Education Project (BEEP). In 1972, Brookline Public Schools and Children's Hospital Medical Center and researchers from the Boston-area universities joined to develop a coordinated plan for physical check-ups and educational programs for young children up to kindergarten age (Figure 8–8). Together, the hospital and school supplied a reassuring support system.

**FIGURE 8–8**
The hospital and school work together to provide for the child's health, education, and development.

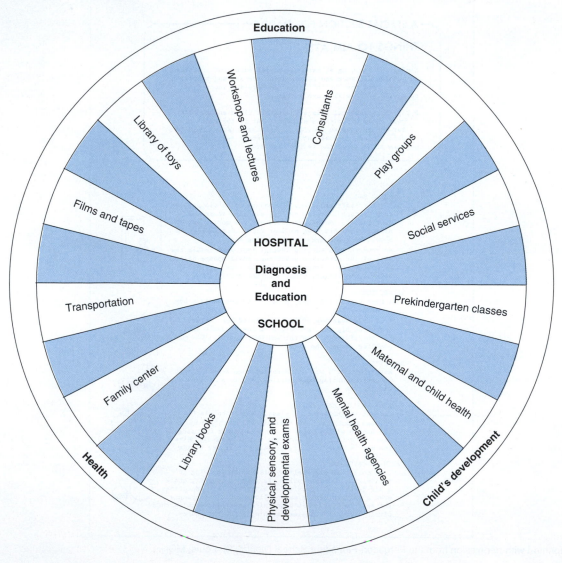

Based on the theory that parents are the child's most influential teachers, BEEP had three interrelated components:

1. *Parent education and support.* Three levels of support were provided, ranging from frequent home visits and meetings to parent-initiated support. Home visits, parent groups, and center visits were available.
2. *Diagnostic monitoring.* Children were periodically screened by staff at Children's Hospital Medical Center from age 2 weeks until entry into kindergarten.
3. *Education and enrichment.* The 2-year-old children attended weekly play group sessions in the BEEP project center.

In addition to these services, the BEEP program offered a parent center; consultants to answer questions; library books and pamphlets, films and videotapes on child development; a series of special events such as workshops, films, and lectures; and transportation for the parents of the children enrolled in BEEP (Pierson, Walker, & Tivnan, 1984). Home visits were reported as being the most valuable in terms of support for the parents. Over 95 percent of the mothers would recommend the BEEP program to their own children (Palfrey, Bronson, Hauser-Cram, & Warfield, 2002).

A study begun in 1996 and published in 2002 found that the young adults who had participated in BEEP had higher incomes and reported higher health ratings and lower levels of depression. They attained more years of education and were more likely to be employed or in school.

## :: MATH AND SCIENCE ASSOCIATIONS THAT SUPPORT PARENT INVOLVEMENT

The National Council of Teachers of Mathematics (NCTM) recommends that parents get involved with their children in their success in and enjoyment of mathematics. They suggest that students discuss their classroom activities and what they have learned with their parents. Parents can help their student if they do the following:

- Provide a place for the student to do homework.
- Participate in parent–teacher conferences.
- Encourage their children to persist, not do the work for them.

- Engage in activities such as games and puzzles during family time.
- Visit mathematics classes when given the opportunity.

### Family Math

The Family Math classes include materials and activities for parents to use while they help their children with mathematics at home. Meetings two to three hours long take place one evening each week for four to six weeks. Children attend the meetings with their parents.

Families can use the Internet to obtain math activities that can be done at home. There is also a book available, *Helping Your Child Learn Math,* which is published by the U.S. Department of Education. Examples of the activities can be found at www.math.com/parents/articles/mathhome.html.

### Family Science

An outgrowth of Family Math, Family Science encourages parents and children to work together on day-to-day science using inexpensive materials available in the home. The program's developers hope that culturally and linguistically diverse children and as well as girls in general—traditionally left behind or discouraged from scientific pursuits—will be encouraged to develop their abilities in math and science if they learn about them in a nonthreatening environment.

### Education Resources Information Center

The Education Resources Information Center (ERIC), located at the University of Illinois under the direction of Lilian G. Katz, was an educational resource for areas of education including elementary and early childhood education. The service commenced in 1967 and continued until December 2003, when a new ERIC was established. At that time all the divisions of ERIC continued as a digital library of education resources under the Institute of Education Sciences of the U.S. Department of Education. The digital library was opened for public use in 2004 with a focus on providing current and archived resources.

The Clearinghouse on Early Education and Parenting (CEEP), part of Early Childhood and Parenting (ECAP), was established within the College of Education at the University of Illinois,

Urbana-Champaign, under the direction of Lilian G. Katz and Dianne Rothenberg (Clearinghouse on Early Education and Parenting, 2011).

## :: TITLE PROGRAMS

### Title I

Federal programs funded under several titles also illustrate innovative use of parents as partners in the educational process. Needs assessments, parent advisory councils, conferences, and home–school activities are included in typical programs. Title I programs, active in most state school systems, heavily emphasize parent involvement, recognizing that the parent is the child's first teacher and that home environment and parental attitude toward school influence a child's academic success. A parent-resource teacher is provided to work solely with parents. Parents, paraprofessionals, teachers, and administrators work together to provide support and education for the children. Parents are trained to instruct their children at home and are also involved in the school program. These successful programs represent the best in curriculum development. Their concern for parent involvement illustrates the significance of parents in the successful education of their children.

### Title I—Section 101

Section 101, Improving the Academic Achievement of the Disadvantaged, reflects the need to ensure high-quality education for all children to have adequate and excellent education. If you want to locate these or other programs throughout the United States, call the U.S. Department of Education at 1-800-USA-LEARN and ask for the most recent publications about families and schools.

Suggestions for changes in Title I were included in the 2001 proposal of the No Child Left Behind Act (NCLB). To meet the goal of reducing the achievement gap between disadvantaged and advantaged students, the report proposed maintaining high standards in reading and math and setting high standards in history and science, providing annual assessments in reading and math for third to eighth grades, reporting results of assessments to parents, and increasing flexibility by reducing the poverty threshold from 50 to 40 percent so that more schools can combine their federal money to improve quality. Federal funds were made available for technical assistance and to provide capacity building to schools that need improvement.

According to NCLB, if an identified school still has not met adequate progress after two years, the district must implement corrective action and offer a public school option to all students in the failing school. If the school fails to make adequate progress after three years, disadvantaged students within the school may use Title I funds to transfer to a higher-performing public or private school, or they may receive supplemental educational services from a provider of choice. All nonpublic providers receiving federal money will be subject to appropriate standards of accountability (U.S. Department of Education, 2001, p. 9).

### Title IV

The purpose of Title IV is "to promote parental choice and to increase the amount of flexible funds available to states and school districts for innovative education programs" (U.S. Department of Education, 2001, p. 18). The proposal promotes charter schools, broadens education savings accounts, expands school choice, consolidates categorical grand programs, and expands private activity bonds to be used for public school construction (U.S. Department of Education, 2001).

## :: SCHOOL AND CENTER-BASED PARENT INVOLVEMENT

### The Minnesota Early Childhood Family Education Program

The State of Minnesota offers support and information for parents and children, birth to kindergarten. Some of the programs offered include:

1. *Early childhood screening* is for children before they enter kindergarten. Because it is important that any potential problems be identified early, it is recommended that screening be done by the time the child is 3.
2. *Early Childhood Family Education* is a program that parents of children, birth until enrollment in kindergarten, can attend for information, activities, and support. A typical day has the parent and child doing an activity, followed by the parent and child doing their own activities, the child active in preschool and the parent attending a parent-education session.

3. *The High-Five* kindergarten is a program for 4-year-olds who will start kindergarten the following year.
4. *Early childhood special education* is for children from birth to kindergarten who have been identified as having a disability.
5. *Parents in Community Action* (PICA) has operated a Head Start program for over 30 years.
6. *Home-based programs* include Way to Grow, a program that builds school readiness for children 3 to 5. It focuses on future school success by focusing on cognitive, emotional, and social development and is delivered through home visits. In addition, Minneapolis offers Home Instruction Program for Preschool Youngsters (HIPPY). See Chapter 9 for a description of HIPPY (Minneapolis Public Schools, 2005).

**Minneapolis.** Minneapolis is a good example of the greater involvement of parents with schools. The Early Childhood Family Education program welcomes the enrollment of all families living in Minneapolis who have children from birth to enrollment in kindergarten. Programs for the children include Early Reading First, a full-year program for children who are 3; Minneapolis Kids Fours Explore is a full-day program for 4-year-olds; and High-Five is a prekindergarten school year for children who are 4 years old. Programs are varied; early childhood special education serves children from birth to kindergarten. Screening is provided to assess if children need a special-education program. The New Families Center is a year-long all-day program for families whose second language is English. There is also the Teenage Pregnant and Parenting Program, which provides services to support teenagers who are pregnant or are already parents. In Minneapolis, pledges or covenants are signed by all involved—students, parents or representatives, teachers and other staff members, the superintendent, school board members, and community members. All participants have specific ways in which they can help (Minneapolis Public Schools, 2006).

## Reading First

Reading First provides funds and tools to states to ensure that children receive effective reading instruction from kindergarten through third grade. The National Reading Panel reported that

Effective reading instruction includes teaching children to break apart and manipulate the sounds in words (phonemic awareness), teaching them that these sounds are represented by letters of the alphabet which can then be blended together to form words (phonics), having them practice what they have learned by reading aloud with guidance and feedback (guided oral reading), and applying reading comprehension strategies to guide and improve reading comprehension. (2000, p. 10)

The program is built on a solid foundation of research and "is designed to select, implement, and provide professional development for teachers using scientifically based reading programs, and to ensure accountability through ongoing, valid and reliable screening, diagnostic and classroom-based assessment" (Ed. Gov, 2004). In some models, parents are approached to help children with specific literacy skills (Griffith, Kimmel, & Biscoe, 2010).

## Institute for Responsive Education

The Institute for Responsive Education (2006) continues with its emphasis on connecting school, family, and community. In April 2005, the program moved to Cambridge College, School of Education, in Cambridge, Massachusetts. Its mission statement states:

The Institute for Responsive Education (IRE) is a research, policy, and advocacy organization that encourages and supports school, family, and community partnerships to enable high quality educational opportunities for all children. We believe that schools, families, and communities all share the responsibility to improve schools and raise educational standards. (Institute for Responsive Education, 2002, p.1)

The various activities of the Institute for Responsive Education include the Parent Leadership Exchange, which provides networking for parent leaders in three New England states; the Boston Parent Organizing Network (BPON); and Family Involvement in After School Study, a study of family centers nationwide. The changes in the Institute illustrate the ebb and flow of family involvement with schools. New programs are developed, flourish, meet the needs of the schools, change the environment, become a part of the total program, or diminish when they are no longer needed, something replaces them, or the funding source is lost (Institute of Responsive Education, 2006).

## National Association of State Boards of Education

The National Association of State Boards of Education (NASBE, 1991, 2006) recommends continual communication between parents and schools, with parent involvement in decision making on program policy, curriculum, and evaluation. The NASBE also encourages more time for teachers to plan and carry out home visits, for home activities and materials to be provided for parents to use with their children, and for schools to provide leadership in developing family support services in collaboration with existing community agencies. They would also like to see businesses encouraged to give parents time off to attend parent–teacher conferences and volunteer in the classroom. The NASBE suggests parents get involved by coming to the classroom to observe and volunteer and to tutor their children at home; strong parent involvement is also important to accommodate the family in before- and after-school programs. Administrators often try to have parents involved in the planning of before- and after-school programs through parent advisory committees, workshops, and orientation sessions, though the task force of the NASBE suggests further in-service training for administrators and teachers on parent involvement. With this mission of cooperation between home and school, the task force supports provision of sufficient staff, training, and time to work together (National Association of State Boards of Education, 2011).

In 2001, NASBE, with financial support from the Kellogg Foundation, started Early Childhood Education Network, a project to increase the ability of six states (Kansas, Illinois, Massachusetts, Louisiana, Ohio, and Wyoming) to integrate early childhood education programs and services. The goal was to help states "increase their ability to create integrated, high-quality early childhood education policies, programs, and services to children" (National Association of State Boards of Education, 2006, p. 1). The results were outstanding, with the states able to define school readiness and unify their standards. It included an outreach to early childhood education programs in higher education and aligned the college course content to the program. In 2006, NASBE received a grant allowing the organization to add five new states to the Early Childhood Education Network (National Association of State Boards of Education, 2006).

## :: PARENT EDUCATION FOR TEENAGERS

According to the Centers for Disease Control or CDC (2011), in 2009 a total of 409,840 infants were born to 15 to 19 year olds. Statistics from the CDC indicate that the U.S. teen rate fell more than one-third from 1991–2005 but then increased by 5 percent. In 2008–2009, the long-term downward trend has resumed. Examining these data shows that programs for teen pregnancy prevention are crucial since teen pregnancy and childbearing increase social and economic costs and the long-term impact on parents and their children (CDC, 2011).

### Teen Pregnancy Prevention 2010–2015

The President's Teen Pregnancy Prevention Initiative focuses on demonstrating the effectiveness of innovative, multicomponent, community-wide initiatives in reducing rates of teen pregnancy and births in communities with the highest rates, with a focus on reaching African American and Latino/Hispanic youth ages 15 to 19 (CDC, 2011). The program goals include the following:

1. Reduce the rates of pregnancies and births to youth in the target areas.
2. Increase youth access to evidence-based and evidence-informed programs to prevent teen pregnancy.
3. Increase linkages between teen pregnancy prevention programs and community-based clinical services.
4. Educate stakeholders about relevant evidence-based and evidence-informed strategies to reduce teen pregnancy and data on needs and resources in target communities.

The goal of prevention programs is to decrease the pregnancy rate and give children opportunity to grow without the stress of having to take care of a child. However, there are programs that are in existence in case pregnancy does occur. Most states have teen parenting programs under their Department of Health and Human Services.

## :: COMPREHENSIVE SERVICE DELIVERY

### Family Support Programs

Three programs—Family Support America (formerly Family Resource Centers), Family and Child Education (FACE), and The National Center for Family Literacy—illustrate the types of services that support centers provide. These three programs were developed because of families' obvious need for support to survive and provide the nurturing environment their children need. The Family Support America is a national coalition of groups that work for resources and provisions to strengthen families. Family and Child Education is a support and literacy program for children who are Native Americans. The National Center for Family Literacy focuses on literacy development for the total family. School personnel are becoming increasingly aware that families are the underlying support for the child and that the school must work with both to be successful in the education of the child.

Premises and principles of family support include the following:

a. Primary responsibility for the development and well-being of children lies within the family, and all segments of society must support families as they rear their children.
b. Ensuring the well-being of all families is the cornerstone of a healthy society and requires universal access to support programs and services.
c. Children and families exist as a part of an ecological and reciprocal system.
d. Child-rearing patterns are influenced by parents' understandings of child development and of their children's unique characteristics, personal sense of competence, and cultural and community traditions and mores.
e. Enabling families to build on their own strengths and capacities promotes the healthy development of children.
f. The developmental processes that make up parenthood and family life create needs that are unique at each stage in the lifespan.
g. Families are empowered when they have access to information and other resources and take action to improve the well-being of children, families, and communities. (Family Support America's Shared Leadership Series, 2000)

The centers focus on families' strengths and respond to parents (be they young or mature) according to their needs, linking them with social services that will help them meet their basic necessities. They help the families cope with stress; they offer prenatal classes, child development, and parent education to help them with their children; they work to prevent crises; they sponsor drop-in services; and they arrange opportunities for parents to develop support networks.

### Family and Child Education (FACE)

In 1990, the Bureau of Indian Affairs, Office of Indian Education, desired an integrated program for early childhood/parental involvement for American Indian families and children. The goals of FACE include the following: to support parents/primary caregivers in their role as their child's first and most influential teacher; to increase family literacy; to strengthen family–school–community connections; to promote the early identification and services to children with special needs; to increase parent participation in their child's learning; to support and celebrate the unique cultural and linguistic diversity of each American Indian community served by the program; and to promote lifelong learning.

The Family and Child Education (FACE) training program provides training sessions and on-site assistance. The program visits include the integration of language and culture in two settings: home and school. Family services include prenatal through 5 years old. The focus is to support parents and their child's first and most influential teacher with a special emphasis in language development. In 2009, FACE services were provided to 2,327 adults and 2,349 children (ages birth to 5 years) from 1,866 families. Seventy percent of adults and children participate in home-based services, 24 percent participate in center-based services, and 4 percent participate in both home- and center-based services (Research Training and Associates, 2009).

### Family Literacy

The federal definition of **family literacy services** is as follows:

Services that are of sufficient intensity in terms of hours and of sufficient duration, to make sustainable changes in a family and that integrate all of the following activities:

a. Interactive literacy activities between parents and their children.
b. Training for parents regarding how to be the primary teacher for their children and full partners in the education of their children.
c. Parent literacy training that leads to economic self-sufficiency.
d. An age-appropriate education to prepare children for success in school and life experiences. (U.S. Department of Health and Human Services, 2000)

The inability to read and write hinders men and women in fulfilling their roles in society and their roles as parents. Parents should become literate not only to ensure self-sufficient employment, but also to engage in interactive literacy activities with their children and to learn how to be the primary teachers for their children so they can become full partners in their child's education—parents who cannot read books or notes their children bring home are unable to collaborate effectively with the school for the betterment of their children's education. Comprehensive family literacy programs and family-centered literacy programs provide the support that parents need to fulfill their parental roles (Dail & Payne, 2010).

The federal government supports family literacy through a few programs, including Title I and Head Start. The Head Start program initiated its focus on family literacy programs in 1992 with three goals: (a) helping parents realize their own needs and working to overcome their own literacy concerns; (b) helping them increase their access to literacy services, programs, and materials; and (c) supporting them in their role as their child's teacher (Potts, 1992). The federal government also offers Even Start, which links parents of children under 8 with combined adult-literacy and preschool programs, with a goal the reduction of illiteracy and poverty (National Even Start Association, 2006).

There are, of course, many programs offered in addition to those available through the federal government. The Education and Human Services Consortium is a coalition interested in connecting families with the services they need, and many non-profit organizations, workplace literacy programs, and colleges and universities also promote adult literacy. Two major nonprofit associations have made great strides in supporting families: Family Support (Family Resource Center) in Chicago spearheaded the move toward more centers, whether federally, state, or privately funded, and the National Center for Family Literacy received a grant from the Kenan Trust in support of its efforts to promote family literacy through programs and training. In addition, the Family Institute for Early Literacy Development, or FIELD, helped bridge the gap between what children learn at home with what they are expected to learn in school (Riojas-Cortez & Flores, 2009). Other studies show how family literacy programs assist individuals to realize the value they have for education and the need to make something of themselves (Prins & Schafft, 2009).

All family literacy programs—whether federal, state, or nonprofit—focus on building family programs based on the strengths of families rather than on their deficits. It recommends that there should be sufficient duration of literacy programs so that the family is supported enough that it enables success. Literacy programs use methods of teaching adults that have been tested over time. Home visits are also used to bring activities and new books to the parents and visit with them on their home territory.

## SUMMARY

Parent involvement is increased when the ecology of the school allows for parents to feel welcomed and valued. School-based programs that involve parents are varied. The Comer process is based on consensus, collaboration, and no fault needed to develop a climate that allows children, parents, and schools to thrive. Effective programs that have a strong parental involvement component include Head Start, Perry Prechool Project, Carolina Abecedarian Project, Project Care, Syracuse Family Development Research, Houston Parent–Child Development Center, Early Training Project, Chicago Child Parent Center, and Oklahoma Pre-K. School-based programs are diversified, but each type of involvement is essential if the needs of families are to be met. Many parent involvement programs begin with grants and develop and change as the needs of the families they serve change. Family literacy programs, particularly for English language learners and other minorities, are crucial in order to help children be successful in school and life.

## SUGGESTED CLASS ACTIVITIES AND DISCUSSIONS

1. Visit a Title I program in a public school. Talk with the principal about the parent involvement specifically developed for the program. Or, if you work in a Title I program, develop a family literacy program.

2. Survey three or four schools that have federal funding. How do the schools differ in their approaches to parent involvement? How are they alike? Are there different responses to the various types of funding, for example, Title I, Title IV-C, Title VII, Follow Through, or Right to Read?

3. Visit schools in different areas and find out how they involve parents. Analyze the different approaches.

4. Design a parent bulletin board that illustrates the various components of the parent program in your classroom.

5. Develop a resource file of games, articles, books, and recycled materials.

6. Develop a workshop in which you have various learning centers—for example, early reading, cognitive, socioemotional development, and language development.

7. Make a universal game board and a series of cards to be used with it.

8. Develop activities that parents can use with their children at home.

9. Search the community for resources that can be used in the school. Include specialists, materials, and places to visit.

## USEFUL WEB SITES

**Clearinghouse on Early Education and Parenting (CEEP): ERIC/EECE Archive of Publications and Resources**

http://ceep.crc.uiuc.edu/eecearchive/

CEEP maintains the ERIC/EECE elementary and early childhood archive.

**Family Support America**

www.familysupportamerica.org/

Family Support America is an organization that is dedicated to providing information to help families survive. Site includes resource centers throughout the United States available for helping parents. Topics of interest include preventing child abuse, stress and children, tips on adoption, day care, education, discipline, divorce, and others.

**National Center for Education Statistics (NCES), U.S. Department of Education**

www.nces.ed.gov/

The NCES has researched and collected data on early childhood education.

**National Center for Family Literacy**

www.famlit.org/

This site provides good tips and help to reduce illiteracy in America.

# Home-Based Programs

*To work with a child and not with the parent is like working with only part of the pieces of a puzzle. It would be like a person who put a puzzle together with a thousand pieces, and then as he finished found the center part missing.*

Winters
*(1988, p. 8)*

*Teachers should explore the various opportunities that can allow them to learn more about their students' life outside of the classroom and to bring their students' life into the classroom.*

Lin & Bates
*(2010)*

*In this chapter you will learn about home-based education, homeschooling, and homework. After completing the chapter, you should be able to do the following:*

- Compare goals and services of several home-based programs.
- Describe a framework for developing activities to be used in a home-based program.
- Develop activities for use in home-based programs.
- Cite practices to avoid when working with parents in the home.
- Identify the reasons for homeschooling.
- Cite the public's response to homeschooling that supports cooperation between the home-schooler and the school.
- Describe the different strategies parents can use to support academic learning at home.

The home is the primary educational setting for children, with parents responsible for nurturing and educating their infants and preschoolers. Some of them share this role with child-care centers and schools and may also work with schools by becoming involved in the school's education program. Still others choose to educate their children at home. Learning at home is one area where parents and school personnel can support children's continued academic development. How can parents be the most helpful? In this chapter, the discussion will center first on children and the home-based offerings that can support the family and last, the move toward homeschooling—in which parents take responsibility for their children's entire education.

## :: ORIGINS OF HOME VISITING

Home visiting originally developed in Europe, mostly in England. Assistance to families was provided by "friendly visitors," church members, and other non-professionals. Florence Nightingale, a nurse recognized for her caring of soldiers during the Crimean War, also was instrumental in promoting health and hygiene in rural areas, villages, and towns. Her efforts led to a school in Liverpool, England, for the training of nurses. She also encouraged health visitors who were not nurses to visit homes in rural areas (Wasik & Bryant, 2001).

When immigrants from southern and eastern Europe began to come in great numbers to the United States in the later 1800s, visiting nurses along with settlement houses became part of the response to "encourage" the new arrivals to use "proper" hygiene and health. The growth of government intervention and services came a bit later, beginning in the 20th century, and parent education with parents attending meetings away from their homes became prominent in the 1920s. The trend toward home visiting was renewed after World War II, and since the 1970s, the programs have moved from working with individuals to working with and empowering families (Wasik & Bryant, 2001). Currently programs such as Early Head Start have a home-visit component for healthy infant development and parenting skills (Roggman, Boyce, & Cook, 2010). Other programs focus on working with parents on couple relationships, father involvement, and parenting interactions to decrease the instances of child maltreatment and strengthen family relationships (Sar, Antle, Bledsoe, Barbee, & Van Zyl, 2010).

## :: HOME-BASED EDUCATION

Imagine yourself as the parent of two preschoolers living in the country at least a mile from the nearest neighbor. Or, pretend that you are a parent in a core-city apartment house with no friends or family living close by. Some parents in urban and suburban areas have no more contact with support networks than those isolated by distance in the country. Immigrant families can face the same sort of challenges, oftentimes living in a different country than their friends and relatives. Both urban and rural residents as well as immigrant families, as the first teachers of their children, need educational support and knowledge to provide an enriched, positive environment for their children.

## :: PROGRAMS THAT WORK

Numerous programs have proved effective in a variety of projects throughout the United States. They range from programs specifically designed to educate children and bring positive parenting practices into the home to those that provide support for the entire family's physical health, mental health, housing, income, child development, and education. Descriptions of selected programs illustrate the scope and variety of parent involvement in the educational process, and families can take from them the ideas and procedures that fit their situation.

Home-based programs were developed on the premise that parents are a child's first and most influential teachers, therefore, parents must be supported in order to reach this potential. Many of these programs were developed to reduce the impact of child abuse by assisting parents to relate constructively to their children and to guide parents to support the physical, emotional, and cognitive development of their children, which is especially important during children's first 3 years, when brain development is most rapid. Programs that help parents during these early years have great benefits for the cognitive and language development of their children.

Home-based programs can assist families with different areas of development.

Home visiting programs provide different services for families in their home. A sample of the home-visiting program models include Parents as Teachers (PAT), Home Instruction Program for Preschool Youngsters (HIPPY), Healthy Families America (HFA), Early Head Start (EHS), Nurse Family Partnership, the Parent–Child Home Program, and the Portage Project.

### Parents as Teachers Program

Parents as Teachers (PAT) program was developed in four districts in Missouri in the early 1980s and extended to the entire state in 1985. By 1999, the program had expanded to 2,197 sites in 49 states, the District of Columbia, and six other countries, serving 500,000 children. In addition to school districts, PAT is offered by churches, hospitals, and social services and as part of Head Start, Even Start, and Family Resource Centers. The program appears to be more effective with very low-income parents (Wager, Spiker, & Linn, 2002). Currently, the PAT program has secured a $14.23 million i3 grant from the U.S. Department of Education to support the BabyFACE project, which provides home visits and family services to high-need Native American families and children (Parents as Teachers, 2011).

PAT program services include four components:

1. Regularly scheduled personal visits by credentialed parent educators, who provide information on the child's development, model and involve parents in age-appropriate activities with the child, and respond to parents' questions and concerns.
2. Group meetings in which parents share insights and build informal support networks.
3. Monitoring of children's progress by both parents and home visitors to detect and treat any emerging problems as early as possible.
4. Linking of families with community services that are beyond the scope of the program (Winter & McDonald, 1997). The following paragraph provides a description of the home visits:

Home visits are usually 1 hour long and are scheduled monthly, biweekly, or weekly, depending on family needs and local program budgetary restrictions. For example, while most enrolled families receive monthly or bimonthly home visits in Missouri, state funds provide for 25 visits per year for high-needs families—that is, families with one or more of the following characteristics: teen parents, single parents, children or parents with disabilities, low educational attainment, English as a Second Language, unemployment, chemical dependencies, foster parents, numerous family relocations, high stress, or involvement with the corrections system or mental health, health, or social service agencies. Weekly visits are conducted at the 22 PAT program sites on Indian reservations which are administered by the Bureau of Indian Affairs. (*The Future of Children*, 1999, pp. 179–180)

Missouri conducted a school-entry-assessment project to study and create a plan in which all children come to school ready to succeed. A School Entry Profile was developed to identify and measure the equities and inequities of early life experiences known to promote school success or difficulty. The profile is organized around seven conceptual areas that reflect dimension of readiness for school. The "areas identified include symbolic development, communication, mathematical/physical knowledge, working with others, learning to learn, physical development and conventional knowledge." Its purpose is to enable educators to address inequities in these areas so all children will have access to opportunities that promote school success (Missouri Department of Elementary and Secondary Education, 1999). Research conducted in 1985 on first-time parents validated the parents' positive responses. It showed that children participating in the Parents as Teachers project scored significantly higher on all measures of verbal ability, intelligence, language ability, achievement, and auditory comprehension than did children in a comparison group. The program proved so successful that it was adopted by the Missouri Department of Elementary and Secondary Education for use by 543 school districts throughout the state. Revisions and updating of the PAT curriculum were accomplished in 1996 in addition to the development of the Born to Learn curriculum. It was field tested and became standard PAT for prenatal to 3 years curriculum for Missouri in 1999 and has now been used in programs in 50 states and seven countries (Parents as Teachers, 2011).

Beginning in the third trimester of pregnancy and continuing until the child is 3, PAT home visitors meet with each family to provide the following:

- Information and guidance to help the parents-to-be prepare for the new arrival.
- Information on child development to foster cognitive, social, motor, and language development. Clearly written handbooks describing what the

parents should expect during each phase of development are provided to parents. The phases are as follows:

Phase 1—prenatal or birth to 6 weeks

Phase 2—6 weeks to 3½ months

Phase 3—3½ months to 5½ months

Phase 4—5½ months to 8 months

Phase 5—8 months to 14 months

Phase 6—14 months to 24 months

Phase 7—24 months to 36 months (Ferguson-Florissant School District, 1989b)

- Periodic hearing and vision checkups for the children.
- Parent resource center at the school that was available for parent meetings.
- Individualized parent conferences each month.
- Monthly group meetings with other parents.

The programs in Missouri and in other states have found that first-time parents are usually very receptive to guidance, as they have no preconceived ideas from their experiences in rearing other children (Wagner, Spiker, & Linn, 2002; Wagner et al., 2003). These programs offer support for new parents, especially those who do not work outside the home and usually have a need to visit and socialize with others. This helps them learn how best to raise the child. Contact and support can also reduce the loneliness of a parent who is solely responsible for an infant.

## HIPPY—Home Instruction Program for Preschool Youngsters

The HIPPY program was developed in 1969 at the Hebrew University of Jerusalem in Israel, and it is now used in at least eight countries. The first U.S. programs were established in 1984. In 1999, there were 121 programs serving 15,000 families in 28 states, Guam, and the District of Columbia. The basic assumptions of the program are that all children can learn and that all parents want the best for their children. The mission of HIPPY is to "help parents empower themselves as their children's first teacher by giving them the tools, skills and confidence they need to work with their children in the home" (Home Instruction for Parents of Preschool Youngsters, 2011).

The skill areas included in the curriculum are tactile, visual, auditory, and conceptual discrimination, in addition to language development, verbal expression, eye–hand coordination, premath concepts, logical thinking, self-concept, and creativity. In 1994, a curriculum for 3-year-olds was added with storybooks and activity packets, so the program now serves 3- to 5-year-olds. The program has a detailed curriculum design, with each activity illustrated. Each year of the 2-year program has nine storybooks, 30 activity packets, 20 manipulative shapes, and weekly instructions for the paraprofessional. Home visitors role play strategies for engaging children in learning activities. There are also group meetings with parents to encourage socialization. A professional coordinates the program, but home visitors are paraprofessionals selected from parents who were in the program. They visit bimonthly or at least 15 times a year to instruct the parents in the use of HIPPY educational materials (*The Future of Children,* 1999). The curriculum focuses on parents working with children using play and hands-on learning (Doyle, 2005). Figures 9–1A and 9–1B illustrate

**FIGURE 9–1A**

*The Cat Who Looked for a House.*

*Source:* Printed with permission. All rights reserved © 1992 NCJW Research Institute for Innovation in Education, School of Education. Hebrew University of Jerusalem, Israel. Published in the United States by the Dushkin Publishing Group, Inc. Revised illustrations by the Averroès Foundation, Amsterdam.

# THE CAT WHO LOOKED FOR A HOUSE (7)

**WEEK: 10**

**DAY: 3**

**ACTIVITY SHEET: 2**

HOME INSTRUCTION PROGRAM FOR PRESCHOOL YOUNGSTERS
HIPPY USA

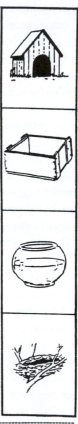

1. (Cut out the animals below and put them on the table.)
   (Point to the animals and to the houses and say):

   **THESE ANIMALS LIVE IN THESE HOUSES.**

2. **I WILL PUT AN ANIMAL NEAR A HOUSE.**

   **YOU TELL ME IF IT IS THE RIGHT HOUSE.**

   **IF NOT, PUT THE ANIMAL NEXT TO A HOUSE THAT'S RIGHT FOR IT.**

3. (Place each animal next to a house which is *not* appropriate for it.)

   **NOW SEE IF I MADE ANY MISTAKES.**
   (The child should be able to rearrange them all.)

4. (Now place 2 correctly and 2 *incorrectly*.)

   **NOW IS EVERY ANIMAL IN THE RIGHT HOUSE?**
   – no.

   **SO PUT EACH ONE WHERE IT BELONGS.**

5. **PASTE EACH ANIMAL NEXT TO ITS HOME.**

   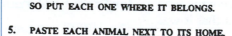

"HIPPY" — Age 4 (1991) 10

**SORTING** (3)

WEEK: 10

DAY: 5

ACTIVITY SHEET: 1

(Materials on the table: an empty shoe box, 4 empty cups, 5 coins, 5 stones, toothpicks, 5 bottle caps and paste.)

1.  (Sit next to a table. Place the 4 cups and the box with all the other objects in it on the table.)

    IN THIS BOX, THERE ARE MANY DIFFERENT THINGS. THEY ARE ALL MIXED TOGETHER. WE WILL ARRANGE THEM.

2.  GIVE ME A TOOTHPICK.
    (Place it in a cup.)

    FIND ALL THE TOOTHPICKS AND PUT THEM IN THIS CUP.

    GIVE ME A COIN.
    (Put it in the second cup.)

    PUT ALL THE COINS IN THIS CUP.
    WHAT IS LEFT IN THE BOX?
    – stones and bottle caps.

    GIVE ME ALL THE BOTTLE CAPS.
    (Place them in the third cup.)

    NOW PUT ALL THE STONES IN THE EMPTY CUP.

3.  (Put all the objects back in the large container.)

    NOW YOU SORT ALL THE THINGS.

    PUT ALL THE THINGS OF ONE KIND IN ONE CUP.
    (When the child has finished sorting the objects into the four cups, ask):

    WHAT DID YOU DO?
    – I arranged the things.
    – I sorted them
    – I put the _____ together, and the _____ together.

the type of study materials offered to parents in the program (Baher, Piotrkowshi, & Brooks-Gunn, 1998; Bar-Hava-Monteith, Harre, & Field, 1999).

## Healthy Families America

Healthy Families America (HFA) replicates the design of Hawaii's Healthy Start program (State of Hawaii, Department of Health, 1997). The HFA program was established by the National Committee to Prevent Child Abuse. The mission of the HFA program is "to prevent the abuse and neglect of our nation's children through intensive home visiting" (Healthy Families America, 2010). The goals of the program include the following:

- To systematically reach out to parents to offer resources and support
- To cultivate the growth of nurturing, responsive, parent–child relationships

- To promote healthy childhood growth and development
- To build the foundations for strong family functioning

These goals support improved parenting skills, enhancement of child health and development, reduction of family stress, and improved family functioning as well as prevention of child abuse and neglect. Recently the program has added "e-parenting," which is a computer-based intervention to augment home visiting. Results show that mothers are utilizing the program in a therapeutic manner (Zero to Three, 2010).

Families are selected primarily through the use of a standardized assessment tool by participating hospitals or physicians, public health nurses, midwives, support groups in areas where access to hospital records is unavailable, or by self or family referral. The HFA staff helps expectant parents and parents of newborns learn how to: properly take care of self during pregnancy, soothe a crying baby, ensure the child receives the appropriate nutrition, promote healthy development and bonding, and assist in creating a safe home environment (Healthy Families America, 2011).

Considering the stress new parents face daily, especially without family/community supports, a key strategy to prevent child abuse and neglect is to provide the support that would otherwise be missing (Daro, McCurdy, Falconnier, & Stojanovic, 2003; Rogers & O'Connor, 2003). Home visitors are trained to provide supportive, culturally appropriate services beginning prenatally or at the birth of a child and continuing until the child is 5. The program begins with level 1, weekly visits; progresses to level 2, which consists of two visits a month; and completes at levels 3 and 4 with monthly or quarterly visits.

Research findings published on the Prevent Child Abuse America Web site, www.preventchildabuse .org, provide results of program outcomes in various state settings. For example, in Pinellas County, Florida, the rate of child maltreatment for participants in the HFA program was 1.6, compared to 4.9 for the county as a whole. In Maryland, there were only two reports of neglect among the 254 families served in 4 years (a rate of 0.8). Results from a study in Alaska show modest benefits to children's cognitive development and behavior as well as an increase in the quality of the home environment (Gomby, 2007).

In general the Healthy Families program has demonstrated the following:

- Mothers achieving higher levels of confidence.
- Home environment observed to be better organized.
- Parents engaged in neglectful behavior less often.
- Parents showing greater acceptance of their children's behavior.
- Significantly lower levels of distress for parents and children.
- Significantly fewer reports of abuse and neglect within the first year of life.

## Early Head Start

Early Head Start (EHS) is a federally funded program that serves low-income pregnant women and families with infants and toddlers. It is designed to serve children until their 3rd birthdays, with transition plans made for preschool services, either in Head Start or other community services for which the families are eligible. Children participating in EHS live in poverty and have at least one of the disability indicators (Peterson, Mayer, Summers, & Luze, 2010).

The EHS program has four service areas in which outcomes are measured: child development, which includes health, language, cognitive and social–emotional development; family development, which includes parenting skill development and economic self-sufficiency; staff development; and family/community partnerships, which include establishing collaborations between the EHS program and other community organizations. Services are provided through home visits by home visitors that represent the parent populations served by the program (Raikes, Green, Atwater, Kisker, Constantine, & Chazan-Cohen, 2006). Program services include the following:

- Weekly home visits that last 90 minutes. Home visitors work with parents to guide them in using daily routines to promote child development. Parents are encouraged to plan each week's activities, which can include cooking to enhance nutrition habits, language and literacy skills, number awareness, and social skills such as turn taking and sharing.
- Screening of children to determine if they are meeting developmental milestones in language, cognitive, and social–emotional areas, physical growth, and nutrition.

- Assessment of the home environment to determine if it is supportive of children's safety, health, and cognitive, language, and social–emotional development.
- Assessment of the children's and families' medical needs.
- Development of family partnership agreements through which parents plan strategies to develop self-sufficiency through participation in education/ training activities, job search strategies, and advocacy skills to attain services needed by their children.
- Assistance to parents in preparing their children for transitioning from the EHS program to preschool programs when their children reach 3 years of age.

Reports from the Early Head Start Research and Evaluation Project (EHSREP) show that when families participate in home-based and center-based approaches or mixed programs, there is a significant positive impact on parents and children through age 3 (Robinson, Klute, Faldowski, Pan, Staerkel, Summers, & Wall, 2009). Twice a month, families have the opportunity to participate in group activities that encourage children and parents to socialize with others and to observe staff modeling appropriate child–adult interactions. Parents also have the opportunity to identify other participants within the program with whom they can develop supportive relationships.

Programming of parent–child socialization activities is decided by a parent committee, which is a subcommittee of the parent policy council, a decision-making group overseeing the EHS program. The EHS program maintains a parent policy council, which is an elected group made up of present and past parents and some community representation. The policy council reviews the EHS budget, hiring and firing of staff, selection of curricula and screening tools to be used by home visitors, annual community needs-assessment activities, and a federally mandated self-evaluation. Participation on the parent policy council provides interested parents with many opportunities to develop skills in public speaking, committee work, business skills, communication skills, and enhanced understanding of the functioning of the program (Lane, Kesker, Ross, et al., 2005; McCallister, Wilson, Green, & Baldwin, 2005).

## Nurse Family Partnership Program

The Nurse Family Partnership Program (formerly the Nurse Home Visitation Program) is a home-visiting nurse program that serves low-income first-time mothers with the goal of the mothers improving their health and social functioning. Public-health nurses begin providing service when mothers are 20 to 28 weeks into their pregnancy. The nurse provides support to the mother through the child's first two years of life. The program was begun as a research project in Elmira, New York, and was expanded to six demonstration cities. In 1999, the National Center for Children, Families, and Communities was established to disseminate the program, which now operates in 22 states. The goals of the program are to do the following:

- Improve prenatal, maternal and early childhood health
- Improve family functioning in health, home, and neighborhood environments
- Build family and friend support networks
- Build parental roles
- Build skills to improve coping with major life events

Home visits target the following content areas:

- Health behaviors that affect preterm delivery, low birth weight, and infant neurodevelopmental impairment, such as tobacco and other substance-abuse usage
- School-dropout prevention
- Welfare dependence
- Unintended subsequent pregnancies

Nurse home visitors follow a structured intervention plan that involves assessing attitudes, skills, knowledge, and support available to the mother in the home environment. Mothers are encouraged to work toward personal goals, attain behavior changes, and cope with challenges. Activities are assigned between home visits. Visits are scheduled to coincide with the progression of the pregnancy and the child's development. Nurse home visitors use the Clinical Information System to track family characteristics, needs, services received, and progress attained by the mother.

A follow-up evaluation has demonstrated several positive outcomes. They include the following:

- A decrease in arrests and convictions of 15-year-old target children.

- A decrease in sexual partners among 15-year-old target children
- Improved birth outcomes
- Reduced child abuse and neglect
- Savings of $4 for every dollar invested due to reduced welfare, fewer arrests, and lower health-care costs. (Karoly, Kilburn, & Cannon, 2005; Williams, 2004)

Studies have shown that the program has helped children born to mothers with low psychological resources not only reduce the use of substances and mental-health problems, but also improve their academic achievement (Kitzman et al., 2010).

### Parent–Child Home Program

The Parent–Child Home Program (PCHP) is a home-based family literacy program that relies on positive verbal interaction between the child 2 to 4 years old and the primary caregiver. This program serves the following families (Parent–Child Home Program, 2011):

- Low income, isolated, and with a history of homelessness
- American born, immigrants and refugees
- Multilingual nonnative English speakers and low-literacy English-speaking families
- Single parent, teen parent, and two-parent families and grandparents raising grandchildren
- Non-educated families, no high school diploma
- Families in need of center-based early childhood experience and parenting resources

The goal of the program is to increase the caregiver's interaction with the child in a natural dialogue that enhances and enriches the child's home environment. By training toy demonstrators who are paraprofessionals with a high school education to demonstrate and model their toys without being didactic, the project facilitates relaxed, verbal interaction between parent and child (Levenstein et al., 1998).

The caregiver may be any adult who has primary nurturing responsibilities for the child. The program is based in the child's home; trained home visitors ("toy demonstrators") come twice weekly for half-hour sessions from the time the child is 2 until the child is 4. The twice-a-week visits to the home are set up at the parent's conve-nience (Levenstein et al., 1998; Nievar, Van Egeren, & Pollard, 2010). During the biweekly visits, the home visitor demonstrates toys and books in a play session with parent and child. Parenting behavior emphasizing verbal interaction is modeled instead of being taught directly. Language interactions are encouraged in the family's native language (Mann, Sandoval, Garcia, & Calderon, 2009). The parent and child participate as they learn through play. Books and toys are given to the families so that the learning can continue. There are no specific tasks other than enjoying the play and resultant verbal interaction. Guide sheets cover such concepts as colors, shapes, and sizes and such cognitive skills as matching, pretending, and differentiating. The program is grounded on constructivist philosophy as stated in the following quote:

> The program's cognitive curriculum was derived from theories and empirical studies of investigators whose work had influenced the program at its inception. At its core are Vygotsky's links between thought and language (Vygotsky, 1962); Bruner's construct of "instrumental conceptualism," the idea that concept formation is fostered in the 2- and 3-year-old child through the child's experience with language (Bruner, 1966); and Sigel's (1971) "distancing hypothesis" in which the promotion of representational competence is given tangible meaning through the child's and parent's play focused around books and 3-dimensional

Children learn through play.

toys as representations of reality, besides being intrinsically motivating curriculum materials. (Levenstein, Levenstein, Shiminski, & Stolzberg, 1998, p. 269)

The method, curricula, and delivery of the program include the following:

- 46 half-hour sessions twice a week spread over 7 months each year for 2 years.
- A guide sheet, a one-page list of concepts, and developmentally appropriate labels for actions or words applied to the toy or book brought by the home visitor to the toddler.
- A 20-item VIP-created instrument called "Child's Behavior Traits," a measure as well as a guide to the child's social–emotional goals.
- A "Parent and Child Together" curriculum of 20 traits that measure and guide positive parent behavior, modeled by the home visitor and achieved by the parent.
- Curriculum materials including 12 illustrated books and 11 toys—with a different set given each year of the 2-year program for a total of 46 books and toys given to the family.
- Parental involvement in the child's play modeled by the home visitor inviting the parent to be involved.
- Home visitor modeling (without directly teaching) positive response to the child and pleasurable reading to the child, encouraging the family's literacy in addition to the child's.
- Sessions arranged at the parents' convenience.
- Program coordinators who are college graduates and work with home visitors to develop necessary nondidactic skills, respect for family privacy and lifestyles, and prepare written reports (Levenstein et al., 1998).

A study (1996) conducted on the Pittsfield, Massachusetts, Parent–Child Home Program (Levenstein et al., 1998) included 123 students who participated as toddlers in the program between 1976–1980. The participants were originally recruited by invitations sent to all parents of children attending Chapter I schools, also termed Title I schools. Those who responded were eligible if they met five of the following eight criteria:

1. Child's IQ score under 100 on the Peabody Picture Vocabulary Test (PPVT)
2. Single-parent family
3. Unemployment of mother
4. Unemployment of father

5. Family receives AFDC payments
6. Parent's education less than 12th grade
7. Family income qualifies for poverty status
8. Older sibling in a Chapter I remedial program (Levenstein et al., 1998)

The study looked at control groups of youngsters who would have been eligible for the Parent–Child Home Program but did not attend. All eligible respondents who were offered the Parent–Child Home Program accepted enrollment.

## Portage Project

The Portage Project was developed in 1969 as a home-based, family-centered demonstration program providing service to children with disabilities and their families. The model worked with children from birth to age 6 and with their families through weekly home visits by a home teacher. The project originally covered 3,600 square miles in south-central Wisconsin (Portage Project, 2011). Successful evaluation of the model and validation by the National Diffusion Network led to other areas setting up the program.

Over the years, the Portage Project has adhered to the principles upon which it was based:

1. Intervention for children with disabilities should begin as early as possible. The earlier work begins, the greater the probability of having a significant effect on the child and the greater the chance that this effect will be maintained over time.
2. Parent/primary caregiver involvement is critical to successful early intervention.
3. Intervention objectives and strategies must be individualized for each child and support the functioning of the family.
4. Data collection is important to reinforce positive change and to make ongoing intervention decisions.

The Portage Project works in collaboration with community agencies to provide comprehensive services to children and families. Referral from individuals and local agencies leads to a play-based assessment conducted by a multidisciplinary team. This process is conducted in the family's home and is designed to provide information on parent–child interaction patterns, parent perceptions, and the developmental functioning level of the child.

If the team, including parents, determines that a child is eligible, the process to develop an Individual

Family Service Plan is initiated. This process includes extensive observation and communication with the family. The plan might include weekly home visits by a member of the Portage Project transdisciplinary staff, therapy or counseling from community providers, consultation with child-care providers or other caregivers, participation in parent support groups or play groups, or other activities requested by the family.

One interventionist is the care coordinator for the family and maintains regular communication with other service providers. This interventionist may be an educator, a speech and language therapist, or a motor specialist, but his or her role in working with families is transdisciplinary.

The Portage Project staff has developed materials to support early childhood programs. These materials include the *Portage Guide to Early Education,* developed in the late 1970s and used in the United States and internationally, and *Growing: Birth to Three* (Portage Project, 2011).

A checklist of 580 developmentally sequenced behaviors for children up to 6 years old is included in The Portage Guide. The behaviors are divided into six areas: infant stimulation, self-help, language, cognition, motor skills, and socialization. Ideas for teaching each of the behaviors are included to assist parents and teachers (see Figure 9–2). The new version of the *Portage Guide* is currently available, both in print and as a Web-based version at www.portageproject.org.

### FIGURE 9–2

Two examples from the card deck of the *Portage Guide* show the types of activities that parents can do with their children at home.

*Source:* From *Portage Project Readings,* by D. Shearer, J. Billingsley, A. Frohman, J. Hilliard, F. Johnson, & M. Shearer, 1976, Portage, WI: Portage Project. Reprinted by permission.

**motor 87**

AGE 3-4

TITLE: Pedals tricycle five feet

WHAT TO DO:

1. If the child cannot reach the pedals, build them up with blocks taped or screwed onto the pedals.
2. Push the child on the tricycle so that he gets the feel of pedaling.
3. Tape the child's feet to the pedals. Move the trike, so that the child can feel how the pedals work. Gradually reduce the amount of tape used. Straps from roller skates may serve the same purpose as tape.
4. Put pressure on the child's knees to help push the pedals down. Continue pushing each knee. Say "up," "down," etc. Decrease aid gradually.
5. Stand about one foot in front of the child on the tricycle. Show the child a goodie and tell him to come and get it. Praise and reward success.
6. Pull trike towards you with rope so child can concentrate on pedaling instead of steering.
7. Put trike in a stand to keep it stationary as child pedals.
8. Put trike on a slight incline so child won't have to use as much pressure at first.

PortageGuide

© 1976 Cooperative Educational Service Agency 12

**motor 88**

AGE 3-4

TITLE: Swings on swing when started in motion

WHAT TO DO:

1. Use a chair swing first that is likely to be found in a playground.
2. Push child in chair swing. Reassure him by keeping close to the swing, touching child often. Do not swing high.
3. Have the child watch other children swinging and show him that their legs move back and forth to make the swing go. Encourage him to lean "back" and "forward."
4. Don't push the child each time the swing comes back to you and tell him to move his legs back and forth with each swing.
5. As he becomes more independent switch to a swing without sides and have the child hold onto the chain. Be sure the swing is low enough for his feet to touch the ground. Continue encouraging him to swing on his own.
6. Stand in front of child and encourage him to reach out to you with the feet each time the swing comes forward to start a pumping motion.

PortageGuide

© 1976 Cooperative Educational Service Agency 12

*Growing: Birth to Three* offers materials to support family-centered interactive intervention. The materials are designed to be used as a package, as each piece contributes to the intervention process. Figure 9–3A describes an On the Move Behavior for children 3 to 6 months, and Figure 9–3B illustrates the Using My Senses Behavior for children 24 to 36 months. The materials are designed to encourage flexibility in working with families as well as act as a stimulus to expand beyond the specific suggested intervention strategies. A brief description of the components of *Growing* follows.

**Ecological Planner.** Part I of the *Ecological Planner* suggests guidelines for observation and communication, provides a way to document

**FIGURE 9–3A**

"On the Move: Three to Six Months." An example of activities from *Growing: Interactions/Daily Routines.*

*Source:* From *Portage Guide to Early Education,* by CESA5, Portage Project, 1998, Portage, WI: Author. Copyright 1998 by the Portage Project. Reprinted with permission.

---

**ON THE MOVE  J14**
**Three To Six Months**

**BEHAVIOR #14:  Maintain Head In Midline When Pulled To Sit**
**AREA:             On The Move**

**Why Is This Important?**

When conscious effort is no longer required to maintain head control, the infant can attend to using her eyes, ears, hands, and mouth to explore the world.

**Commentary:**

*I'm using my neck and tummy muscles to keep my head in a straight line with my body when you pull me up to sit. It requires some effort on my part, since these muscles are not yet that strong. With practice I will become stronger.*

**Information:**

The amount of head lag which the child exhibits when pulled to a sitting position is a good indication of progression in the development of head control. At first, her head will lag behind her trunk when she is pulled up; later she will be able to keep her head in line with her trunk. Finally, she will develop enough strength to pull herself up while gripping your hands.

**Interactive Activities:**

*Engaging:* When I'm sitting on your lap facing you, place your hands over my shoulders with your fingers can supporting my head and my chin tucked. Hold me firmly so my head doesn't fall back. Slowly lower me slightly backward while you sing or talk to me. Watch to see if I can keep my head in line with my trunk; then bring me up again slowly. Repeat this activity several times while we play together. Caution: don't try this activity unless I can maintain head control while in a supported sitting position.

*Expanding:* Place me on my back. Grasp my hands and wrists and slowly pull me up into a sitting position. Please do not move faster than my head control allows. When I can keep my head in line with my trunk, pull me up halfway and let me pull myself the rest of the way. I'm getting so strong!

*Giving Information:* My tummy muscles need to be strong for me to pull myself up into a sitting position. You can help make these muscles stronger by gently rubbing or tickling (if I enjoy this) my tummy. Watch to see if I curl my body into flexion when you stimulate my tummy muscles in this way. Does my head tend to come forward so that my chin tucks down to my chest? Do my legs come up and pull in close to my body? If so, I am strengthening my tummy muscles with this playful activity.

**Daily Routine Activities:**

*Diapering:* If I'm in a playful mood after you change my diaper, try to pull me up into the sitting position. See how much I am able to help you. Make sure to smile and praise me for my attempts.

**Caution:**

Pay attention to the level of head control the child has and do not let her lose head control when you pull her up into a sitting position. It is frightening and potentially harmful to have her head fall back unexpectedly. Be prepared to catch her head when doing "pull to sit" activities.

**FIGURE 9–3B**

"Using my Senses: Twenty-Four to Thirty-Six Months." An example of activities from *Growing: Interactions/Daily Routines.*

*Source:* From *Portage Guide to Early Education,* by CESA5, Portage Project, 1998, Portage, WI: Author. Copyright 1998 by the Portage Project. Reprinted with permission.

**USING MY SENSES   C41**
**Twenty-Four To Thirty-Six Months**

**BEHAVIOR #41:**  Use Vision Effectively To Guide Hands
**AREA:**            Using My Senses

**Why Is This Important?**

This behavior alerts the caregiver to the child's ability to effectively use eye-hand coordination.

**Commentary:**

*What was once a complicated task for me, using my vision to guide what my hands do, is now becoming easier. Watch as I learn to put objects in containers, pegs in holes, and work switches on simple busy boxes. Aren't I clever!*

**Interactive Activities:**

*Turntaking*: The game described in *Playtime* under Daily Routine Activities (see following section) could be lots of fun if we take turns. First, give me a chance to put something in the box, then you take a turn. Pause and wait so that I know it is my turn again.

**Daily Routine Activities:**

*Doing Chores:* As you are taking the clothes off the clothesline, you can occupy me by giving me a plastic milk jug or container with a large opening and some clothespins. Show me how to drop the clothespins into the milk jug, and then see if I will do this by myself.

*Mealtime:* As I begin to use utensils, am I able to scoop up the food, bring my hand all the way to my mouth, and pop it in? This is part of eye-hand coordination. You may need to guide me at first, then slowly let me try on my own.

*Bedtime*: As we look at a book together, see if I can start to flip the pages of the book by myself. Can I focus on the corner, place my hand on it and, with some help from you, turn the page?

*Playtime*: Shape boxes are a good way to help me to practice this skill. Find a shape box with 2 or 3 holes, or you may even want to tape up all but one hole at first. Show me how to drop the shapes in the box, then let me try to do this myself. Be sure to clap or praise all my attempts.

transactions across time, and offers a selection of formats for individualized intervention planning. Part II of the *Ecological Planner* is called the *Developmental Observation Guide.* It provides an in-depth developmentally sequenced series of behaviors that children frequently display from birth through 36 months.

**Nurturing Journals.** These journals are designed for use by parents or primary caregivers. Each book contains open-ended questions or statements to help parents reflect on the process of parenting.

**Interactive Grow Pack.** This section represents the heart of interactive intervention. It offers strategies for interactive communication with parents as well as ways to enhance and encourage mutually satisfying interactions between caregiver and child.

**Interactions and Daily Routines Books.** This collection offers activity suggestions for each skill or behavior listed in the *Developmental Observation Guide.* Activity suggestions are embedded in daily routines, rituals, play, and interactions.

**Master Forms Packet.** This packet of reproducible forms is designed to assist in family-guided intervention. The forms can be used to document communications and observations, develop a family-generated service plan, and develop intervention suggestions responsive to each individual family being served (CESA 5, Portage Project, 1998; CESA 5, Portage Project, 2010).

A variety of home-based programs are operating in the United States and in other countries. The programs included here are just a sample of them. While the basic premise is working with families and children in their own homes, there is great variety in the requirements for staff and the manner in which services are provided.

## A DAY IN THE LIFE OF ONE HOME-BASED PROGRAM

A program initiated in Yakima, Washington, acknowledged the importance of parents as their children's first teachers. Although this home-based program is no longer funded, this article vividly illustrates how home-based programs make a difference in families' lives.

### The winning play at home base[1]

The Rochas's home, neat and attractive, is modest by almost anyone's standards. A few fall flowers brighten the gravel walk, and a small tricycle that has seen better days lies on its side in the grass announcing the presence of at least one preschooler. From under a bush the family's gray-striped cat lifts an eyelid as a visitor approaches.

Mrs. Rochas responds immediately to the knock, hampered only slightly by her 2½-year-old son, Benjie, who manages to cling to her knee while keeping one finger in his mouth.

"Hi, Jean. Come in," says Mrs. Rochas, with a smile almost as wide as the door she swings open to permit her caller to enter the small living room. As Mrs. Rochas gently eases Benjie back toward his toy collection in the corner, she tells Jean that Margaretta, her daughter who is almost 4, is still napping.

"That's fine, don't disturb her," Jean, a paraprofessional parent-educator, replies before she settles on the davenport and begins pulling some materials from her shopping bag—a stack of index cards, several old magazines, a pair of scissors, and a tube of glue.

The casual banter notwithstanding, some serious business is at hand: Mrs. Rochas is about to undergo a lesson that marks the beginning of her second "school year." She is one of 200 parents in Yakima, a central Washington community of 49,000, who are learning how to teach their own preschool children through Project Home Base, a pioneer early childhood education program. Depending on how well she learns her weekly

lessons, she could have a positive and lasting effect on her child's performance in school.

Like many Home Base families, the Rochases were lured to the area from northern California during the previous fall by the promise of better wages in Yakima's fruit industry. Soon afterward they were visited by a representative from the Home Base project, who explained that all parents of children aged 8 months to 4 years in their neighborhood were being given an opportunity for special, federally sponsored training to enable them to help their preschoolers prepare for school. The Rochases were enthusiastic, but even while accepting the invitation Mrs. Rochas had a number of doubts. Among them, her daughter (then 3 years old) did not always "take to strangers" and Benjie was still "just a baby." But as the weeks passed and the home-visitor became a familiar and friendly face, the doubts disappeared.

A half hour goes by and Margaretta awakens from her nap. Still sleepy, she enters the living room to find her mother busily engaged in a game of "Concentration." This particular exercise calls for pasting pictures of similar objects, cut from magazines, onto cards to create a series of pairs. The cards, bearing pictures of various animals and buildings, are then shuffled and placed face down in rows. The game begins with a player picking up a card and trying to match it with a second. If no match results, both cards are returned to their original positions and a second player tries. When all the cards are matched, the player with the most pairs is the winner.

It is important, Mrs. Rochas knows from past experience, that she learn exercises like this one thoroughly before trying them with her children. Then she can become more comfortable in the unfamiliar role of "Teacher."

Before Margaretta plays the game after dinner that day and frequently during the remainder of the week, she will be encouraged to look at the cards and then talk—in complete sentences—about the pictures. As she gains a familiarity, changes are made with the objects pictured and the exercise by adding more cards or, to keep the lessons fresh, changing the object of the exercise to matching pairs of colors rather than pictures. It may be just fun to Margaretta, but while she is playing, she is acquiring some important skills, including the ability to think logically. She is thus preparing to become a better learner when she enters kindergarten the following year.

Little Benjie, meanwhile, is an important part of the action too. Before leaving that afternoon, Jean shows Mrs. Rochas how a small hand mirror and a full-length mirror can transform him into "The Most Wonderful Thing in the World."

Examining his face in the mirror, Benjie is helped to identify his most prominent physical characteristic, such as his curly hair, bright brown eyes, and white teeth. Then

[1]From "Winning Play at Home Base," by V. Hedrich and C. Jackson, 1977, *American Education*, 13(6), pp. 27–30. Revised by J. Popp, Early Childhood Director, Project Home Base, in a personal communication, October, 1987.

he tries to figure out what makes him "special," what makes him different from everyone else in his family. He observes that one eyebrow is straighter than the other, and his ears are round. Then there are all the tricky things he can do with his face: He can squint, wrinkle his nose, and pucker his lips. He is encouraged to talk about how a smile is different from a frown. Before the full-length mirror in the bedroom, Benjie studies his posture and imitates various commonplace activities such as eating a hamburger or kicking a football. He and Margaretta look together into the mirror and discover how their appearances are different and how they are alike. The purpose? To help a child realize he or she is special and to feel good and confident about the discovery.

Although the allotted hour has flown by, Jean takes a few more minutes to discuss some new pamphlets on nutritious snacks for children she has brought along from the County Extension Office and to confirm her appointment for next week.

The exercises for Margaretta and Benjie just described are only two drawn from more than 200 individual "tasks" for various age levels identified and developed by the Home Base staff. Each exercise has a specific goal or aim. There is no special significance attached to the activities' sequence, just that tasks become more complex as the child's needs and intellectual capacity grow. Home Base stresses conversations between parents and their children. There is no special significance attached to the activities' sequence. Tasks become more complex as the child's needs and intellectual capacity grow.

Parents are continually encouraged to adhere closely to a number of effective teaching techniques, such as eliciting questions from the learner, asking questions that have more than one correct answer, asking questions that require more than a one-word reply, praising the learner when he or she does well, urging the child to respond according to evidence instead of guesswork, allowing the child time to think out a problem before receiving assistance, and helping him or her to become familiar with the learning situation and materials.

"As we teach parents what to expect from their children in each situation and how to respond to their child's successes or failures, we find that the parents become stronger and more confident in their teaching role," project director Carol Jackson said. "When they understand the necessity for teaching skills like problem solving, they realize the time is well spent."

Home-visitor's workday may span from 8:30 to 4:00, with about an hour spent at each home. It is an emotionally demanding job and requires a valid driver's license, an available vehicle, and vehicle liability insurance. Fortunately, language problems are minimized because several of the home-visitors are bilingual. Their services are constantly being used to translate tasks into Spanish and to attend meetings to serve as interpreter for Spanish-speaking parents.

A great deal of role playing is used in the training of parent educators. They try out all of the activities scheduled.

Home Base is not without benefit for the rest of the family too. "A father told me that being involved in Home Base has made a difference in his wife," reports another of the parent educators. "She's found out she has ability, and she is using it. Her opinion of herself has been greatly improved."

Keeping an otherwise isolated family in touch with the community is another valuable aspect of the Home Base program. "Instead of my feeling alone and all tied up by my problems," a woman told her visitor, "you help by just being a friend that I can talk to once a week".

The Yakima Home Base program illustrated how schools or centers can use the home as a teaching center. The emphasis was on practices that encourage the child's educational growth: (a) learning communication skills, (b) reasoning logically, (c) developing self-concept, (d) becoming nutritionally aware, (e) using developmental activity sequences, (f) employing effective teaching techniques, (g) using easily obtained play materials, and (h) extending new expertise and knowledge about parenting to other members of the family. This program responded to the individual requirements of the community from which it evolved, but many of the techniques of effective parenting and teaching are appropriate for any home-based program.

While the basic premise of home-based programs is working with families and children in their own homes, there is great variety in the requirements for staff and the manner in which services are provided. Table 9.1 compares the programs to enhance understanding as to who is eligible for service, how the programs operate, and who is responsible for providing services. This information can provide guidance for families if they have the option to choose support from one program or another, and for a community to decide which program to establish. While some of the programs previously mentioned have explicit instructions for delivering services to children and families, the following guide to developing learning activities provides generic guidelines that would result in the home visitor working with the parent to develop a learning environment based on the interests and availability of materials in or near the home.

**TABLE 9.1**

**Comparison of Home-Based Program Descriptions**

| Programs | Populations Served | | Goals | Provider Requirements | | | |
|---|---|---|---|---|---|---|---|
| | Ages | Eligibility Requirements | Schedule | | Background | Training | Materials Used |
| PAT Parents as Teachers | Prenatal to 5 yrs | Child under 3 yrs | Weekly | Child development | Paraprofessional | Program specific | Program materials |
| HIPPY Home Instruction Program for Pre-school Youngsters | 3–5 yrs | Any child and family | 15 × yr | School readiness | Parents | Program specific | Activity packet |
| EHS Early Head Start | Prenatal to 3 yrs | Low income 1+ infant | Weekly | School readiness, family self-sufficiency | Paraprofessional | Developmentally appropriate practice | Home materials |
| PCHP Parent–Child Home Program | 2–4 yrs | Any child & family | 2 × week | Family literacy | Paraprofessional | Program specific | Toys |
| HFA Healthy Families America | Prenatal to 5 yrs | Meets specific criteria | Weekly | Child abuse prevention | Paraprofessional | Program specific | Home materials |
| Nurse–Family Partnership Program | Prenatal to 2 yrs | Low income at-risk mothers | Weekly | Improve family function | Registered nurse | Program specific | Program materials |
| Portage Project | Prenatal to 6 yrs | Children with disabilities | Weekly | Child development | Professional | Program specific | Program materials |

## FIVE-STEP GUIDE TO LEARNING ACTIVITIES

The Florida Parent Education Program developed by Gordon and his colleagues (Gordon & Breivogel, 1976) recommends the following five-step framework in the development of home activities:

### Idea

The concept or idea emerges from the child, parent, home visitor, or special interests of the family. What does the family enjoy? Which experiences have been interesting and fun? What collections, toys, or materials are available around the home? Ideas are also shared among the staff—teachers, other home visitors, and curriculum specialists. When an idea occurs, a memo is jotted down to remind the home visitor of the activity.

### Reason

Each idea is used for a reason. The reasons may range from learning experiences to self-concept development. After ideas are collected, examine the skills that can be associated with each. For example, if the child picks a leaf from one of the trees in the neighborhood, start a collection of fallen leaves that can be classified according to size, color, and shape. The child can make texture and outline rubbings of them. You might ask the child how many kinds of trees are represented by the variety of leaves, and instruct the child to put each kind of leaf in a separate pile and count the kinds. The many learning opportunities available from collecting leaves make this a worthwhile project for as long as the child's interest continues.

### Materials

Implementing a reasonable idea requires available materials. Some experiences can be developed around materials commonly found in the home. If the idea requires special equipment and materials, make sure they are easily obtained. One of the main objectives of home visits is to involve the parent as the teacher. If parents do not realize that they have readily available teaching materials or if the learning activities are not furnished for them, part of the parental autonomy and subsequent success of the program is lost.

### Action

Follow the child's lead and let the activity develop. If the child chooses something to explore that is different from your plans for the activity, vary your plans, take a detour, and enjoy the inquiry and discovery the child is experiencing. Your ideas may be brought up later or eliminated. Remember the objectives of the learning process. If they are being fulfilled, it does not matter which action brought about the learning.

### Extension

Are there other activities related to this idea? If so, expand the action, follow the interest, and extend the learning (Packer, Hoffman, Bozler, & Bear, 1976). Try to help parents see how the activity can be adapted to the child's changing interests and skills. Figure 9–4 illustrates how a garden can be used as a learning experience.

## DEVELOPMENT OF A HOME-ACTIVITIES FILE

The development of a home-activities file depends on the objectives and philosophy of the program. Materials and experiences are based on the home environment, the children's interests, and the parents' enthusiasm. This provides an excellent opportunity to involve parents in creating learning activities for their children. It can also enable the parents to change their approach to childrearing through encouragement and acceptance of their contributions. The idea for a garden described in Figure 9–4 could have originated with a suggestion from a parent.

Throughout the year, home visitors involve parents in teaching their children at home. As the home visitor suggests activities for the child, additional ideas may occur to both the visitor and the parent. In addition, children themselves may elaborate on old ideas or create new activities. The home visitor should bring these ideas back to the office, where they can be classified and cataloged. Parents receive a boost if home visitors recognize their contributions. They will also continue to develop activities for children if they are reinforced. Write down their suggestions and file them for future use or include them in the program for the coming week.

## FIGURE 9–4

*The Utah Home Visitor Guide.* The unit on gardens and vegetables illustrates how ordinary activities around the home can be used for education.

UTAH HOME VISITOR GUIDE
April—1st week

Unit title: Gardens and Vegetables

With the high cost of living, it's important to grow your own fresh vegetables because they are so important in our daily diet. Homegrown vegetables are also healthier (less chemicals and fertilizers) and more nutritious. Families need information on how to store, preserve, and prepare fresh vegetables. Gardening is an excellent learning and sharing experience for families.

Specific objectives:

1. To help parents realize the economical benefits gained through home gardening
2. To give parents help with methods of food preparation and preservation
3. To stress the importance of vegetables to good nutrition

Activities

1. Discussion on growing a garden
   a. Why grow a garden?
   b. How to grow a garden
   c. How to store and preserve food from the garden
   d. Handout on food storage and preserving
   e. How to involve children in gardening
   f. Children will often eat more when they grow the food themselves
   g. Gardening is good exercise and teaches responsibility
   h. Handouts on planting times, spacing, what grows in this area (information from county agents)
2. Choose a garden site
3. Plan a garden
   a. What do you want to grow/like to eat?
   b. How much space, water, and time do you have?
   c. What will grow in your area?
   d. Is this to be a permanent site?
4. If no garden space, use boxes, crates, and flower beds
5. Take fruits and vegetables into home for snack/look, feel, and taste
   a. Cleanliness in handling food
6. Look at seeds and compare or match with vegetable
7. Snack tray of raw vegetables and cottage cheese dip
8. Sprout seeds
9. Plant seeds in plastic bag with wet paper towel
10. Plant seeds in egg carton
11. Grow plants from sweet potato and avocado seeds in water
12. Seed collage
13. Start your own tomato, green pepper, and canta-loupe plants indoors in cardboard cartons
14. Count seeds
15. Pop popcorn
16. Classify vegetables and fruits—cut out pictures from magazines
17. Stories and books
    a. Carrot seed
    b. Turnip seed
    c. Peter Rabbit—Mr. McGregor's Garden
    d. The Little Seed
18. Creative movement—germination and growth of seed
19. Tell parents where to get information and handouts
    a. County extension office
    b. Seed stores
20. Sprinkle grass on wet sponge
21. Print with vegetable or weed leaves
22. Talk about seeds you can eat and eat some for a snack
23. Talk about food that people and animals eat
24. Make a vegetable salad
25. Handouts on vegetables

Follow-up for positive reinforcement:

1. Show seeds—sprouted in bag or planted
2. How do you wash vegetables?
3. What did you decide about your garden?

*Source:* From *Partners with Parents,* by K. D. Hewett et al., for Abt Associates and High/Scope Educational Research Foundation, 1978, Washington, DC: U.S. Department of Health, Education and Welfare, Office of Human Development, Administration for Children, Youth, and Families, Head Start Bureau.

## Parent Involvement During Home Visits

Children learn best when they are actively involved. Piaget (1976) insists that learning stems from the active involvement of the person doing the inventing; once invented, the theory or steps are not forgotten. Piaget recommends "the use of active methods which give broad scope to the spontaneous research of the child or adolescent and require that every new truth to be learned be rediscovered or at least reconstructed by the student and not simply imparted to him" (pp. 15–16). Kamii (1985a, 1985b) recommends a Piagetian approach in constructivism, meaning the belief that children construct their own knowledge if given the opportunity.

Experiential activities that afford children an opportunity to learn by discovery are facilitated best in a relaxed, natural, and rich learning environment. The setting can be either in the home or in the community. It is important to guide and support parents so they can fulfill their role as their child's first teacher–and constant support system—to ensure that children are able to reach their full potential. The steps to developing a home-learning activity, as suggested by Gordon's program in Florida (Gordon & Breivogel, 1976), reflect the use of the natural environment. Most important is the attitude that learning is possible everywhere for the child.

The home is a learning center. Children learn to talk without formal instruction. They learn as they interact with others and participate in interesting events. Through play at home, children become active learners (Parlakian & Lerner, 2010). Learning tasks at home can and should be intriguing rather than simply difficult. For example, a parent who reads stories to children is actually teaching reading—the development of an interest in and love of reading is the first step toward acquisition of proficient reading skills.

## Activities and Resources at Home

Brainstorm for a moment about all the learning opportunities in the home. Record the ideas that can be used during home visits or to share with parents. The following ideas may lead to many more:

- *Art and crafts.* Have tempera paint, watercolors, crayons, chalk, white paper, colored paper, scissors, glue or paste, Play-Doh, and modeling clay available for spontaneous art projects. Draw,

Funds of knowledge include learning opportunities in the home.

paint, or make rubbings and collages. Try painting outdoors with water.

- *Read together.* Children begin learning to read at home. To help children with language and reading development, parents need to talk with and read to their infants. Include a range of literature from nursery rhymes and poems to stories that adults enjoy in their native language. Infants hear the voice, develop sensitivity to the sounds, and set out on their way to literacy. The proximity to the reader helps develop trust and attachment. Read aloud with preschoolers and school-age children. Discover and emphasize the many situations in which children can be engaged in reading and writing.

- *Publishing.* Make a publishing center and include paper, pencils, pens, or computer, and cardboard for backing of books.

For very young children, transcribe their stories for them and let them illustrate the story or book. If children are older, help them brainstorm ideas for a book or make a history book of their family. Let them write in journals or diaries. Encourage them to write to a relative, pen pal, or friend. Create poetry, cinquains, haiku, free verse, rhyming, and limericks. Help them edit their work in a cooperative spirit.

Write a cooperative newsletter for the neighborhood or relatives. Make a form with areas for writings by each person or descriptions of each project. Let someone fill in the information.

- *Games.* Take time to play games. The list is long: Concentration, hopscotch, jacks, jump rope, basketball, table tennis, toss a ball, lotto, Monopoly, word or letter bingo, anagrams, and matching. Games that are culturally appropriate are also recommended, such as *Lotería* for Latino children. Some games are still popular; other games parents need to introduce children to such as jacks, which helps with visual perception.
- *Backyard science.* Examine the ground for insects and vegetation. Examine bugs with a microscope. Classify leaves by shape, size, and color. Categorize plants or animals.
- *Front yard business.* Have a garage sale and let your child be the cashier.
- *Listening center.* Collect read-along books so the child can listen to the books and read along using e-books and Kindle.
- *Music center.* Using iTunes, download music to computer, phones, and other digital devices where the child can listen to various types of music. Use the center for singing, moving, and dancing. If you have songs with written words, the activity can also be a reading experience.
- *Communicate.* Talk with each other. Let children describe all the things that are happening. Help them predict and observe by showing interest in their predictions. Make the home a safe place to express feelings.
- *Homemaking activities.* Chores are not chores if you have fun doing them. Cooking is fun and can be used as an intellectual endeavor as well as a functional activity. Practice mathematics by dividing a recipe in half. Research where and how the ingredients were grown using different Web sites on the Internet.

## Activities Away from Home

Trips around and away from home can also be adventures.

- *Take a walk.* Collect water from a stream or puddle. Examine the water through a microscope when you return home. Describe or draw the creatures found in a drop of water.
- *Visit the library.* Go to the library. Help children get library cards if they don't have them. Choose and check out books. If the library has a story-time or program for older children, attending helps make the library a wonderful place to visit.

Parents can devise a practical educational experience from everyday projects such as planting a garden.

- *Visit a store.* It can be the grocery store, post office, department store, or hardware store. Before going, make out a shopping list together. Keep it simple. Let the child help with selection and cost of the products.
- *Explore museums.* Art, natural history, historical, or other specialty museums may have pictures or artifacts that lend themselves to artwork at home. To increase observation powers, let the child look for something specific, such as a color or materials. Talk about how the art materials were used or which shapes were selected.
- *Visit historical buildings.* Take along paper, pen, and crayons. Draw the shape of the building. Make a crayon rubbing of the placard that tells about the building's dedication.
- *Visit the airport and bus station.* Watch the people. Imagine where they are going. Count the people who walk by. Find out how the station or airport is managed. Note how many buses, trains, or airplanes you can see. How are they different from each other? Compare the costs of the different methods of travel.
- *Go to a garage sale.* Determine how many articles you can buy for $5 or $10.
- *Visit a flea market.* Find out how many different items are sold that are from other countries and other cultures. How many toys can you purchase with $1 or $2?

Using intriguing and exciting activities benefits the family in two ways: learning takes place, and the parent–child relationship is enhanced. This will help parents understand the importance of a rich home environment, but they still need to be reinforced for their positive teaching behaviors. Although good times together may be reinforcement enough, schools can help support productive parent–child interaction by encouraging parents, offering workshops, and supplying home-learning activities.

## Home-Learning Strategies for the Home Visitor

Each home-based program has developed its own approach to home-learning activities. The Portage Project developed a systematic program for its home visitors that can be used by others. HIPPY provides a specific curriculum design with storybooks and activity packets. The Nurse–Family Partnership Program includes a curriculum that emphasizes maternal health, mental health issues, and infant/toddler development. Other programs focus on giving the families support, building family self-sufficiency, and encouraging improved parenting skills.

As parents and home visitors work together to develop the children's curriculum, the following tips will help:

- Choose an emerging skill that the child has shown an interest in or one in which an interest can be developed.
- Choose some skills that the parent considers important.
- Choose a skill the child needs to learn.
- Choose a developmentally appropriate task that is easily accommodated at home (U.S. Department of Health and Human Services, 1985).

In the implementation of a home-based program, both home visitors and parents may develop activities related to individual families or they may be supported by learning activities developed by commercial companies and school districts. Appropriate learning activities can be purchased or found in the library.

Home visitors should remember that the relationship they establish with parents is the most critical means of helping parents support their children's development. They should acknowledge each parent's experience, be respectful at all times, and be a constant learner. While they may establish closer ties with some parents than others, objectivity and an awareness of professional boundaries are of equal importance for all families they serve (U.S. Department of Health and Human Services, 1987). It is also important to provide professional development for the home visitor in order to accomplish his or her job more effectively (Harden, Denmark, & Saul, 2010).

## :: ESTABLISHING A HOME-BASED PROGRAM

Before a program is established, the reasons for and needs of such a program must be examined. The primary goals of home-based programs include the following:

1. To enable parents to become more effective teachers of their children.
2. To support the parents in the roles of caregivers and homemakers.
3. To strengthen the parents' sense of autonomy and self-esteem.
4. To reach the child and family early in the child's formative years.
5. To respond to the family's needs and thus improve the home environment.

Educators look for home-based programs to increase a child's sense of well-being, improve educational success, and help the child realize optimum development. Individual goals for programs vary according to the needs of the area. For instance, an overriding concern in one area may be health; in another, language development; and in still another, nutrition. Although all three are important in varying degrees in every home-based program, the intensity of involvement may vary.

A number of studies have been conducted to determine the effectiveness of home-based programs, since the U.S. Advisory Board on Child Abuse recommended the design and implementation of a national universal home-visiting program. Universal home-visiting was recommended to ensure that support to families would be available to all and, in particular, that universal access would not stigmatize the families most in need. The report also recommended that families should receive support from professionals and paraprofessionals, with weekly services being made available beginning in the neonatal period in a manner that supported positive family interactions. Program evaluation was also recommended to determine the most effective strategies for serving children and families (Krugman, 1993). Subsequent reports have determined that the recommendations have not been realized for many programs. For some programs, the reasons include scarcity of resources and other barriers. For others, outcomes have been child focused or have assessed the home environment but not family functioning. In order to fully determine a program's effectiveness, the long-term impact of family functioning is very important.

The concern for serving families and children in their homes as an intervention strategy has continued. A series of reports and policy briefs titled "Building Community Systems for Young Children" included a policy brief, "Home Visiting: A Service Strategy to Deliver First 5 Results," (Thompson, Kropenske, Heinicke, Gomby, & Halfon, 2003). The policy brief discussed strategies to strengthen program quality. Three principles identified as essential were that (a) interventions should be grounded in research that identify adverse outcomes to be addressed and factors necessary to change the outcome, (b) interventions should be based on theories of behavior change, and (c) interventions should be viewed as relevant and needed by the community. In addition, as in the U.S. Advisory Board recommendations, it was recommended as imperative that programs monitor the implementation of the program services by staff and monitor the impact of the interventions on holistic client outcomes. Program monitoring should be embedded in program implementation efforts in order to support continued funding and to determine what contributes to effective delivery of services to children and families.

## :: DETERMINING THE NEED FOR A PROGRAM

Community groups, schools, and centers should consider the needs of children and their families and the availability of community resources as they determine the need for a home-based program. They should also examine the variety of programs available before embarking on a home-based program.

Home-based programs focus on the socioemotional and academic well-being of children.

The following questions can be used as guidelines for choosing a program:

1. Are there children and families who could be helped by early intervention in the home?
2. What can the community agency or school do in a home-visitation program that cannot be accomplished through other programs?
3. Could early intervention help children go to school?
4. Are there children with disabilities who could be diagnosed and given service before they enter school?
5. Will the preventive program help eliminate later educational problems, offsetting the cost to the public?
6. Will the prevention of later educational problems reduce emotional problems, also offsetting the cost to the public?
7. Are there parents who could be helped by an adult-literacy program?
8. Do parents need support to develop self-sufficiency so they can provide for their children's long-term needs?
9. Are immigrant families in need of resources that will help them improve their quality of life, such as ELL programs for adults or medical services and education for young children?

If "yes" is the answer to most of these questions, the next step is to consider the feasibility of a home-based program. The following questions must be addressed:

1. Has there been a thorough assessment of needs to establish community interest in home-based services?
2. Are there *enough* families in the community who are definitely interested and eligible to participate in a program that emphasizes home visits and the role of the parents?
3. Do staff members already have the skills and interests needed to work effectively with parents in their own homes? If not, does the program have, or can it obtain, the considerable training necessary to prepare staff members for their new roles? Is the staff willing to receive such training? Is the staff culturally and linguistically compatible with families to be served?
4. Can transportation needs be met? Public transportation is often an inefficient mode of travel and is not available in many areas. Home visitors need a car to get around quickly, transport materials, and take parents and children for special services needed from local resource agencies.
5. Will the program include family members who are away from home during the day? The answer to this usually involves meetings and home visits in the evenings and on weekends. In some ways, home-based programs require a staff selflessness and dedication that goes beyond the demands of the workload and schedules of center-based services. (U.S. Department of Health and Human Services, 1985)

Before a questionnaire or needs assessment is devised, data should be gathered from school files, social-service agencies, city surveys, or census reports. Social services will be particularly helpful in determining services and number of children in families. School figures, questionnaires, and surveys will supplement those data so that services can be offered to all those who want or need them. Make every effort to establish a good working relationship with the various agencies. You will need to coordinate your efforts later, and initial communication and rapport are essential to subsequent implementation of the program.

Parents to be served in a home-based program should be actively involved in the initial planning. Many schools and preschool programs have parent advisory councils or citizen advisory councils that can give input on the needs of the community and suggest relevant questions. If a council is not functioning in your area, it may be worth it to start one. You can work through the existing PTO or PTA, or you can establish an entirely new council with the parents you will serve.

The formation or election of the board should be advertised. Parents then have an opportunity to nominate themselves or others, and an election is scheduled to determine who will represent the community on the council. You could advertise the formation of an advisory council by sending notes home with children; explaining the council at meetings of Boy Scouts, Camp Fire Girls, PTA, YMCA, and YWCA; and distributing flyers throughout the community. All nominations should be accepted. Using a democratic process will ensure that everyone has an opportunity to participate in the selection process.

Distinct advantages to using a democratic selection process rather than appointment to an advisory council include: (a) interest in the program is generated and maintained, (b) the parents feel a sense of self-determination and autonomy, (c) the council becomes a source of relevant information and feedback from those affected, and (d) cooperation between school and parents increases.

## Involving Others in the Program

The four components of an effective home-based program are: (a) education, (b) social services, (c) health services (physical and mental health, dental care, nutrition, and safety), and (d) parent involvement. It is only through comprehensive services to children and their families that pervasive family-based problems can be solved. Although the project will be fully responsible for education and parent involvement, social and health services will need the support of other agencies.

## Recruitment of Families

Many families can be identified through cooperative agreements with existing programs, such as Head Start, schools, and social-service agencies. Churches can also help identify families who are in need. Articles in newspapers about the new home-based program will alert other parents, and flyers can be delivered by students. The most effective method, however, is a door-to-door canvass. Home visitors can go from house to house to chat with parents and explain the program and its benefits. This personal approach seems to encourage parents to participate when a notice through the mail may not. Families new to the area or unknown to social agencies probably will be reached only by a door-to-door campaign.

Published articles can increase parents' interest. Curriculum and child development may be communicated through newsletters as well as personal visits. It is also a good idea to combine the two and give the parent a handout at the end of a home visit.

## Selection of Home Visitors

Before selecting home visitors, the choice must be made whether to use professionals, professional parent teachers, paraprofessionals, or volunteers. Although the director, coordinator, and special services specialists will probably be professionals such as therapists for children with special needs, many programs use paraprofessionals or volunteers as the home-visit specialists. Criteria for selection will be determined by the needs of your program.

Five criteria often considered are as follows:

1. Experience, age, and maturity—good judgment and flexibility
2. Race, ethnicity, culture, and language—key consideration should be to the home visitor who has respect for values and beliefs of other cultures
3. Professional education
4. Gender
5. Helping skills (Wasik, 1993)

**Communication Skills.** The skills needed for an effective home visitor program (Figure 9–5) also include collaboration and effective communication in which the home visitor is able to do the following:

1. Listen empathetically
2. Affirm the family
3. Recognize and affirm the family's funds of knowledge
4. Maintain appropriate boundaries
5. Individualize for each family's needs
6. Demonstrate and model effective parenting skills

7. Interpret the purpose of activities and child–parent interactions
8. Problem solve with the parents (Klass, Pettinelli, & Wilson, 1993)

**Recruiting.** When recruiting paraprofessional home visitors, the positions should be advertised throughout the community. Announcements must be clear and include the following:

1. *Explanation of the program.* Explain what your home-based program entails, indicating its goals and objectives.
2. *Job description of the position.* List the duties and responsibilities, workday schedule, salary range, and benefits.
3. *Qualifications required.* Indicate whether high school diploma, college degree, or specific competencies is required. Also include reliable transportation.
4. *Equal opportunity employment announcement.* Make a statement of nondiscrimination.
5. *Instructions for applying.* Give instructions on how to apply, whom to contact, and the deadline for application.
6. *Bilingual ability.* Include a statement in which the qualifications include being bilingual depending on the language spoken in the community (i.e., Spanish/English, Vietnamese/English). This can also include the ability to use sign language.

The announcement should be posted in public places, such as libraries, schools, stores, and social agencies, such as Head Start as well as other Internet Web sites including but not limited to monster.com or Craig's list. Wide dissemination of information about available positions encourages individuals in the community to become involved and alerts others to the upcoming home-based program.

## In-Service Training
## After the Program Has Started

Learning by both the family and the home visitor comes to fruition during the development of the program. During this period, the home visitor responds to the needs, desires, and styles of the parents and children. Close contact with the program's coordinator or trainers supports the home visitor and allows administrators to keep track of

## FIGURE 9–5

A self-evaluation form for home visitors.

| Are YOUR Home Visits Parent-Focused? | | |
|---|---|---|
| • Do you involve the parents in the assessment of the child? | Yes | No |
| • Do you provide the parent with a copy of the checklist for their own use? | Yes | No |
| • When you arrive for the weekly home visit, do you direct your attention and greeting toward the parent? | Yes | No |
| • Do you discuss the previous week's visit and follow up on the weekly activities with the parent? | Yes | No |
| • Does the parent co-plan the activities for the home visit? | Yes | No |
| • Do you make sure that the child is sitting beside the parent? | Yes | No |
| • Does the parent demonstrate EACH new activity? | Yes | No |
| • Do you review each activity with the parent before presenting it? | Yes | No |
| • Do you hand all materials to the parent? | Yes | No |
| • Do you identify and reinforce the parent's teaching strengths? | Yes | No |
| • When the parent has difficulty, do you intervene with the parent rather than the child? | Yes | No |
| • Do you let the parent be the primary reinforcing agent? | Yes | No |
| • Do you help the parent problem solve when problems do arise instead of jumping to the rescue? | Yes | No |
| • Do you work on activities the parent feels are important? | Yes | No |
| • Do you ask the parent to provide as many materials as possible? | Yes | No |
| • Do you give the parent the lead, when appropriate? | Yes | No |
| • Do you incorporate the parent's ideas into each activity? | Yes | No |
| • Do you let the parent present new and exciting experiences? | Yes | No |
| • Do you individualize parent education activities for each parent? | Yes | No |
| • Do you accept the parent's values? | Yes | No |
| • Do you involve the parent in evaluation of the home visit? | Yes | No |

*Source:* From *The Head Start Home Visitor Handbook,* by U.S. Department of Health and Human Services, Office of Human Development Services, Administration for Children, Youth, and Families, Head Start Bureau, 1987, Washington, DC: U.S. Government Printing Office.

what is happening in the field. Reports on each visit, with copies for the home visitor and for the program's administrators or trainers, will enable people from both levels of the program to keep in touch with developments and needs. In doing so, in-service training can be directed to enrich weak areas and clarify procedures. At the end of each visit, home visitors can reflect on the questions presented in Figure 9–5. A home visitor's answers to these questions can also provide the basis for inservice training.

**Small Groups.** Throughout the year, questions and needs for training will arise. Training sessions are more effective when small groups of home visitors—rather than all members of the program—meet together as needs emerge. The individualized meeting is beneficial because the session has been set up especially for the participants, and small numbers allow for a more personalized response by the trainer or coordinator.

**Community Resources.** Although lists of community resources are given to home visitors early in the program, more definite descriptions and procedures are useful when specific problems arise. During the year, specialists from a variety of community agencies can be invited to share their experiences and knowledge of procedures with the staff. Have them come to training meetings, meet the staff, and answer questions concerning use of their programs.

## Program Evaluation

Ongoing evaluations of contacts, visits, and services rendered are essential. Home-visit reports give data that can be used to measure progress. If the home visitor systematically completes each report, the administrator will be able to evaluate progress throughout the training period.

**Parent Questionnaires.** Statements by parents and responses to questionnaires concerning the effect of the program on the child and family are valuable in analyzing the effects of the program. Collect these throughout the program as well as at the completion of the year.

Evaluation is a tool to be used during the development of the program as well as a means to assess accomplishments. Include a variety of evaluations to improve the program and demonstrate its effectiveness.

## :: SCREENING FOR BETTER UNDERSTANDING

As home visitors and parents work with children, they informally assess the child's characteristics and skills. Informal assessments with checklists can be used while the child is playing. It is always best to view the child in a natural setting unrestricted by contrived tasks. A portfolio containing collections of art activities and projects, teacher comments,

Professionals must keep open communication with parents.

and the child's comments can aid in assessing the child's development. These kinds of assessment are essential—they provide the parent and teacher with guidelines for developmentally appropriate activities for each child.

Parent educators also need to be able to recognize if families under their guidance need special help. Screening for potential problems in both the developmental status of children and the children's environment—especially if they are growing up in a low socioeconomic area—will help the parent educator identify problems early and more effectively serve children and their families (Fandal, 1986).

Several instruments are available to screen the developmental progress of children. Two of the most widely used are the Denver Prescreening Developmental Questionnaire and the Denver Developmental Screening Test. There are also standardized methods of assessing the home environment of children, such as the Home Screening Questionnaire and the Home Observation for Measurement of the Environment.

### Home Observation for Measurement of the Environment

The Home Observation for Measurement of the Environment (HOME) Inventory (Figure 9–6) is used by schools, child-care centers, and other social-service agencies to help them determine the quality of the home environment as it relates to the child's development. Current studies using the HOME Inventory show the association between maternal education and reading and math achievement (Zadeh, Farnia, & Ungerleider, 2010).

The HOME Inventory was developed "to get a picture of what the child's world is like from his or her perspective—from where he or she lies or sits or stands or moves about and sees, hears, smells, feels, and tastes that world" (Caldwell & Bradley, 1984, p. 8). In addition to the standardized HOME Inventories for birth to 3-year-olds and 3- to 6-year-olds, an inventory for elementary school children also is available.

When using the program, the interviewer should:

- Know the HOME Inventory well before using it.
- Contact the parents and arrange a visit.
- Visit when the child is awake and available.
- Start the interview with friendly, relaxed interaction.

**FIGURE 9-6**

Home visitors can use the HOME inventory to analyze the family's home environment.

---

HOME Inventory for Families of Infants and Toddlers
Bettye M. Caldwell and Robert H. Bradley

13

Family Name _____ Date _____ Visitor _____

Child's Name _____ Birthdate _____ Age _____ Sex _____

Caregiver for visit _____ Relationship to child _____

Family Composition (Persons living in household, including sex and age of children) _____

Family Ethnicity _____ Language Spoken _____ Maternal Education _____ Paternal Education _____

Is Mother Employed? _____ Type of work when employed _____ Is Father Employed? _____ Type of work when employed _____

Address _____ Phone _____

Current child care arrangements _____

Summarize past year's arrangements _____ Other persons present _____

Caregiver for visit _____

Comments _____

**SUMMARY**

| Subscale | Score | Lowest Middle | Middle Half | Upper Fourth |
|---|---|---|---|---|
| I. Emotional and Verbal RESPONSIVITY of Parent | | 0-6 | 7-9 | 10-11 |
| II. ACCEPTANCE of Child's Behavior | | 0-4 | 5-6 | 7-8 |
| III. ORGANIZATION of Physical and Temporal Environment | | 0-3 | 4-5 | 6 |
| IV. Provision of Appropriate PLAY MATERIALS | | 0-4 | 5-7 | 8-9 |
| V. Parent INVOLVEMENT with Child | | 0-2 | 3-4 | 5-6 |
| VI. Opportunities for VARIETY in Daily Stimulation | | 0-1 | 2-3 | 4-5 |
| TOTAL SCORE | | 0-25 | 26-36 | 37-45 |

For rapid profiling of a family, place an X in the box that corresponds to the raw score on each subscale and the total score.

---

HOME Inventory*

14

Place a plus (+) or minus (-) in the box alongside each item if the behavior is observed during the visit or if the parent reports that the conditions or events are characteristic of the home environment. Enter the subtotal and the total on the front side of the Record Sheet.

I. Emotional and Verbal RESPONSIVITY
1. Parent spontaneously vocalized to child twice.
2. Parent responds verbally to child's verbalizations.
3. Parent tells child name of object or person during visit.
4. Parent's speech is distinct and audible.
5. Parent initiates verbal exchanges with visitor.
6. Parent converses freely and easily.
7. Parent permits child to engage in "messy" play.
8. Parent spontaneously praises child at least twice.
9. Parent's voice conveys positive feelings toward child.
10. Parent caresses or kisses child at least once.
11. Parent responds positively to praise of child offered by visitor.
Subtotal

II. ACCEPTANCE of Child's Behavior
12. Parent does not shout at child.
13. Parent does not express annoyance with or hostility to child.
14. Parent neither slaps nor spanks child during visit.
15. No more than one instance of physical punishment during past week.
16. Parent does not scold or criticize child during visit.
17. Parent does not interfere or restrict child more than 3 times.
18. At least ten books are present and visible.
19. Family has a pet.
Subtotal

III. ORGANIZATION of Environment
20. Substitute care is provided by one of three regular substitutes.
21. Child is taken to grocery store at least once/week.
22. Child gets out of house at least four times/week.
23. Child is taken regularly to doctor's office or clinic.
24. Child has a special place for toys and treasures.
25. Child's play environment is safe.
Subtotal

IV. Provision of PLAY MATERIALS
26. Muscle activity toys or equipment.
27. Push or pull toy.
28. Stroller or walker, kiddie car, scooter, or tricycle.
29. Parent provides toys for child during visit.
30. Learning equipment appropriate to age—cuddly toys or role-playing toys.
31. Learning facilitators—mobile, table and chairs, high chair, play pen.
32. Simple eye-hand coordination toys.
33. Complex eye-hand coordination toys (those permitting combination).
34. Toys for literature and music.
Subtotal

V. Parental INVOLVEMENT with Child
35. Parent keeps child in visual range, looks at often.
36. Parent talks to child while doing household work.
37. Parent consciously encourages developmental advance.
38. Parent invests maturing toys with value via personal attention.
39. Parent structures child's play periods.
40. Parent provides toys that challenge child to develop new skills.
Subtotal

VI. Opportunities for VARIETY
41. Father provides some care daily.
42. Parent reads stories to child at least 3 times weekly.
43. Child eats at least one meal per day with mother and father.
44. Family visits relatives or receives visits once a month or so.
45. Child has 3 or more books of his/her own.
Subtotal

TOTAL SCORE

*For complete wording of items, please refer to the Administration Manual.

Source: From Administration Manual: Home Observation for Measurement of the Environment, by B. M. Caldwell and R. H. Bradley, 1984, Little Rock, AR: University of Arkansas. Reprinted with permission.

A suggested technique for starting the interview is described by the following statement:

> You will remember that we are interested in knowing the kinds of things your baby (child) does when he is at home. A good way to get a picture of what his days are like is to have you think of one particular day—like yesterday—and tell me everything that happened to him as well as you can remember it. Start with the things that happened when he first woke up. It is usually easy to remember the main events once you get started. (Caldwell & Bradley, 1984, p. 3)

The administration and scoring of each item in the inventory are clearly described in the Administration Manuals, so the interviewer can make correct judgments on the scoring of HOME. For example, see Figure 9–6, Item 4, which states, "Parent's speech is distinct and audible." The score on this item is determined by whether the interviewer is able to understand what the parent says. This item should not be interpreted as meaning that dialect usage mandates a negative score; what is important is whether the interviewer can understand and communicate with the parent.

## Home Screening Questionnaire (HSQ)

Coons, Gay, Fandal, Ker, and Frankenburg (1981) and Frankenburg and Coons (1986) recognized the value of an earlier version of the HOME Inventory but were concerned about the length of time needed for a skilled interviewer to make a home visit. Coons et al. developed the Home Screening Questionnaire (HSQ), which could be answered by parents. With the cooperation of the authors of the HOME Inventory, items were selected and turned into two questionnaires that correspond to the two HOME scales (for children from birth to 3 years and those from 3 to 6 years of age). Each takes about 15 minutes for a parent to complete. The questionnaires have been validated as effective screening tools to identify environments that would benefit from a more intensive assessment.

## :: HOMESCHOOLING

**Homeschooling** may be defined as "instruction and learning, at least some of which is through planned activity, taking place *primarily* at home in a family setting with a parent acting as teacher or supervisor of the activity" (Lines, 1991, p. 10). Homeschooling is not new. Many of our nation's early leaders were taught at home. The common school movement began about 1830 and 1840, but it was usual for children to attend for only 3 months out of the year for 3 or 4 years.

The last half of the 19th century saw a greater transformation of schooling. Eighty-six percent of children ages 5 to 14 were attending public schools by 1890 (Carper, 1992). During the 20th century, parents sent their children to public and private schools, and schools became more and more centrally administered. It was not until the 1980s that the increase in homeschooling began to be noticed.

Estimates of the number of children who were being schooled at home in the 1970s ranged from 1,000 to 15,000; in 1983, estimates ranged from 60,000 to 125,000; by 1988, the homeschool "student body" was thought to be 150,000 to 300,000 (Lines, 1991). It increased rapidly in the 1990s—estimates of homeschooled children ranged up to 2 million; but in 1999, the 95 percent confidence interval for the number of homeschoolers was 709,000 to 992,000. Subsequent data gathered have determined that homeschoolers account for 1.7 percent of the students in the United States (Kaplan-Leiserson, 2002; National Center for Education Statistics, 2001). It is anticipated that the number of children homeschooled will increase by 15 percent each year (Kaplan-Leiserson, 2002). The estimate of 1,096,000 homeschooled students shows an increase from 1.7 percent in 1999 to 2.2 percent in 2003 (National Center for Education Statistics, 2007). In 2007, there were 1.5 million students homeschooled in the United States (National Center for Education Statistics, 2011). A report from The National Home Education Research Institute (Ray, 2011) indicates that 2.04 million students were homeschooled in 2010.

## Characteristics of Homeschooling and Homeschooled Children

The majority of the students who are homeschooled are White. Parents make decisions to homeschool based on the quality of local schools, constraints of income, and available leisure time, as well as religious preferences (Isenberg, 2007). In most cases of homeschooling, the mother is the teacher, and she usually teaches her own children, spending 20 to 30 hours each week in school activities. Homeschool teachers are reported to have a more controlling style of teaching than other teachers. They have fewers years of formal education and are more conservative in their political views (Cai, Reeve, & Robinson, 2002). There is no one curriculum that parents use, although they can buy curriculum programs from a variety of organizations.

Testing for academic achievement and effective development has indicated that most homeschooled children do well in academics. Homeschoolers appear to score higher on state-mandated tests, indicating that although some score below average, "a large number test above that mark" (Lines, 1996). Some studies show that homeschooled students have higher SAT and ACT scores as well as grade point averages (Cogan, 2010). In 2002, the average SAT score for public school children was 1020, while it was 1092 for homeschooled children. In 2004, the average ACT score for public school children was 20.9, while it was 22.6 for homeschooled children (Beato, 2005). There also seems to be little risk to their socialization, psychological development, and self-esteem (Lines, 1996; Ray & Wartes, 1991).

In the past decade, proponents have been successful in advocating for homeschool, and state legislatures have been responding to parental demands. When there have been court cases, the proponents of homeschooling are able to rely on court decisions and the Bill of Rights (Guterson, 1992). All states allow homeschooling. Typically, a state's statutes—through a court ruling, an attorney general's opinion, or a regulation that interprets a school attendance law to include homeschooling—consider homeschooling a legitimate option for meeting compulsory education requirements. Because each state regulates homeschooling differently, parents should examine local laws and consult other homeschoolers before proceeding. In every state, parents must, at a minimum, notify a state or local education agency of their intent to educate their children at home and identify the children involved (Lines, 1996).

## Reasons for Homeschooling

The National Center for Education Statistics (2003) indicates that the largest single reason for homeschooling is parents' concern about the environment of the school their child would attend (85 percent). Religious reasons follow (72 percent), with dissatisfaction with the academic instruction being offered making up the third highest reason for selecting homeschooling (68 percent). Figure 9–7 illustrates the reasons that homeschooling parents gave for homeschooling their children. Parents who homeschool do not appear to use

**FIGURE 9–7**

Ten reasons for homeschooling and the percentage of homeschooled students whose parents gave each reason: 1999.

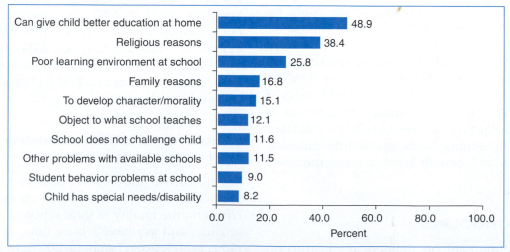

*Note:* Percentages do not add to 100 percent because respondents could give more than one reason.

*Source:* From the *Parent Survey* of the National Household Education Surveys Program, 1999, by the U.S. Department of Education, National Center for Education Statistics.

packaged curricula, as the majority are not certified teachers (Ray, 2010) but many use the Internet as a source for information.

### School–Parent Cooperation

The Cupertino Union School District in California has given parents options for collaboration between public schools and homeschoolers for over 25 years. Parents enroll their child in the district school system, but they educate the child at home. The school receives the revenue from the state, and parents are given curricula, services, materials, software, and money for books. Each family has a resource teacher who holds a conference with them monthly, or more often if desired. They also have access to a library of materials and books for homeschooling. They can use the school's supplies and equipment, and children can be enrolled in extended day class (Berger, 1997; Lamson, 1992).

Another example is the San Diego City School District, which offers support to homeschooled children. The school offers a structured curriculum for families to use. Educators are assigned as home-school teachers, who meet with the families on a trimester basis. Families can contact the teacher assigned to them as often as they desire. Parents can take advantage of services, field trips, special education, and counseling, educating their own children with the support of the school district (Dalaimo, 1996).

In collaboration, schools can furnish resources and services for homeschool families. These may include offering the use of resource centers; enrollment in special classes such as music, art, and science; participation of homeschooled parents in school district programs; advisory and facilitating services; in-service workshops; and participation of homeschooled students in extracurricular activities, summer programs, and large-group or team activities (Knowles, 1989).

By allowing the student to be schooled at home but providing support and an opportunity to participate with other children in activities, the school helps parents achieve their goals of educating their children themselves while giving children opportunities to interact socially with other students. If the child later reenters school, the transition will be easier.

## ∷ SUPPORTING CHILDREN'S LEARNING AT HOME

Children educated out of the home, whether in public or private school, need parental involvement to support their success in developing academic skills. Assisting children with homework is one way to build a bridge between home and school. A U.S. Department of Education report, *What Works: Research About Teaching and Learning* (1986) emphasized that the home environment and homework are essential for children to reach their full potential. Homework varies according to the age of the child. For young children, the home environment, the interaction, and intense work with toys make up the child's learning experience—the home is the child's school and what the child does is homework. Any homework in the early grades should be designed to promote parental involvement (Bailey, 2006). As children get older and the location of school goes outside the home, suddenly what they do at home is not considered school unless they bring home an assignment. But the home is still part of the child's learning experiences, and parents can support children by learning about the child's school experience and what he or she is learning to do. Real-life experiences including funds of knowledge serve as a purposeful context where family literacy and numeracy can take place (Kennedy, 2010).

The need for homework for children in the early grades is questioned by both parents and educators. The Child Study Movement of 1890 and early 1900s believed that children should be children and not start school until they were 7. In the mid-1920s to 1940s, homework was limited or abolished in New York City, Chicago, and San Diego. Reform of homework rather than elimination was the call after World War II. It should be "moderate in amount, creative in purpose and directed to each child's needs" (Winerip, 1999, p. 30). When the Soviet Union launched *Sputnik* in 1957, the educational system felt challenged and set out to educate the young so that the nation could compete. The result was increased homework nationwide (Winerip, 1999). In 1986, the report mentioned earlier, *What Works,* stated that homework "worked." Since then, homework has been seen as necessary and beneficial: "Assignments become common as early as first grade, and some schools require it every day. Parents' grumbling is heard across the land" (Winerip, 1999, p. 32).

Winerip (1999) describes the success that Chinese American parents have in home education. Chinese American children spend an average of 54 minutes each day studying at home, whereas European Americans spend about 6 minutes as indicated in the following statement, "At first and second grade, the Chinese-American families averaged 31 minutes in homework versus 11 for Euro-Americans" (Joshi, 2005, p. 30). Chinese American parents also spent time working with their children on language. Because their parents spoke Chinese at home, the children were behind in their English. The Chinese American parents assigned 15 words each week and by the fourth grade, instead of being behind in English, they were ahead of the European American children (Joshi, 2005, p. 30). Results such as these, even though the work Chinese American children do at home is not assigned by the school, make the demand for homework seem worthwhile.

An alternative to homework has been the development of after-school programs in which children can do schoolwork under supervision and with the help that they might need. This is especially helpful for families in which both parents work. Many after-school programs, however, have been careful to avoid being seen as an extension of the school day. The recurrent concern is how best to support and extend children's learning opportunities.

## Home–School Collaboration

The satisfactory use of homework requires communication and planning on the part of the school and the parent. While homework has long been used as a tool by schools to reinforce classroom instruction, many teachers do not see the opportunity or responsibility to communicate with parents about homework. Much greater cooperation and collaboration will occur if a teacher communicates with parents about the importance of homework. Teachers must reach out to parents, as part of establishing a partnership with them, to find out how the parents respond to the opportunity to support their child's educational growth through homework. Teachers must also determine if parents have the language and educational background to understand information that comes from school. If necessary, written material sent to parents may

need to be translated into the child's home language. If parents are not literate in their first language, school staff needs to attempt to make phone contact to speak with the parents in their first language. In many schools, this may present quite a challenge as many languages may be represented in any particular elementary school. In addition, parents may have disabilities that require alternative methods of communication. If the school has a stated policy about homework, the school staff needs to make this information available to parents in a manner in which parents can understand. If the school leaves homework up to individual teachers, each teacher is responsible for communicating with parents, through translators if necessary, about specific requirements for homework in their classes.

Parents have a shared responsibility to communicate with their child's teacher. They need to ask questions: Will there be homework each night? How long should the average amount of homework take? Will the assignments be explained before the student is sent home with them? Will the student understand the assignment? What are the rules and regulations regarding homework? Can homework be made into "homefun," where both student and parent enjoy the challenge?

If parents resent homework or are not able to assist their children, it can become a negative experience. Instead of strengthening the family, it can become divisive and fail to strengthen the child's academic achievement. At a minimum, parents should be guided by the teacher to talk to their children, in their home language if appropriate, about their school day and what they are learning. This will convey a strong message to children that school is important and that their parents care about their experience.

Homework must be handled with care. The teacher should do the following:

1. Send homework that reinforces or enriches what was learned in class. In either case, the assignment should be something the child is able to accomplish. Assignments that are short and frequent rather than long and infrequent appear to have a more significant effect on the child's learning (Cooper, 1999).
2. Create meaningful assignments. Homework should not be haphazard busy work; instead, it should be well planned and well designed.

Clearly explain the homework assignment. If it is new or extension material, review several of the issues or problems so the student knows what is expected.

3. Explain the rules and regulations of homework. Do you take off points for late homework? Is the homework grade figured into the grade for the grading period?

4. Provide a homework form that the student fills out in class that states the assignment, pages, or work sheets that go along with the homework. This could also include a signature line for the parent to sign so that the teacher knows the parent knows about the assignment.

5. Grade all homework personally. Display homework on the bulletin board to show the student that it is recognized and that it is important. Only assign homework on which students will be given feedback.

6. Communicate with parents to explain the process and respond to any difficulties that the family may be having with the homework.

7. Teach study skills. (Canter & Hausner, 1987; Cooke & Cooke, 1988; Hodapp & Hodapp, 1992; Paulu, 1995; Radencich & Schumm, 1996)

Homework can provide immediate retention of recent learning and can reinforce learning during leisure time. In addition homework can support great self-direction, self-discipline, and time organization. Some children feel that homework should provide them with opportunities to practice areas of weakness and push them to practice what has not been learned (Cushman, 2010).

Homework can have negative outcomes also. It can promote satiation of interest in learning, encourage parental interference in learning, lead to cheating, and can increase the differences between low-income and more affluent students. Teachers and parent must work together to ensure that homework produces positive outcomes and avoids pitfalls.

## How Can Parents Help?

Children of all ages can be helped with their homework. It is important that parents make sure that they observe their children and try to determine if the homework is developmentally appropriate. A rule of thumb is that homework should take about 10 minutes per grade level (Cooper, 2001).

The following tips may be provided to parents by their child's teacher. However, teachers should recognize that parents who live in crowded quarters may not be able to provide a positive environment for homestudy. A staffed study hall for after school might be essential. For homework, parents can help by providing the following:

1. Set up a specific place to study that is
   a. Well lighted.
   b. Quiet, but not too isolated.
   c. Comfortable, with appropriate chair and table.
   d. Equipped with materials—paper, pencils, pens, erasers, pencil sharpener, clock and/or computer.

2. Set aside a regular time for homework, or make a schedule for the week so that parents or children can fill in activities, study periods, dinner time, recreation, and bedtime for each school day.

3. Be supportive and give appropriate help. Parents should not do their children's homework, but parents can engage in problem solving with them, guide them, and help them over the rough spots.
   a. Consider the child's learning style. Does the child learn best through seeing, hearing, or manipulating the material?
   b. Talk about the assignments. Does the child understand the homework? What does the child need in order to complete the work?
   c. Help the child structure the time and assignment, and help the child get started. Recognize that the responsibility for completing the homework belongs to the student.

4. Show interest in and encourage the child's efforts.

5. Be a parent who is both loving and firm.

6. Refer the child to a homework hot line or Web site to get an explanation of the assignment if needed.

7. Contact the teacher if further help is needed. (Canter & Hausner, 1987; Cooke & Cooke, 1988; Hodapp & Hodapp, 1992; Paulu, 1995; Radencich & Schumm, 1996)

The setting for homework should be determined by the learner's preferences and the conditions under which the student learns best (Hong & Milgram, 2000). For example, some learners find background music helpful. Parents may adjust the study area to the child's preference of tempera-ture, lighting, and sound, as "It has been clearly established that higher academic achievement and improved attitude result from tailoring the learning experiences to the cognitive and personal social characteristics of the learner" (Hong & Milgram, p. 17). Training parents on how to work with their children on homework assignments seems to help children with completing their homework, have fewer homework problems, and improve academic performance at least in elementary school (Patall, Cooper, & Robinson, 2008).

Home-based education has many facets and will diversify and increase in the future. Methods may vary as technology advances, but the home is still a primary educator of children.

## SUMMARY

Home-based education, initiated in the 1960s, saw continued and increased use in the 1980s, 1990s, and the 21st century. Programs developed include Parents as Teachers, Home Instruction Program for Preschool Youngsters, Healthy Families America, and Early Head Start, which joined earlier programs such as Portage Project, Parent–Child Home Pro-gram (Verbal Interaction Project), and the Nurse Family Partnership Program.

If the school is interested in developing a home-based program, it should (a) show a need for the program, (b) involve others in planning, (c) develop a parent advisory council, and (d) decide on a pro-gram format.

Home-learning activities to be used by the home visitor and the family can be obtained through de-velopment of individualized activities, commercial offerings, or activities developed by demonstration programs. Use materials that are readily available to the parents because the parent is the primary teacher in the home-based program. The focus in a home-based program is on the parent interacting with and teaching the child after the home visitor is gone. Screening instruments may be selected to guide teachers in their work with parents and children and to serve as a basis for referrals for more thorough evaluation.

Concern about excellence in education has brought added emphasis on homework and the question of what amount shows the greatest benefit. Parents and teachers must work together as partners to support and extend children's learning to ensure their success in school.

## SUGGESTED CLASS ACTIVITIES AND DISCUSSIONS

1. Brainstorm home situations that would be posi-tive experiences for children.
2. Itemize household equipment that can be used as home learning tools. How would you use each?
3. Write role-playing opportunities based on fami-lies in several home situations.
4. Discuss the guidelines related to home visits.
5. Discuss value systems that may vary from your own. How can you work with parents and refrain from infringing on their beliefs?
6. Compare the strengths and weaknesses of home-based programs.
7. Discuss how to establish a working relationship with parents to support out-of-school learning.

## USEFUL WEB SITES

**Early Head Start**
www.acf.hhs.gov/
The Early Head Start site is located within the Head Start Bureau site. Information includes publications, conferences, grant announcements, and research. Links to a variety of Early Head Start resources are provided.

**Healthy Families America**
www.healthyfamiliesamerica.org/
This site provides background information regarding network resources, advocacy activities, and current research. It also provides parenting tips and a link that assists parents in locating programs near their homes.

**HIPPY—Home Instruction Program for Preschool Youngsters**
www.hippyusa.org/
This site provides information regarding the HIPPY model, research, and public policy resources. It also provides a locator link to assist parents in contacting local programs.

### Nurse–Family Partnership Program

www.nursefamilypartnership.org/

Information on the Web site includes recognitions awarded to the program, outcome data, and a program locator for parents. Employment opportunities and newsletter information are also provided.

### Parent–Child Home Program

www.parent-child.org/

This site provides information regarding training events, program news links, and research links. The program mission statement is included.

### Parents as Teachers Program

www.patnc.org/

This site provides parenting tips, announcements for conferences, training, and product sales. It provides links to an advocacy center, contact information, and a locator link for parents.

### Portage Project

www.portageproject.org/

Information included on the site includes links to information regarding a family service credential, a new *Portage Guide*, and training and technical assistance information. Contact information is provided.

# CHAPTER

# 10

# Supporting Families of Children with Special Needs

*Jo Spidel*
*Eugenia H. Berger*
*Mari Riojas-Cortez*

*Respect, empathy, interest, motivation, care, and value create strong partnerships with families of children with special needs.*

Mari Riojas-Cortez

In this chapter on working with parents of children with special needs, you will find information and procedures that will enable you to do the following:

- Summarize historical perspectives of individuals with special needs.
- Identify organizations that provide a variety of resources for children and adults with special needs and their families.
- Examine the development of special education including legislation in the United States.
- Describe different disabilities and create an Individualized Education Program (IEP) and an Individualized Family Service Plan (IFSP).
- Discuss the parents' rights in schools as they relate to special education.
- Discuss special concerns that must be met when working with parents of children with special needs.
- Identify communication strategies that will help teachers work with culturally and linguistically diverse families who have special-needs children.

## :: INFLUENCES FOR THE NEED OF SPECIAL EDUCATION

In American society today, children and adults with special needs are beginning to matter. The government and schools are trying to create environments for children with special needs that allow them to participate in society. Society is learning to accept and understand children and adults who have diverse abilities by increasing awareness and developing policies to protect those who need it the most in order to avoid repeating past negative experiences.

Through history, however, there have been many tales of cruel and inhumane treatment of people with special needs. Recalling the story of *The Hunchback of Notre Dame* quickly brings to mind these cruelties. The Spartans were known to force parents to abandon imperfect babies by leaving them out in the cold (Greenleaf, 1978). There are instances in very early history, however, of people who had a more positive view of those who were different. Hippocrates, who lived around 400 B.C., believed that emotional problems were caused not by

supernatural powers but by natural forces. Plato (375 B.C.) defended those with mental disabilities as not being able to account for their deeds. The temples built by Alexander the Great provided asylum for mentally ill persons. In 90 B.C., Asclepiades made the first attempt at classifying mental illness, advocating humane treatment of those with the illness.

The period of A.D. 1450 to 1700 was an especially difficult time for those who were mentally ill or with other special needs. Belief in demonology and superstition resulted in persecution of those who were mentally ill or developmentally disabled as well as those with any other form of special need. John Locke, concerned about harsh discipline, cultivated the "blank tablet" concept of the newborn's mind to overcome the popular belief that a child was born full of evil ideas. He advocated that children be given empathic understanding (Cook, Tessier, & Armbruster, 1987).

In the late 1700s, Jean Marc Gaspard Itard (1775–1838) sought new methods to teach those with mental challenges. He was a physician and an authority on diseases of the ear and education of the deaf. He found a boy in the forest of Auvergne,

Jo Spidel, M.Ed., was a professional advocate for special education for more than 25 years. She taught, presented papers on, and wrote about special education. Certifications included Learning Disabilities, Behavior Disorders, Mental Retardation, and Director of Special Education. Fifteen years were devoted to teaching in public schools, the last position at Northwest High School in Wichita, Kansas. In addition to teaching, she developed and directed an in-house school for adolescent patients in a psychiatric, drug, and alcohol abuse hospital and served as a case manager for the Kansas Elks Training Center for the Handicapped.

Children with special needs thrive in a playful environment.

France, naked and apparently without upbringing, whom he attempted to raise and educate. He produced behavioral changes in the boy, Victor, but was unable to teach him to talk or to live independently. Itard believed he was a failure, but others followed his methods, which began a movement in treatment and education that had a profound effect on the development of special education (Cook, Klein, & Tessier, 2004; Hallahan & Kauffman, 1997; Reinert, 1987).

## Early Educational Opportunities for Individuals with Special Needs

During the 1800s, residential schools for individuals with special needs began to emerge. The residential schools and asylums that were built in the United States were very much like those in Europe during the 19th century. The first American residential school for those who were deaf was established in 1817 at Hartford, Connecticut, by Thomas Hopkins Gallaudet (1787–1851). Most early schools avoided severely disabled students or those with multiple disabilities and worked only with those who were deaf, blind, or, mentally challenged. Those with more serious disabilities were often not eligible for admission to any school and were often placed in asylums. Private schools were often expensive, and state-operated schools were limited in their facilities (Hallahan & Kauffman, 1990).

The Perkins School for the Blind, founded in Watertown, Massachusetts, was the first school for the blind. Samuel G. Howe (1801–1876) proved that those who were blind could be taught when Laura Bridgemen, who was blind and deaf, was

educated (Hallahan & Kauffman, 1997). Seeking education for his daughter Helen Keller (1880–1968), who was deaf and blind, Arthur H. Keller consulted the director of the Perkins Institution. It was from this institution that Anne Mansfield Sullivan came to teach Helen when Helen was almost 7 years of age (Keller, 1991). The fame of the successful life of this person with disabilities did much to persuade parents and professionals that, indeed, persons with disabilities could be educated.

It was not until the beginning of the 20th century that community-based programs for children with special needs began to appear. Gallaudet College, the only college for those who were deaf, started a teacher training program in the 1890s. In 1904, summer training sessions for teachers of children who were mentally challenged began at the Vineland Training School in New Jersey. The community-based programs, however, often became "sunshine" rooms, in which such activities as arts and crafts were pursued, with little attempt to educate the children. In some cases, expectations were unrealistic and disappointment in the programs ensued. Few parents or professionals were optimistic about educating those who had special needs (Hallahan & Kauffman, 1990). Grassroots organizations also began to emerge and focus on providing support for individuals with special needs and their families.

## Community Organizations Supporting Individuals with Special Needs

Community organizations that have developed to help individuals with special needs have often developed because their families believe in the individual's potential to live a fulfilling and productive life. These families use their funds of knowledge for the benefit of those who need it the most. The families committed to a specific cause often do so because a family member has a particular disability.

The Easter Seals organization has been helping individuals with disabilities and their families for over 90 years. Edgar Allen was a businessman who lost his son in a streetcar accident in 1907 and decided to sell his business and build a hospital in his hometown in Ohio. As he became involved in this endeavor, he realized that children with disabilities were not visible and often hidden from public view. He engaged in a campaign that created what is now one of the exceptional organizations that offers hope and answers to millions of children, adults, and their families affected by a disability. Currently there are more than 550 centers that provide services that are individualized, innovative, family-focused and tailored to meet the specific needs of the communities they serve (Easter Seals, 2011).

Another example of an organization that serves individuals who have special needs and their families is The Joseph Kennedy Jr. Foundation created by the Kennedys, a powerful and influential family with a daughter with a disability. The Foundation's main belief is that "persons with intellectual disabilities have the ability to live, learn, work, recreate, and worship like everyone else . . . but may need assistance to do these things" (The Joseph Kennedy, Jr. Foundation, 2011). The foundation particularly emphasizes the need to assist families by informing them about resources and including children and adults with disabilities in the community. The specific goals of the foundation include the following:

1. Enhance the quality of life of persons with intellectual disabilities and their families.
2. Provide seed funding to capitalize on federal and/or state or local spending on behalf of persons with intellectual disabilities and their families by funding initiatives that evolve beyond where existing programs are going, and do not duplicate public efforts.
3. Increase professional and public awareness of the needs of persons with intellectual disabilities and their families.
4. Work to reduce the incidence of intellectual disabilities (The Joseph Kennedy, Jr. Foundation, 2011).

Special Olympics, established in 1968 by Eunice Kennedy Shriver, is an athletic program for people with intellectual disabilities. It is the world's largest sports program, with 150 countries, 2.25 million athletes and families, and 500,000 volunteers and coaches participating (McCarthy, 2006). Thus, parents, educators, and influential families reinforce the growing concern of all parents of children with disabilities: that their children should have opportunities to develop to their highest potential.

Another example of an organization includes the Association for Retarded Citizens (ARC), previously the National Association for Retarded Children, which was chartered in 1950 and became active in influencing state legislatures and Congress, was created by small group of parents and other concerned individuals to act as voices for change (The Arc, 2011). In 1957, along with other organizations, it supported such important legislative action as the federal establishment of national programs in the field of special education and governmental support of research and leadership training in mental challenges. In 1963, support was extended to other people with special needs, except for people who were gifted, who did not receive support until 1979. The Bureau of Education for the Handicapped was established in 1966. It is important to note that ARC changed its name to "The Arc" in order to change the terminology that is derogatory and demeaning in usage (The Arc, 2011).

More recently, the organization Autism Speaks was created by the grandparents of a child with autism. Bob and Suzanne Wright founded the organization in 2005 when their grandchild was diagnosed with autism. Autism Speaks is the largest nonprofit science and advocacy organization that funds research that focuses on the causes, prevention, treatment, and cure of autism, increasing awareness, of autism spectrum disorders; and advocating for the needs of individuals with autism and their families (Autism Speaks, 2011).

The last example includes the Gordon Hartman Foundation in San Antonio, Texas, which created the only amusement park in the world, Morgan's Wonderland, for children and adults with disabilities and their families (Gordon Hartman Foundation, 2011). The mission of Morgan's Wonderland is to "provide a park that will nurture the minds and bodies of individuals with special needs and their families (Hollingsworth, 2009, p. 24). Gordon Hartman and his wife Maggie were inspired to create a space for children with different abilities and their families to enjoy the benefits of play. The Hartmans have a daughter with physical and cognitive disabilities.

Organizations such as the ones described here have provided children with special needs and their families opportunities to learn to live with their disability and assist the parents to provide a variety of experiences for their children. The government has also ensured that individuals with disabilities are protected. The following section focuses on the development of special-education laws.

## :: LEGISLATION FOR PEOPLE WITH DISABILITIES

Legislation for people with disabilities has been developing since the 1960s. With each new law or amendment to existing legislation, the programs for children and adults with disabilities have become more encompassing. During the 1960s, parents organized advocacy groups that became vocal and attracted enough attention to result in legislation to provide educational support to children with disabilities. In 1971, the Pennsylvania Association for Retarded Children (PARC) won a landmark case against the Commonwealth of Pennsylvania. It was a decision based on the 14th Amendment, which assures all children, including those with disabilities, the right to a free and appropriate education. Decisions such as this one led to the passage of other important laws.

### Vocational Rehabilitation Act of 1973, Section 504

Section 504 of the Vocational Rehabilitation Act of 1973, which relates to nondiscrimination under Federal Grant, P.L. 93-112, required that "no otherwise qualified handicapped individual in the United States shall, solely by reason of his handicap, be excluded from the participation in, be denied the benefits of, or be subjected to discrimination under any program or activity receiving Federal financial assistance" (29 U.S.C. § 794). At the time, Section 504 specifically applied to discrimination in employment. The Rehabilitation Act Amendments of 1974 extended coverage to all civil rights, including education, employment, health, welfare, and other social-services programs.

Under Section 504, all recipients of Department of Education funds that operate public elementary and secondary programs must provide a free appropriate public education (FAPE) to each qualified individual with a disability who is in the recipient's jurisdiction, regardless of the nature or severity of the person's disability (Office of Civil Rights, 2010).

Since the legislation was passed, there has been confusion about implementation and compliance of the regulations. As a result of the confusion, the Office of Civil Rights has issued policies and rulings that clarify many issues.

A person is considered disabled under the definition of Section 504 if the individual:

1. Has a physical or mental impairment that substantially limits one or more of such person's major life activities.
2. Has a record of such impairments.
3. Is regarded as having such an impairment.

*Major life activities* include functions such as caring for oneself, performing manual tasks, walking, seeing, hearing, speaking, breathing, learning, and working. When a condition does not substantially limit a major life activity, the individual does not qualify for services under Section 504.

Much confusion also exists regarding the relationship between Section 504 and special education laws and regulations. It must be emphasized that Section 504 falls under the management of regular education. Students who have disabilities but who do not qualify for special education may still be eligible for accommodations under Section 504.

Section 504, which covers a broader range of disabilities than the special education law, also requires public schools to provide students with a "free appropriate public education" and, in addition, ensures that students with disabilities are afforded an equal opportunity to participate in school programs. A student who is found to be disabled under Section 504 should be served by the resources provided through regular education. The exception to this standard would be a student who has been determined eligible as disabled under the Individuals with Disabilities Education Act (IDEA). Such a student could receive special education services under IDEA and accommodations required under Section 504 of the Rehabilitation Act of 1973.

For students with disabilities or who qualify for Section 504 services, this means that schools are required to make special arrangements so that the students have access to the full range of programs and activities offered, if needed, as determined at a multidisciplinary team meeting to determine students' service needs. At the meeting, the use of "evidence-based assistive technology," as mandated by IDEA 2004, is to be identified, since all students receiving special education services qualify for it (Quinn, Behrmann, Mastropieri, & Chung, 2009). Assistive technology, a means to provide the support needed to increase, maintain, or improve a student's functioning, may include a range of devices, from "low tech," such as a pencil grip, to "high tech," such as a voice synthesizer or Braille reader that helps students with disabilities be successful in the classroom (Dyal, Carpenter, & Wright, 2009; Copenhaver, 2004; Families Together, 1993).

Other students may need technology to provide physical access to the school facilities. An example may include that a student who needs a wheelchair lift on a school bus to get to school must be provided with this technology. Other examples of modifications that might be required under Section 504 include installing ramps into buildings and modifying restrooms to provide access for individuals with physical disabilities.

Determination of a student's eligibility for Section 504 services must be based on the use of tests and other evaluations that evaluate specific areas of need, not solely a single intelligence quotient. They should not be culturally or linguistically biased. Subsequent assessment to determine progress made toward individualized goals should also provide appropriate accommodations so they reflect the student's achievement without the impact of the student's disability (Chicago Office of the Office for Civil Rights, 2005).

Enforcement of Section 504 of the Rehabilitation Act of 1973 in programs and activities that receive funds from the U.S. Department of Education is provided by the Office for Civil Rights (OCR). There are 12 enforcement offices and a headquarters in Washington, D.C. Section 504, like other civil rights laws, is monitored by OCR. It is a goal of OCR to foster partnerships between school districts and parents to address the special education needs of students attending programs that receive federal funds. Enforcement procedures include administrative remedies, a private right of action in federal court, monetary damages, injunctive relief, attorney's fees, and defunding by the U.S. Department of Education (Chicago Office of the Office for Civil Rights, 2005).

## The Americans with Disabilities Act

The Vocational Rehabilitation Act of 1973 was made more comprehensive by the Americans with Disabilities Act of 1990. In it, child-care centers were designated as public accommodations, which must be available to all who desire to use them. They must serve all children, including those who are disabled, unless (a) the child is a direct threat to self or others, (b) the facility cannot provide child care without it being an undue burden, or (c) the child-care center would have to change the services it provides. New updates for this act were passed by Congress and signed by the President in 2008 in relation to student eligibility standards (Zirkel, 2009).

The act specifically defines discrimination, including various types of intentional and unintentional exclusions, such as the following: segregation, inferior or less effective services, benefits, or activities; architectural, transportation, and communication barriers; failure to make reasonable accommodations; and discriminatory qualifications and performance standards. Actions that do not constitute discrimination include unequal treatment unrelated to a disability or that results from legitimate application of qualifications and performance standards necessary and substantially related to the ability to perform or participate in the essential components of a job or activity.

The act stipulates that the Architectural and Transportation Barriers Compliance Board will issue minimum accessibility guidelines. Other regulations will be issued by the attorney general, the U.S. Equal Opportunity Commission, the secretary of Housing and Urban Development, the secretary of Transportation, the Federal Communications Commission, and the secretary of Commerce. The act does not repeal Sections 503 and 504 of the Vocational Rehabilitation Act of 1973, and all regulations issued under those sections remain in full force.

In order to make this act even stronger, the U.S. Department of Justice has revised ADA regulations revising Title I and Title III (U.S. Department of Justice, 2011a). The 2010 ADA Standards for Accessible Design "set minimum requirements for newly designed and constructed or altered State and local government facilities, public accommodations, and commercial facilities to be readily accessible to and usable by individuals with disabilities" (U.S. Department of Justice, 2011b). In addition, the ADA also requires access to medical care and services and the facilities where the care is provided (U.S. Department of Justice, 2011c);

it is not enough for buildings to comply with ADA standards but the entire facility must meet the needs of people with all disabilities.

## Education for All Handicapped Children Act of 1975—P.L. 94-142

The most far-reaching and revolutionary legislation related to education was P.L. 94-142, the Education for All Handicapped Children Act of 1975. All people between the ages of 3 and 18 must be provided with free and appropriate public education (FAPE). The term *appropriate* means suited to the disability age, maturity, and past achievements of the child and parental expectations. The education must be in a program designed to meet the child's needs in the least restrictive environment (Section 504 Regulations). This means that the child will be placed in the classroom that will benefit the child the most (Wagner & Katsiyannis, 2010). If the student would benefit more from a regular classroom, the child is to be placed there.

The terms *mainstreaming* and *inclusion* have become synonymous with placing children with disabilities into the regular classroom. However, meeting the child's needs in the *least restrictive environment* can also refer to moving the child with disabilities out of a regular classroom into a resource room or self-contained special-education room (Rozalski, Stewart, & Miller, 2010). The law requires diagnosis and individualization of the educational program. Legal mandates for more participation of students with disabilities in general education classrooms have prompted teachers to participate in collaborative planning and teaching, particularly for children with special needs who are culturally and linguistically diverse (Nevin, Thousand, & Villa, 2009).

Additional terms that reflect the delivery of services in the least restrictive environment include "pull out" and "push in" services. "Pull out" services are those in which children with similar needs are "pulled out" of their base classroom to meet with a specialist for small-group teaching. "Push in" services are those in which the specialist assigned to children with disabilities works in their base classroom. The specialists work with students with and without disabilities so that children with disabilities are not separated from their peers. Reverse inclusion is a type of program in which typically developing children are brought to the special education classroom for short periods of time to interact with children with disabilities (Schoger, 2006). This type of model ensures that children with

disabilities have an opportunity to interact with others, but it also gives the typically developing children an opportunity to see how special-needs children learn.

## Amendments of 1983—P.L. 98-199

The Education of the Handicapped Act Amendments of 1983, P.L. 98-199, extended fiscal authorization for federal aid to state and local school systems through 1987; improved reporting and information dissemination requirements; increased assistance to children who are deaf and blind; provided grants for transitional programs; and expanded services for children from birth through 5 years of age (*Congressional Record,* 1983).

## Amendments of 1986: Infants and Toddlers with Disabilities—P.L. 99-457

The Education of the Handicapped Act Amendments of 1986, P.L. 99-457, established statewide, comprehensive, coordinated, multidisciplinary, interagency programs of early-intervention services for infants and toddlers with handicaps and their families (*Congressional Record,* 1986). This law addressed easily recognized needs of the very young with disabilities.

However, there are many conditions that are not immediately recognized, so services early in life may be delayed for those with genetic conditions associated with mental challenges, congenital syndromes associated with delays in development, sensory impairments, metabolic disorders, prenatal infections (AIDS, syphilis, cytomegalic inclusion disease), and low birth weight. There are also concerns for infants whose parents are developmentally delayed, have severe emotional disturbances, or are 15 years or younger.

Parents or caretakers may have difficulty finding the programs and services they need to help them care for these young children. These services are provided through the Department of Education in each state, so the first contact should be through the local school. Another group that may be able to offer information about services for rural families is:

American Council on Rural Special Education (ACRES)
Kansas State University
2323 Anderson Avenue, Suite 226
Manhattan, KS 66502
785-53-ACRES
*www.ksu.edu/acres/*

ACRES' goals foster quality services and education for individuals with disabilities who live in rural America. The Web site also offers links to other organizations serving children with disabilities, tips on advocacy, and research related to services to children with disabilities.

P.L. 99-457 provided for public supervision at no cost (except where federal and state laws allow), meeting the needs of handicapped infants and toddlers, family training, counseling, special instruction, physical therapy, stimulation therapy, case management, diagnosis-qualified personnel, and conformation with the Individualized Family Service Plan.

## :: INDIVIDUALS WITH DISABILITIES EDUCATION ACT AMENDMENTS— 1997 P.L. 105-17 AND 2004 P.L. 108-446

This federal law—formerly the Education for All Handicapped Children Act, P.L. 94-142—mandated that all children receive an education regardless of the severity of their disability. An amended IDEA was reauthorized in June 1997 and went into effect on July 1, 1998, and was reauthorized again in 2004 and went into effect July 1, 2005. IDEA '97 and 2004 are organized into four parts: (a) general provisions; (b) school-aged and preschool—3- to 5-year-olds; (c) infants and toddlers, birth through 2; and (d) support. Part C relates to the education of infants and toddlers, birth to age 2 (IDEA, 2011). Although alike in many ways, the differences include "zero reject" in Part B. It requires that there be no exclusion of children ages 3 through 21, and public school systems are responsible for including all these children in an educational program, regardless of the extent or the kind of disability.

Part C for infants gives discretion to the states to develop a program that best serves the needs of infants and toddlers. Each state determines which agency can work most effectively with parents and their infants and toddlers. States use different agencies such as the Departments of Education or Health and Human Services. For infants and toddlers with identified disabilities, there must not be a break in service as they transition from Part C to Part B services.

Terms used in the act include the following:

1. The term *handicapped child* was changed to the *child with disabilities* because it was recognized that the children are handicapped by the limitations placed on them rather than by their abilities. The child has a disability, which may not be a handicap, depending on the situation.

2. All children with disabilities will have an education that is individualized to meet their needs. This is written in an Individualized Education Program (IEP) for children 3 to 21, and in an Individualized Family Service Plan (IFSP) for infants and toddlers (Utah Parent Center, 1997). Teachers, special teachers, administrators, parents, and others who are concerned with the child's education are involved in the development of the IEP. If appropriate, the child is also included. The law provides for a hearing that can be initiated by the parents if they do not agree with the

Educators must communicate effectively with parents of children with special needs.

diagnosis of the child, the placement, and/or the IEP. This is due process, and it is the responsibility of the school to inform the parents of their rights.

The school district is responsible for serving or seeing that children aged 3 to 5 are served in preschools. The primary focus of the IEP is the education of the student, although the family may receive some services. The agenda for the IEP meeting is illustrated in Figure 10–1.

In the birth-to-2 program, an Individualized Family Service Plan (IFSP) is written to serve both student and family. One of the requirements for the IFSP is "to document family concerns, resources, and priorities and to provide the family with services, consistent with members' preferences, so the family can increase its capacity to meet the child's special needs" (Turnbull & Turnbull, 1997, p. 24).

## IDEIA

The Individuals with Disabilities Education Improvement Act, or IDEIA, created new regulations in 2006 that are still in effect. Yell, Katsiyannis, Ryan McDuffie, and Mattocks (2008), provide 20 ways to ensure compliance. Here are a few of their suggestions.

1. Meet the procedural requirements of IDEA
2. Convene legally correct IEP meetings
3. Develop educationally meaningful IEP
4. Conduct relevant assessments
5. Link assessment results to goals and services
6. Develop measurable annual goals
7. Determine how you will measure progress toward the goals and develop a schedule for reporting a student's progress to his or her parents
8. Base services on peer-reviewed research
9. Implement program modifications in the general education classroom
10. Provide related services when necessary

## Development of the Individualized Education Program (IEP)

The development of an Individualized Education Program (IEP) illustrates the goals that schools and parents want for their children with disabilities. Three pages of an IEP for a preschool child who was adopted from China in infancy are illustrated in Figures 10–2A, 10–2B, and 10–2C.

All children (ages 3 through 21) with disabilities receiving any type of special education services

must have an Individualized Education Program prepared especially for them (Christle & Yell, 2010). It must be the product of the joint efforts of members of a child study team, which must include items 1 through 5 of the following:

### Members of the IEP Team

1. Parents of the child with a disability.
2. At least one regular education teacher of the child if the child is participating in the regular classroom environment.
3. At least one special education teacher, or where appropriate, at least one special education provider of such child.
4. A representative of the local educational agency who is (a) qualified to provide, or supervise the provision of, specially designed instruction to meet the unique needs of children with disabilities; (b) knowledgeable about the general curriculum; and (c) knowledgeable about the availability of resources of the local education agency.
5. At least one individual who can relate the evaluation results to the goals and steps of the IEP (Turnbull, Turnbull, & Wehmeyer, 2007).
6. At the discretion of the parent or the agency, other individuals who have knowledge or special expertise regarding the child, including related services personnel as appropriate.
7. Whenever appropriate, the child with the disability ([Section 614(d) (1)(B)] as cited in National Dissemination Center for Children with Disabilities [NICHCY], 2011; Family and Advocates Partnership for Education Project, 2006).

The IEP should accomplish the following:

- The IEP meeting serves as a communication vehicle between parents and school personnel and enables them, as equal participants, to jointly decide what the child's needs are, what services will be provided to meet those needs, and what the anticipated outcomes may be.
- The IEP process provides an opportunity for resolving any differences between parents and school personnel concerning the special education needs of a child with a disability—first, through the IEP meeting, and second, if necessary, through the procedural protections that are available to the parents.

**FIGURE 10–1**
Agenda for IEP meeting.

---

FCPS **FAIRFAX COUNTY PUBLIC SCHOOLS**

**CONFIDENTIAL**

Department of Special Services
**Individualized Education Program**

DRAFT UNTIL IEP
IS SIGNED

### IEP MEETING AGENDA
To be used at initial or annual IEP meetings

Student Name **Periwinkle**          ID # _____          Date of IEP Meeting _____

Check each item after discussed:

I.      ☐    Introduce IEP Team Members

II.     ☐    State Purpose for the Meeting

III.    ☐    Review *Rights and Procedural Safeguards Pertaining to Special Education*

IV.     ☐    Review Information to be Considered by the IEP Team

Parent/family concerns regarding the student's education
Student's strengths and interests in the home, school, and community
Review progress on goals/objectives from current IEP
Review formal or informal assessment results

Additional factors for IEP team consideration (check after discussed):
☐    Impact of student's behavior and is it impeding his/her learning or that of others.
☐    Student's need for instruction in or use of Braille.
☐    Student's language needs, due to limited English proficiency.
☐    Student's communication and/or language needs.
☐    Student's assistive technology needs.
☐    Student's language and communication needs if deaf or hard of hearing.

*Any additional factor(s) that applies to the student must be addressed within the
context of the IEP.

V.      ☐    Identify Student Needs
             —Annual Goals/Short-term Objectives
             —Classroom Accommodations/Curriculum Modifications

VI.     ☐    Determine Student's Participation in Assessment Programs
             —Testing Accommodations
             —Review of Information about State Assessments and Diploma Options
               for Students with Disabilities

VII.    ☐    Discussion and Selection of the Least Restrictive Environment

VIII.   ☐    Summary of Services Required to Meet Student's Areas of Need
             —Transportation Needs

IX.     ☐    Distribution of the ESY Information Form and Copies of the IEP

*Information from the Fairfax County Public Schools student scholastic record is released on the condition that the recipient agrees
not to permit any other party to have access to such information without the written consent of the parent or of the eligible student.*

IEP 301 (06/05) IEP Meeting Agenda                                                            page _____ of _____

---

CONFIDENTIAL

Department of Special Services

# Individualized Education Program

DRAFT UNTIL IEP IS SIGNED

Page _____ of _____

FAIRFAX COUNTY PUBLIC SCHOOLS

**STUDENT**   Periwinkle                                    ID # _____

**4.  Area of Need**   Personal/Social: Play Skills

**5.  Present Level**   Documentation:   Teacher Observation

Periwinkle is now playing beside her classmates in structured play settings. She is beginning to demonstrate independent parallel play. She is also entering into some associative play when the activity is non-threatening to her (ie: free drawing with a friend). She is interested in playing with a wider variety of toys and she is capable of playing with these toys appropriately. She continues to need to broaden her play skills to include pretend play and dramatic play. She needs to acquire skills that will help her join in play with her peers.

How does this area of need impact this student's participation/ progress in the general education curriculum or for preschool children, the child's participation in age appropriate activities?

In order for Periwinkle to have successful relationships with her peers, she needs to acquire appropriate play skills.

**6.  Annual Goal**   What does this student need to know or be able to do?

Periwinkle will exhibit cooperative play skills with three successes of four opportunities as evaluated three times per school year.

**Short-term Objectives**   What short-term objectives indicate progress toward this goal?

With three successes of four opportunities, Periwinkle will:

* exhibit parallel play skills in a variety of play activities.
* take turns with one teacher reminder.
* share toys with her classmates with one teacher reminder.
* clean up her toys/play materials with one teacher reminder.
* exhibit associative play skills in a variety of play activities.

**Progress Comments**

**7.**

How will progress toward this annual goal be measured?

_____ Classroom Participation
_____ Checklists
_____ Classwork
_____ Criterion- referenced Test _____
_____ Homework
_____ Norm- referenced Test _____
_____ Observation
_____ Oral Reports
_____ Special Projects
_____ Tests and Quizzes
_____ Written Reports
_____ Other teacher notes

**Code**

**Date**

| | | | |
|---|---|---|---|
| | | | |
| | | | |

A copy of this form, indicating the student's progress toward this annual goal will be reported to parents at regular scheduled FCPS reporting periods. **The progress codes are: M** The student has met the criteria for this goal/ objective. **SP** The student is making sufficient progress toward achieving this goal/objective within the duration of the IEP. **EP** The student demonstrates emerging skill but may not achieve this goal/objective within the duration of this IEP. **NP** The student has not yet demonstrated progress toward achieving this goal/ objective and may not achieve this goal within the duration of this IEP. **NI** This goal/ objective has not been introduced.

*Information from the Fairfax County Public Schools student scholastic record is released on the condition that the recipient agrees not to permit any other party to have access to such information without the written consent of the parent or of the eligible student.*

**FIGURE 10–2A**

A page of the Individualized Education Program (IEP) for personal/social: play skills.

**CONFIDENTIAL**

Department of Special Services

# Individualized Education Program

DRAFT UNTIL IEP IS SIGNED

FAIRFAX COUNTY PUBLIC SCHOOLS

**STUDENT** Periwinkle                                    ID # _____

**4. Area of Need** Personal/Social: Attention to Task

**5. Present Level**

Documentation:  Teacher Observation

Periwinkle is capable of attending to classroom activities for an age appropriate amount of time. While attending, she will jump up and come up to the teacher, wiggle in her chair, and make comments to her peers. She is easily influenced by her peers and may copy their behavior, not thinking about whether or not the behavior is appropriate.

How does this area of need impact this student's participation/ progress in the general education curriculum or for preschool children, the child's participation in age appropriate activities?

In order for Periwinkle to maximize her opportunities to learn, she needs to attend to a task without being distracted.

**6. Annual Goal** What does this student need to know or be able to do?

Periwinkle will attend to a variety of classroom activities for a 20 minute period, following activity directions with four successes of five opportunities as monitored three times during the school year..

**Short-term Objectives** What short-term objectives indicate progress toward this goal?

With 4 successes of 5 opportunities, Periwinkle will:

* Use appropriate methods of responding as designated by her teacher during classroom activities.
* Participate appropriately, including remaining seated when appropriate, within a classroom activity as directed by the teacher.
* Focus on the content of the activity for a period of 15 minutes with one teacher reminder.
* Refocus on the classroom activity after being distracted by a classmate or any other distraction within the classroom setting.

**Progress Comments**

**7. Progress\***

How will progress toward this annual goal be measured?

____ Classroom Participation
____ Checklists
____ Classwork
____ Criterion- referenced Test ____
____ Homework
____ Norm- referenced Test ____
____ Observation
____ Oral Reports
____ Special Projects
____ Tests and Quizzes
____ Written Reports
____ Other Teacher notes

| Date | | | |
|---|---|---|---|
| Code | | | |
| | | | |
| | | | |
| | | | |

A copy of this form, indicating the student's progress toward this annual goal will be reported to parents at regular scheduled FCPS reporting periods. **The progress codes are: M** The student has met the criteria for this goal/ objective. **SP** The student is making sufficient progress toward achieving this goal/ objective within the duration of the IEP. **EP** The student demonstrates emerging skill but may not achieve this goal/ objective within the duration of this IEP. **NP** The student has not yet demonstrated progress toward achieving this goal/ objective and may not achieve this goal within the duration of this IEP. **NI** This goal/ objective has not been introduced.

*Information from the Fairfax County Public Schools student scholastic record is released on the condition that the recipient agrees not to permit any other party to have access to such information without the written consent of the parent or of the eligible student.*

**FIGURE 10–2B**

A page of the Individualized Education Program (IEP) for personal/social: attention to task skills.

FAIRFAX COUNTY PUBLIC SCHOOLS

CONFIDENTIAL

Department of Special Services
**Individualized Education Program**

DRAFT UNTIL IEP IS SIGNED

**STUDENT** Periwinkle                    ID #

**4. Area of Need** Cognitive

**5. Present Level**

Documentation: Brigance; Classroom Participation

Periwinkle is beginning to rote count, has a concept of the numbers one and two. She is showing emerging skills in counting out objects to four. Peri has a concept of one to one correspondence, but is inconsistent in demonstrating this knowledge. She needs to continue to acquire counting skills and the concept of number.

How does this area of need impact this student's participation/progress in the general education curriculum or for preschool children, the child's participation in age appropriate activities?

In order for Periwinkle to be able to perform classroom activities that require the concept of number, she needs to acquire counting skills.

**6. Annual Goal**

What does this student need to know or be able to do?

Periwinkle will count out five objects from a larger group of objects with three successes of four opportunities as monitored three times per school year.

**Short-term Objectives**

What short-term objectives indicate progress toward this goal?

With three successes of four opportunities, Periwinkle will:

* Rote count to 20.
* Demonstrate a one to one correspondence up to 8.
* Count out three objects from a larger group of objects.
* Answer questions requiring counting objects, etc. up to four objects.

**Progress Comments**

**7. Progress***

How will progress toward this annual goal be measured?

____ Classroom Participation
____ Checklists
____ Classwork
____ Criterion-referenced Test ____
____ Homework
____ Norm-referenced Test ____
____ Observation
____ Oral Reports
____ Special Projects
____ Tests and Quizzes
____ Written Reports
____ Other Teacher notes ____

| Date | | | | | | |
|---|---|---|---|---|---|---|
| Code | | | | | | |
| | | | | | | |

A copy of this form, indicating the student's progress toward this annual goal will be reported to parents at regular scheduled FCPS reporting periods. **The progress codes are: M** The student has met the criteria for this goal/objective. **SP** The student is making sufficient progress toward achieving this goal/objective within the duration of the IEP. **EP** The student demonstrates emerging skill but may not achieve this goal/objective within the duration of this IEP. **NP** The student has not yet demonstrated progress toward achieving this goal/objective and may not achieve this goal within the duration of this IEP. **NI** This goal/ objective has not been introduced.

*Information from the Fairfax County Public Schools student scholastic record is released on the condition that the recipient agrees not to permit any other party to have access to such information without the written consent of the parent or of the eligible student.*

**FIGURE 10–2C**

A page of the Individualized Education Program (IEP) for cognitive skills.

- The IEP sets forth in writing a commitment of resources necessary to enable a child with a disability to receive needed special education and related services.
- The IEP is a management tool to help ensure that each child with a disability is provided special education and related services appropriate to the child's special learning needs.
- The IEP is a compliance and monitoring document that may be used by authorized monitoring personnel from each governmental level to determine whether a child with a disability is actually receiving the free appropriate public education agreed to by the parents and the school.
- The IEP serves as an evaluation device for use in determining the extent of the child's progress toward meeting the projected outcomes (Utah Parent Center, 1997; Gartin & Murdick, 2005; Turnbull, Turnbull, & Wehmeyer, 2007).

Ideally, the IEP:

- Specifies that the assessments yield information that will enable the student to be involved in and progress in the general curriculum or, for preschool children, to participate in appropriate activities.
- Requires that IEPs must now state how the student's disability affects academic achievement and functional performance in the general curriculum (Gartin & Murdick, 2005).
- Requires that annual, measurable academic and functional goals, including benchmarks, be related to helping the child be involved and progress in the general curriculum (Gartin & Murdick, 2005).

- Requires the IEP to state the "supplementary aids and services" needed by the student and the "program modifications or supports for school personnel" so that the student can be involved and progress in the general curriculum and participate in extracurricular and other nonacademic activities.
- Requires IEP teams to consider positive behavioral intervention strategies and supports for students whose behavior impedes their own learning or that of others.
- Requires that the IEP include an "explanation of the extent, if any, to which the child will not participate with nondisabled children in regular class" and in extracurricular and nonacademic activities (Utah Parent Center, 2011).
- Adds the regular education teacher to the IEP team as a required member.
- Requires that the IEP state how the parents will be regularly informed of the student's progress toward the annual goals (as often as parents of other students receive progress reports).
- Allows local districts to use IDEA funds to support students in general education classrooms without concern that students without disabilities might also benefit (PEAK Parent Center, 1997).

(See Figures 10–2A and 10–2B for examples of IEP forms.)

Many requirements must be met when dealing with the child with disabilities. The IEP should be reviewed periodically, and not less than annually, to determine if progress toward the goals is advancing as expected and to reevaluate and assess the

IEPs must avoid jargon and be clearly explained to all parents.

program. The 2004 IDEA reauthorization changed attendance requirements so that all members of the IEP do not need to attend a reevaluation meeting if the area they represent is not being discussed. Administrators and teachers must be aware of all procedures that the schools are responsible for administering. These procedures include the following types of subjects: definitions, opportunity to examine records, independent educational evaluation, prior notice, parent consent, procedures when parent refuses consent, content of notice, formal complaint resolution, impartial due-process hearing, reasonable attorney's fees, impartial hearing officer, appointment of hearing officer, access rights, records, children's rights, and more (Burns, 2006; Family and Advocates Partnership for Education, 2006; Gartin & Murdick, 2005).

### Rights and Responsibilities for Parents—IDEA 2004

IDEA 1997 and 2004 addressed the participation of parents in the development of their child's program. It states that the Local Education Agency (LEA) or the State Education Agency (SEA) will ensure that parents are members of any group that makes decisions on the educational placement of their child. Parents can examine all records and participate in meetings regarding the evaluations, placement, and the free and appropriate public education that the child will receive. Specifications include the following:

- Public agencies must notify parents when the agencies propose or refuse to initiate or change the identification, evaluation, or educational placement of the child or the provision of FAPE to the child.
- Parents have the right to inspect and review all records relating to their child that a public agency collects, maintains, or uses regarding the identification, evaluation, or educational placement of the child or the provision of FAPE to the child.
- Parental consent is required before a child may be evaluated for the first time.
- Parents have the right to obtain an independent educational evaluation (IEE) of their child.
- Parental consent is required for a child's initial special education placement.
- Parents have the right to challenge or appeal any decision related to the identification, evaluation, or educational placement of their child or the provision of FAPE to their child.

- Parents are responsible for notifying the public agency if they plan to remove their child from the public agency for placement in a private school at public expense.
- Parents are responsible for notifying the public agency if they intend to request a due-process hearing (Family and Advocates in Education Project, 2006; PEAK Parent Center, 1997).

**Notification.** There are also procedural safeguards that require written notification to parents prior to any proposed action. The notification must be in the parents' native language or preferred mode of communication—for example, Braille or sign language. There is protection of the child's rights when parents cannot be located.

**Mediation.** If disagreements arise, a mediation system employing a qualified, impartial mediator must be available. Parents may be required to attend a mediation meeting.

**Developmental Delay.** The developmental delay category, previously used for placement of children 3 to 5 years old, was recognized as appropriate for those 3 to 9 and was therefore extended to cover that age group.

**Charter Schools.** Charter schools, new since the original IDEA, were included in the provisions. They must follow the same guidelines as other publicly funded schools.

## ⠶ DEFINITIONS OF SPECIAL-NEEDS TERMINOLOGY

The following descriptions of children with special needs as defined in IDEA (34 Code of Federal Regulations, Section 300.7) clarify those who need special programs. If a student in a classroom fits into any of the following categories, special services should be provided.

1. *Autism.* A developmental disability significantly affecting verbal and nonverbal communication and social interaction, generally evident before age 3, that adversely affects educational performance.
2. *Deafness.* A hearing impairment so severe that a child is impaired in processing linguistic

information through hearing, with or without amplification, which adversely affects educational performance.

3. *Deafness–blindness.* Simultaneous hearing and visual impairments, the combination of which causes such severe communication and other developmental and education problems that a child cannot be accommodated in special-education programs solely for children who are deaf or for children who are blind.

4. *Hearing impairment.* An impairment in hearing, whether permanent or fluctuating, that adversely affects a child's educational performance but is not included under the definition of *deafness.*

5. *Mental disabilities.* Significantly subaverage general intellectual functioning existing concurrently with deficits in adaptive behavior and manifested during the developmental period, which adversely affects a child's educational performance. Another term used is *cognitive disabilities.*

6. *Multiple disabilities.* Simultaneous impairments (such as mental challenges and blindness or mental challenges and orthopedic impairment), the combination of which causes such severe educational problems that the child cannot be accommodated in a special education program solely for one of the impairments. The term does not include children with deafness–blindness.

7. *Orthopedic impairment.* A severe orthopedic impairment that adversely affects a child's educational performance. The term includes impairments caused by a congenital anomaly (e.g., clubfoot or absence of a limb), impairments caused by disease (e.g., poliomyelitis or bone tuberculosis), and impairments from other causes (e.g., cerebral palsy, amputations, or fractures or burns that cause contractures).

8. *Other health impairment.* Having limited strength, vitality, or alertness, due to chronic or acute health problems—such as a heart condition, tuberculosis, rheumatic fever, nephritis, asthma, sickle-cell anemia, hemophilia, epilepsy, lead poisoning, leukemia, or diabetes—that adversely affects a child's educational performance. According to the Office of Special Education and Rehabilitative Services' clarification statement of September 16, 1991, eligible children with Attention Deficit Disorder may also be classified under "other health impairment."

9. *Tourette's syndrome.* A neurological disorder that includes repetitive, involuntary movements or tics. The average age of onset is 7 to 10 years of age. Vocal tics include sniffing, snorting, and barking. Involuntary motor movements include self-harm, such as punching oneself. The movements become worse when there is a high degree of excitement (National Institute of Neurological Disorders and Stroke, 2006).

10. *Emotional disturbance.*
    a. A condition exhibiting one or more of the following characteristics over a long period of time and to a marked degree and that adversely affects educational performance: (a) an inability to learn that cannot be explained by intellectual, sensory, or health factors; (b) an inability to build or maintain satisfactory interpersonal relationships with peers and teachers; (c) inappropriate types of behavior or feelings under normal circumstances; (d) a general pervasive mood of unhappiness or depression; or (e) a tendency to develop physical symptoms or fears associated with personal or school problems.
    b. The term includes children who have schizophrenia. The term does not include children who are socially maladjusted, unless it is determined that they have an emotional disturbance.

11. *Specific learning disabilities.* A disorder in one or more of the basic psychological processes involved in understanding or in using language, spoken or written, that may manifest itself in an imperfect ability to listen, think, speak, read, write, spell, or to do mathematical calculations. The term includes such conditions as perceptual disabilities, brain injury, minimal brain dysfunction, dyslexia, and developmental aphasia. The term does not include children who have learning problems that are primarily the result of visual, hearing, or motor disabilities, of mental or cognitive disabilities, of emotional disturbance, or of environmental, cultural, or economic disadvantage (Hallahan & Kauffman, 2006; NICHCY, 2002).

12. *Speech or language impairment.* A communication disorder, such as stuttering, impaired articulation, a language impairment, or a voice

impairment, that adversely affects a child's educational performance.

13. *Traumatic brain injury*. An acquired injury to the brain caused by an external physical force, resulting in total or partial functional disability or psychosocial impairment, or both, that adversely affects educational performance. The term does not include brain injuries that are congenital or degenerative, nor does it include brain injuries induced by birth trauma.

14. *Visual impairment, including blindness*. A visual impairment that, even with correction, adversely affects a child's educational performance. The term includes both children with partial sight and those who are completely blind (Hallahan & Kauffman, 2006; NICHCY, 1997).

Visually impaired children and youth shall be identified as those whose limited vision interferes with their education and/or developmental progress. Four divisions for the visually impaired shall be made:

*Partially sighted* indicates some type of visual problem has resulted in a need for special education.

*Low vision* generally refers to a severe visual impairment, not necessarily limited to distance vision. Low vision applies to all individuals with sight who are unable to read the newspaper at a normal viewing distance, even with the aid of eyeglasses or contact lenses. They use a combination of vision and other senses to learn, although they may require adaptations in lighting or the size of print and sometimes Braille.

*Legally blind* indicates that a person has less than 20/2000 vision in the better eye or a very limited field of vision (20 degrees at its widest point).

*Totally blind* students learn via Braille or other nonvisual media.

Visual impairment is the consequence of a functional loss of vision, rather than the eye disorder itself. Eye disorders that can lead to visual impairments can include retinal degeneration, albinism, cataracts, glaucoma, and muscular problems that result in visual disturbances, corneal disorders, diabetic retinopathy, congenital disorders, and infection.

15. *Pervasive developmental disorders (PDD)*. A delay in social/language/motor and/or cognitive development. The child may have social development delays and delays in one or more other categories. PDD is a category of delays in different magnitudes and different domains (Council for Exceptional Children, 2011).

## Attention-Deficit Disorder—Attention-Deficit/Hyperactivity Disorder

A policy developed in the 1990s resulted in children with attention-deficit disorder (ADD) or attention-deficit/hyperactivity disorder (AD/HD) being classified under other health impairment, making them eligible to receive special education and related services. *Other health impairment* is defined as "having limited strength, vitality, or alertness, including a heightened alertness to environmental stimuli, that results in limited alertness with respect to the educational environment, that is due to chronic or acute health problems such as asthma, attention deficit disorder or attention deficit hyperactivity disorder, diabetes, epilepsy, a heart condition, hemophilia, lead poisoning, leukemia, nephritis, rheumatic fever, and sickle cell anemia; and adversely affects a child's educational performance" (NICHCY, 2001). A federal policy issued by the Office of Special Education and Rehabilitative Services, U.S. Department of Education, September 16, 1991, specified that a child no longer needs to be labeled as having a specific learning disability or as being seriously emotionally disturbed to receive special education services. Under the policy, a child who is identified as having ADD or AD/HD to the extent that it adversely affects education "performance" can now be served.

Symptoms that are a sign of AD/HD are (a) problems with paying attention, (b) being very active (called *hyperactivity*), and (c) acting before thinking (called *impulsivity*). Three types of AD/HD are

- Inattentive type, in which the person cannot seem to focus on a task or activity.
- Hyperactive-impulsive type, in which the person is very active and often acts without thinking.
- Combined type, in which the person is inattentive, impulsive, and too active.

## :: A BRIEF LOOK AT AUTISM, LEARNING DISABILITIES, AND MENTAL DISABILITY

### Autism

Known as a complex neurobiological disorder, autism impacts communication, behavior, and social relationships. According to the organization Autism Speaks, autism is the fastest-growing serious developmental disability in the United States (Autism Speaks Annual Report, 2008). Currently one in 110 children, mostly boys, are affected by autism. The cause of autism is unknown. Although some organizations and celebrities have blamed vaccines for the development of autism, the American Academy of Pediatrics studies (2011) developed in the United States and Europe yield no evidence. The latest study regarding causes for autism indicates that there is a genetic basis for this disorder (Pinto et al., 2010) but the cause is still unknown.

Currently there are no medical tests to diagnose autism. A developmental pediatrician is the proper professional to diagnose it. In the school districts, licensed school psychologists are also certified to give a variety of assessments to see if the child has an autism disorder. The Modified Checklist for Autism in Toddlers or M-CHAT is a diagnostic tool that can be downloaded free from the Internet for clinical, research, and educational purposes. Parents can complete this diagnostic tool, which focuses on play, social interaction, and communication, but they should still seek an expert for an official diagnosis.

**Characteristics.** Children with autism will vary in intelligence, abilities, and behaviors. While some do not speak, others may have limited language that includes repeated phrases. Children with autism often have difficulty with abstract concepts and have a limited range of interests. They commonly have unusual responses to sensory information such as lights, loud noises, and some textures of food or fabrics. The National Dissemination Center for Children with Disabilities (2011) described the following characteristics of autism:

- Communication problems (e.g., using and understanding language).
- Difficulty in relating to people, objects, and events.
- Unusual play with toys and other objects.

- Difficulty with changes in routine or familiar surroundings.
- Repetitive body movements or behavior patterns.

Autism can be characterized by a broad range of behaviors, which has led diagnosticians to describe autism as a broad-spectrum disorder. This has resulted in the need for teachers and parents to recognize the differences in the needs of children, depending on how their disability manifests itself (Hallahan & Kauffman, 2006).

**Recommendations.** Children with autism respond best in a predictable and consistent program:

> Behavior and communication problems that interfere with learning sometimes require the assistance of a knowledgeable professional in the autism field who develops and helps to implement a plan which can be carried out at home and school. . . . Students learn better and are less confused when information is presented visually as well as verbally. Interaction with nondisabled peers is also important, for these students provide models of appropriate language, social, and behavior skills. To overcome frequent problems in generalizing skills learned at school it is very important to develop programs with parents, so that programs of learning activities, approaches, and experiences can be carried over into the home and community. (NICHCY, 2001, p. 2)

### Learning Disabilities

#### Characteristics

1. Children with learning disabilities are primarily typically developing children. They are not primarily visually impaired, hearing impaired, environmentally disadvantaged, mentally challenged, or emotionally disturbed. In spite of the fact that these children have adequate intelligence, adequate sensory processes, and adequate emotional stability, they do not learn without special assistance.

2. Children with learning disabilities show wide discrepancies of intra-individual differences in a profile of their development. This is often shown by marked discrepancies in one or more of the specific areas of academic learning or a serious lack of language development or language facility. These disabilities may affect the child's behavior in such areas as thinking, conceptualization, memory, language, perception, reading, writing, spelling, or arithmetic.

3. The concept of deviation of a child with learning disabilities implies that the child deviates so markedly from the norm of the child's group as to require specialized instruction. Such specialized instruction required for these children may be of value to other children. However, the population to be served with special education funds authorized for children does not include children with learning problems that are the result of poor instruction or economic or cultural deprivation (Kearns, 1980).

**Signs of Learning Disabilities.** Learning disabilities are generally recognized when the child enters school and specific learning tasks are expected. There is no one sign that says that the child has a learning disability, but you can watch for the difference between what a child accomplishes in school and what that child should be able to do given the child's intellect and ability.

Silver and Hagin (2002) describe and discuss learning disorders, research, and the various curriculum designs used to help students develop. Planning for students requires an understanding of the factors that affect them, including cognitive, emotional, social, neuropsychological, and educational factors.

Identification of the problems that hinder a child's learning need to be analyzed by a specialist, but if a child has several of the following problems, the parent or teacher can assume the child has a learning disability. Clues include the following:

- May have trouble learning the alphabet, rhyming words, or connecting letters to their sounds.
- May make many mistakes when reading aloud, and repeat and pause often.
- May not understand what he or she reads.
- May have real trouble with spelling.
- May have very messy handwriting or hold a pencil awkwardly.
- May struggle to express ideas in writing.
- May learn language late and have a limited vocabulary.
- May have trouble remembering the sounds that letters make or hearing slight differences between words.
- May have trouble understanding jokes, comic strips, and sarcasm.
- May have trouble following directions.
- May mispronounce words or use a wrong word that sounds similar.

- May have trouble organizing what he or she wants to say or not be able to think of the word he or she needs for writing or conversation.
- May not follow the social rules of conversation, such as taking turns, and may stand too close to the listener.
- May confuse math symbols and misread numbers.
- May not be able to retell a story in order (what happened first, second, or third).
- May not know where to begin a task or how to go on from there (NICHCY, 2002b).

## Tips for Teachers and Parents

1. Learn as much about learning disabilities as you can.
2. Observe the child playing and "working." Make note of progress the child has made and tell the child what you have seen. This helps to confirm for the child that you know when he or she works hard or does well. Give positive feedback.
3. Recognize the child's strengths and interests. Find out how the child learns best. Give the child opportunities to use his or her talents and strengths.

### Insights for Teachers and Administrators

1. Review the student's records and ask specialists about the best method for working with the child. This may include the following:
   a. Giving students more time to take tests.
   b. Breaking tasks into smaller units.
   c. Providing directions verbally and in writing (NICHY, 2002b).
   d. Having a peer or classroom assistant take notes or write answers on a test.
   e. Providing tutors in order to individualize teaching.
   f. Providing audio textbooks.
   g. Providing supplementary video materials that relate to the classroom topic.
      For students who have listening difficulties, allow them to use a voice recorder or to borrow notes. For students who have difficulty writing, furnish a computer with specialized software that recognizes speech, and let the student use grammar checks and spell checks on a computer.
2. Teach study skills, organizational skills, and learning strategies. Study various ways to assess a student's learning so that students with learning disabilities can show what they have learned.
3. Communicate and become partners with the parents.

## Tips for Parents

1. Give your child with learning disabilities the opportunity to excel or just enjoy activities outside the classroom, such as dancing, music, sports, or computers. Give your child opportunities to participate in areas of interest or/and talent. Encourage friendships with children whom they meet in these activities.

2. Help your child learn through areas of strengths. Talk with your child's teacher and observe for yourself how the child learns best. Establish a special place where the child can do homework and prioritize its importance.

3. Meet other parents who have children with learning disabilities. Share concerns and successes with others as well as advice and emotional support.

4. Help develop an educational plan for your child with the school. Establish a positive working relationship and communicate regularly with your teacher, discuss questions, and exchange information about successes and progress (NICHCY, 2002b).

### Mental or Cognitive Disability

Mental or Cognitive Disability is diagnosed by determining (a) the ability of a person's brain to learn, think, solve problems, and make sense of the world (called intelligence quotient [IQ] or intellectual functioning); and (b) whether the person has the skills he or she needs to live independently (called adaptive behavior, or adaptive functioning) (NICHCY, 2002a).

The average score of an IQ test is 100, and those classified as mentally challenged score 70 to 75 or below. To look at the skills needed to live independently, the child is compared to others of the same age. The adaptive skills are (a) daily living skills, such as dressing, using the bathroom, and feeding oneself; (b) communication skills—understanding what is said and being able to respond; and (c) social skills with adults, friends, and family (NICHCY, 2002a).

More than 614,000 children ages 6 through 21 with mental disability have need for special education. In fact, "One out of every 10 children who need special education has some form of mental retardation" (NICHCY, 2002a, p. 3).

## Tips for Parents

- Learn about intellectual disabilites in order to give your child the help he or she needs.
- Encourage your child to be independent, learning daily care skills such as dressing, grooming, eating, and using the bathroom.
- Give your child chores, but make the chores one in which she or he can be successful. Use them as teaching tools. For example, in setting the table, have the child count out the number of napkins. Give the child one task at a time and help when assistance is needed.
- Praise, praise, praise when the child has worked hard and accomplished the task. Give feedback and build your child's abilities.
- Have your child join in outside activities, such as scouts, sports, and recreational activities.
- Work with the school and your child's teacher. Apply what he or she is learning at school with activities at home and in the community (NICHCY, 2002a).
- Volunteer in the classroom or in another classroom. See how the teachers work with the children. Contribute to the success of the class by cooperating with the teacher.

### Insights for Teachers and Administrators

- Learn as much as you can about intellectual disabilities. Check with organizations such as NICHCY and the Council for Exceptional Children.
- "Recognize that you can make an enormous difference in this student's life! Find out what the student's strengths and interests are, and emphasize them. Create opportunities for success" (NICHCY, 2002a, pp. 5–6).
- "Be as concrete as possible. Demonstrate what you mean rather than just giving verbal directions. Rather than just relating new information verbally, show a picture. And rather than just showing a picture, provide the student with hands-on materials and experiences and the opportunity to try things out" (NICHCY, 2002a, pp. 5–6). The greater the specificity, the greater the likelihood that the goals can be achieved (Burns, 2006).
- "Break longer, new tasks into small steps. Demonstrate the steps. Have the students do the steps, one at a time. Provide assistance as necessary" (NICHCY, 2002a, pp. 5–6). Make sure to acknowledge the student's strengths as well as needs

when operationalizing steps to reach the student's goals (Burns, 2006).

- Have an IEP that will give the educational goals for the child. Check with the special education teacher for effective ways of teaching this student (NICHCY, 2002a). If possible, observe the special education staff to see for yourself what they do with the child.
- Work with the parents; make a partnership for the welfare of the student.

### Implications of Disabilities on Learning

For years the popular philosophy has been that we could best motivate young people in pleasing and attractive settings. The lesson would stimulate interest, be fun, and be relevant to the learner. Because students enjoyed doing it, they would be willing to learn. This is an excellent theory, and there is no quarrel with its premise. However, we have produced some youths who have not met their potential because, in real life, work is not always pleasing, and for children with disabilities, it is even more of a challenge to achieve.

Work involves diligence, tenacity, endurance, sacrifice, discipline, and repetition. It requires deep concentration and dedication. Work is *not* always fun—it is often boring. Most of us spend our lives doing work. We are willing to make this sacrifice not only for the extrinsic values of status, income, and fringe benefits but also for the intrinsic values of self-worth, dignity, and contribution to society. It is important to help children identify the intrinsic value of what they are learning. It is important for teachers and parents to communicate explicitly with children how what they are learning relates to what is important to them. This will help establish a pattern of lifelong learning—a very valuable lesson indeed.

Children with disabilities often work harder and longer to accomplish what other children do easily and quickly. It is not always easy for them to accept this. It is hard for parents to refrain from expecting the school and the teacher to lighten the load, to expect less because the child has a disability. But this deprives the child of the feeling of accomplishment, of striving for and reaching full potential. The Individualized Education Program provides for the appropriate level of accommodation. Use this tool effectively to ensure that all exceptional children are given the opportunity to reach their goals.

Just as the parent feels warmth and joy at the progress of a child with a disability, so will the professional whose help and guidance leads to better family relations, improved schoolwork, and an ability to participate in life more fully for the child with a disability. It is a worthy and mighty undertaking.

## ⸬ STUDENTS WHO ARE GIFTED AND TALENTED

Students who are gifted and talented have the potential for superior performance. This can include intellectual achievement, special aptitudes, or creative thinking and performing abilities.

The Gifted and Talented Children's Education Act, P.L. 95-561, gave states and local education agencies financial incentives to identify and educate students who are gifted and talented, provide in-service training, and conduct research (Heward & Orlansky, 1988). None of the federal legislation has mandated educational opportunities for children who are gifted. Approximately 30 states mandate educational opportunities for youngsters who are gifted, and other states have legislation permitting establishment of such classes (Karnes & Marquardt, 1997).

The Jacob K. Javits Gifted and Talented Students Education Act of 1988 was followed by the Jacob K. Javits Gifted and Talented Education Act of 1992. In 1998, the Javits Act was the only federal funding earmarked for gifted education. Funding not earmarked for gifted education may be used to benefit students who are gifted. In funding for children with disabilities, meeting the child's needs is required, but children with gifts and talents do not have legislation that requires support. The purpose of the federal acts is to encourage rich education for gifted-and-talented students and to have special programs broadened and expanded into the regular classroom (Boren, 1994).

According to the Council of State Directors of Programs for the Gifted, 20 states administer gifted and talented under special education or exceptional children divisions. Others administer programs under curriculum and instruction, general education, or gifted-and-talented divisions. Twenty-one states provide funding for gifted children; however, most other states do not require school divisions to provide services to children with high abilities (Council of State Directors of Programs for the Gifted, 2002).

According to analysis by the Davidson Institute for Talent Development, more states are offering gifted education. These include the following:

1. Six states offered gifted programming mandated and fully funded: Nebraska, Oklahoma, Alaska, Iowa, Mississippi, and Georgia.
2. Twenty-one states mandated partially funded gifted programs: Montana, Idaho, Wyoming, Utah, Arizona, New Mexico, Kansas, Texas, Arkansas, Louisiana, Tennessee, Kentucky, Ohio, West Virginia, Virginia, Maine, North Carolina, South Carolina, Florida, Maryland, and Hawaii.
3. Four states mandated gifted programs but had no gifted funding available: Oregon, Pennsylvania, Alabama, and New Jersey.
4. Eleven states do not require gifted programs but gifted funding is available: Washington, California, Nevada, Colorado, North Dakota, Minnesota, Wisconsin, Missouri, Indiana, Michigan, and Massachusetts.
5. Eight states do not mandate gifted programs and no gifted funding is available: South Dakota, Illinois, New York, Vermont, New Hampshire, Rhode Island, Connecticut, and Delaware as well as the District of Columbia.

Each state makes its own decision on gifted education, but with the help of foundations and the Jacob K. Javits Gifted and Talented Students Education Act, there is an increase in gifted education. It continues to need support.

The increase of children that speak languages other than English in the education system has created a challenge for educators of gifted and talented children. Children who are second-language learners often are not included in gifted programs because educators may not know how to assess them. Appropriate testing tools, multiple sources of assessment information, and strong parental involvement are strategies educators must use in order to fully meet the needs of gifted second-language learners (Council for Exceptional Children, 2001, 2003).

## :: CHILD FIND PROJECT

Parents of children with special needs want to help their children be successful and get an education but sometimes feel overwhelmed by the challenges a child with special needs has. These are some statements I have heard parents of children with special needs say:

*I don't know how to help my child,*

*I just want to make sure she gets an education.*

*His teacher says that he can do so much more if he could just focus.*

*I don't know who to talk to about his disability.*

*Is there someone who can help me?*

*I don't know what else to do.*

Parents often rely on educators to assist them on how to best help their child by providing them important information regarding their children's rights and strategies to use at home. The majority of parents with special needs children are not familiar with special education programs and very often they have a variety of misconceptions. Teachers and administrators can create a different picture of special education than what it has been historically in order to help children reach their full potential and increase their quality of life (Van Haren & Fiedler, 2008). Special education is truly the means by which public schools can ensure that children reach their learning potential (Friend, 2011).

Concern about reaching parents and their children with disabilities resulted in the federal funding of the Child Find Project. In this program:

All children with disabilities residing in the State, including children with disabilities attending private schools, regardless of the severity of their disabilities, and who are in need of special education and related services are identified, located, and evaluated and a practical method is developed and implemented to determine which children with disabilities are currently receiving needed special education and related services. (NICHCY, 1998; Smith, 2005)

Child Find is designated to locate children with disabilities using any feasible methods available such as door-to-door surveys, media campaigns, dissemination of information from the schools, and home visits by staff and/or volunteers (Cook et al., 2004; Lerner, Mardell-Czudnowski, & Goldenberg, 1987). Figure 10–3 summarizes the special education process starting from Child Find or other referrals to the placement and evaluation team meeting.

In recent years, other names such as Count Your Kid In and Make a Difference have been used to designate this type of program. In many cases, this program is funded by both federal and state

**FIGURE 10–3**
A summary of the special education process.

| | |
|---|---|
| Child Find/Referral | Referral of child for diagnosis may be formal or informal; may come from parent or from others. |
| Assessment/Diagnosis | Multidisciplinary, non-biased comprehensive battery of tests. (Complete reevaluation for classification required every 3 years.) |
| Classification (includes parent) | Team reviews assessment/diagnostic data and classifies for special education based on test results. Parent signature required. |
| IEP Meeting (includes parent) | Individualized Education Plan developed by team. Must be updated yearly, but team or parent may request as needed. Parent signature required. |
| Placement (includes parent) | Team decides placement based on the IEP. Parent signature required. |
| Evaluation Team Meeting | Team evaluates child's total special education program and (includes parent) progress at least yearly. (Teacher evaluates daily as child works on short-term objectives.) |

governments. Preschool screenings have been very successful in finding children in need and informing parents that help is available.

## :: EVALUATION

When parents believe that their child needs special assistance, or if a child is identified through Child Find, the subsequent evaluations must be evaluated in a fair and unbiased manner. Parents must be informed and must give their consent to have the original evaluation.

For initial evaluations:

- Notice must be provided to evaluate a child, and informed consent of parents must be obtained.
- No single procedure shall be the sole criterion for determining eligibility.
- The child must be assessed in all areas of suspected disabilities.
- Determination of eligibility shall be made by a team of qualified professionals and the child's parents. Children are not eligible if the only deciding factor is a limited English proficiency or a lack of math or reading instruction (National Association of State Directors of Special Education, 1997; Turnbull, 2005).

Figure 10–4 illustrates the special education cycle. For insight and a detailed discussion of the major issues in education for children with disabilities, see *Free Appropriate Public Education: The Law and*

*Children with Disabilities* (Turnbull & Turnbull, 1998; Turnbull, Turnbull, Stowe, & Wilcox, 2000). The text discusses the law as well as the zero-reject

**FIGURE 10–4**
The special education cycle.

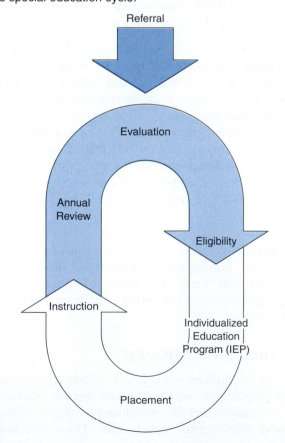

principle, nondiscriminatory evaluation, individualized appropriate education, least-restrictive environment, procedural due process, and parent participation.

## :: REACHING INFANTS AND TODDLERS WITH DISABILTIES

The importance of development while a child is an infant or a toddler is increasingly recognized. Recently developed brain-scan techniques have made it possible to see how synapses and connections develop during the first years of life. If this is a critical time for children without disabilities, one can immediately recognize how important it is for a child with a disability. This is a period in which great change and intervention become crucial (Bruder, 2010).

Child Find, discussed in the previous section, is one method of reaching parents of infants or toddlers with disabilities. Health agencies, doctors, visiting nurses, and hospitals are important sources in finding infants who need services.

## :: PART C OF IDEA 97 AND 2004

Part C of the Individuals with Disabilities Education Act Amendments of 1997 and 2004 focuses on infants and toddlers with disabilities. An at-risk infant or toddler is an individual younger than 3 who would be at risk of experiencing substantial developmental delay if early intervention services were not provided to the individual. Each state sets up its own program, but the program is expected to have the following:

1. A comprehensive child-find system, including a system to make referrals to service providers.
2. An Individualized Family Service Plan, including service coordination.
3. A comprehensive, multidisciplinary evaluation of the infant or toddler with a disability.
4. A family-directed identification of the needs of each family with an at-risk infant or toddler to assist the child's development.
5. A public-awareness program that focuses on early identification of infants and toddlers with disabilities. This emphasizes that hospitals and physicians need to be provided with information about the services so that parents will know about their availability.

6. A comprehensive system of personnel development. Qualified personnel include special educators, speech–language pathologists and audiologists, occupational therapists, physical therapists, psychologists, social workers, nurses, nutritionists, family therapists, orientation and mobility specialists, and pediatricians and other types of physicians. Part C also includes the training of paraprofessionals and primary referral sources—recruitment and retention of early education service providers; early intervention providers, fully and appropriately qualified to provide early intervention; personnel to work in rural and inner-city areas; and personnel to coordinate transition services for infants and toddlers to preschool or other appropriate services. Nothing prohibits the use of paraprofessionals and assistants who are appropriately trained and supervised, and states were given three years to develop the qualified staff.

These services are provided at no cost to families, except where federal or state law provides for a system of payment by families, including a schedule of sliding fees.

### Identifying the Infant and Toddler with Disabilities

The phrase *infant or toddler with a disability* means any child under 3 who needs intervention services because the child is at risk of substantial developmental delays if intervention is not provided to the child. The areas of delay may be in cognitive development, physical development, communicative development, social or emotional development, adaptive development, or a diagnosed physical or mental condition that would probably cause developmental delay (National Association of State Directors of Special Education, 1997).

Conditions that are associated with significant delays in development include the following:

- Chromosomal conditions (such as Down syndrome, Fragile X)
- Congenital syndromes or conditions (such as spina bifida)
- Sensory impairments (such as hearing or visual impairments)
- Metabolic disorders (such as PKU or lactic acidosis)

Children with Down syndrome can live independent and productive lives with the support of their families.

- Prenatal and/or perinatal infections or conditions (such as AIDS, CMV, or exposure to toxic substances)
- Significant medical problems (such as cerebral palsy)
- Low birth weight (less than 1,200 grams, or 2 lb. 10 oz.)
- Postnatal conditions (such as attachment disorder) (Colorado Department of Education, Early Childhood Initiatives, The Arapahoe Early Childhood Network, PEAK Parent Center, The Colorado Consortium of Intensive Care Nurseries, 1997)

## :: THE INDIVIDUALIZED FAMILY SERVICE PLAN AND FAMILY SURVEY

The Individualized Family Service Plan (IFSP) differs from the IEP in format because it is designed to focus on programs for infants and young children. IDEA 97 and 2004 place preschoolers under the school system and do not differentiate between preschooler programs and elementary and secondary programs, which leave the IEP as the format to decide on the child's program. If it appears that a family would benefit from services, it seems appropriate to continue to use the IFSP for that family as was indicated in previous IDEA legislation. Each state may make its own

determination. The intent is the same—to serve individuals with disabilities. The IFSP gives attention to family concerns and needs as well as services for the child.

The IFSP is designed to be flexible, family-focused, and unintrusive for families. It includes the following elements:

1. A statement of the infant's or toddler's present levels of attainment in physical or motor, sensory, cognitive, communication, social–emotional, and adaptive development. The law requires that this statement be based on objective criteria acceptable to both parent and provider.
2. A statement of the family's resources, priorities, and concerns related to enhancing the development of the child with special needs and/or related to broader family issues.
3. A statement of the major outcomes expected for the child and family, including how and when the team will evaluate whether progress is being made and whether changes or updates in outcomes or services are needed.
4. A statement of specific supports and services necessary to meet the unique strengths and needs of the infant/toddler and family, including options and a variety of all community supports and services available.
5. A statement describing the environments in which services will be provided and the location of services.
6. Dates when services will start and how long services will be used.
7. The name of the service coordinator. This person is responsible for seeing that the IFSP is carried out and coordinating the process among all involved parties.
8. The steps to be taken to support the child's transition to home, community, or preschool services, if appropriate (Colorado Department of Education et al., 1997).

The IFSP is evaluated once a year, and the family is provided a review of the plan at six-month intervals or more often, if appropriate, based on the infant's and family's need.

A number of states have established statewide mandated forms for IFSPs. Examples of these forms, and guidance for completing them, can be found at www.nectac.org/topics/families/stateifsp.asp. There are many commonalities between the states, but there are also a few specific individual differences.

### Procedural Rights for Infants and Toddlers

Each state has flexibility in how it sets up Part C for Infants and Toddlers, IDEA 97, and 2004. Most programs should have the following components.

First, a program should have *multidisciplinary evaluations.* A team consisting of the family and two or more qualified professionals looks at how the child is doing in physical or motor, sensory, cognitive, communication, social–emotional, and adaptive development. This evaluation is the procedure used to determine initial and continuing eligibility for services.

Second, an *Individualized Family Service Plan* (IFSP) is needed, consisting of a team of people, including family members, who jointly plan supports and services and identify resources that will meet the family's concerns and priorities about the child's development. This plan is documented.

Other components include a *service coordinator,* who works with the family to identify resources, supports, and services and coordinates agencies and people involved. Parents are given *prior notice* about any changes that service providers want to make, and parents are given the chance to approve or reject those changes.

*Information,* both written and spoken, will be given in the child's native language or, if that is impossible, will be translated orally or by another mode of communication so that parents understand the information. Parents have the right to accept or deny service and must have *informed consent. Confidentiality* is ensured by keeping private any information about the child and the family. Parents will have *access to records* with the ability to change incorrect information.

Support and services are provided in a *natural environment,* the environment typically used for children who are the same age but do not have disabilities. Parents will also have *access to services,* helped by the service coordinator.

Parents may use an *appeals process* to resolve any disagreements they have with providers. The appeals process can involve mediation and due process. Finally, *mediation* will be used to find a solution satisfactory to all involved in the dispute.

Due process is employed in resolving complaints (Colorado Department of Education et al., 1997).

## :: CHILDREN WITH DISABILITIES IN HEAD START AND CHILD CARE

In 1974, with the passage of the Community Services Act (P.L. 96-644), Congress stipulated that 10 percent of Head Start's enrollment must be children with disabilities. Head Start developed procedures and policies to answer the needs of these children by offering individualized and appropriate education. When Early Head Start was initiated, the same requirement for 10 percent enrollment of children with disabilities was mandated for that program.

The Local Education Agency (LEA) is responsible for ensuring that services are provided to children with disabilities from birth to 21 years of age, but it is not responsible for providing all services. IDEA's policy is to ensure that all children with disabilities, beginning as soon as diagnosed for infants and toddlers and continuing through age 21, have the right to a free appropriate education in either public or private institutions. This includes Early Head Start, Head Start, and private child-care facilities. Early Head Start and Head Start facilities were directed to use IDEA's definition of children with disabilities.

The coordinator of services for children with disabilities must have a plan containing the following: (a) procedures for timely screening; (b) procedures for making referrals to the LEA for evaluation; (c) procedures to determine whether there is a need for special education and related services for a child as early as the child's 3rd birthday; (d) provisions to ensure accessibility of the facilities and appropriate special furniture, equipment, and materials as needed; and (e) transition of children from Early Head Start to Head Start or into other appropriate preschool placements.

The Early Head Start and Head Start's service delivery plans must include options to meet the needs and take into consideration the strengths of each child based upon the IFSP or IEP so that a continuum of services available from various agencies is considered.

Eligibility requirements are similar to those cited in the discussion of IDEA 2004, with the addition of developmental delays. These include health impairment, hearing impairment, orthopedic impairment, visual impairment (including blindness), learning disabilities, autism, and traumatic brain injury. The developmental delays are in physical development, cognitive development, communicative development, social–emotional development, or adaptive development as discussed in IDEA 97 and 2004's Part C for Infants and Toddlers.

### Early Head Start and Head Start and Parents

The Early Head Start and Head Start staff must do the following:

1. Support parents of children with disabilities.
2. Provide information to parents on how to foster their child's development.
3. Provide opportunities for parents to observe large-group, small-group, and individual activities described in their child's IFSP or IEP.
4. Provide follow-up assistance and activities to reinforce program activities at home.
5. Refer parents to groups of parents of children with similar disabilities who can provide peer support.
6. Inform parents of their rights under IDEA.
7. Inform parents of resources that may be available from the Supplemental Security Income (SSI) Program; the Early Periodic Screening, Diagnosis, and Treatment (EPSDT) Program; and other sources as well as assist them with initial efforts to access such resources.
8. Identify needs (caused by the disability) of siblings and other family members.
9. Provide information that might help prevent disabilities among younger siblings.
10. Build parents' confidence, skill, and knowledge in accessing resources and advocating to meet the needs of their children (*Federal Register,* 1993).

### Special Quest

In 1997, Special Quest, a partnership between the Hilton Foundation and Early and Migrant Head Start programs, was begun. It is the first public/private partnership with the Administration for Children, Youth, and Families. This partnership was established to improve services to infants and toddlers with disabilities. From 1997 to 2004, in an effort to include Early Head Start administrators, teachers, early-intervention specialists, parents, and community members, 250 teams of service providers met

for four-year intervals to receive training, develop plans, and monitor improvements to the service-delivery systems in their respective communities. In February 2004, the Conrad Hilton Foundation was given an award by the Administration for Children, Youth, and Families (ACF) for its contribution to infants and toddlers (ACF Press Office, 2004).

## ❖ PARENT–SCHOOL PARTNERSHIPS

### Helping Young Children Develop

Developmental delays need special consideration, but very young special-needs children in particular benefit from a nurturing and responsive home or child-care center. Children ages 3 to 5 should attend a good, developmentally appropriate class that has supplemental intervention that meets the needs of each child. They need an appropriate nurturing environment where language, movement, creativity, and discovery support their physical, social–emotional, and cognitive development. Individual concerns for such things as autism, Fragile X, and Down syndrome need to be addressed in relation to appropriate intervention. Because there is not enough space in this text to include all the information and recommendations, care providers should contact the Special Education Early Childhood program and the parent center for children with disabilities in their home state. Call or write the National Dissemination Center for Children with Disabilities (NICHCY). NICHCY can furnish information on each area of the child's disability and can also furnish the names of other references.

**Communicate with the Child.** Communication is how children learn their language, and they must be given opportunities to practice that skill. Talk naturally so the child can understand and develop language. When your child talks, listen. How do you feel when you talk to someone who will not listen to what you are saying? Most adults don't waste time talking to people who do not listen to them. Children don't either. If you want your children to express themselves, let them initiate conversations and respond by giving them your attention.

**Give Praise and Encouragement.** Praise reinforces learning and behaviors, and encouragement helps children continue working. Let children know when you are pleased with what they are doing. We all work for rewards, and praise is one of the most important rewards you can give. Be patient with children. It takes many trials and many errors to learn skills. Adults forget over the years how it was to be a child. If the situation gets out of hand and you become impatient or angry, leave the situation, do something else, and come back to it when you are in control of yourself.

**Never Compare.** Don't compare your children with others. Allow for individuality. Every child is different and has special characteristics that make up his or her personality and no one else's.

**Offer Enrichment Activities.** Help increase your children's knowledge by taking them to places such as zoos, libraries, or airports. Use television as a learning tool by selecting appropriate programs, viewing them together, and discussing them afterward. Another learning experience that is often overlooked is the family mealtime. Sharing experiences, talking about interesting subjects, and improving conversational skills can happen around the dining table.

**Encourage Play.** Play is as important for children with disabilities as it is for children without. It is especially important for children who are deaf or blind. These disabilities do not interfere with the natural phenomenon of learning about the world and growing and developing while doing so. Activities that are appropriate for normal babies are appropriate for the infant with disabilities too. Clapping hands, cooing, playing peekaboo, and cuddling are not only helpful but necessary. Provide the baby or small child with objects to grasp. Firm cushions may be used for crawling babies. Rock children back and forth or play with them on a swing so they will have the experiences needed to develop. Babies and small children must have the opportunity to think, experiment, investigate, and learn about their environment. Of course, infants should never be left unsupervised.

**Read and Talk Together.** Read to your children, have them read to you, and listen to them read. Let them tell you about what they have been reading. Magazines, newspapers, comics, and books can all be used to increase a child's knowledge and reading ability.

For school-age children add the following:

**Develop Good Work Habits.** Set the stage for good homework habits. A well-lighted place to study that is quiet, with room for books, pencils, and papers, helps. Schedule regular home study.

**Get Sufficient Rest.** Set a bedtime and stick to it. Children need a lot of rest to be able to do good mental work. Rest is necessary for proper growth.

**Attend School Regularly.** See that your child attends school regularly and on time. Visit with teachers to learn how your child is getting along in school and listen to what they have to tell you about your child.

## ▪▪ HOW PARENTS CAN HELP THE SCHOOL-AGE CHILD AT HOME

For teachers and parents alike, the goal is to have all children reach their full potential. Students with disabilities may need extra help at home to keep up their schoolwork. Special tutoring by someone outside the family might be very effective. If the parents are planning to work with their child, the following suggestions should help guide them.

### What Parents Can Do

Know your child. You are your child's first teacher and often know better about his or her capabilities than anyone else. Communicate your hopes and plans to your child's teacher.

Actively participate in your child's school. Treat all students and other members of the school community with respect (Educational Resources Information Center, National Library of Education, Office of Educational Research and Improvement, U.S. Department of Education, 1996).

**First, Visit with the Teacher.** Explain that you want to help your child at home with schoolwork. Ask the teacher to explain the material the class will be covering and how assignments should be done. Try to get a schedule for assignments if your child doesn't already have one.

**Set a Definite Time for the Child.** Set a time to work with your child. Go over the day's experiences and listen to how your child felt about them. Discuss how the assignments can be completed and turned in on time.

**Monitor Progress.** Keep a record of the assignments handed in and the scores received, so you can tell how your child is doing in school. If the grades are low or you do not understand them, visit with the teacher to find out exactly what the teacher expects.

**Promote Success.** Your child will be more likely to succeed in home–school collaboration if you do the following:

1. Use a pleasant, firm approach that says, "Yes, this must be done, and we'll do it as quickly and pleasantly as we can."
2. Set up a reward system. Few of us will work hard at a job we do not receive satisfaction from or get paid for. Your praise and approval are the students' pay for a job well done. If they get scolded all the time, they are unlikely to want to work for another scolding.
3. Make sure your child has time for work, play, and rest. There has to be some work, play, and rest in everyone's life. If we do too much of one, the other two will suffer. Parents are the best ones to determine how to keep this balance.

Parents may be the most important force in seeking the correct educational placement for their children. It is important that they are aware of the various ways their children may be served. Different labels for placement may exist in different regions. The *interrelated classroom* is a popular term for a classroom in which children are placed according to their level of academic achievement rather than according to their diagnosed disabilities.

### Parent Involvement in the Classroom

In addition to an advocacy role, parents should also take an active role in the education of their children. Parent involvement in the classroom is an asset that is often overlooked or mismanaged. The parent is involved in planning the IEP and has the right of input and due process. Although parents are aware of these rights, many probably do not feel self-assured enough to fully capitalize on them. They rely on the teacher, the administrator, or the psychologist to keep them informed of what they, as parents, should be doing. Many parents believe the teacher, or some other person in an authority role, knows what is best and that it is up to that person to decide whether the parent can be of assistance.

The counterpart is the teacher who fears parent involvement, perhaps because of misconceptions or a bad experience. Thus, there may be a lack of communication or overt action that prevents application of an influential force—the parents—for the education of the student with disabilities.

**An Example of Parent Involvement.** Precise Early Education for Children with Handicaps (PEECH) involves parents by offering conferences, group meetings, home visits, classroom observations, and a lending library as well as by being receptive to their questions and suggestions. This program integrates children with disabilities in a classroom with children who have no special education needs. The children, ages 3 to 6, attend the program 1/2 a day, 5 days a week (National Dissemination Association & National Diffusion Network, 1993).

Merle Karnes, director of the project, emphasizes the importance of family involvement and the necessity of skillful staff interaction with parents. She finds that parents are interested in their children with disabilities and want to learn how to work with them. Karnes offers the following advice to the professional educator working with these parents: To ensure success in your work with parents, give specific directions and objective feedback on their contributions. Respect them as individuals and be flexible in responding to their needs and value systems. If parents are included in decision making, if the program makes sense to them, if their goals and values are compatible with those of the school, and if they are approached as individuals and are convinced that you, the professional, are interested in helping them, they will join you in developing their abilities and contributing their time. Parents can work effectively in the classroom, and they will extend their newfound understanding to other members of the family. They may become so knowledgeable and skillful that they can reach out to help other parents of children with disabilities.

### How Parents Can Support Children's Schoolwork at Home

Parents may find that a digital voice recorder is one of the most valuable instruments available in helping the student learn at home or at school. With a digital recorder, parents can put exactly what they want in a lesson and determine its format. A set of headphones further enhances the learning situation.

The digital recorder is excellent for recording spelling words and for having children practice taking spelling tests as they would in a classroom. If the children can read the words, have them record the words on the recorder and take them as in a spelling lesson. When the students listen to the words, they automatically monitor the sound of the word, the inflection, and the phrasing. Corrections are made unconsciously as the mind corrects errors that the ear hears.

Another important use is letting children record a reading lesson on the recorder and then asking them to correct their own errors. A chart of the time, number of words read, and errors made can be kept to show progress.

The digital recorder is also valuable for recording messages or giving directions. Instructions on how to set a table, mix pudding, or make a bed can be recorded to give a child valuable experience in learning to follow directions.

### Suggestions for Digital Lessons

1. Make the length of your lesson five minutes shorter than the period you want the lesson to last. This gives flexibility for handling interruptions.
2. Arrange the tasks sequentially. Check the order by doing the lesson once yourself.
3. Speak more slowly than your normal rate of speech. Children with learning disabilities do not process words and thoughts as quickly as most people do. Check to see if children know what the recorder is saying by asking them to repeat what they hear. Be careful not to ask if they understand the information. They may think they do, but testing may reveal they don't.
4. Include a set of questions at the end of the recorded lesson for immediate review of the material. (This is also helpful for the teacher with students who have missed reading lessons or lectures.)

### A Few Things to Remember

When teaching children with disabilities, teachers and parents should follow these suggestions:

1. Encourage correct responses—wrong responses have to be relearned.
2. Use tests as learning instruments. More learning takes place when tests are answered and corrected soon after being given.

3. Learning occurs more effectively when more channels of learning are involved. Involving the visual and hearing channels is more effective than involving just vision or just hearing.
4. Putting what has been learned into action through verbal or physical reaction increases the learning experience.
5. Learning is reinforced by repetition, reviewing often at first and then again at varying intervals.
6. Begin with concrete items and move gradually to teaching abstract concepts. Make sure to model expectations for children that need to learn by observing before they can internalize expectations.
7. Ask the child to help make a "to-do" list so the child begins to practice organizing what needs to be done and the most efficient order in which to do them. The child can dictate them or record them if writing is a problem. Checking off completed tasks is very rewarding.
8. Color-code folders at home and school to help children organize their materials: homework, worksheets, notes, and so forth. Make sure to put the folders in the same place so children can consistently get and put their materials away.
9. Establish a consistent schedule so children can pace themselves and can anticipate how much time it takes to complete tasks. Time management is an issue whether a child has disabilities or not. Help the child become aware of time spent doing tasks by using an egg or clock timer.
10. Children with disabilities, like all children, need downtime. It is important to plan unstructured time that allows the child to make constructive leisure choices. Life is about balancing needs, and an overworked child will be resentful and unproductive. Children should be encouraged to work hard and play hard.

## :: COMMUNICATION BETWEEN PROFESSIONALS AND PARENTS OF CHILDREN WITH DISABILITIES

Teachers may be confronted with dispirited parents experiencing considerable doubt, confusion, and anxiety about their child with a disability and their reactions to her. A troubled parent may enlist the help of a teacher to discuss problems that are related to a child's performance at school or other, more personal concerns that bear a relationship to the child. A parent's inability to cope effectively with a child is often a motivating factor in seeking help. (Seligman, 2000, p. 9)

Parents react differently and sometimes unpredictably to the birth or the diagnosis of a child with a disability. Reactions are a result of feelings; parents may experience frustration, hurt, fear, guilt, disappointment, ambivalence, or despair. For the professional to work effectively with parents of children with disabilities, there must be an ability to recognize these feelings and a willingness to honor them (Chinn, 1984; Chinn et al., 1978). It takes skill, tact, and ingenuity for a professional to communicate with people who have children with different needs. It is also very important to choose the best words to assist in conveying an understanding of parents' feelings. Mistakes to avoid include "talking down" to the parents, assuming an understanding exists where in fact none may, and using jargon or technical language. People First Language (Snow, 2006) offers suggestions for phrases and terms that can facilitate lines of communication.

The professional deals with the child day to day or only occasionally, whereas the parents deal with the child before and after school and on weekends. Parents of a child with a severe disability may be faced with a lifetime of caring for the child. There is a need to offer parents relief from the constant care that is often required. Foster parents, substitute grandparents, and knowledgeable volunteers are becoming more available to give these parents helpful breaks (Chinn, 1984; Chinn et al., 1978).

Parents are receptive to open and direct communication. Messages should be clear and in language the parents can understand. The teacher or professional will deal with a wide variance of language efficiency, so they should acquaint themselves with the parents' backgrounds. Listen to the words parents use to guide how to best communicate information about their child. The professional should also be receptive to clues from the parents to determine if the message is being received and accommodated as intended. Ask a leading question to let the parents express their understanding of the topic being discussed. You might be surprised to find the interpretations are different from what you intended.

The professional should include the support and consultation of the medical and theological professions if the parents exhibit a need for these services.

Be aware of the agencies and organizations that assist parents and professional workers in the community as well as national organizations.

## Ways to Reach Parents

**Daily Log.** Use a form like the one in Figure 10–5 to let the parents know how their child performed in school on a daily basis. The teacher can provide feedback for the parent by writing comments of great things and challenges that faced the child. This is a good way to also keep a record of the progress of the child for later use because it has a space not only for instructional information but also for behavioral information.

**Newsletters.** Use a newsletter to offer tips for parents. There are things that all parents can do to help their children in school that are important to parents of children both with disabilities and without.

**Letters.** Letters are another effective means of communicating an idea or message to parents. Letters should state the concern, then present methods or suggestions for dealing with or changing the situation, include any guidelines or datelines that are pertinent, and finally, end with a conclusion and an offer for assistance if needed. If parents have access to a computer and have an e-mail account, they can readily communicate with their child's teacher without taking too much time. Teachers in return can keep the parent informed by simply sending an e-mail with pertinent information. The use of Facebook and Twitter should be done carefully by special education teachers because there is a great amount of confidential information that should not be shared with the general public. Teachers may want to create a classroom Web site that offers parents an opportunity to look at the information teachers need to share such as suggested activities, homework, and reading lists, among others and also perhaps a blog where parents can communicate with one another and share ideas. The idea of technology for parents of children with special needs is to share resources to help one another help their children.

There are as many ways to write the message you wish to convey as there are teachers. Each will need to adapt the contents to the concerns of the situation.

## FIGURE 10–5

An example of a teacher's daily log.

# Daily Log

**Student:** *Rodrigo*

**Date:** *1-1-09*

**Teacher:** *Mrs. Acosta*

**Teaching Assistant:** *Mr. Jones*

### Instructional

| Workstations | On task | hand/hand | constantly redirected |
|---|---|---|---|
| Sensory | ☑ | ☐ | ☐ |
| Vocational | ☑ | ☐ | ☐ |
| P.E. | ☐ | ☐ | ☑ |
| Library | ☐ | ☐ | ☑ |
| Music | ☐ | ☐ | ☑ |
| Math | ☑ | ☐ | ☐ |
| Reading | ☑ | ☐ | ☐ |
| Language Arts | ☐ | ☑ | ☐ |
| Science | ☐ | ☑ | ☐ |
| Social Studies | ☐ | ☑ | ☐ |

**Comments:** *Good job in math!*

### Breakfast

Ate Well ☐
Ate Little ☑
Did Not Eat ☐

**Comments:**
*Rodrigo drank half of his Pediasure*

### Lunch

Ate Well ☑
Ate Little ☐
Did Not Eat ☐

**Comments:**
*Rodrigo loves his peanut butter sandwich.*

### Behaviors

Excellent ☐          Needs Improvement ☐

Good ☐          Time Out/*Cool out* ☑ *Brief*

**Comments:** *Thought spitting water was funny, so he went to cool out. Did better in the afternoon.*

### Medical

Seizures ☐          Asthma ☐

Meds ☐

Other: ☐          *N/A*

**Comments:**

### My Day Was

Happy ☑ *for the most part*     Not Feeling Well ☐

Good ☐          Not Good ☐

**Comments:** *In the morning we were not communicating, we worked together and Rodrigo accomplished his tasks.*

### Toileting

Urine ☐ ⊘ # of Accidents:

B.M. ☐ ⊘ # of Accidents:

**Comments:**
*Great job!*

### Supplies Needed

Diapers ☐          Wipes ☐          Change of Clothes ☐          Other ☐

Toothbrush ☐          Toothpaste ☐          Other ☐          Other ☐

### My Body

**Comments:** *No marks*

*Rodrigo earned a dollar today because he stayed on task and worked hard.*

*Don't forget picture day tomorrow!*

*Source:* Harlandale Independent School District, San Antonio, Texas, Special Education Department. Data added by author.
Reprinted with permission.

## :: PARENTAL REACTIONS TO DISABILITIES

Parents of a child with a disability typically go through a series of stages in dealing with their concerns. First, they become aware of and recognize the basic problem. Then they become occupied with trying to discover a cause and later begin to look for a cure. Acceptance is the last stage (Chinn, 1984; Chinn et al., 1978). The usual progression to acceptance may vary, but most parents experience guilt and grief before they reach acceptance and compassion.

### Parents' Initial Response

**Denial.** Parents who deny the existence of a child's disability feel threatened. Their security is uncertain, and they are defending their egos or self-concepts. This is a difficult reaction for the professional to deal with. Time, patience, and support will help these parents see that much can be gained through helping children with disabilities realize their potentials.

**Projection of Blame.** A common reaction is to blame the situation on something or someone else—the psychologist, the teacher, the doctor. Often parents' statements begin with "If only. . . ." Again, patience, willingness to listen to the parent, and tact will help the professional deal with a potentially hostile situation.

**Fear.** The parents may not be acquainted with the cause or characteristics of the disability. They may have unfounded suspicions or erroneous information, which causes anxiety or fear. Provide information, but be sure to give the information in amounts the parents can handle. A positive communication process helps the professional judge the time to offer additional information.

**Guilt.** Parents' feelings of guilt—thinking they should have done something differently or believing the disability is retribution for a misdeed—are difficult to deal with. The professional can help by encouraging guilt-ridden parents to channel their energies into more productive activities after genuine communication has been established.

**Grief.** Grief is a natural reaction to a situation that brings extreme pain and disappointment. Parents who have not been able to accept their child as having a disability may become grief stricken. In such a case, it is necessary to allow the parents to go through a healing process before they can learn about their child and how the child can develop.

**Withdrawal.** Being able to withdraw and collect oneself is a healthy, necessary response. It is when one begins to shun others, avoid situations, and maintain isolation that it becomes potentially damaging.

**Rejection.** There are many reasons for rejection and many ways of exhibiting it. It may be subtle, feigning acceptance, or it may be open and hostile. Some forms of rejection are failing to recognize positive attributes, setting unrealistic goals, escaping by desertion, or presenting a favorable impression to others while inwardly rejecting the child.

**Acceptance.** Finally, the reaction of parents may be acceptance that the child has a disability—acceptance of the child and of themselves. This is the goal and realization of maturity. The parents and the child can then grow and develop into stronger, wiser, and more compassionate human beings (Chinn, 1984; Chinn et al., 1978).

Although parents may have some of these feelings, one of the most important components in handling their feelings is the knowledge that there are things they can do to help their child. When parents are able to focus on the positive and able to design a program that will enable their child to develop to full potential, they have a challenge and an answer to the crisis that they may have felt initially. Too often, professionals and friends respond with sympathy rather than suggestions for ways to face the future and meet the challenges.

### Reaching Out with Programs

When parents are confronted with the task of rearing a child with a disability, they need both emotional support and specific information. The first step is the establishment of attachment between father and infant. The second step is the development of parenting qualities in the father. This ability is acquired when the father is able to read cues and understand the baby's behavior. The cues and behavior patterns of a child with a disability may not be the same as those of a typically developing infant. If misinterpreted by the parents, a certain behavior may confuse and frustrate the parents, causing them eventually to withdraw from meaningful relationships. The end result may be that the attachment process between parent and child is disturbed.

Other programs for fathers of children with special needs include the Fathers Network, whose Web site, www.fathersnetwork.org, shares information on fathers and their children. Included are current news articles from sources such as the *Seattle Times*, *Seattle Post Intelligencer*, the *New York Times*, and the Associated Press that provide information pertinent to fathers with children with disabilities. Topics include planning for the future of children with disabilities, experiences of siblings of children with disabilities, and personal experiences of fathers coping with their children's disabilities. An events calendar lists upcoming conferences and seminars offered in Washington State, the Northwest, the rest of the United States, and Canada.

### Students Speak Out

The National Council on Disability (2002) asked youth to respond to questions about their school experiences in IDEA. The questions included were as follows:

1. When you think about your years in school, what comes to mind about special education and related services?

2. If your school was reluctant to provide special-education services because of financial concerns, which services were disputed? Did you receive the services that your IEP team said you needed?

3. If the discipline procedures under IDEA need to be clearer, how would you change the way the discipline policy is explained to students and their parents?

4. How could schools do a better job before students leave high school to help you and other young people with disabilities prepare in areas such as employment, transportation, housing, managing my finances, health care, independent living, connecting to resources in the community, and/or postsecondary (college or vocational) education? (pp. 8–9)

One student's experience was as follows:

I am a 12-year-old who has been diagnosed with Chronic Fatigue Syndrome (CFS) and Postural Orthostatic Tachycardia Syndrome (POTS). I am currently finishing the 6th grade and have been ill with these illnesses for most of my life. By the 3rd grade I was unable to attend school at all and my parents worked with the school to have me classified as Other Health Impaired so that I could receive services under the IDEA. The problem that they had initially was that my test scores showed that I was at the high end of my ability, even though my education was being severely affected by the illness. . . . I have been very fortunate in my school system because once my eligibility was accepted the CSE has been very supportive. They have been very open to our suggestions and those of the tutor to services that may benefit me, and have stuck by my IEP in following through with services. My parents have had to maintain an active role and remind the school of things we needed, such as extra textbooks, or use of a word processor, but the school has accommodated when reminded. Individual teachers have been our great allies and our worst enemies. If they try to understand my illness and limitations they bend over backwards to help me out. But some teachers have been totally unwilling to teach me via a tutor. They will not grade my work and resist modifying my workload. We have been fortunate to be able to find ways to work around these situations. . . . Most of my teachers have been willing to offer help in modifying and consolidating the workload to a manageable level for me to complete. (National Council on Disability, 2002, pp. 11–12, 17)

While not all students interviewed had positive experiences, positive communication that acknowledges an understanding of a student's experience can make a significant impact on a student's performance.

## :: PARENTS SHARE THEIR FEELINGS

Hilaria Bauer is the mother of a young adult with a disability. She shares her feelings and thoughts about this so that others may benefit from her experiences:

Because Asperger's Syndrome was not really coined until the early 80's, we never knew what was wrong with my daughter. We knew she was a bit "different" since she was a toddler, and we took her to many doctors, who diagnosed her from having Cerebral Palsy to Motor Delay, but nobody knew what was really wrong. When she entered school, she had no problems learning to read, but we knew that there was "something." Her fine motor skills never caught up as she developed. She had problems climbing stairs, throwing a ball, and learning how to write. She never learned how to ride a bike. As she grew, she had a very hard time trying to "fit in." She was tested for Special Education services twice and never qualified. She was "high functioning" for her IQ. The school system was not ready to address any of her needs.

Because my daughter did not fit any of the school's labels, we went through a 504 process, to safeguard her rights as a student. Through 504, she was able to obtain some modifications to her school experience, especially when taking a test or completing a project. However, there were no specialized services to help her cope with her condition. Administrators and teachers did not, just like doctors, know what to do with her. She was reading, somewhat writing, and learning all the factual information school imparts, but she was left out of the learning experience whenever abstract concepts were addressed. As she matured, this became painfully real. She was not able to understand literary devices, she was not able to comprehend algebra or other high mathematical concepts, she could not get mature humor. Little by little, her body aged, but her social mind and some of her cognitive skills stayed at the level of someone about 9 or 10 years old.

We learned what her condition was when she entered junior college. At the age of 18, we found out that she had something called Asperger's Syndrome. I became friends with someone who had a Psychiatric Social Work background. In one of my conversations with my friend, I described some of my daughter's symptoms. My friend suggested to have her checked for Asperger's Syndrome. When we took my daughter to a diagnostician, we were finally given a "label." Most people frowned when they saw how happy I was with the "label." For me, it was not knowing what was wrong that prevented us from providing more appropriate help. We read many books about Asperger's, including Songs of the Gorilla Nation by Dr. Dawn Prince-Hughes. Although my daughter didn't have Autism, Asperger's was considered in the same kind of social challenges as Autism. She is now trying to finish her Associate Arts degree from our community college at the age of 26.

The only uncertainty we have for her as an adult are her job prospects. We are committed as parents to provide for her as long as we live; however, we don't know what will happen when we are not around. As of now, she has not been able to hold a steady job. She has tried a couple of things without success, so any conversation around work makes her very anxious. She loves school, she has a couple of acquaintances, and she fulfills all of her responsibilities, at school, home, and church. She is a very caring, responsible, and smart individual. But, as of now, the workplace doesn't appear to be a safe environment for someone who is an adult with a child-like perception.[1]

## Parents of Twin Boys with Cerebral Palsy Share

Bruce and Kelly Stahlman did not expect their twins to be born 3 months early at 28 weeks gestation.

---

[1]Reprinted by permission of Hilaria Bauer, October 25, 2010.

## BRUCE'S LETTER

*Relativity.*

*Whenever we discuss speed or velocity (an object's speed and its direction of motion), we must specify precisely who or what is doing the measuring . . . each observer feels stationary and perceives the other as moving. Each perspective is understandable and justifiable. As there is symmetry between the two space-dwellers, there is, on quite fundamental grounds, no way of saying one perspective is "right" and the other "wrong." Each perspective has an equal claim on truth.* (Greene, 2000, p. 28)

Special needs kids weren't visible during the 60s and 70's when I progressed through public school. Once in a while, you'd see bus No. 16 making an afternoon run, shorter than all the other buses and rumored to be carrying retards. We didn't really understand what that meant, of course, any more than we understood what it meant to be Negro or Jewish or Communist. We gave no thought, shallow or otherwise, to what having a disabled sibling or child might imply.

They'd always been out there, unseen, hidden away by parents and convention, probably ashamed or afraid. More likely out of exhaustion and confusion from having nowhere to turn, no one to help and no one to empathize out of personal experience.

Mike's brother, Tom, had Down's Syndrome. Strong as an ox, he was never without his beloved tinker toy wheel on the end of a coat hanger. We'd always see him while playing cards in Mike's basement. There was a sense of loss, years later, when I heard Tom had passed away. I wish I'd known him better.

Rob was transformed from a cocky high school student to a drooling semi-vegetable as a result of a boating accident. He'd play cards, too, but he was unintelligible most of the time and he moved so slowly. His parents got divorced. I lost track of Rob in short order.

That pretty much covers my formative experience with disabilities. So it's fair to say I wasn't overly prepared for the arrival of our second and third sons, Mark and Eric, 28-week preemies. One alone would have been a shock, two crossed the line into farce. It started with an extended stay in the Intensive Care Nursery. When Eric, the younger twin, finally arrived home he sported a newly repaired heart, apnea monitors, oxygen tanks, and joined his brother in fussing most every night due to their inability to consume enough calories. Sleep deprivation was the worst because it precipitated a cascade of dysfunctionality throughout the house.

I could go on and on. Cerebral palsy is a complicated disorder. Both boys have gastrointestinal tubes for feedings, a regimen of medications and supplements to help with everything from muscle spasm to bowel movement, and a fleet of assistive devices. Hospital trips for specialist review, surgeries, botox injections, and an endless stream of therapist and nursing assistants invading our privacy have become something of a routine that's emotionally draining yet monotonous. A sales professional by training, my wife has become an expert at navigating the private and public health care systems out of necessity, an educational consultant out of conviction and an advocate out of desire.

It would have flatly been impossible to survive this institutionalized anarchy any other way than by simply growing into it, over the years, one day at a time. In the process, the twins have gone from pre-med thesis material to become our sons with rich, individual personalities, idiosyncrasies and foibles just like "normal" kids. While we wish for them more than is presently possible, we take great pride in their many and significant accomplishments: Eric babbling away at dinner and sitting by himself in his red rocker; Mark learning to use his talker; Eric driving his power chair and endlessly playing and rewinding the Lion King with a remote controller all by himself, and Mark laughing hysterically whenever his older brother gets in trouble. We love them as any parent loves his children. We love reading at bedtime, tickling and teasing, going to a baseball game and swimming. And Eric's Make-A-Wish trip to Give Kids the World Village and Disney World in Florida to meet his favorite Radio Disney DJ was one of the most inspirational events of my life.

People in the disability community threw us a lifeline early on by acting as guides through the maze of public services access. It's beyond astonishing that the richest society on earth makes people traverse a gauntlet to receive even the most basic services. It's worse when you realize how many more get no help or respect from agencies purportedly designed for that purpose. In the process, my politics have changed from conservative to liberal. Both my wife and I have served in various charitable capacities to give something back to the community because it's important to remember you're in a lifeboat with others.

Our oldest son, Jay, gets a lot of credit. I assume he's been impacted in ways I can't comprehend, but mainly for the good. He produced a video of his brothers and spent a day in a wheelchair for a school project last year, something that would never have occurred to me when I was his age.

Our marriage has become stronger over the years as we've grown with the family. My wife is fond of saying life is what you do every day. That's true, but I could certainly live without changing my ten-year-olds' diapers, administering tube feeds, doing the "clean and jerk" whenever they need to be moved and watching Barney tapes for the umpteenth million time and counting. This last point is particularly heinous—no parent should be made to endure Barney for ten years without receiving a Congressional medal.

The emotions, surgeries, finances, the life overall certainly isn't what I'd expected or planned. Does God work in mysterious ways? Probably. Do I put more stock in theology versus philosophy? Depends on the day. Are Mark and Eric better off than Chinese, Bosnian, or Rwandan kids with CP? Unquestionably. Do other people see it that way? I guess it's relative.

Bruce R. Stahlman
Littleton, Colorado
September 26, 2002

Kelly follows with a letter that she hopes will clarify the relationship between parent and teacher and help teachers understand parents better.

*A letter to teachers, current and future:*

As a mother of twins with cerebral palsy, I want to thank you for taking the time and making great efforts to care for my children. Without you I would be lost.

Next, I would like to explain, one by one, some of my actions and reactions. Please be patient.

First. After reading the vignette "Story" in the book, *Changed by a Child,* I finally understood why I keep telling you the same story over and over and over. The vignette talks about the excruciating details that I need to convey, because it is all still so real and so raw to me. That, like a spider spinning its web, retelling my story allows me to connect my old life to this new, overwhelming reality.

My story is the vehicle that makes the trip of survival and allows me to cope with the present.

Second. In caring for children with disabilities, a large part of the care is emotional, so the teacher/parent relationship is, by definition, also emotional. We are both investing all that we can into my children, yet we frequently seem to be at odds. Please work WITH me. Give careful consideration to the information that I bring to the table, because it comes as the result of sweat and tears. It is also my role in your system, as a parent, to push the envelope, to be looking ahead, and to be asking for everything that I can to support my child. I will still be here when I am 80 and they are 50, and we shall still be "doing the best we can."

Third. Asking "how are things going" at the start of our meetings gives necessary information. My sleep, the children's health, and life overall will be things that affect our conversation and how effectively I am able to communicate.

Last. Never forget that I am grateful for all that you do. It becomes tiring to always say thank you, because that is the nature of our life. In fact, one of the blessings of a disability is that it frequently brings out the best in others. I never forget a kindness, even years later, but it still gets old saying "thank you" as a way of life. Nevertheless, THANK YOU.

> Kelly of Stahlman
> Mother of 3 sons, Jay, 13,
> Mark and Eric, 10-year-old twins
> with cerebral palsy due to prematurity

Addendum to Bruce Stahlman's letter:

August 16, 2006

Mark and Eric turned 14 this past weekend and their first day of high school is tomorrow. No doubt all parents think time passes quickly, but I still have vivid memories of their stay in the ICCN. They remain great kids with some unique challenges for our family as they inexorably become young adults. These fall into three general categories:

1. Logistic— The physical exertion to move them through space has increased dramatically over time. Simply, they continue to grow and gain weight while my wife and I and the attending CNAs age, so lifting them for wheel chair positioning, hygiene, sleep, etc. while avoiding injury to them and us has become more difficult. We are presently in the final stages of home modification project that involves combining bedrooms; enlarging the bathroom and installing a ceiling lift system to address these concerns. Finally, we continue to explore evolving technology for communication purposes for both boys including Dynavox upgrades for Mark, who is non-verbal, to PC applications for Eric to afford him greater access to the Internet.

2. Behavior— Coupled with the normal hormone changes of adolescence are overlay symptoms of ADD particularly in Eric, the more mobile twin. We suspect there's also a growing psychological awareness of their general situation vis-à-vis other kids, for example, as their older brother enters his junior year of high school. We're seeing a lower tolerance of schedule changes, higher demand for activity repetition, and increased incidence of temper tantrums accompanied by hitting, both outward and self-directed. Behavior modification techniques have been at the forefront of ongoing discussions with school personnel and the CAN, but

results have been mixed. This is a challenging problem given the paradox of life skill training to set appropriate boundaries vs. the need to actively parent through these important years.

3. Medical— My wife estimates each boy has had nine or ten surgeries over the course of their lives and more are on the horizon. Recently some disturbing changes in Eric's spine have been observed and he'll likely require an involved stabilization procedure. Mark will likely have non-weight bearing ankle bones fused to counteract the effects of overpronation. Thankfully, the logistics changes noted about should be a big help here for recuperation and ongoing care.

Of course this type of clinical situation analysis doesn't capture the daily joy of parenting kids with special needs. They are exceptional, funny, loving, and interactive in their own ways, and I can't imagine the family without them.

## A FEW JEWELS FROM THE STAHLMAN FAMILY SURVIVAL SKILLS

*Why me?*

*Why not me?*

*Ignorance is bliss; knowledge is power.*

*Kids with disabilities take much longer to go to the next stage. They wear you out. Patience and endurance are required, with lots of support!*

*In some ways it gets easier; in some ways it gets harder, and in some ways it just gets different as you go through stages and ages.*

*God never gives you more than you can handle. He did at our house! The miracle is to watch God's grace at work in the midst of all the chaos.*

*My kids teach the art of being with the gift of presence, the miracle of doing, and the priority of having.*

*No matter where you are, someone is better off and someone is worse off.*

*Equipment is the quintessential mixed blessing:*

*It can be social barrier which prevents the community from seeing the child/person, a management nightmare and just plain awkward while being vital to the child's participation in life. My greatest nightmare is that Eric and Mark will learn the low expectation of observing life instead of participating in it.[2]*

---

[2]Reprinted by permission from Bruce and Kelly Stahlman (2002, 2006).

## 1 Out of 110: A Father's Perspective

Armando is a father of three with his middle child diagnosed with autism. Here he shares his experience as a father of a child with autism.

My Rodrigo is a 7-year-old diagnosed with autism and sensory processing dysfunction. At 11 months Rodrigo stopped eating solid foods, cried constantly, and played with his toys differently than other children such as lining up toys and fixation with items other than toys such as leafs. My wife and I were given a packet of resources and were told to go and find help but we did not know where to begin. Although Rodrigo has gone through speech, occupational, and applied behavior analysis therapy, it is what I do with him that I can see making a difference for him. To have a child with a disability is to know him as my boy. When I say my boy it means a love from my heart. My Rodrigo is the son I have always wanted, and his disability is to overcome what the world has put in front of him, and my job is to not allow for anyone's prejudice, skewed ideas, ignorance, limits, and their own life, keep my boy from reaching his own potential. He is my inspiration to become the best father, role model, friend, teacher, coach, and a shelter when he is tired and wants to be next to his dad. I am proud of him and want him to always know that wherever we go he will always be with us. No matter what the future brings Rodrigo will always be my boy and I want to be in his world and make the world a better place for him and others.

Armando Cortez
San Antonio, Texas
November 1, 2010

Rodrigo's father shared that his son is in second grade in an autistic unit because he is able to learn his academic content more effectively in a setting with fewer children and with a teacher who has special education certification. He is able to go to inclusion twice a day every day—once during physical education for motor development and socialization and once in the general second-grade classroom for science and social studies. His father explains that the special education teachers as well as the inclusion teachers want to do more for him because he is a "smart boy."

## :: CONCERNS FOR THOSE WHO WORK WITH CHILDREN WITH DISABILITIES

### Burnout

*Burnout* is a term applied to the loss of concern and emotional feeling for people you work with or live with (Maslach, 1982). Both teachers and parents experience burnout. It is felt most when what you are trying to do seems unproductive or when you think you have few alternatives that would change or improve the course of events. This frustration can lead to a feeling of being trapped. It can happen to any teacher and any parent. The obligations of teaching and parenting are similar. Both are in an authoritarian role and are responsible for setting up the child's program. Balancing the student's needs with time constraints, the mechanical constraints of running a classroom or a home, and the constraints of the personal needs of the authoritarian figure is a role for a magician. Indeed when parents and teachers are successful, the result does seem to be magical. Both teacher and parent know, however, that their success was produced by hard work, good planning, cooperation, and perseverance.

Those who set high standards and aim for perfection are more likely to experience burnout, as are

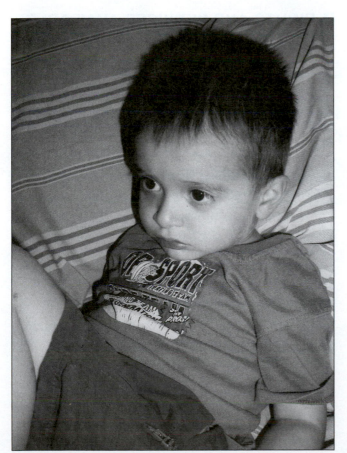

Parents are the best advocates for children with autism.

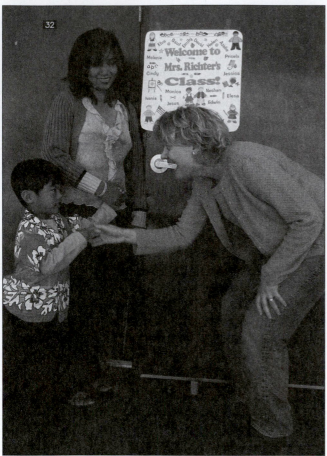

Working with children of special needs requires teachers to maintain a positive attitude.

those who feel a need to be in control. Feelings of anger, guilt, depression, self-doubt, and irritability are symptoms of burnout. When these occur, take a hard look at what is really going on and what needs to be going on. Are you neglecting yourself? Are the things you want to do essential? Do some things need to be changed? Learn to accept the fact that change can occur. Be willing to give yourself and others credit where credit is due. Build in rewards so that you and others feel good about what you are doing. Always have some goals that are short term and accessible. Nothing feels better than success. This is one of the best methods to combat burnout. Remember, burnout is reversible.

## Depression and Suicide

People who parent or work with exceptional children need to know that these children are in a high-risk group for depression and suicide. Children

with learning disabilities are particularly at risk because of the frustration they often encounter in trying to learn. Children with giftedness are also at risk because they often find it difficult to feel comfortable in the school and home environment.

Parents and teachers must recognize the child's symptoms of depression and impending suicide and be willing to take appropriate action. Generally, the child will be depressed or irritable, lacking enjoyment in usually pleasurable activities. Changes in weight, appetite, or eating habits may be signals. Sleeplessness, hyperactivity, loss of energy, and/or fatigue are also signals that something is wrong. Loss of self-esteem and feelings of inadequacy or decreased ability to concentrate should alert teachers and parents to a very real need for help. Thoughts of death or suicide should not be taken lightly. Recognize these as very serious symptoms and get professional help. Mental-health centers and public schools have programs for crisis intervention and can give guidance and help in a time of need.

## :: RIGHTS AND SERVICES AVAILABLE TO PARENTS

Many parents of children with exceptionalities are unaware of the rights they have and the services available to them. The Buckley Amendment, described here, is a right for all parents, but it is especially important for parents who have children with disabilities.

### Family Educational Rights and Privacy Act (FERPA)—The Buckley Amendment

The Buckley Amendment, written for all citizens, greatly affected record keeping for people with disabilities. Please refer to Chapter 12 for a description of FERPA.

### How to File a Complaint of Discrimination

Filing a complaint of discrimination for children with disabilities can help advocate for those who need it the most. If parents and friends of the disabled do not stand up for these rights, they will be lost. Whenever discrimination occurs, it hurts not just the people involved but our nation as well. Complaints should be directed first to the person in charge. If a satisfactory conclusion is not reached, take the complaint to the next higher level of responsibility. Follow the chain of command. If this is not satisfactory, contact the regional Office of Civil Rights (OCR) for your area. The following items are important to include in a complaint:

- Your name and address (a telephone number where you can be reached during business hours is helpful but not required).
- A general description of the person or class of people injured by the alleged act or acts (names are not required).
- The name and location of the institution that allegedly committed the discriminatory act or acts.
- A description of the alleged discriminatory act(s) in sufficient detail to enable OCR to understand what occurred, when it occurred, and the basis for the alleged discrimination—race, color, national origin, sex, disability, age, or the Boy Scouts of America Equal Access Act—(Office for Civil Rights, 2007).

Each state has Parent Training and Information Centers that provide training and information to parents of children with disabilities. A directory is listed on *Exceptional Parent Magazine's* Web site, *www.eparent.com*.

## :: WORKING WITH CULTURALLY AND LINGUISTICALLY DIVERSE FAMILIES OF CHILDREN WITH DISABILITIES

Culturally and linguistically diverse children, particularly those of African American, Latino, and Native America descent, are often overrepresented in special education classrooms and are underrepresented in gifted-and-talented programs (Cartledge, Gardener, & Ford, 2009). For many culturally and linguistically diverse (CLD) families, the school system is very overwhelming, as many have had negative experiences or are not familiar with the system (Harry, 2008). When a child with special needs is involved, the situation very often becomes more distressing because not only are parents learning to help their child but they are learning to accept the child's disability.

Teachers complain that CLD parents are not involved in their child's education, but very often parents feel disrespected and belittled in the meetings that they attend (Lo, 2008). This results in outcomes that do not consider the cultural values of the family (Sheehy, Ornelles, & Noonan, 2009); thus, children

suffer cultural and language loss. Cultural reciprocity allows for educators and parents to share information about cultural values and beliefs to promote effective communication and collaboration (Sheehy et al., 2009). Becoming linguistically competent for teachers helps increase communication and break down cultural barriers (Columna, Senne, & Lytle, 2009).

Culturally relevant pedagogy helps teachers include culturally and linguistically diverse parents in the educational decisions that affect their child. A teacher must gain a family's trust in order to successfully work with their child (Pewewardy & Fitzpatrick, 2009). The following list includes issues faced by CLD families in schools (Cartledge et al., 2009, pp. 136–139) and suggestions for teachers:

*Perceptions*—Very often families face negative perceptions from teachers and administrators. SUGGESTION—Discover the family's funds of knowledge by getting to know the family and the child. Avoid making judgments about the family and focus on the child's needs.

*Trust*—Parents do not trust educators, and educators feel that parents are not involved enough because they don't care. SUGGESTION—Create an ecology of trust by inviting parents to visit their child's classroom often. Allow them to stay and observe the different techniques that you use as a teacher so that they can use them at home. Make them feel welcome.

*Adaptation to the child's special needs*—CLD families appear to have less of a "grief cycle"—they seem to be more resilient in accepting their child's disability. SUGGESTION—form a parent support group in which parents can talk with one another. Let parents guide the meeting and learn to listen.

*Goals for their child*—Every family has different goals for their children. SUGGESTION—Respect parents' wishes and work with them to help the child be successful in your classroom without infringing in the parents' cultural beliefs.

*Parenting issues*—Usually referred to as *parenting styles*, many CLD families' approaches differ from families with a European background. SUGGESTION—Be understanding of the different parenting styles. Learn from the parent the type of values they have and see how those affect the child.

*Economic issues*—Because a large number of CLD families are poor, they have to work hard to provide for their children, and that means that many must find support systems, such as caregivers. Very often grandparents and other extended family members help to take care of the child while the parents work. SUGGESTION—Provide parents with a list of resources that they can use. This list can be derived from the United Way directory or from the school district.

*Cultural discontinuities*—CLD parents need to communicate with teachers and other professionals that work with their child, particularly in their native language. Parents want professionals to value and respect their culture including their language and not to have deficit views. SUGGESTION—Develop respect for families' funds of knowledge and cultural traditions by discovering reasons why families practice what they do. Dismiss deficit thinking. Find qualified translators (rather than the children) for parent conferences, particularly for Admission, Review, and Dismissal (ARD) meetings.

## SUMMARY

Parents, teachers, and other professionals are effective forces in influencing the life of the exceptional child. It is important that all be able and willing to work together for the benefit of the child with disabilities. Special educational terms, once crude, have been replaced with more inclusive educational terms.

During the 20th century, the special education movement grew, and in 1971, the Pennsylvania Association for Retarded Children (PARC) won a court case against the Commonwealth of Pennsylvania, affirming the right of all children to a free and appropriate education. This included children with disabilities. The Vocational Rehabilitation Act of 1973, the Education of All Handicapped Children Act of 1975 (P.L. 94-142), the Education of the Handicapped Act Amendments of 1983 (P.L. 98-199), Americans with Disabilities Act, Individuals with Disabilities Education Act, and IDEA 97 are some of the far-reaching laws passed in the last quarter of the century.

From the Education of All Handicapped Children Act of 1975 to IDEA 97 (P.L. 105-17) and IDEA 04 reauthorization, the Individualized Education Program (IEP) and the Individualized Family Service Program (IFSP) have been instrumental in addressing the needs of children with disabilities. They are plans developed by the parents, the child, teachers (special and regular), administrators, psychologists, and any others involved with the child's education. The plans ensure a continuum of services appropriate to age, maturity, handicapping condition, achievements, and parental expectations. The child or student with a disability includes those with autism, deafness, deafness–blindness, hearing impairments, intellectual disabilities, multiple disabilities, orthopedic impairments, other health impairments (including ADD and AD/HD), emotional disturbances, learning disabilities, speech or language impairments, traumatic brain injury, and visual impairments. For children 3 to 9 years old, developmental delays are also used for placement. IDEA 97 and 04 also provide for due process—the right to a hearing—if parents disagree with the educational placement.

Parents have been effective forces in securing this legislation. Parents should and do have an important role in the life and education of their exceptional children. The parent's role begins as one of nurturing in the home but can become an effective force in the school as the parent supports the teacher at home as a tutor or at school as a volunteer. Value parents' funds of knowledge to help in the development of their child with special needs.

## SUGGESTED CLASS ACTIVITIES AND DISCUSSIONS

1. Write a brief review of the development of special education.
2. Describe in your own words what *least restrictive* means.
3. List and describe briefly the 13 categories of exceptional students.
4. A *staffing* refers to the meeting that takes place when an exceptional student's IEP is developed or changed. Who is included on the IEP team? What are their responsibilities?
5. *Mainstreaming* and *inclusion* are terms used quite frequently. Read carefully about them and write in your own words what you think they mean.
6. List ways that the general classroom can adapt to and support a child with a disability.
7. Study the legislation that has developed for children with disabilities. How has it progressed? List changes.

8. Choose one of the problems a parent of an exceptional child may encounter and describe how you as a professional would try to help that parent. Examples may include a parent who is an English language learner or one who has a disability well.

## USEFUL WEB SITES

### Autism Speaks
www.autismspeaks.org
This organization is dedicated to increasing awareness of autism spectrum disorders.

### Council for Exceptional Children
www.cec.sped.org/
Provides updates on legislation related to children with special needs and their families, resource information related to specific disabilities, and links to organizations serving children with special needs and their families.

### Individuals with Disabilities Education Act (IDEA 2004)
http://idea.ed.gov/
This Web site contains information about the law that ensures services for individuals with disabilities.

### Morgan's Wonderland
www.morganswonderland.com
Located in San Antonio, Texas, it is the world's first ultra accessible family fun park designed specifically for children and adults with special needs and their family members.

### National Association for Parents with Children in Special Education
www.napcse.org/

This site provides resources to help ensure that children receive special education services in and out of school.

### National Council on Disabilities
www.ncd.gov/
The council is an independent federal agency that makes recommendations to the President. The council Web site provides resource information and links to agencies and programs, including contact information for legislators and state vocational and rehabilitation agencies.

### National Dissemination Center for Children with Disabilities (NICHCY)
www.nichcy.org/
Provides resource information of agencies serving children with disabilities, including phone numbers, addresses, and e-mail addresses. Links are provided to information regarding specific disabilities.

### Special Quest
www.specialquest.org/
Provides information related to infants and toddlers with special needs, especially those being served by early-intervention programs and Early Head Start. Resources and links for families and providers are also provided.

### U.S. Department of Health and Human Services
www.hhs.gov/autism/
Provides different resources for parents, educators, and other professionals regarding autism.

### Wrightslaw Special Education Law and Advocacy
www.wrightslaw.com
The leading Web site about special education law and advocacy.

# CHAPTER 11

# The Abused Child

*Then there is the pain. A breaking and entering when even the senses are torn apart. The act of rape on an eight-year-old body is the matter of the needle giving because the camel can't. The child gives, because the body can, and the violator cannot.*

Angelou (2002, p. 76)

John Lennon's song "Imagine" talks about living life in peace. Living in peace is something we all want, not only those unfortunate to be going through wars. Many children face a war of abuse and the offenders are usually those who they trust and love. Over the years we have heard about mothers drowning their children while battling depression, other parents who are under the influence of drugs killing their infant children, and other offenders, including educators and members of the clergy, who take advantage of their role and treat children in the most horrendous manner. Imagine if we, as educators and parents, would advocate for those children who are suffering from child abuse and neglect.

## ∷ DEFINING CHILD ABUSE

What is child abuse? According to the Child Abuse Prevention and Treatment Act of 1974, or P.L. 93-247 (1977), it is "The physical or mental injury, sexual abuse, negligent treatment or maltreatment of a child under the age of 18 by a person who is responsible for the child's welfare under circumstances which indicate that the child's health or welfare is harmed or threatened thereby" (p. 1826). The Centers for Disease Control and Prevention (2011) define child maltreatment as "any acts or series of acts of commission or omission by a parent or other caregiver (e.g., clergy, coach, teacher) that results in harm, potential for harm, or threat of harm to a child."

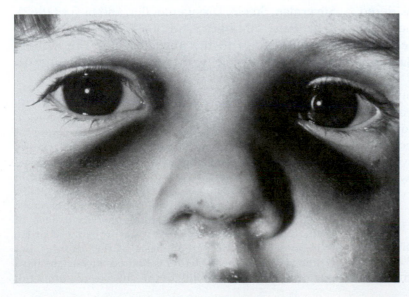

It is difficult to understand this kind of physical abuse against children.

It is estimated that approximately 300 million children around the world are subject to many types of abuse and maltreatment. UNICEF works diligently to eradicate violence and abuse from the lives of children around the world (UNICEF, 2011). It is the responsibility of parents and other caregivers to protect children from abuse, neglect, maltreatment, and oppression. Failure to do so results in a society without compassion, morals, or ethical standards. A family's funds of knowledge can help prevent child abuse and neglect.

## :: BACKGROUND

For centuries child abuse and neglect have been prevalent in many societies. In fact, child abuse used to be considered quite normal (deMause, 1988). The child was considered property of the father to be worked, sold, loved, or killed as the father willed. In the 1500s, a case of child abuse was reported when authorities began to be suspicious of two parents who claimed that their son was a "monster," taking him from town to town and making considerable amounts of money. The parents were found guilty and were put to death for the atrocity that they had committed with their son (Kompanje, 2007). In the 1800s it was common for children to work 12 hours a day under the threat of beatings. They were cheap and useful laborers. Children "continued to be the property of their parents who could choose to beat them, neglect them, or send them out to work" (Crosson-Tower, 2002, p. 4). Actions that would be called child abuse today were overlooked or considered to be the parent's right to discipline. The child had no rights (Crosson-Tower, 2002; Gelles & Lancaster, 1987; Helfer & Kempe, 1987; Jalongo, 2006; Nagi, 1977).

It was not until 1874, in New York City, that the first case of abuse was reported. It involved a 9-year-old girl, Mary Ellen, who was beaten daily by her parents and was severely undernourished when found by church workers. Because there were no agencies to deal with child abuse, the workers turned to the American Society for the Prevention of Cruelty to Animals.

One year later the New York Society for the Prevention of Cruelty to Children was organized (Fontana & Besharov, 1979; Lazoritz, 1990). The Children's Division of what is now the American Humane Association began addressing the issues in 1878 (American Humane Association, 1998). There were other early indications of growing concern for children. National groups such as the Child Study Association of America and the National Congress of Parents and Teachers were formed. Mounting concern over working conditions and care of children culminated in 1909 in the first White House Conference on Children, which resulted in the 1912 legislation establishing the Children's Bureau.

What happened between 1913 and recent decades to focus attention on the child at risk? Dr. John Caffey, a radiologist, began collecting data that indicated child abuse in the early 1920s, but he was not supported in his beliefs by his associates. Thus, it was not until after World War II that he published the first of several studies relating to fractures in young children (American Humane Association, 1978; Elmer, 1982). Caffey's first medical paper, written in 1946, reported the histories of six traumatized infants and questioned the cause of their injuries. In it he reported that fractures of the long bones and subdural hematomas occurring concurrently were not caused by disease.

Dr. Frederick Silverman, who had been a student of Caffey's, followed in 1953 with an article that indicated that skeletal trauma in infants could be the result of abuse (American Humane Association, 1978; Elmer, 1982). Reports began appearing more frequently (Altman & Smith, 1960; Bakwin, 1956; Fisher, 1958; Silver & Kempe, 1959; Woolley & Evans, 1955), but it was an article by Kempe, Silverman, Steele, Droegemueller, and Silver (1962), "The Battered-Child Syndrome," that brought national attention to the abused child. The authors began their article with the following charge to physicians:

> The battered-child syndrome, a clinical condition in young children who have received serious physical abuse, is a frequent cause of permanent injury or death. The syndrome should be considered in any child exhibiting evidence of fracture of any bone, subdural hematoma, failure to thrive, soft tissue swellings or skin bruising, in any child who dies suddenly, or where the degree and type of injury is at variance with the history given regarding the occurrence of the trauma. Psychiatric factors are probably of prime importance in the pathogenesis of the disorder, but knowledge of these factors is limited. Physicians have a duty and responsibility to the child to require a full

evaluation of the problem and to guarantee that no expected repetition of trauma will be permitted to occur. (Kempe et al., p. 17)

The article described the status of child abuse in the nation and pointed out the effectiveness of X-ray examinations in determining abuse. The term *battered* came from the description of bruises; lacerations; bites; brain injury; deep body injury; pulled joints; burns and scalds; fractures of arms, legs, skull, and ribs; and other injuries that resulted from beating, whipping, throwing the child about, or slamming the child against something. Fontana (1973b) described battering by parents as follows:

Parents bash, lash, beat, flay, stomp, suffocate, strangle, gut-punch, choke with rags or hot pepper, poison, crack heads open, slice, rip, steam, fry, boil, dismember. They use fists, belt buckles, straps, hairbrushes, lamp cords, sticks, baseball bats, rulers, shoes and boots, lead or iron pipes, bottles, brick walls, bicycle chains, pokers, knives, scissors, chemicals, lighted cigarettes, boiling water, steaming radiators, and open gas flames. (pp. 16–17)

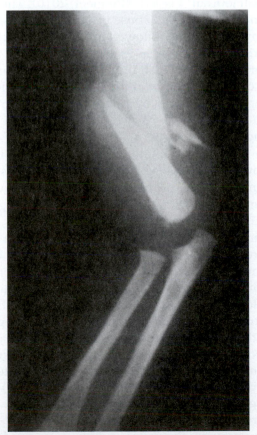

When X-rays became available, doctors began noticing recurring breaks that revealed abuse.

## National Response

The term *battered* and the picture it evoked aroused the nation. By 1967, all 50 states had legislation to facilitate the reporting of child abuse. There was, however, no provision for the coordination of procedures, nor was there a standard definition of abuse and neglect. Other conditions that precluded standardized reporting included the inconsistent ages of children covered by law, hesitation of professional and private citizens to report cases, different systems of official record keeping, and varied criteria on which to judge abuse.

## National Center on Child Abuse and Neglect

The National Center on Child Abuse and Neglect (NCCAN) was created in 1974 by P.L. 93-247. The NCCAN disseminates information through the Clearinghouse on Child Abuse and Neglect.

After the establishment of NCCAN, regional centers on child abuse were funded. Their purpose was to conduct research to determine the cause of child abuse and neglect, its identification and prevention, and the incidence of child abuse in the nation. Reporting of child abuse and neglect has been conducted by a variety of organizations. From 1973 until 1986, the American Association for Protecting Children (now the American Humane Association) supplied data on abuse and neglect. The National Committee for the Prevention of Child Abuse did a survey of the 50 states in 1991. At that time, NCCAN established the National Child Abuse and Neglect Data System (NCANDS) to be responsible for providing comprehensive data on abuse and neglect.

Reports by states have always been voluntary. Each state develops its own procedures for analyzing and reporting, but because it is important to have data that are useful throughout the United States, NCANDS provides forms for states to use. These forms ask for report source; number of investigations; number of children by disposition; victim data that includes the type of maltreatment, age, gender, and ethnicity; number of victims from each home; number of victims removed from homes; number of victims for whom court action was initiated; number of victims who died; number of victims and families who received additional services; and the relationship of the victim to the perpetrator

(U.S. Department of Health and Human Services, Children's Bureau, 1998).

## Domestic Violence

Domestic violence is considered a major health problem that affects tens of millions of families (Smith Slep & O'Leary, 2009). Very often victims of domestic violence are victims of abuse or their children are victims of abuse. A very useful online tool that helps individuals find out more information regarding domestic violence is the course on family violence found on the *childabuse.com* Web site: *www.childabuse.com/familyviolence/preventfamilyviolence.html*. This course helps professionals and others discover useful strategies to combat family violence, which leads to abuse. Another resource is the National Domestic Violence Hotline (1-800-799-SAFE or 1-800-799-7233), which provides crisis intervention to victims of domestic violence (The National Domestic Violence Hotline, 2011).

### Effects of Domestic Violence on Children.

Medically fragile infants appear to be at high risk of abuse, particularly if their family has a history of social problems including domestic violence, mental illness, or substance abuse (Fullar, 2008). Studies have shown how children are at high risk of maltreatment when parents psychologically abuse each other (Chang, Theodore, Martin, & Runyan, 2008). It is imperative, therefore, to provide resources and crisis intervention to families who are experiencing domestic violence so that children and their parents do not become yet another statistic.

## Child Abuse Around the World

Around the world many children endure all kinds of abuse including maltreatment, neglect, exploitation, physical labor, commercial sex exploitation, child wedlock, child soldiering, and child trafficking (UNICEF, 2010). Those who are the most vulnerable are very young children and children with disabilities. UNICEF reports that there is a higher incidence of mortality (80 percent) for those children who have a disability, particularly in poor countries.

It is important for all nations around the world to help fight child abuse because its existence ails society and its citizens. The Convention on the Rights of the Child created by UNICEF and adopted by the United Nations General Assembly appears to be the only international human rights treaty that has almost universal ratification, except in Somalia and the United States, which appear to be working toward formally approving it (Svevo-Cianci & Lee, 2010). Difficulty arises when some cultural practices are abusive and lead to neglect of children. This can be considered the "dark side of culture," and unfortunately, it is present in all cultures in all countries. The voice of children in this case should be heard rather than keeping traditions that hurt them. The journal *Child Abuse and Neglect* provides an international and multidisciplinary perspective on child abuse and neglect.

There are many articles that describe different instances of child abuse and neglect in other countries, and many times measures are taken by different entities to help stop child abuse and neglect. For example, in Saudi Arabia, it was not until 1990 that the first case of child abuse was reported in a medical journal (Eissa & Almuneef, 2010). The most common type of child abuse in Saudi Arabia is listed as physical abuse followed by neglect, with the majority of the children abused being males about 5 years of age. In Australia, it is estimated that the most common form of abuse is emotional followed by neglect (Goebbels, Nicholson, Walsh, & DeVries, 2008). For many Gypsy children in Albania, trafficking appears to be a major incidence of child abuse since it is connected to contextual issues of poverty, internal and external migrations, discrimination, and problems with the legal system (Gjermeni, VanHook, Gjipali, Xhillari, Lungu, & Hazizi, 2008).

Similarly, children who live in the streets in India endure all kinds of abuse, with young males being reported being abused more than young females (Mathur, Rathore, & Mathur, 2009). Other children who look for a better place to live outside of their country end up being abused by the caregivers who they begin to trust, as shown in an example of sexual maltreatment of unaccompanied asylum-seeking minors from the Horn of Africa to the United Kingdom (Lay & Papadopoulos, 2009).

Neglect and corporal punishment are two issues related to abuse that seem to be prevalent in many countries. For instance, in a study conducted in Botswana, Mexico, and Vietnam, it was found that parents leave their children home alone many times not by choice but out of necessity (Ruiz-Casares & Heymann, 2009). Many countries, including Mauritania, Kenya, Barbados, Thailand, and Tanzania (among others), are seeking to change attitudes and implement positive discipline rather than corporal punishment (UNICEF, 2010).

The examples provided here represent a small fraction of the global epidemic of child abuse. There are many organizations that are working closely with many governments to stop child abuse.

## Who Are the Victims?

Child abuse strikes children at all ages, but those who are the youngest seem to be the most at risk. Childhelp indicates that 5.8 million children were involved in 3.2 million child abuse reports and allegations (Childhelp, 2011). It is estimated that child abuse is reported every 10 seconds. Neglect is the most frequent type of abuse followed by physical abuse. In 2007, the National Child Abuse and Neglect Data System (NCANDS) reported an estimated 1,760 child deaths due to abuse (Child Welfare Information Gateway, 2010). Figure 11–1 shows the maltreatment types of victims, and Figure 11–2 shows the maltreatment types of child fatalities for 2008.

It is also important to recognize that although some children overcome barriers related to child abuse and neglect, the majority suffer many consequences through adulthood (Zielinski, 2009). Support systems such as the extended family must be agents of change and help when their members are involved in the cycle of child abuse.

## Who Are the Abusers?

In most of the reports from NCANDS, over 80 percent of abusers are the victim's parents. Harsh discipline seems to be prevalent in abusive parents (Belsky, Conger, & Capaldi, 2009), particularly those with substance abuse problems (Baily, Hill, Oesterle, & Hawkins, 2009). Perpetrators of maltreatment are defined by most states as parents and other caregivers including other relatives, foster parents, and babysitters. Figure 11–3 indicates that 81.2 percent of the perpetrators are parents, a statistic that also shows the effect of domestic violence. If children see and live violence, more than likely they will become victims of violence.

**FIGURE 11–1**
Maltreatment types of victims, 2008.

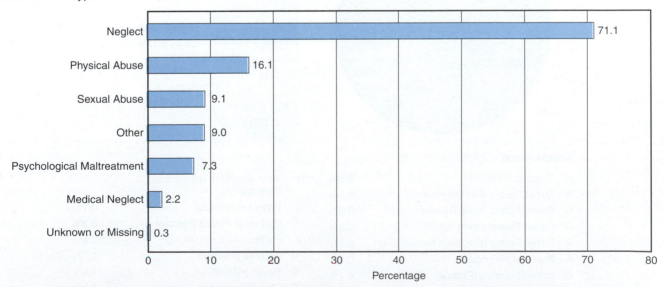

*Source:* From *Child Maltreatment 2008,* by the U.S. Department of Health and Human Services, Administration for Children and Families, Children's Bureau, 2010. Retrieved from www.acf.hhs.gov/programs/cb/stats_research/index.htm#can.

## FIGURE 11–2
Maltreatment types of child fatalities, 2008.

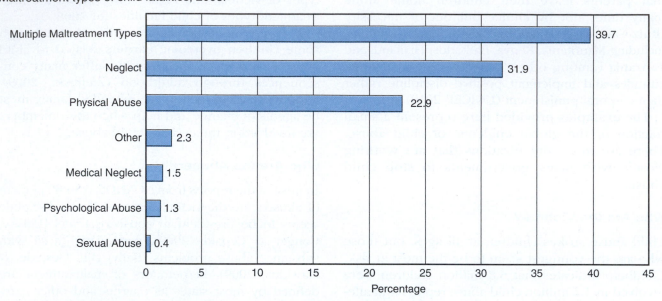

*Source:* From *Child Maltreatment 2008,* by the U.S. Department of Health and Human Services, Administration for Children and Families, Children's Bureau, 2010. Retrieved from www.acf.hhs.gov/programs/cb/stats_research/index.htm#can.

## FIGURE 11–3
Victims by perpetrator relationship, 2008.

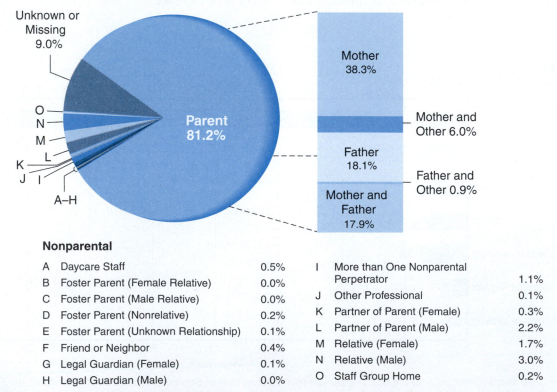

### Nonparental

| | | | | | |
|---|---|---|---|---|---|
| A | Daycare Staff | 0.5% | I | More than One Nonparental Perpetrator | 1.1% |
| B | Foster Parent (Female Relative) | 0.0% | J | Other Professional | 0.1% |
| C | Foster Parent (Male Relative) | 0.0% | K | Partner of Parent (Female) | 0.3% |
| D | Foster Parent (Nonrelative) | 0.2% | L | Partner of Parent (Male) | 2.2% |
| E | Foster Parent (Unknown Relationship) | 0.1% | M | Relative (Female) | 1.7% |
| F | Friend or Neighbor | 0.4% | N | Relative (Male) | 3.0% |
| G | Legal Guardian (Female) | 0.1% | O | Staff Group Home | 0.2% |
| H | Legal Guardian (Male) | 0.0% | | | |

*Source:* From *Child Maltreatment 2008,* by the U.S. Department of Health and Human Services, Administration for Children and Families, Children's Bureau, 2010. Retrieved from www.acf.hhs.gov/programs/cb/stats_research/index.htm#can.

## :: CHILD ABUSE CATEGORIES

### Neglect

Child neglect occurs when there is failure to care for the child's basic needs. Physical neglect is the area most frequently identified, but there are also educational and emotional neglect. Neglect may also include medical neglect, abandonment, or not allowing a runaway to return home. The parents are not always indifferent. Instead, they may not recognize the importance of medical care or a developmental environment, or they may be incapable of furnishing them. For example, young children under the age of 3 who have been severely neglected may have serious language delays because of the lack of interaction in the environment (Sylvestre & Mérette, 2010).

**Physical neglect** refers to the parents' failure to provide the necessities—adequate shelter, care and supervision, food, clothing, and protection. Physical neglect is the most common type of child abuse, accounting for more than half of maltreatment. The child shows signs of malnutrition, usually is irritable, and may need medical attention. The child often goes hungry and lacks supervision after school. The parents are either unable or unwilling to give proper care. In this type of neglect, parents can also refuse to provide the basic necessities (American Humane Association, 2011).

**Educational neglect** occurs when parents permit chronic truancy, fail to make sure their child attends school, or fail to tend to any special educational needs of the child. Both physical neglect and educational neglect result in the child's inability to develop fully.

**Emotional neglect** includes refusal to provide psychological help if the child needs it, exposure of the child to abuse of someone else (e.g., spousal abuse in the child's presence), and permission for use of drugs and alcohol by the child (U.S. Department of Health and Human Services, 1992).

Parents may be psychologically unavailable to the child, ignoring their child's need for comfort. This results in some children failing to thrive. The child does not continue to grow or develop at a rate expected for their age (Brier, Berliner, Bulkley, Jenny, & Reid, 1996).

### Physical Abuse

The **physically abused** child shows signs of injury—welts, cuts, bruises, burns, or fractures. Educators should be aware of repeated injuries, untreated injuries, multiple injuries, and new injuries added to old. Multiple maltreatment often occurs in a child who suffers abuse or neglect. Although emotional maltreatment can be isolated, instances of physical abuse or neglect usually are accompanied by emotional abuse.

**Recognizing Physical Abuse.** Although many bruises and abrasions are accidental, others give cause for the teacher to believe that they were intentionally inflicted. Bruises are the most common symptoms of physical abuse. Other signs include welts, lumps, or ridges on the body, usually caused by a blow; burns, shown by redness, blistering, or peeling of the skin; fractured bones; scars; lacerations or torn cuts; and abrasions.

Head Start personnel are given guidelines with four criteria for identifying abuse of the preschool child. These guidelines are useful for detection of abuse in children of any age. The first is location of the injury. As illustrated in Figure 11–4, bruises on the knees, elbows, shins, and—for the preschool child—the forehead are considered normal in most circumstances. If bruises are "found on the back, genital area, thighs, buttocks, face or back of legs, one should be suspicious" (U.S. Department of Health, Education and Welfare, 1977, p. 67).

The second criterion is evidence of repetition of injury. A significantly large number of bruises or cuts and injuries in various stages of healing should be suspect. There are instances, however, when repetition could be accidental: The child could be accident prone, so the correlation between the injury and an explanation of its cause—the fourth criterion, described later—needs to be kept in mind.

The third criterion is the injury. If it is obvious that the bruise, cut, or burn was inflicted by an object, such as a belt, stick, or cigarette, the caregiver or teacher should suspect abuse. It is also important to work with a child protection team to confirm the severity of the injury, which many times goes untreated (Lane, Dubowitz, & Langenberg, 2009).

The fourth criterion is the correlation between the injury and the explanation given by the child or the parent. The accident as described should be likely to produce the resultant injury. For example, could round burns shaped like the end of a cigarette be caused by the child playing too near the stove?

**FIGURE 11–4**
Comparison of typical and suspicious bruising areas.

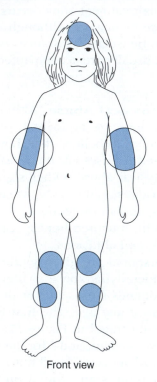
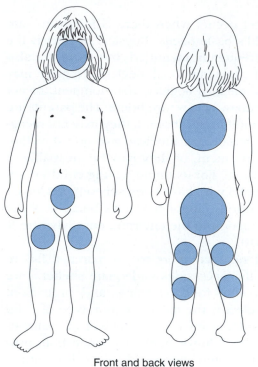

Front view                                                      Front and back views

Normal bruising areas                                          Suspicious bruising areas

*Note:* The bruises children receive in play are depicted on the left. The bruises on the right would not normally happen in everyday play.

*Source:* From *Child Abuse and Neglect: A Self-Instructional Text for Head Start Personnel,* by U.S. Department of Health, Education and Welfare, Head Start Bureau and Children's Bureau, 1977, Washington, DC: U.S. Government Printing Office.

Parents who were victims of maltreatment as children are more likely to resort to abuse when confronted with other risk factors (Horton & Cruise, 2001). In ascertaining the extent of suspected physical abuse, the teacher should not remove any of the child's clothing. That should be done only by such personnel as a nurse or doctor who would undress a child as part of their professional responsibilities.

After reviewing the four criteria and checking school policy—the suspicious placement of injury, the severity and repetition of injuries, evidence of infliction by an object, and inconsistent explanation (or consistent if the child reports the abuse)—the educator must report a suspected injury to the appropriate authorities.

**Shaken Baby Syndrome.** Parent educators and teachers should discuss shaken baby syndrome with parents and those who care for infants, because violent shaking is extremely dangerous for infants and young children. Children under 2 have undeveloped neck muscles, and sudden motion can result in the brain pulling away and tearing blood vessels and brain cells. The force with which an angry person might shake a child is five to 10 times greater than if the child had simply fallen (American Humane Association, 2001). Even pushing a young child on a swing is cause for concern. Is the baby able to hold its head upright? Is the head bobbing back and forth? If it is, the jarring of the brain might cause injury. Tossing a baby in the air results in jarring and should be avoided. It is estimated that about 300 babies die each year due to this syndrome (National Center on Shaken Baby Syndrome, 2011).

Shaken baby syndrome appeared in medical literature about 1972 and has since been recognized as a cause of injury or death for young children. In the United States every year, 1,200 to 1,400 children are shaken, and 25 percent to 30 percent die as a

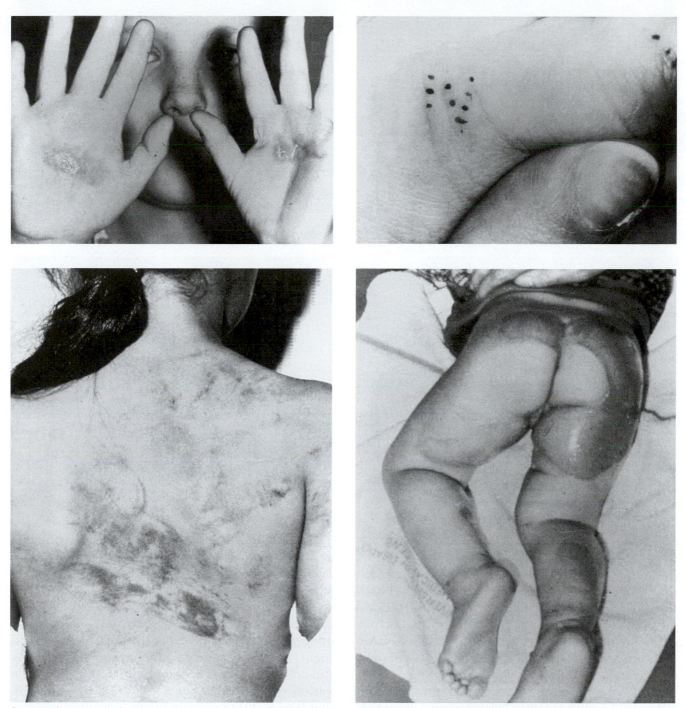

Cigarette burns on the hands or body, puncture wounds, scald marks, and bruises are recognizable signs of physical abuse.

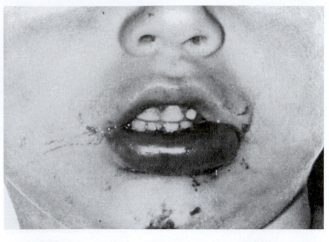

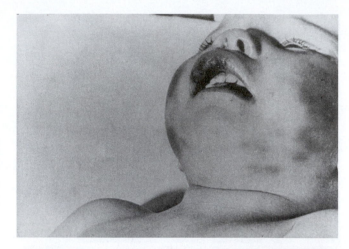

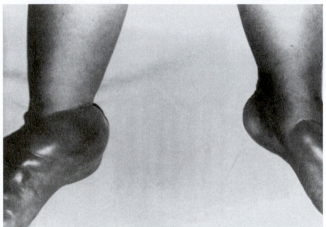

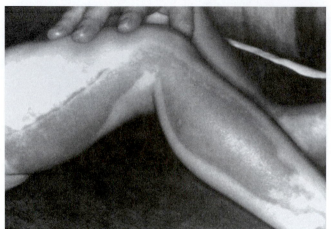

Scalded and battered, these children were victims of child abuse.

result (National Center on Shaken Baby Syndrome, 2006). Shaking can cause subdural hemorrhage, brain swelling, and damage that may also result in developmental delays, intellectual disability, blindness, paralysis, or hearing loss (American Humane Association, 2001).

Shaking usually occurs when a frustrated caregiver loses control with a crying child. Parents and caregivers need to know that it is all right for a baby to cry if the caregiver checks and knows that all the child's needs are met. It is also very important to acknowledge that some children cry more than others, particularly newborns between 1 month and 4 months of age (Barr, Rivara, Barr, Cummings, Taylor, Lengua, & Benitz, 2009). When this is the case, respite needs to be given to caregivers so they can maintain control of their own emotions. Three states (Texas, New York, and Utah) have legislation regarding the prevention of shaken baby syndrome.

Training regarding the dangers of shaking infants and young children is mandatory for caregivers to maintain their license (National Center on Shaken Baby Syndrome, 2006).

The Period of PURPLE Crying is a prevention program that includes an 11-page booklet and 10-minute DVD to be given to new parents. The focus is to help parents understand the reasons for an infant's cry. It is culturally sensitive to a variety of groups (National Center on Shaken Baby Syndrome, 2011).

## Emotional Abuse

Compared to physical neglect and abuse, it is more difficult to identify **emotional neglect and abuse**, defined as a "pattern of behavior that can seriously interfere with a child's positive emotional development" (American Humane Association, 1992c).

Parents of emotionally abused children are usually overly harsh and critical. They withhold love and acceptance and do not give the child either physical or verbal encouragement and praise. Although they expect performance, they do not support the child's endeavors. While physical abuse damages a child's body, emotional abuse damages a child's psyche: "Children who are constantly shamed, terrorized, humiliated, or rejected suffer at least as much if not more than if they had been physically assaulted" (American Humane Association, 1992b, p. 1). Patterns can include the following:

- Terrorizing.
- Continued rejection of the child.
- Refusal to provide needed nurturance.
- Refusal to provide help for a child's psychological problems.
- Lack of needed mental or physical stimulation.
- Forced involvement with drugs, criminal activities, and other corruptive forces.

Children who are not nurtured and who live in an emotionally insecure environment may show signs of low self-esteem, slow educational growth, and insecurity (Dowling, 2010). Egeland (1988) reported on the Minnesota Mother–Child Project, a longitudinal study that worked with at-risk children and their families. In the 267 families, 44 children were identified as maltreated during their first 2 years of life. The researchers assessed four maltreatment groups: physical abuse, neglect, verbal rejections, and psychological unavailability at 12, 18, 24, 41, and 54 months. The infancy period was examined in relation to attachment, the "relationship that the infant develops a sense of trust and confidence" (p. D-12). The children were followed through the periods until they were in school. At each level it was apparent that psychological unavailability affects the child's development, self-esteem, and confidence. The children who were neglected (psychological unavailability) displayed greater problems in attention. They were

> uninvolved, reliant, lacking creative initiative, and having much more difficulty comprehending the day-to-day schoolwork than children in the control group. They were impatient, disrespectful, expressed anxiety about their schoolwork and were more likely to make irrelevant response in the classroom. . . . On the individual scales, the neglected children were rated as anxious, withdrawn, unpopular, aggressive, and obsessive-compulsive. Not

> only did they present far more problems than children in the control group, but they also presented more problems than children in the physical abuse group. (Egeland, 1988, p. D-15)

The difficulty of identifying psychological unavailability and emotional neglect makes it doubly difficult for the schools to respond to the concern. It also is impossible for teachers to overcome a student's childhood devoid of emotional security. However, there are incidents and examples of teachers who have had a positive effect on children who were emotionally neglected:

> I don't think my fourth-grade teacher, Mr. Evans, had any idea what an impact he had on my life. He was my father's opposite and taught me much about how men could be. He was consistent and concerned while my father was drunk or ignoring me. He praised me while my father criticized. He prized my mind and my accomplishments; my father cared only about abusing my body. I learned a great deal from that teacher about who I was and that I was an important person. I think I became a teacher myself to be like him, so that I could make a difference for some other child. (Tower, 1992, p. 57)

As shown in this example, teachers have a great deal of power over how the students in their classes feel about themselves. Children's self-confidence and self-esteem can be either enhanced or diminished. They can either feel good about themselves or view themselves as incapable, unlikable people.

## Sexual Abuse

Sexual abuse is defined under the Child Abuse Prevention and Treatment Act (CAPTA) as follows:

- The employment, use, persuasion, inducement, enticement, or coercion of any child to engage in, or assist any other person to engage in, any sexually explicit conduct or simulation of such conduct for the purpose of producing a visual depiction of such conduct.
- The rape, and in cases of caretaker or interfamilial relationships, statutory rape, molestation, prostitution, or other form of sexual exploitation of children, or incest with children. (NCCAN, 2001, p. 2)

Categories of sexual abuse include the following:

1. *Incest.* Physical sexual activity between members of the extended family.
2. *Pedophilia.* Sexual preference by an adult for prepubertal children.

3. *Exhibitionism.* Exposure of genitals to someone of the opposite gender.
4. *Molestation.* Fondling, touching, masturbation, or kissing child, especially on breast and/or genital areas.
5. *Sexual intercourse (statutory rape).* Includes penile–vaginal intercourse, fellatio (oral–genital contact), and sodomy (anal–genital contact).
6. *Rape.* Sexual intercourse or attempted sexual intercourse without consent.
7. *Sexual sadism.* Infliction of bodily harm for sexual gratification.
8. *Child pornography.* Photographs, videos, or films showing sexual acts featuring children.
9. *Child prostitution.* Children in sex acts for profit. (Kempe & Kempe, 1984)

Sexual conduct becomes abuse when activities are instigated through trickery or force with the instigator—one who has caretaking relations with the child or has age and maturational advantage over the child. The situation includes a perpetrator who has a power advantage over a child (Finkelhor, 1994; Putman, 2009) physically and mentally. Most sexual abuse is committed by someone who is close to the child, placing the child at high risk for repeat attacks.

Abuse may be categorized as contact and noncontact sexual abuse. Contact includes touching sexual parts of a child's body or having the child touch parts of the sexual partner's body, which may include penetration (into the vagina, mouth, or anus) and nonpenetration. Nonpenetration contact involves fondling, kissing, or touching sexual parts of the body by either the child or the partner.

Noncontact sexual abuse may involve exhibitionism, voyeurism, or the making of pornographic materials, and it may also include verbal harassment (Finkelhor, 1994). An estimated 300,000 children are involved in child pornography.

Sexual abuse is difficult to detect. About 80 percent of the offenders are known to the family or are family members. The victims are most often girls (77 percent) ranging from infants to adolescents (U.S. Department of Health and Human Services, Children's Bureau, 1998).

Although historically most societies have had taboos against such behavior, sexual abuse and incest have always existed. But sexual abuse generally has been concealed, mythicized, or ignored. Not until the late 1970s and early 1980s did its existence become realistically recognized. Even then, most people gathering information on the problem believed that, as in reported incidents of other kinds of child abuse, only the tip of the iceberg had been revealed.

Incest and other sexual abuse occur in all socioeconomic groups, and, therefore, teachers in all schools or child-care settings should be aware of the indicators. Sexually abused children often exhibit some of the following physical and behavioral characteristics (Krugman, 1986; Riggs, 1982):

### Physical signs

- Bruises or bleeding in external genitalia or anal area
- Uncomfortable while sitting
- Difficulty walking
- Pregnancy
- Torn, bloody, or stained underclothing
- Sexually transmitted disease

### Behavioral signs

- Appetite disorders
- Phobias
- Guilt
- Temper tantrums
- Neurotic and conduct disorders
- Truancy
- Suicide attempts
- Confides with teacher or nurse that he or she has been sexually mistreated
- Reports by other children that their friend is being sexually mistreated
- Displays precocious sexual behavior and/or knowledge
- Unwilling to change for gym
- Withdrawn, engages in fantasy
- Depressed, sad, and teary eyed
- Confused about own identity
- Frequent absences justified by male caregiver or parent
- Acts out in a seductive manner
- Reluctant to go home
- Young child regresses to earlier behavior by thumb sucking, bed wetting, difficulty in eating, sleeping, and fear of the dark
- Older child turns to drugs, tries to run away, and has difficulty doing schoolwork

Concern about sexual abuse has steadily risen because of its deleterious effects on the child and, later, the adult. Psychological and emotional reactions are common. Children feel trapped, confused, betrayed, and disgraced. Many feel confused by the loyalty they feel toward their perpetrator and the pain he or she is causing them (Child & Adolescent Psychiatry, 2008). They may have fears, phobias, somatic complaints, mood changes, anxieties, hysterical seizures, multiple personalities, or nightmares (Rafanello, 2010). They may become prostitutes, self-mutilating, or suicidal. At school they may show developmental lags, communication problems, and apparent learning deficiencies (Finkelhor, 1986; Krugman, 1986; Ryan, 1989; Wodarski & Johnson, 1988).

Child sexual abuse has been reported up to 80,000 times a year but the majority of child sexual abuse still goes unreported (Child & Adolescent Psychiatry, 2008). Figure 11–5 provides parents with ideas for talking with children about sexual abuse and for choosing a safe preschool or child care center.

Boys and girls have similar responses to sexual abuse, both long term and short term, including fears, sleep problems, and distractedness (Finkelhor, 1990). Whereas boys may act out more aggressively, girls may act more depressed. The differences show boys are less symptomatic when evaluated by teachers and parents, but the same when evaluated by themselves.

Children who are being sexually abused often go through five phases: (a) secrecy; (b) helplessness; (c) entrapment and accommodation; (d) delayed, conflicted, and unconvincing disclosure; and (e) retraction (Summit, 1983). To understand a child's predicament, one must understand the helplessness the child feels in responding to the adult who is more physically powerful and supposedly more knowledgeable. The adult first approaches the child with the need for secrecy: "Everything will be all right if you do not tell. No one else will understand our secret." "Your mother will hate you." "If you tell, it will break up the family." "If you tell, I'll kill your pet." "If you tell, I'll spank you."

Whatever the secret, the child is in a no-win position. The child fears being hurt if he or she tells the secret. When the child does tell, the reaction is often disbelief. "Unless the victim can find some permission and power to share the secret and unless there is the possibility of an engaging, non-punitive response" the child may spend a life of "self-imposed exile from intimacy, trust and self-validation" (Summit, 1983, p. 182).

The teacher or child caregiver who suspects sexual abuse must report those suspicions—social service and child protection agencies are established in every state. In Texas, for example, the law protects children by providing a process that includes involvement of different agencies in order to keep them safe (Texas Attorney General, 2011).

The teacher's role is a supportive one. Continue to have normal expectations for the child, keep a stable environment for the child, and do not make the child feel ostracized or different. Treat the child with understanding, be sensitive to the child's needs, and help build the child's self-esteem. Several programs have been developed to help the child develop defenses against personal abuse.

Reviewers and teachers have asked for more help in responding to a child who shares about an abusive situation. An article by Austin (2000) gives suggestions to help teachers respond to a sexually abused child. The topics include the following:

- Remain calm and reassuring. Speak quietly; do not panic.
- Take the child to a private place like the nurse's office.
- Position yourself at the child's eye level.
- Speak on the child's level. Use language the child understands.
- Listen intently.
- Take the child seriously.
- Obtain only the information necessary to make a report.
- Do not put words in the child's mouth.
- Do not use words that the child has not already used. (Don't use words describing the sex that are not in the child's vocabulary.)
- Allow the child to have feelings.
- Reassure the child that the abuse is not his or her fault.
- Start your conversation with general open-ended questions and allow the child to tell the story without interrupting.
- Do not condemn the abuser.
- Let the child know that he or she is not alone and that you are willing to help.
- Do not touch the child without permission.
- Tell the truth—do not make promises you will not be able to keep.

**FIGURE 11–5**

Tips for parents for preventing sexual abuse.

*Source:* From *Child Sexual Abuse Prevention: Tips for Parents,* by U.S. Department of Health and Human Services, Administration for Children, Youth and Families, National Center on Child Abuse and Neglect, 1986, Washington, DC: U.S. Government Printing Office.

**Listen and Talk to Your Children**

Perhaps the most critical child sexual prevention strategy for parents is good communication with your children. This is not only challenging to every parent but also can be difficult, especially for working parents and parents of adolescents.

☐ Talk to your child every day and take time to really listen and observe. Learn as many details as you can about your child's activities and feelings. Encourage him or her to share concerns and problems with you.

☐ Explain to your children that their bodies belong only to them alone and that they have the right to say no to anyone who might try to touch them.

☐ Tell your child that some adults may try to hurt children and make them do things the child doesn't feel comfortable doing. Often these grownups call what they're doing a secret between themselves and the child.

☐ Explain that some adults may even threaten children by saying that their parents may be hurt or killed if the child ever shares the secret. Emphasize that an adult who does something like this is doing something that is wrong.

☐ Tell your child that adults whom they know, trust and love or someone who might be in a position of authority (like a babysitter, an uncle, a teacher or even a policeman) might try to do something like this. Try not to scare your children—emphasize that the vast majority of grownups never do this and that most adults are deeply concerned about protecting children from harm.

**Choosing a Preschool or Child Care Center**

Although the vast majority of this nation's preschools and child care centers are perfectly safe places, recent reports of child sexual abuse in these settings are a source of great concern to parents.

☐ Check to make sure that the program is reputable. State or local licensing agencies, child care information and referral services, and other child care community agencies may be helpful sources of information. Find out whether there have been any past complaints.

☐ Find out as much as you can about the teachers and caregivers. Talk with other parents who have used the program.

☐ Learn about the school or center's hiring policies and practices. Ask how the organization recruits and selects staff. Find out whether they examine references, background checks, and previous employment history before hiring decisions are made.

☐ Ask whether and how parents are involved during the day. Learn whether the center or school welcomes and supports participation. Be sensitive to the attitude and degree of openness about parental participation.

☐ Ensure that you have the right to drop in and visit the program at any time.

☐ Make sure you are informed about every planned outing. Never give the organization blanket permission to take your child off the premises.

☐ Prohibit in writing the release of your child to anyone without your explicit authorization. Make sure that the program knows who will pick up your child on any given day.

**If You Think That Your Child Has Been Abused...**

☐ Believe the child. Children rarely lie about sexual abuse.

☐ Commend the child for telling you about the experience.

- Tell the child about the process, that others will be told about the abuse.
- Thank the child for confiding in you.
- Help the child devise a safety plan if abuse occurs again. Have the child tell someone immediately—a reliable person at home or a teacher or school professional.
- Assure the child that she or he will remain with someone safe until authorities come. Do not allow the child to return to the home of the abuser.

## :: RESPONSIBILITY TO REPORT

School personnel and child-care staff members have more than a moral responsibility to report suspected abuse. Reporting abuse helps with the early detection and even prevention of abuse (Goebbels, Nicholson, Walsh, & DeVries, 2008). Laws in each state require them to report it (Horton & Cruise, 2001; U.S. Department of Health and Human Services, 2010). Some states identify categories of school personnel such as teachers, psychologists, or administrators; others have a general category of school personnel (see Figure 11–6).

Four categories of professional-mandated reporting are medical, legal, and human-service professionals, and educators (Lowenthal, 2001). No states require proof of the abuse before reporting, and the reporters must report if they have suspicions of maltreatment. Teachers, child-care professionals, and others who report in good faith are immune from legal action.

**FIGURE 11–5**
(Continued)

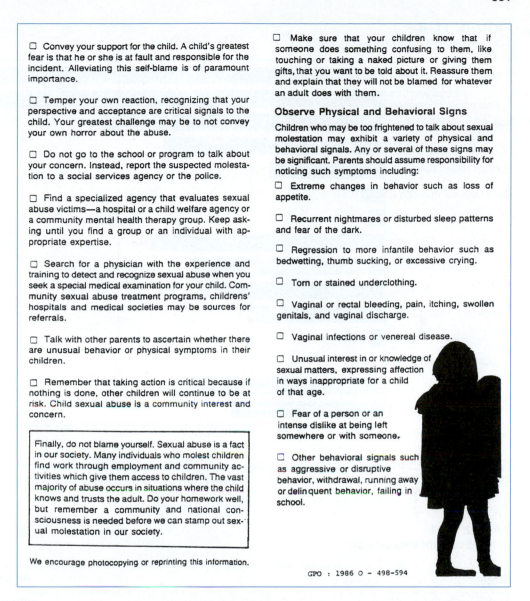

☐ Convey your support for the child. A child's greatest fear is that he or she is at fault and responsible for the incident. Alleviating this self-blame is of paramount importance.

☐ Temper your own reaction, recognizing that your perspective and acceptance are critical signals to the child. Your greatest challenge may be to not convey your own horror about the abuse.

☐ Do not go to the school or program to talk about your concern. Instead, report the suspected molestation to a social services agency or the police.

☐ Find a specialized agency that evaluates sexual abuse victims—a hospital or a child welfare agency or a community mental health therapy group. Keep asking until you find a group or an individual with appropriate expertise.

☐ Search for a physician with the experience and training to detect and recognize sexual abuse when you seek a special medical examination for your child. Community sexual abuse treatment programs, childrens' hospitals and medical societies may be sources for referrals.

☐ Talk with other parents to ascertain whether there are unusual behavior or physical symptoms in their children.

☐ Remember that taking action is critical because if nothing is done, other children will continue to be at risk. Child sexual abuse is a community interest and concern.

Finally, do not blame yourself. Sexual abuse is a fact in our society. Many individuals who molest children find work through employment and community activities which give them access to children. The vast majority of abuse occurs in situations where the child knows and trusts the adult. Do your homework well, but remember a community and national consciousness is needed before we can stamp out sexual molestation in our society.

We encourage photocopying or reprinting this information.

☐ Make sure that your children know that if someone does something confusing to them, like touching or taking a naked picture or giving them gifts, that you want to be told about it. Reassure them and explain that they will not be blamed for whatever an adult does with them.

**Observe Physical and Behavioral Signs**

Children who may be too frightened to talk about sexual molestation may exhibit a variety of physical and behavioral signals. Any or several of these signs may be significant. Parents should assume responsibility for noticing such symptoms including:

☐ Extreme changes in behavior such as loss of appetite.

☐ Recurrent nightmares or disturbed sleep patterns and fear of the dark.

☐ Regression to more infantile behavior such as bedwetting, thumb sucking, or excessive crying.

☐ Torn or stained underclothing.

☐ Vaginal or rectal bleeding, pain, itching, swollen genitals, and vaginal discharge.

☐ Vaginal infections or venereal disease.

☐ Unusual interest in or knowledge of sexual matters, expressing affection in ways inappropriate for a child of that age.

☐ Fear of a person or an intense dislike at being left somewhere or with someone.

☐ Other behavioral signals such as aggressive or disruptive behavior, withdrawal, running away or delinquent behavior, failing in school.

GPO : 1986 O - 498-594

Schools are essential agencies in the reduction of the national crisis of child abuse and neglect.

## Reporting Child Abuse and Neglect

The nonprofit organization Childhelp provides the National Child Abuse Hotline, which is dedicated to the prevention of child abuse (Childhelp, 2010). This hotline serves the United States, its territories, and Canada. It is staffed 24 hours a day seven days a week by crisis professional counselors. With the use of translators, counselors are able to provide assistance in 170 languages. The Childhelp Web site also provides information regarding how to report child abuse and what to expect after reporting. The Web site also has a link for children who are being abused so that the children can contact Childhelp directly. According to Childhelp, every year over 3 million reports of child abuse are made. There are more cases of child neglect reported than any of the other types of child abuse.

The Child Welfare Information Gateway gives information to help prevent child abuse. This organization is a service of the U.S. Department of Health and Human Services, which also provides links to the Statewide Automated Child Welfare Information System (SACWIS). Table 11.1 shows information by state agencies for reporting child abuse. The information is also provided in Spanish. When a child is in immediate danger, everyone is required to call 911.

## FIGURE 11–6

Sources of child abuse reporting, 2008.

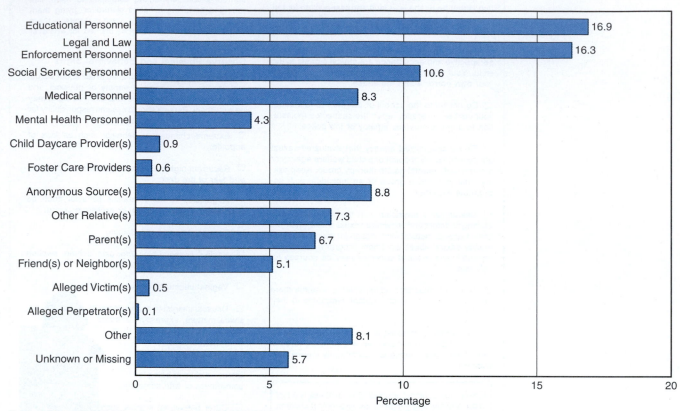

*Source:* From *Child Maltreatment 2008,* by the U.S. Department of Health and Human Services, Administration for Children and Families, Children's Bureau, 2010. Retrieved from http://www.acf.hhs.gov/programs/cb/stats_research/index.htm#can.

## TABLE 11.1

**Child abuse hotlines by state.**

| State | Agency | Phone Number |
| --- | --- | --- |
| Alabama | Alabama Child Protective Services | (334) 242-9500 |
| Alaska | State of Alaska Office of Children's Services | 1-800-478-4444 |
| Arizona | The Childhelp Children's Center of Arizona | (888) SOS-CHILD (767-2445) |
| California | California Department of Social Services | 1-800-422-4453 |
| Colorado | Colorado Department of Human Services Division of Child Welfare | (303) 866-5932 |
| Connecticut | Connecticut Department of Children and Families | (800) 842-2288 |
| Delaware | Delaware Services for Children, Youth and their Families | (800) 292-9582 |
| District of Columbia | District of Columbia Child and Family Services Agency | (202) 671-SAFE 7233 |
| Florida | Florida Department of Children and Families | (800) 96-ABUSE (962-2873) |

| State | Agency | Phone Number |
|---|---|---|
| Georgia | Georgia Department of Human Resources Division of Family & Children Services | Emergency 911 Non emergency Child Protective Services 404-651-9361 |
| Hawaii | Hawaii Child Welfare Services | (808) 832-5300 |
| Idaho | Idaho Department of Health and Welfare | (800) 926-2588 |
| Illinois | Illinois Department of Children and Family Services | Local (217) 524-2606 (800) 25-ABUSE (252-2873) |
| Indiana | Indiana Department of Child Services | (800) 800-5556 |
| Iowa | Iowa Department of Human Services | (800) 362-2178 |
| Kansas | Kansas Department of Social and Rehabilitation Services www.srs.ks.gov | (800) 922-5330 |
| Kentucky | Kentucky Cabinet for Health and Family Services www.chfs.ky.gov/dcbs/dpp/childsafety.htm | (800) 752-6200 |
| Louisiana | Office of Community Services www.dss.louisiana.gov | Contact the local Office of Community Services Parish Offices www.dss.state.la |
| Maine | Children's Services www.maine.gov/portal/family/children.htm | (800) 452-1999 24 hour hotline |
| Maryland | Department of Human Resources/ Social Services Administration www.dhr.state.md.us/cps/address.php | (410) 767-7112 Each county has different numbers to report child abuse. All counties have after hour phone services. |
| Massachusetts | Family Services www.mass.gov | Child-At-Risk Hotline 1-800-792-5200 |
| Michigan | Department of Human Services www.michigan.gov/dhs/ | 1-800-942-4357 Statewide 24/7 |
| Minnesota | Department of Human Services Contact social service agency or the police. Number for each county is located on www.minnesotahelp.info Key words "child abuse reporting" | Child Abuse hotlines provided by county |
| Mississippi | Mississippi State Department of Health | 24 hour hotline 800-222-8000 |
| New Mexico | Children, Youth and Families Department | 800-797-3260 |
| New Hampshire | Bureau of Child Protection www.dhhs.state.nh.us | 1-800-894-5533 or (603) 271-6556 Monday–Friday 8–4:30 Call 911 on weekends and holidays |

*(Continued)*

303

**TABLE 11.1**
(*Continued*)

| State | Agency | Phone Number |
|---|---|---|
| New Jersey | Department of Children and Families<br>www.state.nj.us/dcf/abuse/how/ | 1-877- NJ -ABUSE<br>(1-877-652-2873) |
| New York | Office of Children and Family Services<br>www.ocfs.state.ny.us/main/cps<br>Information in Spanish, Chinese, Russian and Arabic | 1-800-342-3720 |
| North Carolina | Division of Social Services<br>www.ncdhhs.gov/dss/local | Each county has a different phone number. See county directory at Web site. |
| North Dakota | Department of Human Services<br>www.nd.gov/dhs/locations/countysocialserv/index | Each county has a different phone number. See county directory at Web site. |
| Ohio | Department of Job and Family Services<br>http://jfs.ohio.gov/county/cntydir.stm | Each county has a different phone number. See county directory at Web site. |
| Oklahoma | Department of Human Services<br>www.okdhs.org/programservices | 1-800-522-3511 |
| Oregon | Department of Human Services<br>www.oregon.gov/DHS/children/abuse | Each county has a different phone number. See county directory at Web site. |
| Pennsylvania | Department of Public Welfare | 800-932-0313<br>(TDD: 866-872-1677) |
| Rhode Island | Department of Children, Youth and Families | 1 (800) RI-CHILD<br>1 (800) 742-4453 |
| South Carolina | Department of Social Services Division of Child Protective and Preventive Services | 803-734-5670 |
| South Dakota | Child Protective Services | (605) 773-3227 |
| Tennessee | Department of Human Services Child Protective Services | (615) 313-4746 |
| Texas | | 800-252-5400 |
| Utah | | 800-678-9399 |
| Vermont | Department of Social and Rehabilitation Services | 802-241-2131 |
| Virginia | | 800-552-7096 |
| Washington | | 800-562-5624 |
| West Virginia | | 800-352-6513 |
| Wisconsin | Department of Health and Social Services | 608-266-3036 |
| Wyoming | | 307-777-7922 |

## :: THE SCHOOL SYSTEM AND CHILD ABUSE

Although some children recover from maltreatment without serious consequences, the evidence is clear that maltreatment often has deleterious effects on children's mental health and development, both short and long term (Child Welfare Information Gateway, 2009). The quality of life that a child is entitled to is one without suffering inflicted by others. Although most victims of serious and fatal child abuse are very young, to regard older children and adolescents as invulnerable to the severe consequences of abuse and neglect is a mistake.

Because of required school attendance and an increase in the use of child-care centers, caregivers and teachers have an expanded opportunity for contact with families and children. These professionals work closely with children and families over extended periods. In so doing, they are also the people most able to detect and prevent abuse and neglect. The responsibilities are great, but an affirmative response by schools is vital to the well-being of thousands of children throughout the United States.

School has not always been recognized as an important agency in the detection of child abuse, but with more than 70 percent of the children who are abused or neglected having contact with schools or child-care centers, the school's role in detecting and preventing child abuse is vital. Through Parents as Teachers, Early Head Start and Head Start, and private and public preschool programs, it has become easier to detect abuse of 2- to 6-year-olds.

### Better Information and Education on Reporting

The U.S. Advisory Board on Child Abuse and Neglect (1995) made 27 recommendations for responding to this crisis. Recommendation D-4a refers to Child Protection and the Schools as follows:

#### Strengthening the Role of Elementary and Secondary Schools in the Protection of Children

The Federal Government should take all necessary measures to ensure that the nation's elementary and secondary schools, both public and private, participate more effectively in the prevention, identification, and treatment of child abuse and neglect. Such measures should include knowledge building, program development,

program evaluation, data collection, training, and technical assistance. The objective of such measures should be the development and implementation by State Educational Agencies (SEAs) in association with Local Educational Agencies (LEAs) and consortia of LEAs, of:

- Inter-agency multidisciplinary training for teachers, counselors, and administrative personnel on child abuse and neglect;
- Specialized training for school health and mental health personnel on the treatment of child abuse and neglect;
- School-based, inter-agency, multidisciplinary supportive services for families in which child abuse or neglect is known to have occurred or where children are at high risk of maltreatment, including self-help groups for students and parents of students;
- Family life education, including parenting skills and home visits, for students and/or parents; and
- Other school-based inter-agency, multidisciplinary programs intended to strengthen families and support children who may have been subjected to maltreatment, including school-based family resource centers and after-school programs for elementary and secondary school pupils which promote collaboration between schools and public and private community agencies in child protection. (p. 164)

Both public and private schools are considered essential to the child-protection system and have responsibilities to effectively provide for the children who attend schools.

The school professionals must consider legal considerations (mandated reporting), ethical considerations (confidentiality), and moral considerations (commitment to the child's well-being) (Horton & Cruise, 2001). When a professional reports suspicions of maltreatment, "families may move away from the school or at least cancel their children's participation in any counseling relationships" (p. 55). The parents may feel that their belief and trust in the school have been destroyed. Reporting, however, may prevent severe physical injury, psychological harm, or inadequate nourishment and health care. However, "reports may protect children from severe physical injury or even death. Psychological suffering may be lessened and dysfunctional patterns interrupted. Families may get needed services" (p. 56).

The school must serve as a defense against child abuse in three basic ways: (a) as a referral agency to child protection agencies—reporting suspected abuse is required by law; (b) as an educational institution offering parent education, family-life education, and home visitations to adults and students; and (c) as a support system for families and as a collaborator with other agencies in providing a total protection system.

### Internet Safety

In recent years children using the Internet have become vulnerable to pedophiles and pornographers. Children can inadvertently become exposed by simply typing the word *legs,* for LEGOS. Several steps must be taken to protect children by teachers, parents, and children themselves. It has been recommended that preventive software such as filtering, monitoring, or blocking be installed as an Internet safety plan for children, particularly those younger than 15 years of age (Ybarra, Finkelhorn, Mitchell, & Wolak, 2009). First, parents and teachers must monitor children's use of the computer. At school, teachers can set up safe Web sites that control what children will be able to access. Parents can contact their Internet service providers to block certain materials from coming into a child's computer. The filtering programs can also restrict personal information from being sent online. In addition, children can be guided to discriminate between appropriate sites and those that make them feel uncomfortable. All three steps are necessary to safeguard children (Kids Health, 2006).

## :: BULLYING AND VIOLENCE IN SCHOOLS

**Bullying** refers to "repeated, unprovoked, harmful actions by one child or children against another" (Bullock, 2002, p. 130). Bullying can be physical or emotional. The emotional bullying includes teasing, threatening, taunting, calling names, or starting negative rumors about someone. Equally devastating is being rejected and excluded from other groups of children (Banks, 1997; Bullock, 2002; Garrity, Baris, & Porter, 2000).

Physical bullying can include hitting, pushing, rough and intimidating actions, jabbing, or shoving (Bullock, 2002; Garrity et al., 2000). There is a difference between girl bullying and boy bullying. Boys use more physical strength along with verbal aggression, whereas girls add social intimidation to verbal aggression.

Two types of victims are chosen by the aggressor. One is the passive victim who seems to be helpless and unable to fight back. Afraid and alone, the child is an easy victim of the aggressor. The victim may convey his or her vulnerability through body language.

The second type of victim is the child who is a provocative victim. This child is impulsive, acts without thinking, and responds to the attack by fighting back (Bullock, 2002; Garrity et al., 2000). "Soon the bully has far more children on his or her side and the victim feels even more helpless. When a scene such as this plays itself out day after day, the victimized child grows more miserable, desperate, and incapable of handling the situation. If the cycle has grown this serious, it will not turn itself around without adult help" (Garrity et al., 2000, p. 7).

Bullies tend to be children whose parents use physical discipline; these children strike back physically to handle problems. They may break school rules and are oppositional to authority (Banks, 1997). Bullies enjoy dominating others; they also have little empathy for others. As mentioned, boy bullies usually have physical strength that helps them dominate others. Girls use their ability to control other girls through intimidation and exclusion.

Research conducted by Arseneault et al. (2006) examined the impact of early school bullying experiences on the mental health of 5- and 7-year-olds. The results indicated that there was a long-term impact, both socially and cognitively, on children's development, even years after the experience. It was recommended that programs targeted to meet the mental-health needs of children should include bullying as a risk factor.

Work by the National Youth Violence Prevention Resource Center (2006) indicates that bullying has long-term consequences on children's behavior. If bullying behavior continues into the teen years, they (especially boys) are more likely to be involved in vandalism, truancy, and drug abuse into adulthood. Sixty percent of bullies have at least one criminal conviction by age 24. Victims of bullies are more likely to do poorly in school and have a number of behavior problems. They generally have few friends and poor peer relationships. Some victims have been driven to suicide. Observers of bullying are also victims. They feel helpless and experience guilt. They may be drawn into bullying themselves or avoid relationships with the bullied victims.

## Awareness of Abuse, Child to Child

Another area of concern that has been evident in schools and playgrounds for many years, but which is most often overlooked as a process of growing up, is degradation of one child by another whether it is defined as bullying or teasing. Research by the Family and Work Institute, conducted from October to December 2001 on children grades five through 12, found that 67 percent of the children in the study experienced being teased or negatively gossiped about during a one-month span. The study cannot say which came first, the being hurt or hurting, but 68 percent of those who were gossiped about or teased in the month turned around and did the same to others. Sixty-one percent of the Colorado students in the study had been rejected or ignored, and 32 percent had been bullied (Galinsky & Salmond, 2002). More children are bullied, hit, kicked, and shoved between fifth and eighth grade than high school, where there is more gossip and students are more often teased.

Programs designed to reduce devastating experiences for children in school need to be implemented in schools. Action steps to end violence include the following:

1. Help establish norms where differences are not put down but are celebrated.
2. Work toward the creation of a civil society where there is more caring and respect.
3. Improve the relationships that children have in all aspects of their lives—at home and at school.
4. Include young people's views of how to end violence in violence prevention efforts.
5. Establish, invest in, and evaluate violence prevention efforts as well as positive youth development efforts (Galinsky & Salmond, 2002).
6. Do *not* victimize the child who has already been bullied and victimized.

**Can Teachers Make a Difference?** Teachers are extremely important to a child's feeling adequate, competent, and cared for. One way teachers can lose this and add to a child's insecurity is by using children as scapegoats in a class. They control the rest of the class by focusing on one or two children who are targeted for discipline and negative reinforcement. I have observed classrooms in which teachers cause emotional abuse in their efforts to control the classroom. Teachers can have an attitude toward a child that fosters prejudice and discrimination against that child by the child's classmates. They do not recognize that they are, in effect, emotionally abusing the child. Their actions are not occasional disciplinary decisions; they are caused by a repeated pattern as described by James Garbarino, past Executive Director of the Erikson Institute, as "the chronic pattern that erodes and corrodes a child . . . that persistent, chronic pattern of behavior toward a child" (American Humane Association, 1992c, p. 2).

Garbarino was speaking about parents and children, but this chronic pattern is also damaging when it is used in the schools. An occasional loss of control by parents (or teachers) does not indicate emotional abuse. Human beings may lose control and say hurtful things, but the person who consistently destroys a child's self-esteem is the one who is being extremely hurtful to the child and is emotionally abusing the child.

## Programs to Combat Bullying and Violence in Schools

The National Education Association Professional Library has published teacher guides to prevent bullying and sexual harassment. The one for students kindergarten through grade three is titled *Quit It*. Educational Equity Concepts, Inc., Wellesley College Center for Research on Women, and the NEA Professional Library cooperated in producing the teacher's guide, which discusses procedures and activities in detail (Froschi, Sprung, & Mullin-Rindler, 1998).

The second guide, *Bullyproof: A Teacher's Guide on Teasing and Bullying,* was developed for fourth- and fifth-grade students and was a joint publication of the Wellesley College Center and NEA Professional Library (Stein, 1996). One activity illustrates an example of a letter written to the person who is bullying. Lesson 8, which is one or two class sessions, is titled "What Are Your Rights?" and is a review and discussion of sexual harassment and relevant laws. Lesson 10, an action alert, allows the students to brainstorm to answer how to end bullying and teasing among the students. The guides include materials, a teacher's guide, and many references (Stein & Sjostrom, 1994).

The third guide, titled *Flirting or Hurting? A Teacher's Guide to Student-to-Student Sexual Harassment in Schools,* gives examples and discussion points to clarify what sexual harassment is and what can be done if a student thinks he or she is being harassed (Stein & Sjostrom, 1994).

The International Bullying Prevention Association also provides conferences, resources, and training to guide adults in effective strategies to develop environments to protect victims of bullying. The organization also recognizes the need to guide and redirect children that bully others, so they have the chance to develop constructive interpersonal relations (International Bullying Prevention Association, 2006).

## :: CORPORAL PUNISHMENT IN SCHOOLS

Does there seem to be an element of inconsistency in our work to eliminate abuse in the schools with the policy of corporal punishment still in place in many schools? Every industrialized country in the world prohibits school corporal punishment except the United States and one state in Australia (Center for Effective Discipline, 2006). The paddle is the primary instrument of physical discipline in the schools that still have corporal punishment. In the United States, 301,016 students were physically punished in the 2002–2003 school year. Teachers in Texas account for 19 percent of all school paddlings in the country (U.S. Department of Education, 2005). African American students received 38 percent of paddlings though they make up only 17 percent of the population.

By 2007, 29 states and the District of Columbia had banned corporal punishment: Alaska, California, Connecticut, Delaware, Hawaii, Illinois, Iowa, Maine, Maryland, Massachusetts, Michigan, Minnesota, Montana, Nebraska, Nevada, New Hampshire, New Jersey, New York, North Dakota, Oregon, Pennsylvania, Rhode Island, South Dakota, Utah, Vermont, Virginia, Washington, West Virginia, and Wisconsin. Many cities in states that have not abolished corporal punishment have abolished the practice in their schools (Center for Effective Discipline, 2007; U.S. Department of Education, 2005). In general, schools have been alarmingly slow to join

the national movement to reduce abuse—a movement that began in the 1960s and has continued into the 21st century. Thus, schools perpetuate the use of force to discipline children.

Parents can impact the school culture to protect their children from corporal punishment. According to the Center for Effective Discipline (2006), parents can do the following:

1. Get a copy of the school's discipline code to determine school policy.
2. Write a letter requesting that their child not be physically punished and if possible have the child's pediatrician sign the letter.
3. If the child has a disability, ask to have a statement included in the IEP that prohibits the child from receiving corporal punishment.
4. If a child is injured, take the child to a physician or emergency room and ask that pictures be taken of the injury.
5. Talk with the child to make sure he or she doesn't feel to blame for the punishment.
6. Organize a ban in the school district on corporal punishment.

Parents and educators working together can make a difference in ensuring that children experience human treatment in their school settings.

## :: WHO REPORTS MALTREATMENT CASES?

Cases of child maltreatment are reported by both nonprofessionals and professionals. Educators have become much more aware of their responsibility, and most reports come from this group (16.5 percent in 2004), as shown in Figure 11–6. Professionals—including educators as well as law enforcement, social services, and medical personnel—made 55.7 percent of the reports. Friends and family members reported 19.6 percent of the cases (U.S. Department of Health and Human Services, 2004). Situations related to teachers and schools are described in *Child Abuse and Neglect: A Shared Community Concern* (U.S. Department of Health and Human Services, 1992). Two examples follow.

### REPORT

When Cindy was 8 years of age, her teacher called Child Protection Services (CPS). Cindy was the only child in her family who wore old, tattered clothing to school and was not given the same privileges and opportunities as her brothers and sisters. The other children were allowed to join in after-school activities; however, Cindy was not allowed to participate in any outside activities. Cindy became very withdrawn at school. She stopped speaking in class and would not engage in play activities with her classmates. Her academic performance declined rapidly. Finally, Cindy became incontinent and had "accidents" in class.

REASONS

The reasons the teacher reported this case to CPS were

- Serious differential treatment of one child in the family.
- Marked decline in academic performance and class participation.
- Incontinence.

REPORT

Susan, age 7, was in her first-grade class when her teacher noticed that she had difficulty sitting and had some unusually shaped marks on her arm. Susan was sent to the school nurse to be examined. The nurse noted approximately 12 linear and loop-shaped marks on her back and buttocks. These marks ranged in length from 6 to 10 inches. The nurse believed that the marks were inflicted by a belt and belt buckle. The marks were purple, blue, brown, and yellow, indicating that the bruises were sustained at different times. Susan said she did not know how she got the bruises. The nurse spoke with the principal, who called CPS.

REASONS

The school principal reported this case to CPS because

- The child had sustained a physical injury.
- The bruises were inflicted at different times, perhaps days apart. (Even if the bruises had been inflicted at one time, this case should still be reported. The fact that the bruises were in different stages of healing raises greater concern for the child's safety.)
- The nurse's clinical opinion was that the injuries were inflicted by a belt and belt buckle. (U.S.

Department of Health and Human Services, 1992)

Indicators that a child has the potential need for protections is described in Figure 11–7.

## :: BEHAVIORS AND ATTITUDES OF PARENTS AND CHILDREN THAT MAY INDICATE CHILD ABUSE

Specialists working with child abuse have also developed some guidelines to help educators determine the existence of child abuse (Fontana, 1973a; Helfer & Kempe, 1987). The following are modified from publications by Head Start, the U.S. Department of Health and Human Services, and the American Humane Association.

### The Child of Preschool Age

1. Does the child seem to fear his or her parents?
2. Does the child miss preschool or the child-care center often?
3. Does the child bear evidence of physical abuse? Are there signs of battering, such as bruises or welts, belt or buckle marks, cuts, or burns?
4. Does the child exhibit extreme behavior changes? Is the child very aggressive at times and then fearful, withdrawn, and/or depressed?
5. Does the child have sores, bruises, or cuts that are not adequately cared for?
6. Does the child come to school inadequately dressed? Does the child look uncared for?
7. Does the child take over the parent role and try to "mother" the parent?
8. Does the child seem to be hungry for affection?

### The Child of Elementary School Age

1. Does the child exhibit behavior that deviates from the norm? Is the child (a) aggressive, destructive, and disruptive or (b) passive and withdrawn? The first may be a child who is shouting for help, demanding attention, and striking out, whereas the second may be out of touch with reality, remote, submissive, and subdued, but crying for help in another way.
2. Does the child miss classes, or is the child often tardy? Does the child come to school too early and stay around after hours? In the first

**FIGURE 11–7**

Indicators of a child's potential need for protection.

|  | *Physical Indicators* | *Behavioral Indicators* |
|---|---|---|
| **Physical Abuse** | • Unexplained bruises (in various stages of healing), welts, human bite marks, bald spots<br>• Unexplained burns, especially cigarette burns or immersion burns (glovelike)<br>• Unexplained fractures, lacerations or abrasions | • Self-destructive<br>• Withdrawn and aggressive—behavioral extremes<br>• Uncomfortable with physical contact<br>• Arrives at school early or stays late as if afraid to be at home<br>• Chronic runaway (adolescents)<br>• Complains of soreness or moves uncomfortably<br>• Wears clothing inappropriate to weather, to cover body |
| **Physical Neglect** | • Abandonment<br>• Unattended medical needs<br>• Consistent lack of supervision<br>• Consistent hunger, inappropriate dress, poor hygiene<br>• Lice, distended stomach, emaciated | • Regularly displays fatigue or listlessness, falls asleep in class<br>• Steals food, begs from classmates<br>• Reports that no caretaker is at home<br>• Frequently absent or tardy<br>• Self-destructive<br>• School dropout (adolescents) |
| **Sexual Abuse** | • Torn, stained, or bloody underclothing<br>• Pain or itching in genital area<br>• Difficulty walking or sitting<br>• Bruises or bleeding in external genitalia<br>• Venereal disease<br>• Frequent urinary or yeast infections | • Withdrawal, chronic depression<br>• Excessive seductiveness<br>• Role reversal, overly concerned for siblings<br>• Poor self-esteem, self-devaluation, lack of confidence<br>• Peer problems, lack of involvement<br>• Massive weight change<br>• Suicide attempts (especially adolescents)<br>• Hysteria, lack of emotional control<br>• Sudden school difficulties<br>• Inappropriate sex play or premature understanding of sex<br>• Threatened by physical contact, closeness |
| **Emotional Maltreatment** | • Speech disorders<br>• Delayed physical development<br>• Substance abuse<br>• Ulcers, asthma, severe allergies | • Habit disorders (sucking, rocking)<br>• Antisocial, destructive<br>• Neurotic traits (sleep disorders, inhibition of play)<br>• Passive and aggressive—behavioral extremes<br>• Delinquent behavior (especially adolescents)<br>• Developmentally delayed |

*Source:* From *Guidelines for Schools to Help Protect Abused and Neglected Children,* by the American Association for Protecting Children (n.d.), Denver, CO: American Humane Association. Reprinted with permission. Adapted in part from *Early Childhood Programs and the Prevention and Treatment of Child Abuse and Neglect* (The User Manual Series), by D. D. Broadhurst, M. Edmunds, and R. A. MacDicken, 1979, Washington, DC: U.S. Department of Health, Education, and Welfare.

instance, the child's behavior suggests problems at home. In the second, the child may be pushed out in the morning and have nowhere to go after school.

3. Does the child bear evidence of physical abuse? Are there obvious signs of battering: bruises, belt or buckle marks, welts, lacerations, or burns?
4. Does the child lack social skills? Is the child unable to approach other children and play with them?
5. Does the child have learning problems that cannot be diagnosed? Does the child underperform? If intelligence tests show average academic ability and the child is not able to do the work, there may be problems at home.
6. Does the child show great sensitivity to others' feelings? Does the child get upset when another person is criticized? Abused children often have to "mother" their abusive parents, and some are overly sensitive to the feelings of others.
7. Does the child come to school inadequately dressed? Is the child unwashed and uncared for? These may be signs of neglect.
8. Does the child seem tired or fall asleep in class?
9. Does the child appear undernourished? Does the child attempt to save food? Is there real poverty in the home, or do the parents not care?
10. Does the child seem to be afraid of his or her parents?

### The Secondary-Level Student

Most of the traits just mentioned are relevant to detection of abuse in the middle school and high school student, but there are additional signs to watch for in the upper levels. In addition to evidence of physical abuse, neglect, truancy, and tardiness, the older student may experience the following:

1. Does the student have to assume too much responsibility at home?
2. Does the parent expect unrealistic and overly controlled behavior?
3. Does the student have difficulty conforming to school regulations and policies?
4. Does the student have problems communicating with his or her parents?
5. Does the student have a history of running away from home or refusing to go home?
6. Does the student act out sexually?
7. Does the student lack freedom and friends?

## :: WHY DO ABUSE AND NEGLECT CONTINUE TO HAPPEN?

The National Center on Child Abuse and Neglect identified the following factors to determine which contribute to ongoing abuse and neglect of children:

- *Family income.* Children who come from families with incomes below the poverty level are seven times more likely to be abused than those at a higher income level.
- *Gender.* A child's gender has no effect on whether the child is neglected. However, girls are more likely to be abused than boys. The rate of sexual abuse is three times higher for girls than for boys.
- *Family size.* Children in families with four or more children are more likely to be neglected or abused.
- *Race or ethnicity.* There was no significant difference among children of different ethnic groups.
- *Type of community.* Abuse and neglect occur in rural, suburban, and urban communities (U.S. Department of Health and Human Services, 1992).
- *Exposure to violence.* Personal experience and exposure to media reports, television programs, Internet, and movies expose the child and the school to excessive violence.

### Characteristics and Risk Factors of Abusive Parents

Three approaches for understanding abusive parents have been investigated: the psychological model, the sociological model, and the parent–child interaction model.

In the psychological model, lack of empathy distinguishes the abusive parent. In the sociological model, cultural attitudes toward violence, social stress, family size, and social isolation are factors that relate to child abuse. Prevention and treatment based on the sociological model focus on the effect the community and society have on the family. Environmental stress is a sociological risk factor in abuse of children. Stress from poverty or in the workplace may cause anxiety in parents, and they may lash out at their child.

In the parent–child interaction model, the parents lack skill in interacting with their children, disciplining them, and teaching them appropriate behavior (Wiehe, 1989). Parents may have had inadequate exposure to positive parenting and lack information on child development. If raised by maladaptive parents or if raised with cultural beliefs that are compatible with mistreatment, the parent may not be capable of adapting to the child's needs.

The U.S. Department of Health and Human Services (1992) offered these reasons as to why parents may be more likely to abuse their children:

Parents may be more likely to maltreat their children if they abuse drugs or alcohol (alcoholic mothers are three times more likely and alcoholic fathers are eight times more likely to abuse or neglect their children than are nonalcoholic parents); are emotionally immature or needy; are isolated, with no family or friends to depend on; were emotionally deprived, abused or neglected as children; feel worthless and have never been loved or cared about; or are in poor health. Many abusive and neglectful parents do not intend to harm their children and often feel remorse about their maltreating behavior. However, their own problems may prevent them from stopping their harmful behavior and may result in resistance to outside intervention. It is important to remember that diligent and effective intervention efforts may overcome the parents' resistance and help them change their abusive and neglectful behavior.

Children may be more likely to be at risk of maltreatment if they are unwanted, resemble someone the parents dislike, or have physical or behavioral traits which make them different or especially difficult to care for.

- *Family interactions.* Each member of a family affects every other member of that family in some way. Some parents and children are fine on their own, but just cannot get along when they are together, especially for long periods of time. Some characteristics commonly observed in abusive or neglectful families include social isolation and parents turning to their children to meet their emotional needs.
- *Environmental conditions.* Changes in financial condition, employment status, or family structure may shake a family's stability. Some parents may not be able to cope with the stress resulting from the changes and may experience difficulty in caring for their children. (U.S. Department of Health and Human Services, 1992, p. 5)

The National Center on Child Abuse and Neglect suggests these guiding principles:

- Child maltreatment is a family problem. Consequently our treatment efforts must focus on the family as a whole as well as the individual family members. Treatment must be provided to abused and neglected children as well as their parents. Unless children receive the support and treatment for the trauma they have suffered, they may suffer permanent physical, mental, or emotional handicaps, and as adults they may continue the cycle of abuse with their own family or other children. In addition, abused and neglected children are more likely than other children to have substance abuse problems.
- Although we cannot predict with certainty who will abuse or neglect their children, we do know the signs indicating *high risk*. People at high risk include parents who abuse drugs and alcohol, young parents who are ill-prepared for the parenting role, families experiencing great stress who have poor coping skills and have no one to turn to for support, and parents who have difficulty with or who have not developed an emotional bond with their infant. We need to be alert to these and other high risk indicators and offer assistance, support, counseling, and/or parent education to families at risk before their children are harmed.
- Families at risk may be most receptive to help soon after the birth of their first child.
- Child sexual abuse prevention programs aimed at school-aged children appear to be useful in helping children avoid sexually abusive situations and to say no to inappropriate touch by adults. However, prevention programs must be carefully examined and selected. These programs must be responsive to the learning capacities and developmental stages of the children involved. Inappropriately designed programs may frighten young children or fail to teach them what they can do to protect themselves.
- Volunteers can be very effective with some abusive and neglectful parents—especially with those parents who are experiencing stress, who have been emotionally deprived, and who lack knowledge of child development and effective parenting skills. Volunteers must be carefully screened, trained, and supervised.

Clearly, if we are going to stop child abuse and neglect and help the child victims and their families, we all must work together. Efforts must occur at the Federal, State, and local levels. (U.S. Department of Health and Human Services, 1992, pp. 10–11)

The following behavioral characteristics can help the professional determine the likelihood of abuse or neglect:

1. Do the parents fail to show up for appointments? Do they stay away from school? When

they come to school, are they uncooperative and unresponsive?

2. Do the parents have unrealistically high expectations for themselves and their child? Do the parents describe the child as "different" or "bad"?

3. Do the parents have expectations for the child that are inconsistent or inappropriate for the child's age?

4. Do the parents become aggressive or abusive when school personnel want to talk about the child's problems?

5. Do the parents isolate themselves? Do they know other parents in the school? Are they known by other parents?

6. Do they lack knowledge of child development and the child's physical and psychological needs?

7. Do the parents report that they were abused or neglected as children?

8. Do the parents refuse to participate in school events?

9. Do the parents ignore the child and avoid touching?

10. Do the parents show little interest in the child's activities or concern for the child's well-being?

## Why Is There Abuse?

Children learn parenting patterns from their parents (Iverson & Segal, 1990). With few exceptions, abusive parents experienced some form of maltreatment when young (Steele, 1986). These parents did not have a childhood that allowed them to become independent, productive, functioning adults. Generally they had to disregard their own needs and desires for the wishes of an authority figure. They were unable to develop inner controls and looked to outside figures for direction. Such parents also exhibit dependence on others in their search for love and affection. They are still affected by maternal deprivation. Abusive parenting may include the following:

1. *Inappropriate expectations.* Abusive parents often perceive the child's abilities to be greater than they are, and they expect children to take on responsibilities that are not appropriate for their ages. These parents may have expectations such as toilet training the child at 6 to 12 months, talking by age 2, and taking on housekeeping chores at an early age. Young or inexperienced parents, who do not know child development, may interpret an infant or toddler's appropriate behavior as stubbornness and rebellion. Combine this with a belief that physical punishment will help the child behave, and you have the conditions for abuse. Children in these families develop a poor self-concept and feel incapable, unacceptable, and worthless (Bavolek, 1989; Hamilton, 1989).

2. *Lack of empathy.* Abusive parents often did not experience loving care when they were growing up, so they do not have a model to follow. They cannot change their own personality traits until they receive the support and love they need. These parents usually have dependency needs and are unable to empathize with their children. The child's basic needs are ignored. Such parents may justify cruel and abusive behaviors under the guise of teaching and guiding their children. Mothers who were brought up by uncaring, inattentive mothers will tend to mother their own children in the same way. Their children grow up with a low sense of self-esteem and inadequate identity (Bavolek, 1989; Hamilton, 1989; Steele, 1986, 1987).

3. *Belief in physical punishment.* Abusive parents often believe that physical punishment is necessary to rear their children without spoiling them. This is a common belief in the United States, but abusive parents go to extremes and believe that babies and children should not be allowed to get away with anything. They punish to correct perceived misbehavior or inadequacy on the part of their child. The child does not live up to expectations and is considered "bad." The parents think they have the moral duty to correct their child's behavior any way they choose.

4. *Parent–child role reversal.* In these abusive families, children are looked upon by the parents as providing the love and support that the parent needs. The parent is like a needy child, so the child must play the role of the adult. If the child is able to take on some of the parental roles, abuse may be avoided, but only at the expense of the child's normal development. This is destructive to children—they do not go through normal developmental stages, do not develop their own identities, and see themselves as existing to meet the needs of their parents (Bavolek, 1989; Hamilton, 1989).

5. *Social isolation.* Social isolation is recognized by most child abuse researchers as a factor that perpetuates neglect and abuse. Either the absence of social support or inability to accept any support has the same effect. The abusive family isolates itself, attempts to solve its problems alone, and avoids contact with others. Isolation is a defense against being hurt and rejected. Although abusive parents may act self-sufficient and sure of themselves, they are dependent, frightened, and immature. Cross-cultural research indicates that child maltreatment occurs less often in cultures with multiple caregivers, including extended families (Hamilton, 1989).

6. *Difficulty experiencing pleasure.* In other abusing families, the parents do not enjoy life. Their social relationships are minimal and unrewarding. They do not feel competent, have difficulty planning for the future, and do not trust their own performances. Children in these families exhibit similar behavior.

7. *Intergenerational ties.* Although a history of maltreatment and lack of parenting skills set the scene for more neglect and abuse, the "majority of maltreated children do not maltreat their own children" (Hamilton, 1989, p. 38). According to Vondra and Toth (1989), one-third of the maltreated are abusive to their children (p. 13). If abuse and neglect are viewed in a broad sense, however, an alarming number of parents did not receive adequate parenting or develop a positive attachment to their parents and other loved ones and thus have a difficult time providing the kind of environment that nourishes and cares for a child adequately (Steele, 1986).

The American Association for Protecting Children, a division of the American Humane Association, has developed a flyer that briefly describes parental attitudes, the child's behavior, and the child's appearance. This flyer, illustrated in Figure 11–5, succinctly focuses on the highlights of the foregoing discussion. Schools may purchase this flyer from the American Humane Association for a nominal fee and distribute it to staff and teachers.

## :: DEVELOPMENT OF POLICIES

School districts and child-care centers need to develop the policies and training programs vital to successful child abuse intervention. If there is no policy, the teacher should see the school nurse, psychologist, director, counselor, social worker, or principal, depending on the staffing of the school. Even in a school district with a policy statement, each school or child-care center should have one person who is responsible for receiving reports of child abuse. Making one person responsible results in greater awareness of the problem of abuse and facilitates reporting. It is also helpful to establish a committee to view evidence and support the conclusions of the original observer. A written report contains the details of the situation.

All states require reporting of suspected child abuse. Evidence of violent physical abuse must be reported immediately. If school officials refuse to act, you should call social services, law enforcement, or a family crisis center. The person making the report should have the right to remain anonymous. When reporting in good faith, the person reporting is protected by immunity described in state legislation. Colorado law, for example, specifically states: "Any person participating in good faith in the making of a report or in a judicial proceeding held pursuant to this title shall be immune from any liability, civil or criminal, that otherwise might result by reason of such reporting" (Denver Public Schools, 1992).

## Needs Assessment

Schools and child-care centers first must determine the prevention and protection delivery systems that are already available in the community. They should consider social-service departments, child-protection teams, child-welfare agencies, law enforcement, juvenile court system, Head Start, child-care centers, hospitals, clinics, public-health nurses, mental-health programs, public and private service groups, fundraising agencies such as United Way, and service organizations that might be unique to their community.

Following assessment of the community, the schools and child-care centers have to determine their roles in an integrated approach to abuse and neglect. Communication lines must be kept open at all times. A representative of the schools should serve on the child-protection team. One role that is mandated is identification of abuse and neglect. Other roles will be individualized according to the needs of the community, the resources in the schools and child-care centers, and the commitment of the personnel.

## Policy

Child abuse is found in all socioeconomic groups in the United States, so all school districts must be prepared to work with interdisciplinary agencies in the detection and prevention of this national social problem.

Policies should be written in compliance with the requirements of each state's reporting statute, details of which may be learned by consulting the state's attorney general. Because reporting is required in all states, the policy should include a clear statement of reporting requirements. The policy should also inform school personnel of their immunity and legal obligations. Dissemination of the policy should include the community as well as all school employees. Not only is it important that the community realize the obligation of the school or child-care center to report suspected abuse or neglect, it also is vital that the community become aware of the extent of the problem.

## :: COMMUNICATION WITH FAMILIES

Just as there are varieties and levels of abuse and neglect, there should be variations in the school's interaction with parents. Child-care workers and school personnel who want to help an abused child must exercise good judgment. Their first response may be to want to call the parent to determine how the injury occurred, but in the case of violent abuse, the child may be in danger of being permanently injured or killed. With serious abuse, do not call the parents or try to handle the situation by yourself. Contact the appropriate authorities immediately. Calling the family to discuss the problem not only fails to help the family, but also may precipitate more abuse. In addition the family may become alarmed and move away. Then the child may be abused for many more months before a new school or center detects the problem.

When the problem appears to be neglect rather than abuse, as when a child comes to school hungry or inappropriately dressed, a supportive visit or call to the family is in order. The school can provide emotional support and food and clothing. Working *with* parents shows them they are not alone with their overwhelming problems. If providing services is beyond the capability of the school, or if the family needs professional help, social services should be called.

## How to Talk with Children and Parents

When planning to talk with the parents and/or children of suspected abuse or neglect, plan a productive meeting focused first on the needs of the family and how the school might be able to help them. Although you should report your concerns of abuse to the authorities first if there is obvious suspected abuse, offering support to the family is always appropriate.

Care must be taken in talking with or interviewing children or parents. The conversation should take place in a private, relaxed, and comfortable atmosphere. Children should not feel threatened, nor should they be pressed for information or details they do not want to reveal. Parents should be aware of the school's legal obligation to report suspected neglect and abuse. If they believe the school is supportive of the family, the interaction between parents and school will be more positive. Tower (1992) provides some guidelines:

### *When Talking with the Child*

#### *Do:*

Make sure the interviewer is someone the child trusts.
Make sure the educator is the most competent person in the school to talk with children.
Conduct the interview in private.
Sit beside the child, not across a table or desk.
Tell the child that the interview is confidential, but that child abuse and neglect must be reported.
Conduct the interview in language the child understands.
Ask the child to clarify words or terms that you do not understand.
Tell the child if any future action will be required.

#### *Don't:*

Allow the child to feel "in trouble" or "at fault."
Disparage or criticize the child's choice of words or language.
Suggest answers to the child.
Probe or press for answers the child is unwilling to give.
Display horror, shock, or disapproval of parents, the child, or the situation.
Pressure or force the child to remove clothing.
Conduct the interview with a group of interviewers.
Leave the child alone with a stranger (e.g., a CPS worker).

### When Talking with the Parents

#### Do:

Select the person most appropriate to the situation.

Conduct the interview in private.

Tell the parents why the interview is taking place.

Be direct, honest, and professional.

Tell the parents the interview is confidential.

Reassure the parents of the support of the school.

Tell the parents if a report has been made or will be made.

Advise the parents of the school's legal responsibilities to report.

#### Don't:

Try to prove abuse or neglect; that is not an educator's role.

Display horror, anger, or disapproval of parents, the child, or the situation.

Pry into family matters unrelated to the specific situation.

Place blame or make judgments about the parents or child.

## ⠿ PROGRAMS TO PREVENT ABUSE

### Parent Education

Parent education can be delivered in high school, provided by hospitals when parents have their first child, offered through adult education, or provided by social services. The STEP, Parent Effectiveness Training, and Active Parenting courses have been effective. Building Family Strengths programs reinforce the positive aspects of a family. Specially designed programs are also appropriate.

### Caring Programs

Home visitation programs have demonstrated that early intervention is effective. First-time parents are especially receptive to help from visiting nurses or nonprofessionals who model, support, and help them with their infant (Justice & Justice, 1990). Programs that were developed to offer this support included the Prenatal/Early Infancy Project in Rochester, New York; the Pre-School Intervention Program in Bloomfield, Connecticut; MELD in Minnesota; the Parents as Teachers program; and Healthy Start. The emphasis in the last three programs—MELD, Parents as Teachers, and Healthy Start—is broader than home visitations for parenting skills, but the programs include these areas and demonstrate that larger groups can benefit from a national response. In Great Britain, newborns and their parents are visited by public-health nurses. Although the parents do not have to accept the visit, most do, and after the initial visit there are follow-ups with periodic assessments of intellectual, emotional, and physical development.

**The Community Caring Project.** The Community Caring Project, a joint project of the Center and the Junior League of Denver is based on the concept of intervention. It provides support and parenting skills to new mothers. These mothers, selected from four hospitals in the Denver area, are matched with a community volunteer, who offers assistance, modeling, and education to the new mothers.

The Caring Program is an offshoot of programs developed by researchers at the University of Colorado Medical School. Mothers who are at high risk for abnormal parental practices (following observations made during and after labor and delivery) are offered special programs. When identified as high risk, the family receives a pediatric follow-up by a physician, lay health visitor, and/or public-health nurse.

### Support Offered by Schools

The position statement by the American School Counselor Association supports programs to help eliminate child abuse. The association hopes to provide children with coping skills; help teachers understand abuse; provide continued counseling to the child and the family; and offer workshops for parents that focus on handling anger, parenting skills, and methods of discipline other than corporal punishment (American School Counselor Association, 1988). Some of the school-based programs include life-skills training, socialization skills, problem solving, and coping skills (Tower, 1992).

If the public were aware of how essential it is for teenagers who have not received these skills at home to be able to learn and model life skills, there would not be the demand to eliminate these types of courses. Although academic basics (reading, writing, and arithmetic) are essential, the focus away from life skills could be detrimental to the next generation. Offering of workshops or courses on conflict resolution, consequences of actions, and seeking alternatives should be recognized as essential. It should be possible for schools to provide all the needed academic skills as well as the necessary skills for parenthood, self-protection, and life skills.

Many schools are developing family resource centers. Offerings for parents who are no longer students include parent education and family literacy.

## Checklist for Schools and Centers

Having a checklist available for teachers and administrators helps the school or center maintain accountability for preventing child abuse and neglect. Public schools should work with their school district's office to ensure that they are following the appropriate policy.

The following questions can be used to create a checklist:

- Does the school have a policy on reporting child abuse and neglect?
- Did the school do a needs assessment that shows the resources in your area and the status of child abuse and neglect in the school district?
- Does the school or center coordinate activities and resources with other social agencies?
- Does the school or center hold periodic meetings for improved communication and coordination among agencies?
- Does someone in the school district serve on the child protection team?
- Does the school or center have a training program?
- Do parents feel welcome in the school?
- Does the school or center have a parent education program for parents of preschoolers?
- Does the school or center have a parent education program for parents of infants and toddlers?
- Is the PTA or any other parent group involved with the school or center in a meaningful way for parents?
- Is there a parent resource room in the school?
- Do parents feel welcome to visit the school?
- Is there regular contact with parents, the teacher, and the school or center? Do the teachers have frequent communication with parents when there is something good to report?

## Rights of the Child

The U.S. Advisory Board on Child Abuse and Neglect (1993), using statements (shown in italics) taken from the United Nations Convention on the Rights of the Child (United Nations, 1989), declares the following rights for the child:

Respect for the inherent dignity and inalienable rights of children as members of the human community requires protection of their integrity as persons.

Children have a right to protection *from all forms of physical or mental violence, injury or abuse, neglect or negligent treatment, maltreatment or exploitation, including sexual abuse, while in the care of parent(s), legal guardian(s) or any other person who has the care of the child, including children residing in group homes and institutions* (art. 19, 1).

Children have a right to *grow up in a family environment, in an atmosphere of happiness, love and understanding* (preamble).

The several Governments of the United States share a profound responsibility to ensure that children enjoy, at a minimum, such protection of their physical, sexual, and psychological security.

The several Governments of the United States bear a special duty to refrain from subjecting children in their care and custody to harm.

Children have a right to be treated with respect as individuals, with due regard to cultural diversity and the need for culturally competent delivery of services in the child protection system.

Children have a right to *be provided the opportunity to be heard in any judicial and administrative proceedings* affecting them (art. 12), with ample opportunity for representation and for provision of procedures that comport with the child's sense of dignity.

The duty to protect the integrity of children as persons implies a duty to prevent assaults on that integrity whenever possible. (p. 84)

## :: PROGRAMS AFTER RECOGNIZING ABUSE

Professionals who work with the abusive parent must first understand themselves and their values so they can come to peace with their feelings toward abuse and neglect of children. To help the family, professionals should not have a punitive attitude toward the parents. It may help to remember that many abusive or neglectful parents are rearing their children the same way they were reared. It is a lifelong pattern that must be broken (Bavolek, 1989; Reppucci, Britner, & Woolard, 1997; Steele, 1987; Vondra & Toth, 1989).

Although the parents may resist intrusion or suggestion, they desperately need help in feeling good about themselves. They need support, comfort, and someone they can trust and lean on. They need someone who will come when they have needs. Instead of criticism, they need help and assurance that they are worthwhile. Because they are unable to cope with their child, someone must help them understand the child. Parents need to feel valuable and adequate.

## Parents Anonymous

Parents Anonymous (2006) is a self-help program that gives parents the chance to share their feelings with others who have had similar experiences. Parents can use Parents Anonymous (PA) and its crisis-intervention hotlines without fear of public disclosure.

The members help one another avoid abuse by providing the opportunity to talk out problems. Each group has a group facilitator who is trained in Parents Anonymous standards and practices. They also have a parent group leader, selected by the group. Weekly meetings are held and both the group leader and group facilitator are available between the weekly meetings. PA believes that abuse happens because parents have unresolved issues about their own childhood, stressful current problems and unmet needs, and a precipitating crisis that brings about the abuse.

## Community Help

Help from social services or nonprofit organizations may include treatment that is offered by parent-aides, homemakers, and health visitors (Hamilton, 1989). The helper may serve as an advocate for the family to get the extra assistance it needs. This might include family therapy (Pardeck, 1989), assertiveness training, Healthy Start, Parents as Teachers, Community Resource Centers, Family Resource Centers, and Building Family Strengths programs. These programs try to bolster the positive elements in the family and eliminate the destructive elements.

Many abusive parents want help. When they reveal their desires, they indicate that they want another parent to help them develop childrearing skills through modeling and friendship. Professionals can give them psychiatric help and other support, but because these parents may have missed a childhood with nurturing parents, their greatest need is the opportunity to have an active experience with a nurturing model. The importance of bonding and of a close relationship between parent and infant has been recognized as necessary for the child's emotional and physical growth. Severe deprivation can result in failure to thrive and marasmus (Skeels & Dye, 1939; Spitz, 1945). Failure to develop close and trusting bonds as infants and children results later in parents who need special help in learning to relate to their own child. These parents are still looking for someone to mother them. The supportive help of another parent can function as a nurturing model for both parent and child.

## Preschool Settings

Youngsters who have been abused adapt in two ways, according to Pearl (1988). They either internalize and over control their behavior, or they externalize and under control their actions. Children in the first category will be easy to overlook—their behavior is often fearful, withdrawn, depressed, and shy. The externalized child will demand attention, be aggressive, and act out (Pearl, 1988; Steele, 1986). Both types of children have low self-esteem. Aggressive, externalized children see themselves as unlovable and bad. The withdrawn child tries to please but feels little pleasure. Abused children will scan their surroundings often, avert their eyes, and stare away to avoid eye contact. Preschool teachers can help both types of children if they do the following:

1. Use a quiet, clear voice.
2. Have good eye contact.
3. Stand near the child when giving directions.
4. Use body language that says the same thing as the oral message.
5. Give directions that tell the child the appropriate behavior using specific instructions.
6. Set limits and have expectations for behavior.
7. Accept all feelings, but be consistent with behavioral expectations (Pearl, 1988).

## SUMMARY

The wave of child abuse cases reveals a phenomenon that is not new. Child abuse has been with society since very early times, but it was not recognized as a problem until the second half of the 20th century, and no concerted effort was made to stem the crisis until the 1960s.

Legislation requires schools to report cases of abuse and neglect. Schools work with children more than any other agency, so they need to be in the forefront in preventing child abuse.

Child abuse and neglect include physical, sexual, and emotional abuse. It is important to note the characteristics of families who tend to be abusive, ways to identify the abused or neglected child, and psychological characteristics of abusive parents and abused children in order to keep children safe. Prevention programs provide ideas about how to work with families that have experienced abuse and/or neglect.

Ways schools can work to help potentially abusive parents are discussed. Recognition of and response to the problem by financial support from the school, parent-education groups, school curricula, resource rooms, crisis nurseries, and/or parent-to-parent support groups are necessary.

SUGGESTED CLASS ACTIVITIES AND DISCUSSIONS

1. Attend a meeting of the Child Protection Council or similar group. What is the composition of the council—for example, doctors, educators, social workers, or judges? How does the wide spectrum of specialists show the need for cooperation among agencies working with families?
2. Go to the UNICEF Web site and explore different videos that deal with child abuse around the world. Think about how volunteers, particularly those who are teachers or going to be teachers, can help this organization with this epidemic.
3. Based on the information you have read in this chapter, create a public service announcement in which you talk about a type of abuse and provide local, state, and national resources that can be helpful for families.
4. Visit with the director of a women's shelter and ask questions regarding how they serve families who are victims of domestic violence. Remember to use pseudonyms to protect everyone's identity.
5. Working in four groups, students create four scenarios that deal with child abuse. The students dramatize each scenario and ask the audience to help find solutions and sources.
6. Read an article from one of the volumes of the journal *Child Abuse and Neglect* (www .sciencedirect.com/science/journal/01452134) that focuses on helping families who are victims of abuse. Write a one-page paper that discusses those efforts.

USEFUL WEB SITES

**Child Welfare Information Gateway**
http://childwelfare.gov/
This Web site provides links and resources for professionals, parents, and community personnel on child abuse and neglect. It provides toll-free phone numbers for crisis and abuse.

**Child Welfare League of America (CWLA)**
www.cwla.org/
CWLA is the oldest and largest membership-based child welfare organization. It was established to promote the well-being of children, youth, and families.

**i-SAFE**
www.isafe.org/
This is a nonprofit organization that works to protect online experiences of youth worldwide. Programs are offered to teach children Internet safety in school. The Web site includes a calendar of events, educational resources, and outreach resources.

**National Data Analysis System**
http://ndas.cwla.org/
This site provides reports and links to child abuse data from nationwide and state-by-state perspectives.

# Assisting Parents with Child Advocacy

*G. R. Berger*
*Clark E. Myers*
*Eugenia Hepworth Berger*
*Mari Riojas-Cortez*

*A strong effective, independent voice for all children of America.*

Children's Defense Fund
*(2011)*

*In this chapter you will find guidelines regarding how to assist parents in engaging in different aspects of advocacy for their children. By the end of the chapter, you should be able to do the following:*

- Define advocacy.
- Identify advocacy issues for young children and their families.
- Describe the power of advocacy and collaboration with parents.
- Provide steps for advocacy.

## :: CHILD ADVOCACY

As we think of advocacy, we must return to one of the ideas that this book is based on, which is **funds of knowledge.** Parents advocate for their children by teaching them about their cultural capital and how to best use it for their development; they give them their voice. We also have to recall the Ecological Systems Theory in which different systems work together to help children achieve optimal potential. Understanding our role in child advocacy as educators and parents will help us fight for our children, but we must work together and give children a voice.

### What Is Advocacy?

**Advocacy** is the strong belief and active involvement for a cause. Child advocacy grows from an emotional involvement in the lives of children, a caring, a recognition of need, and a willingness to do something about that need. On both an individual level (micro) and a social level (macro), the opportunity for advocacy is ever present for teachers. It is there when the teacher assesses the children's abilities and life situations. How can children be protected so that they grow into productive adults, particularly those who come from culturally and linguistically diverse backgrounds? How can children be enabled to achieve their potential? How can parents advocate for the healthy development of their children?

Through the ages there have been movements to help the child, although sometimes the answers seemed to remove children's rights rather than help them. Concern about children and how they should be reared continued throughout the 20th century. The civil rights movement and the rights of people

The rights that guard these children are derived from the U.S. Constitution, the Bill of Rights, social customs, legislation, and rulings of state and federal courts.

with disabilities focused on fair and equal treatment and provided the foundation for important laws that protect our children today.

Currently the Children's Defense Fund (2011), founded and headed by Marion Edelman, advocates vehemently for children's rights. The United Nations Children's Fund, or UNICEF, also works for children's rights around the world. Other associations—such as the Center on Families, Communities, Schools, and Children's Learning; Family Resource Coalition; Institute for Responsive Education; National Center for Family Literacy; The National Children's Advocacy Center; The Child Welfare League of America; The National Association for the Advancement of Colored People; National Council of La Raza; National Immigration Law Center; and National Parent and Teacher Association—work to provide equal educational opportunities for all children regardless of ability, ethnicity, or gender. Other early childhood organizations, such as the National Association for the Education of Young Children (NAEYC), have specific advocacy based on public policy, such as NAEYC Children's Champions, which addresses advocacy at the national level but that has tremendous impact at all levels.

## A Sleeping Giant: The Child Advocate

The issues of the new century vividly illustrate why children need advocates. The growing demand for quality child care and green spaces to play, along with increases in poverty, homelessness, and reports of incest and child abuse shout to the public. These social problems need a great deal of action to overcome the obstacles that children face. But children also need advocates at a personal level. For example, educators need the tools to advocate for parents, particularly those who are English language learners (Campos, Delgado & Soto Huerta, 2011). Children face many challenges, and they need teachers and parents to work together to help them meet their individual needs and create opportunities for a healthy development. Both teachers and parents must stand up for the children and advocate at all levels. If they do not, who will?

## Levels of Advocacy

Advocacy can be done on the case or class level, at administrative or legislative levels, or on the public level (Kieff, 2010).

**Case or Class Action.** Advocates may work with individual cases or in class actions. The individual

Organizations that advocate for families and their children must work together to meet their needs.

or case advocate works on behalf of a specific child. The class or social advocate works for a whole group of children who need special or basic services (e.g., the Children's Defense Fund works for child rights). Lay advocates must obtain the necessary services and help. When legal issues and court cases are involved, legal counsel from a lawyer (a professional advocate) is needed. The Family Leave Bill, which languished but was finally passed by Congress and signed into law by President Clinton, is an example of the persistence demanded of those who advocate for families. President Obama's fatherhood initiative promotes responsible parenting (U.S. Department of Health and Human Services, 2011), another example of advocacy for children.

**Administrative or Legislative Levels.** Advocates can bring change at the administrative and legislative levels by working toward change in regulations and guidelines at the administrative level or toward change in the laws through legislative advocacy (Goffin & Lombardi, 1988).

**Advocacy on the Public Level.** Individuals work together and separately to advocate on the public level. Most successful advocacy requires a broad-based approach, whether it is achieved through the responses of many individuals, the advocacy work of professional organizations, or the lobbying efforts of political action committees.

## :: THE CHILD ADVOCATE

Often children need someone to have a voice for them (Oliver & Dalrymple, 2008). The advocate must grasp the needs of the child, the resources available within the school system, and the alternative resources outside the school system. Advocates may be involved at many levels:

1. *Leaders*—people with vision who help keep advocacy efforts on track.
2. *Advisers*—people who share their expertise with advocates and policymakers.
3. *Researchers*—people who collect data and synthesize research reports to support advocacy efforts.
4. *Contributors*—people who make phone calls, stuff letters, and make visits or write letters to legislators. (National Association for Education of Young Children, 2004)

## Making a Personal Contribution

The most common kind of advocacy is one that many teachers and parents do every day. If parents and teachers look upon positive intervention that helps children live full and meaningful lives as advocacy and recognize that children cannot advocate for themselves, they will accept the responsibility and challenge of advocacy as a necessary role. Individual advocates who work for children in their own child-care programs or classrooms can have a huge effect on children's lives. If everyone who works or lives with a child would assume the important role of an advocate for the child, the lives of all children would be improved.

Together parents and teachers can advocate for those issues that best address their children's needs. For instance, the organization Zero to Three and the NAEYC's award-winning journal *Young Children* (Zero to Three, 2010) indicate that a major issue facing many families includes early care and education, particularly quality child care. Zero to Three provides parents with publications that give tips regarding child care. For parents who have no access to the Internet, teachers can share this information with them by holding monthly meetings or outlining important information for parents to read. They can also have a news wall including information and a variety of activities that parents can do for advocacy.

Parents and teachers can advocate on a personal level in the following ways:

| Parents | Teachers |
|---|---|
| Use funds of knowledge to provide a stimulating environment where children grow and play. | Acknowledge the family's funds of knowledge and how those help children with their development. |
| Spend time with children, listening to what concerns or interests them. | Provide a stimulating environment where children are free to speak and adults listen. |
| All children have the right to an education. Speak to teachers and administrators when that is not happening. | Maintain educational and social equity for culturally and linguistically diverse children. |
| Develop a love for the environment by taking children to parks and other natural areas where they can play. | Seek out interesting excursions and activities that will benefit the child. |

| Parents | Teachers |
|---|---|
| Look for resources for children who have special needs. Ask the teacher and/or social worker for help. | Determine the most appropriate education for a child with special needs. |
| Report physical, sexual, and emotional abuse. | Report physical, sexual, and emotional abuse. |
| Attend meetings and speak out on issues. | Attend meetings and speak out on issues. |
| Become active in your community. | Become active in professional organizations. |
| Write and contact your legislator. | Write and contact your legislator. |

### Qualifications for Personal Advocates

Essentially what qualifies a person to be a good child advocate is the intrinsic quality of being truly motivated to help children. The help must be systematic, knowledgeable, and thorough. The advocate must be committed to finding out all the needs of the child or children being helped. Although it is time consuming and difficult, advocacy, when supported by the best available data, is most beneficial to the community, parents, and schools. For advocates, becoming change agents in the lives of children is the ultimate goal (McDonald, 2010).

## :: PREPARING FOR ADVOCACY

### Procedure

Teachers advocate for their students when they see that the children's needs are met. At times this seems to be just part of the role of a teacher. At other times, objectives and preparation must be established to advocate effectively.

To achieve their objectives, advocates must systematically study and proceed with a sound foundation. They first list the needs of the child and justify these needs by making certain they have been professionally determined. They read the literature and speak to experts in the field so that their views are supported by reputable observations. Good advocates make sure their positions are based not on their own beliefs alone but on the true needs of the child, the group of children, and society at large.

Parents are their child's first advocates. No one can escape the responsibility of being an advocate.

The following guidelines describe the steps to take when working on an individual advocacy case:

1. *Know your facts.* Be sure they are correct. Find out who, what, where, when, and why.
2. *Know the rights.* This includes the rights of the child, the parent, or other parties in the case. Contact an advocacy organization or lawyer if you have any questions.
3. *Know the policy.* Make sure you know the policies and procedures that relate to the problem. Get it in writing; don't accept just an oral version.
4. *Keep accurate notes.* Document as much evidence as possible. Date everything. Remember when notes kept as a personal memory aid are not educational records and when educational records must be shared.
5. *Discuss various options.* Do not tell the young person or parent what to do. Rather, let the people you are helping choose the option and

course of action that is wisest and that they are willing to live with.

6. *Never go alone to a meeting with officials.* Unless it is an unusual circumstance, take the young person, the parent, or another concerned person with you.

7. *Keep to the point when meeting with officials.* Be firm but not antagonistic and keep focused on the problem and the need to resolve it. Steer clear of personality conflicts.

8. *Follow channels.* Don't go over someone's head without first talking to that person about the problem. It is wise to let the person know you are dissatisfied with the result of your meeting and that you intend to go to the next person in authority.

9. *Send a letter.* If appropriate, send a letter to indicate your understanding of what took place at a meeting with officials or administrators. (Fernandez, 1980)

### Help Parents Become Advocates and Active Partners in the Schools

How can professionals ensure that parents will feel empowered and become involved? The following suggestions are adapted from a book on community mobilization from the Families and Work Institute (Dombro, O'Donnell, Galinsky, Melcher, & Farber, 1996):

- If you provide ongoing support to parents from the beginning—showing respect, using a buddy system, encouraging them to ask questions, and introducing them into the school program—you will promote feelings of competence and empowerment. The parents will be more comfortable and confident and will see how they can contribute.

- Help parents see that they are important as part of the organization. Parents come to the table with different skills and experiences. "When parents define roles with which they are comfortable, they are more likely to be effective and remain involved in the process" (Dombro et al., 1996).

- Parents have unique skills, but you can offer them training and workshops to develop their skills and leadership potential.

- Recognize that parents have limited time. If possible, reimburse them for expenses such as transportation or try to assist with their transportation needs so they can participate. Provide child care to permit parents with younger children to attend

Parents use their funds of knowledge to advocate for their children.

meetings. Reach out to single parents with their special needs and help them get representation in the political process.

If you include parents as partners in the education process, you are advocating for them and their children.

### Steps to Take for Public Advocacy

These are the basic steps involved in advocacy at the public level:

1. *Write to federal officials.* Individual letters written by constituents are more effective than form letters with many signatures. You can also use e-mail and telephone contact. Send letters about national issues and legislation to the following addresses:

President of the United States: The White House, 1600 Pennsylvania Ave., Washington, DC 20500. Telephone: (202) 456-1414

Representatives: The Honorable *(name)*, U.S. House of Representatives, Washington, DC 20515.

Senators: The Honorable *(name)*, U.S. Senate, Washington, DC 20515.

For representatives' and senators' telephone numbers and e-mail addresses, call the Capitol switchboard, 202–224–3121, or go to www .house.gov or www.senate.gov.

2. *Talk with and write to state legislators.* On the state level, write or call your state representative or state senator. Work with your representative before the assembly or legislature meets if you or your group has a bill that you want introduced.

If you plan to write to your state representative or senator, there are a few tips to follow:

- State your purpose in the first paragraph, including the number of the legislation, such as HR _____ or S _____.
- Be courteous, but to the point.
- Address only one issue in the letter.
- Follow up your letter with a phone call (Children's Defense Fund, 2006).

If you will be communicating with the media remember to do the following:

- Know what you want to say.
- Say it well by using a brief but powerful anecdote.
- Say it clearly. Avoid jargon.
- Say it again, clearly and simply (National Association for the Education of Young Children, 2004).

NAEYC's Take Action link www.naeyc.org/ policy/action connects you to your legislator where you can write a personal message regarding an action item. You can also use a form letter provided by NAEYC.

3. *Get involved before elections.* Campaign for legislators who agree with your position on child care, families, and children.
4. *Stay involved after elections.* After an election, invite elected officials to meet with your organization.
5. *Join professional organizations in your region.* For example, the National Association for the Education of Young Children, the Council for Exceptional Children, the National Association for Children with Learning Disabilities, your local Association for the Education of Young Children, and the National Council on Family Relations.
6. *Get firsthand experience.* Visit child-care centers, homeless shelters, schools, and other facilities.

## Possible Advocacy Topics

Parents and educators can develop a list of possible topics to advocate for their children. Usually those topics have some type of immediate impact on young children and their families. For example, parents of children with autism can advocate for sensory rooms in public libraries so that children with autism can also enjoy this community organization. Another important topic that many working parents highly need is universal prekindergarten. Universal prekindergarten is a topic of high debate but one that can help alleviate many problems for working families (Casto & Sipple, 2009). Activities that families can do to advocate for green space include planting trees and working with government officials to stop unplanned development. Families can organize to plant trees and prevent from unplanned development to occur. A similar issue is the need to create accessible play environments for all children. Many children in the inner city do not enjoy the benefits of playgrounds because their families are afraid to take them to the park because of unforeseen dangers. A final issue may be to advocate for the rights of immigrants (Olson, 2009). Very often we forget that many of us also came to the U.S. to pursue a dream and that others may also have that dream. Immigrants have the right to appropriate education, health care, and jobs. Together we can make the U.S. an even better place to live so that we can turn our advocacy lens to the rest of the world.

## :: ADVOCACY FOR CHILDREN AROUND THE WORLD

Europe has been a leader in advocacy for children. The Council of Europe has been active since after World War II with over 50 years of work, much of it concerned with children and their rights. European countries also adopted the United Nations Convention on the Rights of the Child, and there is movement in recognizing the need for rights for children. The United States has tended to be slower than western Europe in implementing legislation and policies to support and protect children but is now making many of the same policy changes. As of 2008, there are 29 states that have banned corporal punishment. The remaining 21 states do not prohibit corporal punishment, and the majority of the children affected are African Americans and children with disabilities (Duper & Montgomery Dingus, 2008).

## Office of Children's Ombudsman in the United States

In the United States, many individual states are in the process of creating ombudsmen offices for hearing child-related concerns based on the European model (see Table 12.1). Michigan is one such state. The mission statement for Michigan's ombudsman is as follows:

### Mission of the Office of Children's Ombudsman

The mission of the office of the Children's Ombudsman is to assure the safety and wellbeing of Michigan's children in need of foster care, adoption, and protective services and promote public confidence in the child welfare system. This will be accomplished through independently investigating complaints, advocating for children, and recommending changes to improve law policy and practice for the benefit of current and future generations. (Office of Children's Ombudsman, 2011)

Many other states have ombudsmen for children in one form or another. The remaining states have offices dealing with family issues but not specifically for children.

## European Network

*Ombudsman* is a Scandinavian word first used in the current form in Sweden when Sweden ruled much of Scandinavia. The root is from Old Norse and means *representative*. The word is commonly used today to mean a people's advocate in dealing with government. In Sweden an Ombudsman was first appointed in 1809. In 1919 Finland adopted the idea, but it was not until after 1954, when Denmark established an Ombudsman's Office, that the idea of an Ombudsman started to attract world-wide attention. (Office of the Ombudsman, 1998, p. 2)

The European Network of Ombudsmen for Children (ENOC) reports on the achievements of the nations in Europe. This includes Austria, Belgium, Denmark, France, Georgia, Hungary, Iceland, Lithuania, Macedonia, Northern Ireland, Norway, Poland, Portugal, Romania, Russia (Volgograd), and Sweden. Some nations, such as Finland, Norway, and

Sweden, have had ombudsman systems for many years. Other countries, having adopted the United Nations Convention on the Rights of the Child, are developing their children's ombudsman program.

In Finland the ombudsman is the legal aspect of the Mannerheim League for Child Welfare, a private advocacy group. In Norway the system was created by national legislation. In Sweden it was run by Radda Barnen (Save the Children), a large, private organization until 1993, when Sweden established an Office of Children's Ombudsman (Mork, 1998; Rauche-Elnekave, 1989). In each of these countries, in addition to working on behalf of individual children, the ombudsmen work toward betterment for groups of children and answer general complaints.

**Norway.** Two countries that have highly developed systems of ombudsmanship—a comprehensive child advocacy office include Norway and Sweden. Norway's involvement with families reaches back several centuries. In 1621, a Norwegian law required parents to find a useful occupation for their children. If the children were found idle, public guardians would take over the responsibility of the parents. Now Norway has one of the first national ombudsman programs for children—the Ombudsman for Children office, established in 1981 (Flekkoy, 1989), and is by law regarded as independent, non-partisan, and politically neutral (Barneombudet, 2002, p. l).

The Ombudsman for Children advocates for children's education based on international conventions, including the United Nations Convention on the Rights of the Child. Children have rights to education, rights in education, and rights through education. The rights to education include the following: (a) the right of refugees to obtain education without regard to the length of their stay in the country or their legal status, (b) the right to a religious and moral education (Norway has a state church), and (c) the right to come and go to school without extra costs—"right to go to school in the closest environment" (Hauge, 1998, p. 53).

These three rights in education provide for quality of education with stimulating education and child care. These rights also include the right to be protected from bullying or abuse by teachers, with the right to complain and to have the situation resolved in a "secure procedure" (Hauge, 1998, p. 53).

## TABLE 12.1
Child advocates by state.

| State | Ombudsmen or advocate | Within state divisions of children and family services | Independent ombudsmen for children's issues* |
|-------|----------------------|-------------------------------------------------------|---------------------------------------------|
| AL | | | |
| AK | Yes | | |
| AZ | Yes | | |
| AR | Yes | Yes | |
| CA | Yes, and by county | Yes | |
| CO | | | |
| CT | Yes | | Yes |
| DE | Yes | | Yes |
| FL | Yes | | |
| GA | Yes | | Yes |
| HI | Yes | Yes | Yes |

*The ombudsmen or offices that represent children's issues may be responsible for other tasks not involving children.

| Ombudsmen or offices that represent children* or Offices of the Child Advocate | For children but not ombudsmen |
|---|---|
| | Dept. of Children's Affairs www.dca.state.al.us/ |

Office of the Ombudsman
Anchorage, AK 99510–2636
www.state.ak.us/local/akpages/LEGISLATURE/ombud/home.htm

Arizona Ombudsman/Citizen's Aide Office
Phoenix, AZ 85014
www.azleg.state.az.us/ombudsman/default.htm

Office of Youth Advocate (re:Children)
Division of Children and Families
Dept. of Human Services
Little Rock, AR 72203–1437
www.arkansas.gov/dhhs/chilnfam/

California's programs administered by the 58 individual counties. Example:
LA County Dept. of Ombudsman
Los Angeles, CA 90020
www.childsworld.ca.gov/
Example: LA County:http://ombudsman.lacounty.info/default.asp

Colorado is a state-supervised, county-administered system for social services, including child welfare services.

Complaint Resolution Process
Colorado Dept. of Social Services
Denver, CO 80203
www.cdhs.state.co.us/

The Office of the Child Advocate
Hartford, CT 06106
www.ct.gov/oca/site/default.asp

The Office of the Child Advocate
Wilmington, DE 19801
www.courts.delaware.gov/childadvocate/index.htm

Florida Statewide Advocacy Council
Tallahassee, FL 32308
www.floridasac.org

The Office of the Child Advocate
Macon, GA 31210–2591
www.state.ga.us/gachildadvocate/

Office of the Ombudsman
Honolulu, H1 96813
www.ombudsman.state.hi.us

*(Continued)*

**TABLE 12.1**
**Child advocates by state.** *(Continued)*

| State | Ombudsmen or advocate | Within state divisions of children and family services | Independent ombudsmen for children's issues* |
|-------|----------------------|-------------------------------------------------------|---------------------------------------------|
| ID | | | |
| IL | Yes | Yes | |
| IN | | | |
| IA | Yes | | |
| KS | Yes | Yes | |
| KY | Executive order | Yes | |
| LA | Yes | Yes | |
| ME | | | Yes (state contract) |
| MD | | | |
| MA | Yes | Yes | |
| MI | Yes | | Yes |

*The ombudsmen or offices that represent children's issues may be responsible for other tasks not involving children.

| Ombudsmen or offices that represent children* or Offices of the Child Advocate | For children but not ombudsmen |
|---|---|
| | Traditional State Services by Regions<br>Boise, ID 83704<br>www.state.id.us/ |

Advocacy Office (Ombudsperson's Office) for Children and Families, DCFS
Springfield, IL 62701
www.state.il.us/dcfs/index.html

Proposed Child Advocate Bureau, within the Indiana Dept. of Administration
www.state.in.us/

Office of Citizens' Aide/Ombudsman
Des Moines, IA 50319
www.legis.state.ia.us/ombudsman/

Ombudsman Program Social & Rehabilitation Services (re: children)
Topeka, KS 66606
www.srskansas.org

The Office of the Ombudsman Cabinet for Health and Family Services
Frankfort, KY 40621
www.chfs.ky.gov/omb/

Family Ombudsman Office of Youth Development
Baton Rouge, LA 70896
www.oyd.louisiana.gov

Maine Children's Alliance
Ombudsman Program
Augusta, ME 04330-7037
www.maineChildrensalliance.org/am/publish/ombudsman.shtml

Governor's Office for Children, (also for Youth & Families)
Baltimore, MD 21201
www.ocyf.state.md.us

Governor's Office of Constituent Services
Dept. of Social Services
Ombudsman State House
Boston, MA 02133
www.mass.gov/gov

Children's Ombudsman
Lansing, MI 48909
www.michigan.gov/oco

*(Continued)*

## TABLE 12.1

**Child advocates by state.** *(Continued)*

| State | Ombudsmen or advocate | Within state divisions of children and family services | Independent ombudsmen for children's issues* |
|-------|----------------------|--------------------------------------------------------|----------------------------------------------|
| MN | Yes | | |
| MS | | | |
| MO | Yes | Yes | |
| MT | | | |
| NE | Yes | | Yes |
| NV | | | |
| NH | Yes | Yes | |
| NJ | Yes | | Yes |
| NM | Executive order | Yes | |
| NY | By county | | |

*The ombudsmen or offices that represent children's issues may be responsible for other tasks not involving children.

| Ombudsmen or offices that represent children* or Offices of the Child Advocate | For children but not ombudsmen |
|---|---|
| Ombudsman for Mental Health and Mental Retardation (re: children)<br>Governor's Office St. Paul, MN 55101<br>www.ombudmhmr.state.mn.us/contact/ombuds.htm | |
| | Family and Children's Services,<br>Mississippi Dept. of Human Services<br>Jackson, MS 39202<br>www.mdhs.state.ms.us/index.html |
| Office of Child Advocate<br>Jefferson City, MO 65102<br>www.oca.mo.gov | |
| Dept. of Family Services<br>Helena, MT 59604<br>www.dphhs.mt.gov | |
| State Ombudsman's Office<br>Lincoln, NE 68509-4712<br>www.nebRaskalegislature.gov/web/public/ombudsman | |
| | Domestic Violence Ombudsman<br>Office of the Attorney General, Nevada<br>Dept. of Justice Carson City Office<br>Carson City, NV 89701-4717<br>www.ag.state.nv.us/menu/action_bttn/units/domestic/ombud.htm |
| New Hampshire Dept. of Health and Human Services Ombudsman<br>Concord, NH 03301<br>www.dhhs.state.nh.us/DHHS/OMBUDSMAN/default.htm | |
| Child Advocate<br>Trenton, NJ 08625<br>www.childadvocate.nj.gov | |
| Social Services Client Relations Liaison (re: children)<br>Children Youth & Families<br>Santa Fe, NM 87502<br>www.newmexico.gov | |
| Public Advocate for the City of New York<br>New York, NY 10007<br>www.pubadvocate.nyc.gov | |

*(Continued)*

**TABLE 12.1**
Child advocates by state. *(Continued)*

| State | Ombudsmen or advocate | Within state divisions of children and family services | Independent ombudsmen for children's issues* |
|---|---|---|---|
| NC | Yes | Yes | |
| ND | | | |
| OH | By county | | |
| OK | Yes | Yes | |
| OR | Yes | Yes | |
| PA | | | |
| RI | Yes | | Yes |
| SC | Yes | Yes | |

*The ombudsmen or offices that represent children's issues may be responsible for other tasks not involving children.

| Ombudsmen or offices that represent children* or Offices of the Child Advocate | For children but not ombudsmen |
| --- | --- |

North Carolina Dept. of Health and Human Services
(NCDHHS)
Ombudsman Program
Raleigh, NC 27699–2001
www.dhhs.state.nc.us/ocs/ombudsman.htm

The public child welfare system in North Dakota is county administered and state supervised.
www.nd.gov/humanservices/services/childfamily/

Executive Director/Ombudsman,
Citizens of Cuyahoga County
Cleveland, OH 44113;
Children's Ombudsman/Lucas County,
Toledo, OH 43624
www.co.lucas.oh.us/index.aspx?NID=160

Advocate General
Office of Client Advocacy,
Office of Advocate Defender,
Oklahoma Dept. of Human Services
Oklahoma City, OK 73125
www.okdhs.org/divisionsoffices/oca/

Oregon Dept. of Human Services
Salem, OR 97301–1097
www.oregon.gov/DHS/aboutdhs/gao.shtml

Governor's Cabinet and Commission for Children
and Families
Harrisburg, PA 17105–2675
www.pachildren.state.pa.us/ccf/site/default.
asp?dsftns=32261

Office of the Child Advocate
Providence, RI 02903
(ABA Model Legislation)
www.state.ri.us/govtracker/index.php?page=
DetailDeptAgency&eid=3867

Governor's Office of Children's Affairs
Columbia, SC 29201,
and Governor's Office of Ombudsman
Columbia, SC 29201
www.govoepp.state.sc.us/ca/

*(Continued)*

**TABLE 12.1**
**Child advocates by state.** *(Continued)*

| State | Ombudsmen or advocate | Within state divisions of children and family services | Independent ombudsmen for children's issues* |
|-------|-----------------------|--------------------------------------------------------|----------------------------------------------|
| SD    |                       |                                                        |                                              |
| TN    | Yes                   |                                                        | Yes                                          |
| TX    | Yes                   | Yes                                                    |                                              |
| UT    |                       | Yes                                                    |                                              |
| VT    |                       |                                                        |                                              |
| VA    |                       |                                                        |                                              |
| WA    | Yes                   |                                                        | Yes                                          |
| WV    | Yes                   | Yes                                                    |                                              |
| WI    |                       |                                                        |                                              |
| WY    |                       | Yes                                                    |                                              |

*Source:* National Conference of State Legislatures; Web sites for individual states.

*The ombudsmen or offices that represent children's issues may be responsible for other tasks not involving children.

## Ombudsmen or offices that represent children* or Offices of the Child Advocate

## For children but not ombudsmen

South Dakota Dept. of Social Services
Pierre, SD
57501-5070
www.dss.sd.gov/cps/

Gerald Papica or Michael Cash,
Ombudsman for Children and Families,
Tennessee Commission on Children and Youth
Nashville, TN 37243–0800
www.tennessee.gov/tccy/ombuds.html

Texas Health and Human Services Commission
Office of the Ombudsman
Austin, TX 78708
www.hhs.state.tx.us/OMB

Office of Child Protection Ombudsman
Salt Lake City, UT 84145–0500
www.ocpo.utah.gov

Vermont Agency of Human Service
Waterbury, VT 05671-0204
www.vermont.gov/health-safety/children.html

Virginia Dept. of Social Services
Richmond, VA 23219
www.dss.state.va.us/family/children.html

Office of the Family and Children's Ombudsman
Tukwila, WA 98188
www.governor.wa.gov/ofco/index.html

Office of the Ombudsman for Behavioral Health
Charleston, WV 25305
www.wvdhhr.org/bhhf/ombudsman.asp

Office of the Milwaukee Ombudsman for Child Welfare
Milwaukee, WI 53202
www.ombudsmanmilw.org

Wyoming Dept. of Family Services
Ombudsman Division
Cheyenne, WY 82002
www.dfsweb.state.wy.us

The rights through education include participation and democracy. Schools have a dialectic process leading to democracy and school development with input from the children.

The ombudsman has particularly focused on:

*Environment:* learning environment; increased opportunities of growth and learning, directly and indirectly.

*Participation:* children's competence; participation in school-democracy and in the community.

*Equality:* equal access to schooling and to quality in education by means of participation.

**Sweden.** The Office of Children's Ombudsman, referred to in Swedish as *Barnombudsmanner* (BO), was established in Sweden in 1923 and followed the United Nations Convention on the Rights of the Child for the purpose of ensuring children's rights (Children's Ombudsman in Sweden, 1998) as the following quote shows, "The Ombudsman has the task of ensuring that the Rights of the Child [are] respected, as well as promoting good formative condition, a good psychosocial environment and a good standard of child safety" (Mork, 1998, 21).

**Austria.** The Federal Youth Welfare Act of 1989 was established through child-welfare legislation. By 2002, each of the nine provinces of Austria had an ombudsman for children and youth. Each office is in direct contact with children and young people: "We provide information and give advice, we mediate between them and the parents or other professionals. We try to represent their interest, to find amicable solutions. We help them to solve their problems" (Centre for Europe's Children, 2001b, p. 3). Notice that like the United States, there are provincial ombudsmen for children but, unlike the United States, also a federal ombudsman.

**France.** The French ombudsman for children was established March 6, 2000, as an independent agency vested with authority to defend and promote children's rights as defined by law or an international agreement such as the United Nations Convention of the Rights of the Child (Centre for Europe's Children, 2001a).

## Latin America

Although Latin American countries do not have an Office of Ombudsman for Children, children's rights are advocated by either a broader ombudsman office or a commissioner for human rights. Honduras has a National Commissioner for Human Rights Office. Costa Rica has an Ombudsman Office for the Inhabitants of the Republic. Guatemala has an Ombudsman Office for the Rights of the Child within the Human Rights Ombudsman Office. In Colombia, within the Defensoria del Pueblo, there is a delegate for Children, Women, and Seniors. Panama has an Office of the General Ombudsman. Ecuador and Peru have Commissions of State, which include a defender of children. Mexico's National Commission of Human Rights includes Coordination of Woman, the Child and the Family (Centre for Europe's Children, 2001d). Latin America has begun to recognize the special needs and rights of women and children, but much greater development needs to be accomplished.

## Ombudsmanship

The United Nations Convention on the Rights of the Child has made a strong impact on the development of programs concerned about children's rights and their need to be protected. The need for protection ranges from slavery and sexual violence to provision of a home and nourishment. In addition, the European Network of Ombudsmen for Children (ENOC) is working to end all corporal punishment of children in Europe. ENOC states: "Hitting children is disrespectful and dangerous. Children deserve at least the same protection from violence that we as adults take for granted for ourselves" (Centre for Europe's Children, 2001b, p. 3).

In 2006, the Council of Europe launched a three-year campaign to increase protection of children affected by violence. This followed a summit of heads of state in May 2005. The European Community contemplated appointing a European Defender of the Rights of the Child as the highest-level coordinator. Also in 2006, the Department of Freedom, Security and Justice of the European Commission circulated a draft of the Communication on the Rights of the Child. Maintaining rights of children throughout

The Buckley Amendment (Family Educational Rights and Privacy Act) gives this child's parents the right to see her school records.

the world is a goal that all nations and all citizens should applaud and serve.

## SUMMARY

Legal rights and responsibilities of parents, students, and professional educators are crucial to the success of advocacy. Criticisms of schools make cooperation between home and schools even more essential than in previous times.

Rights and responsibilities of parents and students are expressed on the following topics: suspension and expulsion, speech and expression, flag saluting and reciting the Pledge of Allegiance, racial discrimination, sex discrimination, students with disabilities and special education, corporal punishment, and the Buckley Amendment on open-record policy.

Three levels of advocacy involvement between home and school include the following: (a) development and periodic review of a code of rights and responsibilities for each class, school, or local school district; (b) election of and active involvement with a parent or citizen advisory council; and (c) implementation of the educational program in a classroom community. Development of a code involves identification of interests, research and gathering of background material, formulation of a draft code, feedback, approval, implementation, and review.

Parents and teachers must advocate for children's rights. This can be accomplished by organizing, planning, and advocating for a more caring and healthy environment. Parents and schools working together can provide a wholesome, intellectually stimulating, and challenging environment for families and children.

Ombudsman programs for children have been recognized as needed in Sweden for over 200 years. Many countries have developed ombudsman programs. Since 1950, programs have been developed in the United States.

### SUGGESTED CLASS ACTIVITIES AND DISCUSSIONS

1.  Discuss what free speech is and how the boundaries are defined.
2.  Discuss the rights parents and students have to see school records.
3.  Discuss the concept that rights are also accompanied by responsibilities.
4.  How have schools responded to the need to eliminate racial discrimination? Investigate the changes that have occurred in schools in your area because of affirmative action.
5.  Contact a school in your area and find out what alternative education programs exist.
6.  Follow the legislative action in your state, choose a bill that you strongly support, and advocate for its passage.
7.  Brainstorm and come up with a list of needs that should be addressed by an advocate or advocacy groups.
8.  Research the status of the United Nations Convention on the Rights of the Child in the United States.
9.  Design an ombudsman program for children. What would be needed?

## USEFUL WEB SITES

**Child Advocate**

www.childadvocate.net/

The goal of this Web site is to develop resources for advocacy for children and parents. It seeks to address educational, legal, and medical issues and to support local, state, and national legislative action.

**Child Welfare League of America (CWLA)**

www.cwla.org/advocacy/advocacyresources.htm/

The CWLA provides links to other advocacy organizations and government sites, advocacy tips, links to nonpartisan, nonprofit voter information with factual information about elected officials, and a link to a youth policy action center, which is a resource that helps youth and concerned adults contact elected officials about programs and initiatives related to children and families.

**Children's Defense Fund**

www.childrensdefense.org/

This site provides information that assists concerned adults with contacting legislators regarding current and pending legislation, data regarding the status of children in the United States and the world, and resources available to assist advocacy initiatives for children and families.

The rights that guard these children are derived from the U.S. Constitution, the Bill of Rights, social customs, legislation, and rulings of state and federal courts.

# References

Ainsworth, M. D. (1973). The development of infant–mother attachments. In B. M. Caldwell & H. N. Ricciuti (Eds.), *Review of child development research*. Chicago: University of Chicago Press.

Akers, P. (2005). Conferencing the SMART way. *Principal, 84*(3), 47.

Alanis, I. (2011). Learning from each other: Bilingual pairs in dual-language classrooms. *Dimensions of Early Childhood, 39*(1).

Altman, D. H., & Smith, R. L. (1960). Unrecognized trauma in infants and children. *Journal of Bone and Joint Surgery, 42A*(1), 407–413.

Amato, P. R. (1994). Life-span adjustment of children to their parents' divorce. *The Future of Children: Children and Divorce 4*(1), 143–164.

American Academy of Child & Adolescent Psychiatry. (2004, July). *Stepfamily problems*. Retrieved from http://www.aacap.org/publications/factfam/stepfmly.htm

American Association for Protecting Children. (n.d.). *Guidelines for schools to help protect abused and neglected children*. Denver, CO: American Humane Association.

American Humane Association. (1978). *National analysis of official child neglect and abuse reporting*. Denver, CO: Author.

American Humane Association. (1992a, October). *Fact sheet: Child abuse and neglect data*. Englewood, CO: Author.

American Humane Association. (1992b, July). *Fact sheet: Shaken baby syndrome*. Englewood, CO: Author.

American Humane Association. (1998). *Children's division*. Englewood, CO: Author.

American Humane Association. (2001). *Fact sheet: Shaken baby syndrome*. Retrieved from http://www.americanhumane.org/children/factsheets/shake.htm

American School Counselor Association. (1988). The school counselor and child abuse/neglect prevention. *Elementary School Guidance & Counseling, 22*(4), 261–263.

Angelou, M. (2002). *I know why the caged bird sings*. New York: Random.

Annie E. Casey Foundation. (2005). *Kids count indicator brief: Reducing the teen birth rate*. Baltimore: Author.

Anonymous. (2009). Chasing the Dream. *Harvard Educational Review, 79*(2), 325–326. (Document ID: 1791294071. Retrieved from Research Library).

Applbaum, R. L., Bodaken, E. M., Sereno, K. K., & Anatol, K. W. E. (1979). *The process of group communication* (2nd ed.). Palo Alto, CA: Science Research Associates.

Araujo, B. E. (2009). Best practices in working with linguistically diverse families. *Intervention in School and Clinic, 45*(2), 116–123.

Arseneault, L., Walsh, E., Trzesniewski, K., Newcombe, R., Caspi, A., & Muffit, T. (2006). Bullying victimization uniquely contributes to adjustment problems in young children: A nationally representative cohort study. *Pediatrics, 118*(1), 130–138.

Asher, L. J., & Lenhoff, D. R. (2001). Family and medical leave: Making time for family is everyone's business. *The Future of Children: Caring for Infants and Toddlers, 11*(1), 115–121.

Austin, J. S. (2000). When a child discloses sexual abuse: Immediate and appropriate teacher responses. *Childhood Education, 77*(1), 2–5.

Autism Speaks. (2008). *Autism Speaks Annual Report, 2008*. Retrieved from http://www.autismspeaks.org/annual_report.php

Bailey, J. A., Hill, K. G., Oesterle, S., & Hawkins, J. D. (2009). Parenting practices and problem behavior across three generations: Monitoring, harsh discipline, and drug use in the intergenerational transmission of externalizing behavior. *Developmental Psychology, 45*(5), 1214–1226. doi: 10.1037/a0016129

Bakwin, H. (1956). Multiple skeletal lesions in young children due to trauma. *Journal of Pediatrics, 49*(1), 7–15.

Ballantine, J. H. (1999/2000, Winter). Figuring the father factor. *Childhood Education, 76*(2), 104–105.

Banks, J. A. (1991). *Teaching strategies for ethnic studies* (5th ed.). Boston: Allyn & Bacon.

Banks, J. A. (1997). *Teaching strategies for ethnic studies* (6th ed.). Boston: Allyn & Bacon.

Banks, J. A. (2003). *Teaching strategies for ethnic studies* (7th ed.). Boston: Allyn & Bacon.

Banks, J. A. (Ed.) (2004). *Diversity and citizenship education*. San Francisco: Jossey-Bass.

Banks, J. A. (Ed.), & Banks, C. (Assoc. Ed.). (2001). *Handbook of research on multicultural education*. San Francisco: Jossey-Bass.

Barneombudet. (2002). *The ombudsman for children in Norway*. Retrieved from http://www .barneombudet.no/html/english/ factsheet.html

Barr, R. G., Rivara, F. P., Barr, M., Cummings, P., Taylor, J., Lengua, L. J., & Benitz, M. (2009). Effectiveness of educational materials designed to change knowledge and behaviors regarding crying and shaken-baby syndrome in mothers of newborns: A randomized, controlled trial. *Child: Care, Health and Development, 35*(4), 587–588.

Barr, R. G., Rivara, F. P., Barr, M., Cummings, P., Taylor, J., Lengua, L. J., & Meredith-Benitz, E. (2009). Effectiveness of educational materials designed to change knowledge and behaviors regarding crying and shaken-baby syndrome in mothers of newborns: A randomized, controlled trial. *Pediatrics, 123*(3), 972–980. doi: 10.1542/peds.2008–0908

Barton, P. E. (2002, January). *Raising achievement and reducing gaps*. Retrieved from http://www.negp.gov

Bassuk, E. L. (1991). Homeless families. *Scientific American, 264*(6), 66–74.

Bassuk, E., & Rubin, L. (1987). Homeless children: A neglected population. *American Journal of Orthopsychiatry, 57*(22), 279–285.

Bavolek, S. J. (1989). Assessing and treating high-risk parenting attitudes. *Early Child Development and Care, 42*, 99–111.

Beal, G., Bohlen, J. M., & Raudabaugh, J. N. (1962). *Leadership and dynamic group action*. Ames: Iowa State University.

Beato, G. (2005). Homeschooling alone. *Reason, 36*(11), 32–39.

Becker, H. J. (2000, Fall/Winter). Who's wired and who's not: Children's access and use of computer technology. *The Future of Children: Children and Computer Technology, 10*(2), 44–75.

Bekerman, Z. (2009). The complexities of teaching historical conflictual narratives in integrated Palestinian-Jewish schools in Israel. *International Review of Education, 55*(2/3), 235–250.

Bell, R. Q., & Harper, L. V. (1980). *Child effects on adults*. Lincoln: University of Nebraska Press.

Belsky, J., Conger, R., Capaldi, D. M., (2009). Intergenerational transmission of parenting: Introduction to the special section. *Developmental Psychology, 45*(5). doi: 10.1037/a0016245

Benne, K. D., & Sheets, P. (1948). Functional roles of group members. *Journal of Social Issues, 4*(2), 41–49.

Berger, E. H. (1968). *Mature beginning teachers: Employment, satisfaction, and role analysis*. Unpublished doctoral dissertation, University of Denver.

Berger, E. H. (1996a). Don't leave them standing on the sidewalk. *Early Childhood Education Journal, 24*(2), 131–133.

Berger, E. H. (1996b). Communication: The key to parent involvement. *Early Childhood Education Journal, 23*(3), 179–183.

Berger, E. H. (1997). Home schooling. *Early Childhood Education Journal, 24*(3), 205–208.

Berger, E. H. (1998). Reaching parents through literacy. *Early Childhood Education Journal, 25*(3), 211–215.

Berrueta-Clement, J. R., Schweinhart, L. J., Barnett, W. S., Epstein, A. S., & Weikart, D. P. (1984). *Changed lives: The effects of the Perry Preschool Program on youths through age 19*. Monograph of the High/Scope Educational Research Foundation, No. 8. Ypsilanti, MI: High/Scope Press.

Bigner, J. J. (1985). *Parent–child relations*. New York: Macmillan.

Bjorklund, G., & Burger, C. (1987). Making conferences work for parents, teachers, and children. *Young Children, 42*(2), 26–31.

Bloom, B. S. (1964). *Stability and change in human characteristics*. New York: Wiley.

Bloom, B. S. (1981). *All our children learning*. New York: McGraw-Hill.

Bloom, B. S. (1986). The home environment and school learning. In Study Group of National Assessment of Student Achievement, *The nation's report card*. Washington, DC: U.S. Department of Education. (ERIC Document Reproduction Service No. ED279663).

Bloome, D. (2007). Words are power. *Language Arts, 85*(2), 48–152.

Bolívar, J. M., Chrispeels, J. H. (2011). Enhancing parent leadership through building social and intellectual capital. *American Educational Research Journal, 48*(1), 4–38.

Borchers, T. (1999). *Small group communication:* Roles in groups. Retrieved from http://www.abacon .com/commstudies/groups/roles .html

Boren, S. (1994). *Education of the gifted and talented reauthorization fact sheet*. Washington, DC: U.S. Department of Education. (ERIC Document Reproduction Service Nos. ED371526 and EC303113).

Boute, G. S., & Strickland, J. (2008). Making African American culture and history central to early childhood teaching and learning. *The Journal of Negro Education, 77*(2), 131–132.

Bowlby, J. (1966). *Attachment*. New York: Basic Books.

Bowlby, J. (1982). *Maternal care and mental health*. New York: Schocken Books.

Bowlby, J. (1988). *A secure base*. New York: Basic Books.

Boyer, E. L. (1995). *The basic school: A community for learning*. Princeton, NJ: Carnegie Foundation for the Advancement of Teaching.

Brazelton Institute. (2005). *The Newborn Behavioral Observation system: What is it?* Retrieved from http://www.touchpoint.brazelton-institute.com/clnbas.html

Brazelton, T. B. (1987). *Working and caring*. Reading, MA: Addison-Wesley.

Brazelton, T. B., & Greenspan, S. I. (2000). *The irreducible needs of children: What every child must have to grow, learn, and flourish*. Cambridge, MA: Perseus.

Brazelton, T. B., & Greenspan, S. I. (2001). The irreducible needs of children. *Young Children, 56*(2), 6–14.

Brazelton, T. B., & Yogman, M. W. (1986). *Affective development in infancy*. Norwood, NJ: Ablex.

Brier, J., Berliner, L., Bulkley, J. A., Jenny, C., & Reid, T. (1996). *The APSAC handbook on child maltreatment*. Thousand Oaks, CA: Sage.

Brim, O. (1965). *Education for child rearing*. New York: Free Press.

Bronfenbrenner, U. (1979). *The ecology of human development*. Cambridge, MA: Harvard University Press.

Bronfenbrenner, U. (1986). Ecology of the family. Research perspectives. *Developmental Psychology, 22,* 723–742.

Brooks, K., & Karathanos, K. (2009). Building on cultural and linguistic capital of English learner (EL) students. *Multicultural Education, 16*(4), 47–51.

Buell, M. J., Hallam, R. A., & Beck, H. L. (2001, May). Early Head Start and child care partnerships: Working together to serve infants, toddlers, and their families. *Young Children, 56*(3), 7–12.

Bullock, J. R. (2002). Bullying among children. *Childhood Education, 78*(3), 130–133.

Burns, E. (2006). *IEP-2005. Writing and implementing individualized education programs (IEPs)*. Springfield, IL: Charles Thomas Ltd.

Buysse, V., Castro, D. C., & West, T. (2005). Addressing the needs of Latino children: A national survey of state administrators of early childhood programs. *Early Childhood Research Quarterly, 20*(2), 146–163.

C. Henry Kempe National Center for the Prevention and Treatment of Child Abuse and Neglect. (n.d.). *Kempe Center programs*. Denver, CO: Author.

Caffey, J. (1946). Multiple fractures in long bones of infants suffering from chronic subdural hematoma. *American Journal of Roentgenology, 56,* 163–173.

Cai, Y., Reeve, J., & Robinson, D. T. (2002). Homeschooling and teaching style: Comparing motivational styles of homeschool and public school teachers. *Journal of Educational Psychology, 94*(2), 372–380.

Caldwell, B. (1968). The fourth dimension in early childhood education. In R. Hess & R. Bear (Eds.), *Early education: Current theory, research, and action*. Chicago: Aldine.

Caldwell, B. M. (1989). Achieving rights for children: Role of the early childhood profession. *Childhood Education, 66*(1), 4–7.

Caldwell, B. M. (1991). Continuity in the early years: Transitions between grades and systems. In S. L. Kagan (Ed.), *The care and education of America's young children: Obstacles and opportunities. Ninetieth yearbook of the National Society for the Study of Education*. Chicago: University of Chicago Press.

Caldwell, B. M., & Bradley, R. H. (1984). *Administration manual: Home observation for measurement of the environment*. Little Rock: University of Arkansas.

Campbell, F. A., Wasik, B. H., Pungello, E., Burchinal, M., Barbarin, O., Kainz, K., Sparling, J. J., & Ramey, C. T. (2008). Young adult outcomes from the Abecedarian and care early childhood educational interventions. *Early Childhood Research Quarterly, 23,* 452–466.

Campos, D., Delgado, R., & Soto Huerta, M. E. (2011, July, forthcoming). *Reaching out to Latino parents of English learners*. Alexandria, VA: ASCD.

Cancian, M., & Danziger, S. (2009). Changing poverty and changing antipoverty policies. *Focus, 26*(2), 1–5.

Cancian, M., & Reed, D. (2009). Family structure, childbearing, and parental employment: Implications for the level and trend in poverty. *Focus, 26*(2), 21–26.

Cannella, G. S. (2002). *Deconstructing early childhood education: Social justice & revolution*. New York: Peter Lang.

Canter, L., & Hausner, L. (1987). *Homework without tears*. New York: Harper & Row.

Carlson, C. I. (1992). Single-parent families. In M. E. Procidano & C. B. Fisher (Eds.), *Contemporary families: A handbook for school professionals*. New York: Teachers College Press.

Carnegie Corporation of New York. (1994). *Starting points: Meeting the needs of our youngest children*. New York: Author.

Carper, J. C. (1992). Home schooling: History and historian: The past and present. *The High School Journal, 75*(4), 252–257.

Cartledge, G. Y., Gardener, R. III., & Ford, D. Y. (2009). *Diverse learners with exceptionalities: Culturally responsive teaching in the inclusive classroom*. Ohio: Merrill.

Casper, L. M. (1997, November). Who's minding our preschoolers? Fall 1994 (Update). *Current Population Reports* (P70–62). Washington, DC: Bureau of the Census.

Casper, L. M., & Bianchi, S. M. (2002). *Continuity & change in the American family*. Thousand Oaks, CA: Sage.

Casper, L. M., & Bryson, K. R. (1998, March). *Coresident grandparents and their grandchildren: Grandparent maintained families*. Washington, DC: Population Division, U.S. Bureau of the Census. Retrieved from http://www.census.gov/population/www/documentation/twps0026.html

Casper, V., Cooper, R. M., & Finn, C. D. (2003). Culture and caregiving: Goals, expectations, & conflict. *Zero to Three, 25*(3), 4–54.

Casto, H. G., & Sipple, J. W. (2009). Who and what influences school leaders' decisions: An institutional analysis of the implementation of universal prekindergarten. *Educational Policy, 25,* 134–165.

Cataldo, C. Z. (1987). *Parent education for early childhood*. New York: Teachers College Press.

Center for Effective Discipline. (2000, July). *Facts about corporal punishment*. Retrieved from http://www.stophitting.com/disatschool/facts.php

Center for Effective Discipline. (2006, July). *Facts about corporal punishment worldwide.* Retrieved from http://www.stophitting.com/disatschool/facts.php

Center for Effective Discipline. (2007). U.S.: *Corporal punishment and paddling statistics by state and race.* Retrieved from http://www.stophitting.com/disatschool/statesBanning.php

Center for Family Strengths. (1986). *Building family strengths: A manual for facilitators.* Lincoln, NE: University of Nebraska.

Centers for Disease Control. (2006a). *Youth violence: Fact sheet.* Retrieved from http://cdc.gov/hcipe/factsheets/yvfacts.htm

Centers for Disease Control. (2006b). *Child maltreatment: Fact sheet.* Retrieved from http://cdc.gov/hcipc/fctsheets/yvfacts.htm

Centers for Disease Control. (2011). *Teen pregnancy prevention 2010–2015.* http://www.cdc.gov/TeenPregnancy/PreventTeenPreg.htm

Centre for Europe's Children. (2001a, December 13). *Annual report on the activities of the French ombudsman for children/Defenseur des enfants.* Retrieved from http://www.ombudsnet.org/Ombudsmen/France/Activities_00_01.htm

Centre for Europe's Children. (2001b, December 13). *Austrian report for the annual meeting of ENOC.* Retrieved from http://www.ombudsnet.org/Ombudsmen/Austria/austria.htm

Centre for Europe's Children. (2001c, December 13). *Standards for human rights.* Retrieved from http://www.ombudsnet.org/WhatsNew.htm

Centre for Europe's Children. (2001d, March 30). *Latin America.* Retrieved from http://www.ombudsnet.org/ombudsmen/RestOfWorld/LatinAmerica/LatinAmerica.htm

Centre for Europe's Children. (2002, April 4). *History of the office.* Retrieved from http://www.ombudsnet.org/ombudsmen/Hungary/hungary.htm

CESA 5, Portage Project. (1998). *Growing: Interactions/daily routines.* Portage, WI: Author.

Chang, J. J., Theodore, A. D., Martin, S. L., & Runyan, D. K. (2008). Psychological abuse between parents: Associations with child maltreatment from a population-based sample. *Child Abuse & Neglect, 32,* 819–829.

Chazan-Cohen, R., Raikes, H., Brooks-Gunn, J., Ayoub, C., Pan, B. A., Kisker, E. E., Roggman, L., & Fuligni, A. S. (2009). Low-income children's school readiness: Parent contributions over the first five years. *Early Education and Development, 20*(6), 958–977.

Chicago Longitudinal Study. (2004). *Parent program.* Retrieved from http://www.waisman.wisc.edu:8000/cls/parent.htm

Chicago Office of the Office for Civil Rights. (2005). *Protecting students with disabilities.* Chicago: Author.

Child Abuse Prevention and Treatment Act of 1974. (1977). *United States Code, 1976, The Public Health and Welfare, Section 5101* (Vol. 10). Washington, DC: U.S. Government Printing Office.

Child Trends Data Bank. (2004). *Number and rate of victims of child maltreatment, 2002.* Retrieved from http://www.childtrendsdatabank.org

Child Welfare Information Gateway. (2003). *Child fatalities resource listing.* Retrieved from http://www.childwelfare.gov/pubs/reslit/rl_dsp.cfm?subjiD[equals]1

Child Welfare Information Gateway. (2010). *About us.* Retrieved from http://www.childwelfare.gov/

Children's Defense Fund. (1989). *A vision for America's future.* Washington, DC: Author.

Children's Defense Fund. (1992). *The state of America's children, 1991.* Washington, DC: Author.

Children's Defense Fund. (1997). *The state of America's children: Yearbook 1997.* Washington, DC: Author.

Children's Defense Fund. (1998). *The state of America's children: Yearbook 1998.* Washington, DC: Author.

Children's Defense Fund. (2001). *Children in the states.* Washington, DC: Author.

Children's Defense Fund. (2005). *State of America's children, 2005.* Retrieved from http://www.childrensdefensefund.org

Children's Defense Fund. (2010). *State of America's children, 2008.* Retrieved from http://www.childrensdefensefund.org

Children's Defense Fund. (2011).

Children's Ombudsman in Sweden. (1998). *Children's ombudsman in Sweden report.* Retrieved from http://www.bo.se/eng/engelsk.asp

Chinn, P. C. (Ed.). (1984). *Education of culturally and linguistically exceptional children.* Reston, VA: Council for Exceptional Children.

Chinn, P. C., Winn, J., & Walters, R. H. (1978). *Two-way talking with parents of special children: A process of positive communication.* St. Louis, MO: C. V. Mosby.

Christle, C. A., & Yell, M. L. (2010). Indi-vidualized education programs: Legal requirements and research findings. *Exceptionality, 18*(3), 109–123.

Civil Rights Act of 1964, 42 U.S.C. 601, 78 Stat. 252; 2000d. Cited in the *Federal Register, 45*(92).

Clark, E. R., & Flores, B. B. (2001). Who am I? The social construction of ethnic identity and self-perceptions of bilingual preservice teachers. *The Urban Review, 33*(2), 69–86.

Cochran, M., & Dean, C. (1991). Home–school relations and the empowerment process. *Elementary School Journal 91*(3), 261–269.

Cogan, M. (2010). Exploring academic outcomes of homeschooled students. *Journal of College Admission, 208,* 18–25.

Colorado Department of Education, Early Childhood Initiatives, The Arapahoe Early Childhood Network, PEAK Parent Center, & The Colorado Consortium of Intensive Care Nurseries. (1997). *From one parent to another.* Denver, CO: Author.

Columna, L., Senne, T. A., & Lytle, R. (2009). Communicating with

Hispanic parents of children with and without disabilities. *Journal of Physical Education, Recreation, & Dance, 80*(4), 1–58.

Comenius, J. A. (1967). *The great didactic of John Amos Comenius* (M. W. Keatinge, Ed. & Trans.). New York: Russell & Russell. (Original work published 1657.)

Comer, J. P. (1988). Educating poor minority children. *Scientific American, 259*(5), 42–48.

Comer, J. P. (1997). *Waiting for a miracle.* New York: Dutton.

Comer, J. P. (2004). *Leave no child behind: Preparing today's youth for tomorrow's world.* New Haven: Yale University Press.

*Congressional record.* (1983). 98th Congr., Vol. 129, pt. 24: 33310–33329, 98–199.

Consortium for Longitudinal Studies. (1983). *As the twig is bent.* Hillsdale, NJ: Erlbaum.

Cook, R. E., Klein, M. D., & Tessier, A. (2004). *Adapting early childhood curricula for children in inclusive settings* (6th ed.). Upper Saddle River, NJ: Merrill/Prentice Hall.

Cook, R. E., Tessier, A., & Armbruster, V. B. (1987). *Adapting early childhood curricula for children with special needs* (2nd ed.). Upper Saddle River, NJ: Merrill/Prentice Hall.

Cooke, G., & Cooke, S. (1988). Homework that makes a difference in children's learning. Personal communication.

Coons, C. E., Gay, E. C., Fandal, A. W., Ker, C., & Frankenburg, W. K. (1981). *Home screening questionnaire.* Denver, CO: JFK Child Development Center.

Cooper, H. (1994, Summer). *Homework research and policy: A review of the literature.* Center for Applied Research and Education Improvement. Retrieved from http://education.umn.edu/carei/ Reports/Rpractice/Summer94/ homework.htm

Cooper, H. (2001). Homework for all. *Educational Leadership, 58*(7), 34–38.

Cooper, J. M. (1999). *Classroom teaching skills* (6th ed.). Boston: Houghton Mifflin.

Copenhaver, J. (2004). *Assistive technology for students with disabilities: Information for parents and educators.* Logan, UT: U.S. Department of Education.

Council for Exceptional Children. (2000). *Pervasive developmental disorders (PDD).* Retrieved from http://www.cec.sped.org

Council for Exceptional Children. (2001). *Nurturing young children.* Retrieved from http://www.cec .sped.org

Council for Exceptional Children. (2002). *Public policy and legislative information: IDEA reauthorization recommendations.* Retrieved from http://www.cec.sped.org/pp/

Council for Exceptional Children. (2003). *GT-English as a second language.* Retrieved from http:// www.cec.sped.org

Council for Exceptional Children. (2011). *Exceptionality area.* Retrieved from http://www.cec .sped.org

Council of State Directors of Programs for the Gifted. (2001–2002). *State of the states.* Dr. Kristy Ehlers, State Director, Gifted and Talented Education. Oklahoma Department of Education.

Crosbie-Burnett, M., & Giles-Sim, J. (1994). Adolescent adjustment and step-parenting styles. *Family Relations, 43*(4), 394–399.

Crosbie-Burnett, M., & Skyles, A. (1989). Stepchildren in schools and colleges: Recommendations for educational policy changes. *Family Relations, 38*(1), 59–64.

Crosson-Tower, C. (2002). *Child abuse and neglect* (5th ed.). Boston: Allyn & Bacon.

Cummins, J. (1979). Cognitive/ academic language proficiency, linguistic interdependence, the optimum age and some other matters. *Working Papers on Bilingualism, 19,* 121–129.

Cupoli, J. M., & Sewell, P. M. (1988). One thousand fifty-nine children with a chief complaint of sexual abuse. *Child Abuse and Neglect, 12*(2), 151–161.

Currie, J. (2000). *Early childhood intervention programs: What do we know?* Retrieved from http:// www.jcir.org/wpfiles.currie. EARLYCHILDHOOD.Psd

Cushman, K. (2010). Show us what homework is for. *Educational Leadership, 68*(1), 74–78.

Dalaimo, D. M. (1996). Community home education: A case study of public school-based home schooling program. *Education Research Quarterly, 19*(4), 3–21.

Daro, D., McCurdy, K., Falconier, L., & Stajanovie, D. (2003). Sustaining new parents in home visitation services: Key participation and program factors. *Child Abuse and Neglect, 27*(10), 1101–1126.

Darragh, J. (2009). Informal assessment as a tool for supporting parent partnerships. *Exchange, 31*(3), 22–25.

Davidson Institute for Talent Development. (2007). *Genius denied: How to stop wasting our brightest young minds.* Retrieved from http://www.geniusdenied .com/Policies/StatePolicy.aspx

Delpit, L. (1996). *Other people's children: Cultural conflict in the classroom.* New York: New Press.

deMause, L. (Ed.). (1974). *The history of childhood.* New York: Psychohistory Press.

deMause, L. (Ed.). (1988). *The history of childhood: The untold story of child abuse.* New York: Harper & Row.

DeNavas-Walt, C., Proctor, B. D., & Smith, J. C. (2010). Income, poverty, and health insurance coverage in the United States: 2009. *Current Population Reports,* U.S. Census Bureau.

Denver Public Schools, Emily Griffith Opportunity School. (n.d.). *Parent education and preschool department leadership handbook.* Denver, CO: Author.

Denver Public Schools. (1998). *Child abuse bulletin.* Denver, CO: Author.

Denver Public Schools. (n.d.). *For VIPs only. Volunteers in public schools.* Denver, CO: Author.

Derman-Sparks, L. (2004). Culturally relevant anti-bias education with young children. In W. G. Stephan and W. P. Viogt (Eds.), *Education programs for improving intergroup relations* (pp. 19–37). New York: Teachers College Press.

Derman-Sparks, L., & A.B.C. Task Force. (1989). *Anti-bias curriculum: Tasks for empowering young children.* Washington, DC: National Association for the Education of Young Children.

Dewey, J. (1916). *Democracy and education: An introduction to the philosophy of education.* New York: Macmillan.

Diamond, A. (2009). The interplay of biology and the environment broadly defined. *Developmental Psychology, 45*(1), 1–8.

Diffily, D. (2004). *Teachers and families working together.* Boston: Allyn & Bacon.

Dinkmeyer, D., & McKay, G. D. (1989). *STEP: Systematic training for effective parenting.* Circle Pines, MN: American Guidance Service.

Dinkmeyer, D., McKay, G. D., & Dinkmeyer, D., Jr. (1997). *Parent's handbook. Systematic training for effective parenting.* Circle Pines, MN: American Guidance Service.

Dinkmeyer, D., McKay, G. D., Dinkmeyer, J. S., & Dinkmeyer, D., Jr. (1992). *Teaching and leading children.* Circle Pines, MN: American Guidance Service.

Dombro, A. L., O'Donnell, N. S., Galinsky, E., Melcher, S. G., & Farber, A. (1996). *Community mobilization: Strategies to support young children and their families.* New York: Families and Work Institute.

Dowling, M. (2010). *Young children's personal, social & emotional development* (3rd ed.). Los Angeles: SAGE.

Dunlap, K. M. (2000). *Family empowerment: One outcome of parental participation in cooperative preschool education.* New York: Garland.

Duper, D. R., & Montgomery Dingus, A. E. (2008). Corporal punishment in U.S. public schools: A continuing challenge for school social workers. *Children & Schools, 30*(4), 243–250.

Dutro, E., Kazemi, E., Balf, R., & Lin, Y. S. (2008). "What are you and where are you from?": Race, identity, and the vicissitudes of cultural relevance. *Urban Education, 43,* 269–300.

Dyal, A., Carpenter, L. B., & Wright, J. V. (2009). Assistive technology: What every school leader should know. *Education, 129*(3), 556–560.

Earls, F. (2002, January). Studying the causes of delinquency and violence. *In panel: The effect of emotions: Laying the groundwork in childhood.* Retrieved from http://www.lcweb.loc.gov/loc/brain/emotion/Earls.html

Eddowes, E. A. (1992). Children and homelessness: Early childhood and elementary education. In E. H. Stronge (Ed.), *Educating homeless children and adolescents: Evaluating policy and practice.* Newbury Park, CA: Sage.

Ed.gov. (2004). *Reading first purpose.* Retrieved from http://www.ed.gov/print/programs/readingfirst/index.html

Education Commission of the States. (1996). *Bridging the gap between neuroscience and education.* Denver, CO: Author.

Educational Resources Information Center, U.S. Department of Education. (1996, Fall). Inclusion. *ERIC Review, 4*(3).

Egeland, B. (1988). The consequences of physical and emotional neglect on the development of young children. In U.S. Department of Health and Human Services, Children's Bureau, *National Center on Child Abuse and Neglect: Research symposium on Child Neglect,* February 23–25. (D-10–D-21)

Eissa, A. M., & Almuneef, M. (2010). Child abuse and neglect in Saudi Arabia: Journey of recognition to implementation of national prevention strategies. *Child Abuse & Neglect, 34*(1), 28–33.

Ek, L. D., Machado-Casas, M., Sánchez, P., & Smith, H. (2011, forthcoming). Aprendiendo de sus comunidades/Learning from their communities: Bilingual teacher candidates use research to explore language views and the literacy environments of urban Latino neighborhoods. In V. Kinlock (Ed.), *Critical perspectives on education in urban settings.* New York: Teachers College Press.

Elmer, E. (1982). Abused young children seen in hospitals. In S. Antler (Ed.), *Child abuse and child protection: Policy and practice.* Silver Springs, MD: National Association of Social Workers.

Elmore, M. (2008). Effective parent conferences. *Principal Leadership (Middle School Ed.), 8*(6), 7–8.

Enciso, P., Katz, L., Kiefer, B. Z., Price-Dennis, D., & Wilson, M. (2007). Common threads in the fabric of education. *Language Arts, 84*(6), 508–509.

Epstein, J. L. (1986). Parents' reactions to teacher practices of parent involvement. *The Elementary School Journal, 86*(3), 277–294.

Epstein, J. L. (1987a). Parent involvement: What research says to administrators. *Education and Urban Society, 19*(2), 119–136.

Epstein, J. L. (1987b). What principals should know about parent involvement. *Principal, 66*(3), 6–9.

Epstein, J. L. (1994). Theory to practice: School and family partnerships lead to school improvement and student success. In C. L. Fagnano & B. Z. Werber (Eds.), *School, family, and community interaction: A view from the firing lines.* Boulder, CO: Westview Press.

Epstein, J. L. (1995b). School/family/community partnerships: Caring for the children we share. *Phi Delta Kappan, 76*(9), 701–712.

Epstein, J. L. (1996). Perspective and previews on research and policy for school, family and community partnerships. In A. Booth & J. F. Dunn (Eds.), *Family-school links: How do they affect educational outcomes?* Mahwah, NJ: Erlbaum.

Epstein, J. L. (2001). *Schools, family, and community partnerships: Preparing educators and improving schools.* Boulder, CO: Westview Press.

Epstein, J. L. (2005a). *Developing and sustaining research-based programs of school, family, and community partnerships: Summary of five years of NNPS research.* Retrieved from http://www.csos.jhu.edu/p2000/Research%20Summary.pdf

Epstein, J. L. (2005b). Attainable goals? The spirit and letter of the No Child Left Behind Act on parental involvement. *Sociology of Education, 78,* 179–182.

Epstein, J. L. (2006). Families, schools, and community partnerships. *Young Children, 61*(1), 40.

Epstein, J. L. (2008). Improving family and community involvement in secondary schools. *The Education Digest, 73*(6), 9–12.

Epstein, J. L., & Sheldon, S. B. (2002). Present and accounted for: Improving student attendance through family and community involvement. *Journal of Educational Research, 95,* 308–318.

Erikson, E. (1986). *Childhood and society.* New York: W. W. Norton.

Esparza, R. (2007). Personalizing my school: Perfect parent attendance. *School Administrator, 64*(8), 1–2.

Families and Work Institute. (1994). *Employers, families, and education: Facilitating family involvement in learning.* New York: Author.

*Families together.* (1993, Summer). Newsletter. Topeka, KS: Author.

Family and Advocates Partnership for Education Project, 2006.

Family and Advocates Partnership for Education Project. (2006). *The IEP process.* Minneapolis, MN: Pacer Center.

Family and Child Education. (2002). *Family and child education (FACE).* Retrieved from http://www.famlit.org/faqs/faqface.html

Family Resource Coalition. (1993a). *Family support programs and family literacy.* Chicago: Author.

Family Resource Coalition. (1993b). *Family support programs and the prevention of alcohol and other drug abuse (AOD).* Chicago: Author.

Family Resource Coalition. (1993c). *Family support programs and school readiness.* Chicago: Author.

Family Resource Coalition. (1993d). *Family support programs and school-linked services.* Chicago: Author.

Family Support America's Shared Leadership Series. (2000). *From many voices: Consensus what American needs for strong families and communities.* Chicago: Family Support America.

Fandal, A. (1986, February). Personal correspondence. Denver: University of Colorado Medical Center.

*Federal Register.* (1990, May 9). *Part II Department of Education, 45*(92), 30918–30965.

*Federal Register.* (1993, January 21). *Part VI Department of Health and Human Services: Administration for Children and Families, 58*(12), 1304–1305, 1308.

*Federal Register.* (2006). Rules and regulations assistance to states for the education of children with disabilities and preschool grants for children with disabilities. *Department of Education, 71*(156), 46544.

Fenichel, E., & Mann, T. L. (2001). Early Head Start for low-income families with infants and toddlers. *The Future of Children: Caring for Infants and Toddlers, 11*(1), 135–141.

Ferguson-Florissant School District. (1989b). *Parents as first teachers.* Ferguson, MO: Author.

Fernandez, H. C. (1980). *The child advocacy handbook.* New York: The Pilgrim Press.

Fields-Smith, C., & Neuharth-Pritchett, S. (2009). Families as decision-makers: When researchers and advocates work together. *Childhood Education, 85*(4), 237–242.

Fierman, A. H., Dreyer, B. P., Quinn, L., Shulman, S., Courtland, C. D., & Guzzo, R. (1991). Growth delay in homeless children. *Pediatrics, 88*(5), 918–925.

Finkelhor, D. (1986). *A sourcebook on child sexual abuse.* Beverly Hills, CA: Sage.

Finkelhor, D. (1990). Early and long-term effects of child sexual abuse: An update. *Professional Psychology: Research and Practice, 21*(5), 325–330.

Finkelhor, D. (1994). Current information on the scope and nature of child sexual abuse. *The Future of Children: Sexual Abuse of Children, 4*(2), 31–53.

Fisher, M. (1933). Parent education. In *Encyclopedia of the social sciences* (Vol. 2). New York: Macmillan.

Fisher, S. H. (1958). Skeletal manifestations of parent-induced trauma in infants and children. *Southern Medical Journal,* 956–960.

Flores, B. B., Clark, E. R., Guerra, N., Casebeer, C. M., Sánchez, S. V., & Mayall, H. (2010). Measuring the psychosocial characteristics of teacher candidates through the Academic Self-Identity: Self-Observation Yearly (ASI SOY) Inventory. *Hispanic Journal of Behavioral Sciences, 32*(1), 136–163. Retrieved from *http://dx.doi.org/10.1177/0739986309353029.*

Flynn, G., & Nolan, B. (2008). What do school principals think about current school–family relationships? *NASSP Bulletin, 92*(3), 173–190.

Fontana, V. (1973a). The diagnosis of the maltreatment syndrome in children. *Pediatrics, 51,* 780–782.

Fontana, V. (1973b). *Somewhere a child is crying.* New York: Macmillan.

Fontana, V. J., & Besharov, D. J. (1979). *The maltreated child: The maltreatment syndrome in children.* Springfield, IL: Charles C. Thomas.

Frankenburg, W. K., & Coons, C. E. (1986). HOME screening questionnaire: Its validity in assessing home environment. *Journal of Pediatrics, 108,* 624–626.

Freeman, D. E., & Freeman, Y. S. (2001). *Between worlds: Access to second language acquisition.* Portsmouth, NH: Heinemann.

Friend, M. (2011). *Special education: Contemporary perspectives for school professionals* (3rd ed.). Upper Saddle River, NJ: Pearson

Froschi, M., Sprung, B., & Mullin-Rindler, N. (1998). *Quit it: A teacher's guide on teasing and bullying for use with students in grades K–3.* Washington, DC: NEA Professional Library.

Fullar, S. A. (2008). Babies at double jeopardy. *Zero to Three, 28*(6), 25–32.

Galinsky, E. (1987). *The six stages of parenthood*. Reading, MA: Addison-Wesley.

Galinsky, E., & Salmond, K. (2002, July). *Youth & violence*. Denver: Colorado Trust and Families and Work Institute.

Gallick, B., & Lee, L. (2009). "Cheesy pizza": The pizza project. *Early Childhood Research & Practice, 11*(2).

Gamble, T. K., & Gamble, M. (1982). *Contacts: Communicating interpersonally*. New York: Random House.

Garrett, S. (2004). *Oklahoma #1 in pre-kindergarten program participation*. Retrieved from http://www.sde.state.ok.us/pro/prek/default.htm

Garrity, C., Baris, M., & Porter, W. (2000). *Bully proofing your child: A parent's guide*. Longmont, CO: Sopris West.

Gartin, B., & Murdick, N. (2005, November/December). IDEA 2004: the IEP. *Remedial and Special Education, 26*(6), 327–332.

Geertz, C. (1973). *The interpretation of cultures*. New York: Basic Books.

Gelles, R. J., & Lancaster, J. B. (Eds.). (1987). *Child abuse and neglect: Biosocial dimensions*. New York: Aldine de Gruyter.

Geneva, G. (2010). Acting on beliefs in teacher education for cultural diversity. *Journal of Teacher Education, 61*(1–2), 143–152.

Gjermeni, E., VanHook, M. P., Gjipali, S., Xhillari, L., Lungu, F., & Hazizi, A. (2008). Trafficking of children in Albania: Patterns of recruitment and reintegration. *Child Abuse & Neglect, 32*(10), 941–980.

Goebbels, A. F., G., Nicholson, J. M., Walsh, K., & DeVries, H. (2008). Teachers' reporting of suspected child abuse and neglect: Behaviour and determinants. *Health Education Research, 23*(6), 941–951.

Goffin, S. G., & Lombardi, J. (1988). *Speaking out: Early childhood advocacy*. Washington, DC: National Association for the Education of Young Children.

Goldhaber, J., & Smith, D. (2002). The development of documentation strategies to support teacher reflection, inquiry, and collaboration. In V. R. Fu, A. N. Stremmel, & L. T. Hill, (Eds.). *Teaching and learning: Collaborative exploration of the Reggio Emilia approach*. Upper Saddle River, NJ: Merrill/Prentice Hall.

Goldman, L. (2005, November). Child health and the environment, a review of evidence. *Zero to Three, 26*(2), 11–19.

Goldman-Rakic, P. (1996). What can neuroscience contribute to education? In *Education Commission of the States: Bridging the gap between neuroscience and education*. Denver, CO: Author.

Gomby, D. S. (2007). The promise and limitations of home visiting: Implementing effective programs. *Child Abuse & Neglect, 31*(8), 793–799.

Gonzalez, V., Yawkey, T. D., & Minaya-Rowe, L. (2006). *English-as-a-second-language (ESL) teaching and learning: Pre-K-12 classroom applications for students' academic achievement and development*. Upper Saddle River, NJ: Pearson.

Goodykoontz, B., Davis, M. D., & Gabbard, H. F. (1947). Recent history and present status in education for young children. In *National Society for the Study of Education, 46th yearbook, part II*. Chicago: National Society for the Study of Education.

Gordon, I. J., & Breivogel, W. F. (Eds.). (1976). *Building effective home–school relationships*. Boston: Allyn & Bacon.

Gordon, T. (1975). *P.E.T.: Parent effectiveness training*. New York: Wyden.

Gordon, T. (2000). *P.E.T.: Parent effectiveness training: The proven program for raising responsible children*. New York: Three Rivers Press.

Gormley, W. T., Jr., Gayer, T., Phillips, D., & Dawson, B. (2004). *The effects of universal pre-k on cognitive development*. Retrieved from http://www.crocus.georgetowm.edu/reports/oklahoma9z.pdf

Grall, T. S. (2009). *Custodial mothers and fathers and their child support: 2007*. U.S. Census Bureau.

Gray, S. W., & Klaus, R. A. (1965). An experimental preschool program for culturally deprived children. *Child Development, 36*(4), 887–898.

Gray, S. W., Ramsey, B. K., & Klaus, R. A. (1982). *From 3 to 20: The early training project*. Baltimore: University Park Press.

Green, S. (2002, October). Involving fathers in children's literacy development: An introduction to fathers reading every day (FRED) program. *Journal of Extension*. Retrieved from http://www.joe.org/joe/2002october/iw4.shtml

Greenleaf, B. (1978). *Children through the ages: History of childhood*. New York: McGraw-Hill.

Greenspan, S. (2002, January). *Emotional origins of intelligence. Special presentation*. Retrieved from http://www.lcweb.loc.gov/loc/brain/emotion/Greenspan.html

Griffin, D., & Steen, S. (2010). School–family–community partnerships: Applying Epstein's theory of the six types of involvement to school counselor practice. *Professional School Counselor, 13*(4), 218–226.

Griffith, P. L., Kimmel, S. J., & Biscoe, B. (2010). Teacher professional development for at-risk preschoolers: Closing the achievement gap by closing the instruction gap. *Action in Teacher Education, 31*(4), 41–53.

Gruenberg, B. C. (Ed.). (1927). *Outlines of child study*. New York: Macmillan.

Guo, Y. (2009). Communicating with parents across cultures: An investigation of an ESL parents' night. *Journal of Educational Thought, 43*(2), 171–190.

Gutek, G. L. (1968). *Pestalozzi and education*. New York: Random House.

Guterson, D. (1992). *Family matters: Why homeschooling makes sense*. New York: Harcourt Brace Jovanovich.

Hallahan, D. P., & Kaufman, J. M. (1997). *Exceptional learners: Introduction to special education* (7th ed.). Boston: Allyn & Bacon.

Hallahan, D. P., & Kauffman, J. M. (2006). *Exceptional learners: Introduction to special education* (10th ed.). Boston: Allyn & Bacon.

Halme, N., Astedt-Kurk, P., & Tarkka, M. T. (2009). Fathers' involvement with their preschool-age children: How fathers spend time with their children in different family structures. *Child Youth Care Forum, 8,* 103–119. DOI 10.1007/s10566-009-9069-7

Hamilton, L. R. (1989). Child maltreatment: Prevention and treatment. *Early Child Development and Care, 42,* 31–56.

Handel, G. (Ed.). (1988). *Childhood socialization.* New York: Aldine de Gruyter.

Hanson, R. A. (1975). Consistency and stability of home environmental measures related to IQ. *Child Development, 46*(2), 470–480.

Harden, B. J., Denmark, N., & Saul, D. (2010). Understanding the needs of staff in Head Start programs: The characteristics, perceptions, and experiences of home visitors. *Children & Youth Services Review, 32*(3), 371–390.

Harris, A., & Goodall, J. (2008). Do parents know they matter? Engaging all parents in learning. *Educational Research, 50*(3), 277–289.

Harris Helm, J., & Katz, L. (2010). *Young investigators: The project approach in the early years.* New York: Teachers College Press.

Harry, B. (2008). Collaboration with culturally and linguistically diverse families: Ideal versus reality. *Exceptional Children, 74*(3), 372–388.

Hauge, E. (1998). Promoting children's interests and rights in education. In A. Curtis (Ed.), *International Journal of Early Childhood: 50th anniversary issue OMEP, 30*(1), 52–55.

Helfer, R. E. (1975). *The diagnostic process and treatment programs.*

Washington, DC: U.S. Department of Health, Education and Welfare.

Helfer, R. E., & Kempe, R. S. (Eds.). (1987). *The battered child* (4th ed.). Chicago: University of Chicago Press.

Helm, J., Huebner, A., & Long, B. (2000). Quiltmaking: Perfect project for preschool and primary. *Young Children, 5*(3), 44–49.

Helm, J. H., & Lang, J. (2003). Overcoming the ill effects of poverty. In C. Copple (Ed.), *A world of difference* (pp. 94–98). Washington DC: National Association for the Education of Young Children.

Hernandez, D. J., Denton, N. A., & Macartney, S. (2009). School-age children in immigrant families: Challenges and opportunities for America's schools. *Teachers College Record 111*(3), 616–658.

Hernandez-Sheets, R. (2005). *Diversity pedagogy: Examining the role of culture in the teaching-learning process.* Upper Saddle River, NJ: Pearson.

Hess, R. D., & Holloway, S. D. (1984). Family and school as educational institutions. In R. D. Parke, R. N. Emde, H. P. McAdoo, & G. P. Sackett (Eds.), *Review of child development research: Vol. 7. The family.* Chicago: University of Chicago Press.

Heward, W. L. (1992). *Exceptional children: Introduction to special education* (4th ed.). Upper Saddle River, NJ: Merrill/Prentice Hall.

Heward, W. L. (2006). *Exceptional children: An introduction to special education* (8th ed.). Upper Saddle River, NJ: Merrill/Prentice Hall.

Heward, W. L., & Orlansky, M. D. (1988). *Exceptional children: An introductory survey of special education* (3rd ed.). Upper Saddle River, NJ: Merrill/Prentice Hall.

Hewett, V. M. (2001, Winter). Examining the Reggio Emilia approach to early childhood education. *Early Childhood Education Journal, 28*(4), 95–99.

Hill, R. (1960). The American family today. In E. Ginsberg (Ed.), *The nation's children.* New York: Columbia University Press.

Hodapp, A. F., & Hodapp, J. B. (1992). Homework: Making it work. *Intervention in School and Clinic, 27*(4), 233–235.

Hollingsworth, J. C. (2009). Morgan's Wonderland: An oasis of fun and accessibility for children with special needs and their families. *The Exceptional Parent Magazine.* http://www.eparent.com

Hong, E., & Milgram, R. M. (2000). *Homework: Motivation and learning preference.* Westport, CT: Bergin & Garvey.

Honig, A. S., Lally, J. R., & Mathieson, D. H. (1982). Personal-social adjustment of school children after five years in a family enrichment program. *Child Care Quarterly, 11*(2), 138–146.

Honigsfeld, A. (2009). ELL programs: Not "one size fits all." *Kappa Delta Pi Record, 45*(4), 166–171.

Horn, W. F. (1997, July, August). You've come a long way, daddy. *Policy Review,* No. 84, 24–30.

Horton, C. B., & Cruise, T. K. (2001). *Child abuse and neglect.* New York: Guilford Press.

Howard, T. C. (2003). Culturally relevant pedagogy: Ingredients for critical teacher reflection. *Theory into Practice, 42*(3), 195–202.

Hulit, L. M., Howard, M. R., Fahey, K. R. (2011). *Born to Talk: An Introduction to Speech and Language Development* (5th ed.). Upper Saddle River, NJ: Pearson.

Hunt, J. M. (1961). *Intelligence and experience.* New York: Wiley.

Huttenlocher, P. (1979). Synaptic density in human frontal cortex—developmental changes in effects of aging. *Brain Research, 163,* 195–205.

Hymes, J. L., Jr. (1974). *Effective home–school relations.* Sierra Madre: Southern California Association for the Education of Young Children.

Hymes, J. L., Jr. (1987). *Early childhood education: The year in review: A look at 1986.* Carmel, CA: Hacienda Press.

Institute for Children, Poverty & Homelessness. (2011). *Quick facts.* http://www.icphutsa.org

Institute for Responsive Education. (2006). *IRE: Connecting school, family and community.* Retrieved from http://www.responsiveeducation.org

Interagency Council on Homelessness. (2010). *Opening doors: Federal strategic plan to prevent and end homelessness: 2010.*

International Bullying Prevention Association. (2006). *Our mission.* Retrieved from http://stopbullyingworld.com/

Isenberg, E. J. (2007). What have we learned about homeschooling? *Peabody Journal of Education, 82*(2–3), 387–409.

Iverson, T. J., & Segal, M. (1990). *Child abuse and neglect: An information and reference guide.* New York: Garland.

Jackson, B. L., & Cooper, B. S. (1992). Involving parents in improving urban schools. *NAASP Bulletin, 76*(543), 30–38.

Jalongo, M. R. (2006). The story of Mary Ellen Wilson: Tracing the origins of child protection in America. *Early Childhood Education Journal, 34*(1), 1–4.

Johnson, D. L., Walker, T. B., & Rodríguez, G. G. (1996). Teaching low-income mothers to teach their children. *Early Childhood Research Quarterly, 11*(1), 101–114.

Joshi, A. (2005). Understanding Asian Indian families—facilitating meaningful home-school relations. *Young Children, 60*(3), 75–78.

Justice, B., & Justice, R. (1990). *The abusing family.* New York: Plenum Press.

Kagan, S. L., & Zigler, E. F. (1987). *Early schooling.* New Haven: Yale University Press.

Kamii, C. (1985a). Leading primary education toward excellence: Beyond worksheets and drills. *Young Children, 40*(6), 3–9.

Kamii, C. (1985b). *Young children reinvent arithmetic.* New York: Teachers College Press.

Kaplan-Leiserson, E. (2002). Education evolution: How many other institutions look exactly as they did 40 years ago? *T&D, 56*(4), 16–18.

Karnes, F. A., & Marquardt, R. (1997, February). *Know your legal rights in gifted education.* Reston, VA: The ERIC Clearinghouse on Disabilities and Gifted Education, The Council for Exceptional Children.

Karoly, L. A., Kilburn, R., & Cannon, J. (2005). *Early childhood inter-ventions: Proven results, future promise.* Santa Monica, CA: Rand Books & Publication.

Katz, L. G. (n.d.). Clearinghouse on early education and parenting. *The Project Approach Catalog: The Importance of Projects.* Retrieved from http://ceep.crc.ululc.edu eecearchive/books/projappl/initial.html#incorporating

Kearns, P. (Ed.). (1980). *Your child's right for a free public education: Parent's handbook.* Topeka: Kansas Association for Children with Learning Disabilities.

Keller, H. (1957). *The open door.* Garden City, NY: Doubleday.

Keller, H. (1991). *The story of my life: With her letters (1887–1901) and supplementary account of her education including passages from the reports and letters of her teacher, Anne Mansfield Sullivan.* CA: Temecula American Biography Series, Reprint Services Co.

Kelley, M. L. (1990). *School–home notes: Promoting children's classroom success.* New York: Guilford Press.

Kempe, C. H., & Kempe, R. (1984). *The common secret: Sexual abuse of children and adults.* San Francisco: W. H. Freeman.

Kempe, C. H., Silverman, F. N., Steele, B. F., Droegemueller, W., & Silver, H. (1962). The battered-child syndrome. *Journal of the American Medical Association, 181,* 17–24.

Kennedy, A. (2010). Family support for early literacy and numeracy: Examining events in the home and community. *Exchange, 32*(1), 18–22.

Kids Count. (2004). *Kids Count state-level data outline: Children in povety.* Retrieved from http://www.aecf.org

Kids Health. (2006). *Internet safety.* Retrieved from http://kidshealth.org/kid/

Kieff, J. (2010). Informed Advocacy in Early Childhood Care and Education: Making a Difference for Young Children and Families. Upper Saddle River, NJ: Pearson.

King, C. E. (1962). *The sociology of small groups.* New York: Pageant Press.

Kitzman, H. J., Olds, D. L., Cole, R. E., Hanks, C. A., Anson, E. A., Arcoleo, K. J., Luckey, D. W., Knudtson, M. D., Henderson, C. R. Jr, & Holmberg, J. R. (2010). Enduring effects of prenatal and infancy home visiting by nurses on children. Follow-up of a randomized trial among children at age 12 years. *Archives of Pediatrics & Adolescent Medicine, 164*(5), 412–418.

Klass, C., Pettinelli, D., & Wilson, M. (1993). Home visiting: Building linkages. Personal correspondence.

Klein, T., Bittel, C., & Molnar, J. (1993). No place to call home: Supporting the needs of homeless children in the early childhood classroom. *Young Children, 48*(6), 22–31.

Knopf, H. T., & Swick, K. J. (2007). Using our understanding of families to strengthen family involvement. *Early Childhood Education Journal, 35*(5), 419–427.

Knowles, J. G. (1989, January). Cooperating with home school parents: A new agenda for public schools? *Urban Education, 23*(4), 392–411.

Koch, P. K., & McDonough, M. (1999, March). Improving parent–teacher conferences through collaborative conversations. *Young Children, 54*(2), 11–15.

Kompanje, E. J. O. (2007). A case of malingering by proxy described in 1593. *Child Abuse & Neglect, 31*(9), 1013–1017.

Krashen, S. D. (1981). *Principles and practice in second language acquisition.* English Language Teaching Series. London: Prentice Hall International (UK) Ltd.

Kristensen, N., & Billman, J. (1987). Supporting parents and young children. *Childhood Education, 63*(4), 276–282.

Kroth, R. L., & Edge, D. (2007). Parent–teacher conferences. *Focus on Exceptional Children, 40*(2), 1–8.

Krugman, R. D. (1986). Recognition of sexual abuse in children. *Pediatrics in Review 8*(1), 25–30.

Krugman, R. D. (1993). Universal home visiting: A recommendation from the U.S. Advisory Board on Child Abuse and Neglect. *The Future of Children, 3*(3), 185–201.

Krugman, R. D., & Krugman, M. K. (1984). Emotional abuse in the classroom. *American Journal of Diseases of Children, 138,* 284–286.

LaConte, R. T. (1981). *Homework as a learning experience.* Washington, DC: National Education Association of the United States.

Ladson-Billings, G. (1995). Toward a theory of culturally relevant pedagogy. *American Educational Research Journal, 32*(3), 465–491.

Lally, J. R. (2001). Infant care in the United States and how the Italian experience can help. In L. Gandini & C. P. Edwards (Eds.), *Bambini: The Italian approach to infant/toddler care.* New York: Teachers College Press.

Lamb, M. E. (Ed.). (1997). *The role of the father in child development.* New York: Wiley.

Lamson, P. A. (1992). Home schooling: A choice the Cupertino district supports. *The School Administrator, 49*(1), 26–27.

Lane, J., Kesker, E. E., Ross, C., et al. (2005). The effectiveness of Early Head Start for 3-year old children and their parents. *Developmental Psychology, 41*(6), 885–902.

Lane, W. G., Dubowitz, H., & Langenberg, P. (2009). Screening for occult abdominal trauma in children with suspected physical abuse. *Pediatrics, 124*(6), 1595–1602.

Lay, M., & Papadopoulos, I. (2009). Sexual maltreatment of unaccompanied asylum-seeking minors from the Horn of Africa: A mixed method study focusing on vulnerability and prevention. *Child Abuse & Neglect, 33.*

Lazar, I., Darlington, R., Murray, H., Royce, J., & Snipper, A. (1982). Lasting effects of early education: A report from the Consortium for Longitudinal Studies. *Monographs of the Society for Research in Child Development, 47*(2–3).

Lazoritz, S. (1990). Whatever happened to Mary Ellen? *Child Abuse and Neglect, 14*(2), 143–149.

Lee, S. M. (1998, June). Asian Americans: Diverse and growing. *Population Bulletin, 53*(2).

Leon, K., & Cole, K. (2004, March). *Helping children understand divorce.* University of Missouri Extension. Retrieved from http://muextension.missouri.edu/xplor/hesguide/humanrel/gh600.htm

Lerner, J., Mardell-Czudnowski, C., & Goldenberg, D. (1987). *Special education for the early childhood years.* Upper Saddle River, NJ: Prentice Hall.

Levenstein, P. (1988). *Messages from home: The mother-child program.* Columbus: Ohio State University Press.

Levenstein, P., Levenstein, S., Shiminski, J. A., & Stolzberg, J. E. (1998). Long-term impact of a verbal interaction program for at-risk toddlers: An exploratory study of high school outcomes in a replication of the mother-child home program. *Journal of Applied Developmental Psychology, 19*(2), 267–285.

Levine, J. A., Murphy, D. T., & Wilson, S.(1993). *Getting men involved: Strategies for early childhood programs.* New York: Scholastic.

Lewis, J. K. (1992). Death and divorce: Helping students cope in single-parent families. *NASSP Bulletin, 76*(543), 55–60.

Lin, M., Bates, A. B. (2010). Home visits: How do they affect teachers' beliefs about teaching and diversity? *Early Childhood Education Journal, 38*(3), 179–185.

Lin, M., Lake, V. E., & Rice, D. (2008). Teaching anti-bias curriculum in teacher education programs: What and how. *Teacher Education Quarterly, 35*(2), 187–200.

Lines, P. (1991). Home instruction: The size and growth of the movement. In J. Van Galen & M. A. Pitman (Eds.), *Home schooling: Political, historical, and pedagogical perspective* (pp. 9–42). Norwood, NJ: Ablex.

Lines, P. (1996). *Homeschooling.* Washington, DC: Office of Educational Research and Improvement, U.S. Department of Education. (ERIC Document Reproduction Service No. ED965033)

Litcher, D. T., & Crowley, M. (2002, June). Poverty in America: Beyond welfare reform. In *Population Bulletin 57.* Washington DC: Population Reference Bureau.

Little Soldier, L. (1985). To soar with the eagles: Enculturation and acculturation of Indian children. *Childhood Education, 62*(2), 185–191.

Lo, L. (2008). Chinese families' level of participation and experiences in IEP meetings. *Preventing School Failure, 53*(1), 21–27.

Locke, J. (1989). *Some thoughts concerning education* (J. W. Yolton & J. S. Yolton, Eds.). Oxford: Clarendon.

Loucks, H. (1992). Increasing parent/family involvement: Ten ideas that work. *NASSP Bulletin, 76*(543), 19–23.

Malaguzzi, L. (1993, November). For an education based on relationships. *Young Children, 49*(1), 9–12.

Manning, B. H. (1985). Conducting a worthwhile parent-teacher conference. *Education, 105*(4), 342–348.

Manning, D. T., & Wootten, M. D. (1987). What stepparents perceive schools should know about blended families. *The Clearing House, 60*(5), 230–235.

Margolis, H., & Brannigan, G. G. (1986). Relating to angry parents. *Academic Therapy, 21*(3), 343–346.

Martin, A., Ryan, R. M., & Brooks-Gunn, J. (2010). When fathers' supportiveness matters most: maternal and paternal parenting and children's school readiness. *Journal of Family Psychology, 24*(2), 144–155.

Marvasti, A., & McKinney, K. D. (2004). *Middle eastern lives in America*. Lanham, MD: Rowman & Littlefield.

Maslach, C. (1982). *Burnout: The cost of caring*. Upper Saddle River, NJ: Prentice Hall.

Mathur, M., Rathore, P., & Mathur, M. (2009). Incidence, type and intensity of abuse in street children in India. *Child Abuse & Neglect, 33*(12), 907–913.

McCallister, C., Wilson, P., Green, B., & Baldwin, J. (2005). "Come take a walk": Listening to Early Head Start parents on school readiness as a matter of child, family and community health. *American Journal of Public Health, 95*(4), 617–626.

McCarthy, M. L. (2006). The context and process for performance evaluations: Necessary preconditions for use of performance evaluations as a measure of performance—A critique of Perry. *Research on Social Work Practice, 16*(4), 419–423.

McCormick, L., & Holden, R. (1992). Homeless children: A special challenge. *Young Children, 47*(6), 61–67.

McDonald, L. (2010). Advocacy in reading: To be or not to be an advocate? *Reading Improvement, 47*(2), 71–73.

Mead, M., & Wolfenstein, M. (1963). *Childhood in contemporary cultures*. Chicago: University of Chicago Press.

MELD. (1988). *MELD's Young Moms (MYM): Information and support for teen mothers*. Minneapolis, MN: Author.

MELD. (1990). *Blending information and support for parents*. Minneapolis, MN: Author.

MELD. (2006). *What is MELD?* Retrieved from http://www.meld .org

Meyer v. Nebraska, 262 U.S. 390, 399 (1923).

Meyer, D. R., & Wallace, G. (2009). Poverty level and trends in comparative perspective. *Focus, 26*(2), 7–13.

Meyerhoff, M. K., & White, B. L. (1986). New parents as teachers. *Educational Leadership, 44*(3), 42–46.

Meyers, K., & Pawlas, G. (1989). Simple steps assure parent-teacher conference success. *Instructor, 99*(2), 66–67.

Michael, S., Dittus, P., & Epstein, J. L. (2007). Family and community involvement in schools: Results from the school health in policies and programs of study 2006. *Journal of School Health, 77*(8).

Michel, G. J. (1996). *Building schools: The new school and community relations*. Lancaster, PA: Technomic.

Miller, S., Wackman, S., Nunnally, E., & Miller, P. (1988). *Connecting with self and others*. Littleton, CO: Interpersonal Communication Programs.

Minneapolis Public Schools. (2006). *School readiness*. Retrieved from http://schoolchoice.mpls.k12. mn.us/School_Readiness.html

Missouri Department of Elementary and Secondary Education. (1999). *School entry assessment project*. Jefferson City, MO: Author.

Moles, O. C. (1987). Who wants parent involvement? Interest, skills, and opportunities among parents and educators. *Education and Urban Society, 19*(2), 137–145.

Moles, O. C. (Ed.). (1996a). *Reaching all families: Creating family-friendly schools*. Washington, DC: U.S. Department of Education, Office of Educational Research and Improvement.

Moles, O. C. (1996b). New national directions in research and policy. In A. Booth & J. F. Dunn (Eds.), *School–family links: How do they affect educational outcomes?* Mahwah, NJ: Erlbaum.

Mork, O. (1998). Playing processes—Art processes. In A. Curtis (Ed.), *International Journal of Early Childhood: 50th Anniversary Issue OMEP 30*(1), 20–26.

MSU Extension. (1999). *Group effectiveness: Understanding group member roles*. Retrieved from http://www.msue.msu.edu/msue/ imp/modii/ii719202.html

Nagi, S. Z. (1977). *Child maltreatment in the United States*. New York: Columbia University Press.

Napier, R. W., & Gershenfeld, M. K. (1981). *Groups, theory, and experience* (2nd ed.). Boston: Houghton Mifflin.

National Association for the Education of Young Children (2004). *NAEYC affiliate public policy tool kit, 2004*. Retrieved from http://www.naeyc .org

National Association for the Education of Young Children (NAEYC) & National Association of Early Childhood Specialists in State Depart-ments of Education. (1991). Guidelines for appropriate curriculum content and assessment in programs serving children ages 3 through 8. *Young Children, 46*(3), 21–38.

National Association of Elementary School Principals. (1990). *Early childhood education and the elementary school principal: Standards for quality programs for young children*. Alexandria, VA: Author.

National Association of State Boards of Education (NASBE). (1988). *Right from the start*. Alexandria, VA: Author.

National Association of State Boards of Education. (1991). *Caring communities: Supporting young children and families*. Alexandria, VA: Author.

National Association of State Boards of Education. (2001). *NASBE Projects: Early Childhood Education Network*. Alexandria, VA: NASBE.

National Association of State Boards of Education. (2006). *NASBE awarded grant to replicate successful early childhood learning strategies*. Alexandria, VA: NASBE.

National Association of State Directors of Special Education. (1997). *1997 amendments to the Individuals with Disabilities Education Act*. Washington, DC: Author.

National Center for Children in Poverty. (2006b). *Basic facts about low income children: Birth to age 18*. Retrieved from http://www.nccp.org/fac.html

National Center for Children in Poverty. (2006c). *Basic facts about low income on children in the U.S.* Retrieved from http://www.nccp.org/fact.html

National Center for Education Statistics. (2001, March). *National assessment of educational progress history—Time spent on homework.* Retrieved from http://nces.ed.gov/nationsreportcard/ushistory/findhomework.asp

National Center for Education Statistics. (2002). *Children's reading and mathematics achievement in kindergarten and first grade.* Retrieved from http://nces.ed.gov/pubs2002/kindergarten/5.asp?nav[equals]1

National Center for Education Statistics. (2007). *1.1 million homeschooled students in the United States in 2003.* Retrieved from http://nces.ed.gov/nhes/homeschool

National Center for Family Literacy. (2002). *Family and child education (FACE).* Retrieved from http://www.famlit.org/faqs/faqface.html

National Center for Family Literacy. (2005). *Family literacy programs targeting Hispanics prove successful.* Louisville KY: Author.

National Center on Child Abuse and Neglect (NCCAN). (2001). *Child abuse and neglect state statutes elements: Definitions of child abuse and neglect.* Retrieved from http://www.calib.com/nccanch/pubs/stats01/define/indes.cfm

National Center on Shaken Baby Syndrome. (2006). *Prevention and legislation.* Retrieved from http://www.dontshake.com

National Child Abuse and Neglect Data System (NCANDS). (2002, April). *Summary of key findings from calendar year 2000.* Washington, DC: U.S. Department of Health and Human Services, Children's Bureau, Administration on Children, Youth and Families, National Clearinghouse on Child Abuse and Neglect Information. Retrieved from http://www.calib.com/nccanch/pubs/factsheets/canstats.cfm

National Council on Disability. (2002, July). *Individuals with Disabilities Education Act reauthorization: Where do we really stand?* Retrieved from http://www.ncd.gov/newsroom/publications/synthesis_07–05–02.html

National Dissemination Association & National Diffusion Network. (1993). *Educational programs that work.* Longmont, CO: Sopris West.

National Dissemination Center for Children with Disabilities. (2010). *Autism spectrum disorders. Disability fact sheet #1.* http://www.nichcy.org/disabilities/specific/pages/autism.aspx

National Dissemination Center for Children with Disabilities. (2011). *All about the IEP.* www.nichy.org/educatechildren/ieppages

National Information Center for Children and Youth with Disabilities, Early Childhood Research Network. (1996). Characteristics of infant child care: Factors contributing to positive caregiving. *Early Childhood Research Quarterly, 11,* 269–306.

National Information Center for Children and Youth with Disabilities. (1997). *NICHCY documents on disabilities.* Washington, DC: Author.

National Information Center for Children and Youth with Disabilities. (1998). IDEA amendments of 1997. *NICHCY News Digest 26* (Rev. ed.). Washington, DC: Author.

National Information Center for Children and Youth with Disabilities. (2000, February). *Reading and learning disabilities.* Retrieved from http://www.nichy.org/pubs/factshe/fs17text.htm

National Information Center for Children and Youth with Disabilities. (2001, December). *Attention deficit/hyperactivity disorder (AD/HD).* Retrieved from http://www.nichcy.org/pubs/factshe/fs19txt.htm

National Information Center for Children and Youth with Disabilities. (2002a, January). *Mental retardation.* Retrieved from http://www.nichcy.org/pubs/factshe/fa8txt.htm

National Information Center for Children and Youth with Disabilities. (2002b, April). *Learning disabilites.* Retrieved from http://www.nichcy.org/pubs/factshe/fs7txt.htm

National Institute of Neurological Disorders and Stroke. (2006). *What is Tourette syndrome?* Retrieved from http://www.hinds.nih.gov.disorders/tourette/detail_tourette.htm

National Law Center on Homelessness & Poverty. (2002a). *Homelessness and poverty in America.* Retrieved from http://www.nlchp.org/FA_HAPIA/

National Law Center on Homelessness & Poverty. (2002b). *McKinney-Vento 2001 reauthorization—at a glance.* Retrieved from http://www.nlchp.org/FA_Education/mckinneyGlance.cfm

National Law Center on Homelessness and Poverty. (2004, July). *Key data concerning homeless persons in America.* Retrieved from http://www.nlchp.org

National Society for the Study of Education. (1929). *Twenty-eighth year book. Preschool and parent education (parts 1 and 2).* Bloomington, IL: Public School Publishing.

National Youth Violence Prevention Resource Center. (2006). Retrieved from http://www.safeyouth.org/scripts/teens/bullying.asp

Nelson, S. W., & Guerra, P. L. (2010). Empowered parents partner with schools to meet student needs. *Journal of Staff Development, 31*(1), 67–68.

Nevin, A. I., Thousand, J. S., & Villa, R. A. (2009). Collaborative teaching for teacher educators—what does the research say? *Teaching and Teacher Education, 25,* 569–574.

Newman, F. (1996). Introduction. In *Education Commission of the States, Bridging the gap between neuroscience and education.* Denver, CO: Author.

Newman, L. (1996). Response. In *Education Commission of the States, Bridging the gap between neuroscience and education.* Denver, CO: Author.

Nievar, A. M., Van Egeren, L. A., & Pollard, S. (2010). A meta-analysis of home visiting programs: Moderators of improvement in maternal behaviors. *Infant Mental Health Journal, 31*(5), 499–520.

Nimnicht, G. P., & Brown, E. (1972). The toy library: Parents and children learning with toys. *Young Children, 28*(2), 110–116.

Nuñez, R. D. (1996). *The new poverty: Homeless families in America.* New York: Plenum Press.

Nuñez, R. D. (2004). *A shelter is not a home . . . Or is it? Lessons from family homelessness in New York City.* Retrieved from http://www.homesforthehomeless.com

O'Callaghan, J. B. (1993). *School-based collaboration with families.* San Francisco: Jossey-Bass.

O'Connell, M., & Bloom, D. E. (1987). Juggling jobs and babies: America's child care challenge. *Population Bulletin,* No. 12. Washington, DC: Population Reference Bureau.

Office of Children's Ombudsman (2011). Mission statement. Retrieved from http://www.michigan.gov/oco/0,1607,7-133-3196---,00.html

Office of Civil Rights. (2010). *Free and appropriate education for students with disabilities: Requirements under Section 504 of The Rehabilitation Act of 1973.* U.S. Department of Education, http://www2.ed.gov/about/offices/list/ocr/docs/edlite-FAPE504.html

Office of Civil Rights, U.S. Department of Education. (2007). *How to file a discrimination complaint with the Office for Civil Rights.* Retrieved from http://www.ed.gov/about/offices/list/ocr/docs/howto.html

Oliver, C., & Dalrymple, J. (eds). (2008). *Developing advocacy for children and young people: Current issues in research policy and practice.* London: Jessica Kingsley Publishers.

Olson, L. (2009). The role of advocacy in shaping immigrant education: A California case-study. *Teachers College Record, 111*(3), 817–850.

Osborn, D. K. (1991). *Early childhood education in historical perspective* (3rd ed.). Athens, GA: Education Associates. P.L., 94-142, Part B of the Education of All Handicapped Children Act, Title 20 of the *United States Code,* Sections 1400–1420. Regulations, Title 34 of the *Code of Federal Regulations,* Sections 300.1–300.754 and Appendix C, IEP Notice of Interpretation.

Ovando, C. J., Combs, M. C., Collier, V. P. (2006). Bilingual and ESL classrooms: Teaching in multicultural contexts (4th ed.). Dubuque, IA: McGraw-Hill

Packer, A., Hoffman, S., Bozler, B., & Bear, N. (1976). Home learning activities for children. In I. Gordon & W. F. Breivogel (Eds.), *Building effective home–school relationships.* Boston: Allyn & Bacon.

Palfrey, J., Bronson, M. B., Hauser-Cram, P., & Warfield, M. E. (2002). *Beepers come of age. The Brookline early education project follow-up study.* Retrieved from http://www.bc.edu/bc_org/avp/soe/beep/bpmajorfindings.htm

Papernow, P. (1998). *Becoming a stepfamily. Patterns of development of remarried families.* Mahwah, NJ: Analytic Press.

Papernow, P. L. (1993). *Becoming a stepfamily.* San Francisco: Jossey-Bass.

Pardeck, J. T. (1989). Family therapy as a treatment approach to child maltreatment. *Early Child Development and Care, 42,* 151–157.

Parents Anonymous. (1985). *The program development manual.* Los Angeles: Author.

Parents Anonymous. (2006). *Strengthening families around the world.* Retrieved from http://www.parents anonymous.org

Parents as Teachers National Center. (2002). *What's new.* Retrieved from http://www.patnc.org/forpatprograms-whatsnew.asp

Parents as Teachers National Center. (2006). *Fact sheet.* Retrieved from http://www.parentsasteachers.org/site/pp.asp?c[equals]eklRLcMZJxE&B[equals]1802131

Parlakian, R., & Lerner, C. (2010). Beyond twinkle, twinkle: Using music with infants and toddlers. *Young Children, 65*(2), 14–19.

Patall, E. A., Cooper, H., & Robinson, J. C. (2008). Parent involvement in homework: A research synthesis. *Review of Educational Research, 78*(4), 1039–1101.

Paulu, N. (1995). *Helping your child with homework for parents of elementary and junior high school-aged children.* Washington, DC: Office of Educational Research and Improvement, U.S. Department of Education.

PEAK Parent Center. (1997). *IDEA 97 and the tie to the general curriculum: Module 9–1.* Colorado Springs, CO: Parent Education and Assistance for Kids (PEAK).

Pearl, P. (1988). Working with preschool-aged child abuse victims in group settings. *Child and Youth Care Quarterly, 17*(3), 185–194.

Pennsylvania Department of Public Instruction. (1935). *Parent education. Bulletin 86.* Harrisburg: Author.

Perez, B. (2004). *Becoming biliterate: A study of two-way bilingual immersion education.* New York: Routledge.

Peterson, C. A., Mayer, L. M., Summers, J. A., & Luze, G. J. (2010). Identifying and preventing disabilities among vulnerable children. *Early Childhood Education Journal, 37,* 509–517.

Pewewardy, C., & Fitzpatrick, M. (2009). Working with American Indian students and families: Disabilities, issues, and interventions. *Intervention in School and Clinic, 45*(2), 91–98.

Piaget, J. (1976). *To understand is to invent.* New York: Penguin Books.

Piazza, G. (2007). On the wave of creativity: Children expressive language and technology. *International Journal of Education Through Art, 3*(2), 103–121. doi:10.1386/etz.3.2103

Pierson, D. E., Walker, D. K., & Tivnan, T. (1984). A school-based program from infancy to kindergarten for children and their parents. *The Personnel and Guidance Journal, 62*(8), 448–455.

Pinto, D., Pagnamenta, A. T., Klei, L., Anney, R., et al. (2010). Functional impact of global rare copy number variation in autism spectrum disorders. *Nature, 466,* 368–372. PMID 20531469.

Plato. (1953). *The dialogues of Plato* (4th ed., B. Jowett, Trans.). London: Oxford University Press. (Original work published 1871.)

Pomerantz, E. M., Moorman, E. A., & Litwack, S. D. (2007). The how, whom, and why of parents' involvement in children's schooling: More is not necessarily better. *Review of Educational Research, 77,* 373–410.

Popkin, M. H. (2002). *Active parenting now.* Marietta, GA: Active Parenting. Retrieved from http://www.activeparenting.com/xapn.htm

Portage Project Outreach. (2000). *Portage Project of Cooperative Education Agency #5: Final report.* Portage, WI: Author.

Potts, M. (1992, March). Strengths model. *National Center for Family Literacy, 4*(1), 5.

Powell, D. R. (1986). Parent education and support programs. *Young Children, 41*(3), 47–53.

Powell, D. R., Son, S-H., File, N., & San Juan, R. R. (2010). Parent–school relationships and children's academic and social outcomes in public school pre-kindergarten. *Journal of School Psychology, 48,* 269–292.

Prins, E., Schaff, K. A. (2009). Individual and structural attributions for poverty and persistence in family literacy programs: The resurgence of the culture of poverty. *Teachers College Record, 111*(9), 2280–2310.

Promising Practices Network. (n.d.). *Syracuse family development research program.* Retrieved from http://www.promisingpractices.net/program.asp? programid[equals]133#overview

Putman, S. E. (2009). The monsters in my head: Posttraumatic stress disorder and the child survivor of sexual abuse. *Journal of Counseling and Development, 87*(1), 80–89.

Quinn, B. S., Behrmann, M., Mastropieri, M. A., & Chung, Y. (2009). Who is using assistive technology in schools? *Journal of Special Education Technology, 24*(1), 1–13.

Radencich, M. C., & Schumm, J. S. (1996). *How to help your child with homework* (2nd ed.). Minneapolis, MN: Free Spirit.

Rafanello, D. (2010). Child sexual abuse prevention and reporting: It's everyone's responsibility *Exchange, 32*(1), 50–53.

Raikes, H., Green, B. L., Atwater, J., Kisker, E., Constantine, J., & Chazan-Cohen, R. (2006). Involvement in Early Head Start home visiting services: Demographic predictors and relations to child and parent outcomes. *Early Childhood Research Quarterly, 21,* 2–24.

Rauche-Elnekave, H. (1989). Advocacy and ombudswork for children: Implications of the Israeli experience. *Child Welfare, 68*(2), 101–112.

Ray, B. D. (2011). 2.04 million homeschool students in the United States in 2010. National Home Education Research Institute. Retrieved from http://www.nheri.org

Ray, B. D., & Wartes, J. (1991). The academic achievement and affective development of home-schooled children. In H. Van Galen & M. A. Pitman (Eds.), *Home schooling: Political, historical, and pedagogical perspective* (pp. 43–62). Norwood, NJ: Ablex.

Ray, K., & Smith, M. C. (2010). The kindergarten child: What teachers and administrators need to know to promote academic success in all children. *Early Childhood Educational Journal, 38*(1), 5–18.

Reppucci, N. D., Britner, P. A., & Woolard, J. L. (1997). *Preventing child abuse and neglect through parent education.* Baltimore: Brookes.

Riggs, R. C. (1982). Incest: The school's role. *The Journal of School Health, 52,* 365–370.

Riojas-Cortez, M. (2001). Preschoolers' funds of knowledge displayed through sociodramatic play episodes in a bilingual classroom. *Early Childhood Education Journal, 29,* 35–40.

Riojas-Cortez, M. (2008). Trying to fit in a different world. Acculturation of Latino families with young children in the United States. *International Journal of Early Childhood Education, 40*(1).

Riojas-Cortez, M., & Flores, B. B. (2009). Sin olvidar a los padres: Families as collaborators within the school and university partnership. *Journal of Latinos in Education, 8*(3), 231–239.

Riojas-Cortez, M., & Flores, B. B. (2009). Supporting preschoolers' social development in school through funds of knowledge. *Journal of Early Childhood Research, 7*(2), 185–199.

Riojas-Cortez, M., Flores, B. B, & Clark, E. R. (2003). Los niños aprenden en casa: Valuing and connecting home cultural knowledge with the school's early childhood education program. *Young Children, 58*(6), 78–83.

Riojas-Cortez, M., Flores, B. B., Smith, H. H., & Clark, E. R. (2003). Cuéntame un cuento: Bridging family oral traditions with school literacy. *Language Arts, 81*(1), 62–71.

Riojas-Cortez, M., Huerta, M. E., Flores, B. B., Clark, E. R., & Pérez, B. (2007). Using cultural tools to develop scientific literacy of young Mexican American preschoolers. *Early Child Development and Care, 178*(5), 527–536.

Robinson, J. L, Klute, M. M., Faldowski, R., Pan, B., Staerkel, F., Summers, J. A., & Wall, S. (2009). Mixed approach programs in the Early Head Start research and evaluation project: An in-depth view. *Early Education & Development, 20*(6), 893–919.

Rogers, C. (1983). *Freedom to learn for the '80s.* Upper Saddle River, NJ: Merrill/Prentice Hall.

Rogers, C., & Freiberg, H. J. (1994). *Freedom to learn* (3rd ed.). Upper Saddle River, NJ: Merrill/Prentice Hall.

Rogers, P., & O'Connor, R. E. (2003). How to build a better mother: A successful program prevents child abuse by teaching the art of being a mother. *People Weekly, 59*(15), 137.

Rotter, J. C., & Robinson, E. H. (1986). *Parent-teacher conferencing: What research says to the teacher.* Washington, DC: National Education Association of the United States.

Rousseau, J. J. (1979). *Emile: Education* (A. Bloom, Trans.). New York: Basic Books. (Original work published 1762.)

Rozalski, M. E., Stewart, A., & Miller, J. (2010). How to determine the least restrictive environment for students with disabilities. *Exceptionality, 18*(3), 151–163.

Ruiz-Casares, M., & Heymann, J. (2009). Children home alone unsupervised: Modeling parental decisions and associated factors in Botswana, Mexico, and Vietnam. *Child Abuse & Neglect, 33*(5), 312–323.

Rutter, M. (1981). *Maternal deprivation reassessed.* Harmondsworth, England: Penguin Books.

Rutter, M. (1985). Family and school influences on cognitive development. *Journal of Child Psychology and Psychiatry, 26*(5), 683–704.

Ryan, C. S., Casas, J. F., Kelly-Vance, L., Ryalls, B. O., & Nero, C. (2010). Parent involvement and views of school success: The role of parents' Latino and White American cultural orientations. *Psychology in the Schools, 47*(4), 391–405.

Ryan, G. (1989). Victim to victimizer: Re-thinking victim treatment. *Journal of Interpersonal Violence, 4*(3), 325–341.

Sanders, M. G. (1999). Schools' programs and progress in the National Network of Partnership Schools. *Journal of Educational Research, 92*(4), 220–229.

Sar, B. K., Antle, B. F., Bledsoe, L. K., Barbee, A. P., & Van Zyl, M. A. (2010). The importance of ex-panding home visitation services to include strengthening family relationships for the benefit of children. *Children & Youth Services Review, 32*(2), 198–205.

Saylor, R. S. (2007). Take the time to communicate with parents: Build a relationship of respect and cooperation with students' families. *American Teacher, 92*(2), 7.

Schacht, P. M., Cummings, E. M., & Davis, P. T. (2009) Fathering in family context and child adjustment: A longitudinal analysis. *Journal of Family Psychology, 23*(6), 790–797.

Schecter, S. R., & Sherri, D. L. (2009). Value added? Teachers' investments in and orientations toward parent involvement in education. *Urban Education, 44*(1), 59–87.

Schlossman, S. L. (1976). Before Home Start: Notes toward a history of parent education in America, 1897–1929. *Harvard Educational Review, 46*(3), 436–467.

Schoger, K. D. (2006). Reverse inclusion: Providing peer social interaction opportunities to students placed in self-contained special education classrooms. *Teaching Exceptional Children Plus, 2*(6), Article 3. Retrieved from http://escholarship.bc.edu/education/tecplus/vol12/iss6/art3/

Schorr, L. B., & Schorr, D. (1988). *Within our reach: Breaking the cycle of disadvantage.* New York: Doubleday.

Schweinhart, L. J. (2009). Designing a curriculum for EC teachers and caregivers. *Exchange, 31*(2), 34–37.

Section 504 Regulations, Title 34 of the Federal Regulations, Sections 104.1–104.61, and Appendix A: Analysis of Final Regulations (29 U.S.C. § 794).

Seeley, D. S. (1989). A new paradigm for parent involvement. *Educational Leadership, 47*(2), 46–48.

Seligman, M. (2000). *Conducting effective conferences with parents of children with disabilities.* New York: Guilford Press.

Shatkin, G., & Gershber, A. I. (2007). Empowering parents and building communities: the role of school-based councils in educational governance and accountability. *Urban Education, 42*(6), 582–615.

Shaw, D. S. (1992). The effects of divorce on children's adjustment. In M. E. Procidano & C. B. Fisher (Eds.), *Contemporary families: A handbook for school professionals.* New York: Teachers College Press.

Sheehy, P., Ornelles, C., & Noonan, M. J. (2009). Biculturalization: Developing culturally responsive approaches to family participation. *Intervention in School and Clinic, 45*(2), 132–139.

Shipman, V. C., Boroson, M., Bidgeman, B., Gart, J., & Mikovsky, M. (1976). *Disadvantaged children and their first school experiences.* Princeton, NJ: Educational Testing Service.

Shonkoff, J. P., & Phillips, D. H. (2000). *From neurons to neighborhoods: The science of early childhood development.* Washington, DC: National Academy Press.

Shore, R. (1997). *Rethinking the brain.* New York: Families and Work Institute.

Silver, A. A., & Hagin, R. A. (2002). *Disorders of learning in childhood.* New York: Wiley.

Silver, H. K., & Kempe, C. H. (1959). Problems of parental criminal neglect and severe physical abuse of children. *American Journal of Diseases of Children, 95,* 528.

Silverman, F. (1953). Roentgen manifes-tations of unrecognized skeletal trauma in infants. *American Journal of Roentgenology, 69,* 413–427.

Simmons, T., & Dye, J. L. (2003, October). *Grandparents living with grandchildren: 2000.* Washington, DC: U.S. Department of Commerce, Economics and Statistics Administration, U.S. Census Bureau.

Skeels, H. (1966). *Adult status of children with contrasting early life experiences: A follow-up study.*

In Monographs of the Society for Research in Child Development (Vol. 31). Chicago: University of Chicago Press.

Skeels, H. M., & Dye, H. B. (1939). A study of the effects of differential stimulation on mentally retarded children. *Proceedings and Addresses of the American Association on Mental Deficiency, 44,* 114–136.

Smith Slep, A. M., & O'Leary, S. G. (2009). Distinguishing risk profiles among parent-only, partner-only, and dually perpetrating physical aggressors. *Journal of Family Psychology, 23*(5), 705–16.

Smith, T. (2005, November/December). IDEA 2004: Another round in the reauthorization process. *Remedial and Special Education, 26*(6), 314–320.

Smith, V. (1986). Listening. In O. Hargie (Ed.), *A handbook of communication skills* (pp. 246–265). Washington Square: New York University Press.

Snow, K. L. (2006). Measuring school readiness: Conceptual and practical considerations. *Early Education and Development, 17*(1), 7–41.

Soley, G., & Hannon, E. E. (2010). Infants prefer the musical meter of their own culture: A cross-cultural comparison. *Developmental Psychology, 46*(1), 286–292.

Soska, K. C., Adolph, K. E., & Johnson, S. P. (2010). Systems in development: Motor skill acquisition facilitates three-dimensional object completion. *Developmental Psychology, 46*(1), 129–138.

Spidel, J. (1980, March). *Exceptional students in the regular classroom: How we help them learn.* Paper presented at Showcase Kansas, Wichita State University, Wichita, KS.

Spitz, R. A. (1945). Hospitalism: An inquiry into the genesis of psychiatric conditions in early childhood. In A. Freud et al. (Eds.), *The psychoanalytic study of the child* (Vol. 2). New York: International Universities Press.

Spitz, R. A. (1965). *The first year of life.* New York: International Universities Press.

Spock, B. (1957). *Baby and child care.* New York: Pocket Book.

Spodek, B. (Ed.). (1982). *Handbook of research on early childhood education.* New York: Free Press/Macmillan.

Stahlman, B. R. (2002). Personal communication.

Stahlman, K. (2002). Personal communication.

State of Hawaii, Department of Health. (1997, October). *Innovations in American government recognizes Hawaii's Healthy Start for program excellence.* Honolulu: Author.

Steele, B. F. (1986). Notes on the lasting effects of early child abuse throughout the life cycle. *Child Abuse and Neglect, 10,* 283–291.

Steele, B. F. (1987). C. Henry Kempe memorial lecture. *Child Abuse and Neglect, 11,* 313–318.

Stein, N. (1996). *Bullyproof: A teacher's guide on teasing and bullying for use with fourth and fifth grade students.* Washington, DC: Wesley College Center for Research on Women and NEA Professional Library.

Stein, N., & Sjostrom, L. (1994). *Flirting or hurting? A teacher's guide to student-to-student sexual harassment in schools (grades 6 through 12).* Washington, DC: NEA Professional Library.

Stendler, C. B. (1950). Sixty years of child training practices. *Journal of Pediatrics, 36*(1), 122–134.

Stephens, K. (2007). Parent meetings: Creative ways to make them meaningful. *Exchange, 175.*

Stronge, J. H. (Ed.). (1992). *Educating homeless children and adolescents: Evaluating policy and practice.* Newbury Park, CA: Sage.

Stronge, J. H., & Helm, V. A. (1991). Legal barriers to the education of homeless children and youth: Residency and guardianship issues. *Journal of Law & Education, 20*(2), 201–218.

Suárez-Orozco, C., Gaytán, F. X., Bang, H. J., Pakes, J., O'Connor, R., & Rhodes, J. (2010). Academic trajectories of newcomer immigrant youth. *Developmental Psychology, 46*(3), 602–618.

Summit, R. C. (1983). The child sexual abuse accommodation syndrome. *Child Abuse and Neglect, 7,* 177–193.

Svevo-Cianci, K., & Lee, Y. (2010). Twenty years of the Convention of Rights of the Child: Achievements in and challenges for child protection implementation, measurement and evaluation around the world. *Child Abuse & Neglect, 34*(1), 1–4.

Swick, K. J. (1983, April). Parent education: Focus on parents' needs and responsibilities. *Dimensions,* 9–12.

Swick, K. J. (1986). Parents as models in children's cultural development. *The Clearing House, 60*(2), 72–75.

Swick, K. J. (1997). A family–school approach for nurturing caring in young children. *Early Childhood Education Journal, 25*(2), 151–154.

Swick, K. J. (1999). Empowering homeless and transient children/families: An ecological framework for early childhood education. *Early Childhood Education Journal, 26*(3), 195–201.

Swick, K. J. (2001). Nurturing decency through caring and serving during the early childhood years. *Early Childhood Education Journal, 23*(2), 131–137.

Swick, K. J., Da Ros, D. A., & Kovach, B. A. (2001). Empowering parents and families through a caring inquiry approach. *Early Childhood Education Journal, 29*(1), 65–71.

Swick, K., & Williams, R. (2006). An analysis of Bronfenbrenner's bio-ecological perspective for early childhood educators: Implications for working with families experiencing stress. *Early Childhood Education Journal, 33*(5), 371–378.

Sylvestre, A., & Mérette, C. (2010). Language delay in severely neglected children: A cumulative or specific effect of risk factors? *Child Abuse and Neglect, 34*(6), 414–428.

Taylor, K. W. (1981). *Parent and children learn together: Parent cooperative nursery schools.* New York: Teachers College Press.

Tebes, J. K., Grady, K., & Snow, D. L. (1989). Parent training in decision-making facilitation: Skill acquisition and relationship gender. *Family Relations, 38*(3), 243–247.

The Arc. (2011). http://www.thearc.org/

The Children's Ombudsman. (1998). *The children's ombudsman in Sweden.* Retrieved from http://www.bo.se/eng/engelsk.asp

Thompson, L., Kropenske, V., Heinicke, C., Gomby, D., & Halfon, N. (2003, July). *Home visiting: A service strategy to delivery first 5 results.* Policy Brief Number 15, Building Community Systems for Young Children, Los Angeles: UCLA Center for Healthier Children, Families and Communities, California Policy Research Center.

Thornton, A., & Freedman, D. (1983). The changing American family. *Population Bulletin, No. 38,* 4. Washington, DC: Population Reference Bureau.

Tower, C. C. (1992). *The role of educators in the protection and treatment of child abuse and neglect.* Washington, DC: U.S. Department of Health and Human Services, National Center on Child Abuse and Neglect.

Trawick-Smith, J. W. (2010). *Early childhood development: A multicultural perspective* (5th ed.). Upper Saddle River, NJ: Pearson.

Turbiville, V., Umbarger, G. T., III, & Guthrie, A. C. (2000, July). Fathers' involvement in programs for young children. *Young Children, 55*(4).

Turnbull, A. P., & Turnbull, H. R., III. (1997). *Families, professionals, and exceptionality: A special partnership* (3rd ed.). Upper Saddle River, NJ: Merrill/Prentice Hall.

Turnbull, A., Turnbull, R., & Wehmeyer, M. L. (2007). *Exceptional lives: Special education in today's schools.* Upper Saddle River, NJ: Pearson Merrill Prentice Hall.

Turnbull, H. R., Turnbull, A. P., Stowe, M. J., & Wilcox, B. (2000). *Free appropriate public education.* Denver: Love.

UNICEF. (2006). *State of the world's children 2006.* Retrieved from http://www.childinfo.org

UNICEF. (2010). The state of the world's children special edition: Celebrating 20 years of the convention on the rights of the child. Retrieved from http://www.unicef.org/publications

United Nations. (1989). *United Nations convention on the rights of the child.* New York: Author.

University of North Carolina FPG Child Development Institute. (2004). *The Carolina Abecedarian Project.* Retrieved from http://www.childcareresearch.org/location/ccrca4716

U.S. Advisory Board on Child Abuse and Neglect. (1990, August). Department of Health and Human Services: Office of Human Development Services, Child Abuse and Neglect. *Critical first steps in response to a national emergency.* Washington, DC: U.S. Government Printing Office.

U.S. Advisory Board on Child Abuse and Neglect. (1993, April). In Department of Health and Human Services, Administration for Children and Families, *The continuing child protection emergency: A challenge to the nation.* Washington, DC: U.S. Government Printing Office.

U.S. Bureau of the Census. (1991). *The census and you, 26*(12). Washington, DC: U.S. Government Printing Office.

U.S. Bureau of the Census. (1995, June). *Who receives child support? Statistical briefs* (SB 95–16). Washington, DC: Author.

U.S. Bureau of the Census. (1997, Spring). *Who's minding the kids? Child care arrangements.* Retrieved from http://www.census.gov/prod/w2002pubs/p70–86.pdf

U.S. Bureau of the Census. (1998). Money income in the United States: 1997 (with separate data on valuation of noncash benefits). *Current Population Reports* (P60–200). Washington, DC: U.S. Government Printing Office.

U.S. Census Bureau. (2000a). *Current Population Reports* (P20–515) and unpublished data. Households, families, sub/families and married couples: 1980 to 2000. Retrieved from http://www.census.gov/prod/2001pubs/statab/sec01.pdf

U.S. Census Bureau. (2000b). *Current population survey (March 1950–2000). Poverty rates by race and Hispanic origin: 1959 to 2000.* Retrieved from http://www.census.gov/hhes/poverty/poverty00/povrac00.html

U.S. Census Bureau. (2000c). *Historical poverty tables.* Retrieved from http://www.census.gov/hhes/poverty/hispov/hispov4.html

U.S. Census Bureau. (2000d). *Income and poverty, 2000.* Retrieved from http://www.census.gov/hhes/income/income001/prs01/asc.html

U.S. Census Bureau. (2000e). *Real median household income holds steady between 1999 and 2000.* Retrieved from http://www.census.gov/hhes/www/img/incpov00/fig01

U.S. Census Bureau. (2000f). *The American Indian and Alaska native population.* Washington, DC: Author.

U.S. Census Bureau. (2001, April 25). Administrative and Customer Services Division, Statistical Compendia Branch. *Population by race and Hispanic/Latino status.* Retrieved from http://www.census.gov/statab/www/partla.html

U.S. Census Bureau. (2001, July). *Population briefing: National population estimates for July, 2001.* Retrieved from http://www.census.gov/popest/data/national/popbriefng.php

U.S. Census Bureau, U.S. Department of Commerce News. (2001, September 25). *Nations household income stable in 2000. Poverty rate virtually equals record low. Census Bureau Reports.* Retrieved from http://www.census.gov/PressRelease/www/2001/cb01–158.html

U.S. Census Bureau. (2002). *Historical poverty tables*. Retrieved from http://www.census.gov/hhes/poverty/hispoolfamindex.html

U.S. Census Bureau. (2004). *ACS congressional toolkit*. Washington, DC: Author.

U.S. Census Bureau. (2005a). *American fact finder. Ancestry for People with One or More Ancestry Categories Reported*. Retrieved from http://factfinder.census.gov

U.S. Census Bureau. (2005b, August 15). *2005 American community survey data*. Retrieved from http://factfinder.census.gov

U.S. Census Bureau. (2005c). *Income, poverty and health insurance coverage in the U.S. 2005*. Retrieved from http://www.census.gov

U.S. Census Bureau. (2010). *Publications*. Retrieved from http://www.census.gov/

U.S. Census Bureau. (2011). *American fact finder*. Retrieved from http://factfinder.census.gov/home/saff/aff_transition.html

U.S. Department of Commerce, U.S. Bureau of the Census. (2000). *Statistical abstract of the United States, education*. Washington, DC: Author.

U.S. Department of Education. (n.d.). *Involving fathers at school*. Adapted from *Fathers involvement in children's learning*. Retrieved from http://www.teachersfirst.com/fathers.html

U.S. Department of Education. (1980, May 9). Establishment of Title 34, Section 504, Rehabilitation Act of 1973, Rules and Regulations. *Federal Register 45*(92), 30937–30938.

U.S. Department of Education. (1986). *What works: Research about teaching and learning*. Washington, DC: U.S. Government Printing Office.

U.S. Department of Education. (1987). *Schools that work: Educating disadvantaged children*. Washington, DC: U.S. Government Printing Office.

U.S. Department of Education. (1991a). *America 2000: An education strategy*. Washington, DC: U.S. Government Printing Office.

U.S. Department of Education. (1991b). *Preparing young children for success: Guideposts for achieving our first national goal*. Washington, DC: Author.

U.S. Department of Education. (1993). *Goals 2000: Educate America*. Washington, DC: Author.

U.S. Department of Education. (1994). *Strong families, strong schools: Building community partnerships for learning*. Washington, DC: Author.

U.S. Department of Education. (1996, October 3). *United States Department of Education news: Riley announces $17 million in support for charter schools*. Washington, DC: Author.

U.S. Department of Education. (1997). *America goes back to school: The partnership for family involvement in education*. Washington, DC: Author.

U.S. Department of Education, Office of Intergovernmental and Interagency Affairs. (1998a). Partnership for family involvement in education. *Community Update*. Washington, DC: Author.

U.S. Department of Education, Office for Civil Rights. (n.d.). *Student assignment in elementary and secondary schools and Title IX*. Washington, DC: Author.

U.S. Department of Education, Office for Civil Rights, 2002 Elementary and Secondary School Civil Rights Compliance Report. (2005, November). *Corporal punishment in U.S. public schools, 2002–2003 school year*. Washington, DC: U.S. Government Printing Office.

U.S. Department of Education, Office of Educational Research and Improvement, Office of Educational Technology. (1997). *Parents' guide to the Internet*. Washington, DC: Author.

U.S. Department of Education, Office of Intergovernmental and Interagency Affairs. (1998b). America's public opinion on education and budgets. *Community Update*. Washington, DC: Author.

U.S. Department of Education, Office of Intergovernmental and Interagency Affairs. (2002, January/February). No child left behind plan becomes law. *Community Update*. Washington, DC: Author.

U.S. Department of Education, Office of Intergovernmental and Interagency Affairs, Educational Partnerships and Family Involvement Unit. (2003). *Reading tips for parents*. Washington, DC: Author.

U.S. Department of Education, Office of Special Education and Rehabilitative Services. (1997, September). *Resource 10–4*. Washington, DC: Author.

U.S. Department of Education, Office of the Secretary. (2001, February). *No child left behind*. Washington, DC: Author.

U.S. Department of Education, Title I of the Elementary and Secondary Education Act of 1965. (2002). *Improving the academic achievement of the disadvantaged*. Washington, DC: Author.

U.S. Department of Health and Human Services. (2002). *Head Start promoting early childhood development*. Retrieved from http://www.hhs.gov/news/press/2002pres/headstart.html

U.S. Department of Health and Human Services. (2010). *Families*. Retrieved from http://www.hhs.gov/children/index.html

U.S. Department of Health and Human Services. (2011). *Promoting responsible fatherhood*. http://www.fatherhood.hhs.gov/

U.S. Department of Health and Human Services, Administration for Children and Families. (2000). *Information memorandum: Family literacy services in Head Start and Early Head Start programs*. Retrieved from http://www.headstartinfo.org/publications/im00/m00_25.htm

U.S. Department of Health and Human Services, Administration for Children and Families. (2004). *Child maltreatment. 2002.*

Washington, DC: U.S. Government Printing Office.

U.S. Department of Health and Human Services, Administration for Children and Families, Administration on Children, Youth and Families, Children's Bureau. (2010). *Child maltreatment 2008.* Retrieved from http://www.acf.hhs.gov/programs/cb/stats_research/index.htm#can

U.S. Department of Health and Human Services, Administration for Children and Families, Administration on Children, Youth and Families, National Center on Child Abuse and Neglect. (1992, March). *Child abuse and neglect: A shared community concern.* Washington, DC: U.S. Government Printing Office.

U.S. Department of Health and Human Services, Administration for Children, Youth and Families, (2004). *Child maltreatment,* 2002. Washington, DC: U.S. Government Printing Office.

U.S. Department of Health and Human Services, Children's Bureau. (1998). *Child maltreatment 1996: Reports from the states to the National Child Abuse and Neglect Data System.* Washington, DC: U.S. Government Printing Office.

U.S. Department of Health and Human Services, Office of Human Development Services. (1985). Administration for Children, Youth and Families, Head Start Bureau. *A guide for operating a home-based child development program.* Washington, DC: U.S. Government Printing Office.

U.S. Department of Health and Human Services, Office of Human Development Services. (1987). Administration for Children, Youth and Families, Head Start Bureau. *The Head Start home visitor handbook.* Washington, DC: U.S. Government Printing Office.

U.S. Department of Health, Education and Welfare. (1962). *Your child from one to six.* Washington, DC: U.S. Government Printing Office.

U.S. Department of Health, Education and Welfare. (1974). *Home Start/Child and family resource programs. Reports of a joint conference—Home Start, child, and family resource programs.* Washington, DC: U.S. Government Printing Office.

U.S. Department of Health, Education and Welfare, Children's Bureau. (1949). *Your child from 6 to 12.* Washington, DC: U.S. Government Printing Office.

U.S. Department of Health, Education and Welfare, Head Start Bureau, Children's Bureau, Administration for Children, Youth and Families, Office of Human Development. (1977). *Child abuse and neglect: A self-instructional text for Head Start personnel* (Publication No. OHDS 8–31103). Washington, DC: U.S. Government Printing Office.

U.S. Department of Health, Education and Welfare, Office of Human Development. (1978). Administration for Children, Youth and Families; Head Start Bureau. *Partners with parents.* Kathryn D. Hewett et al. for Abt Associates and High/Scope Educational Research Foundation. Washington, DC: U.S. Government Printing Office.

U.S. Department of Health, Education and Welfare, Office of Human Development Services. (1979). *The rights and responsibilities of students: A handbook for the school community.* Washington, DC: U.S. Government Printing Office.

U.S. Department of Justice. (2011a). *Americans with Disabilities Act of 1990, as amended.* http://www.ada.gov

U.S. Department of Justice. (2011b). *2010 ADA standards for accessible design.* http://www.ada.gov

U.S. Department of Justice. (2011c). *Access to medical care for individuals with mobility disabilities.* Retrieved from http://www.ada.gov

U.S. General Accounting Office. (1992, August). Report to the chairman, Oversight of Government Management Subcommittee, U.S. Senate Committee on Governmental Affairs. *Child abuse: Prevention programs need greater emphasis.*

*Appendix I: Hawaii's Healthy Start program.* Washington, DC: Author.

Utah Parent Center. (1997). *Parents as partners in the IEP process: Information booklet.* Salt Lake City, UT: Author.

Utah Parent Center. (2011). http://www.utahparentcenter.org

Valdés, G. (1996). *Con respeto: Bridging the distances between culturally diverse families and schools.* New York: Teachers College Press.

Valencia, R. (2002). *Chicano school failure and success: Past, present, and future.* New York: Routledge/Falmer.

Van Haren, B., & Fiedler, C. R. (2008). Support and empower families of children with disabilities. *Intervention in School and Clinic, 43*(4), 231–235.

Villegas, A. M., & Lucas, T. (2007). The culturally responsive teacher. *Educational Leadership, 64*(6), 28–33.

Vincent, C. E. (1951). Trends in infant care ideas. *Child Development, 22*(3), 199–209.

Visher, E. B. (2001). *A systemic examination of stepfamily relationships.* First Annual Ohio State University Extension Family Life Electronic Inservice. Columbus, OH. Ohio State University.

Visher, E. B., & Visher, J. S. (1979). *Stepfamilies: A guide to working with stepparents and stepchildren.* Secaucus, NJ: Citadel Press.

Vondra, J. I., & Toth, S. L. (1989). Child maltreatment research and intervention. *Early Child Development and Care, 42,* 11–24.

Wagner, J. Y, Katsiyannis, A. (2010). Special education update: Implications for school administrators. *NASSP Bulletin, 94*(1), 40–52.

Wagner, M., Spiker, D., Inman, M., Linn, D., et al. (2003). Dimensions of parental engagement in home visiting programs, exploratory study. *Topics in Early Childhood Special Education, 4,* 171–188.

Wallerstein, J. (1985). Effect of divorce on children. *The Harvard Medical School Mental Health Letter, 2*(3).

Walsh, M. E. (1992). *Moving to nowhere*. Westport, CT: Auburn.

Warner, I. (1991). Parents in touch: District leadership for parent involvement. *Phi Delta Kappan, 73*(5), 372–375.

Wasik, B. H. (1983). *Teaching parent problem-solving skills: A behavioral-ecological perspective*. American Psychological Association Meeting, Anaheim, CA.

Wasik, B. H. (1993). Staffing issues for home visiting programs. *The Future of Children: Home Visiting, 3*(3), 140–157.

Wasik, B. H., & Bryant, D. M. (2001). *Home visiting: Procedures for helping families* (2nd ed.). Thousand Oaks, CA: Sage.

Weigel, D. J. (2008). The concept of family: An analysis of lay people's views of family *Journal of Family 29(11), 1426–1447*.

Wherry, J. H. (2009). Enter the new generation of parents. *Principal, 52*.

White, B. L., Kaban, B. T., Attanucci, J., & Shapiro, B. B. (1973). *Experience and environment: Major influences on the development of the young child* (Vol. 1). Upper Saddle River, NJ: Prentice Hall.

Wiehe, V. R. (1996). *Working with child abuse and neglect: A primer*. Thousand Oaks, CA: Sage.

Williamson, R., & Blackburn, B. R. (2010). Supporting student learning. *Principal Leadership, 10*(8), 65–67.

Winter, M., & McDonald, D. (1997). Parents as Teachers: Investing in good beginnings for children. In G. Albee & T. Gullotta (Eds.), *Primary prevention works* (pp. 119–145). Thousand Oaks, CA: Sage.

Winters, D. G. (1988). *Parents: The missing link in education reform* (Hearing before the Select Committee on Children, Youth, and Families. House of Representatives 100th Congress. November 16, 1987). Washington, DC: U.S. Government Printing Office.

Wodarski, J. S., & Johnson, S. R. (1988). Child sexual abuse: Contributing factors, effects and relevant practice issues. *Family Therapy, XV*(2), 157–173.

Wolfenstein, M. (1953). Trends in infant care. *American Journal of Orthopsychiatry, 23*(1), 120–130.

Wong-Fillmore, L. (1991). When learning a second language means losing the first. *Early Childhood Research Quarterly, 6,* 323–346.

Woolley, P. V., Jr., & Evans, W. A. (1955, June). Significance of skeletal lesions in infants resembling those of traumatic origin. *Journal of American Medical Association,* 539–543.

Ybarra, M. L., Finkelhorn, D., Mitchell, K. J., & Wolak, J. (2009). Associations between blocking, monitoring, filtering software on the home computer and youth-reported unwanted exposure to sexual material online. *Child Abuse & Neglect, 33*(12), 857–860.

Young, D., & Behounek, L. (2008). Kindergarten students use PowerPoint to lead conferences. *Principal, 87*(5), 58–59.

Youngblade, L. M., & Belsky, J. (1989). Child maltreatment, infant–parent attachment security, and dysfunctional peer relationships in toddlerhood. *Topics in Early Childhood Special Education, 9*(2), 1–15.

Youngquist, J., & Martínez-Griego, B. (2009). Learning in English learning in Spanish: A Head Start program changes its approach. *Young Children*. Retrieved from http://www.naeyc.org/yc.

Zadeh, Z. Y., Farnia, F., & Ungerleider, C. (2010). How home enrichment mediates the relationship between maternal education and children's achievement in reading and math. *Early Education & Development, 21*(4), 568–594.

Zero to Three. (2001). *Brain wonders*. Retrieved from http://zerotothree.org/brainwonders/faq.html

Zero to Three. (2010). *Parenting infants and toddlers today: Key findings from a Zero to Three 2099 National Parents Survey*. Retrieved from http://www.zerotothree.org

Zielinsky, D. S. (2009). Child maltreatment and adult socioeconomic well-being. *Child Abuse and Neglect, 33*(10), 666–678.

Zirkel, P. A. (2009). What does the law say? New Section 504 student eligibility standards. *Teaching Exceptional Children, 41,* (4), 68–71.

# Index